Mastercam. 2017

Mill Essentials Training Tutorial

To order more books:

Call 1-800-529-5517 or

Visit www.emastercam.com or

Contact your Mastercam dealer

Mastercam 2017 Mill Essentials Training Tutorial

Copyright: 1998 - 2017 In-House Solutions Inc. All rights reserved

Software: Mastercam 2017

Author: Mariana Lendel

ISBN: 978-1-77146-527-4

Date: June 23, 2016

Notice

In-House Solutions Inc. reserves the right to make improvements to this manual at any time and without notice.

Disclaimer Of All Warranties And Liability

In-House Solutions Inc. makes no warranties, either express or implied, with respect to this manual or with respect to the software described in this manual, its quality, performance, merchantability, or fitness for any particular purpose. In-House Solutions Inc. manual is sold or licensed "as is." The entire risk as to its quality and performance is with the buyer. Should the manual prove defective following its purchase, the buyer (and not In-House Solutions Inc., its distributer, or its retailer) assumes the entire cost of all necessary servicing, repair, of correction and any incidental or consequential damages. In no event will In-House Solutions Inc. be liable for direct, indirect, or consequential damages resulting from any defect in the manual, even if In-House Solutions Inc. has been advised of the possibility of such damages. Some jurisdictions do not allow the exclusion or limitation of implied warranties or liability for incidental or consequential damages, so the above limitation or exclusion may not apply to you.

Copyrights

This manual is protected under International copyright laws. All rights are reserved. This document may not, in whole or part, be copied, photographed, reproduced, translated or reduced to any electronic medium or machine readable form without prior consent, in writing, from In-House Solutions Inc.

Trademarks

Mastercam is a registered trademark of CNC Software, Inc.

Microsoft, the Microsoft logo, MS, and MS-DOS are registered trademarks of Microsoft Corporation; N-See is a registered trademark of Microcompatibles, Inc.; Windows 7 and Windows 8 are registered trademarks of Microsoft Corporation.

Tutorial	Geometry Functions	Toolpath Creation
#1	Rectangle. Circle Center Point. Chamfer Entities.	Facing Toolpath. Circle Mill Toolpath. Contour Toolpath. Spot Drill Toolpath. Drill Toolpath. 2D Contour (Chamfer Toolpath).
#2	Rectangle. Polygon. Fillet Entities. Circle Center Point. Line Endpoints - Vertical. Trim Divide. Rectangular Shapes.	Setup 1 Slot Mill Toolpath. 2D HS Dynamic Mill Toolpath. Contour Toolpath. 2D HS Dynamic Contour Toolpath. Setup 2 Facing Toolpaths.
#3	Polar Arcs. Circle Center Point. Line Tangent. Fillet Entities. Mirror. Arc Tangent to Two Entities. Trim 3 Entities. Ellipse. Offset. Letters. Bounding Box. Translate.	2D High Speed Area Mill Toolpath. 2D HS Dynamic Mill Toolpath. Pocket with Island Toolpath. Pocket Remachine Toolpath.
#4	Circle Center Points. Line Tangent. Mirror. Arc Tangent. Arc Polar. Trim. Fillets. Rotate. Translate. Solids Extrude.	Setup 1 2D High Speed Area Mill Toolpath. 2D HS Dynamic Mill Toolpath. Transform Toolpath. Pocket Toolpath. Drill Toolpath. Circle Mill Toolpath. Contour (Chamfer Toolpath). Setup 2 2D HS Dynamic Mill Toolpath.

Tutorial	Geometry Functions	Toolpath Creation
#5	Import a SolidWorks file. Translate 3D.	Setup 1 - Top Tool Planes. 2D HS Area Mill Toolpath. 2D HS Area Mill Rest Toolpath. Setup 2 - Front Tool Plane. Drill Toolpath. Setup 3 - Left Tool Plane. Slot Mill Toolpath.
#6	Rectangle. Circle Center Point. Arc Tangent to 1 Entity. Line Parallel. Chamfer. Line Polar. Trim.	2D HS Dynamic Mill Toolpath. 2D HS Core Mill Toolpath. 2D HS Blend Mill Toolpath. 2D HS Peel Mill Toolpath.
#7	Circle Center Point. Line Tangent. Line Parallel. Rectangular Shapes. Trim. Fillet Chains. Solids Extrude. Solids Chamfer. Solids Fillet.	2D HS Area Mill Toolpath. Feature Based Drilling Toolpath. 2D HS Area Mill Toolpath. Pocket Toolpath. 2D Contour Toolpath.

MASTERCAM SHORTCUTS

Function	Keyboard Shortcut	Function	Keyboard Shortcut
Analyze entities	F4	Mastercam version, SIM serial number	Alt+V
AutoSave	Alt+A	Motion controller rotation point	Alt+F12
C-Hook or user app	Alt+C	Pan	Arrow keys
Configure Mastercam	Alt+F8	Paste from clipboard	Ctrl+V
Copy to clipboard	Ctrl+C	Redo an event that has been undone	Ctrl+Y
Cut to clipboard	Ctrl+X	Repaint	F3
Delete entities	F5	Rotate	Alt+Arrow keys
Drafting global options	Alt+D	Select all	Ctrl+A
Exit Mastercam	Alt+F4	Selection grid parameters	Alt+G
Fit geometry to screen	Alt+F1	Shading on/off	Alt+S
Gview–Back	Alt+3	Show/hide all axes (WCS, Cplane, Tplane)	Alt+F9
Gview–Bottom	Alt+4	Show/hide coordinate axes	F9
Gview–Front	Alt+2	Show/hide displayed toolpaths	Alt+T
Gview–Isometric	Alt+7	Show/hide Operations Manager panel	Alt+O
Gview–Left	Alt+6	Undo the last creation or event	Ctrl+U, Ctrl+Z
Previous Plane	Alt+P	Unzoom to 80% of original	Alt+F2
Gview–Right	Alt+5	Unzoom to previous or 50% of original	F2
Gview–Top	Alt+1	Zoom around target point	Ctrl+F1
Help	Alt+H	Zoom with window selection	F1
Hide entities	Alt+E	Zoom/unzoom by 5%	Page Up/Page Down
Levels Manager	Alt+Z		
Main attributes, set from entity	Alt+X		

CUSTOMIZE MASTERCAM

Create Your Own Keyboard Shortcuts

- Right mouse click in the **Ribbon.**
- **Customize the Ribbon.**
- **Keyboard shortcuts,** select **Customize** button.

- Select the **Category.**

- Select a command and under **Press new shortcut key** enter the key combinations you want to assign to it.

Customize Quick Access Toolbar

- Right mouse click on a command in the **Ribbon.**
- Select **Add to Quick Access Toolbar.**

Customize the Ribbon

- Right mouse click in the **Ribbon.**
- Select **Customize the Ribbon.**
- Select a Mastercam command.
- Select a **Tab** or create a **New Tab.**
- Press **Add** button.

Customize the right-click menu

- Right mouse click in the **Ribbon.**
- Select **Customize the Ribbon.**
- Select **Context Menu.**
- Select the **Category** and then the command that you want to add.
- Once you click on the **Add** button the function will be added to the **Right mouse button menu.**

WAYS TO GET THE MOST FROM MASTERCAM

Mastercam Training

In-House Solutions offers unsurpassed industrial training for Mastercam and Octopuz. We have training facilities in a number of cities across Canada and some of our courses can also be offered onsite, depending on trainer availability. Learn more at **eMastercam.com/store**.

Our library of **Mastercam Training Solutions** consists of several product lines that cater to any learning style. Learn Mastercam at your own pace with our **Training Tutorials**, teach your students with the help of our **Instructor Kits**, learn the theory behind Mastercam with our **Handbooks**, get projects à-la-carte with our **Single Projects**, let our instructors show you best practices with our **Video Training** or go digital with our **eBooks**.

Mastercam Community

eMastercam is the one-stop web resource for Mastercam users. People from all over the world visit the site whether they are teaching, learning or working with Mastercam daily. Members can post questions, comments or share projects and success stories. Visit eMastercam.com and sign up for your free account today!

For downloaded pdf please visit

www.emastercam.com/qrc

Table of Contents

GETTING STARTED

Objectives:

✓ Starting Mastercam.
✓ The student will learn about the Graphical User Interface.
✓ The student will learn how to navigate through Mastercam.

STEP 1: STARTING MASTERCAM

For Windows 7

- ◆ Select the **Start** button.
- ◆ Select **All Programs** and click on **Mastercam 2017**.

For Windows 8

- ◆ Select **Start** button.
- ◆ Click on the drop down arrow to open **Apps**.
- ◆ Find and click on **Mastercam 2017**.

For Windows 10

- ◆ Select **Start** button.
- ◆ Click on the drop down arrow to open **Apps**.
- ◆ Find and click on **Mastercam 2017**.

- ◆ To start the software, from **Desktop**, click on the shortcut icon as shown.

STEP 2: GUI - GRAPHICAL USER INTERFACE

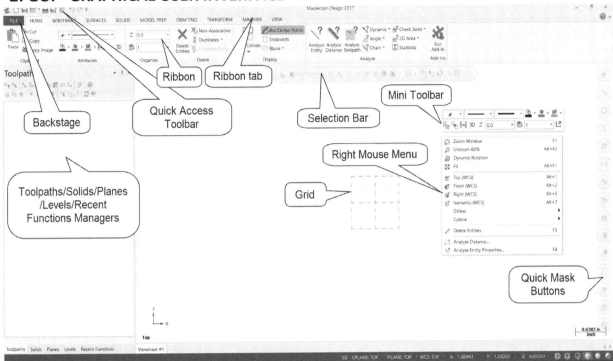

Quick Access Toolbar	**QAT** contains a fully customizable set of functions that can be quickly accessed by the user.
Backstage (FILE)	Allows you to manage the files. You can insert information about the file, start a new file, open an existing one or merge files together. You can also save, convert or print files as well as access the help resources.
Tabs	Contains all the functionality within Mastercam.
Ribbon	Displays the commands available for a selected Tab.
Selection Bar	Allows you to set the AutoCursor modes and to switch between wireframe or solid selections.
Quick Mask Buttons	Let you select all entities of a specific type. Clicking on the left side of the button or right side of the button toggles between select all or only.
Right Click Menu	Right mouse button menu allows quick access to functions such as zoom, graphic views or recent functions used. A mini toolbar will also appear that allows you to quickly change the attributes.
Toolpaths/Solids/ Planes Manager	Lists the history of the toolpath operations and solids.
Graphics Window	Workspace area in Mastercam where the geometry is displayed.
Scale	Shows you a scale of the object on the screen.
View Port XYZ Axes	Informs you which Graphics view, WCS and Tool plane/Construction plane you are working in.
WCS: TOP T/Cplane:	Displays the current WCS and T/Cplane information.

STEP 3: NAVIGATE THROUGH MASTERCAM

In this step, you will learn how to use the menu functions in Mastercam to create geometry.

3.1 Using the Wireframe tab to select the command to create Line Endpoint

- ◆ Left click on **WIREFRAME.**
- ◆ Left click on the **Line Endpoints** icon as shown in Figure: 3.1.1.

Figure: 3.1.1

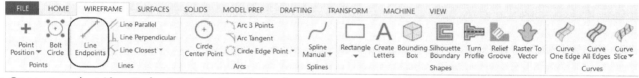

- ◆ Once you select **Line Endpoints**, the **Line Endpoints** panel appears on the screen as shown.

Sketching a line

◆ To sketch a line, left click on two locations on the screen.

Creating a line knowing the endpoint coordinates

◆ To make a line knowing the two endpoint coordinates, press **Space bar** and in the coordinates field that opens in the upper left corner, enter the coordinates of the first endpoint as shown.

> 0,1

◆ Press **Enter** to continue.
◆ Press again the **Space bar** and enter in the coordinates of the second endpoint and then press **Enter**.

Creating a line knowing an endpoint, the length and the angle

◆ You can also press **Space bar** and enter the coordinates of the first endpoint, then enter the **Length** and **Angle** if necessary.
◆ To continue making lines, choose the **OK and Create New Operation** button from the dialog box or press

Enter.

◆ To exit the current command, select the **OK** button or press the **Esc** button.

◆ To undo the last command, from the **QAT** (Quick Access Toolbar) select the **Undo** button. ↰ The **Undo** button can be used to go back to the beginning of geometry creation or to the last point of the saved file.

Mastercam also has a **Redo** button ↱ for your convenience.

3.2 Function Prompt

Prompts the user to execute a command.

◆ Example: this prompt is used in the **Line Endpoints** command. Specify the first endpoint

STEP 4: SET THE ATTRIBUTES

Mastercam attributes are point style, line style, line thickness, color and levels. Before starting to create geometry, you should set the attributes.

4.1 Attributes

Point Style	Displays and sets the system's point style.
Line Style	Displays and sets the system's line style.
Line Width	Displays and sets the current system's line width.
Color	Assigns the current color to wireframe, solid and surface entities. To change the current color, click in the specific color field and select a color from the color pallet. To change an existing geometry color, select the geometry first and then click in the color field and select a color from the color pallet.
Clear Color	When performing a transform function (Xform), Mastercam creates a temporary group from the originals (red) and a result (purple) from the transformed entities. These system groups appear in the Groups dialog box. However, they stay in effect only until you use the **Clear Colors** function or perform another transform function.
2D / 3D Construction Mode	Toggles between 2D and 3D construction modes. In 2D mode, all geometry is created parallel to the current Cplane at the current system Z depth. In 3D mode, you can work freely in various Z depths, unconstrained by the current system Z depth and Cplane setting.
Z Depth	Sets the current construction depth. To set this, click the drop down arrow and pick one from the most recently used list or click the **Z:** label and pick a point in the graphics window to use the Z depth values based on the selected entity.
Level	Sets the main level you want to work with in the graphics window. To change the current working level. type the level number in the box.

Change the Wireframe Color

- Click on the drop down arrow next to the **Wireframe Color** field as shown.

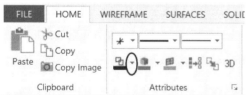

- Select the desired color from the dialog box as shown in <u>Figure: 4.1.1</u>.

Figure: 4.1.1

• Select the **OK** button to exit the command and begin creating geometry in the color of your choice.

> **NOTE:** Any geometry on your screen will remain in the previous system color. This change will only affect the geometry you create going forward.
> To change the color of existing geometry, select the entities first and then click on the drop down arrow next to the **Wireframe Color** and select the desired color.
> The same method can be applied for any other attribute that you want to set or change.

STEP 5: MANAGER PANELS

5.1 The Toolpaths Manager

The **Toolpaths Manager** displays all the operations for the current part. You can sort, edit, regenerate, verify and post

any operation as shown in Figure: 5.1.1. For more information on the **Toolpaths Manager**, please refer to **General Notes**

or click on the **Help** icon.

Figure: 5.1.1

◆ The **Toolpaths Manager, Solids Manager**, or **Planes Manager** can be hidden to gain more space in the graphics area for creating geometry. Use **Auto Hide** icon to close all **Toolpaths, Solids, Planes** and **Levels Manager** panels.

◆ The panels will be hidden to the left of the graphics window as shown.

◆ To un-hide them, click on one of the managers to open it and then click again on the **Auto Hide** icon a shown.

◆ Selecting the **X** (**Close** icon) instead of the **Auto Hide**, you will close the manager panel. To re-open them, from the **VIEW** tab, select **Toolpaths, Solids, Planes** or **Levels** as shown.

STEP 6: SET THE GRID

Before beginning to create geometry, it is highly recommended to enable the **Grid**. The grid will show you where the origin is and the orientation of the grid gives you a quick preview of the plane you are working in.

FILE
- ◆ **Configuration**.
- ◆ Select **Screen** from the configuration **Topics.**
- ◆ Select the plus sign (+) beside **Screen** as shown in Figure: 6.0.1.

Figure: 6.0.1

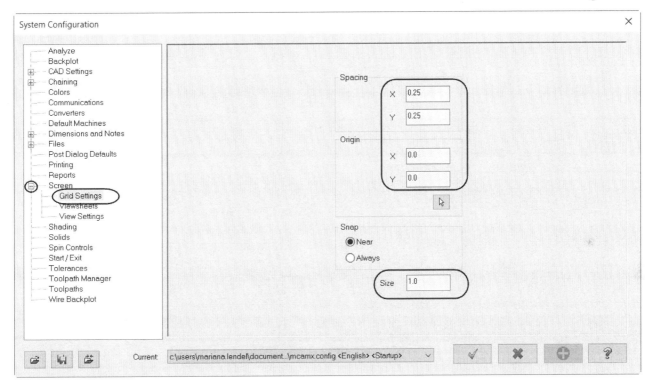

- ◆ In **Grid Settings**, change the **Spacing** to **X = 0.25** and **Y = 0.25**.
- ◆ Set the **Size** to **1.0.**

- ◆ Choose the **OK** button to exit.
- ◆ Select the **Yes** button to save the settings in the **System Configuration**.
- ◆ To see the **Grid** in the graphics window, from the **VIEW** tab, enable **Show Grid** as shown.

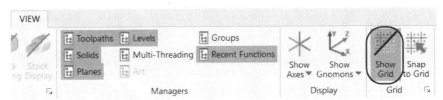

◆ The grid should look as shown.

TUTORIAL #1

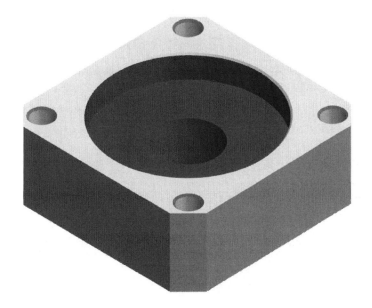

OVERVIEW OF STEPS TAKEN TO CREATE THE FINAL PART:

From Drawing to CAD Model:
* The student should examine the drawing on the following page to understand what part is being created in the tutorial.
* From the drawing we can decide how to create the geometry in Mastercam.

Create the 2D CAD Model used to generate Toolpaths from:
* The student will create the Top 2D geometry needed to create the toolpaths.
* Geometry creation commands such as Rectangle, Circle Center Point and Chamfer Entities will be used.

Create the necessary Toolpaths to machine the part:
* The student will set up the stock size to be used and the clamping method used.
* A Facing toolpath will be created to machine the top of the part.
* A Circle Mill toolpath will remove the material inside of the large hole.
* A Drilling toolpath will be created to spot drill the four holes.
* A Drilling toolpath will be created to machine the through holes.
* A Contour toolpath with 2D Chamfer option will be used to chamfer the top of the pocket.

Backplot and Verify the file:
* The Backplot will be used to simulate a step-by-step process of the tool's movements.
* The Verify will be used to watch a tool machine the part out of a solid model.

Post Process the file to generate the G-code:
* The student will then post process the file to obtain an NC file containing the necessary code for the machine.

 This tutorial takes approximately an hour and a half to complete.

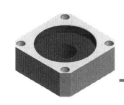

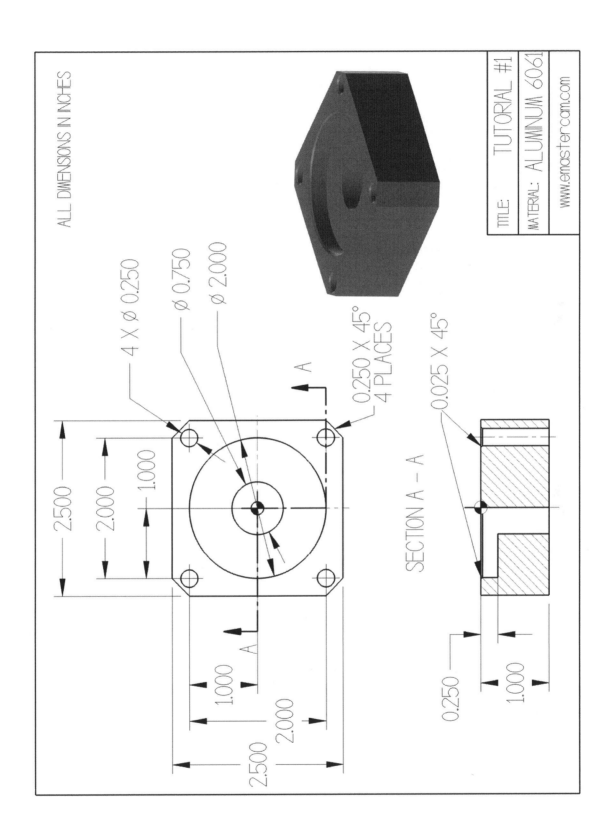

ALL DIMENSIONS IN INCHES

4 X Ø 0.250

Ø 0.750

Ø 2.000

0.250 X 45°
4 PLACES

0.025 X 45°

SECTION A – A

2.500

2.000

1.000

A

A

1.000

2.000

2.500

0.250

1.000

TITLE: TUTORIAL #1

MATERIAL: ALUMINUM 6061

www.emastercam.com

GEOMETRY CREATION

STEP 1: SETTING UP THE GRAPHICAL USER INTERFACE

Please refer to the **Getting Started** section to set up the graphical user interface. In this step, you will learn how to hide the manager panels to gain more space in the graphics window.

◆ Use **Auto Hide** icon to hide all **Manager** panels.

◆ The panels will be hidden to the left of the graphics window as shown.

NOTE: To un-hide them temporally, you can click on one of the Managers to open it as shown.

While creating the geometry, keep the Manager panels hidden. This ensures more space in the graphics window for the geometry.

STEP 2: CREATE TWO RECTANGLES

In this step, you will learn how to create a rectangle given the width, the height, and the anchor position.
You will create the 2.5" by 2.5" rectangle with the center anchor in the Origin.

Step Preview:

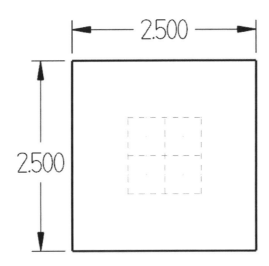

2.1 Create a 2.5" by 2.5" Rectangle

WIREFRAME

♦ From the **Shapes** group, select **Rectangle**.

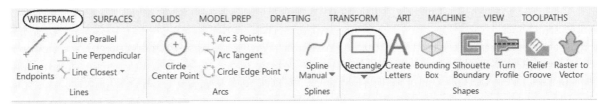

◆ In the **Rectangle** panel, enter the **Width** and **Height** and enable **Anchor to center** as shown.

NOTE: Make sure that **Create surface** is not selected. **Anchor to center** sets the base point of the rectangle to its center and draws the rectangle outward from the center.
Create surface creates a surface inside of the rectangle. Surface creation and Surface toolpath are covered in Mill Level 3.

◆ Select the position of the base point as shown.

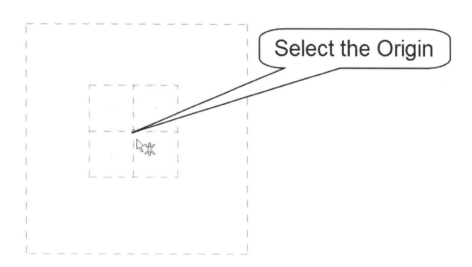

Select the Origin

◆ A preview of the geometry should look as shown.

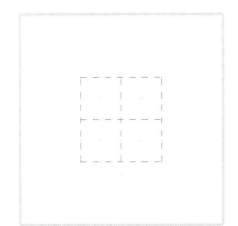

NOTE: The geometry should appear in cyan blue color which is the color for the live entities.
While the rectangle is live, you can adjust the dimensions or select a new base point.

◆ Select the **OK** button to exit the **Rectangle** command.
◆ The geometry should look as shown.

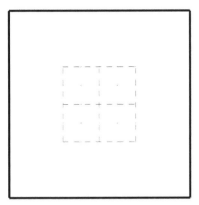

NOTE: While creating geometry for this tutorial, if you make a

mistake, you can undo the last step using the **Undo** icon. ↰
You can undo as many steps as needed. If you delete or undo a

step by mistake, just use the **Redo** icon. ↱ To delete unwanted geometry, select the geometry first and then press **Delete** from the keyboard. To zoom or un-zoom, move the cursor in the center of the geometry and scroll up or down the mouse wheel.

STEP 3: CREATE THE 1/4" DIAMETER CIRCLES

In this step, you will create circles for which you know the diameter and the locations. To use **Circle Center Point**, you need to know the center point and the radius or the diameter of the circle. To complete this step, you will need to know the **Cartesian Coordinate System**. A **Cartesian Coordinate System** is a coordinate system that specifies each point uniquely in a plane by a pair of numerical coordinates, which are the signed distances from the point to two fixed perpendicular directed lines, measured in the same unit of length as shown in Figure: 3.0.1.

Figure: 3.0.1

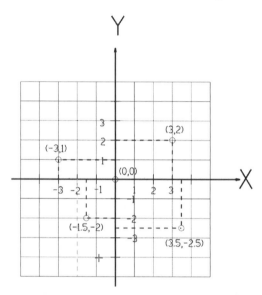

Step Preview:

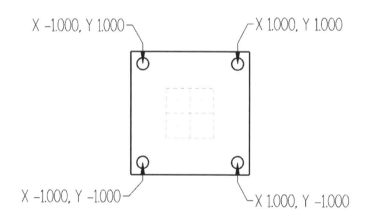

WIREFRAME

♦ From **Arcs** group, select **Circle Center Point.**

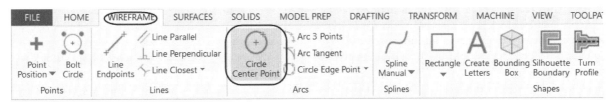

♦ Enter the **Diameter 0.25** in the panel as shown.
♦ To create all four circles, click on the locker icon to lock the value.

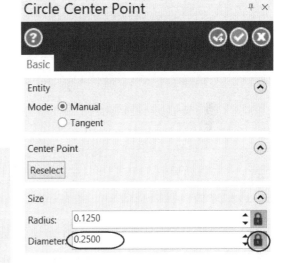

> **NOTE:** When entering the coordinates for the center point, the first value is the **X** coordinate value, then the **Y** value followed by the **Z** value only if it is different from zero. The coordinate values are separated with commas. You do not need to use the coordinate labels if you enter the values in this order.

♦ [Enter the center point]: Press **Space bar** from the keyboard and the field where you can type the coordinates will open at the upper left side of the graphics window as shown.

♦ Type **1, 1** as shown.

1,1

- Press **Enter** and the circle will be placed as shown.

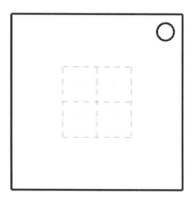

- [Enter the center point]: Press **Space bar** again and enter **1, -1**.
- Press **Enter** to place the circle.
- [Enter the center point]: Press **Space bar** again and enter **-1, 1**.
- Press **Enter** to place the circle.
- [Enter the center point]: Press **Space bar** again and enter **-1, -1**.
- Press **Enter** to place the circle.

- Once complete choose the **OK** button to exit the command.
- The geometry should look as shown.

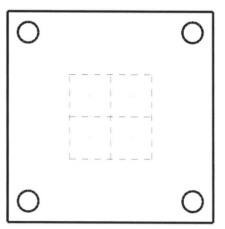

STEP 4: CREATE THE 2.0" AND 0.75" DIAMETER CIRCLES

In this step, you will use the same **Circle Center Point** to create circles that you know the diameters and the locations.

Step Preview:

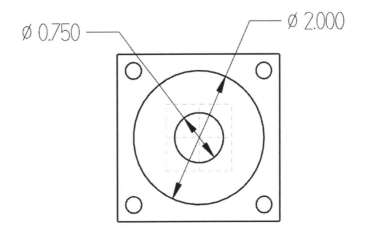

WIREFRAME

◆ From **Arcs** group, select **Circle Center Point.**

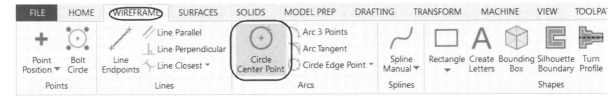

◆ Enter the **Diameter 0.75** in the panel and disable the locker icon as shown.
◆ Press **Enter** to see the circle preview.

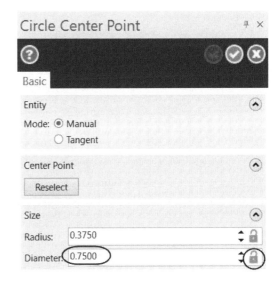

◆ [Enter the center point]: Move the cursor to the center of the rectangle until the cursor cue tip changes to the

Origin as shown.
◆ Click to select the **Origin**.

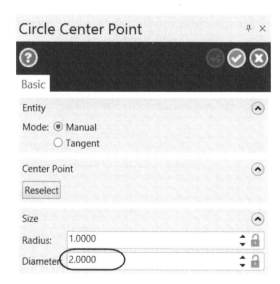

◆ Press **Enter** again to finish the circle.

> **NOTE:** While the circle is live, cyan color, the circle diameter and its location can be modified. To avoid this, you need to press **Enter** to finish the circle.

◆ In the **Circle Center Point** panel, in the **Diameter** field, type **2.0** and press **Enter**.
◆ The panel should look as shown.

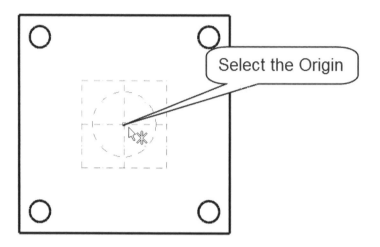

◆ [Enter the center point]: Select the **Origin** as shown.

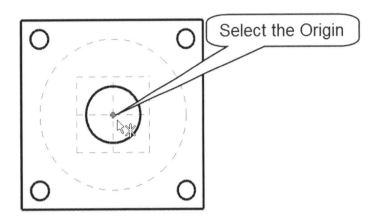

Select the Origin

NOTE: Because the center of the 0.75" diameter circle is in the **Origin**, you could also select the point when the cursor center cue tip appears as

shown.

◆ Once complete, choose the **OK** button to exit the command.
◆ The geometry should look as shown.

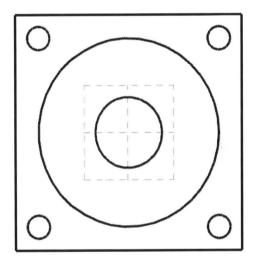

STEP 5: CREATE THE CHAMFERS

In this step, you will create 45 degree chamfers at the corner of the rectangles. You will use the **Chamfer Entities** command.

Step Preview:

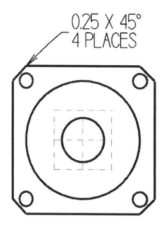

WIREFRAME

* From **Modify** group, select **Chamfer Entities**.

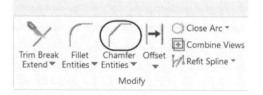

◆ In the **Chamfer Entities** panel, make sure that **1 Distance** and **Trim entities** are enabled and the **Distance** is set to **0.25** as shown.

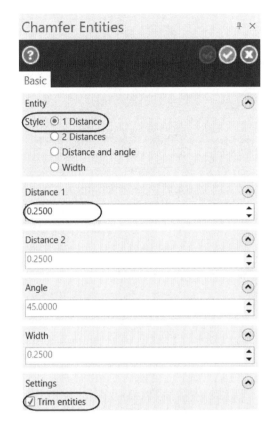

◆ Select the lines as shown.

NOTE: A preview of the chamfer should appear when you hover the cursor above the second line (Entity B).

◆ The geometry should look as shown.

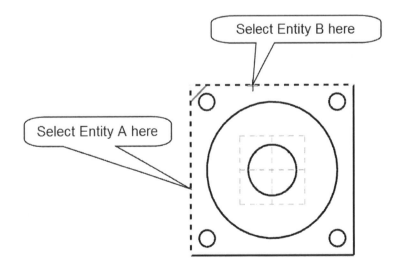

• The part will appear as shown.

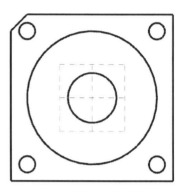

• Follow the same steps to chamfer the rest of the corners.
• The geometry should look as shown when completed.

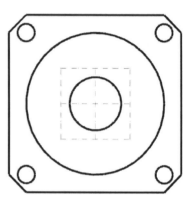

• Select the **OK** button to exit the command.

STEP 6: SAVE THE FILE

FILE
• **Save As.**

> **NOTE:** You can also click on the **Save As** icon from the **Quick Access Toolbar**.

• Click on the **Browse** icon as shown.
• Find a location on the computer to save your file. File name: "Your Name_1".

> **NOTE:** It is highly recommended to save the file from time to time when going through the tutorial.
> Click on the **Save** icon from the **Quick Access Toolbar** at the upper left corner to save the file.

TOOLPATH CREATION

SUGGESTED FIXTURE:

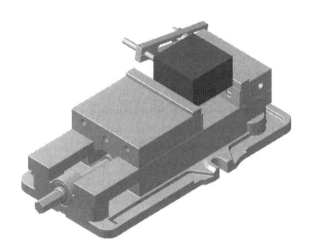

SETUP SHEET:

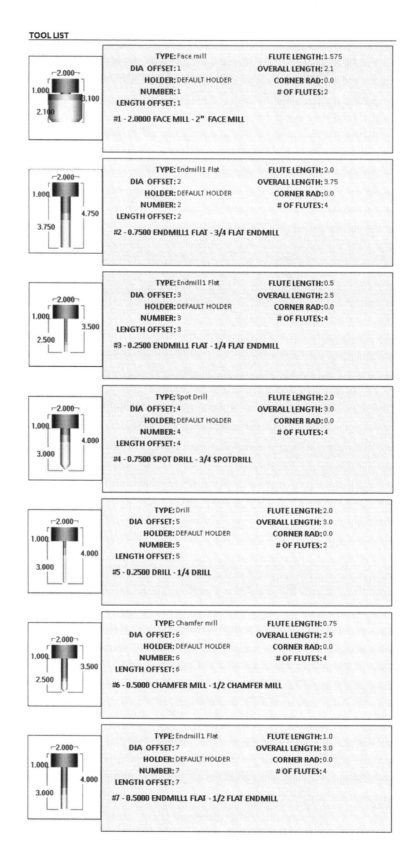

TOOL LIST

TYPE: Face mill | FLUTE LENGTH: 1.575
DIA OFFSET: 1 | OVERALL LENGTH: 2.1
HOLDER: DEFAULT HOLDER | CORNER RAD: 0.0
NUMBER: 1 | # OF FLUTES: 2
LENGTH OFFSET: 1

#1 - 2.0000 FACE MILL - 2" FACE MILL

TYPE: Endmill1 Flat | FLUTE LENGTH: 2.0
DIA OFFSET: 2 | OVERALL LENGTH: 3.75
HOLDER: DEFAULT HOLDER | CORNER RAD: 0.0
NUMBER: 2 | # OF FLUTES: 4
LENGTH OFFSET: 2

#2 - 0.7500 ENDMILL1 FLAT - 3/4 FLAT ENDMILL

TYPE: Endmill1 Flat | FLUTE LENGTH: 0.5
DIA OFFSET: 3 | OVERALL LENGTH: 2.5
HOLDER: DEFAULT HOLDER | CORNER RAD: 0.0
NUMBER: 3 | # OF FLUTES: 4
LENGTH OFFSET: 3

#3 - 0.2500 ENDMILL1 FLAT - 1/4 FLAT ENDMILL

TYPE: Spot Drill | FLUTE LENGTH: 2.0
DIA OFFSET: 4 | OVERALL LENGTH: 3.0
HOLDER: DEFAULT HOLDER | CORNER RAD: 0.0
NUMBER: 4 | # OF FLUTES: 4
LENGTH OFFSET: 4

#4 - 0.7500 SPOT DRILL - 3/4 SPOTDRILL

TYPE: Drill | FLUTE LENGTH: 2.0
DIA OFFSET: 5 | OVERALL LENGTH: 3.0
HOLDER: DEFAULT HOLDER | CORNER RAD: 0.0
NUMBER: 5 | # OF FLUTES: 2
LENGTH OFFSET: 5

#5 - 0.2500 DRILL - 1/4 DRILL

TYPE: Chamfer mill | FLUTE LENGTH: 0.75
DIA OFFSET: 6 | OVERALL LENGTH: 2.5
HOLDER: DEFAULT HOLDER | CORNER RAD: 0.0
NUMBER: 6 | # OF FLUTES: 4
LENGTH OFFSET: 6

#6 - 0.5000 CHAMFER MILL - 1/2 CHAMFER MILL

TYPE: Endmill1 Flat | FLUTE LENGTH: 1.0
DIA OFFSET: 7 | OVERALL LENGTH: 3.0
HOLDER: DEFAULT HOLDER | CORNER RAD: 0.0
NUMBER: 7 | # OF FLUTES: 4
LENGTH OFFSET: 7

#7 - 0.5000 ENDMILL1 FLAT - 1/2 FLAT ENDMILL

STEP 7: SELECT THE MACHINE AND SET UP THE STOCK

In Mastercam, you select a **Machine Definition** before creating any toolpath. The **Machine Definition** is a model of your machine's capabilities and features. It acts like a template for setting up your machine. The machine definition ties together three main components: the schematic model of your machine's components, the control definition that models your control capabilities, and the post processor that will generate the required machine code (G-code). For a Mill Level 1 exercise (2D toolpaths), we need just a basic machine definition.

> **NOTE:** For the purpose of this tutorial, we will be using the **Default Mill** machine.

7.1 Unhide the Toolpaths Manager panel

• From the left side of the graphics window, click on the **Toolpaths** tab as shown.

• Pin the **Toolpaths Manager** by clicking on the **Auto Hide** icon as shown.

7.2 Select the machine

MACHINE

• From the **Machine Type** group, select the drop down arrow below **Mill.**
• Select the **Default.**

> **NOTE:** Once you select the **Mill Default**, the **Ribbon bar** changes to reflect the toolpaths that could be used with **Mill Default**.

* Select the plus sign (+) in front of **Properties** in the **Toolpaths Manager** to expand the **Toolpaths Group Properties.**

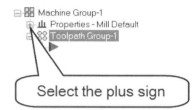

* Select **Tool settings** to set the tool parameters.

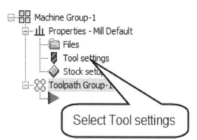

◆ Change the parameters to match the screen shot as shown.

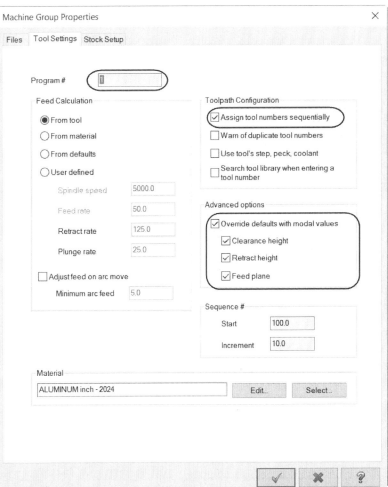

Program # is used to enter a number if your machine requires a number for a program name.

Assign tool numbers sequentially allows you to overwrite the tool number from the library with the next available tool number. (First operation tool number 1; second operation tool number 2, etc.).

Warn of duplicate tool numbers allows you to get a warning if you enter two tools with the same number.

Override defaults with modal values enables the system to keep the values that you enter.

Feed Calculation set to **From tool** uses feed rate, plunge rate, retract rate, and spindle speed from the tool definition.

◆ Select the **Stock Setup** tab to define the stock.
◆ Select the **All Entities** button near the bottom of the **Stock Setup** page as shown.

◆ In the **Stock Setup**, enter in the **Z** field **1.1** and the **Z Stock Origin 0.1**. Make sure that the rest of the parameters are as shown in Figure: 7.2.1.

Figure: 7.2.1

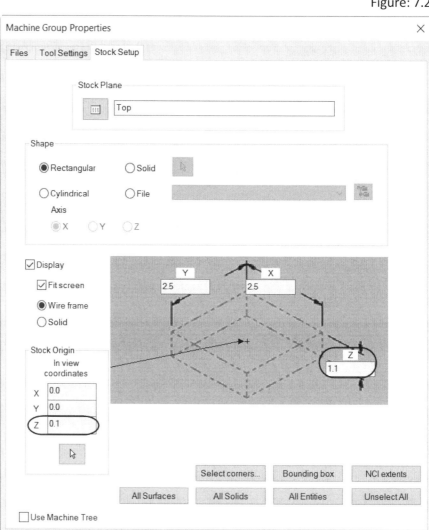

The X, Y, Z values in the graphics area are the dimensions of the stock model. They are always positive values.

The **Stock Origin** values adjust the positioning of the stock, ensuring that you have an equal amount of extra stock around the finished part. In the graphics, the plus sign (+) shows you where the stock origin is. The default position is the middle of the stock.

Display options allow you to set the stock as **Wireframe** and to fit the stock to the screen. (Fit Screen)

> **NOTE:** The **stock** model that you create can be displayed with the part geometry when viewing the file or the toolpaths, during backplot, or while verifying toolpaths.

+ Select the **OK** button to exit **Machine Group Properties**.
+ From the **VIEW** tab, select the **Isometric** view as shown.

+ From the same **VIEW** tab, select the **Fit** icon to fit the drawing to the screen.
+ The stock model will appear as shown.

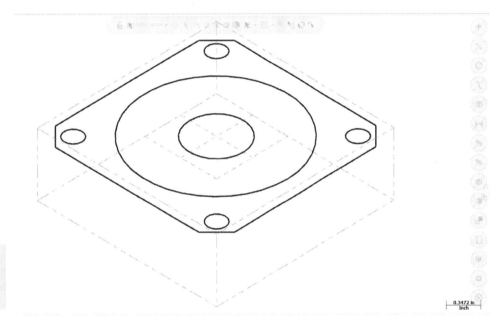

> **NOTE:** The stock is not geometry and cannot be selected.

+ Select the **Top** view from the **VIEW** tab and if needed, the **Fit** icon again to see the part from the top.

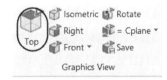

STEP 8: FACE THE PART

A **Facing** toolpath quickly removes material from the top of the part to create an even surface for future operations.

Toolpath Preview:

TOOLPATHS

◆ From the **2D** group, select **Face** as shown.

◆ If a prompt appears to ask you to **Enter new NC name**, select the **OK** button to accept the default.

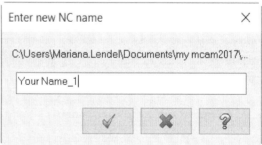

◆ When the chaining dialog box appears, choose the **OK** button to use the defined stock and exit the **Chaining** dialog box.

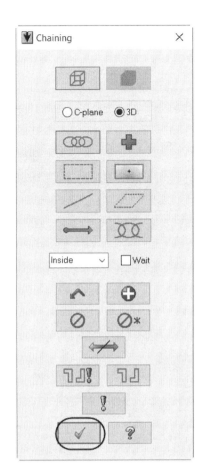

> **NOTE:** Mastercam will create the **Facing** toolpath defined from the stock setup.
>
> For more information on the **Chaining** button and **Options**, click on the
>
> **Help** button.

* In the **Toolpath Type** page, the **Facing** icon will be automatically selected.

Contour   Pocket   Facing   Slot Mill

> **NOTE:** Mastercam updates the pages as you modify them and then marks them, in the **Tree View list**, with a green check mark. Pages that are not enabled are marked with a red circle and slash.

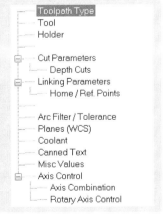

8.1 Select a 2.0" Face Mill from the library and set the Tool parameters

◆ Select **Tool** from the **Tree View list**.
◆ Click on the **Select library tool** button.

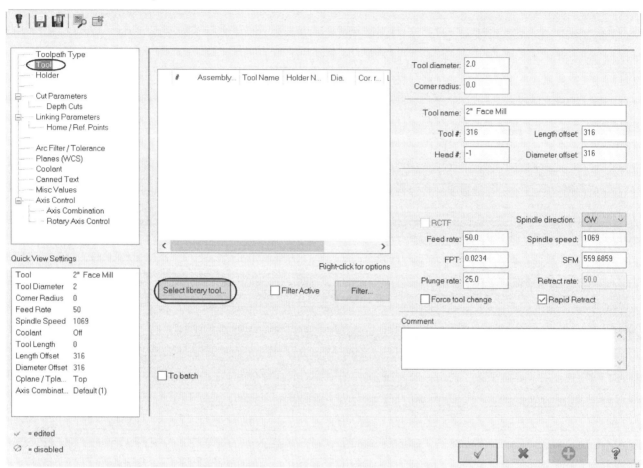

◆ To be able to see all of the tools from the library, disable **Filter Active**.

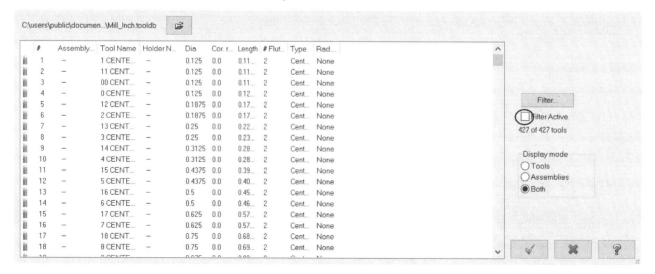

◆ Select the **2" Face Mill (#322)** as shown.

315	—	1 INCH B...	—	1.0	0.5	2.0	4	End...	Full
316	—	1-1/2 BAL...	—	1.5	0.75	2.75	4	End...	Full
317	—	2 INCH B...	—	2.0	1.0	2.75	4	End...	Full
318	—	1/4 CHA...	—	0.25-...	0.0	0.5	4	Cha...	None
319	—	1/2 CHA...	—	0.5-45	0.0	0.75	4	Cha...	None
320	—	3/4 CHA...	—	0.75-...	0.0	1.0	4	Cha...	None
321	—	1 INCH C...	—	1.0-45	0.0	1.0	4	Cha...	None
322	—	2" FACE	—	2.0	0.0	1.575	2	Fac...	None
323	—	2-1/2" FA...	—	2.5	0.0	1.575	4	Fac...	None

◆ Select the tool in the **Tool Selection** page and then select the **OK** button to exit.

◆ Input a comment and make all the necessary changes, as shown in Figure: 8.1.1.

Figure: 8.1.1

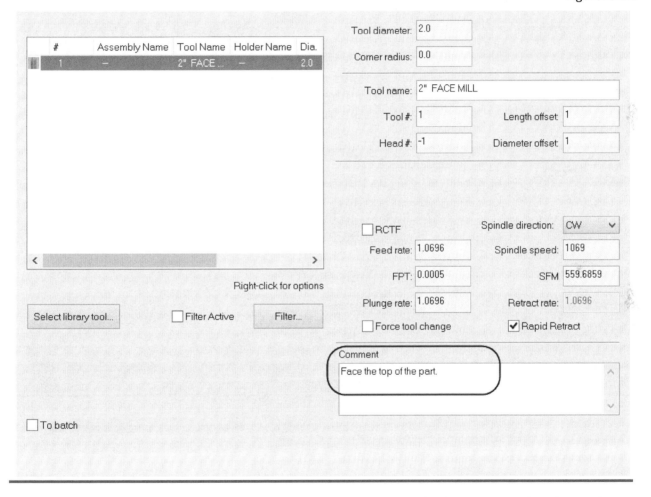

In the **Comment** field, enter a comment to help identify the toolpath in the **Toolpaths Manager** such as the one shown above.

NOTE: The **Feed rate, Plunge rate, Retract rate**, and **Spindle speed** are based on the tool definition as set in the **Tool Settings**. You may change these values as per your part material and tools.

NOTE: If by mistake you click the **OK** button, the toolpath will be generated without all the parameters set properly. To return and set the parameters, click on the **Parameters** in the **Toolpaths Manager** as shown below.

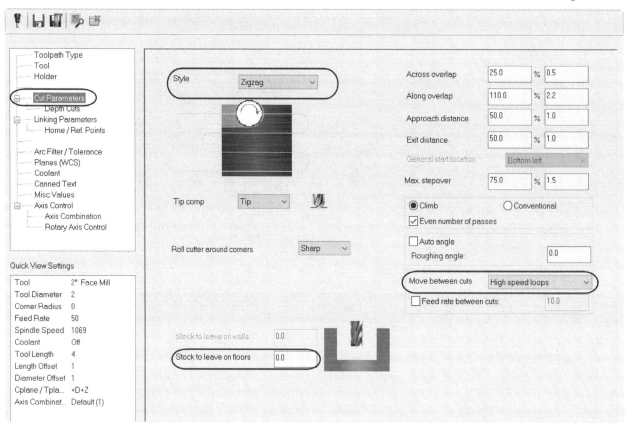

♦ Select **Cut Parameters** and make the necessary changes as shown in Figure: 8.1.2.

Figure: 8.1.2

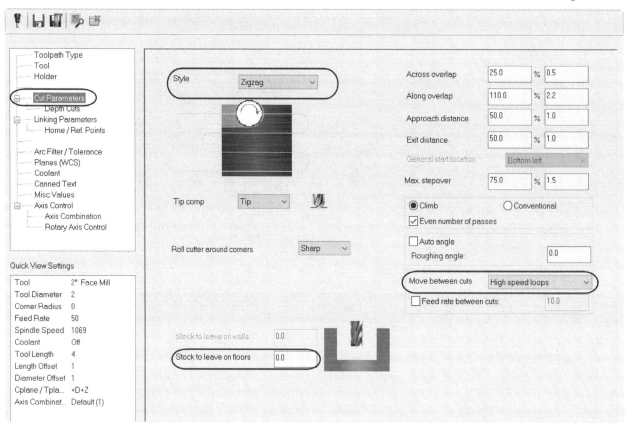

The **Style** (facing cutting method) **Zigzag** creates a back and forth cutting motion.

Move between cuts determines how the tool moves between each cut. This is only available if you select the zigzag cutting method.

High speed loops create 180 degree arcs between each cut.

◆ Select the **Linking Parameters** page and make the necessary changes as shown in <u>Figure: 8.1.3</u>.

Figure: 8.1.3

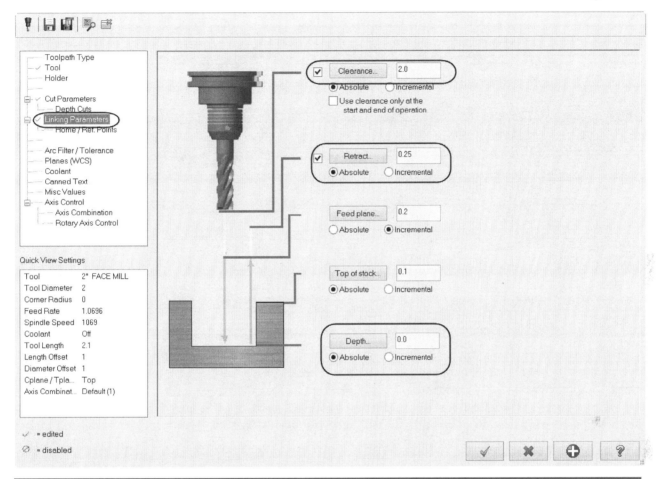

Clearance sets the height at which the tool moves to and from the part.

Retract sets the height to which the tool moves up before the next tool pass.

Feed plane sets the height to which the tool rapids before changing to the plunge rate to enter the part.

Top of stock sets the height of the material in the Z axis.

Depth determines the final machining depth that the tool descends into the stock.

NOTE: The **Top of stock** is set to **0.1"** because the **Stock Origin** was set to **0.1"** above the origin. The depth is set to **0.0"** because this is the finish depth. The majority of the values are set to absolute (measured from Z zero which is set at the top of the finished part). **Feed plane** set to incremental is measured from the **Top of stock**.

8.2 Preview the Toolpath

• To quickly check how the toolpath will be generated, select the **Preview toolpath** icon as shown.

• To hide the dialog box, click on the **Hide dialog** icon as shown.

• To see the part from an **Isometric** view, right mouse click in the graphics window and select **Isometric** as shown.

🔍	Zoom Window
🔍	Unzoom 80%
🔄	Dynamic Rotation
⛶	Fit
📦	Top (WCS)
📦	Front (WCS)
📦	Right (WCS)
📦	Isometric (WCS)
✏	Delete Entities
⌐?	Analyze Distance...
⌐?	Analyze Entity Properties...

• The toolpath should look as shown.

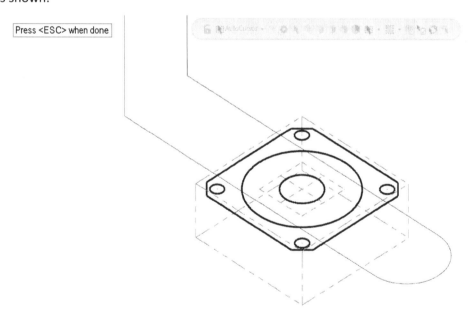

Press <ESC> when done

• Press **Esc** key to exit the preview.

NOTE: If the toolpath does not look as shown in the preview, check your parameters again.

• Select the **OK** button to exit the **Facing Parameters**.

NOTE: If you exit the toolpath in the middle of setting the parameters, in the **Toolpaths Manager**, you will have a red **X** on the **Face Toolpath** as shown in Figure: 8.2.1. This shows that you modified the toolpath and you need to update it. You will have to select the **Regenerate all dirty operations** icon each time you change something in the toolpath parameters.

Figure: 8.2.1

STEP 9: CIRCLE MILL THE LARGE HOLE

Circle Mill Toolpaths remove circular pockets based on a single point. You can select either point entities or center points of arcs. Mastercam will then pocket out a circular area of the diameter and to the depth that you specify.

Toolpath Preview:

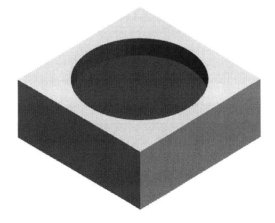

9.1 Drill Point Selection

♦ Press **Alt** + **T** to remove the toolpath display.

TOOLPATHS

♦ From the **2D** group, click on the drop down arrow until the **Circle Mill** toolpath appears as shown.
♦ Click on the **Circle Mill** icon.

♦ From the **Drill Point Selection**, click on **Entities.**

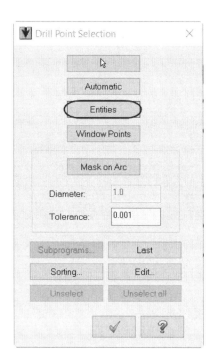

♦ Select the **2.0"** diameter circle as shown.

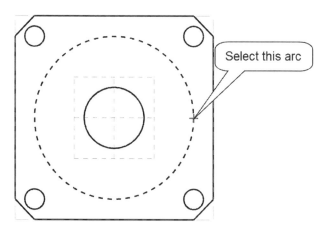

Select this arc

- Click on the **End Selection** button or press **Enter** to finish the selection.

- Select the **OK** button to exit **Drill Point Selection**.
- In the **Toolpath Type** page, the **Circle Mill** icon will be selected.

Drill   Circle Mill   Point   Helix Bore   Thread Mill

9.2 Select a 3/4" Flat Endmill from the library and set the Tool parameters

- Select **Tool** from the **Tree View list**.
- Click on **Select library tool** button.

- To be able to see all the tools from the library, disable **Filter Active**.

- Scroll down and select the **3/4" Flat Endmill (#294)** as shown.

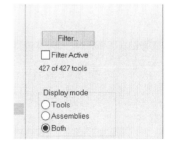

289	–	7/16 FLAT ENDMILL	–	0.4375	0.0	0.8	4	End...	None
290	–	1/2 FLAT ENDMILL	–	0.5	0.0	1.0	4	End...	None
291	–	17/32 FLAT ENDMILL	–	0.5312	0.0	1.0	4	End...	None
292	–	5/8 FLAT ENDMILL	–	0.625	0.0	1.5	4	End...	None
293	–	23/32 FLAT ENDMILL	–	0.71...	0.0	1.5	4	End...	None
294	–	3/4 FLAT ENDMILL	–	0.75	0.0	2.0	4	End...	None
295	–	13/16 FLAT ENDMILL	–	0.8125	0.0	2.0	4	End...	None
296	–	7/8 FLAT ENDMILL	–	0.875	0.0	2.0	4	End...	None
297	–	1 INCH FLAT ENDMILL	–	1.0	0.0	2.0	4	End...	None
298	–	1-3/16 FLAT ENDMILL	–	1.1875	0.0	2.0	4	End...	None
299	–	1-1/2 FLAT ENDMILL	–	1.5	0.0	2.5	4	End...	None
300	–	2 INCH FLAT ENDMILL	–	2.0	0.0	2.75	4	End...	None

- Select the tool in the **Tool Selection** page and then select the **OK** button to exit.

◆ Input a comment and make all the necessary changes, as shown in Figure: 9.2.1.

Figure: 9.2.1

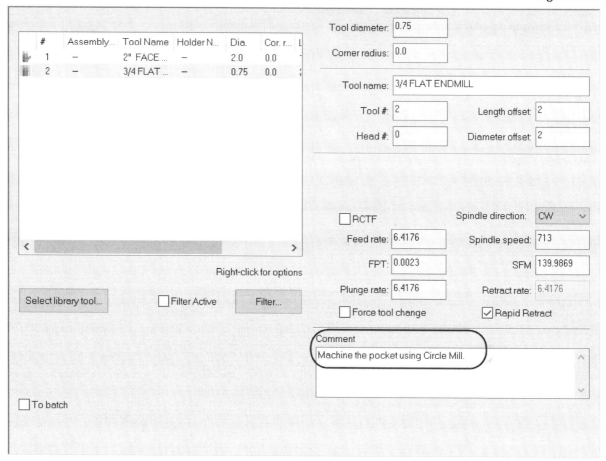

NOTE: The **Feed rate**, **Plunge rate**, **Retract rate**, and **Spindle speed** are based on the tool definition as set in the **Tool Settings**. You may change these values as per your part material and tools.

9.3 Cut Parameters

♦ From the **Tree View list**, select **Cut Parameters** and ensure the settings appear as shown in <u>Figure: 9.3.1</u>.

Figure: 9.3.1

Toolpath Type
Tool
Holder
— Cut Parameters
    ✓ Roughing
    ⊘ Finishing
        ⊘ Transitions
    Depth Cuts
    ⊘ Break Through
Linking Parameters
    Home / Ref. Points

Planes (WCS)
Coolant
Canned Text
Misc Values

Compensation type	Computer		Circle diameter	2.0
Compensation direction	Left			
Tip comp:	Tip		Start angle	90.0

| Stock to leave on walls | 0.0 |
| Stock to leave on floors | 0.0 |

Quick View Settings

Tool	3/4 FLAT ENDMILL
Tool Diameter	0.75
Corner Radius	0
Feed Rate	6.4176
Spindle Speed	713
Coolant	Off
Tool Length	3.75
Length Offset	2

9.4 Roughing

♦ From the **Tree View list**, select **Roughing** and enable it. Set the **Stepover** to **50%**, enable **Helical Entry**, and specify the other parameters as shown in <u>Figure: 9.4.1</u>.

Figure: 9.4.1

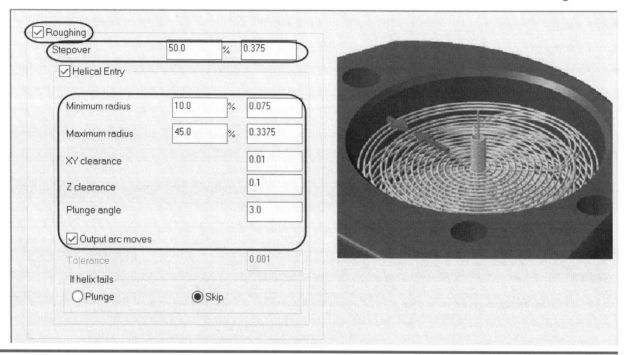

Stepover sets the distance between cutting passes in the X and Y axes as a percentage of the tool diameter.

Helical Entry creates a helix at the center of the circle to begin the roughing motion. If this option is turned off, the tool plunges to start the toolpath.

NOTE: The images in the toolpaths change depending on the parameter that you last selected in the page.

9.5 Depth Cuts

- From the **Tree View list**, select **Depth Cuts**. On the **Depth Cuts** page, enable **Depth cuts** and set the **Max rough step** to **0.5** and enable **Keep tool down**.
- Make any necessary change as shown in <u>Figure: 9.5.1</u>.

Figure: 9.5.1

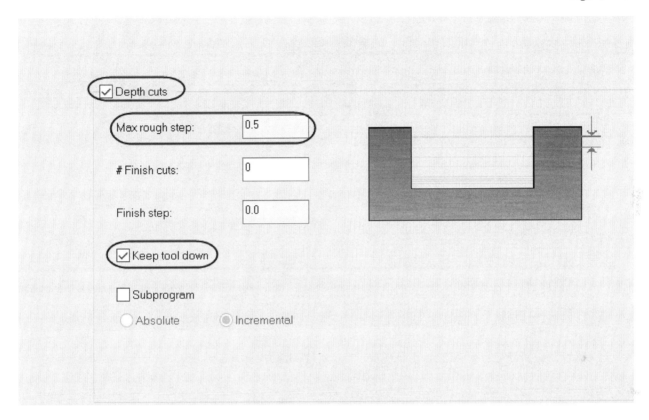

Depth Cuts sets the steps the tool takes along the **Z axis.** Mastercam will take the total depth and divide it into separate depth cuts. Mastercam never performs unequal depth cuts.

Max rough step sets the maximum amount of material removed in the Z axis with each rough cut. Mastercam will calculate equal rough cuts no larger than the maximum rough step until it reaches the final Z depth.

Keep tool down determines whether or not to retract the tool between depth cuts.

9.6 Linking Parameters

- ◆ Select **Linking Parameters** from the **Tree View list**.
- ◆ Change the **Top of stock** to **0.0** and set the **Depth** to **-0.25.** Ensure all the values are set the same as shown in Figure: 9.6.1.

Figure: 9.6.1

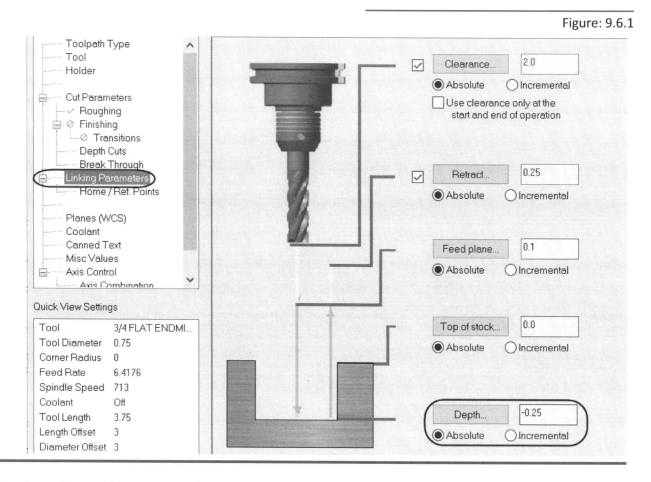

Absolute values are always measured from the origin 0,0,0.

Incremental values are relative to other parameters or chained geometry.

9.7 Preview the Toolpath

◆ To quickly check how the toolpath will be generated, select the **Preview toolpath** icon as shown.

◆ To hide the dialog box, click on the **Hide dialog** icon as shown.
◆ To see the part from an **Isometric** view, right mouse click in the graphics window and select **Isometric** as shown.

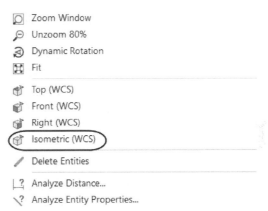

◆ The toolpath should look as shown.

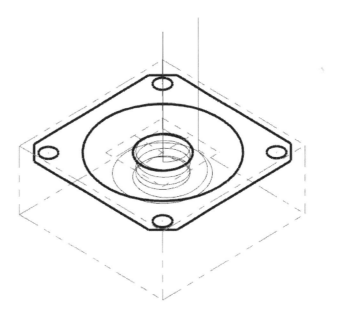

◆ Press **Esc** key to exit the preview.

> **NOTE:** If the toolpath does not look as shown in the preview, check your parameters again.

◆ Select the **OK** button to exit the **Circle Mill** parameters.

STEP 10: BACKPLOT THE TOOLPATHS

Backplotting shows the path the tools take to cut the part. This display lets you spot errors in the program before you machine the part. As you backplot toolpaths, Mastercam displays additional information such as the X, Y, and Z coordinates, the path length, the minimum and maximum coordinates, and the cycle time.

* Make sure that the toolpaths are selected (signified by the green check mark on the folder icon). If both operations are not selected, choose the **Select all operations** icon.

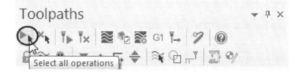

* Select the **Backplot selected operations** button.

* In the **Backplot** panel, enable **Display with color codes**, **Display tool** and **Display rapid moves** icons as shown.

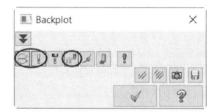

* To see the part from an **Isometric** view, right mouse click in the graphics window and select **Isometric** as shown.

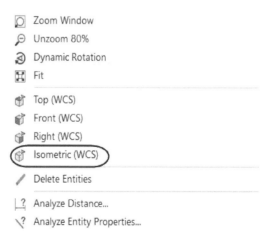

* To fit the workpiece to the screen, if needed, right mouse click in the graphics window again and select the **Fit**.

* You can step through the **Backplot** by using the **Step forward** ▶▶ or **Step back** ◀◀ buttons.

* You can adjust the speed of the backplot.

Mill Essentials Training Tutorial *Mastercam.* 2017

◆ Select the **Play** button to run **Backplot**.
◆ The toolpath should look as shown in Figure: 10.0.1.

Figure: 10.0.1

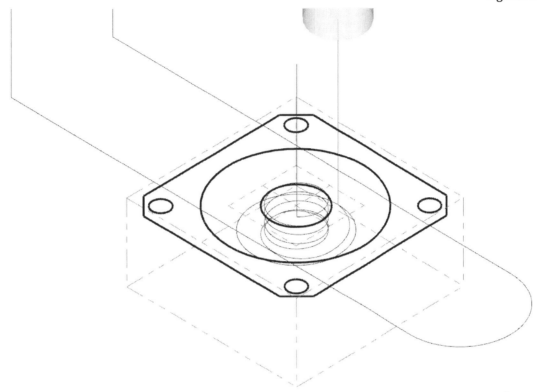

◆ Select the **OK** button to exit **Backplot**.

STEP 11: SIMULATE THE TOOLPATH IN VERIFY

Verify Mode shows the path the tools take to cut the part with material removal. This display lets you spot errors in the program before you machine the part. As you verify toolpaths, Mastercam displays additional information such as the X, Y, and Z coordinates, the path length, the minimum and maximum coordinates, and the cycle time. It also shows any collision between the workpiece and the tool.

- From the **Toolpaths Manager**, select **Verify selected operations** icon as shown.

> **NOTE:** Mastercam launches a new window that allows you to check the part using **Backplot** or **Verify.**

- In **Mastercam Simulator**, **Verify** should be enabled and change the settings as shown.

- Select the **Play** button to run **Verify.**
- The part should appear as shown in Figure: 11.0.1.

Figure: 11.0.1

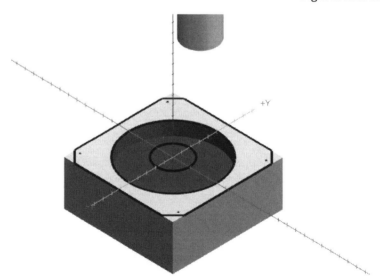

> **NOTE:** To rotate the part, move the cursor to the center of the part and click and hold the mouse wheel and slowly move it in one direction.
>
> To zoom in or out, hold down the mouse wheel and scroll up or down as needed.

◆ Right mouse click in the graphics window and select **Isometric**. Then right mouse click again and select **Fit** to see the part in the original position.

◆ To check the part step-by-step, click first on the **Reset simulation** icon.

◆ Click on the **Step Forward** to see the tool moving one step at a time.

◆ The part should look as shown after several steps.

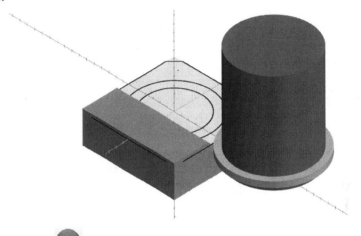

◆ Click on the **Step Forward** until the toolpath is completed.

◆ To go back to Mastercam window, minimize **Mastercam Simulator** window as shown.

STEP 12: CIRCLE MILL THE INSIDE HOLE

Circle Mill Toolpaths remove circular pockets based on a single point. You can select either point entities or center points of arcs. Mastercam will then pocket out a circular area of the diameter and to the depth that you specify.

Toolpath Preview:

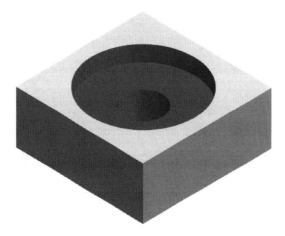

12.1 Drill Point Selection

• Hover the cursor in the **Toolpaths Manager** and press **T** to remove the toolpath display.

TOOLPATHS

• From the **2D** group, click on the **Circle Mill** icon.

• From the **Drill Point Selection**, click on **Entities.**

Mill Essentials Training Tutorial   *Mastercam*.2017

◆ Select the **0.75"** diameter circle as shown.

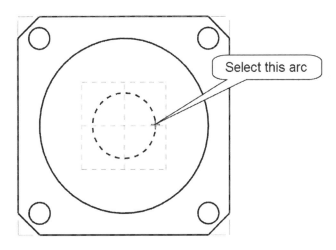

Select this arc

◆ Click on the **End Selection** button or press **Enter** to finish the selection. End Selection

◆ Select the **OK** button to exit **Drill Point Selection**. ✓

◆ In the **Toolpath Type** page, the **Circle Mill** icon will be selected.

Drill   Circle Mill   Point   Helix Bore   Thread Mill

12.2 Select a 1/4" Flat Endmill from the library and set the Tool parameters

◆ Select **Tool** from the **Tree View list**.

◆ Click on **Select library tool** button. Select library tool...

◆ To be able to see all the tools from the library, disable **Filter Active**.

Filter...

☐ Filter Active

427 of 427 tools

◆ Scroll down and select the **1/4" Flat Endmill (#285)** as shown.

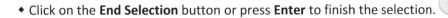

	278	–	1 INCH COUNTERSINK ...	–	1.0	0.0	2.0	2	CSink	None
	279	–	1/32 FLAT ENDMILL	–	0.03...	0.0	0.375	4	End...	None
	280	–	1/16 FLAT ENDMILL	–	0.0625	0.0	0.375	4	End...	None
	281	–	3/32 FLAT ENDMILL	–	0.09...	0.0	0.375	4	End...	None
	282	–	1/8 FLAT ENDMILL	–	0.125	0.0	0.375	4	End...	None
	283	–	5/32 FLAT ENDMILL	–	0.15...	0.0	0.375	4	End...	None
	284	–	3/16 FLAT ENDMILL	–	0.1875	0.0	0.4375	4	End...	None
	285	–	1/4 FLAT ENDMILL	–	0.25	0.0	0.5	4	End...	None
	286	–	5/16 FLAT ENDMILL	–	0.3125	0.0	0.75	4	End...	None
	287	–	3/8 FLAT ENDMILL	–	0.375	0.0	0.75	4	End...	None

Filter...

☐ Filter Active
427 of 427 tools

Display mode
○ Tools
○ Assemblies

◆ Select the tool in the **Tool Selection** page and then select the **OK** button to exit. ✓

• Input a comment and make all the necessary changes, as shown in Figure: 12.2.1.

Figure: 12.2.1

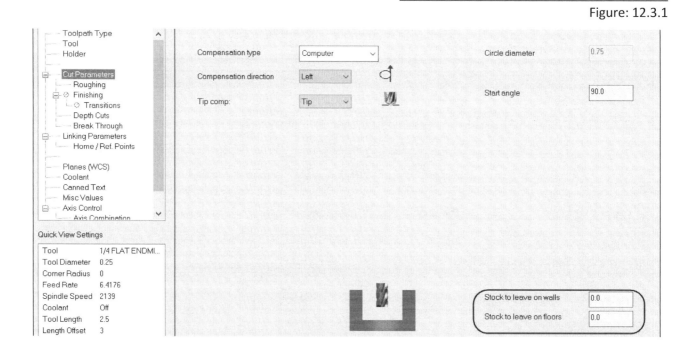

12.3 Cut Parameters

• From the **Tree View list**, select **Cut Parameters** and ensure the settings appear as shown in Figure: 12.3.1.

Figure: 12.3.1

12.4 Roughing

• From the **Tree View list**, select **Roughing** and enable it. Set the **Stepover** to **50%**, enable **Helical Entry**, and specify the other parameters as shown in Figure: 12.4.1.

Figure: 12.4.1

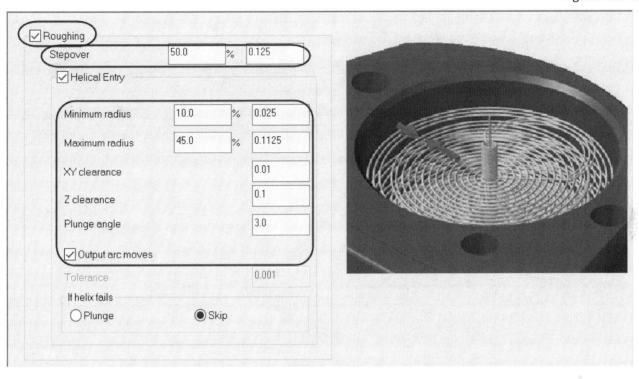

Stepover sets the distance between cutting passes in the X and Y axes as a percentage of the tool diameter.

Helical Entry creates a helix at the center of the circle to begin the roughing motion. If this option is turned off, the tool plunges to start the toolpath.

NOTE: The images in the toolpaths change depending on the parameter that you last selected in the page.

12.5 Depth Cuts

♦ Make any necessary change as shown in <u>Figure: 12.5.1</u>.

Figure: 12.5.1

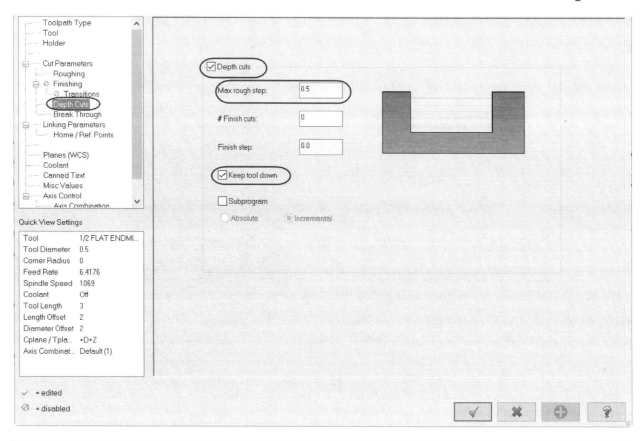

Depth Cuts sets the steps the tool takes along the **Z axis.** Mastercam will take the total depth and divide it into separate depth cuts. Mastercam never performs unequal depth cuts.

Max rough step sets the maximum amount of material removed in the Z axis with each rough cut. Mastercam will calculate equal rough cuts no larger than the maximum rough step until it reaches the final Z depth.

Keep tool down determines whether or not to retract the tool between depth cuts.

12.6 Set the Break Through

◆ From the **Tree View list**, select **Break Through** and set the parameters to completely cut through the material by an amount that you specify as shown in Figure: 12.6.1.

Figure: 12.6.1

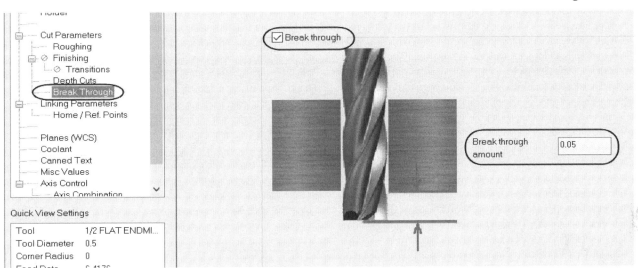

12.7 Linking Parameters

- ◆ Select **Linking Parameters** from the **Tree View list**.
- ◆ Change the **Top of stock** to **-0.25** and set the **Depth** to **-1.0**. Ensure all the values are set the same as shown in <u>Figure: 12.7.1</u>.

Figure: 12.7.1

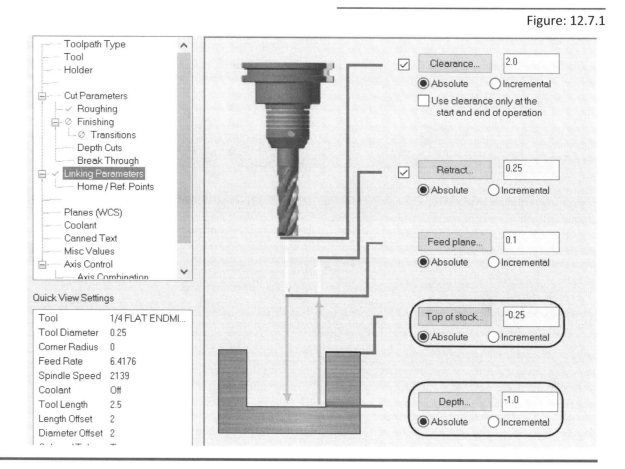

Absolute values are always measured from the origin 0,0,0.

Incremental values are relative to other parameters or chained geometry.

12.8 Preview the Toolpath

♦ Select the **Preview toolpath** icon as shown.

♦ Click on the **Hide dialog** icon as shown.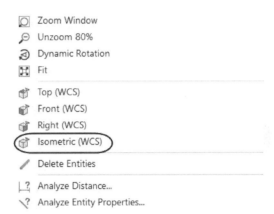

♦ To see the part from an **Isometric** view, right mouse click in the graphics window and select **Isometric** as shown.

    ⌑ Zoom Window
    🔍 Unzoom 80%
    🔄 Dynamic Rotation
    ▦ Fit

    📦 Top (WCS)
    📦 Front (WCS)
    📦 Right (WCS)
    📦 Isometric (WCS)

    ✎ Delete Entities

    ⌊? Analyze Distance...
    ↘? Analyze Entity Properties...

♦ The toolpath should look as shown.

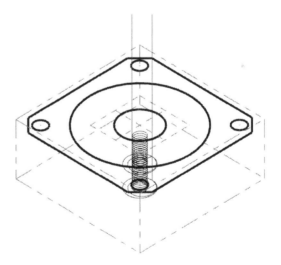

♦ Press **Esc** key to exit the preview.

NOTE: If the toolpath does not look as shown in the preview, check your parameters again.

♦ Select the **OK** button to exit the **Circle Mill** parameters.

12.9 Verify the Toolpaths

◆ From the **Toolpaths Manager**, click on the **Select all operations** icon.

◆ Click on the **Verify selected operation** icon.

◆ For information on how to set the **Verify** parameters and how to simulate the toolpath, please check **page 52**.

◆ Disable **Wireframe** as shown.

◆ Select the **Play** button as shown.

◆ The part will appear as shown in Figure: 15.10.1.

Figure: 12.9.1

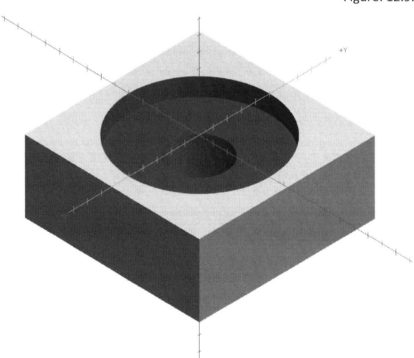

◆ To go back to Mastercam window, minimize **Mastercam Simulator** window as shown.

STEP 13: SPOT DRILL THE 0.25" HOLES

Spot Drilling the holes allows you to start the hole. In this operation, we will use the spot drill to chamfer the hole before drilling it.

Toolpath Preview:

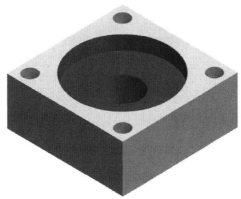

* Select all toolpaths and press **T** to remove the toolpath display if needed.

TOOLPATHS
* In the **2D** group, select the **Drill** icon as shown.

* In the **Drill Point Selection** panel, choose the option **Mask on Arc**.

> **NOTE: Mask on Arc** is a tool for selecting arcs whose diameters match the one that you select within a specified tolerance.

♦ Hover the cursor above the center of the geometry and scroll down the mouse wheel to unzoom the geometry as shown in Figure: 13.0.1.
♦ Select one of the four arcs as shown in Figure: 13.0.1.
♦ Left click in the upper left corner of the graphics window, hold the left button down and drag a rectangle to the lower right corner of the part to include all entities, as shown in Figure: 13.0.1.

Figure: 13.0.1

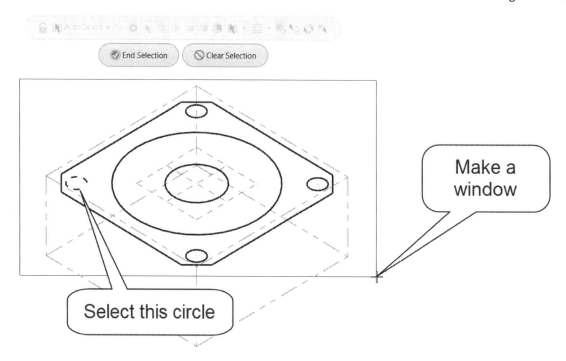

Make a window

Select this circle

♦ Release the left mouse button and click it again once you have created a window encompassing the entire part.

NOTE: All the arcs inside of the window will be selected. Once you hit the **Enter** key or **End Selection** button, only the circles with the same diameter as the original selected circle will be selected.

♦ Click on the **End Selection** button or press **Enter** to finish the selection.

♦ Select the **OK** button in the **Drill Point Selection** panel to accept the 4 drill points.
♦ In the **Toolpath Type** page, the **Drill** toolpath should already be selected.

Drill Circle Mill Point Helix Bore Thread Mill

13.1 Select a 3/4" Spot Drill from the library and set the Tool Parameters

◆ Select **Tool** from the **Tree View list**.

◆ Click on the **Select library tool** button. Select library tool...
◆ To view only the spot drill, select the **Filter** button.

◆ Under **Tool Types,** select the **None** button to unselect any unwanted tool.
◆ Hover the cursor over each icon and the tool type will be displayed; choose the **Spot Drill** icon as shown in Figure: 13.1.1.

Figure: 13.1.1

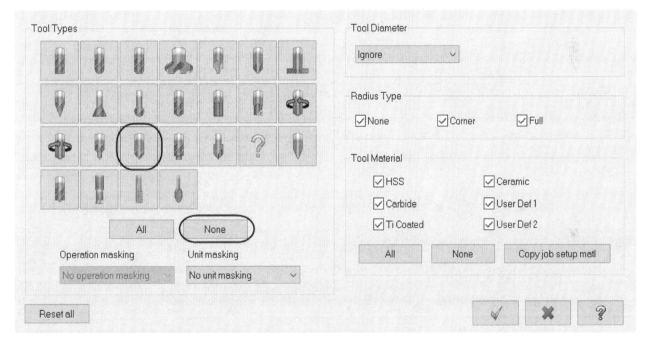

◆ Select the **OK** button to exit the **Tool List Filter** panel.
◆ At this point you should only see **Spot Drills**.
◆ From that list select the **3/4" Spot Drill** as shown.

#	Assembly...	Tool Name	Holder N...	Dia.	Cor. r...	Length	# Flut...	Type	Rad....
21	–	1/8 SPOT...	–	0.125	0.0	2.0	2	Spot...	None
22	–	1/4 SPOT...	–	0.25	0.0	2.0	2	Spot...	None
23	–	3/8 SPOT...	–	0.375	0.0	2.0	4	Spot...	None
24	–	1/2 SPOT...	–	0.5	0.0	2.0	2	Spot...	None
25	–	3/4 SPOT...	–	0.75	0.0	2.0	4	Spot...	None
26	–	1. SPOT...	–	1.0	0.0	2.0	4	Spot...	None

◆ Select the tool in the **Tool Selection** page and then select the **OK** button to exit.

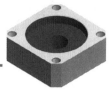

◆ Input a comment and make the necessary changes to the **Tool** page as shown in Figure: 13.1.2.

Figure: 13.1.2

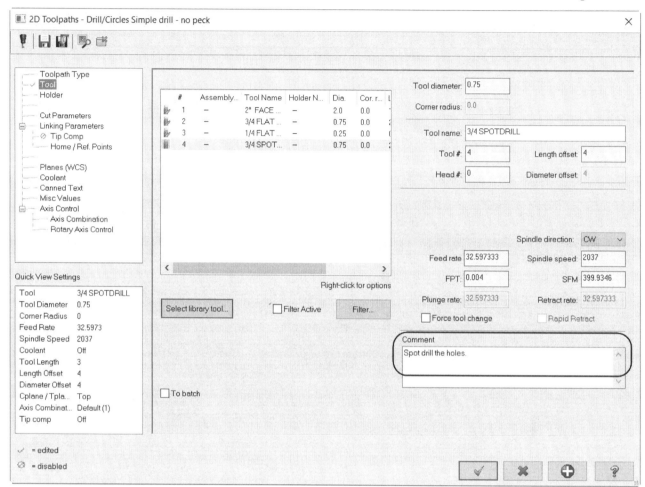

Mill Essentials Training Tutorial
*Mastercam.*2017

13.2 Set the Cut Parameters

◆ Select **Cut Parameters** and make sure the parameters are set as shown in Figure: 13.2.1.

Figure: 13.2.1

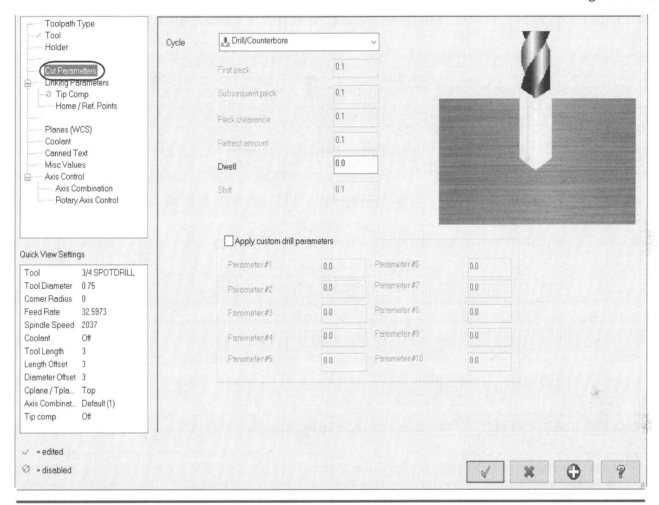

Drill/Counterbore is recommended for drilling holes with depths of less than three times the tool's diameter.

Dwell sets the amount of time in seconds that the tool remains at the bottom of a drilled hole.

13.3 Linking Parameters

♦ Choose **Linking Parameters** and ensure **Clearance** is enabled. Set the **Top of stock** and the **Depth** to **Absolute** and **0.0** as shown.
♦ Select the **Calculator** icon on the right hand side of the **Depth** icon as shown.

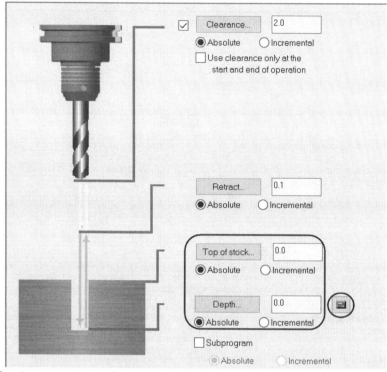

♦ To generate a **0.025** chamfer, input the following equation in the **Finish diameter** area: **0.25 + 0.05** (diameter of the finished hole + 2 X the chamfer size) and hit **Enter** to calculate the **Depth**, as shown in Figure: 13.3.1. Make sure that **Add to depth** is enabled.

Figure: 13.3.1

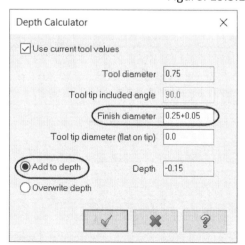

♦ Select the **OK** button to exit the **Depth Calculator**.

♦ You will now see the **Depth** for this spot drilling operation is updated after we specify the finish diameters of the holes including the chamfer. Change the rest of the parameters as shown in <u>Figure: 13.3.2</u>.

Figure: 13.3.2

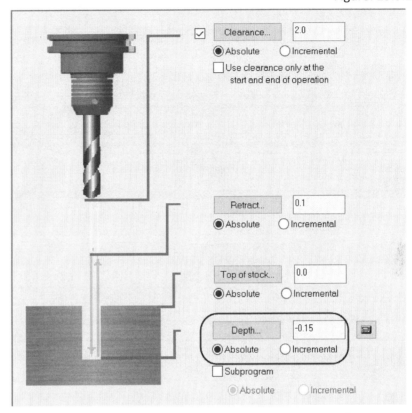

13.4 Preview the Toolpath

♦ To quickly check how the toolpath will be generated, select the **Preview toolpath** icon as shown.

♦ See **page 40** to review the procedure.

◆ The toolpath should look as shown.

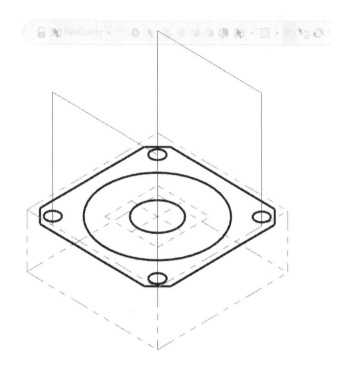

◆ Press **Esc** key to exit the preview.

> **NOTE:** If the toolpath does not look as shown in the preview, check your parameters again.

◆ Select the **OK** button to exit the toolpath parameters.

13.5 Verify the toolpaths

◆ From the **Toolpaths Manager**, click on the **Select all operations** icon.

◆ Click on the **Verify selected operation** icon.
◆ See **page 52** to review the procedure.

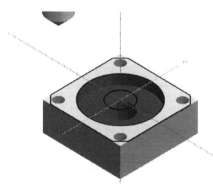

◆ To go back to the Mastercam window, minimize the Mastercam Simulator window as shown.

STEP 14: DRILL THE 0.25"HOLES

In this step, we will drill the holes to a specified depth.

Toolpath Preview:

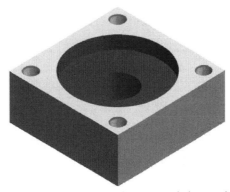

♦ Move the cursor in the **Toolpaths Manager** and press **Alt + T** until the toolpath display is removed.

TOOLPATHS

♦ From the **2D** group, select **Drill**.

♦ In the **Drill Point Selection** panel, choose the option **Last**.

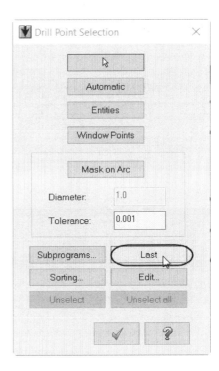

◆ This option will automatically select the 4 holes from the previous drill operation.

◆ Select the **OK** button in the **Drill Point Selection** panel to accept the 4 drill points.

◆ In the **Toolpath Type** page, the **Drill** toolpath will be selected as shown in <u>Figure: 14.0.1</u>.

Figure: 14.0.1

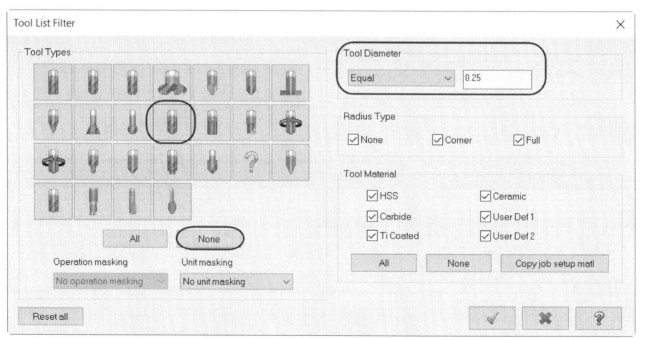

14.1 Select a 1/4" Drill from the library and set the Tool Parameters

◆ Select **Tool** from the **Tree View list**.

◆ Click on the **Select library tool** button. `Select library tool...`

◆ To view only the drill tools, select the **Filter** button.

◆ Under **Tool Types**, select the **None** button and then choose the **Drill** icon. Under **Tool Diameter** section, select **Equal** and input a value of **0.25.**

◆ Select the **OK** button to exit the **Tool List Filter** panel.

◆ At this point you should see a **1/4" Drill**.

#	Assembly...	Tool Name	Holder N...	Dia.	Cor. r...	Length	# Flut...	Type	Rad...
124	–	1/4 DRILL	–	0.25	0.0	2.0	2	Drill	None

◆ Select the tool in the **Tool Selection** page and then choose the **OK** button to exit.
◆ Make the necessary changes to the **Tool** page as shown in Figure: 14.1.1.

Figure: 14.1.1

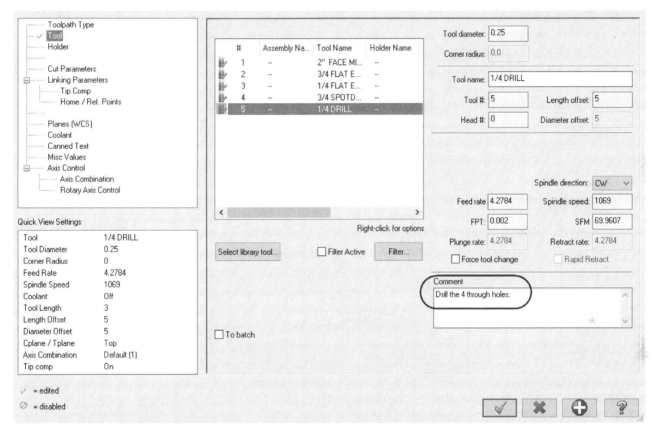

14.2 Cut Parameters

• Select **Cut Parameters** and change the drill **Cycle** to **Drill/Counterbore** as shown in <u>Figure: 14.2.1</u>.

Figure: 14.2.1

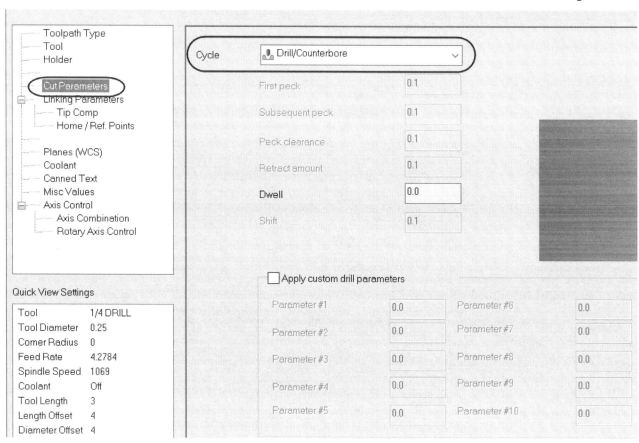

14.3 Linking Parameters

♦ Choose **Linking Parameters** and set the **Top of stock** to **0.0**. Input a **Depth** value of **-1.0** as shown in
Figure: 14.3.1.

Figure: 14.3.1

Toolpath Type
Tool
Holder

Cut Parameters
Linking Parameters
Tip Comp
Home / Ref. Points

Planes (WCS)
Coolant
Canned Text
Misc Values
Axis Control
Axis Combination
Rotary Axis Control

Quick View Settings

Tool	1/4 DRILL
Tool Diameter	0.25
Corner Radius	0
Feed Rate	4.2784
Spindle Speed	1069
Coolant	Off
Tool Length	3
Length Offset	4
Diameter Offset	4
Cplane / Tpla...	Top

☑ Clearance... 2.0
● Absolute ○ Incremental
☐ Use clearance only at the
start and end of operation

Retract... 0.1
● Absolute ○ Incremental

Top of stock... 0.0
● Absolute ○ Incremental

Depth... -1.0
● Absolute ○ Incremental

☐ Subprogram
● Absolute ○ Incremental

14.4 Set the Tip Compensation

◆ Select **Tip Comp** and enable it.
◆ Set the **Breakthrough amount** to **0.05** as shown in Figure: 14.4.1.

Figure: 14.4.1

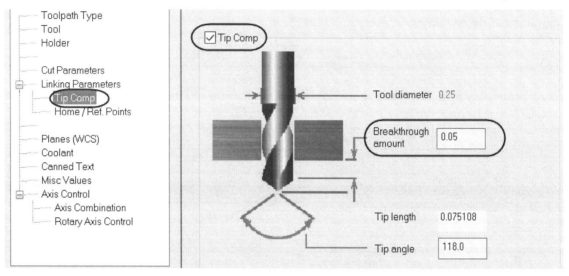

14.5 Preview the Toolpath

◆ To quickly check how the toolpath will be generated, select the **Preview toolpath** icon as shown.

◆ See **page 40** to review the procedure.
◆ Use the mouse wheel to slightly rotate the part.

♦ The toolpath should look as shown.

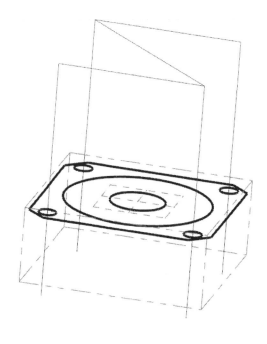

♦ Press **Esc** key to exit the preview.

> **NOTE:** If the toolpath does not look as shown in the preview, check your parameters again.

♦ Select the **OK** button to exit the **2D Toolpaths - Drill/Circles Simple drill - no peck** parameters.

14.6 Verify the toolpaths

♦ From the **Toolpaths Manager**, click on the **Select all operations** icon.

♦ Click on the **Verify selected operation** icon.
♦ To **Verify** the toolpaths, see **page 52** to review the procedure.

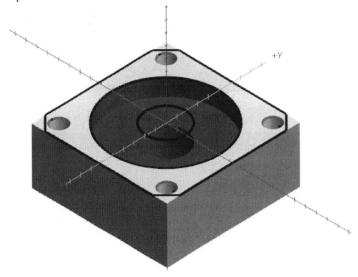

♦ To rotate the part, click in the center of the part with the mouse wheel. Hold down the mouse wheel and slightly drag the cursor to rotate.

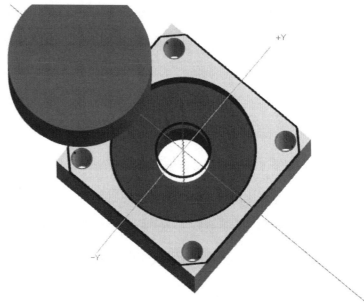

♦ To go back to the Mastercam window, minimize the **Mastercam Simulator** window as shown.

STEP 15: CHAMFER THE LARGE HOLE

Chamfer Toolpath automatically cuts a chamfer around a contour using a chamfer mill.

Toolpath Preview:

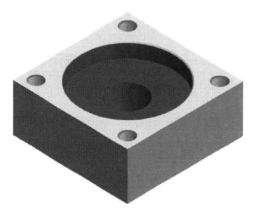

15.1 Chain selection

A **chain of entities** consists of one or more entities linked together in order and direction. The distance between the endpoints of two consecutive entities of the chain has to be equal or less than the chaining tolerance (0.0001"). In an open chain, the start point is placed at the end of the chain closest to the selection point and the chain direction points to the opposite end of the chain. See **Help** for more information on chaining.

♦ Hover the cursor in the **Toolpaths Managers** and press **T** to remove the toolpath display.

TOOLPATHS
♦ From the **2D** group, click on the upper arrow until the **Contour** toolpath appears as shown.
♦ Click on the **Contour** icon.

♦ Leave the default settings in the **Chaining** dialog box as shown.

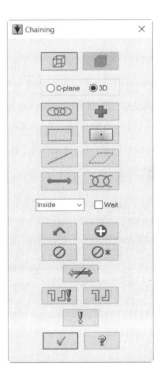

NOTE: The **Chain** button ⬭⬭⬭ is enabled in the **Chaining** dialog box. This lets you chain the entire contour by clicking on one entity.

• Select the chain and ensure the chaining direction is the same as shown in <u>Figure: 15.1.1</u>.

Figure: 15.1.1

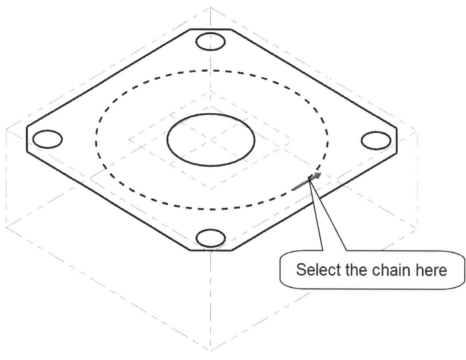

Select the chain here

• Select the **OK** button to exit the **Chaining** dialog box.
• In the **Toolpath Type** page, the **Contour** toolpath should already be selected.

Contour   Pocket   Facing   Slot Mill

15.2 Select a 1/2" Chamfer Mill from the library and set the Tool parameters

• Select **Tool** from the **Tree View list**.

• Click on the **Select library tool** button. Select library tool...
• To be able to see just the spot drill, select the **Filter** button.

Filter...

☑ Filter Active

427 of 427 tools

- Under **Tool Types,** select the **None** button and then choose the **Chamfer mill** Icon.

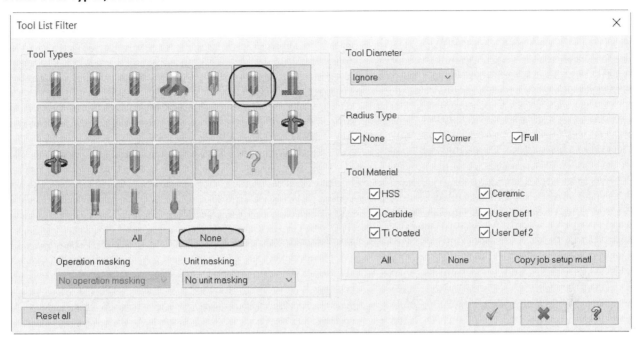

- Select the **OK** button to exit the **Tool List Filter** panel.
- At this point you should only see a list of chamfer mills.
- From the **Tool Selection** list, select the **1/2" Chamfer Mill**.

#	Assembly Name	Tool Name	Holder Name	Dia.	Cor. rad.	Length	# Flutes	Type	Ra...
318	–	1/4 CHA...	–	0....	0.0	0.5	4	Ch...	No...
319	–	1/2 CHA...	–	0....	0.0	0.75	4	Ch...	No...
320	–	3/4 CHA...	–	0....	0.0	1.0	4	Ch...	No...
321	–	1 INCH C...	–	1....	0.0	1.0	4	Ch...	No...

- In the **Tool Selection** page, choose the **OK** button to exit.
- A warning message might appear on the screen telling that the tool selected is not defined as being capable of both roughing and finishing.

NOTE: The chamfer mill is defined for finish operation only. For chamfer toolpath, we only need a finish operation.

- Select the **OK** button to continue.

15.3 Select the 1/2" Chamfer Mill from the list and set the Tool Parameters

◆ Select **Tool** from the **Tree View list**.

◆ Input a comment and make the necessary changes as shown in Figure: 15.3.1.

Figure: 15.3.1

Tree View	Tool Table	Parameters

Tree View:
- Toolpath Type
- Tool
- Holder
- Cut Parameters
  - ⊘ Depth Cuts
  - Lead In/Out
  - ⊘ Break Through
  - ⊘ Multi Passes
  - ⊞ ⊘ Tabs
- Linking Parameters
  - Home / Ref. Points
- Arc Filter / Tolerance
- Planes (WCS)
- Coolant
- Canned Text
- Misc Values
- ⊞ Axis Control

Tool Table:

#	Assembly...	Tool Name	Holder N...	Dia.	Cor. r...	L
1	–	2" FACE ...	–	2.0	0.0	
2	–	3/4 FLAT ...	–	0.75	0.0	
3	–	1/4 FLAT ...	–	0.25	0.0	
4	–	3/4 SPOT...	–	0.75	0.0	
5	–	1/4 DRILL	–	0.25	0.0	
6	–	1/2 CHA...		0.5-45	0.0	

Right-click for options

Select library tool...   ☐ Filter Active   Filter...

☐ To batch

Tool diameter: 0.5
Corner radius: 0.0

Tool name: 1/2 CHAMFER MILL

Tool #: 6   **Length offset:** 6
Head #: 0   **Diameter offset:** 6

Spindle direction: CW

Feed rate: 8.5568   **Spindle speed:** 1069
FPT: 0.002   **SFM:** 559.6859
Plunge rate: 8.5568   **Retract rate:** 8.5568
☐ Force tool change   ☐ Rapid Retract

Comment
Chamfer the outer circle.

Quick View Settings

Tool	1/2 CHAMFER ...
Tool Diameter	0.5
Corner Radius	0
Feed Rate	8.5568
Spindle Speed	1069
Coolant	Off
Tool Length	2.5
Length Offset	6
Diameter Offset	6
Cplane / Tpla...	Top
Axis Combinat...	Default (1)

15.4 Cut Parameters

◆ Select the **Cut Parameters** page and change the **Contour type** to **2D chamfer**.
◆ Input a **Width** of **0.02** and a **Tip offset** of **0.05** as shown in Figure: 15.4.1.

Figure: 15.4.1

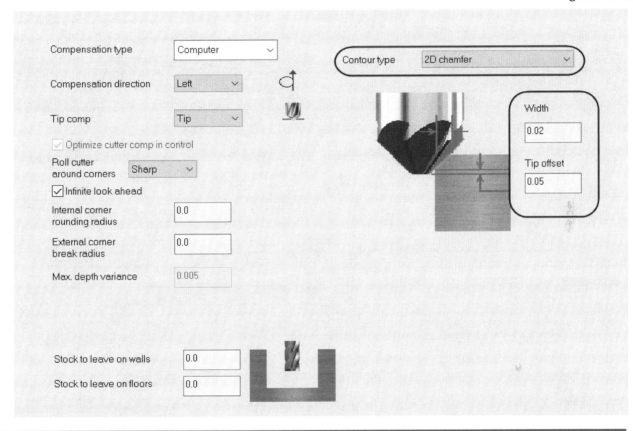

2D chamfer cuts chamfers around a contour.

Width sets the chamfer width. Mastercam measures the width from the chained geometry adjusted by the cut depths defined on the **Linking Parameters** page.

Tip offset is an amount to ensure that the tip of the tool clears the bottom of the chamfer.

15.5 Depth Cuts

◆ Select **Depth Cuts** and disable it as shown in Figure: 15.5.1.

Figure: 15.5.1

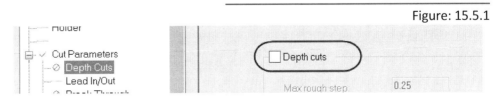

15.6 Lead In/Out

◆ From the **Tree View list**, select **Lead In/Out**. Change the **Lead In/Out** parameters and input an **Overlap** value as shown in Figure: 15.6.1.

Figure: 15.6.1

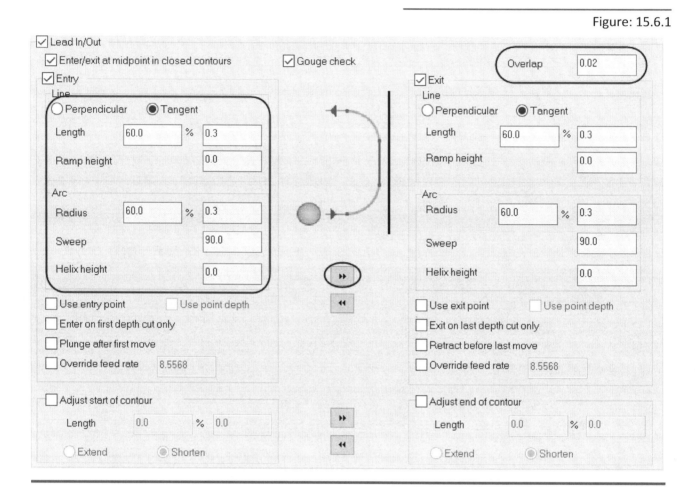

Lead In/Out allows you to select a combination of a Line and an Arc at the beginning and/or end of the contour toolpath for a smooth entry/exit while cutting the part.

Length is set to 60% of the tool diameter to ensure that the linear movement is greater than the tool radius in case **Cutter Compensation** in **Control** was used.

Radius is set to 60% of the tool diameter to ensure that the arc movement is greater than the tool radius to generate an arc output.

Overlap sets how far the tool goes past the end of the toolpath before exiting for a cleaner finish.

15.7 Multi Passes

◆ Select **Multi Passes** from the **Tree View list**. Disable **Multi Passes** as shown in Figure: 15.7.1.

Figure: 15.7.1

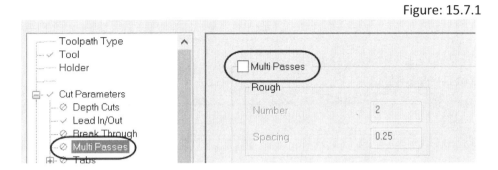

15.8 Linking Parameters

◆ Select **Linking Parameters** from the **Tree View list**. Set the **Top of stock** to **0.0** and the **Depth** to **0.0** as shown in Figure: 15.8.1.

Figure: 15.8.1

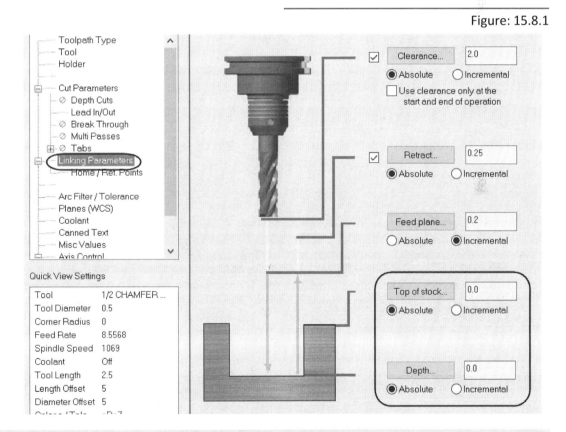

> **NOTE:** The depth of the chamfer is based on the **Width** and **Tip Offset** set in the **Cut Parameters** page. This is why we set the depth here to zero.

15.9 Preview the Toolpath

◆ To quickly check how the toolpath will be generated, select the **Preview toolpath** icon as shown.

◆ See **page 40** to review the procedure.
◆ The toolpath should look as shown.

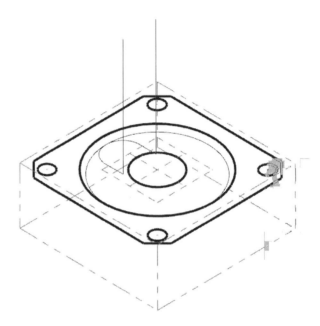

◆ Press **Esc** key to exit the preview.

NOTE: If the toolpath does not look as shown in the preview, check your parameters again.

◆ Select the **OK** button to exit the **2D Toolpaths - Contour** parameters.

15.10 Verify the Toolpaths

- From the **Toolpaths Manager**, click on the **Select all operations** icon.
- Click on the **Verify selected operation** icon.
- For information on how to set the **Verify** parameters and how to simulate the toolpath, please check **page 52**.
- The part will appear as shown in Figure: 15.10.1.

Figure: 15.10.1

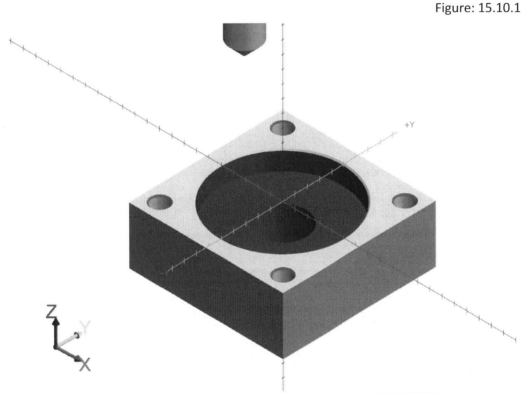

- To go back to Mastercam window, minimize **Mastercam Simulator** window as shown.

STEP 16: MACHINE THE CHAMFERS AT THE CORNERS USING CONTOUR TOOLPATH

In this step, you will machine the corners of the part using **Contour Toolpath**.

Toolpath Preview:

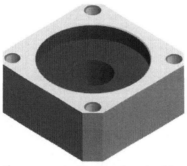

- ◆ To remove the toolpath display, hover the cursor in the **Toolpaths Manager** and press **T** until the toolpaths disappear.

TOOLPATHS
- ◆ From the **2D** group, select **Contour** as shown.

- ◆ To select only one entity at a time, select the **Single** button in the **Chaining** dialog box as shown below.

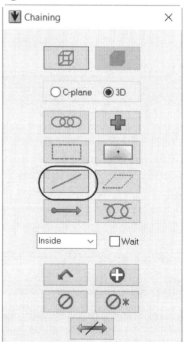

♦ Right mouse click in the graphics window and select the **Top** view as shown.

🔍	Zoom Window
🔍	Unzoom 80%
🔄	Dynamic Rotation
⊞	Fit
📦	Top (WCS)
📦	Front (WCS) Top (WCS)
📦	Right (WCS)
📦	Isometric (WCS)

♦ Select the chains and ensure the chaining direction is the same as shown in Figure: 16.0.1.

> **NOTE:** Select the contour as shown in Figure: 16.0.1 to ensure that the chaining directions for all four chains are correct. Use the **Reverse** button to flip the chains if needed. The green color arrow shows the chain's start location and the red color arrow shows the end of the chain. The chain selection arrows will disappear when you select the next chamfer.

Figure: 16.0.1

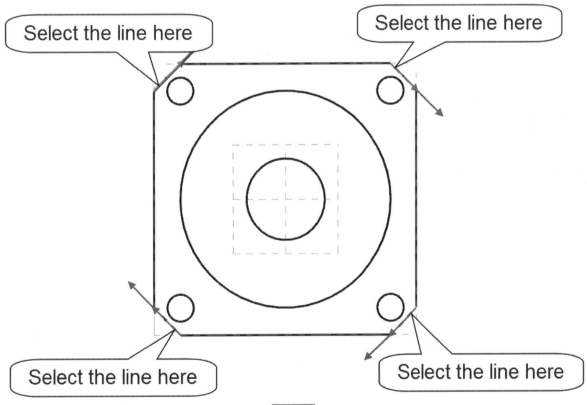

♦ Select the **OK** button to exit the **Chaining** dialog box.

◆ In the **Toolpath Type** page, the **Contour** toolpath will be selected.

Contour   Pocket   Facing   Slot Mill

16.1 Select a 1/2" Flat Endmill and set the Tool parameters

◆ Select **Tool** from the **Tree View list**.

◆ Click on **Select library tool** button. [Select library tool...]

◆ To be able to see all the tools from the library, disable **Filter Active**.

◆ Scroll down and select the **1/2" Flat Endmill (#290)** as shown.

◆ Select the tool in the **Tool Selection** page and then select the **OK** button to exit.

◆ Make all the necessary changes as shown in Figure: 16.1.1.

Figure: 16.1.1

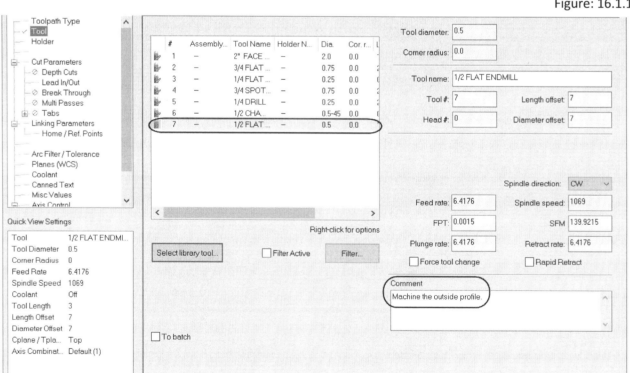

16.2 Cut Parameters

• Select the **Cut Parameters** page and change the **Contour type** to **2D** as shown in Figure: 16.2.1.

Figure: 16.2.1

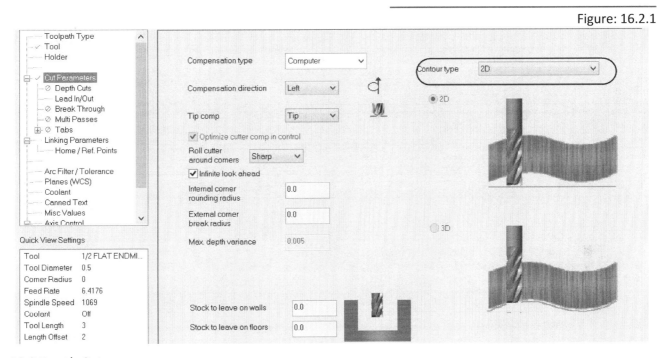

16.3 Depth Cuts

• Select **Depth Cuts** and enable it as shown in Figure: 16.3.1.
• Make sure that the parameters are set as shown in Figure: 16.3.1.

Figure: 16.3.1

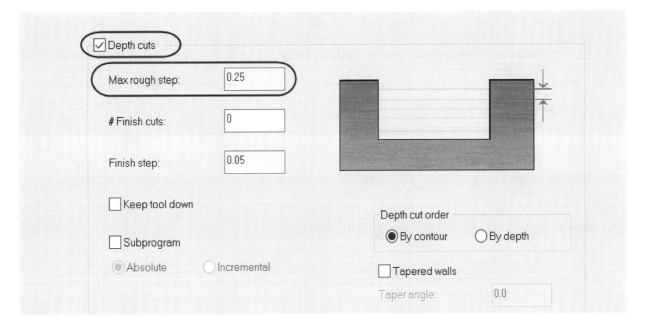

16.4 Lead In/Out

◆ Select **Lead In/Out** from the **Tree View list**. Make sure the parameters are set as shown in Figure: 16.4.1.

Figure: 16.4.1

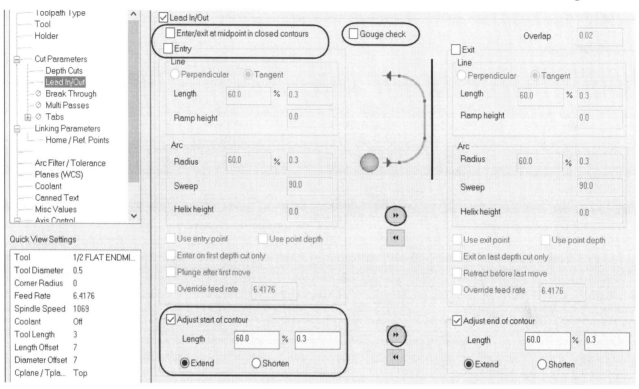

Adjust start/end of contour moves the starting/ending position in open contours by adding (**Extend**) or removing (**Shorten**) the specified length.

16.5 Linking Parameters

◆ Select **Linking Parameters** from the **Tree View list**. Set the **Top of stock** and the **Depth** as shown in
Figure: 16.5.1.

Figure: 16.5.1

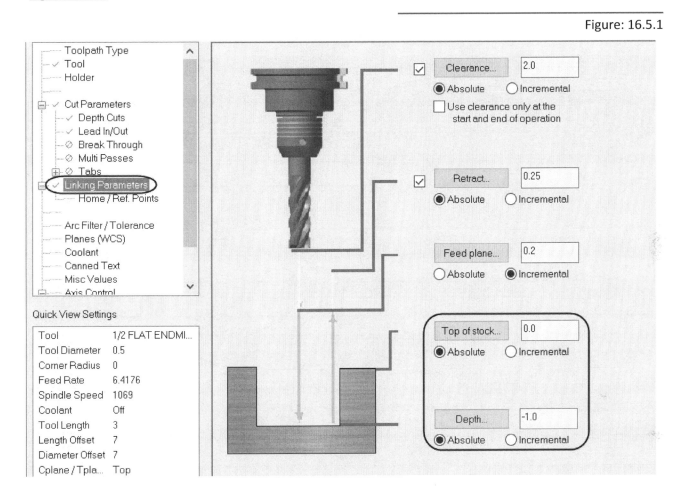

16.6 Preview the Toolpath

◆ To quickly check how the toolpath will be generated, select the **Preview toolpath** icon as shown.

◆ See **page 40** to review the procedure.
◆ The toolpath should look as shown.

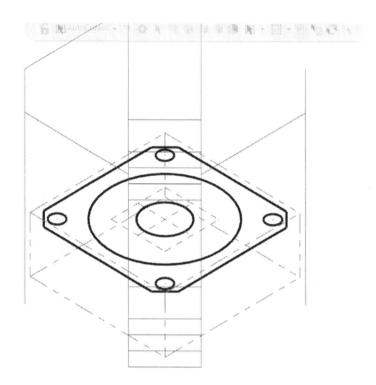

◆ Press **Esc** key to exit the preview.

> **NOTE:** If the toolpath does not look as shown in the preview, check your parameters again.

◆ Select the **OK** button to exit **2D Toolpaths - Contour**.

16.7 Verify the toolpaths

◆ To **Verify** the toolpaths, see **page 52** to review the procedure.

◆ Ensure all operations are selected; if not, use the button **Select all operations** in the **Toolpaths Manager.**

◆ To change the graphics view in the **Mastercam Simulator**, right mouse click in the graphics window and select **Isometric**.

◆ Your part will appear as shown.

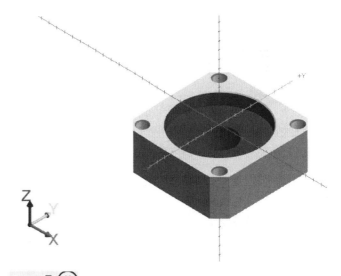

◆ To exit **Mastercam Simulator**, click on the **Close** icon.

STEP 17: POST THE FILE

♦ Ensure all operations are selected; if not, use the button **Select all operations** in the **Toolpaths Manager.**
♦ Select the **Post selected operations** icon from the **Toolpaths Manager** as shown.

> **NOTE:** The HLE/Demo version of Mastercam does not support post processing. The **G1** button does not work and no G-code can be created in the HLE/Demo version.

♦ In the **Post processing** window, make necessary changes according to Figure: 17.0.1.

Figure: 17.0.1

NC file enabled allows you to keep the NC file and to assign the same name as the MCAM file.

Edit enabled allows you to automatically launch the default.

♦ Select the **OK** button to continue.
♦ Save the NC file.

◆ A window with **Mastercam Code Expert** will be launched and the NC program will appear as shown in Figure: 17.0.2.

Figure: 17.0.2

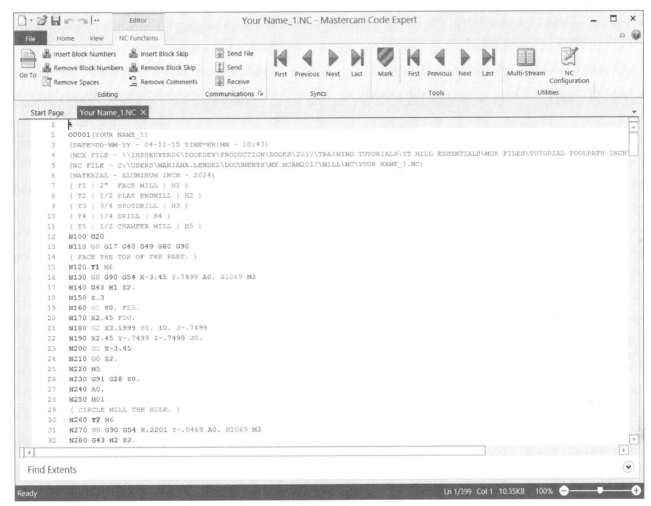

◆ Select the "**X**" box at the upper right corner to exit the editor.

STEP 18: SAVE THE UPDATED MCAM FILE

REVIEW EXERCISE - STUDENT PRACTICE

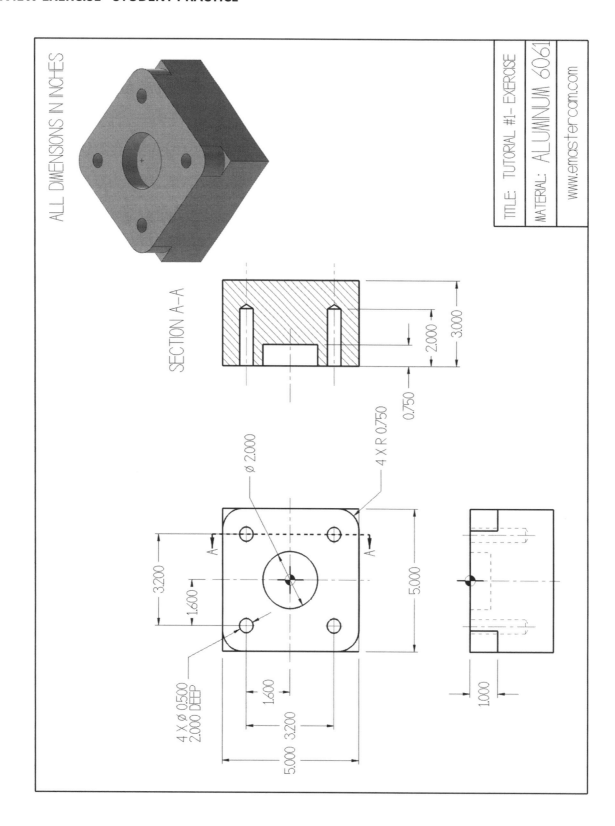

ALL DIMENSIONS IN INCHES

TITLE: TUTORIAL #1- EXERCISE

MATERIAL: ALUMINUM 6061

www.emastercam.com

SECTION A-A

3.000

2.000

0.750

Ø 2.000

4 X R 0.750

3.200

1.600

5.000

4 X Ø 0.500
2.000 DEEP

1.600

5.000   3.200

1.000

A

A

Mill Essentials Training Tutorial

Mastercam. 2017

CREATE THE GEOMETRY FOR TUTORIAL #1 EXERCISE

Use these commands from the Wireframe tab to create the geometry.
- Rectangle.
- Fillet Entities.
- Line Endpoints.
- Line Parallel.
- Circle Center Points.
- Trim.

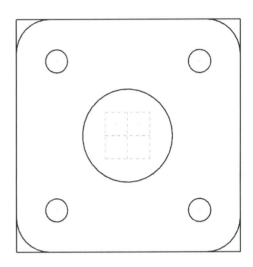

CREATE THE TOOLPATHS FOR TUTORIAL #1 EXERCISE

Create the Toolpaths for Tutorial #1 Exercise as per the instructions below.

Set the machine properties including the stock.

Remove the material on the outside of the part Contour (2D).
- Use a **1/2" Flat Endmill**.
- Based on your chaining direction, ensure the **Compensation direction** is set correctly.
- Enable **Depth Cuts** and set the **Max rough step** to **0.25"**.
- **Lead In/Out** set **Length** and **Radius** to **60%** with a **90** degree sweep.
- No **Break Through**, **Multi Passes**.
- Set the depth according to the drawing.

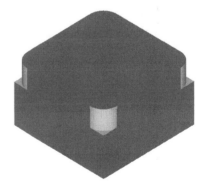

Spot drill the holes.
- Use a **3/4" Spot Drill**.
- Set the **Cycle** to **Drill/Counterbore** and set a **Dwell** to **1.0** second.
- Use the depth calculator to set a **0.05"** chamfer on the hole.

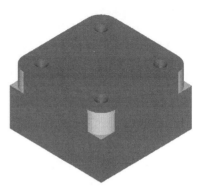

Drill the holes.
- Use a **1/2" Drill**.
- Set the **Cycle** to **Peck Drill** and set your peck values.
- Set the depth according to the drawing.

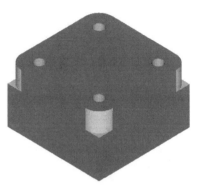

Remove the material in the center of the part using Circle Mill toolpath.
- Use a **1/2" Flat Endmill**.
- Choose to leave no stock on the walls.
- The **Entry Motion** will be **Helix**.
- Enable **Roughing** and set the parameters.
- Enable **Depth Cuts** and set the **Max rough step** to **0.5"** and enable **Keep tool down.**
- Set the depth according to the drawing.

NOTES:

TUTORIAL #1 QUIZ

• What is a Contour Toolpath used for?

• What is a Facing Toolpath used for?

• What does a Circle Mill Toolpath allow you to do?

• What does Backplot do?

• What does Verify allow you to do?

TUTORIAL #2

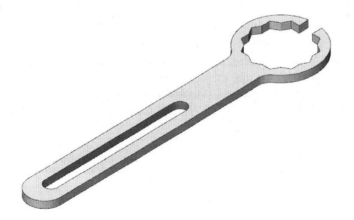

OVERVIEW OF STEPS TAKEN TO CREATE THE FINAL PART:

From Drawing to CAD Model:
* The student should examine the drawing on the following page to understand what part is being created in the tutorial.
* From the drawing we can decide how create the geometry in Mastercam.

Create the 2D CAD Model used to generate Toolpaths from:
* The student will create the Top 2D geometry required to create the toolpaths.
* Geometry creation commands such as Rectangle, Polygon, Fillet Entities, Fillet Chain, Arc Circle Center Point, Line Endpoints, Rectangular Shapes, and Trim will be used.

Create the necessary Toolpaths to machine the part:
* The student will set up the stock size to be used and the clamping method used.

Setup 1
* A Slot Mill toolpath will be created to machine the slot.
* 2D High Speed Dynamic Mill toolpath will be created to rough out the outside profile.
* A Contour toolpath will be created to finish the outside profile.
* 2D High Speed Dynamic Contour Mill toolpath will be created to machine the small radii.

Setup 2
* A Facing toolpath will be used to face the bottom of the part.

Backplot and Verify the file:
* The Backplot will be used to simulate a step-by-step process of the tool's movements.
* The Verify will be used to watch a tool machine the part out of a solid model.

Post Process the file to generate the G-code:
* The student will then post process the file to obtain an NC file containing the necessary code for the machine.

 This tutorial takes approximately two hours to complete.

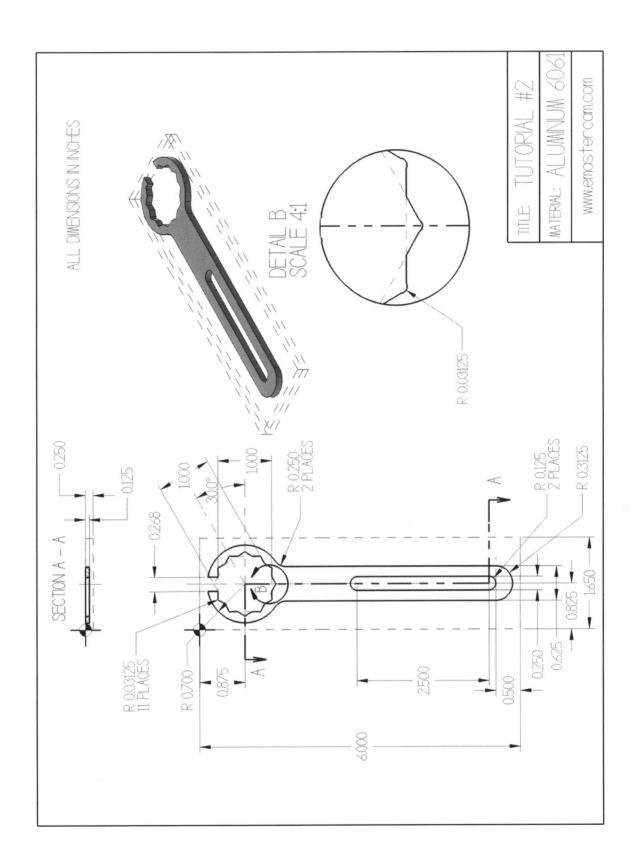

ALL DIMENSIONS IN INCHES

DETAIL B
SCALE 4:1

R 0.03125

SECTION A – A

0.250

0.125

1.000

30.0°

1.000

0.268

R 0.250
2 PLACES

A

R 0.125
2 PLACES

R 0.3125

1.650

0.825

0.250

0.625

0.500

2.500

R 0.03125
11 PLACES

R 0.700

0.875

A

B

6.000

TITLE: TUTORIAL #2

MATERIAL: ALUMINUM 6061

www.emastercam.com

GEOMETRY CREATION

STEP 1: SETTING UP THE GRAPHICAL USER INTERFACE

Please refer to the **Getting Started** section to set up the graphical user interface. If the manager panels are hidden by default in your graphics window, you may skip this step.

* Use **Auto Hide** icon to hide all **Manager** panels.

* The panels will be hidden to the left of the graphics window as shown.

* To un-hide them temporally, click on one of the managers to open it as shown.

STEP 2: CREATE A RECTANGLE

In this step, you will learn how to create a rectangle given the width, the height, and the anchor position.

Step Preview:

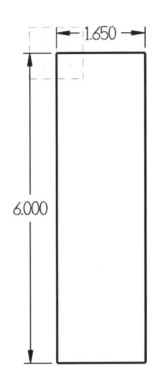

WIREFRAME
- From the **Shapes** group, select **Rectangle** as shown.

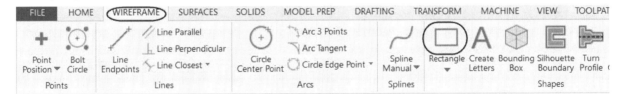

- Enter the **Width 1.65** and the **Height -6.0** as shown.

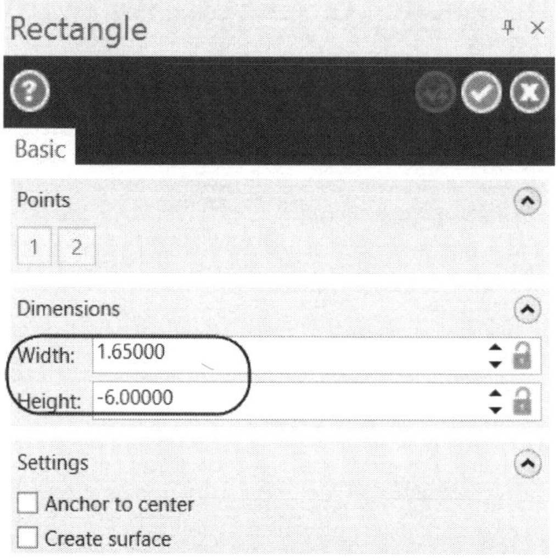

> **NOTE:** The **Anchor to center** and the **Create surface** icons should not be selected in this step.

- Press **Enter** after typing the values to see a preview of the rectangle.
- To select the position of the base point, from the **General Selection** toolbar, click on the drop down arrow next to the **AutoCursor** as shown.

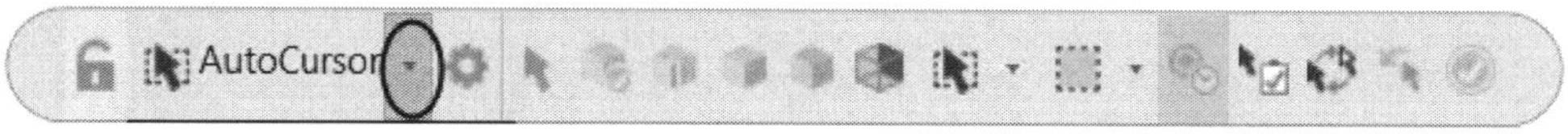

- From the fly-out menu, select **Origin**.

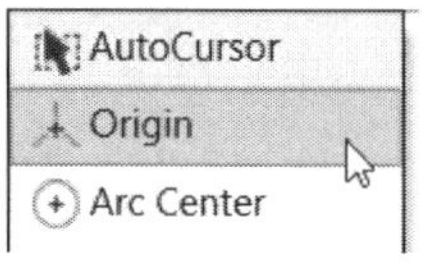

- Select the **OK** button to exit the **Rectangle** command. 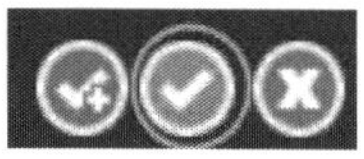
- Press **Alt + F1** to fit the drawing to the screen. Use the mouse wheel to zoom and unzoom if needed.

> **NOTE:** While creating the geometry for this tutorial, if you make a mistake, you can undo the last step using the **Undo** icon. You can undo as many steps as needed. If you delete or undo a step by mistake, just use the **Redo** icon. To delete unwanted geometry, select the geometry first and then press **Delete** from the keyboard.

STEP 3: CREATE TWO POLYGONS

In this step, you will learn how to create two six sided polygons. To create a Polygon, you need to specify the number of sides, the radius of the arc based on which polygon is created and how it is measured (Corner or Flat), and the center point.

Step Preview:

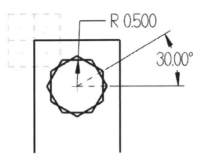

3.1 Create the straight polygon

WIREFRAME

• From the **Shapes** group, click on the drop down arrow next to **Rectangle** and select **Polygon** as shown.

• Change the settings in the dialog box to create a six sided polygon with the arc radius **0.5"** measured to the flats as shown in Figure: 3.1.1.

Figure: 3.1.1

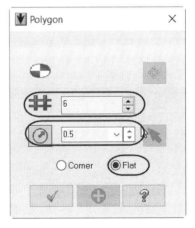

• Press **Enter** to set the parameters.

◆ [Select position of base point]: Press the **Space bar** and enter the coordinates as shown.

$$\boxed{0.825,-0.875}$$

NOTE: When entering the coordinates for the center point, the first value is the **X** coordinate value, then the **Y** value follow by the **Z** value only if it is different from zero. The coordinate values are separated by a comma. You do not need to use the coordinate labels if you enter the values in this order.

◆ Press **Enter** to see the polygon created in the windows graphics as shown.

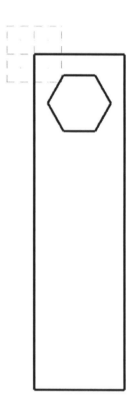

◆ Select the **Apply** button to continue with the same command.

3.2 Create the 30 degrees rotated polygon

◆ Expand the dialog box by selecting the arrow at the top-left corner as shown.

♦ Re-enter the arc radius **0.5** (although the value is still showing in the panel) and enter the rotation angle **30** degrees as shown in <u>Figure: 3.2.1</u>.

Figure: 3.2.1

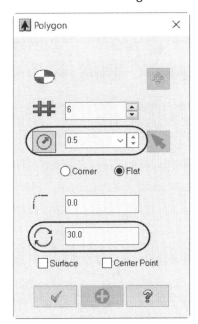

♦ [Select position of base point]: Press the **Space bar** and enter the coordinates as shown.

0.825,-0.875

• Press **Enter** to see the polygon created in the windows graphics as shown.

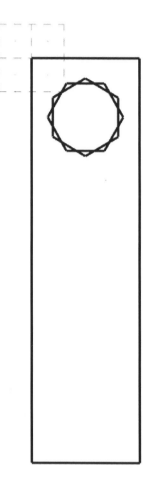

• Select the **OK** button to exit the command.

STEP 4: USE TRIM DIVIDE TO CLEAN THE POLYGONS

In this step, you will learn how to trim the geometry using the **Divide** option. **Divide** allows you to trim an entity into two disjointed segments by removing the segment that lies between two dividing intersections. It also allows you to delete entities based on the nearest intersection. Always select the segment in the area that should be removed.

Step Preview:

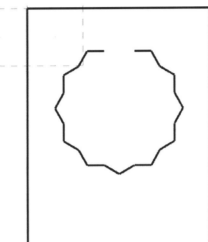

- ♦ To have a better view of the area on which we are working, zoom in by moving the cursor as shown and then scroll up the mouse wheel.
- ♦ The geometry should look as shown.

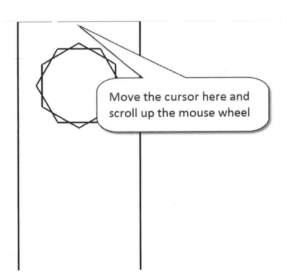

Move the cursor here and scroll up the mouse wheel

WIREFRAME

• From the **Modify** group, select **Trim Break Extend** as shown.

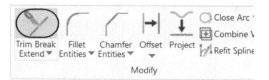

• Make sure the **Mode** is set to **Trim** and enable the **Divide/delete** as shown.

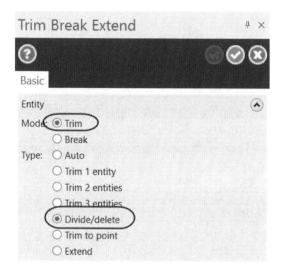

• Select the lines as shown in Figure: 4.0.1.

Figure: 4.0.1

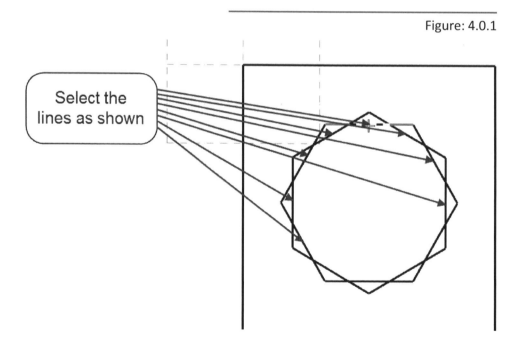

Select the lines as shown

NOTE: When hovering above the line, you will notice that the line changes to a hidden line style. This is a preview of what is going to be deleted and lets you select another segment of the line if necessary.

◆ Repeat the step selecting the lines as shown in <u>Figure: 4.0.2</u>.

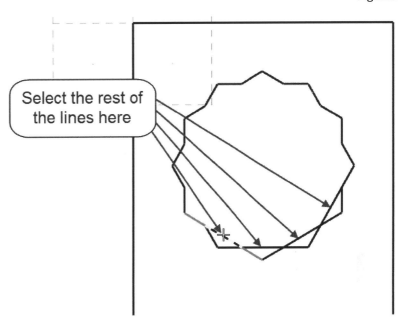

◆ Your drawing will appear as shown.

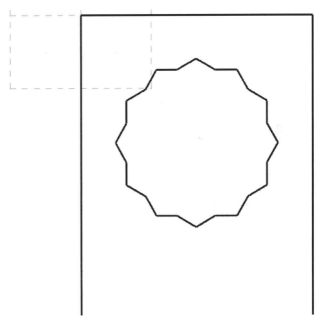

• Select the lines shown in <u>Figure: 4.0.3</u> to delete them using **Divide**.

Figure: 4.0.3

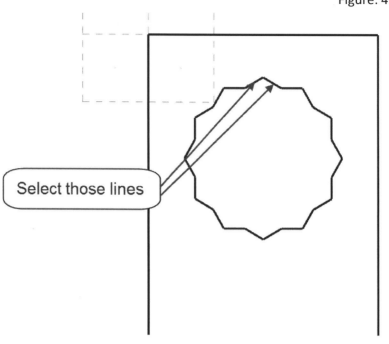

Select those lines

• The geometry should look as shown.

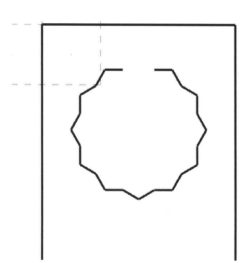

• Select the **OK** icon to exit the command.

STEP 5: CREATE THE CLEARANCE STYLE ARCS

In this step, you will learn how to use the **Fillet Chains** command to create the clearance style arcs with the 0.035 radius.

Step Preview:

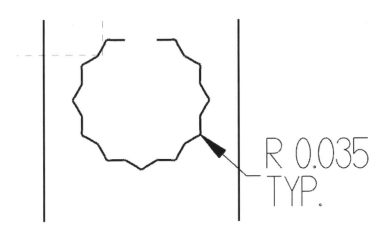

WIREFRAME

◆ From the **Modify** group, select the drop down arrow next to **Fillet Entities** and select **Fillet Chains** as shown.

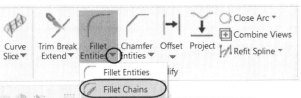

◆ The **Chaining** dialog box appears on the screen as shown.

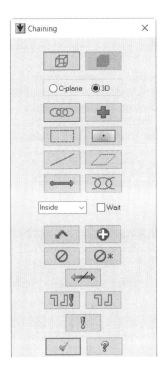

• [Select chain1]: Select the chain as shown in Figure: 5.0.1.

Figure: 5.0.1

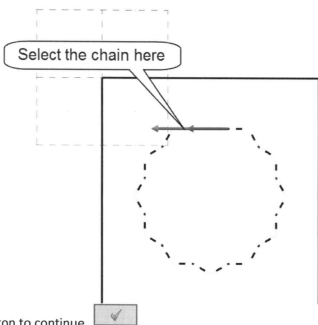

Select the chain here

• From the **Chaining** dialog box, select the **OK** button to continue.
• In the **Fillet Chains** panel, enable **Clearance** and enter the **Radius 0.035** as shown.

NOTE: Clearance style creates fillets inside the contour corners so that the tool can reach completely into the corners to remove the material.

• **Trim entities** should be selected as shown.

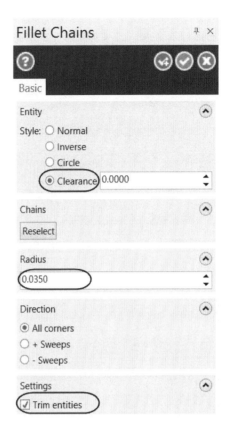

Fillet Chains

Basic

Entity
Style: ○ Normal
○ Inverse
○ Circle
● Clearance 0.0000

Chains
Reselect

Radius
0.0350

Direction
● All corners
○ + Sweeps
○ - Sweeps

Settings
☑ Trim entities

• Select the **OK** icon to exit the command.
• The drawing will appear as shown.

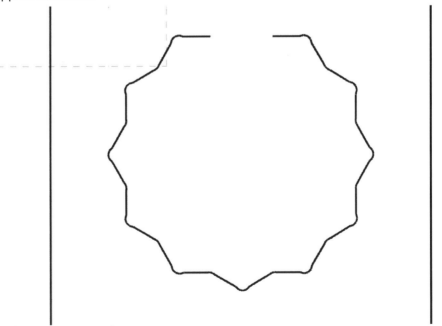

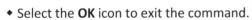

• Press **Alt** + **F1** to fit the geometry to the screen.

STEP 6: CREATE CIRCLES

In this step, you will create two circles given the radii and the center locations.

Step Preview:

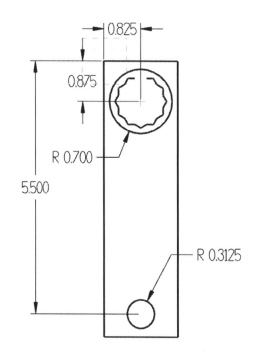

WIREFRAME

* From the **Arcs** group, select **Circle Center Point** as shown.

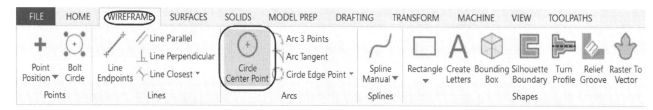

◆ Enter the **Radius 0.7** in the panel as shown.

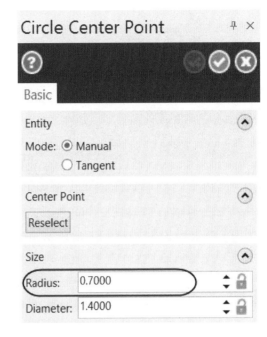

◆ Press **Enter**.
◆ Press the **Space bar** from the keyboard and the field where you can type the coordinates will open at the upper left side of the graphics window.
◆ Enter the values as shown.

◆ Press **Enter** and the circle will be placed as shown.

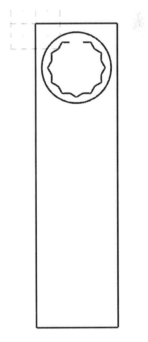

◆ Press another **Enter** to finish the circle and to continue in the same command.

* Input the **Radius 0.3125** in the panel as shown.

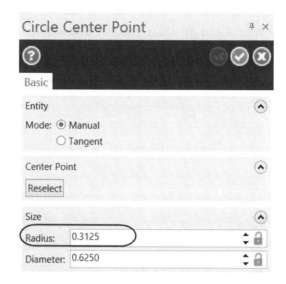

* Press the **Space bar** again.
* Enter the coordinates **0.825, -5.5** and hit **Enter** on the keyboard once again.

* Once completed, choose the **OK** button to exit the command.
* To see the entire geometry in the graphics window, press **Alt + F1**.
* The geometry should look as shown.

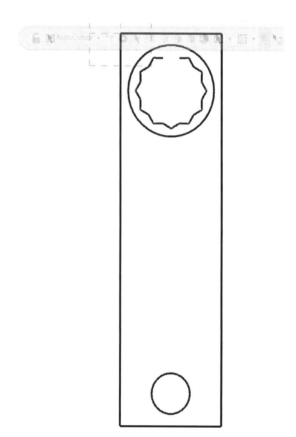

STEP 7: CREATE THE VERTICAL LINES

In this step, you will learn how to create vertical lines.

Step Preview:

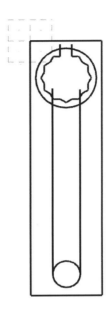

WIREFRAME

* From the **Lines** group, select **Line Endpoints**.

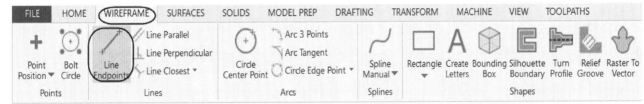

* Enable the **Vertical** button as shown.

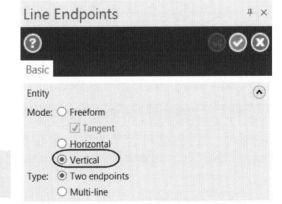

NOTE: Once this icon has been selected, you will only be able to create vertical lines.

◆ [Specify the first endpoint]: Select the **Endpoint** as shown in Figure: 7.0.1.

Figure: 7.0.1

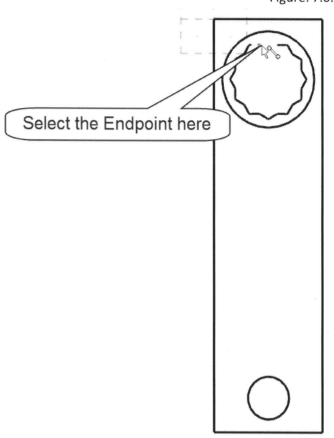

◆ [Specify the second endpoint]: Select a point above the circle to create a vertical line as shown in Figure: 7.0.2.

Figure: 7.0.2

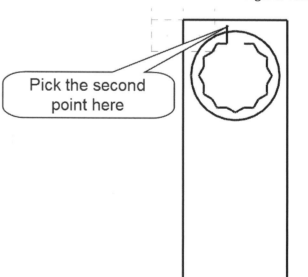

◆ Repeat this same step creating the second line as shown in <u>Figure: 7.0.3</u>.

Figure: 7.0.3

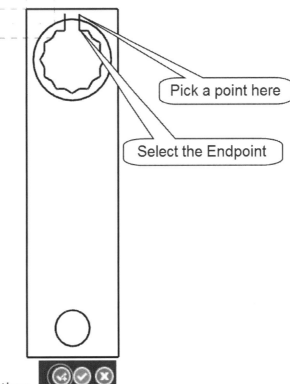

Pick a point here

Select the Endpoint

◆ Choose the **OK and Create New Operation** button to continue.

♦ [Specify the first endpoint]: Select the **Quadrant** as shown in <u>Figure: 7.0.4</u>.

Figure: 7.0.4

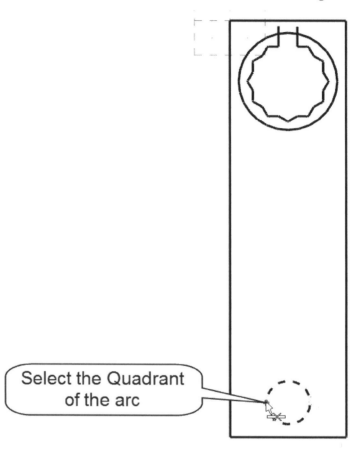

Select the Quadrant
of the arc

◆ [Specify the second endpoint]: Select a point inside the polygon shape to create a vertical line as shown in
Figure: 7.0.5.

Figure: 7.0.5

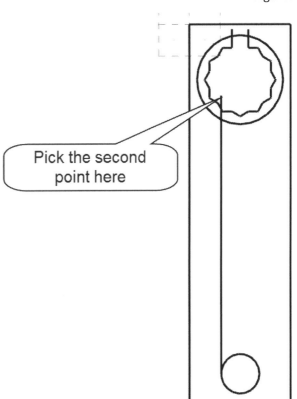

Pick the second
point here

• Repeat this same step creating the second line as shown in Figure: 7.0.6.

Figure: 7.0.6

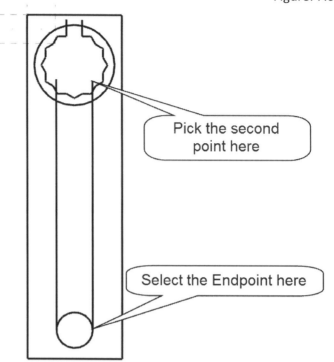

• Select the **OK** button once complete.

STEP 8: USE TRIM DIVIDE TO CLEAN THE GEOMETRY

Step Preview:

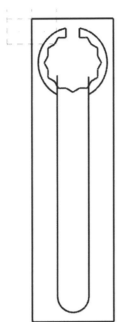

• To have a better view of the area on which we are working, zoom in by placing the cursor as shown and then scroll up the mouse wheel.

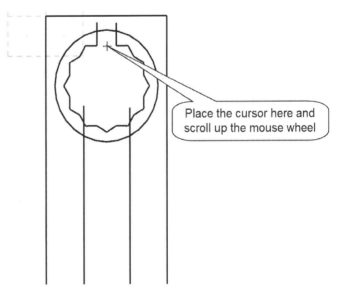

Place the cursor here and scroll up the mouse wheel

WIREFRAME

♦ From the **Modify** group, select **Trim Break Extend**.

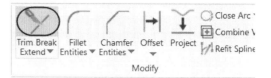

♦ Ensure the **Mode** is set to **Trim** and enable **Divide/delete** as shown.

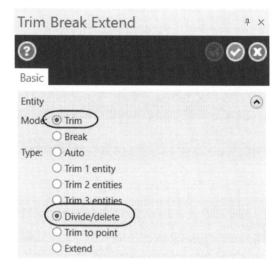

♦ Select the lines and the arcs as shown in <u>Figure: 8.0.1</u>.

Figure: 8.0.1

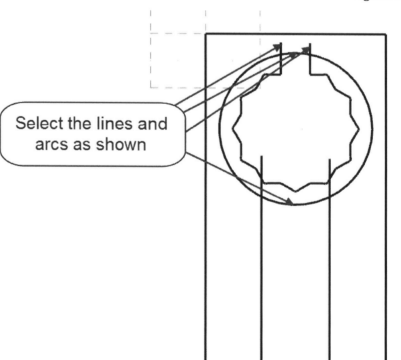

Select the lines and arcs as shown

♦ Press **Alt + F1** to fit the geometry into the graphics window.

• Repeat the step selecting the lines as shown in Figure: 8.0.2.

Figure: 8.0.2

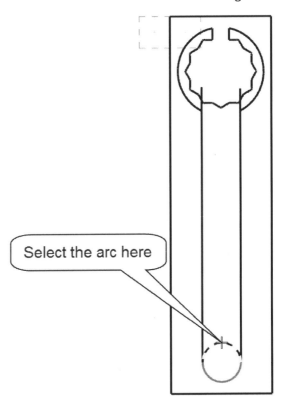

Select the arc here

• Select the **OK** icon to exit the command.
• The geometry should look as shown.

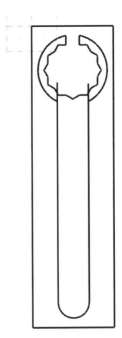

STEP 9: CREATE FILLETS

Fillets are used to round sharp corners.

Step Preview:

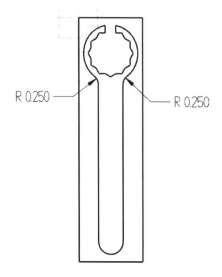

R 0.250 — — R 0.250

WIREFRAME

• From the **Modify** group, select **Fillet Entities.**

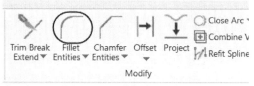

• Enter a fillet radius of **0.25**. Ensure the fillet style is set to **Normal** and **Trim entities** is enabled as shown.

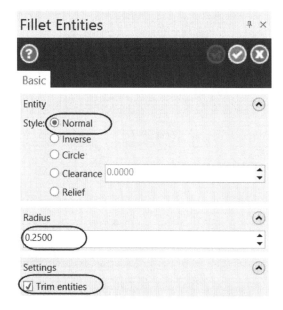

♦ [Select an entity]: Select **Entity A** as shown in Figure: 9.0.1.
♦ [Select another entity]: Select **Entity B** as shown.

Figure: 9.0.1

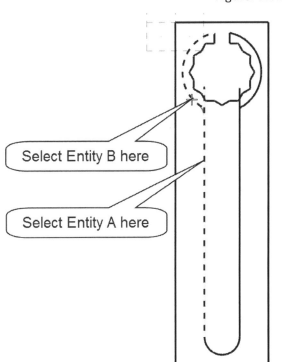

- [Select an entity]: Select **Entity C** as shown in Figure: 9.0.2.
- [Select another entity]: Select **Entity D** as shown.

Figure: 9.0.2

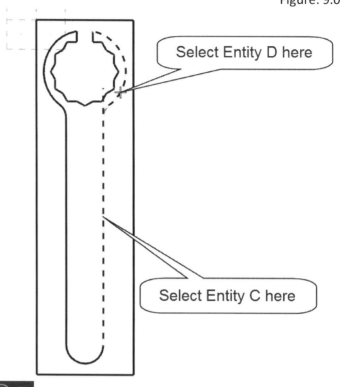

Select Entity D here

Select Entity C here

- Select the **OK** button to exit the command.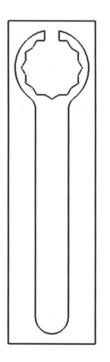
- The geometry should look as shown.

STEP 10: CREATE THE RECTANGULAR SHAPE

Create the **Obround Shape** which consists of 2 straight lines and two 180 degrees arcs at the ends using the **Rectangular Shapes** command.

Step Preview:

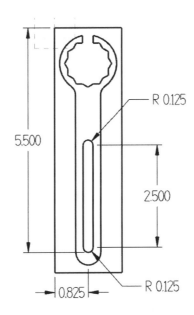

WIREFRAME

♦ Click on the drop down arrow below **Rectangle** and select **Rectangular Shapes**.

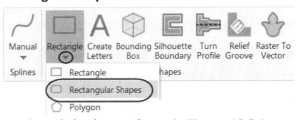

♦ Enter the **Width** and the **Height** in the **Rectangular Shapes Options** dialog box as shown in Figure: 10.0.1.

> **NOTE:** Mastercam can perform basic math functions as shown in Figure: 10.0.1.

Figure: 10.0.1

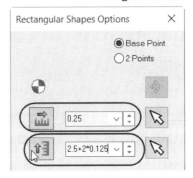

• Set the rest of the parameters as shown in Figure: 10.0.2.

Figure: 10.0.2

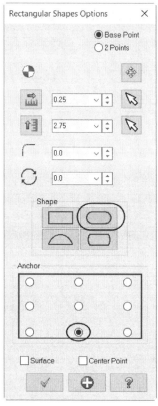

• [Select position of base point]: Press the **Space bar** and enter the values **0.825,-5.5** as shown.

0.825,-5.5

• Press **Enter** to place the obround shape.

• Select the **OK** button to exit the **Rectangular Shapes Options** dialog box.

◆ The geometry should look as shown.

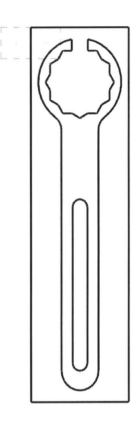

STEP 11: SAVE THE FILE

FILE
◆ **Save As.**

◆ Click on the **Browse** icon as shown.
◆ Find a location on the computer to save your file. File name: "Your Name_2".

TOOLPATH CREATION - SETUP 1

SUGGESTED FIXTURE:

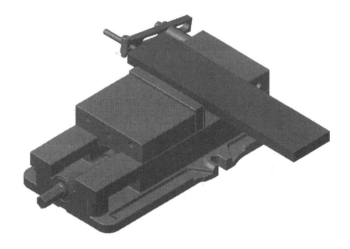

NOTE: In order to machine this part, we will have 2 setups and output 2 NC files. To view the second setup, see **page 195**.

SETUP SHEET:

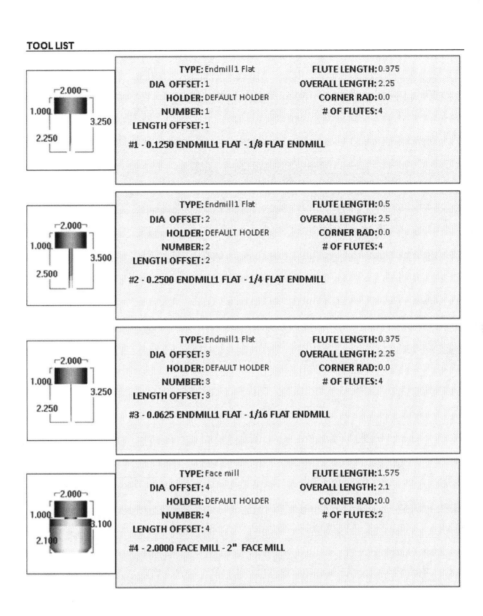

TOOL LIST

TYPE: Endmill1 Flat	**FLUTE LENGTH:** 0.375
DIA OFFSET: 1	**OVERALL LENGTH:** 2.25
HOLDER: DEFAULT HOLDER	**CORNER RAD:** 0.0
NUMBER: 1	**# OF FLUTES:** 4
LENGTH OFFSET: 1	

#1 - 0.1250 ENDMILL1 FLAT - 1/8 FLAT ENDMILL

TYPE: Endmill1 Flat	**FLUTE LENGTH:** 0.5
DIA OFFSET: 2	**OVERALL LENGTH:** 2.5
HOLDER: DEFAULT HOLDER	**CORNER RAD:** 0.0
NUMBER: 2	**# OF FLUTES:** 4
LENGTH OFFSET: 2	

#2 - 0.2500 ENDMILL1 FLAT - 1/4 FLAT ENDMILL

TYPE: Endmill1 Flat	**FLUTE LENGTH:** 0.375
DIA OFFSET: 3	**OVERALL LENGTH:** 2.25
HOLDER: DEFAULT HOLDER	**CORNER RAD:** 0.0
NUMBER: 3	**# OF FLUTES:** 4
LENGTH OFFSET: 3	

#3 - 0.0625 ENDMILL1 FLAT - 1/16 FLAT ENDMILL

TYPE: Face mill	**FLUTE LENGTH:** 1.575
DIA OFFSET: 4	**OVERALL LENGTH:** 2.1
HOLDER: DEFAULT HOLDER	**CORNER RAD:** 0.0
NUMBER: 4	**# OF FLUTES:** 2
LENGTH OFFSET: 4	

#4 - 2.0000 FACE MILL - 2" FACE MILL

STEP 12: SELECT THE MACHINE AND SET UP THE STOCK

In Mastercam, you select a **Machine Definition** before creating any toolpath. The **Machine Definition** is a model of your machine's capabilities and features. It acts like a template for setting up your machine. The machine definition ties together three main components: the schematic model of your machine's components, the control definition that models your control capabilities, and the post processor that will generate the required machine code (G-code). For a Mill Level 1 exercise (2D toolpaths), we just need a basic machine definition.

NOTE: For the purpose of this tutorial, we will be using the **Default Mill** machine.

12.1 Unhide the Toolpaths Manager panel and lock it

• The **Toolpaths Manage**r will be hidden to the left of the graphics window as shown.

Toolpaths Solids Planes Levels Recent Functions

• To lock it, click on the **Toolpaths** tab and then click on the **Auto Hide** icon a shown.

• The **Manager** panels will be translated to the lower left corner of the graphics window.

Toolpaths

Toolpaths Solids Planes Levels Recent Functions

12.2 Select the machine

MACHINE

• From the **Machine Type** group, click on the drop down arrow below **Mill** and select the **Default.**

> **NOTE:** Once you select the **Mill Default**, the **Ribbon bar** changes to reflect the toolpaths that could be used with **Mill Default.**

• Select the plus sign (+) in front of **Properties** in the **Toolpaths Manager** to expand the **Toolpaths Group Properties.**

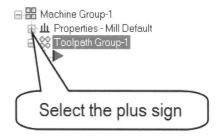

• Select **Tool settings** to set the tool parameters.

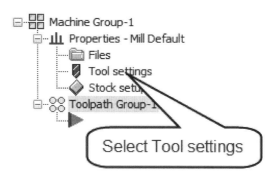

◆ Change the parameters to match the screen shot as shown in <u>Figure: 12.2.1</u>.

Figure: 12.2.1

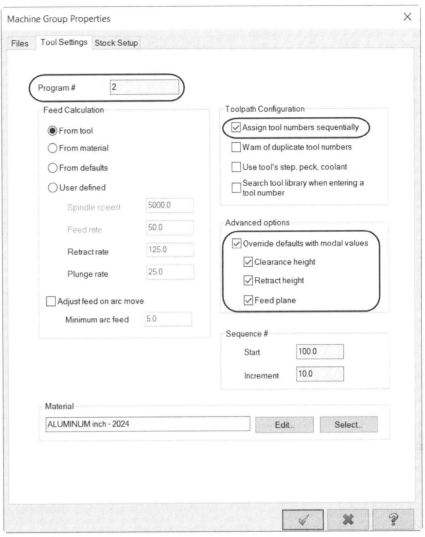

Program # is used to enter a number if your machine requires a number for a program name.

Assign tool numbers sequentially allows you to overwrite the tool number from the library with the next available tool number. (First operation tool number 1; second operation tool number 2, etc.)

Warn of duplicate tool numbers allows you to get a warning if you enter two tools with the same number.

Override defaults with modal values enables the system to keep the values that you enter.

Feed Calculation set to **From tool** uses feed rate, plunge rate, retract rate and spindle speed from the tool definition.

◆ Select the **Stock Setup** tab to define the stock.
◆ Select the **All Entities** button near the bottom of the **Stock Setup** page as shown.

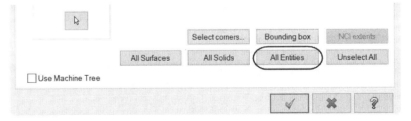

◆ In the **Stock thickness**, enter **0.25** as shown in Figure: 12.2.2. This will add **0.125"** of stock on the bottom of the model.

◆ Click in the graphics area at the upper left corner to move the arrow where the origin is set and then change the **Stock Origin** values to zero as shown in Figure: 12.2.2.

Figure: 12.2.2

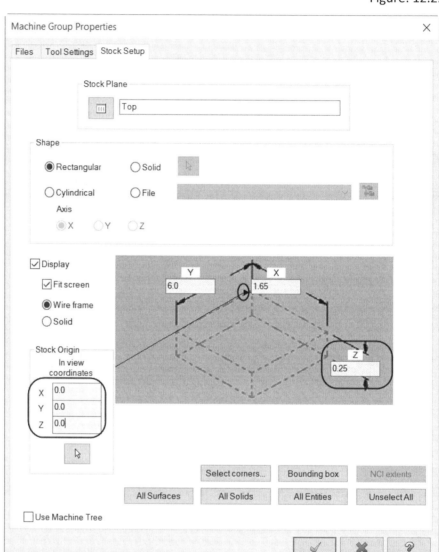

The **Stock Origin** values adjust the positioning of the stock, ensuring that you have an equal amount of extra stock around the finished part.

Display options allow you to set the stock as **Wireframe** and to fit the stock to the screen. (Fit Screen)

◆ Select the **OK** button to exit **Machine Group Properties**.

◆ Right mouse click in the graphics window and select the **Isometric** view to see the stock.

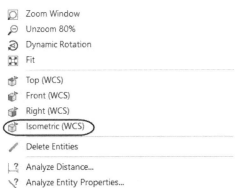

◆ Press **Alt + F1** to fit the drawing to the screen.
◆ The stock model will appear as shown.

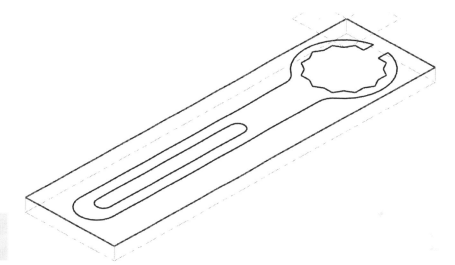

NOTE: The stock is not geometry and cannot be selected.

◆ Right mouse click again and select the **Top** view from the list to see the part from the top.

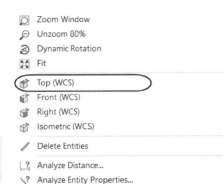

NOTE: There will not be a facing toolpath because the stock is already to size.

STEP 13: SLOT MILLING

Slot Mill toolpath allows Mastercam to efficiently machine obround slots. These are slots that consist of 2 straight lines and two 180-degree arcs at the ends.

Toolpath Preview:

TOOLPATHS

* From the **2D** group, select the **Expand gallery** arrow as shown.

* Select the **Slot Mill** as shown.

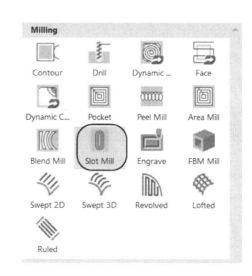

• If a prompt appears to ask you to **Enter new NC name**, select the **OK** button to accept the default.

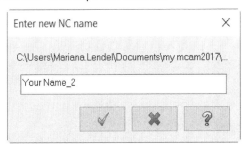

• When the **Chaining** dialog box appears, leave the settings as shown.

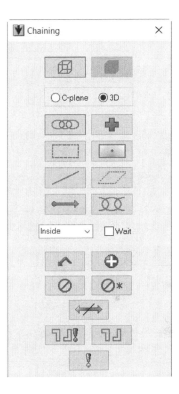

◆ Select the chain as shown in Figure: 13.0.1.

Figure: 13.0.1

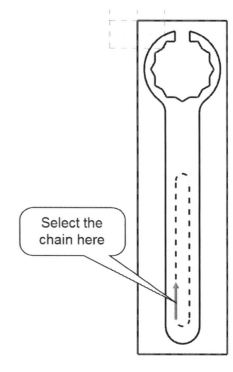

Select the
chain here

◆ Choose the **OK** button to exit the **Chaining** dialog box.
◆ In the **Toolpath Type** page, the **Slot Mill** icon will be selected.

Contour   Pocket   Facing   Slot Mill

NOTE: Mastercam updates the pages as you modify them and then marks them in the **Tree View list** with a green check mark. Pages that are not changed are marked with a red circle and slash.

13.1 Select a 1/8" Flat Endmill and set the Tool Parameters

- Select **Tool** from the **Tree View list**.
- Click on the **Select library tool** button.

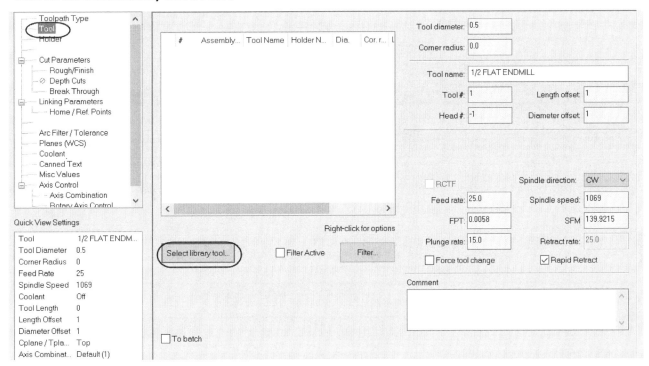

- Select the **Filter** button.

- Select the **None** button and then under **Tool Types**, choose the **Flat Endmill** icon.

- Under **Tool Diameter**, select **Equal** and input a value **0.125** as shown in Figure: 13.1.1.

Figure: 13.1.1

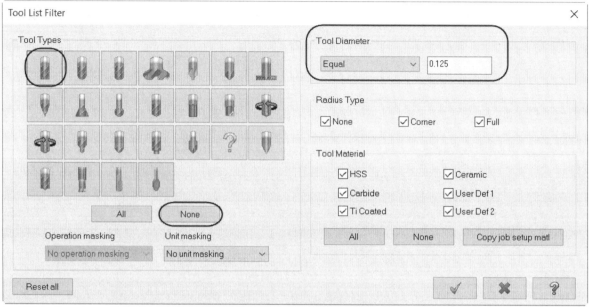

- Select the **OK** button to exit the **Tool List Filter.**
- In the **Tool Selection** panel you should only see a **1/8" Flat Endmill**.

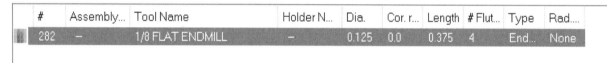

#	Assembly...	Tool Name	Holder N...	Dia.	Cor. r...	Length	# Flut...	Type	Rad....
282	–	1/8 FLAT ENDMILL	–	0.125	0.0	0.375	4	End...	None

- Select the **1/8" Flat Endmill** in the **Tool Selection** page and then select the **OK** button to exit.

◆ Make all the necessary changes as shown in Figure: 13.1.2.

Figure: 13.1.2

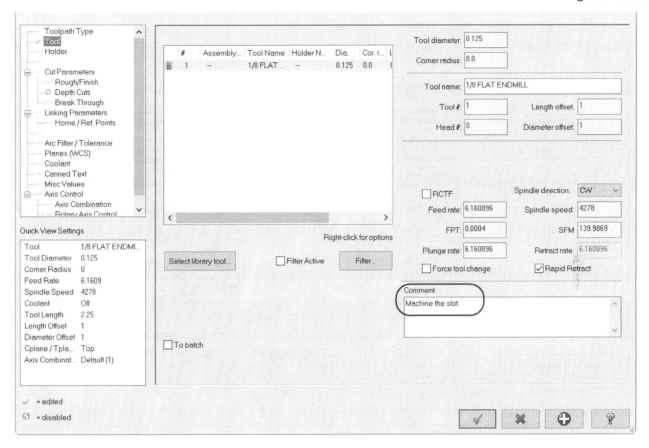

The **Feed rate**, **Plunge rate**, **Retract rate** and **Spindle speed** are based on the tool definition as set in the **Tool Settings**. You may change these values as per your part material and tools.

In the **Comment** field, enter a comment to help identify the toolpath in the **Toolpaths Manager** such as the one shown above.

13.2 Cut Parameters

• From the **Tree View list**, select **Cut Parameters** and make the necessary changes as shown in Figure: 13.2.1.

Figure: 13.2.1

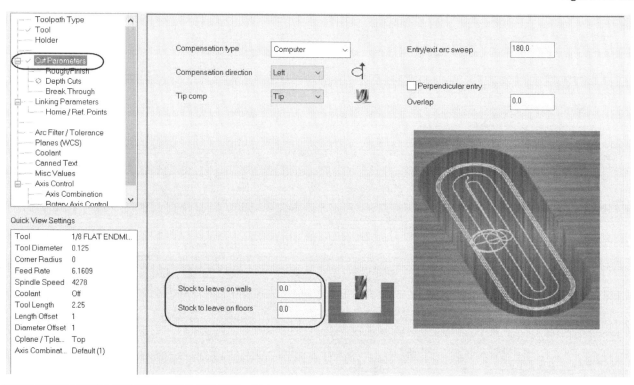

Compensation type allows you to choose how you want to handle cutter compensation. The computer sets Mastercam to compute the compensated toolpath and does not output control codes for compensation.

Entry/exit arc sweep sets the included angle of each entry and exit arc. If the entry/exit arc sweep is less than 180 degrees, the system applies an entry/exit line.

Perpendicular entry enters the toolpath perpendicular to the first tool move.

13.3 Rough/Finish

◆ Select **Rough/Finish** and make necessary changes as shown in <u>Figure: 13.3.1</u>.

Figure: 13.3.1

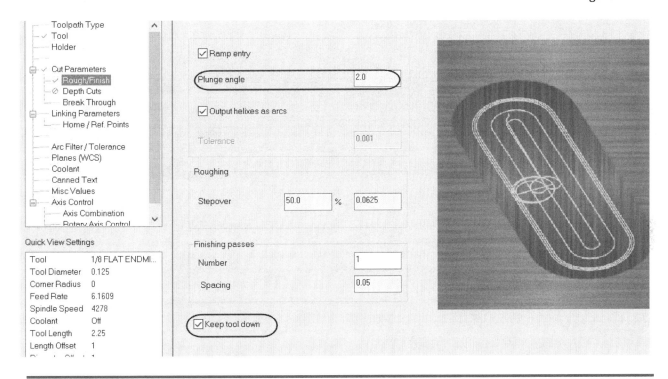

Ramp entry creates a smoother entry motion rather than plunging directly.

Plunge angle sets the angle of descent for the entry move and determines the pitch. A smaller plunge angle means that the entry move takes longer to descend in the Z axis. A recommended angle is 3 to 5 degrees.

Output helixes as arcs writes the entry helix to the NCI file as arcs. Using this option can create shorter NC files. If you turn off this option, the helix breaks into linear segments in the NCI file.

Roughing Stepover sets the distance between cutting passes in the X and Y Axes. Enter a percentage of the tool diameter or a distance.

Finish passes allows you to set the finish cuts for the toolpath. This **Number** multiplied by the finish **Spacing** value equals the total amount of stock cut by the finish passes. Setting the number of finish cuts to 0 creates no finish cuts.

Keep tool down enabled does not allow the tool to retract between multipasses.

13.4 Depth Cuts

- Choose **Depth Cuts** from the **Tree View list**. Enable **Depth cuts**. Input a **Max rough step** of **0.1**.
- Enable the option **Keep tool down** as shown in <u>Figure: 13.4.1</u>.

Figure: 13.4.1

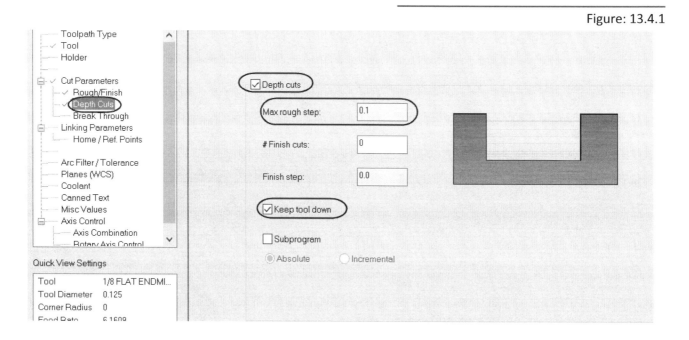

13.5 Break Through

• Select **Break Through** from the **Tree View list**. Enable this option and input a **Break through amount** of **0.1** as shown in Figure: 13.5.1.

Figure: 13.5.1

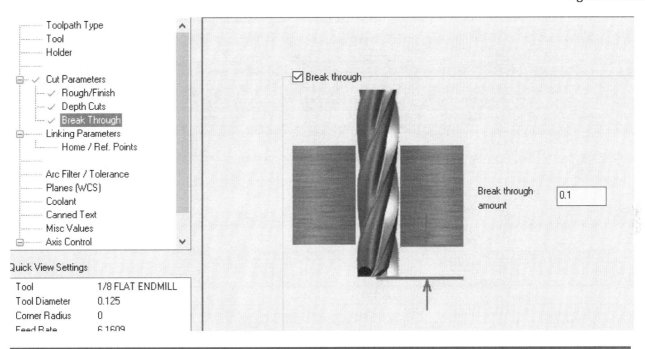

Break Through allows you to specify an amount by which the tool will completely cut through the material. This value is always a positive number.

13.6 Linking Parameters

♦ Select **Linking Parameters** and make the necessary changes as shown in <u>Figure: 13.6.1</u>.

Figure: 13.6.1

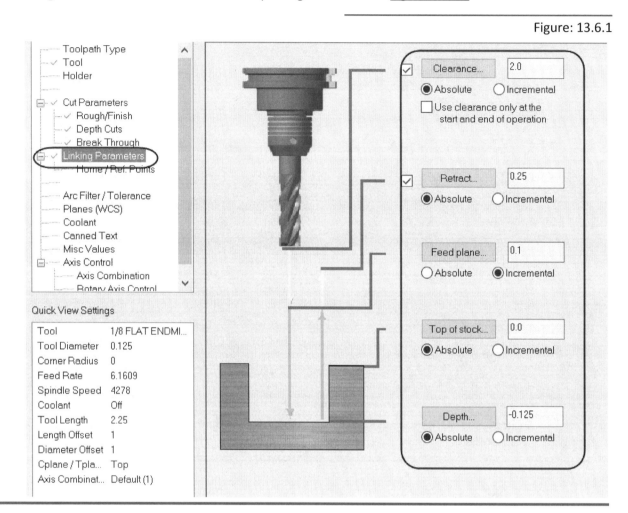

Clearance sets the height at which the tool moves to and from the part.

Retract sets the height to which the tool moves up to before the next tool pass.

Feed plane sets the height to which the tool rapids to before changing to the plunge rate to enter the part.

Top of stock sets the height of the material in the Z axis.

Depth determines the final machining depth that the tool descends into the stock.

13.7 Preview the Toolpath

◆ To quickly check how the toolpath will be generated, select the **Preview toolpath** icon as shown.

◆ To hide the dialog box, click on the **Hide dialog** icon as shown.
◆ To see the part from an **Isometric** view, right mouse click in the graphics window and select **Isometric**.

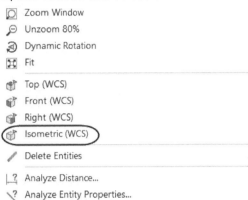

◆ The toolpath should look as shown.

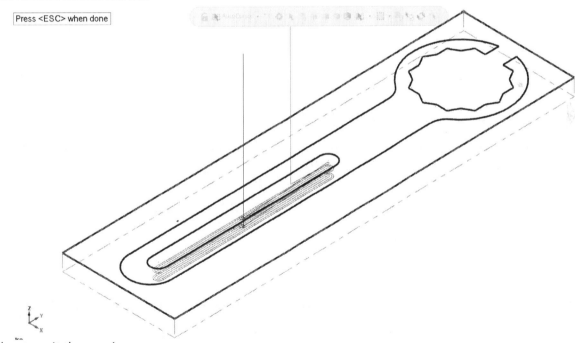

◆ Press **Esc** key to exit the preview.

NOTE: If the toolpath does not look as shown in the preview, check your parameters again.

◆ Select the **OK** button to exit the **Slot Mill** parameters.

STEP 14: BACKPLOT THE TOOLPATHS

Backplotting shows the path the tools take to cut the part. This display lets you spot errors in the program before you machine the part. As you backplot toolpaths, Mastercam displays additional information such as the X, Y, and Z coordinates, the path length, the minimum and maximum coordinates, and the cycle time. It also shows any collision between the workpiece and the tool.

* Make sure that the toolpaths are selected (signified by the green check mark on the folder icon). If the operation is not selected, choose the **Select all operations** icon.

* Select the **Backplot selected operations** button.

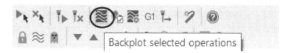

* In the **Backplot** dialog box, enable **Display with color codes**, **Display tool** and **Display rapid moves** icons as shown.

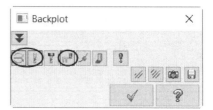

* To fit the workpiece to the screen, if needed, right mouse click in the graphics window again and select **Fit**.

* You can step through the **Backplot** by using the **Step forward** ▶▶ or **Step back** ◀◀ buttons.

* You can adjust the speed of the backplot. ▲

* Select the **Play** button to run **Backplot**. ⊙ ■ ◀◀ ◀◀ ▶▶ ▶▶ ✎ ✐

◆ The toolpath should look as shown in Figure: 14.0.1.

Figure: 14.0.1.

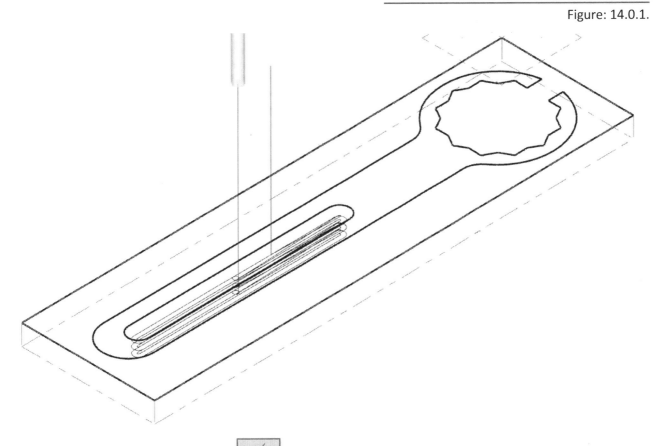

◆ Select the **OK** button to exit **Backplot**.

STEP 15: SIMULATE THE TOOLPATH IN VERIFY

Verify Mode shows the path the tools take to cut the part with material removal. This display lets you spot errors in the program before you machine the part. As you verify toolpaths, Mastercam displays additional information such as the X, Y, and Z coordinates, the path length, the minimum and maximum coordinates, and the cycle time. It also shows any collision between the workpiece and the tool.

◆ From the **Toolpaths Manager**, select **Verify selected operations** icon as shown.

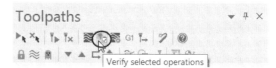

> **NOTE:** Mastercam launches a new window that allows you to check the part using **Verify.**

◆ Select the **Play** button to run **Verify.**
◆ The part should appear as shown in <u>Figure: 15.0.1</u>.

Figure: 15.0.1

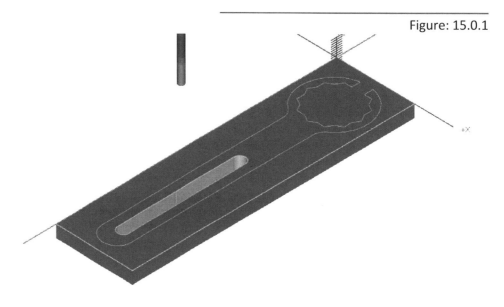

◆ To go back to the Mastercam window, minimize the **Mastercam Simulator** window as shown.

STEP 16: ROUGH THE OUTSIDE USING HIGH SPEED DYNAMIC MILL

In this step, you will machine the outside profile using **2D HS Dynamic Mill toolpath**.

Dynamic Mill toolpath machines cores or pockets using the entire flute length. The Toolpath supports many powerful entry methods, including a customized entry method. Entry methods and micro lifts support custom feeds and speeds to optimize and generate safe tool motion.

The toolpath depends on the **Machining strategy** that you choose in the **Chain Options**. If the strategy chosen is **From outside**, the toolpath starts at the outmost chain and works its way in, taking on the final shape of the part as it approaches the final pass. You can also machine pockets, in which case the strategy selected is **Start inside,** which keeps the tool inside the machining regions.

Toolpath Preview:

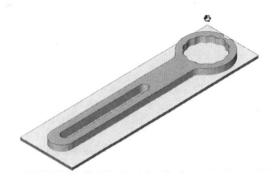

16.1 Chain selection

• Press **T** to remove the toolpath display.

TOOLPATHS

• In the **2D** group, click on the **Expand gallery** arrow as shown.

• Select the **Dynamic Mill** icon as shown.

- In the **Chaining Options** dialog box, under **Machining regions,** click on the **Select machining chains** button as shown to define the area to be machined.

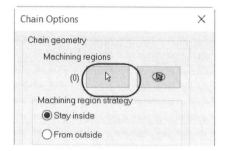

- The **Chaining** dialog box will open and leave the **Chain** button enabled as shown.

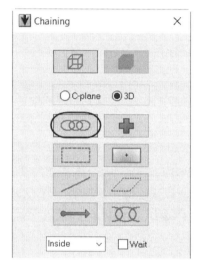

- Right mouse click in the graphics window and select the **Top** view.

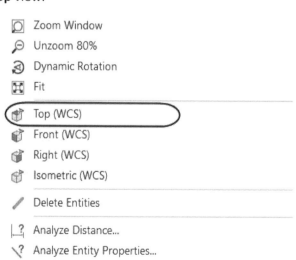

◆ [2D HST machining chain 1]: Select the rectangle as shown in <u>Figure: 16.1.1</u>.

Figure: 16.1.1

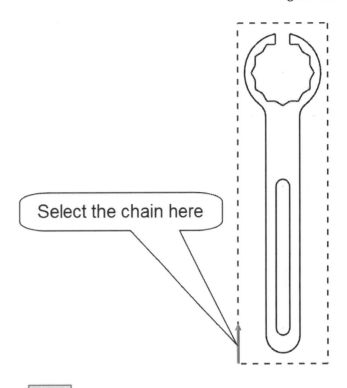

◆ Select the **OK** button to exit the **Chaining** dialog box.

◆ To start the toolpath from the outside, in the **Machining region strategy**, make sure that **From outside** is enabled.

◆ In the **Avoidance regions**, click on the **Select avoidance chains** button as shown.

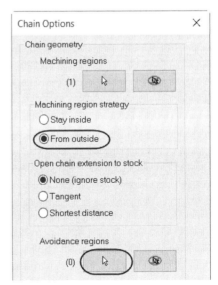

◆ [Select 2D HST avoidance chain 1]: Select the profile as shown in Figure: 16.1.2.

Figure: 16.1.2

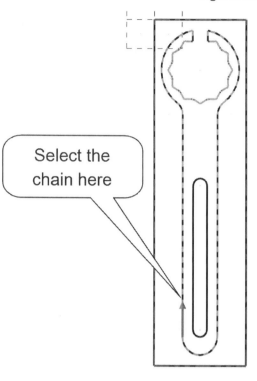

◆ Select the **OK** button to exit the **Chaining** dialog box.

◆ Select the **OK** button to exit the **Chain Options** panel.

◆ In the **Toolpath Type** page, **Dynamic Mill** will be selected as shown in Figure: 16.1.3.

Figure: 16.1.3

16.2 Preview Chains

The **Preview Chains** function is intended to give the user a quick visual representation of how Mastercam sees the various pieces of geometry that have been selected, how they interact with one another and a general overview of how the toolpath will be calculated with the selections presently made.

♦ Click on the **Color** icon to see the legend for **Preview chains** as shown.

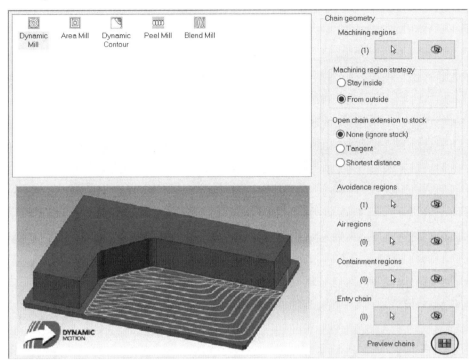

♦ The **Preview Chains Colors** dialog box should look as shown.

The **Material region** and **Material crosshatch** are the two colors that are used to define the material to be cut. The default colors are red for the background and black for the crosshatch.

The **Motion region** displays the area that Mastercam is making available to the toolpath for motion if it needs it. The color to represent it is dark blue. The primary reason for the display of the entire available (but not necessarily used) Motion region is to help the user visualize how the tool may move near or interact with any adjacent geometry.

The **Tool containment** is what you have selected as the Containment region in the chain geometry. If you have not selected a containment region, it will default to the outside of the Motion region since that is currently the default area the toolpath is being contained to. The color used to represent the Tool containment is yellow.

♦ Select the **OK** button to exit **Preview Chains Colors**.

• Select the **Preview chains** button as shown.

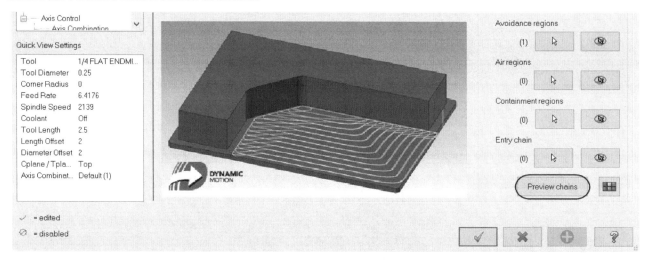

• Select the **Hide dialog** button to see the preview in the graphics window.
• The **Preview chains** should look as shown.

• Press **Esc** key to return to the toolpath parameters.
• Click on the **Preview chains** button again to clear the Preview chains display.

16.3 Select a 1/4" Flat Endmill from the library and set the Tool Parameters

◆ Select **Tool** from the **Tree View list**.
◆ Click on the **Select library tool** button.

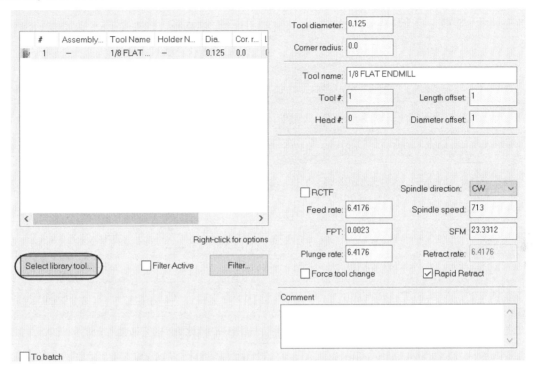

◆ Select the **Filter** button.

- Select the **None** button and then under **Tool Types** choose the **Flat Endmill** Icon.
- Under **Tool Diameter**, select **Equal** and input a value **0.25** as shown in <u>Figure: 16.3.1</u>.

Figure: 16.3.1

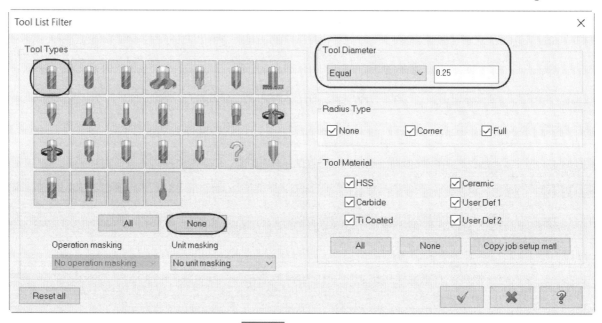

- Select the **OK** button to exit the **Tool List Filter.**
- In the **Tool Selection** panel you should only see a **1/4" Flat Endmill**.

#	Assembly...	Tool Name	Holder N...	Dia.	Cor. r...	Length	# Flut...	Type	Rad....
285	–	1/4 FLAT ...	–	0.25	0.0	0.5	4	End...	None

- Select the **1/4" Flat Endmill** in the **Tool Selection** page and then select the **OK** button to exit.

◆ Make all the necessary changes as shown in <u>Figure: 16.3.2</u>.

Figure: 16.3.2

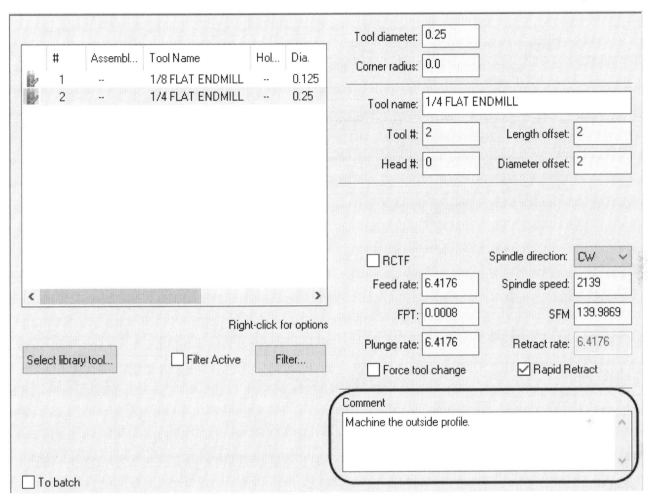

16.4 Set the Cut Parameters

♦ From the **Tree View list**, select **Cut Parameters**. Change the settings as shown in <u>Figure: 16.4.1</u>.

Figure: 16.4.1

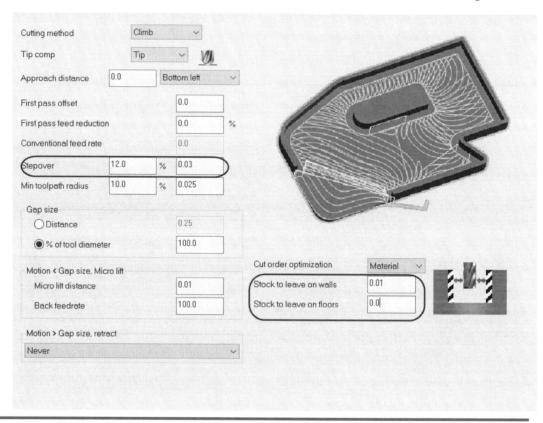

Stepover sets the distance between cutting passes in the X and Y axes.

Approach distance adds the specified absolute distance to the beginning of the toolpath's first cut.

First pass offset offsets out the machining region with a user defined distance for the tool to safely engage from the outside off the material.

First pass feed reduction allows you to slow the feed for the first pass on machining region material approached from the outside.

Min toolpath radius reduces sharp corner motion between cut passes.

Micro lift distance enters the distance the tool lifts off the part on the back moves. Microlifts are slight lifts that help clear chips and minimize excessive tool heating.

Back feedrate controls the speed of the backfeed movement of the tool.

Motion > Gap Size, retract controls retracts in the toolpath when making a non-cutting move within an area where the tool can be kept down or microlifted.

16.5 Set the Entry Motion

- From the **Tree View list**, select and enable **Entry Motion**.
- Entry motion configures an entry method for the dynamic mill toolpath, which determines not only how and where the tool enters the part, but also the cutting method/machining strategy used by the toolpath. Set the **Entry method** to **Helix only** as shown in <u>Figure: 16.5.1</u>.

Figure: 16.5.1

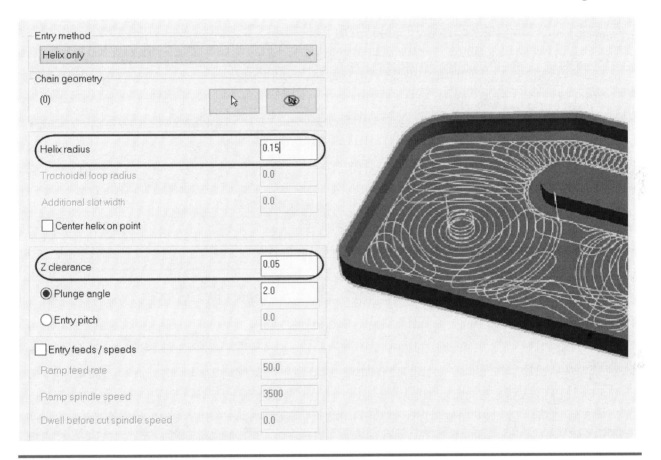

Entry method set to **Helix only** creates a helical entry into the part.

16.6 Set the Break through

♦ From the **Tree View list**, select and enable **Break Through** to cut completely through the material by an amount that you specify as shown in <u>Figure: 16.6.1</u>.

Figure: 16.6.1

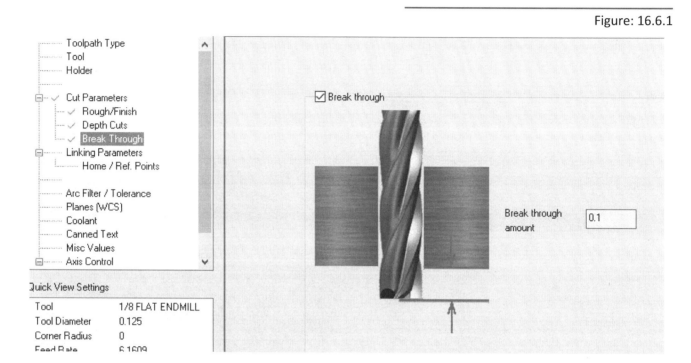

16.7 Set the Linking Parameters

• Select **Linking Parameters**. Make sure the **Depth** is set to **-0.125**, **Absolute**, and the other parameters are set to the same values as shown in Figure: 16.7.1.

Figure: 16.7.1

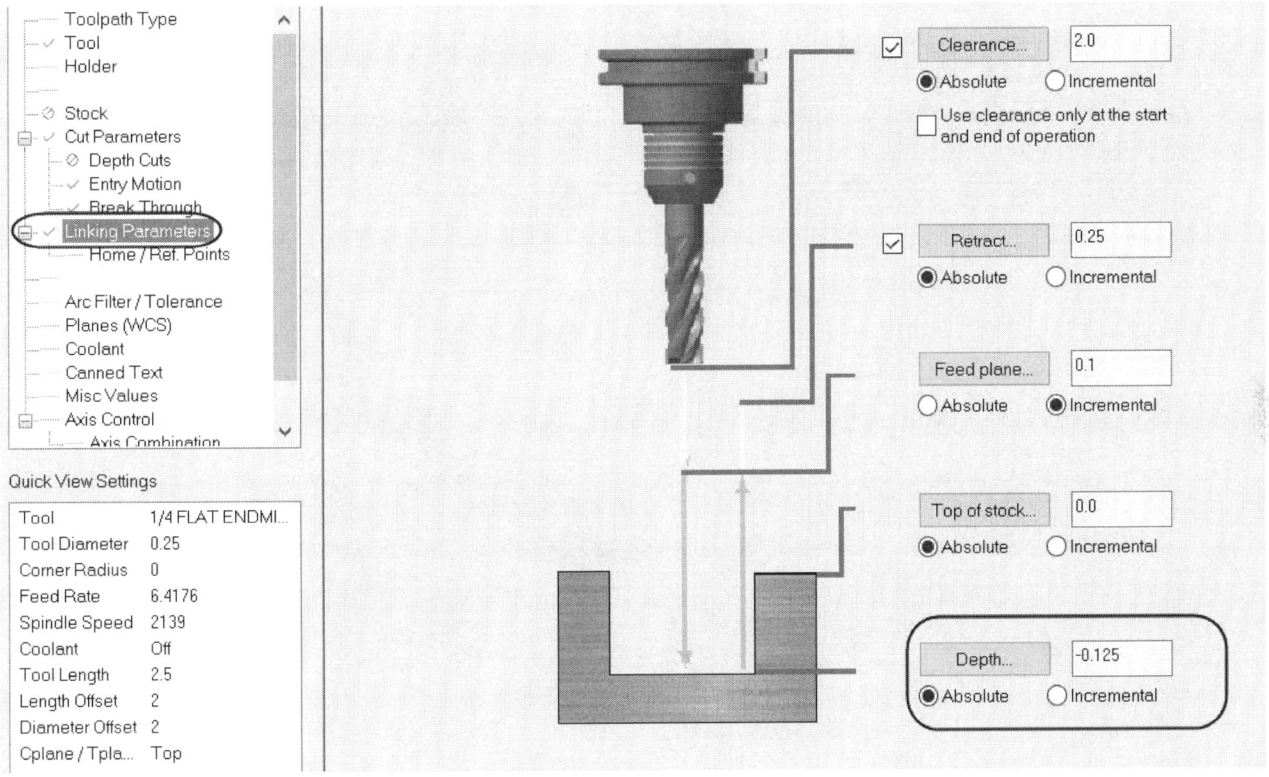

16.8 Preview the Toolpath

♦ To quickly check how the toolpath will be generated, select the **Preview toolpath** icon as shown.

♦ See **page 157** to review the procedure.
♦ The toolpath should look as shown.

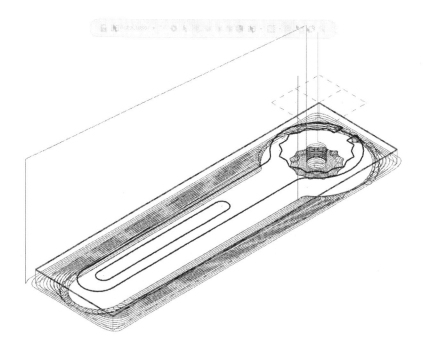

♦ Press **Esc** key to exit the preview.

> **NOTE:** If the toolpath does not look as shown in the preview, check your parameters again.

♦ Select the **OK** button to generate the toolpath.
♦ To remove the toolpath display, press **T** or click on the **Toggle display on selected operations**.

16.9 Verify the toolpath

♦ From the **Toolpaths Manager**, click on the **Select all operations** icon before clicking on the **Verify** button.

♦ Follow **Mastercam Simulation** procedures as shown on **page 160**.
♦ The part will appear as shown in Figure: 16.9.1.

Figure: 16.9.1

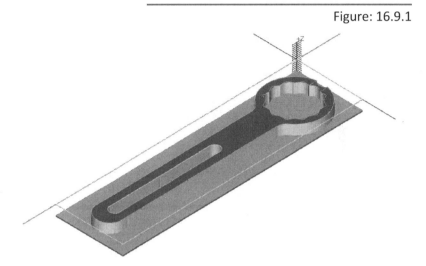

♦ To go back to the Mastercam window, minimize the **Mastercam Simulator** window as shown.

STEP 17: FINISH THE OUTSIDE PROFILE USING CONTOUR TOOLPATH

Contour toolpaths remove material along a path defined by a chain of curves. **Contour** toolpaths only follow a chain; they do not clean out an enclosed area.

Toolpath Preview:

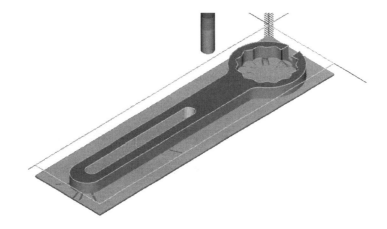

17.1 Chain selection

TOOLPATHS

♦ From the **2D** group, select **Contour** icon.

♦ Leave the **Chain** button enabled in the **Chaining** dialog box as shown.

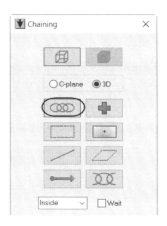

◆ Change the graphic view to **Top** and select the profile as shown in Figure: 17.1.1.

Figure: 17.1.1

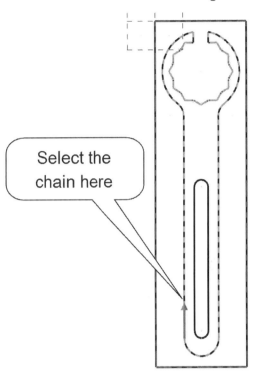

Select the
chain here

◆ Select the **OK** button to exit the **Chaining** dialog box.
◆ In the **Toolpath Type** page, the **Contour** icon will be selected as shown.

Contour   Pocket   Facing   Slot Mill

17.2 Select a 1/4" Flat Endmill from the list and set the Tool page parameters

♦ From the **Tree View list**, select **Tool** and make all the necessary changes as shown in Figure: 17.2.1.

Figure: 17.2.1

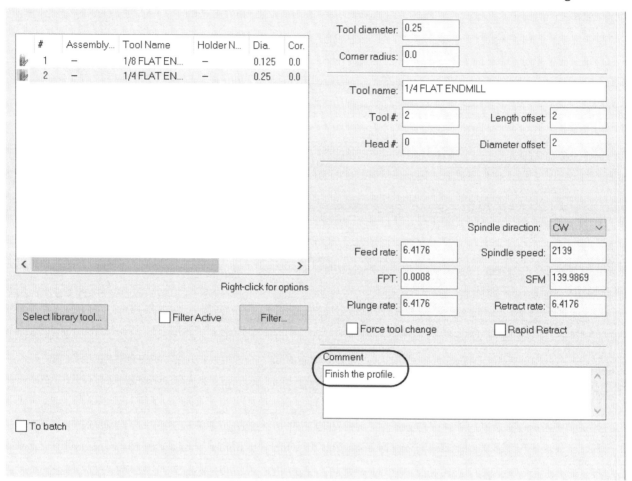

17.3 Cut Parameters

◆ From the **Tree View list**, select **Cut Parameters** and ensure the settings appear as shown in Figure: 17.3.1.

Figure: 17.3.1

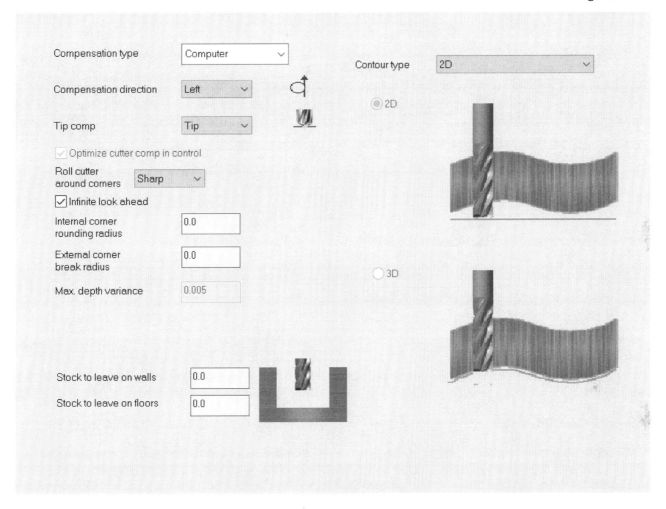

NOTE: For more information regarding these parameters ,please check **Step 15** in **Tutorial #1**.

17.4 Lead In/Out

◆ Select **Lead In/Out** from the **Tree View list**.
◆ Change the parameters as shown in Figure: 17.4.1.

Figure: 17.4.1

☑ Lead In/Out
  ☑ Enter/exit at midpoint in closed contours   ☑ Gouge check   Overlap `0.0`

☑ Entry			☑ Exit		
Line			**Line**		
○ Perpendicular	● Tangent		○ Perpendicular	● Tangent	
Length	`60.0`	% `0.15`	Length	`60.0`	% `0.15`
Ramp height		`0.0`	Ramp height		`0.0`
Arc			**Arc**		
Radius	`60.0`	% `0.15`	Radius	`60.0`	% `0.15`
Sweep		`90.0`	Sweep		`90.0`
Helix height		`0.0`	Helix height		`0.0`

  ☐ Use entry point   ☐ Use point depth   ☐ Use exit point   ☐ Use point depth
  ☐ Enter on first depth cut only   ☐ Exit on last depth cut only
  ☐ Plunge after first move   ☐ Retract before last move
  ☐ Override feed rate `6.4176`   ☐ Override feed rate `6.4176`

  ☐ Adjust start of contour   ☐ Adjust end of contour
    Length `0.0` % `0.0`   Length `0.0` % `0.0`
    ○ Extend   ● Shorten   ○ Extend   ● Shorten

17.5 Break Through

◆ From the **Tree View list**, select **Break Through** and make the necessary changes according to Figure: 17.5.1.

Figure: 17.5.1

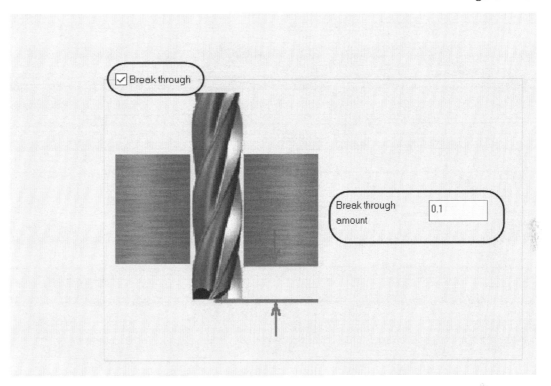

17.6 Linking Parameters

♦ Select **Linking Parameters** and input the **Depth** as shown as shown in Figure: 17.6.1.

Figure: 17.6.1

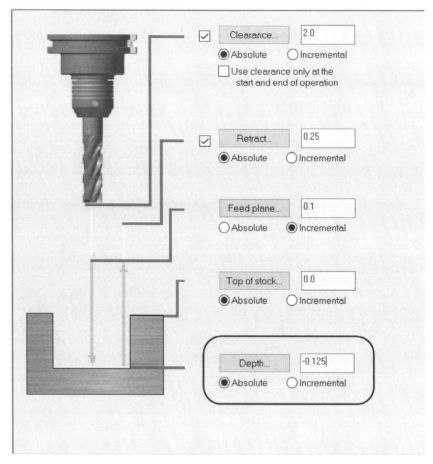

17.7 Preview the Toolpath

♦ To quickly check how the toolpath will be generated, select the **Preview toolpath** icon as shown.

♦ See **page 157** to review the procedure.

- ◆ The toolpath should look as shown.

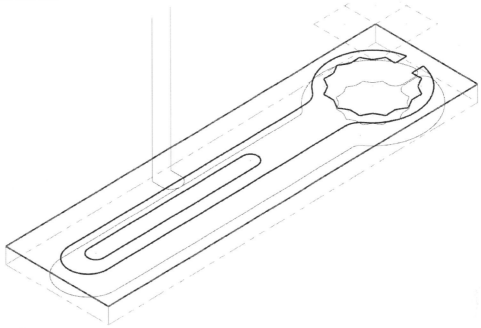

- ◆ Press **Esc** key to exit the preview.

> **NOTE:** If the toolpath does not look as shown in the preview, check your parameters again.

- ◆ Once completed select the **OK** button to generate the toolpath.

17.8 Backplot and Verify the toolpaths

- ◆ To **Backplot** and **Verify** the toolpaths, see **page 158** to review the procedures.
- ◆ To select all the operations, from the **Toolpaths Manager**, click on the **Select all operations** icon.

- ◆ After running **Verify,** the part should look as shown.

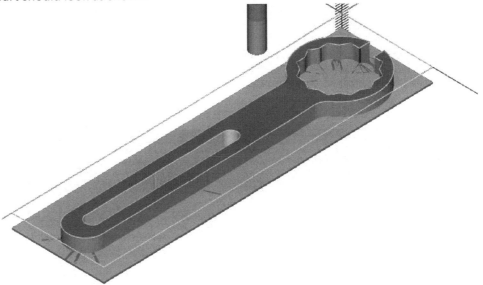

STEP 18: CLEAN THE INSIDE SHAPE USING 2D HS DYNAMIC CONTOUR

2D HS Dynamic Contour toolpath utilizes the entire flute length of the cutting tools and is used to mill material off walls. It does support both closed or open chains.

Toolpath Preview:

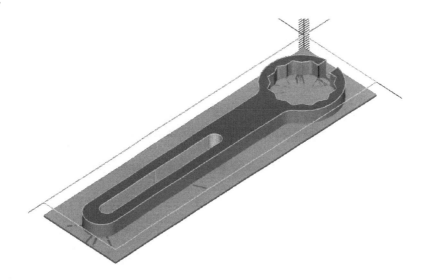

TOOLPATHS

• From the **2D** group, click on the downward arrow until you see the **Dynamic Contour** icon and select it.

18.1 Select the Geometry

• In the **Chain Options** panel, in the **Machining regions**, click on the **Select machining chains** button as shown.

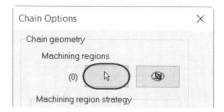

• Enable the **Partial** button in the **Chaining** dialog box as shown.

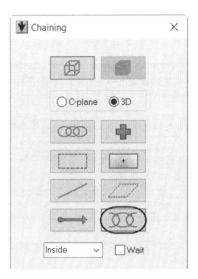

• Select the first entity of the chain as shown in Figure: 18.1.1. Make sure that the arrows are pointing

downward as shown. Otherwise, select the reverse button from the **Chaining** dialog box.

Figure: 18.1.1

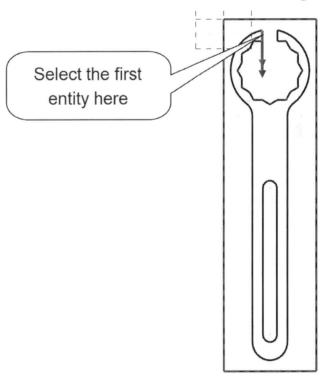

Select the first
entity here

• Select the last entity of the chain as shown in <u>Figure: 18.1.2</u>.

Figure: 18.1.2

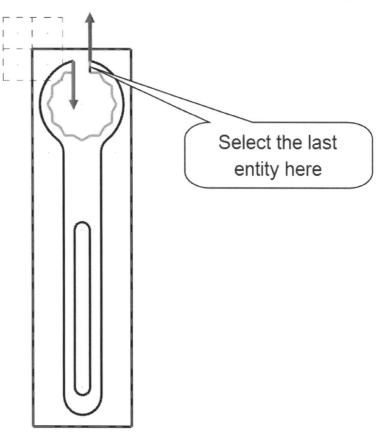

Select the last entity here

• Choose the **OK** button to exit the **Chaining** dialog box.

• Select the **OK** button to exit the **Chain Options** dialog box and to continue.
• On the **Toolpath Type** page, **Dynamic Contour** should already be selected.

18.2 Select a 1/16" Flat Endmill

+ Select **Tool** from the **Tree View** list.
+ Click on **Select library tool** button.

+ Select the **Filter** button.

+ Select the **None** button and then under **Tool Types** choose the **Flat Endmill** icon.
+ Under tool diameter pick **Equal** and input a value **0.0625** as shown in Figure: 18.2.1.

Figure: 18.2.1

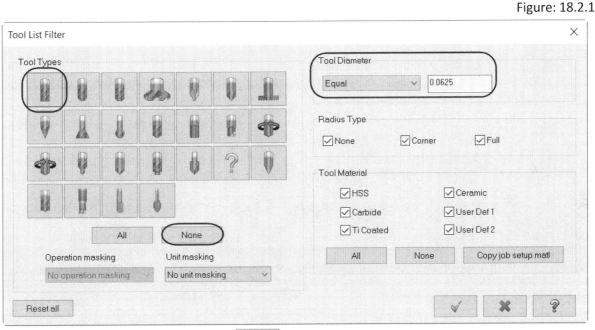

+ Select the **OK** button to exit the **Tool List Filter.**
+ In the **Tool Selection** dialog box you should only see a **1/16" Flat Endmill**.

#	Assembly...	Tool Name	Holder Name	Dia.	Cor. r...	Length	# Flut...	Type	Rad....
280	--	1/16 FLAT ENDMILL	--	0.0625	0.0	0.375	4	End...	None

+ Select the **1/16" Flat Endmill** in the **Tool Selection** page and then select the **OK** button to exit.

◆ Make any other changes as shown in Figure: 18.2.2.

Figure: 18.2.2

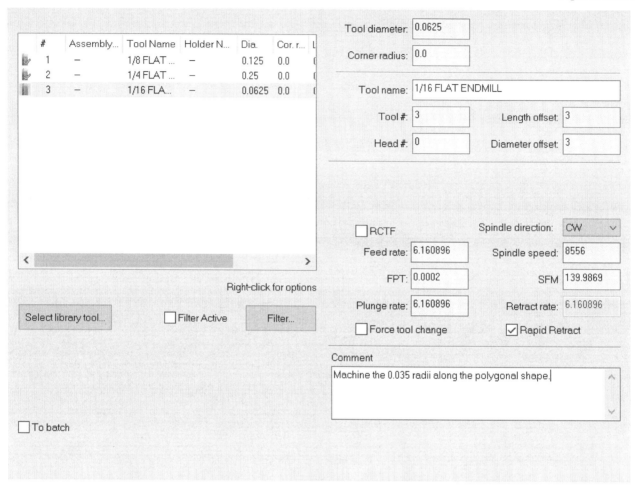

18.3 Cut Parameters

◆ From the **Tree View list**, select **Cut Parameters** and ensure the parameters are the same as in Figure: 18.3.1.

Figure: 18.3.1

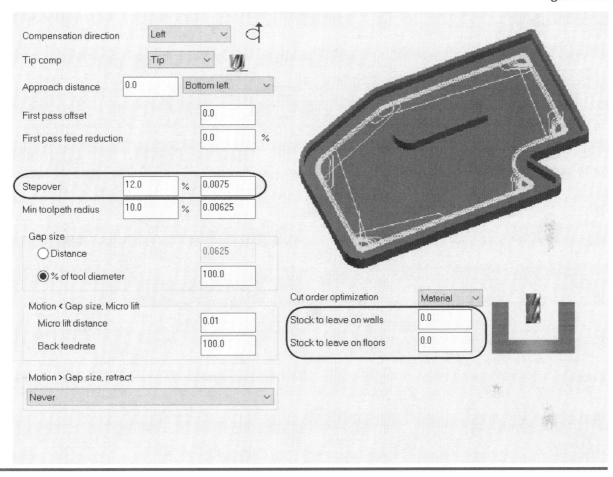

Compensation direction offsets the tool to the **Left** in our case.

Approach distance adds the specified absolute distance to the beginning of the toolpath's first cut.

First pass offset offsets out the machining region with a user defined distance for the tool to safely engage from the outside in the material.

First pass feed reduction allows you to slow the feed for the first pass on machining region material approached from the outside.

Stepover sets the distance between cutting passes in the X and Y axes. Enter a percentage of the tool diameter or an absolute distance.

Min toolpath radius sets the minimum toolpath radius used in combination with the **Microlift distance** and **Back feedrate** parameters to calculate 3D arc moves between cut passes.

18.4 Contour Wall

♦ From the **Tree View list**, select **Contour Wall** and ensure your parameters appear as shown in Figure: 18.4.1.

> **NOTE:** The graphics in the toolpath pages are changing based on the parameter field you click on. Your graphic might look different.

Figure: 18.4.1

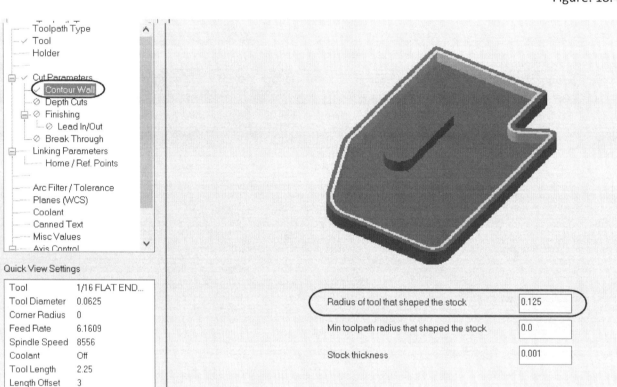

Radius of tool that shaped the stock is the radius of the tool used in a toolpath that already cuts this area. Mastercam calculates the stock to remove along the contour wall using the stock thickness (required) and, if provided, the **Radius of the tool that shaped the stock** and the **Toolpath radius that shaped the stock**.

In your case, in the previous contour operation you used a 0.25" Flat Endmill and no toolpath radius was required in the toolpath. As no stock was left in the contour, the stock thickness is the value of the toolpath tolerance.

18.5 Depth Cuts

◆ From the **Tree View list**, choose **Depth Cuts** and enable it. Input a **Max rough step** of **0.05** as shown in
Figure: 18.5.1.

Figure: 18.5.1

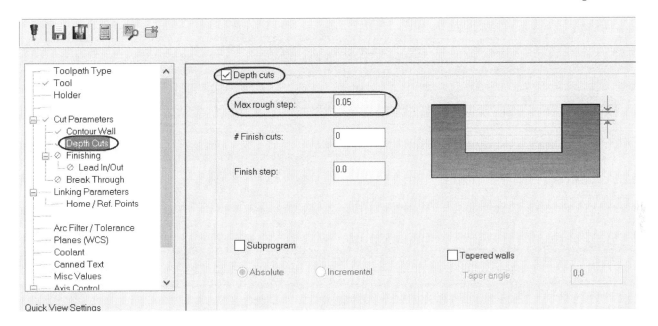

18.6 Break Through

◆ From the **Tree View list**, select **Break Through** and make the necessary changes as shown in Figure: 18.6.1.

Figure: 18.6.1

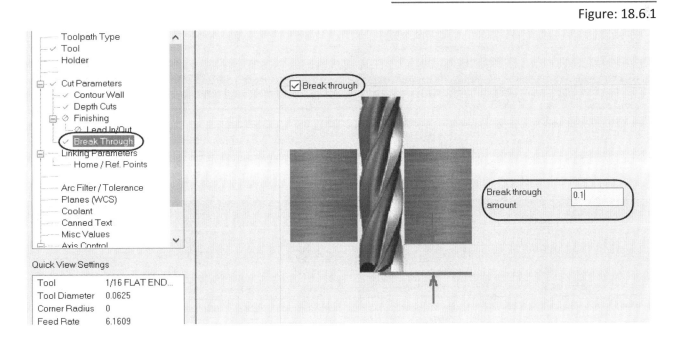

18.7 Linking Parameters

• Select **Linking Parameters** from the **Tree View list**.
• Set the **Depth** to **-0.125** as shown in Figure: 18.7.1.

Figure: 18.7.1

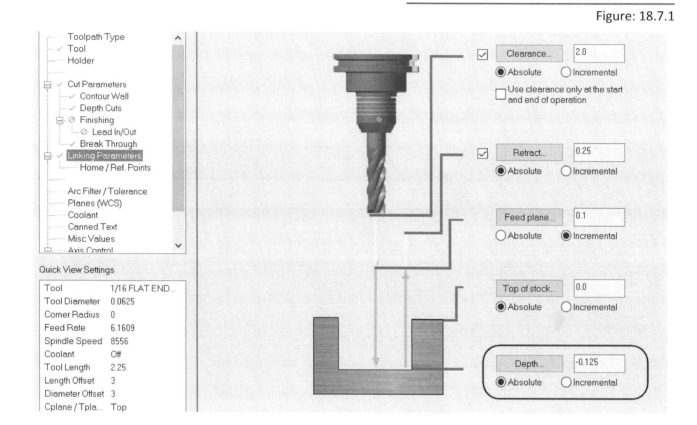

18.8 Preview the Toolpath

◆ To quickly check how the toolpath will be generated, select the **Preview toolpath** icon as shown.

◆ See **page 157** to review the procedure.
◆ The toolpath should look as shown.

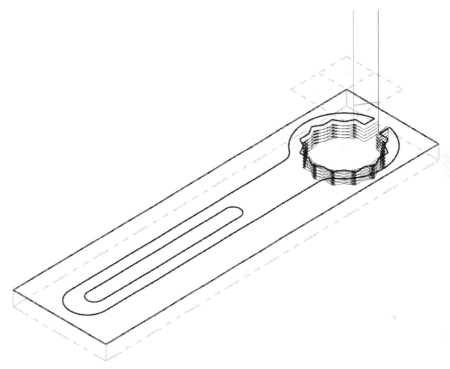

◆ Press **Esc** key to exit the preview.

| **NOTE:** If the toolpath does not look as shown in the preview, check your parameters again.

◆ Select the **OK** button to exit the **Dynamic Contour** parameters.

18.9 Backplot and Verify

- To **Backplot** and **Verify** your toolpath, see **page 158** to review the procedures.
- To select all the operations, from the **Toolpaths Manager**, click on the **Select all operations** icon.

- The part should look as shown.

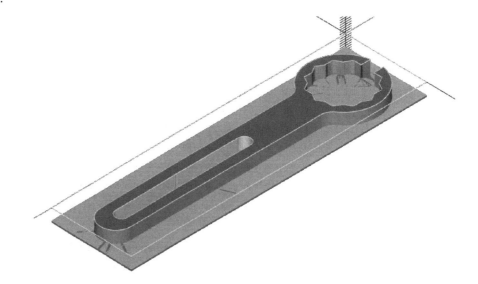

TOOLPATH CREATION - SETUP 2

SUGGESTED FIXTURE:

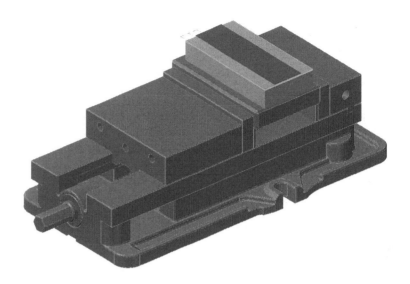

| NOTE: In order to machine this part, we will have 2 setups and output 2 NC files.

SETUP SHEET:

TOOL LIST

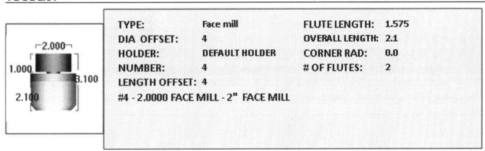

TYPE:	Face mill	FLUTE LENGTH:	1.575
DIA OFFSET:	4	OVERALL LENGTH:	2.1
HOLDER:	DEFAULT HOLDER	CORNER RAD:	0.0
NUMBER:	4	# OF FLUTES:	2
LENGTH OFFSET:	4		

#4 - 2.0000 FACE MILL - 2" FACE MILL

STEP 19: CREATING AND RENAMING TOOLPATH GROUPS

To machine the part in two different setups, we will need to have two separate programs. To be able to post process the operations of each setup separately, we will create them under different toolpath groups with different NC names.

19.1 Rename the current Toolpath Group - 1 and NC file

- Click once on the **Toolpath Group - 1** to highlight it and then click on it again to rename it "Setup #1" as shown in Figure: 19.1.1.

Figure: 19.1.1

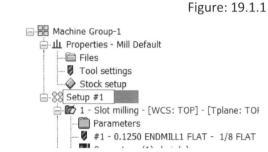

- Right mouse click on the **Setup #1 Toolpath group** and select **Edit selected operations** and then select **Change NC file name.**

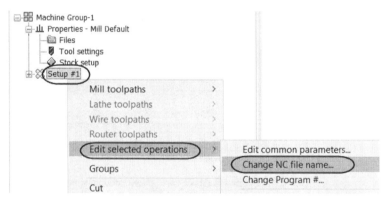

- Enter the new NC name: **Setup #1.**

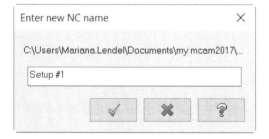

- Select the **OK** button to accept the new **NC name**.

19.2 Create a new Toolpath Group

◆ Right mouse click on the **Machine Group-1** and select **Groups** and then **New Toolpath group** as shown.

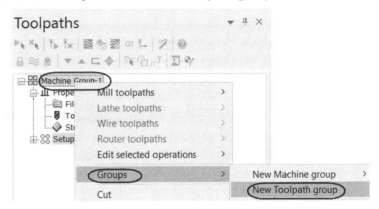

◆ Rename the toolpath group "**Setup #2**" as shown in the previous step.

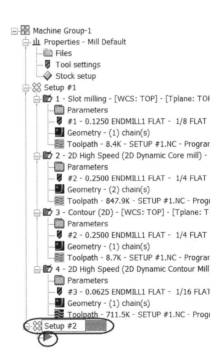

NOTE: The red insert arrow controls where the new operation will be inserted. In our case it should be located below the Setup #2 group.

◆ If the insert arrow needs to be relocated, from the **Toolpaths Manager**, click on the **Move insert arrow down** icon.

STEP 20: SET WCS TO BOTTOM

Work coordinate system (WCS) is the active coordinate system in use by Mastercam at any given time. The WCS contains the orientation of the X-Y-Z axes plus the location of the zero point (the origin). This tells Mastercam how your part is positioned or oriented in the machine.

Construction plane (Cplane) is the plane in which the geometry is created.

Tool plane (Tplane) is the plane normal to Z or to the vertical tool axis in which the tool moves. When creating a toolpath, both **Cplane** and **Tplane** should be set to the same plane. If the Tplane is different than the **WCS,** the post will produce a rotary motion code. By setting the **Cplane**, **Tplane** and **WCS** to one plane, no rotary move will be generated in the code which is what you want when machining parts with multiple setups.

In this step you will set the **WCS**, the **Construction plane (Cplane)** and the **Tool plane (Tplane)** to a new plane that can be defined using existing geometry. In our case, we will define the plane using two lines.

 ♦ Select **Planes** tab located at the bottom left corner.

◆ To create a new plane based on existing geometry, click on the + sign as shown.

◆ Select **From Geometry** as shown.

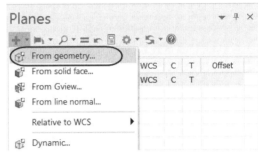

◆ Right mouse click in the graphics window and select the **Isometric** view.

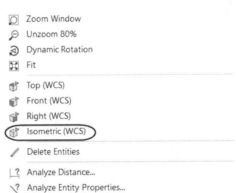

- Select the first line along the X axis of the new view and then select the line along the Y axis of the new view as shown in <u>Figure: 20.0.1</u>.

Figure: 20.0.1

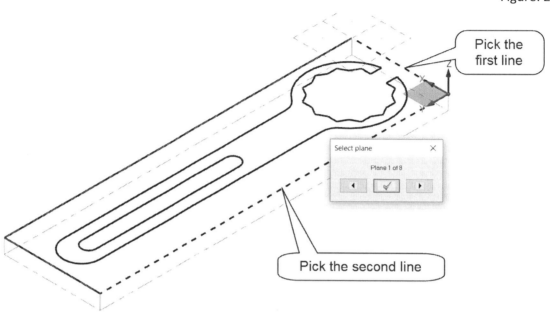

- In **Select plane**, click on the **Next plane** button until the axes are oriented as shown in <u>Figure: 20.0.2</u>.

Figure: 20.0.2

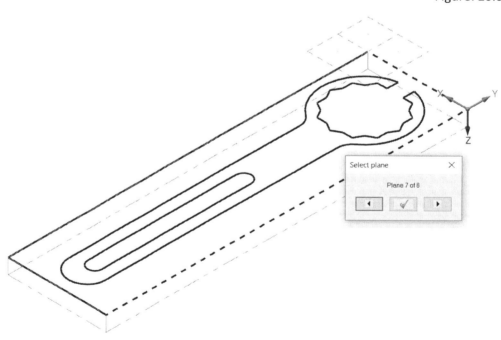

- From the **Select plane,** click on the **OK** button to continue.

- In the **New Plane** dialog box, in the **Name** field, input **Setup 2 Plane** as shown. Make sure that the **X coordinate** for the **Origin** is **-1.65**.

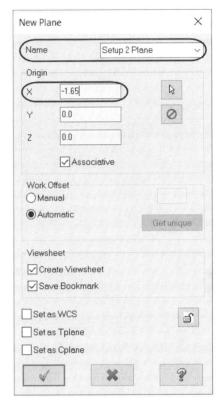

- Select the **OK** button to continue.

- Now we set the **Work Coordinate System (WCS)**, **Tool plane**, and **Construction plane** to the newly created **Setup 2 Plane** by clicking on the equal icon, with **Setup 2 Plane** highlighted in blue, as shown in Figure: 20.0.3.
- Set the **Origin Z** to **0.125**as shown in Figure: 20.0.3.

Figure: 20.0.3

- Right mouse click and select the **Isometric** view to see the part in its new orientation.

• The part should look as shown.

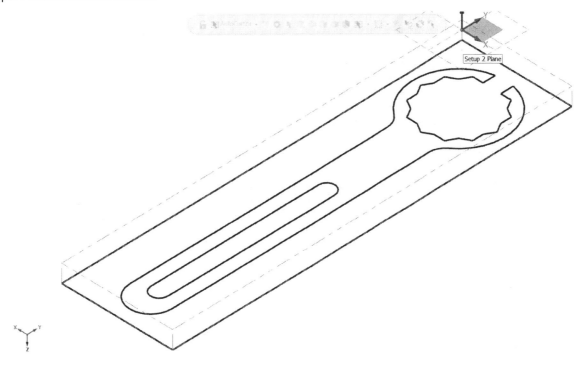

• Select the **Toolpath** tab to open the **Toolpaths Manager**.

| NOTE: **Z zero** is at **0.125** below the stock.

STEP 21: FACE THE PART

A **Facing** toolpath quickly removes material from the top of the part to create an even surface.

Toolpath Preview:

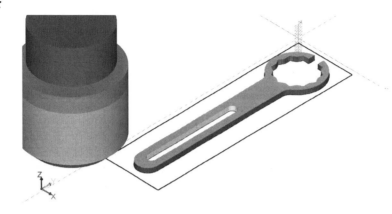

TOOLPATHS

* From the **2D** group, click on the upper arrow until you see the **Face** icon and select it as shown.

* When the **Chaining** dialog box appears, choose the **OK** button to use defined stock and exit the **Chaining** dialog box.

> **NOTE:** Mastercam will create the **Facing** toolpath defined from the stock setup.

* In the **Toolpath Type** page, the **Facing** icon will be automatically selected.

Contour   Pocket   Facing   Slot Mill

21.1 Select a 2.0" Face Mill from the library and set the Tool parameters

* Select **Tool** from the **Tree View list.**

* Click on the **Select library tool** button. Select library tool...
* To be able to see all the tools from the library, disable **Filter Active**.
* Select the **2" Face Mill** as shown.

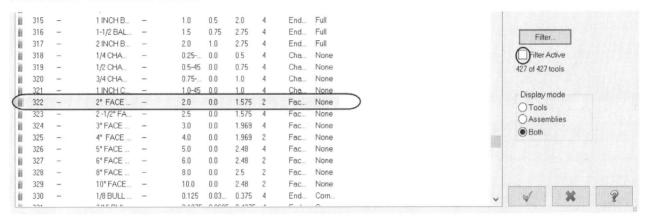

* Select the tool in the **Tool Selection** page and then select the **OK** button to exit.

• Make all the necessary changes as shown in Figure: 21.1.1.

Figure: 21.1.1

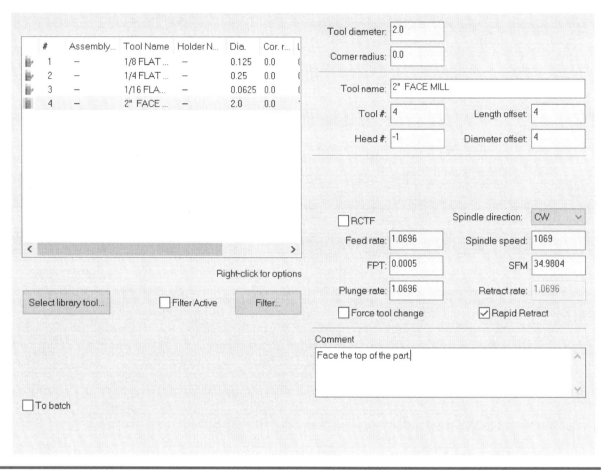

The **Feed rate**, **Plunge rate**, **Retract rate** and **Spindle speed** are based on the tool definition as set in the **Tool Settings**. You may change these values as per your part material and tools.

In the **Comment** field, enter a comment to help identify the toolpath in the **Toolpaths/ Toolpaths Manager** such as the one shown above.

● Select **Cut Parameters** and make the necessary changes as shown in Figure: 21.1.2.

Figure: 21.1.2

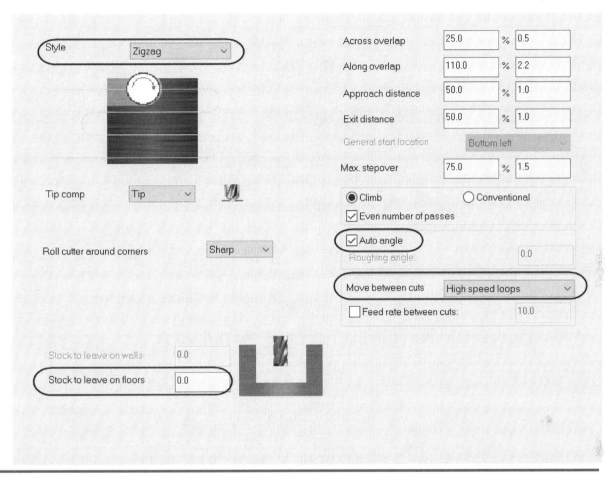

The **Style** (facing cutting method) **Zigzag** creates a back and forth cutting motion.

Auto angle determines the angle to machine along the larger side of the stock.

Move between cuts determines how the tool moves between each cut. This is only available if you select the zigzag cutting method.

High speed loops creates 180 degrees arcs between each cut.

◆ Select the **Linking Parameters** page and make the necessary changes as shown in Figure: 21.1.3.

Figure: 21.1.3

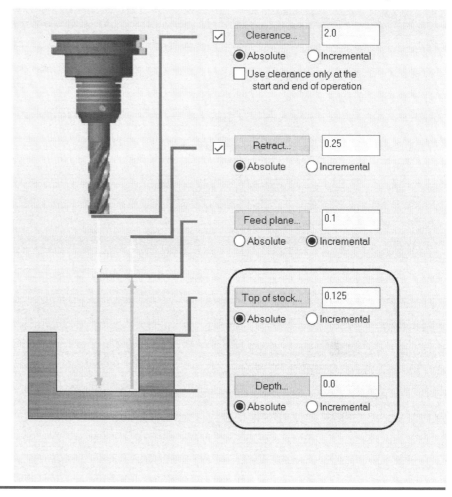

Clearance sets the height at which the tool moves to and from the part.

Retract sets the height to which the tool moves up before the next tool pass.

Feed Plane sets the height to which the tool rapids before changing to the plunge rate to enter the part.

Top of stock sets the height of the material in the Z axis.

Depth determines the final machining depth that the tool descends into the stock.

NOTE: The top of stock is set to **0.125"** because in our **Setup 2 Plane** we have the **Origin Z** value set to **0.125"** above the first setup origin. The depth is set to **0.0"** because this is the depth of the finish part we want the tool to go to.

21.2 Preview the Toolpath

- To quickly check how the toolpath will be generated, select the **Preview toolpath** icon as shown.

- See **page 157** to review the procedure.
- The toolpath should look as shown.

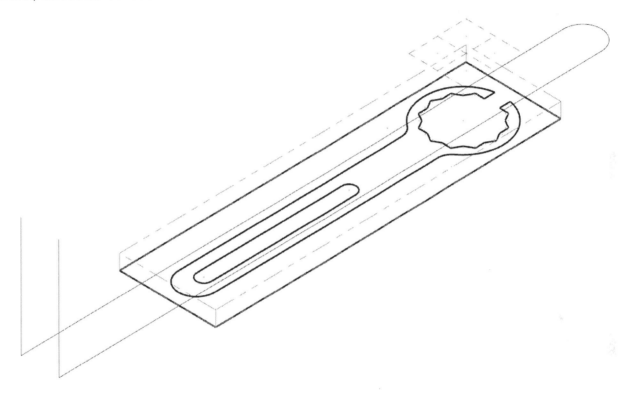

- Press **Esc** key to exit the preview.

> **NOTE:** If the toolpath does not look as shown in the preview, check your parameters again.

- Select the **OK** button to exit the **2D Toolpaths - Facing** parameters.
- To **Backplot** and **Verify** your toolpath, see **page 158** to review the procedures.
- To select all the operations, from the **Toolpaths Manager**, click on the **Select all operations** icon.

• The toolpaths should look as shown.

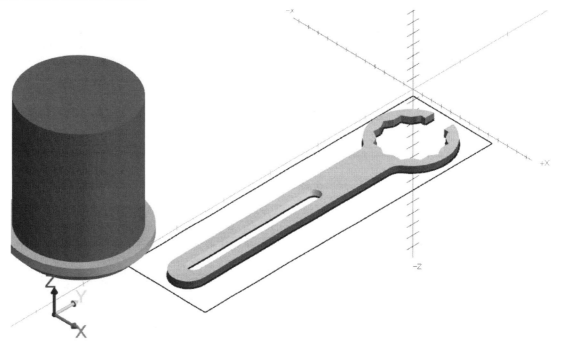

• To exit the **Mastercam Simulator**, click on the **Close** icon.

STEP 22: RENAME THE NC FILE

The Facing operation in Setup #2 kept the NC name from Setup #1. We need to rename this operation.

* Right click on **Setup #2** group, choose the option **Edit selected operations** and then select **Change NC file name**.

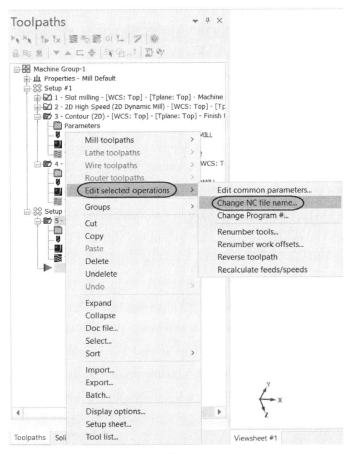

* When the **Enter new NC name** panel appears, enter **"Setup #2"** in the input field.

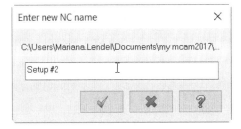

* Select the **OK** button to apply the change and exit the panel.

♦ As a result, you should see **Setup #2.NC** in the last item of text for Operation #5.

STEP 23: POST THE FILE

♦ Ensure all operations are selected; if not, use the button **Select all operations** in the **Toolpaths Manager.**

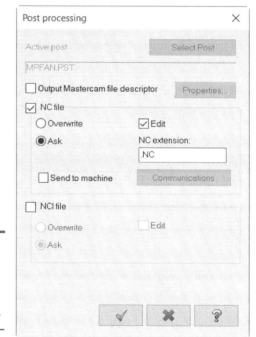

♦ Select the **Post selected operations**  button from the **Toolpaths Manager.**
♦ In the **Post processing** window, make the necessary changes as shown in Figure: 23.0.1.

Figure: 23.0.1

NC File enabled allows you to keep the NC file and to assign the same name as the MCAM file.

Edit enabled allows you to automatically launch the default editor.

♦ Select the **OK** button to continue.
♦ Save Setup #1 NC file.
♦ Save Setup #2 NC file.

♦ A window with the **Mastercam Code Expert** will be launched, and the NC program will appear as shown in
Figure: 23.0.2.

Figure: 23.0.2

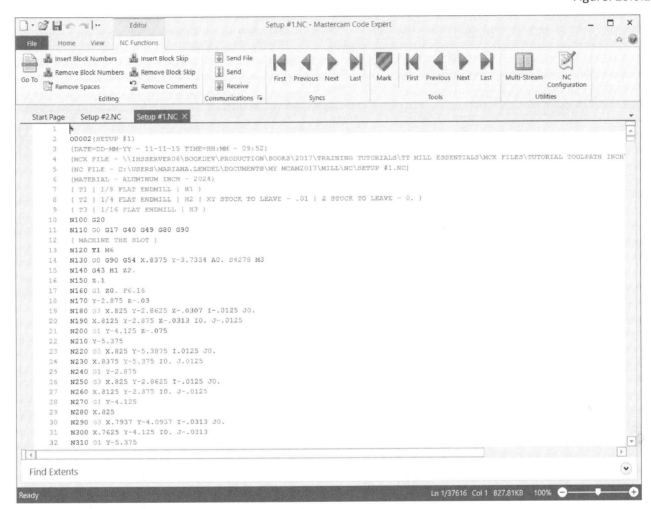

♦ Select the **"X"** at the upper right corner to exit the editor.

STEP 24: SAVE THE UPDATED MCAM FILE

REVIEW EXERCISE - STUDENT PRACTICE

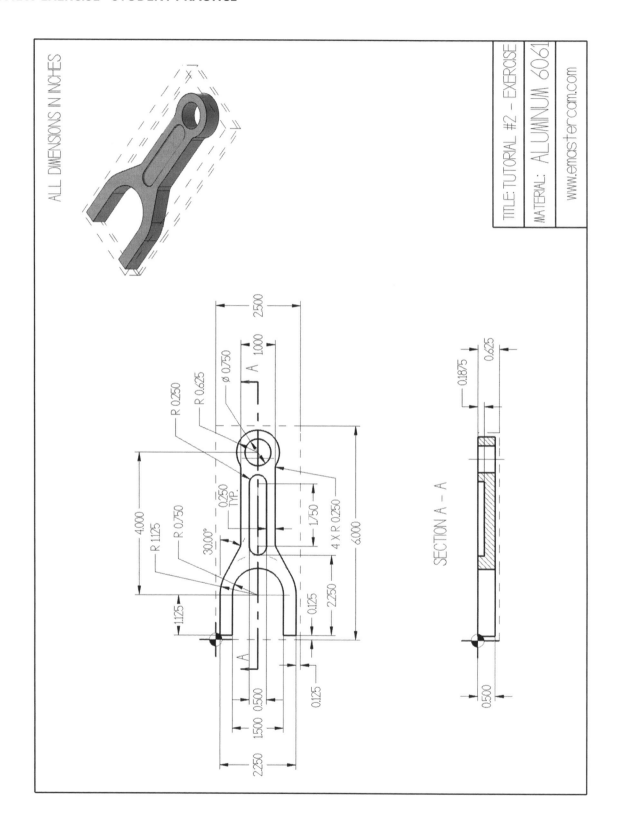

ALL DIMENSIONS IN INCHES

TITLE: TUTORIAL #2 - EXERCISE
MATERIAL: ALUMINUM 6061
www.emastercam.com

SECTION A – A

CREATE THE GEOMETRY FOR TUTORIAL #2 EXERCISE

Use these commands to create the geometry:
- Rectangular Shapes.
- Circle Center Point.
- Line Endpoints (Vertical and Horizontal).
- Line Tangent.
- Use Break Two Pieces.
- Line Parallel.
- Fillet Entities.

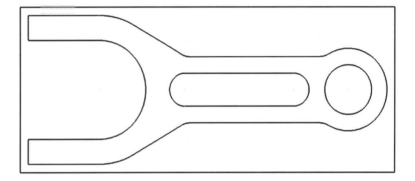

CREATE THE TOOLPATHS FOR TUTORIAL #2 EXERCISE

Create the Toolpaths for Tutorial #2 Exercise as per the instructions below.

Setup #1
Set the machine properties including the stock setup.

Remove the material in the slot using Slot Mill.
* Use a **1/4" Flat Endmill**.
* **Stock to leave on walls/floors = 0.0**.
* Set the **Depth** according to the drawing.

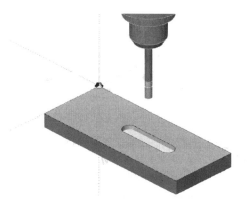

Circle Mill the 3/4" Hole.
* Choose a **3/8" Flat Endmill**.
* **Stock to leave on walls/floors = 0.0**.
* Enable **Roughing**.
* Set appropriate Depth of cuts and **Break through amount**.
* Input a **Depth** according to the drawing.

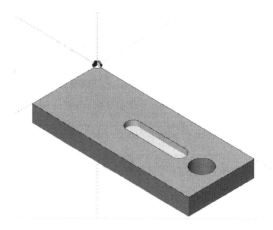

Rough the outside profile using 2D HS Dynamic Mill.
* Select the outside rectangle in the **Machining regions**.
* Enable **From outside**.
* Select the profile in the **Avoidance regions**.
* Use a **1/2" Flat Endmill**.
* Leave stock on the wall only.
* Set the **Depth** according to the drawing.

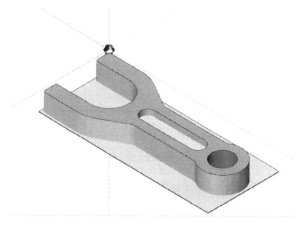

Finish the outside profile using Contour.

◆ Use a **1/2" Flat Endmill**.

◆ Set the final **Depth** according to the drawing.

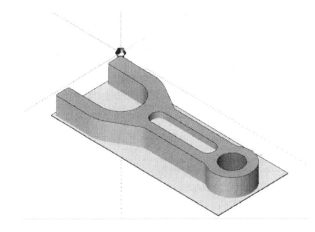

Setup #2.

◆ Rename the previous Toolpath Group Setup #1.

◆ Rename all the existing operation NC file Setup #1.

◆ Create a new Toolpath Group and rename it Setup #2.

Use the Plane Manager and set the Setup #2 plane.

◆ Use **Geometry** to define the plane.

◆ Set **WCS**, **Cplane** and **Tplane** to the new view.

◆ Set the **Z** origin to **-0.5**.

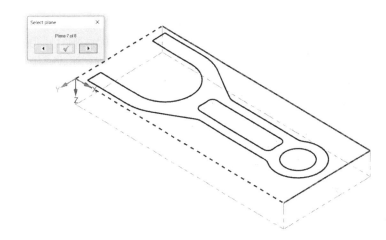

Face the part.

◆ Select the **2" Face Mill** from the **Tool** page.

◆ **Stock to leave on floors** = **0.0**.

◆ Set the **Depth** according to the drawing.

NOTES:

TUTORIAL #2 QUIZ

- What does Slot Mill toolpath do?

- What does 2D HS Dynamic Mill do?

- What does the 2D HS Dynamic Contour Mill do?

- What is the process used to be able to post different operations as different programs?

TUTORIAL #3

OVERVIEW OF STEPS TAKEN TO CREATE THE FINAL PART:

From Drawing to CAD Model:
* The student should examine the drawing on the following page to understand what part is being created in the tutorial.
* From the drawing we can decide how to create the geometry in Mastercam.

Create the 2D CAD Model used to generate Toolpaths from:
* The student will create the Top 2D geometry needed to create the toolpaths.
* Geometry creation commands such as Arc Polar, Circle Center Point, Line Tangent at an Angle, Mirror, Arc Tangent, Ellipse, Letters and Translate will be used.

Create the necessary Toolpaths to machine the part:
* The student will set up the stock size to be used and the clamping method used.
* A 2D High Speed Area Mill toolpath will be created to remove the material from the outside step.
* A 2D High Speed Dynamic Mill toolpath will be created to remove the outside material.
* A Pocket Island Facing toolpath will be created to machine the pocket and face the letters.
* A Pocket Remachining toolpath will be used to machine the remaining material.

Backplot and Verify the file:
* The Backplot will be used to simulate a step-by-step process of the tool's movements.
* The Verify will be used to watch a tool machine the part out of a solid model.

Post Process the file to generate the G-code:
* The student will then post process the file to obtain an NC file containing the necessary code for the machine.

 This tutorial takes approximately two hours to complete.

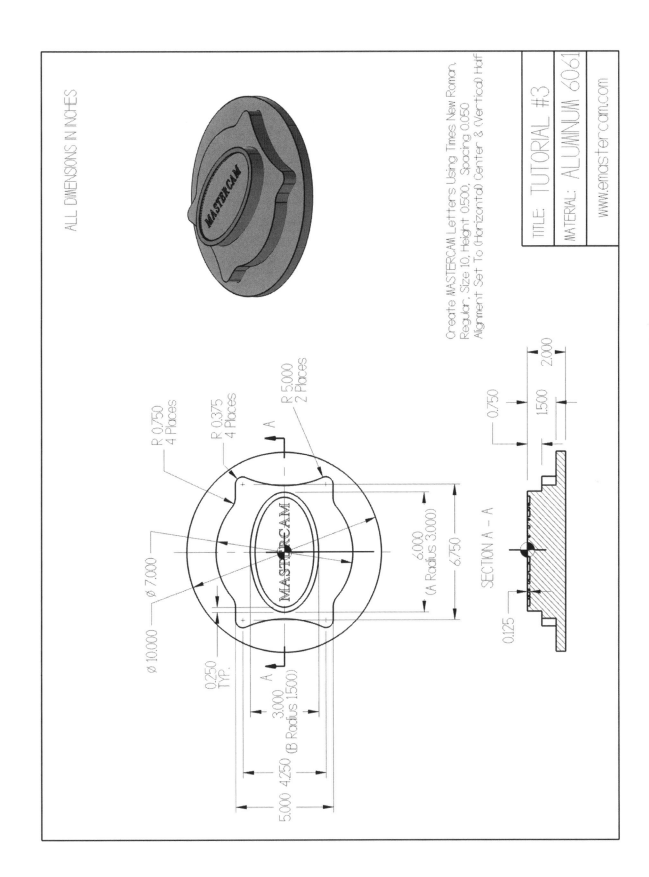

ALL DIMENSIONS IN INCHES

Create MASTERCAM Letters Using Times New Roman,
Regular, Size 10, Height 0.500, Spacing 0.050
Alignment Set To (Horizontal) Center & (Vertical) Half

TITLE: TUTORIAL #3

MATERIAL: ALUMINUM 6061

www.emastercam.com

R 0.750
4 Places

R 0.375
4 Places

R 5.000
2 Places

Ø 7.000

Ø 10.000

0.250
TYP.

3.000
(B Radius 1.500)

5.000   4.250

A

A

6.000
(A Radius 3.000)

6.750

SECTION A – A

0.750

2.000

1.500

0.125

GEOMETRY CREATION

STEP 1: SETTING UP THE GRAPHICAL USER INTERFACE

Please refer to the **Getting Started** section to set up the graphical user interface.

> **NOTE:** In the next few steps you will create a quarter of the entire geometry. You will then use the Mirror command to generate the rest.

STEP 2: CREATE TWO POLAR ARCS

In this step you will create two arcs using arc polar command. To create an arc polar, you need to know the radius, the start angle, the end angle, and the center point of the arc.

Step Preview:

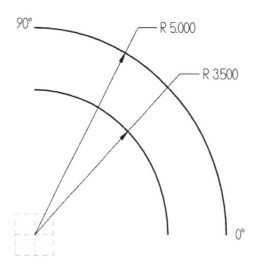

2.1 Create the 10.0" diameter arc

WIREFRAME

♦ From the **Arcs** group, click on the drop down arrow next to **Circle Edge Point** and select **Arc Polar** as shown.

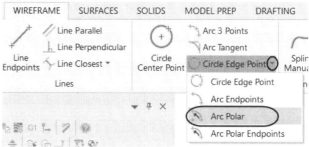

◆ [Enter the center point]: Select the Origin as shown in Figure: 2.1.1.

Figure: 2.1.1

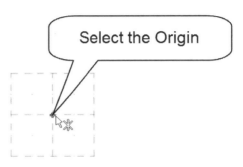

Select the Origin

◆ Make sure that when selecting the origin, the visual cue of the cursor changes as shown.
◆ Change the values in the **Arc Polar** panel as shown.

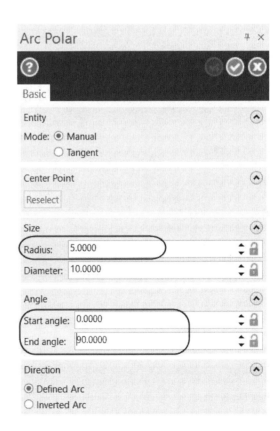

◆ Press **Enter**.
◆ Press **Alt** + **F1** to fit the geometry in the graphics window.

◆ Your drawing will appear as shown.

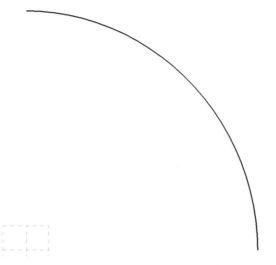

◆ Select the **OK and Create New Operation** button to continue with the same command.

> **NOTE:** While creating the geometry for this tutorial, if you make a mistake, you can undo the last step using the
>
> **Undo** icon. ↰ You can undo as many steps as needed. If you delete or undo a step by mistake, just use the
>
> **Redo** icon. ↱ To delete unwanted geometry, select the geometry first and then press **Delete** from the keyboard.

2.2 Create the 7.0" diameter arc

◆ [Enter the center point]: Select the center point of the arc as shown in <u>Figure: 2.1.1</u>.

Figure: 2.2.1

Select the center point

♦ Enter the values in the panel as shown.

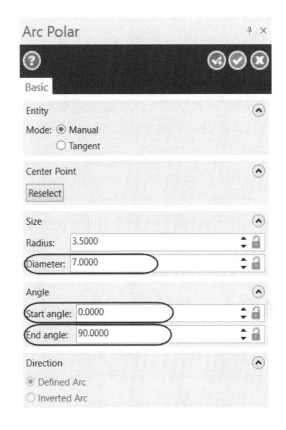

♦ The drawing will appear as shown.

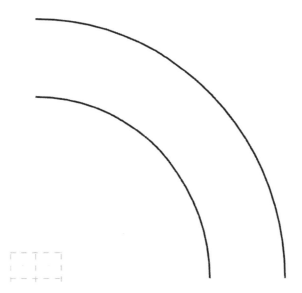

♦ Choose the **OK** button to exit the command.

STEP 3: CREATE A CIRCLE

In this step you will learn how to create a circle given the radius and the center point.

Step Preview:

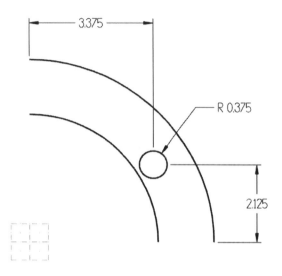

WIREFRAME

• From the **Arcs** group, select **Circle Center Point** as shown.

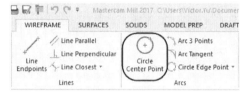

• Enter the **Radius 0.375** in the **Circle Center Point** panel as shown. Press **Enter**.

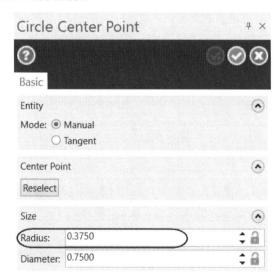

* Press **Space bar** and enter the coordinates of **3.375, 2.125** as shown.

3.375,2.125

* Hit **Enter** on your keyboard to position the arc.

* Select the **OK** button to exit the command.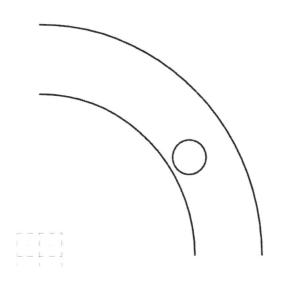
* The drawing should look as shown.

STEP 4: CREATE A LINE TANGENT TO THE CIRCLE

In this step you will use the **Create Line Endpoint** command to create a line tangent to the circle at a 180 degree angle. Mastercam angles are measured counter clockwise and will always total 360 degrees.

Step Preview:

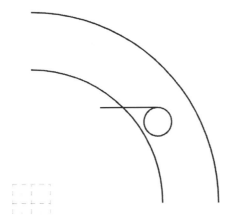

WIREFRAME

♦ From the **Lines** group, select **Line Endpoints** as shown.

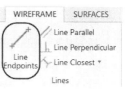

♦ In the panel, make sure that the **Tangent** button is enabled and enter the **Angle 180** as shown.

♦ [Specify the first point]: Select the arc as shown in <u>Figure: 4.0.1</u>. Make sure that only the arc as a whole is

selected and the quadrant point sign does not appear while selecting the arc.

Figure: 4.0.1

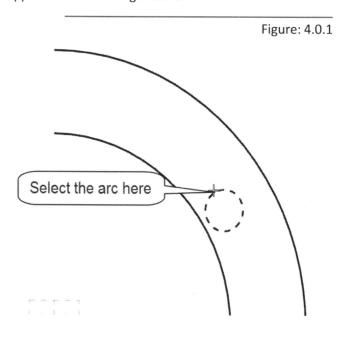

Select the arc here

• Sketch the line by moving the cursor to the left of the arc and click to select the second endpoint as shown in <u>Figure: 4.0.2</u>.

Figure: 4.0.2

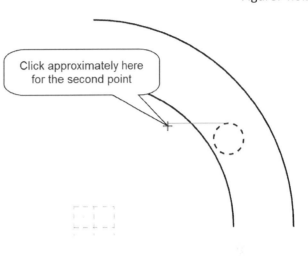

• Select the **OK** button to exit the command.
• The geometry should look as shown.

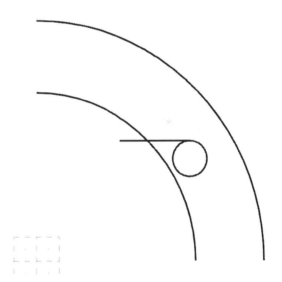

STEP 5: CREATE A FILLET

In this step you will use the **Create Fillet Entities** command to create a fillet with the radius 0.75. Fillets are used to round sharp corners.

Step Preview:

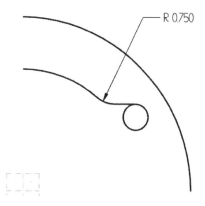

— R 0.750

WIREFRAME

♦ From the **Modify** group, select **Fillet Entities**.

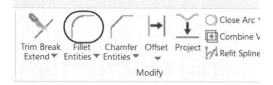

♦ Enter a fillet radius of **0.75**. Ensure the fillet style is set to **Normal** and **Trim entities** is enabled as shown.

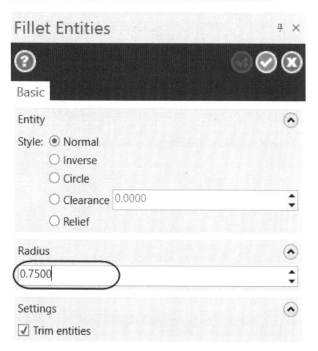

◆ [Select an entity]: Select Entity A as shown in <u>Figure: 5.0.1</u>.
◆ [Select another entity]: Select Entity B as shown in <u>Figure: 5.0.1</u>.

Figure: 5.0.1

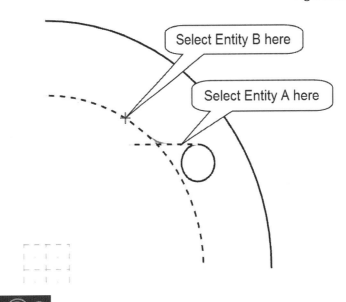

◆ Select the **OK** button to exit the command.
◆ The geometry should look as shown.

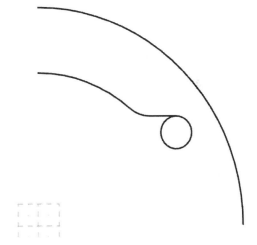

STEP 6: MIRROR THE GEOMETRY

In this step you will **Mirror** the inside geometry about the X axis.

Step Preview:

TRANSFORM

* From the **Position** group, select **Mirror** as shown.

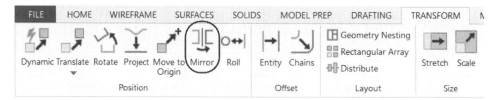

◆ [Mirror: select entities to mirror]: Make a Window around the entire geometry as shown in Figure: 6.0.1.

Figure: 6.0.1

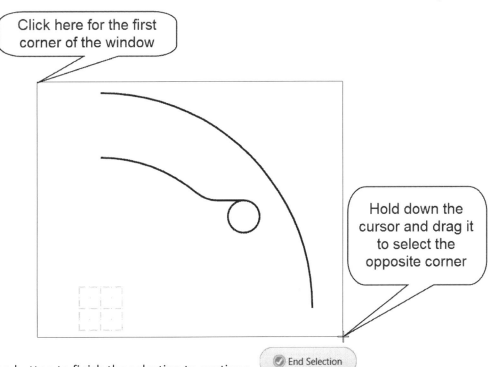

Click here for the first corner of the window

Hold down the cursor and drag it to select the opposite corner

End Selection

◆ Click on the **End Selection** button to finish the selection to continue.

• Select the option to mirror the entities about the **X axis** as shown in Figure: 6.0.2.

Figure: 6.0.2

• Select the **OK** button to exit the **Mirror** dialog box.
• Press **Alt + F1** to fit the drawing in the graphics window.
• The geometry should look as shown.

• Right mouse click in the graphics window and from the **Mini toolbar** select **Clear Colors** to return the colors to the original system colors.

STEP 7: CREATE AN ARC TANGENT TO TWO ENTITIES

In this step you will learn how to create an arc tangent to 2 arcs.

Step Preview:

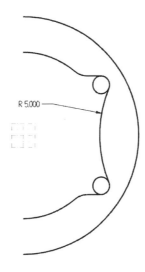

R 5.000

WIREFRAME

• From the **Arcs** group, select **Arc Tangent**.

• In the **Mode**, select the **Arc two entities** and enter the radius, as shown.

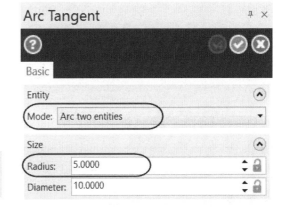

NOTE: To see a comprehensive description of the other tangent options, hover the cursor above the **Mode** field.

• [Select the entity that the arc is to be tangent]: Select Entity A as shown in Figure: 7.0.1.
• [Select the entity that the arc is to be tangent]: Select Entity B as shown in Figure: 7.0.1.

Figure: 7.0.1

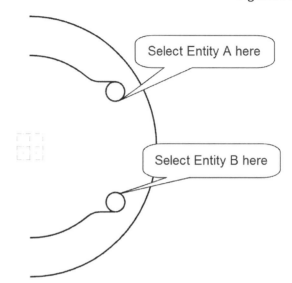

• [Select the fillet to use]: Select the arc as shown in Figure: 7.0.2.

Figure: 7.0.2

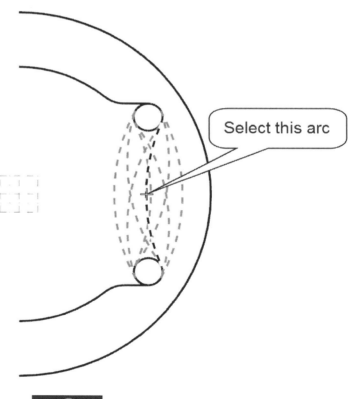

• Select the **OK** button to exit the **Arc Tangent** panel.

◆ The geometry should look as shown.

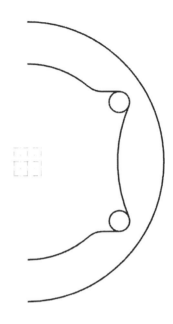

STEP 8: TRIM THE GEOMETRY USING TRIM 3 ENTITIES COMMAND

In this step you will use the **Trim Three Entities** command to clean the geometry. The first two entities that you select are trimmed to the third, which acts as a trimming curve. The third entity is then trimmed to the first two.

This function is useful for trimming two lines to a circle that is tangent to both lines. The arc is selected as the last entity, and the results vary depending on whether you choose to keep the top or the bottom of the arc.

Step Preview:

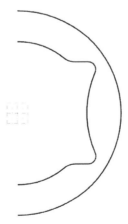

WIREFRAME

- From the **Modify** group, select **Trim Break Extend** icon as shown.

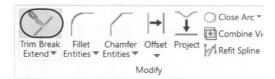

> **NOTE:** If you click on the lower part of the icon the drop down arrow will be activated and a list of options starting with the **Trim Break Extend** will open. Select the **Trim Break Extend** from the list.

- In the **Trim Break Extend** panel, select **Trim 3 entities** as shown.

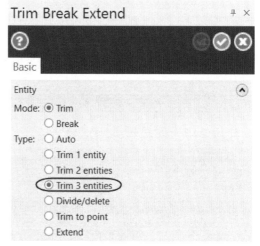

- [Select the first entity to trim/extend]: Select Entity A as shown in Figure: 8.0.1.
- [Select the second identity to trim/extend]: Select Entity B as shown in Figure: 8.0.1.
- [Select the entity to trim/extend to]: Select Entity C as shown in Figure: 8.0.1.

Figure: 8.0.1

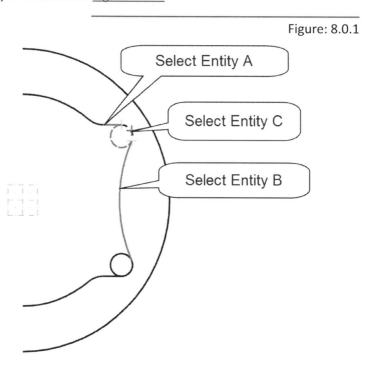

◆ The geometry should look as shown.

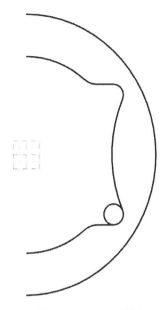

◆ Following the previous steps, similarly, you may trim the other circle at the bottom. The outcome will be as shown in the figure to the right.

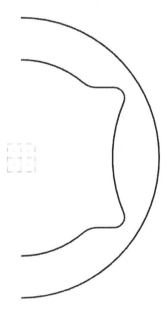

◆ Select the **OK** button to exit the command.

STEP 9: MIRROR THE GEOMETRY

In this step you will **Mirror** the inside geometry about the Y axis.

Step Preview:

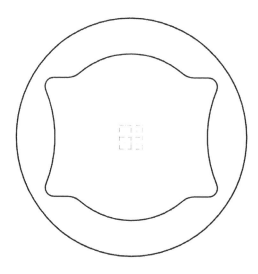

TRANSFORM

◆ From the **Position** group, select **Mirror**.

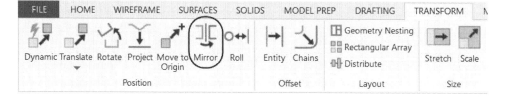

♦ [Mirror: select entities to mirror]: To select the entire geometry, hold down the **Shift** key and click on both contours as shown in <u>Figure: 9.0.1</u>.

Figure: 9.0.1

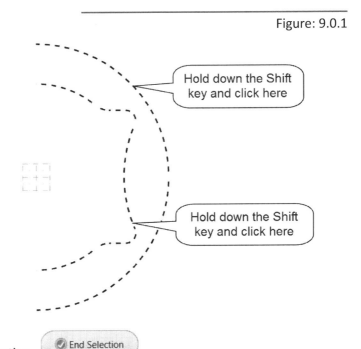

Hold down the Shift key and click here

Hold down the Shift key and click here

NOTE: By holding the **Shift** key and selecting one entity of a chain, Mastercam selects all the other entities that are in the same chain.

♦ Click on the **End Selection** button to finish the selection.   End Selection
♦ Select the option to mirror the entities about the **Y axis** as shown in <u>Figure: 9.0.2</u>.

Figure: 9.0.2

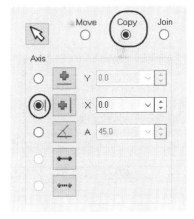

♦ Select the **OK** button to exit the **Mirror** dialog box.

* The geometry should look as shown.

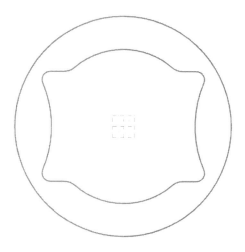

* Right mouse click in the graphics window and from the **Mini Toolbar**, select **Clear Colors** to return the colors to the original system colors.

STEP 10: CREATE THE ELLIPSES

In this step you will learn how to create an ellipse given the point of origin, A radius, and B radius.

Step Preview:

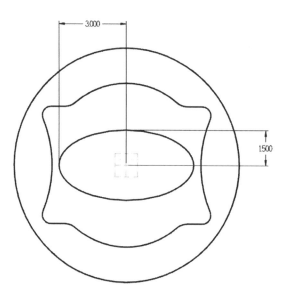

WIREFRAME

• From the **Shapes** group, click on the drop down arrow under **Rectangle** and select **Ellipse**.

• Select the **Origin** as the position of base point.

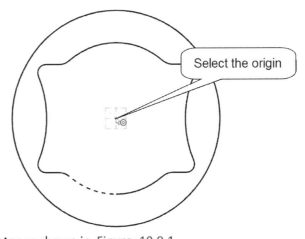

Select the origin

• Enter an **A radius** of **3.0**, a **B radius** of **1.5** and press **Enter** as shown in Figure: 10.0.1.

Figure: 10.0.1

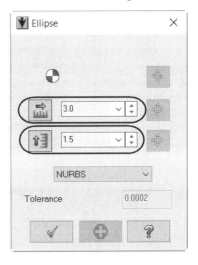

• Select the **OK** button to exit the **Ellipse** command.

STEP 11: OFFSET THE ELLIPSE

In this step you will offset the ellipse with a given distance.

Step Preview:

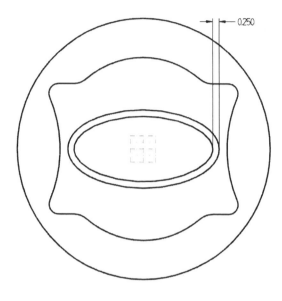

TRANSFORM
+ From the **Offset** group, select **Entity**.

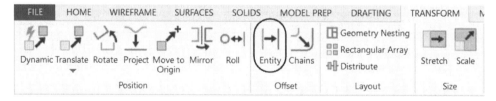

♦ [Select the line, arc, spline or curve to offset]: Select the ellipse as shown in <u>Figure: 11.0.1</u>.
♦ [Indicate the offset direction]: Click inside of the ellipse as shown in <u>Figure: 11.0.1</u>.

Figure: 11.0.1

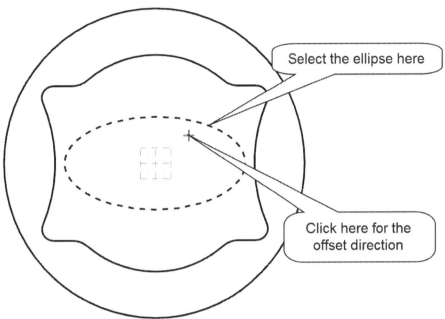

Select the ellipse here

Click here for the offset direction

♦ Change the distance in the **Offset** dialog box to **0.25** and leave **Copy** enabled as shown in <u>Figure: 11.0.2</u>.

Figure: 11.0.2

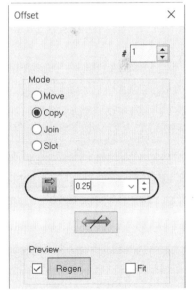

♦ Select the **OK** button to exit the **Offset** dialog box.
♦ Right mouse click in the graphics window and from the **Mini toolbar** select **Clear Colors** to return the colors to the original system colors.

• The geometry should look as shown.

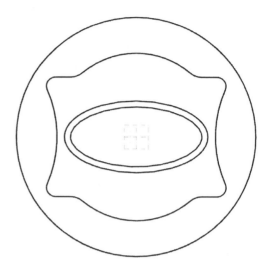

STEP 12: ADD THE TEXT

In this step you will create the **Letters**, then by using **Bounding box,** you will create a point at the center of these letters. You will then use the **Translate** command to move the letters to the center of the part.

Creating letters uses lines, arcs and, **NURBS** splines. There are various fonts found in this command as well. When using **TrueType** fonts, the height of the letters may not match the value you entered for the letter height because Mastercam scales the letters based on all the information encoded into the **TrueType** font.

Step Preview:

12.1 Change the wireframe color to red

HOME

- From the **Attributes** group, click on the drop down arrow next to the **Wireframe color** and select color red as shown.

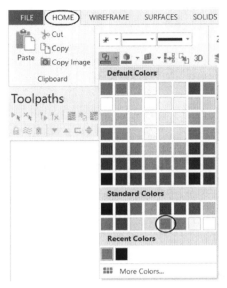

12.2 Create the letters

WIREFRAME

- From the **Shapes** group, select **Create Letters** as shown.

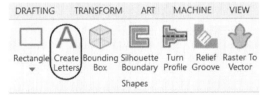

- When the **Create Letters** panel appears, leave the default settings and select **TrueType(R)** as shown in Figure: 12.2.1.

Figure: 12.2.1

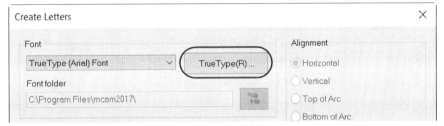

- Scroll down the **Font** list and find the font **Times New Roman**.

◆ Select **Bold** for the **Font style** as shown in <u>Figure: 12.2.2</u>.

Figure: 12.2.2

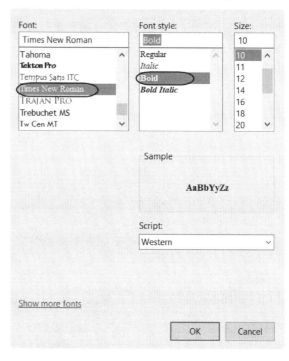

◆ Select the **OK** button. OK
◆ Input the word **MASTERCAM** in the field under **Letters** as shown in <u>Figure: 12.2.3</u>.

Figure: 12.2.3

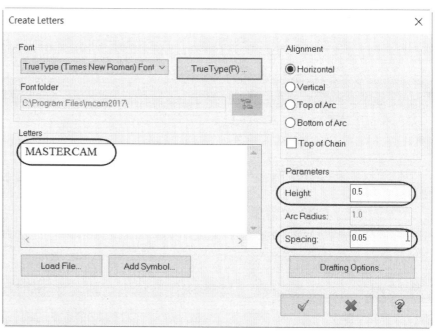

◆ Change the **Height** to **0.50** and the **Spacing** to **0.05**.

- Select the **OK** button.
- [Enter the starting location]: Select a point to the right of the part as the text starting location as shown in Figure: 12.2.4.

Figure: 12.2.4

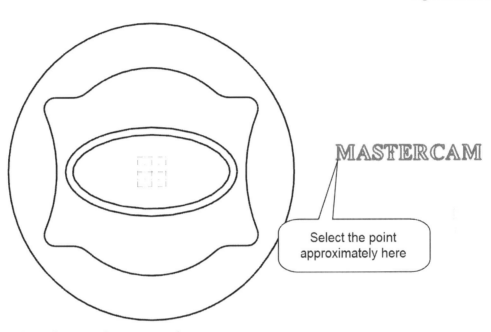

Select the point approximately here

- Press the **Esc** key on your keyboard to exit the command.

NOTE: Next we will move the text within the part.

- Press **Alt + F1** to fit the geometry in the graphics window if needed.

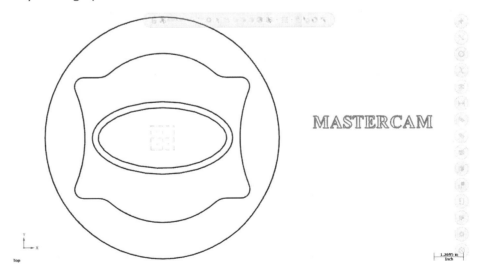

12.3 Move the letters using Translate

• Make a window outside the letters, as shown in <u>Figure: 12.3.1</u>.

Figure: 12.3.1

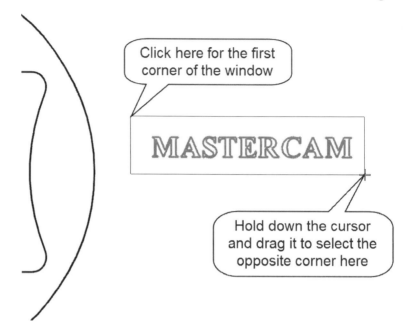

Click here for the first corner of the window

MASTERCAM

Hold down the cursor and drag it to select the opposite corner here

TRANSFORM

• From the **Position** group, select **Translate** icon as shown.

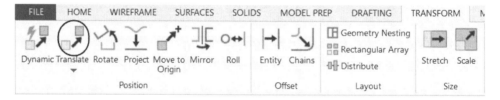

◆ When the **Translate** dialog box appears, select the **Move** button and then choose the **FROM point** icon as shown in Figure: 12.3.2.

Figure: 12.3.2

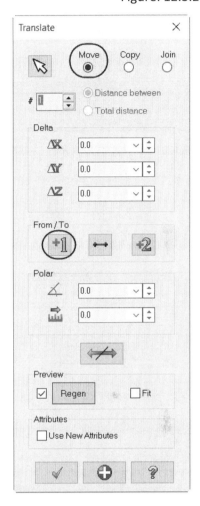

● Move the cursor close to the midpoint of the letters and scroll the mouse up to zoom in as shown in
<u>Figure: 12.3.3</u>

Figure: 12.3.3

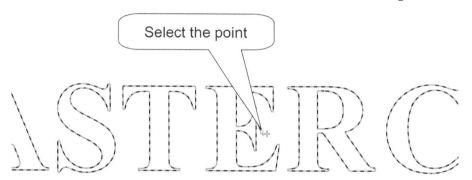

● [Select the point to translate from]: Select the center point that appeared automatically once you selected the
FROM point icon.

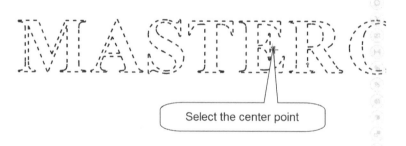

● [Select the point to translate to]: Click on the drop down arrow next to **AutoCursor** and then select **Origin**.

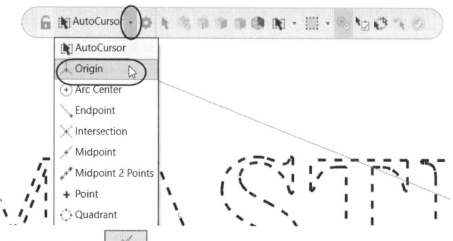

● Select the **OK** button in the **Translate** dialog box.

- Press **Alt + F1** to see the geometry.
- Right mouse click in the graphics window and from the **Mini toolbar** select **Clear Colors** to return the colors to the original system colors.

- Once complete, the geometry should look as shown.

STEP 13: SAVE THE FILE

FILE
- **Save As.**

- Click on the **Browse** icon as shown.
- Find a location on the computer to save your file. File name: "Your Name_3".

TOOLPATH CREATION

SUGGESTED FIXTURE:

SETUP SHEET:

TOOL LIST

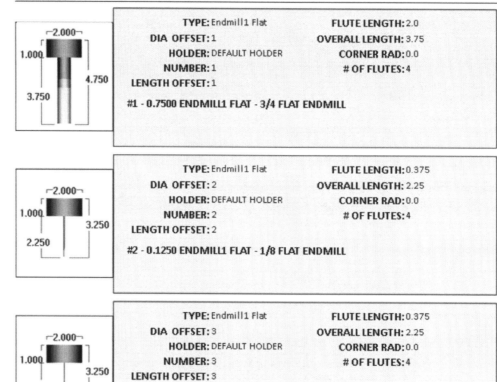

TYPE: Endmill1 Flat	**FLUTE LENGTH:** 2.0
DIA OFFSET: 1	**OVERALL LENGTH:** 3.75
HOLDER: DEFAULT HOLDER	**CORNER RAD:** 0.0
NUMBER: 1	**# OF FLUTES:** 4
LENGTH OFFSET: 1	

#1 - 0.7500 ENDMILL1 FLAT - 3/4 FLAT ENDMILL

TYPE: Endmill1 Flat	**FLUTE LENGTH:** 0.375
DIA OFFSET: 2	**OVERALL LENGTH:** 2.25
HOLDER: DEFAULT HOLDER	**CORNER RAD:** 0.0
NUMBER: 2	**# OF FLUTES:** 4
LENGTH OFFSET: 2	

#2 - 0.1250 ENDMILL1 FLAT - 1/8 FLAT ENDMILL

TYPE: Endmill1 Flat	**FLUTE LENGTH:** 0.375
DIA OFFSET: 3	**OVERALL LENGTH:** 2.25
HOLDER: DEFAULT HOLDER	**CORNER RAD:** 0.0
NUMBER: 3	**# OF FLUTES:** 4
LENGTH OFFSET: 3	

#3 - 0.0313 ENDMILL1 FLAT - 1/32 FLAT ENDMILL

STEP 14: SELECT THE MACHINE AND SET UP THE STOCK

In Mastercam, you select a **Machine Definition** before creating any toolpath. The **Machine Definition** is a model of your machine's capabilities and features. It acts like a template for setting up your machine. The machine definition ties together three main components: the schematic model of your machine's components, the control definition that models your control capabilities, and the post processor that will generate the required machine code (G-code). For a Mill Level 1 exercise (2D toolpaths), we just need a basic machine definition.

> **NOTE:** For the purpose of this tutorial, we will be using the Default milling machine.

14.1 Unhide the Toolpaths manager panel

+ From the left side of the graphics window, click on the Toolpaths tab as shown.

+ Pin the **Toolpaths Manager** by clicking on the **Auto Hide** icon as shown.

14.2 Select the machine

> **NOTE:** Select the **Mill Default** only if there is no **Machine Group** in the **Toolpaths Manager**.

MACHINE
+ From the **Machine Type** group, click on the drop down arrow below **Mill** and select the **Default**.

> **NOTE:** Once you select the **Mill Default** the ribbon bar changes to reflect the toolpaths that could be used with **Mill Default**.

♦ Select the plus sign (+) in front of **Properties** in the **Toolpaths Manager** to expand the **Toolpaths Group Properties.**

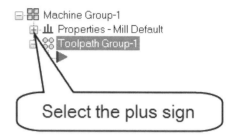

♦ Select **Tool settings** to set the tool parameters.

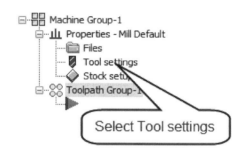

◆ Change the parameters to match the screenshot as shown in <u>Figure: 14.2.1</u>.

Figure: 14.2.1

Program # is used to enter a number if your machine requires a number for a program name.

Assign tool numbers sequentially allows you to overwrite the tool number from the library with the next available tool number. (First operation tool number 1; Second operation tool number 2, etc.)

Warn of duplicate tool numbers allows you to get a warning if you enter two tools with the same number.

Override defaults with modal values enables the system to keep the values that you enter.

Feed Calculation set to **From tool** uses feed rate, plunge rate, retract rate and spindle speed from the tool definition.

Machine Group Properties

Files | Tool Settings | Stock Setup

Program # [3]

Feed Calculation
- ● From tool
- ○ From material
- ○ From defaults
- ○ User defined
  - Spindle speed [5000.0]
  - Feed rate [50.0]
  - Retract rate [125.0]
  - Plunge rate [25.0]
- ☐ Adjust feed on arc move
  - Minimum arc feed [5.0]

Toolpath Configuration
- ☑ Assign tool numbers sequentially
- ☐ Warn of duplicate tool numbers
- ☐ Use tool's step, peck, coolant
- ☐ Search tool library when entering a tool number

Advanced options
- ☑ Override defaults with modal values
  - ☑ Clearance height
  - ☑ Retract height
  - ☑ Feed plane

Sequence #
- Start [100.0]
- Increment [10.0]

Material
[ALUMINUM inch - 2024] Edit.. Select..

- Select the **Stock Setup** tab to define the stock.
- Select the **Cylindrical Shape** and enter the values as shown in Figure: 14.2.2.

Figure: 14.2.2

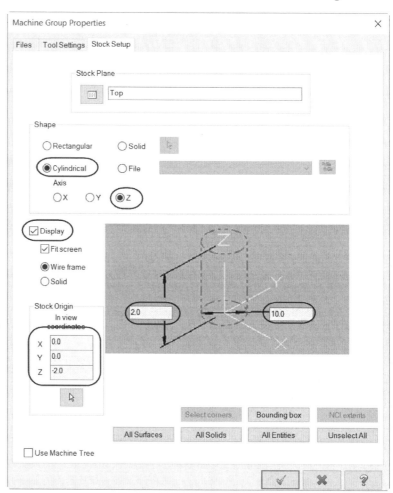

The **Stock Origin** values adjust the positioning of the stock, ensuring that you have an equal amount of extra stock around the finished part.

Display options allow you to set the stock as Wireframe and to fit the stock to the screen. (Fit Screen)

- Select the **OK** button to exit the **Machine Group Properties**.
- Right mouse click in the graphics window and select the **Isometric** view to see the stock.

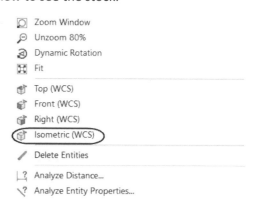

◆ The stock model will appear as shown.

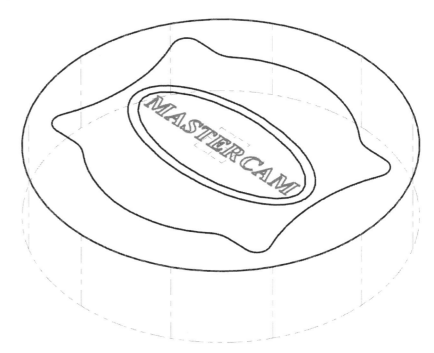

NOTE: The stock is not geometry and cannot be selected.

◆ Right mouse click in the graphics window and select the **Top** view to see the part from the top.

NOTE: There will not be a facing toolpath because the stock is already set to size.

STEP 15: 2D HIGH SPEED AREA MILL

2D High Speed Area Mill generates the free-flowing motion needed to machine features, such as standing bosses and cores or pockets in a single operation. With **Area Mill High Speed,** smaller depth of cuts are recommended, versus **Dynamic Mill** in which the depth cuts can be the size of the flute.

The toolpath depends on the **Machining strategy** that you choose in the **Chain Options**. If the strategy chosen is **From outside**, the toolpath starts at the outmost chain and works its way in, taking on the final shape of the part as it approaches the final pass. You can also machine pockets, in which case the strategy selected is **Start inside** which keeps the tool inside the machining regions.

Toolpath Preview:

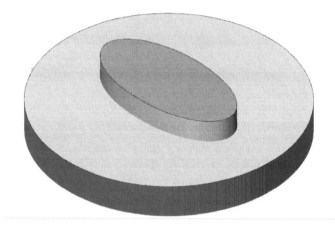

TOOLPATHS

◆ From the **2D** group, select the **Expand gallery** arrow.

◆ Select the **Area Mill** icon as shown.

♦ If a prompt appears, enter new **NC name** and select the **OK** button to accept the default.

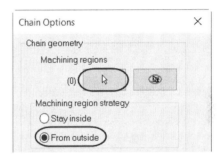

♦ In the **Chain Options,** enable **From outside** and click on the **Select machining chains** button in the **Machining regions** as shown.

♦ Leave the default settings in the **Chaining** dialog box.

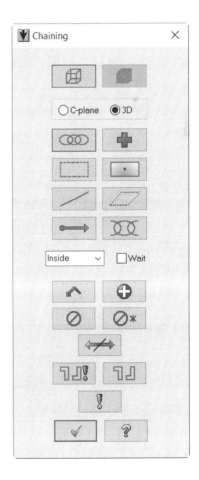

• [Select 2D HST machining chain 1]: Select the first chain as shown in <u>Figure: 15.0.1</u>.

Figure: 15.0.1

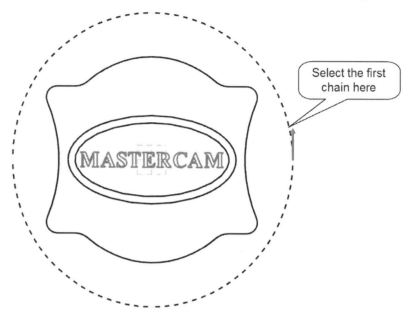

Select the first chain here

• Select the **OK** button to exit the **Chaining** dialog box. ✓
• From the **Chain Options**, click on the **Select avoidance chains** button in the **Avoidance regions** as shown.

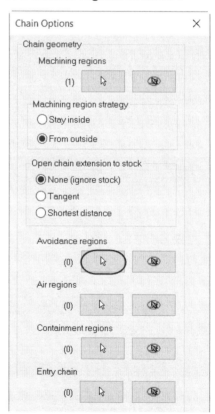

◆ [Select 2D HST avoidance chain 1]: Select the chain as shown in Figure: 15.0.2.

Figure: 15.0.2

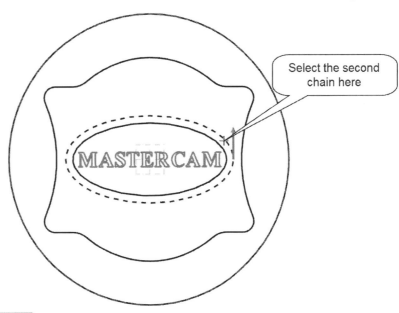

Select the second chain here

◆ Choose the **OK** button to continue.

◆ Select the **OK** button to exit the **Chain Options** panel.

◆ In the **Toolpath Type** page, **Area Mill** will be selected as shown.

Dynamic Mill   Area Mill   Dynamic Contour   Peel Mill   Blend Mill

NOTE: Mastercam updates the pages as you modify them and then marks them, in the **Tree View** list, with a green check mark. Pages that are not changed are marked with a red circle and slash.

15.1 Preview Chains

The **Preview Chains** function is intended to give the user a quick visual representation of how Mastercam sees the various pieces of geometry that have been selected, how they interact with one another and a general overview of how the toolpath will be calculated with the selections presently made.

• Click on the **Color** icon to see the legend for **Preview chains** as shown.

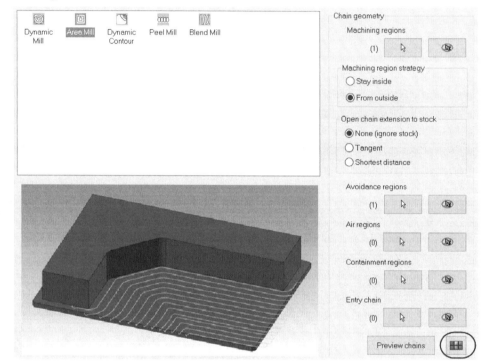

♦ The **Preview Chains Colors** dialog box should look as shown.

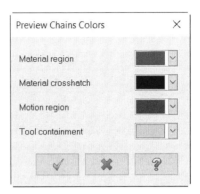

The **Material region** and **Material crosshatch** are the two colors that are used to define the material to be cut. The default colors are red for the background and black for the crosshatch.

The **Motion region** displays the area that Mastercam is making available to the toolpath for motion if it needs it. The color to represent it is dark blue. The primary reason for the display of the entire available (but not necessarily used) **Motion region** is to help the user visualize how the tool may move near or interact with any adjacent geometry.

The **Tool containment** is what you have selected as the containment region in the chain geometry. If you have not selected a containment region, it will default to the outside of the **Motion region** since that is currently the default area the toolpath is being contained to. The color used to represent the **Tool containment** is yellow.

♦ Select the **OK** button to exit **Preview Chains Colors**.
♦ Select the **Preview chains** button as shown.

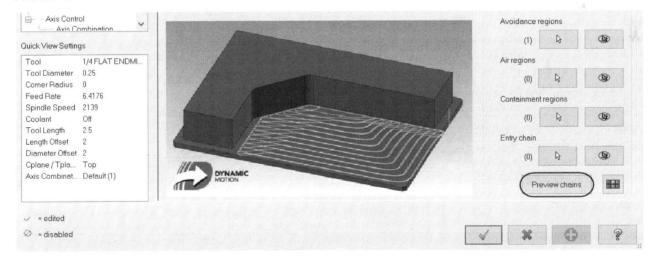

♦ Select the **Hide dialog** button to see the preview in the graphics window.

• The **Preview chains** should look as shown.

• Press **Esc** key to return to the toolpath parameters.
• Click on the **Preview chains** button again to clear the **Preview chains** display.

15.2 Select a 3/4" Flat Endmill from the Tool Library and set the Tool Parameters

• From the **Tree View list**, select **Tool**.

• Click on the **Select library tool** button.
• Select the **Filter** button.

• Select the **None** button and then under **Tool Types,** choose the **Endmill1 Flat** icon.

* Under **Tool Diameter**, select **Equal** and input a value of **0.75** as shown in <u>Figure: 15.2.1</u>.

Figure: 15.2.1

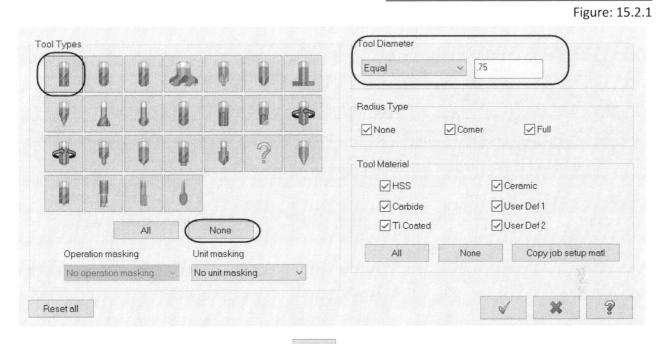

* Select the **OK** button to exit the **Tool List Filter**.
* In the **Tool Selection** panel you should only see a **3/4" Flat Endmill**.

#	Assembly...	Tool Name	Holder Name	Dia.	Cor. r...	Length	# Flut...	Type	Rad....
294	–	3/4 FLAT ENDMILL	–	0.75	0.0	2.0	4	End...	None

* Select the **3/4" Flat Endmill** in the **Tool Selection** page and then select the **OK** button to exit.

♦ Make all the necessary changes as shown in Figure: 15.2.2.

Figure: 15.2.2

2D High Speed Toolpath - Area Mill ✕

Toolpath Type
✓ Tool
Holder

◇ Stock
Cut Parameters
◇ Depth Cuts
◇ Trochoidal Motion
Transitions
◇ Break Through
Linking Parameters
HST Leads
Home / Ref. Points

Arc Filter / Tolerance
Planes (WCS)
Coolant
Canned Text
Misc Values

#	Assembly...	Tool Name	Holder N...	Dia.	Cor. r...	L
1	--	3/4 FLAT ...	--	0.75	0.0	

Quick View Settings

Tool	3/4 FLAT ENDMI...
Tool Diameter	0.75
Corner Radius	0
Feed Rate	6.4176
Spindle Speed	713
Coolant	Off
Tool Length	3.75
Length Offset	1
Diameter Offset	1
Cplane / Tpla...	Top
Axis Combinat...	Default (1)

Right-click for options

Select library tool... ☐ Filter Active Filter...

☐ Tool inspection / change

⦿ 0.0 Inches
Force retract every
◯ 0.0 Minutes

☐ To batch

Tool diameter: 0.75

Corner radius: 0.0

Tool name: 3/4 FLAT ENDMILL

Tool #: 1   Length offset: 1

Head #: 0   Diameter offset: 1

☐ RCTF   Spindle direction: CW ⌄

Feed rate: 6.4176   Spindle speed: 713

FPT: 0.0023   SFM: 139.9869

Plunge rate: 6.4176   Retract rate: 6.4176

☐ Force tool change   ☑ Rapid Retract

Comment
Machine the elliptical shape as a boss.

✓ = edited
◇ = disabled

✓ ✖ ✚ ?

Tool inspection/change forces a retract move at set intervals so that your machine operator can inspect the tool. When the tool reaches an inspection point, it retracts and rapids off the part to the clearance plane.

15.3 Set the Cut Parameters

• Select **Cut Parameters** and enable **Corner rounding**. Make all the necessary changes as shown in Figure: 15.3.1.

Figure: 15.3.1

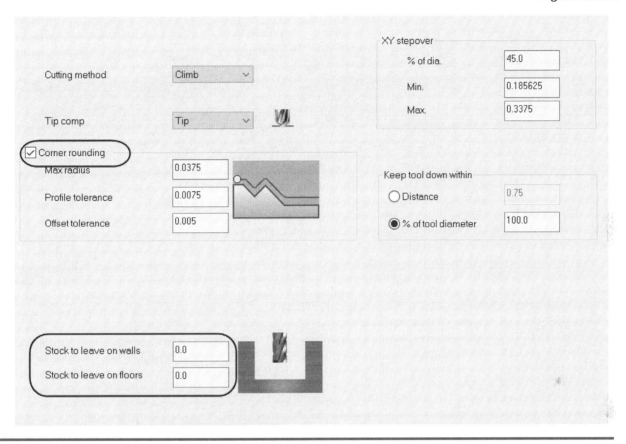

Corner rounding replaces sharp corners with arcs for faster and smoother transitions in tool direction.

Max radius is the largest arc that you allow Mastercam to insert to replace a corner. Larger arcs will create a smoother toolpath but with greater deviation from the originally programmed toolpath.

Profile tolerance represents the maximum distance that the outermost profile of a toolpath created with a corner rounding can deviate from the original toolpath.

Offset tolerance represents the maximum distance that a profile of a toolpath created with corner rounding can deviate from the original toolpath. This is the same measurement as the profile tolerance but is applied to all the profiles except the outermost one.

XY stepover expresses the maximum XY stepover as a percentage of the tool diameter. Mastercam will use the largest value possible that does not leave unwanted upstands of material between the passes.

Keep tool down within keeps the tool down if the distance from the end pass to the start of the next pass is less than the value here. Mastercam will not create a retract move as defined on the linking parameters page. Instead, the tool will stay down and move directly between the passes at the feed rate.

15.4 Set the Depth Cuts Parameters

♦ Select **Depth cuts** and make the necessary changes as shown in Figure: 15.4.1.

Figure: 15.4.1

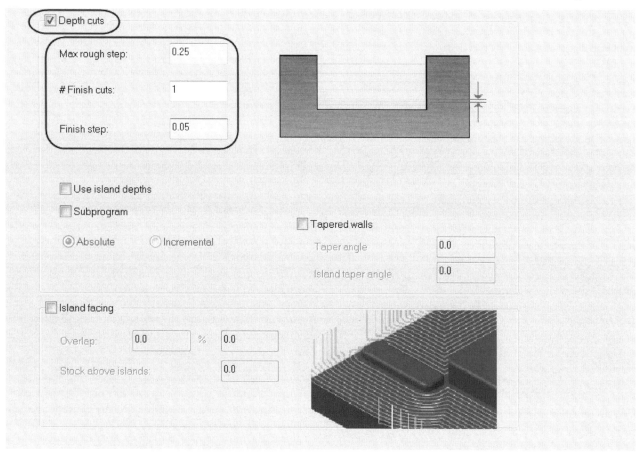

15.5 Set the Transitions Parameters

* Select **Transitions,** under the **Entry method** section, select **Entry helix** and enter a **Radius** of **0.25**.
* Make sure that the value in **Skip pockets smaller than** is set to **0.55** as shown in <u>Figure: 15.5.1</u>.

Figure: 15.5.1

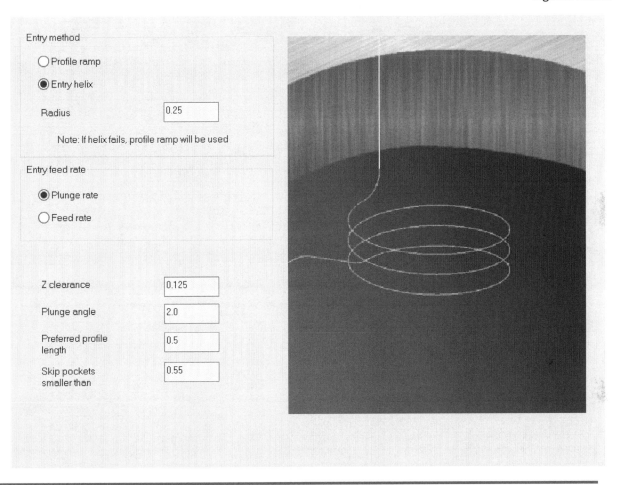

Entry method sets the entry move that the tool makes as it transitions to new Z depths. If you choose to create a helical entry and there is not enough room, Mastercam creates a ramp entry instead.

Entry feed rate sets the rate that the tool feeds into the material.

Z clearance is extra height used in the ramping motion down from a top profile. It ensures the tool has fully slowed down from the rapid speeds before touching the material.

Plunge angle sets the angle of descent for the entry move, and determines the pitch. A smaller plunge angle means that the entry move takes longer to descend in the Z axis.

15.6 Set the Linking Parameters

• Select **Linking Parameters** and make the necessary changes as shown in Figure: 15.6.1.

Figure: 15.6.1

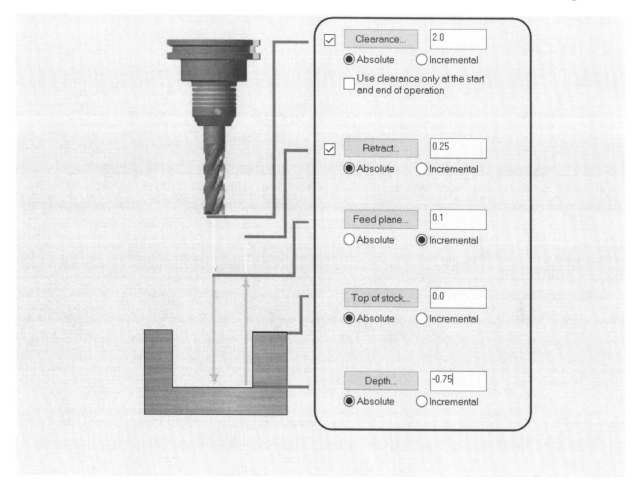

Mill Essentials Training Tutorial *Mastercam.* 2017

15.7 Set the HST Leads

◆ From the **Tree View list**, select **HST Leads** and make any necessary changes as shown in Figure: 15.7.1.

Figure: 15.7.1

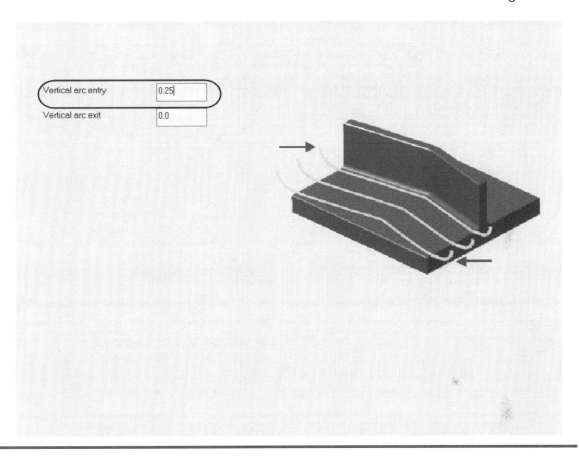

HST Leads page allows you to specify an entry and exit arc radius value for the **2D High Speed Toolpaths**. The arc is created vertically to lead on and off the material.

15.8 Set the Arc Filter / Tolerance

- Choose **Arc Filter / Tolerance** from the **Tree View list**.
- Select **Line/Arc Filter Settings** as shown in Figure: 15.8.1.
- Select the **OK** button to accept the warning and make the necessary changes as shown in Figure: 15.8.1.

Figure: 15.8.1

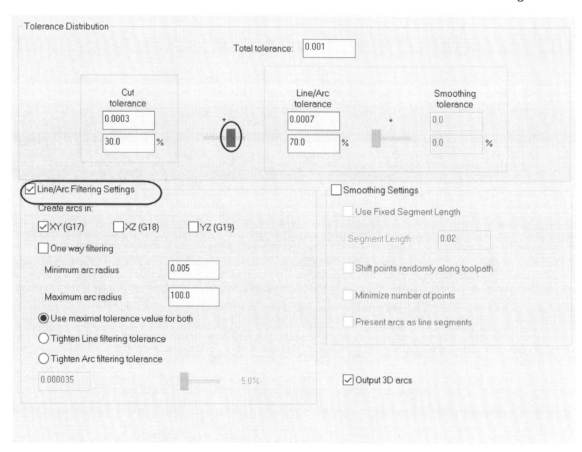

Tolerance Distribution allows you to dynamically adjust the toolpath's total tolerance. Total tolerance is the sum of the cut tolerance and the line/arc and smoothing tolerances. Move the sliders between the **Cut tolerance**, **Line/Arc tolerance** and/or **Smoothing tolerance** fields. The ratios update in 5% increments and the toolpath's total tolerance remains at its current value.

Line/Arc Filtering Settings allows you to activate Line/Arc filtering for the toolpath and apply the settings you define in this section to the toolpath refinement. Toolpath filtering lets you replace multiple very small linear moves — within the filter tolerance — with single arc moves to simplify the toolpath. Smoothing distributes a toolpath's node points, avoiding the clustering and grouping of points that can cause marks and other imperfections.

Create arcs in creates arcs in the selected plane. Your post processor must be able to handle arcs and output the code G17, G18, G19 to select this option.

15.9 Preview the Toolpath

♦ To quickly check how the toolpath will be generated, select the **Preview toolpath** icon as shown.

♦ To hide the dialog box, click on the **Hide dialog** icon as shown.

♦ To see the part from an **Isometric** view, right mouse click in the graphics window and select **Isometric** as shown.

> Zoom Window
> Unzoom 80%
> Dynamic Rotation
> Fit
>
> Top (WCS)
> Front (WCS)
> Right (WCS)
> Isometric (WCS)

♦ The toolpath should look as shown.

Press <ESC> when done

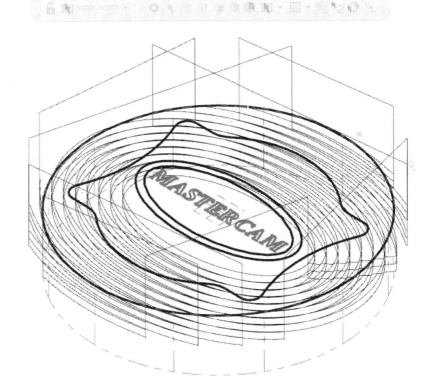

♦ Press **Esc** key to exit the preview.

NOTE: If the toolpath does not look as shown in the preview, check your parameters again.

♦ Select the **OK** button to exit the **2D High Speed Toolpath - Area Mill**.

STEP 16: BACKPLOT THE TOOLPATHS

Backplotting shows the path the tools take to cut the part. This display lets you spot errors in the program before you machine the part. As you backplot toolpaths, Mastercam displays additional information such as the X, Y, and Z coordinates, the path length, the minimum and maximum coordinates and the cycle time.

* Make sure that the toolpaths are selected (signified by the green check mark on the folder icon). If the operation is not selected, choose the **Select all operations** icon.

* Select the **Backplot selected operations** button.

* In the **Backplot** dialog box, enable **Display with color codes**, **Display tool** and **Display rapid moves** icons as shown.

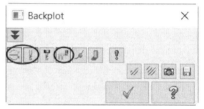

* To see the part from an **Isometric view**, right mouse click in the graphics window and select **Isometric** as shown.

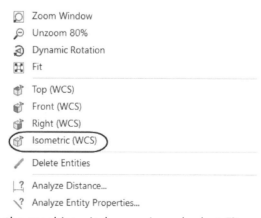

* To fit the workpiece to the screen, if needed, right mouse click in the graphics window again and select **Fit**.

* You can step through the **Backplot** by using the **Step forward** ▶▶ or **Step back** ◀◀ buttons.

* You can adjust the speed of the backplot. ▲

- Select the **Play** button to run **Backplot**.
- After **Backplot** is completed, the toolpath should look as shown.

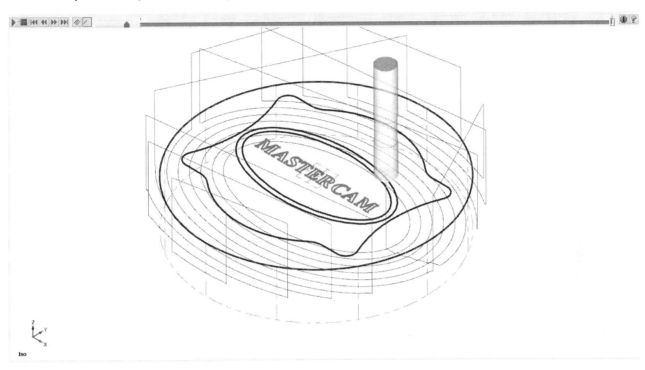

- Select the **OK** button to exit **Backplot** dialog box.

STEP 17: SIMULATE THE TOOLPATH IN VERIFY

Verify shows the path the tools take to cut the part with material removal. This display lets you spot errors in the program before you machine the part. As you verify toolpaths, Mastercam displays additional information such as the X, Y, and Z coordinates, the path length, the minimum and maximum coordinates and the cycle time. It also shows any collision between the workpiece and the tool.

♦ From the **Toolpaths Manager**, select **Verify selected operations** icon as shown.

NOTE: Mastercam launches a new window that allows you to check the part using **Backplot** or **Verify**. For more information on how to set and use **Backplot** and **Verify**, please check **Tutorial 1 page 50**.

♦ Change the settings for the **Visibility** and **Focus** as shown in Figure: 17.0.1.

Figure: 17.0.1

♦ Select the **Play** button to run **Verify**.
♦ The part should appear as shown in Figure: 17.0.2.

Figure: 17.0.2

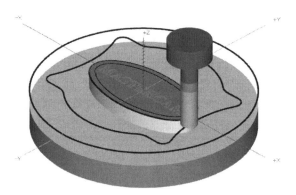

♦ To go back to the Mastercam window, minimize the **Mastercam Simulator** window as shown.

STEP 18: 2D HIGH SPEED DYNAMIC MILL

In this step you will machine the outside profile using **2D HS Dynamic Mill** toolpath which machines pockets, material that other toolpaths left behind, and standing bosses or cores using the entire flute length.

The toolpath supports many powerful entry methods, including a customized entry method. Entry methods and micro lifts support custom feeds and speeds to optimize and generate safe tool motion.

The toolpath depends on the **Machining strategy** that you choose in the **Chain Options**. If the strategy is **From outside**, the toolpath starts at the outmost chain and works its way in taking on the final shape of the part as it approaches the final pass. You can also machine pockets with the strategy set to be **Start inside**, which keeps the tool inside the machining regions.

Toolpath Preview:

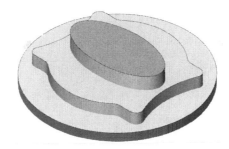

18.1 Chain Selection

- To remove the toolpath display, press **Alt + T** or click on the **Toggle display on selected operations** in the **Toolpaths Manager**.

TOOLPATHS

- In the **2D** group, click on the **Expand gallery** arrow as shown.

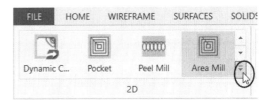

- Select the **Dynamic Mill** icon as shown.

* In the **Chain Options** dialog box, **Machining regions**, enable **From outside** and click on the **Select machining chains** button as shown.

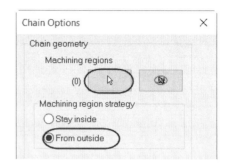

* Leave the default setting in the **Chaining** dialog box.
* Right mouse click in the graphics window and select **Top** view.
* [Select 2D HST machining chain 1]: Select the first chain as shown in Figure: 18.1.1.

Figure: 18.1.1

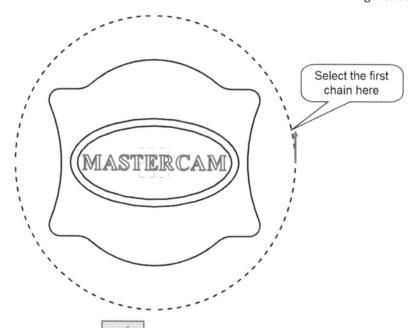

* Select the **OK** button to exit the **Chaining** dialog box.

◆ In the **Chain Options** panel, **Avoidance regions**, click on the **Select avoidance chains** button as shown.

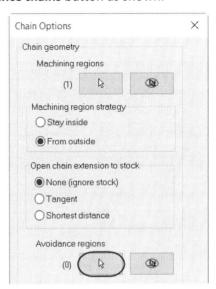

◆ [Select 2D HST avoidance chain 1]: Select the chain as shown in Figure: 18.1.2.

Figure: 18.1.2

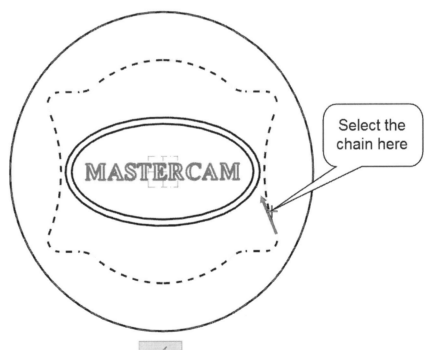

Select the chain here

◆ Select the **OK** button to exit the **Chaining** dialog box.

◆ Select the **OK** button to exit the **Chain Options** panel.

- In the **Toolpath Type** page, the **Dynamic Mill** should already be selected as shown.

Dynamic Mill   Area Mill   Dynamic Contour   Peel Mill   Blend Mill

18.2 Preview Chains

- Select the **Preview chains** button as shown.

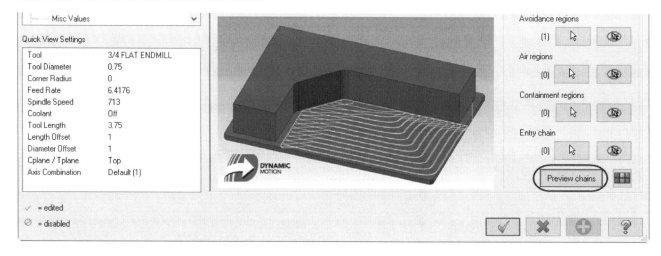

- See **page 164** to review the procedure.
- The **Preview chains** should look as shown.

- Press **Esc** key to return to the toolpath parameters.

◆ Click on the **Preview chains** button again to clear the **Preview chains** display.

18.3 Select the existing 3/4" Flat Endmill from the list and set the Tool Parameters

◆ From the **Tree View list**, select **Tool**.
◆ Make all the necessary changes as shown in Figure: 18.3.1.

Figure: 18.3.1

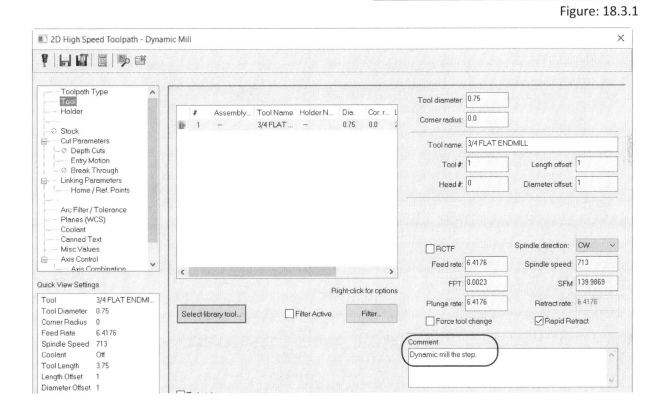

18.4 Set the Cut Parameters

• From the **Tree View list**, select **Cut Parameters**. Input a **Stepover** value of **12%** and make the changes as shown.

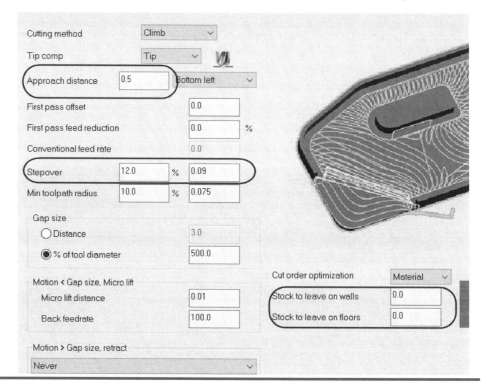

Approach distance is available only when open pocket machining is selected. It adds the specified absolute distance to the beginning of the toolpaths first cut.

First pass offset offsets out the machining region with a user defined distance for the tool to safely engage from the outside in the material.

First pass feed reduction allows you to slow the feed for the first pass on machining region material approached from the outside.

Stepover sets the distance between cutting passes in the X and Y axes.

Toolpath radius reduces sharp corner motion between cut passes.

Micro lift distance enter the distance the tool lifts off the part on the back moves. Microlifts are slight lifts that help clear chips and minimize excessive tool heating.

Back feedrate controls the speed of the backfeed movement of the tool.

Retract controls retracts in the toolpath when making a non-cutting move within an area where the tool can be kept down or microlifted.

Cut order optimization defines the cut order Mastercam applies to different cutting passes in the **Dynamic Mill Toolpath**.

18.5 Disable the Depth cuts parameters

◆ From the **Tree View list,** select the **Depth Cuts** and make sure **Depth cuts** is disabled as shown.

18.6 Set the Entry Motion

◆ From the **Tree View list**, select **Entry Motion**.
◆ Input a **Z clearance** of **0.05** and a **Plunge angle** of **2.0** degrees.
◆ Enable **Entry feeds / speeds** and set a **Ramp feed rate** of **10.0 inch per minute**, a **Ramp spindle speed** of **4000** RPM and **Dwell before cut spindle speed** of **3.0** seconds as shown in Figure: 18.6.1.

Figure: 18.6.1

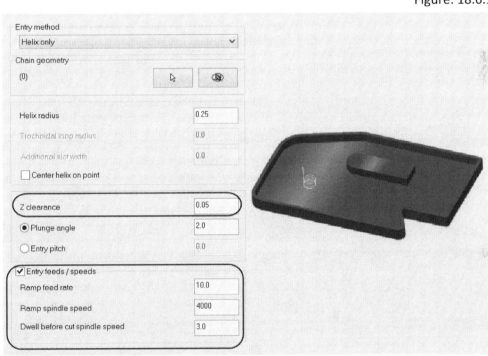

Entry method defines the entry point and cutting strategy used to create the toolpath.

Z clearance adds an extra height used in the ramping motion down from a top profile. It ensures that the tool has fully slowed down from rapid speeds before touching the material.

Plunge angle sets the angle of descent for the entry move, and determines the pitch.

Rapid feed rate overrides the feed rate set on the tools page and uses the specified feed rate for entry ramps into the material.

Ramp spindle speed overrides the spindle speed set in the tools page and uses the specified spindle speed for entry ramps into the material.

18.7 Set the Linking Parameters

♦ Select **Linking Parameters** and input the **Depth** as shown in Figure: 18.7.1.

Figure: 18.7.1

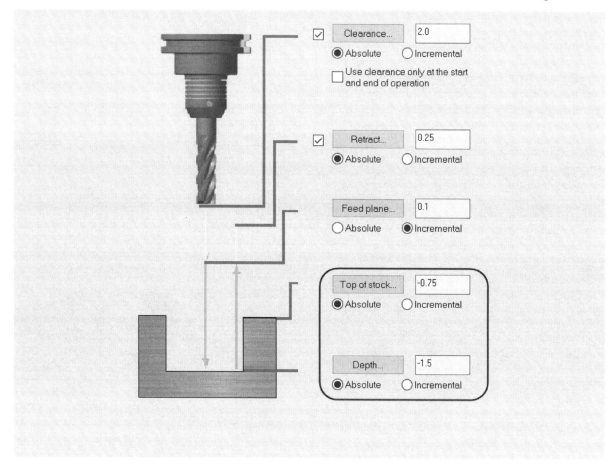

18.8 Preview the Toolpath

◆ To quickly check how the toolpath will be generated, select the **Preview toolpath** icon as shown.

◆ See **page 157** to review the procedure.
◆ The toolpath should look as shown.

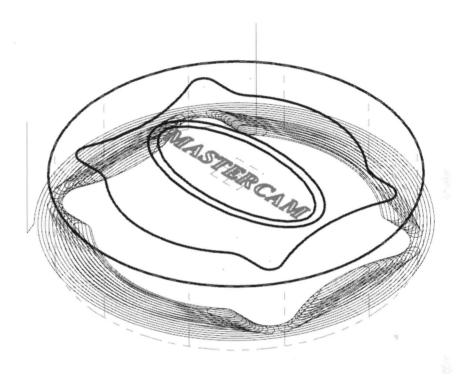

◆ Press **Esc** key to exit the preview.

> **NOTE:** If the toolpath does not look as shown in the preview, check your parameters again.

◆ Once complete, select the **OK** button to generate the toolpath.

18.9 Backplot the toolpath

♦ To **Backplot** the toolpath, see **page 50** to review this procedure.

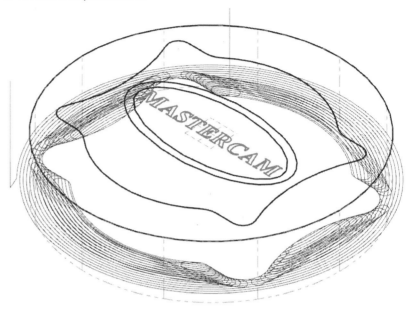

♦ Select the **OK** button to exit **Backplot**.

18.10 Simulate the toolpaths using Verify

♦ To select all operations, in the **Toolpaths Manager**, click on the **Select all operation** icon.

♦ To **Verify** the toolpath, see **page 52**.

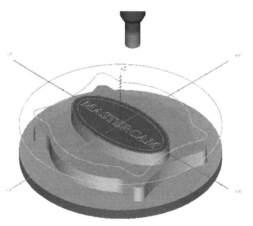

♦ To go back to the Mastercam window, minimize the **Mastercam Simulator** window as shown.

STEP 19: POCKET

In this step, you will use a **Pocket** toolpath to remove the material inside of the inner ellipse leaving the letters as islands.

Toolpath Preview:

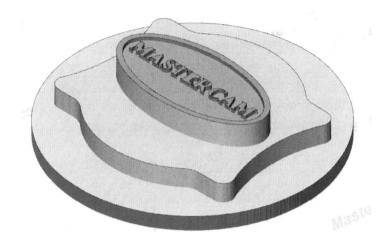

+ Press **T** to remove the toolpath display.

TOOLPATHS
+ From the **2D** group, select the **Expand gallery** arrow as shown.

+ Select the **Pocket** icon as shown.

19.1 Select the Geometry

♦ Right mouse click and select the **Top** graphics view.
♦ In the **Chaining** dialog box select the **Window** chaining option.

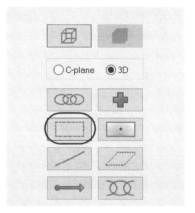

♦ Create a window around the letters and the inner ellipse as shown in <u>Figure: 19.1.1</u>.

NOTE: Make sure that the window is big enough to include the inside ellipse but avoid parts of the outside ellipse.

Figure: 19.1.1

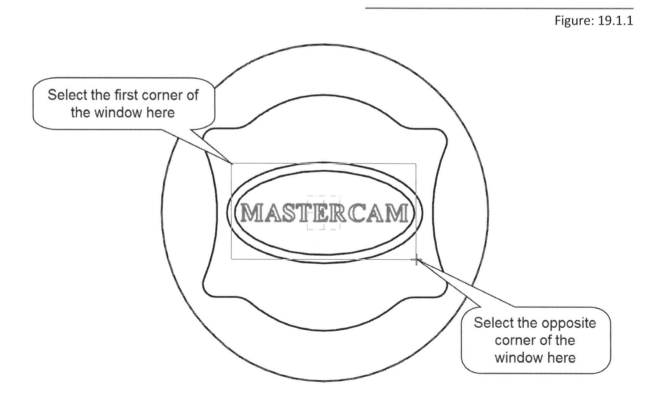

◆ [Sketch approximate start point]: Select an approximate starting point near the bottom of the letter "M" as shown in Figure: 19.1.2.

Figure: 19.1.2

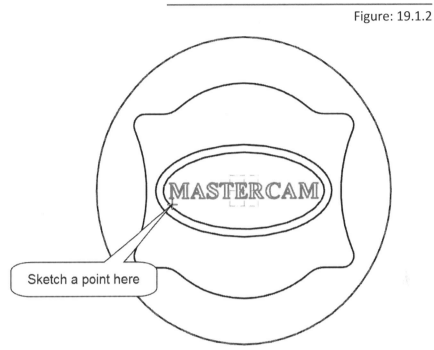

Sketch a point here

◆ The geometry should be selected as shown.

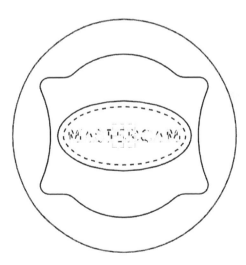

◆ Choose the **OK** button to exit the **Chaining** dialog box.
◆ On the **Toolpath Type** page, **Pocket** will be selected.

Contour

Pocket

Facing

Slot Mill

19.2 Select a 1/8" Flat Endmill from the library and set the Tool Parameters

◆ Select **Tool** from the **Tree View list**.

◆ Click on the **Select library tool** button.
◆ Select the **Filter** button.

◆ Select the **None** button and then under **Tool Types** choose the **Endmill1 Flat** icon.
◆ Under **Tool Diameter**, select **Equal** and input a value of **0.125** as shown in Figure: 19.2.1.

Figure: 19.2.1

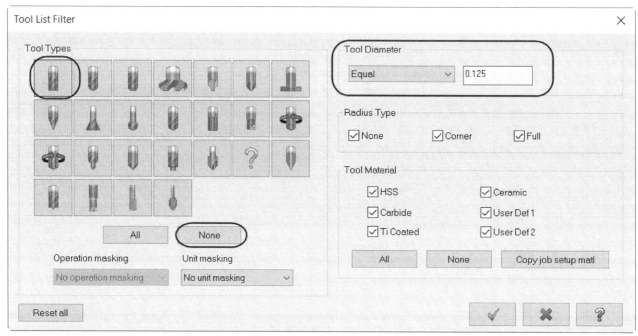

◆ Select the **OK** button to exit the **Tool List Filter**.
◆ In the **Tool Selection** panel you should only see a **1/8" Flat Endmill**.

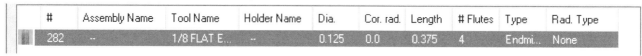

#	Assembly Name	Tool Name	Holder Name	Dia.	Cor. rad.	Length	# Flutes	Type	Rad. Type
282	--	1/8 FLAT E...	--	0.125	0.0	0.375	4	Endmi...	None

◆ Select the **1/8" Flat Endmill** in the **Tool Selection** page and then select the **OK** button to exit.

◆ Make all the necessary changes as shown in <u>Figure: 19.2.2</u>.

Figure: 19.2.2

#	Assembly...	Tool Name	Holder N...	Dia.	Cor. r...	L
1	–	3/4 FLAT ...	–	0.75	0.0	
2	–	1/8 FLAT ...	–	0.125	0.0	

Right-click for options

Select library tool...   ☐ Filter Active   Filter...

☐ To batch

Tool diameter: 0.125

Corner radius: 0.0

Tool name: 1/8 FLAT ENDMILL

Tool #: 2   Length offset: 2

Head #: 0   Diameter offset: 2

☐ RCTF   Spindle direction: CW

Feed rate: 6.160896   Spindle speed: 4278

FPT: 0.0004   SFM: 139.9869

Plunge rate: 6.160896   Retract rate: 6.160896

☐ Force tool change   ☐ Rapid Retract

Comment
Pocket the inside of the ellipse leaving the letters as islands.

19.3 Set the Cut Parameters

♦ From the **Tree View list**, select **Cut Parameters** and ensure **Pocket type** is set to **Standard** as shown in Figure: 19.3.1.

Figure: 19.3.1

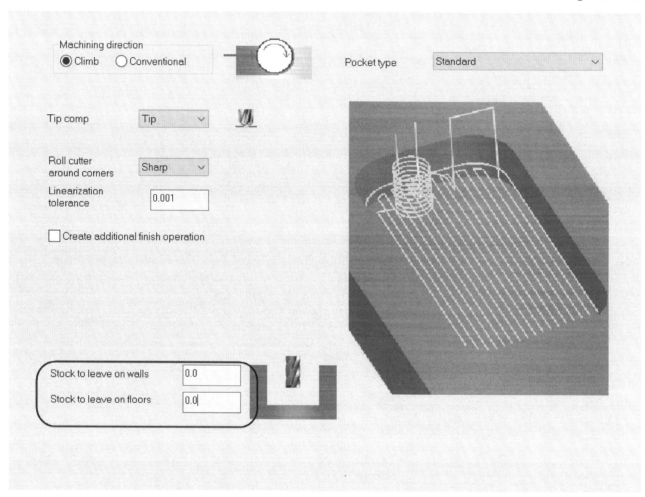

NOTE: **Pocket** set to **Standard** will machine the inside of the ellipse leaving the letters as islands with heights at the same level as the top of the pocket.

19.4 Set the Roughing Parameters

- From the **Tree View list**, select **Roughing**.
- Enable **Roughing** and ensure your parameters appear as shown in Figure: 19.4.1.

Figure: 19.4.1

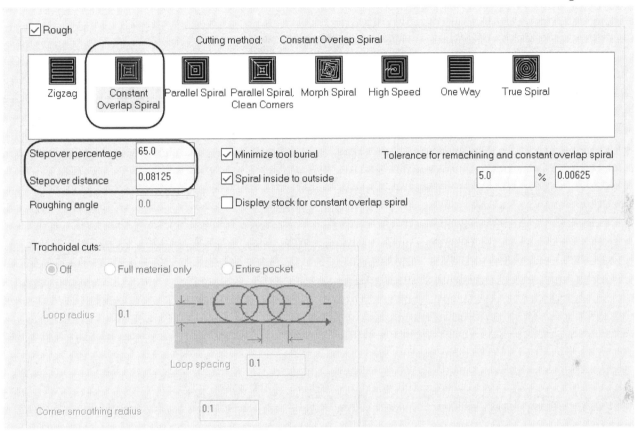

Constant Overlap Spiral creates one roughing pass, determines the remaining stock and recalculates based on the new stock amount. This process repeats until the pocket is cleared.

19.5 Set the Entry Motion

◆ Choose **Entry Motion** from the **Tree View list.** Ensure your settings appear as shown in <u>Figure: 19.5.1</u>.

Figure: 19.5.1

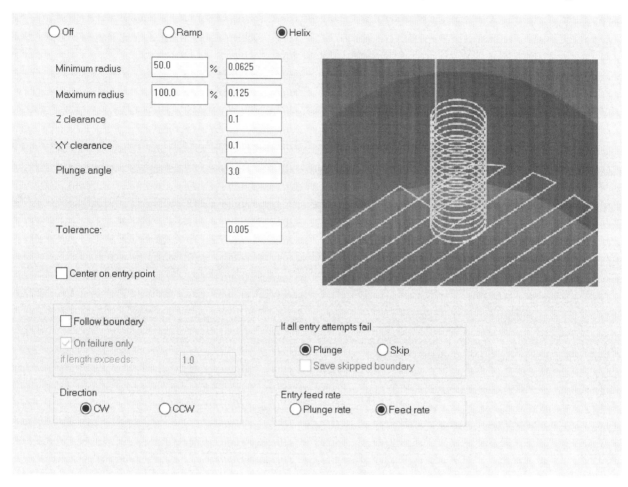

Minimum radius sets the smallest possible radius for the entry helix.

Maximum radius sets the largest possible radius for the entry helix.

19.6 Set the Finishing Parameters

◆ Select **Finishing** and ensure your options appear as shown in <u>Figure: 19.6.1</u>.

Figure: 19.6.1

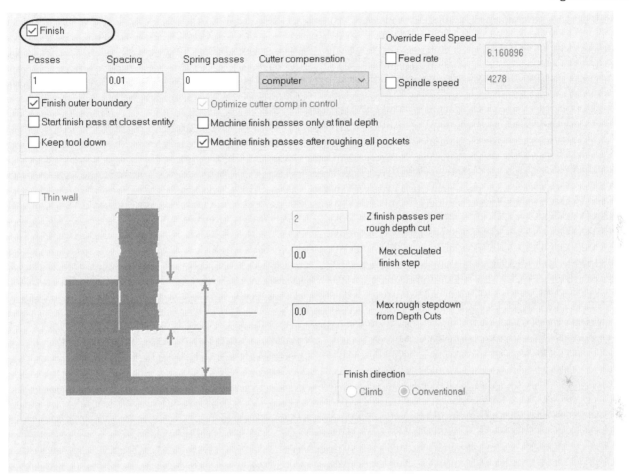

19.7 Set the Lead In/Out Parameters

◆ Select **Lead In/Out** from the **Tree View list**. Set the length and arc percentage to **60%** and input an **Arc Sweep** of **90** degrees as shown in Figure: 19.7.1.

Figure: 19.7.1

☑ Lead In/Out

Overlap | 0.0 |

☑ Entry

Line
○ Perpendicular   ● Tangent

| Length | 60.0 | % | 0.075 |

| Ramp height | | | 0.0 |

Arc

| Radius | 60.0 | % | 0.075 |

| Sweep | | | 90.0 |

| Helix height | | | 0.0 |

☐ Use entry point
☐ Use point depth
☐ Enter on first depth cut only
☐ Plunge after first move
☐ Override feed rate   6.160896

☑ Exit

Line
○ Perpendicular   ● Tangent

| Length | 60.0 | % | 0.075 |

| Ramp height | | | 0.0 |

Arc

| Radius | 60.0 | % | 0.075 |

| Sweep | | | 90.0 |

| Helix height | | | 0.0 |

☐ Use exit point
☐ Use point depth
☐ Exit on last depth cut only
☐ Retract before last move
☐ Override feed rate   6.160896

->
<-

19.8 Setup Depth Cuts Parameters

• Select **Depth Cuts** and enable this option. Set the **Max rough step** to **0.05** as shown in Figure: 19.8.1.

Figure: 19.8.1

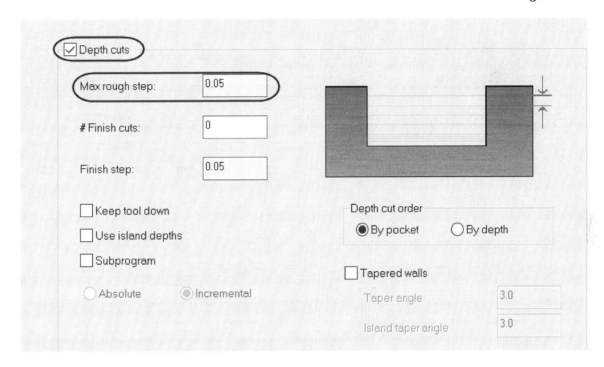

19.9 Set the Linking Parameters

♦ Choose **Linking Parameters** and input a final **Depth** of **-0.125** as shown in <u>Figure: 19.9.1</u>.

Figure: 19.9.1

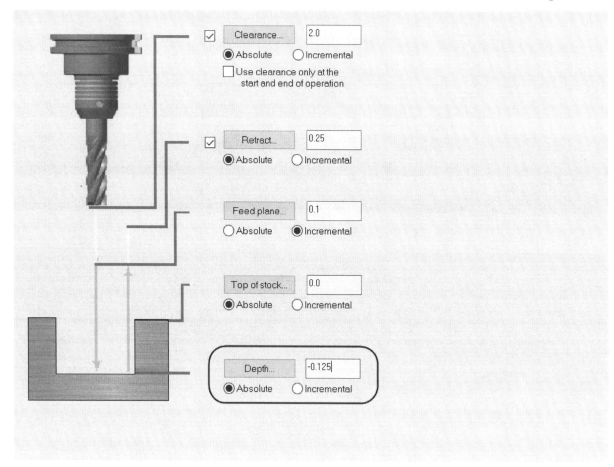

19.10 Preview the Toolpath

◆ To quickly check how the toolpath will be generated, select the **Preview toolpath** icon as shown.

◆ See **page 157** to review the procedure.
◆ The toolpath should look as shown.

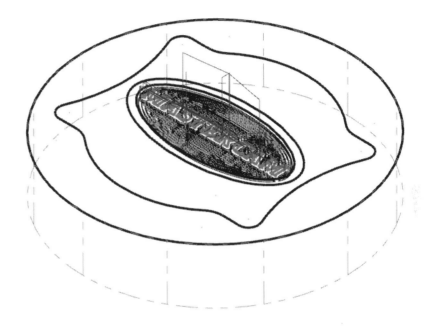

◆ Press **Esc** key to exit the preview.

> **NOTE:** If the toolpath does not look as shown in the preview, check your parameters again.

◆ Select the **OK** button to exit the **2D Toolpath - Pocket** parameters.

19.11 Backplot and Verify the toolpath

◆ To **Backplot** and **Verify** your toolpath, see **page 50** to review these procedures.

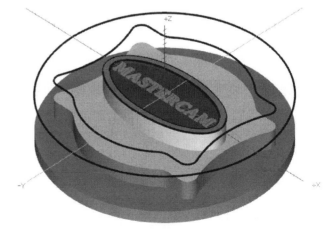

> **NOTE:** To better see the machined part, make the tool invisible by clicking twice on the square in front of the **Tool** in the **Visibility** area.

STEP 20: POCKET REMACHINING

Pocket Remachining is only used with closed chains. It calculates areas where the pocket roughing tool could not machine the stock and creates a remachining pocket toolpath to clear the remaining material.

Toolpath Preview:

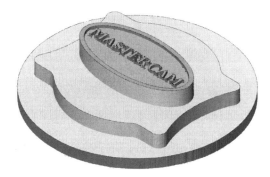

20.1 Select the Geometry

TOOLPATHS
* From the **2D** group, select **Pocket**.

* When the **Chaining** dialog box appears choose the **Last** button to reselect the chains used in the previous toolpath.

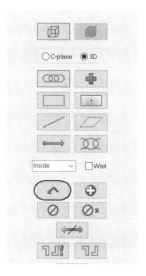

* Select the **OK** button to exit the chaining dialog box.

- On the **Toolpath Type** page, **Pocket** will be selected.

Contour   Pocket   Facing   Slot Mill

20.2 Select a 1/32" Flat Endmill from the library and set the Tool Parameters

- Select **Tool** from the **Tree View list**.

- Click on the **Select library tool** button.

- Select the **Filter** button.

- Select the **None** button and then under **Tool Types** choose the **Endmill1 Flat** icon.
- Under **Tool Diameter**, select **Equal** and input a value of **0.03125.** Make all the necessary changes as shown in Figure: 20.2.1.

Figure: 20.2.1

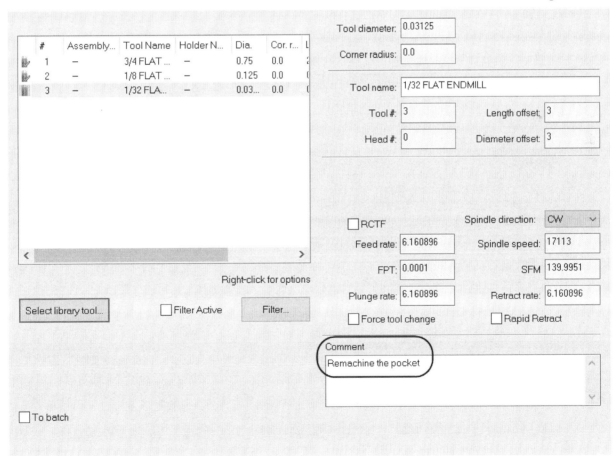

20.3 Set the Cut Parameters

◆ Select **Cut Parameters** and change the **Pocket type** to **Remachining.**

NOTE: The standard pocket removes the material inside of a closed boundary while the remachining pocket removes only the remaining material that a previous toolpath could not clean due to the tool size.

◆ Ensure your settings appear as shown in Figure: 20.3.1.

Figure: 20.3.1

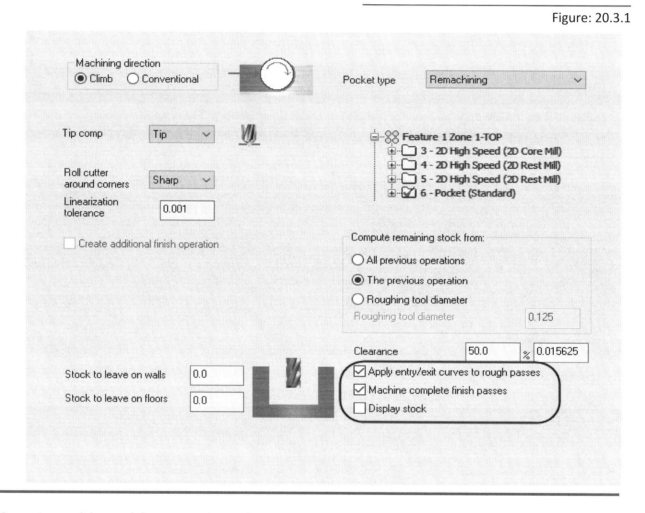

Compute remaining stock from set to **The previous operation** determines remaining stock for remachining by calculating stock removed during the previous toolpath.

Clearance extends the remachining toolpath at the beginning and end to prevent cusps of material from being left behind.

20.4 Set the Roughing Parameters

♦ Choose **Roughing** and change the **Stepover percentage** to **55** as shown in Figure: 20.4.1.

Figure: 20.4.1

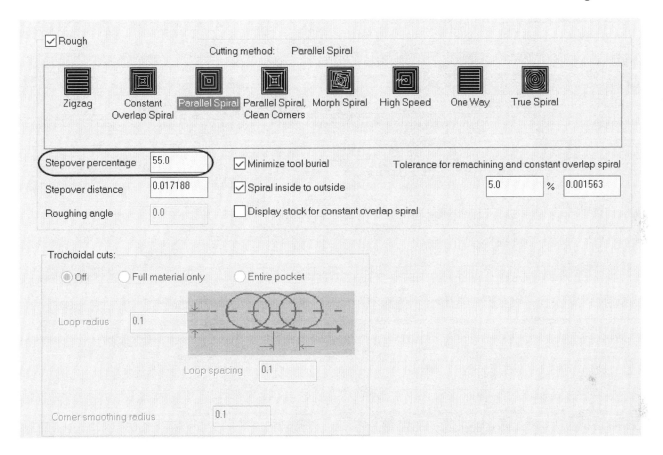

NOTE: The **Cutting method** is defined by the **Pocket type** and cannot be modified for **Remachining**. The **Finishing**, **Lead In/Out** and **Depth Cuts** parameters are the same as the previous toolpath. Therefore, we do not need to view them.

20.5 Set the Linking Parameters

♦ Choose **Linking Parameters** and set the **Depth** to **-0.125** as shown in Figure: 20.5.1.

Figure: 20.5.1

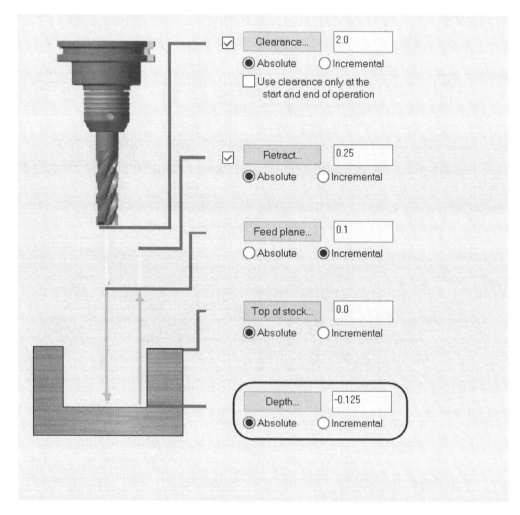

Mill Essentials Training Tutorial *Mastercam.* 2017

20.6 Preview the Toolpath

◆ To quickly check how the toolpath will be generated, select the **Preview toolpath** icon as shown.

◆ See **page 157** to review the procedure.
◆ The toolpath should look as shown.

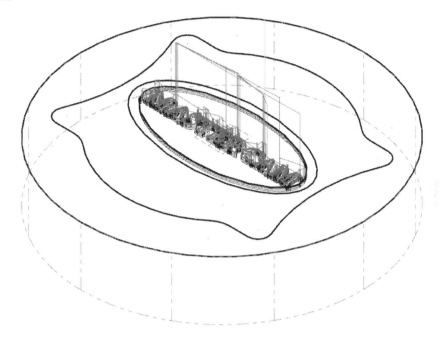

◆ Press **Esc** key to exit the preview.

> **NOTE:** If the toolpath does not look as shown in the preview, check your parameters again.

◆ Select the **OK** button to exit the **2D Toolpaths - Pocket**.

20.7 Backplot and Verify the toolpaths

♦ To **Backplot** and **Verify** your toolpath, see **page 50** to review these procedures.

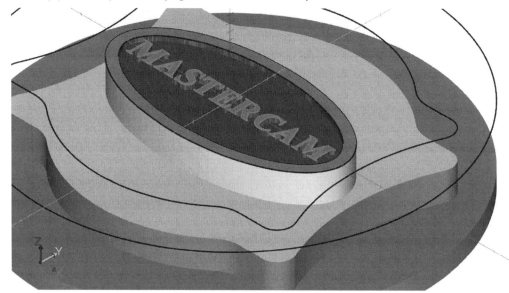

♦ Select the close button at the top-right corner to exit the **Mastercam Simulator**.

STEP 21: POST THE FILE

◆ Ensure all operations are selected. If they are not, use the button **Select all operations** in the **Toolpaths Manager.**

◆ Select the **Post selected operations** button from the **Toolpaths Manager.** G1

◆ In the **Post processing** window, make the necessary changes as shown in <u>Figure: 21.0.1</u>.

Figure: 21.0.1

NC File enabled allows you to keep the NC file and to assign the same name as the MCAM file.

Edit enabled allows you to automatically launch the default editor.

◆ Select the **OK** button to continue.

◆ Save the NC file.

♦ A window with **Mastercam Code Expert** will be launched and the NC program will appear as shown in Figure: 21.0.2.

Figure: 21.0.2

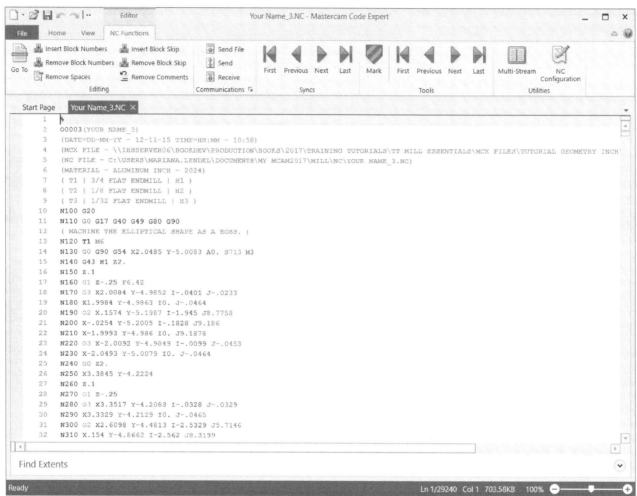

♦ Select the **"X"** box at the upper right corner to exit the editor.

STEP 22: SAVE THE UPDATED MCAM FILE

REVIEW EXERCISE - STUDENT PRACTICE

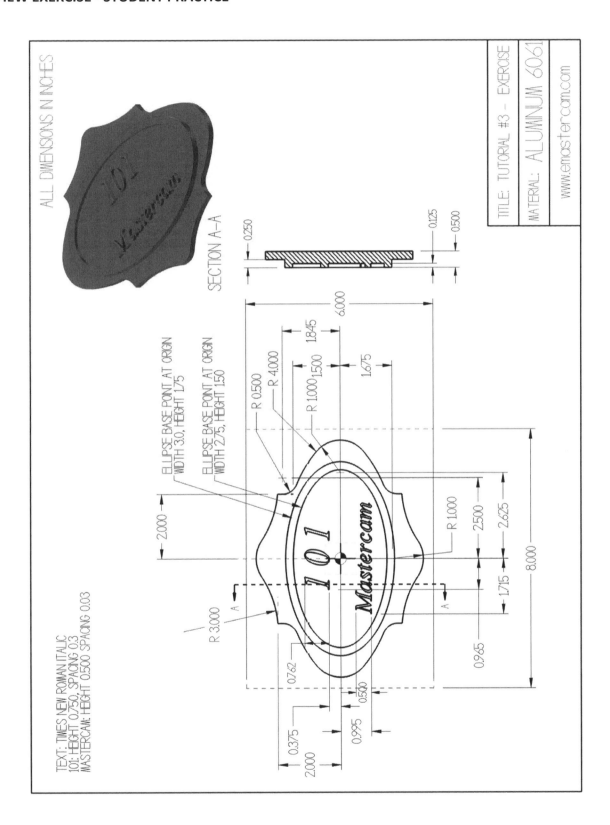

CREATE THE GEOMETRY FOR TUTORIAL #3 EXERCISE

Use these commands to create the geometry:
- Arcs Circle Center Point.
- Line Endpoints - Horizontal.
- Arc Tangent 2 Entities.
- Arc one point.
- Trim Break Extend.
- Mirror.
- Ellipse.
- Create Letters.

CREATE THE TOOLPATHS FOR TUTORIAL #3 EXERCISE

Create the Toolpaths for Tutorial #3 Exercise as per the instructions below.

Set the machine properties including the stock setup.
- Remove the material around the part using **2D HS Area Mill**.
- Use a **1" Flat Endmill**.
- Enable **Corner rounding**.
- Set the **Entry method**.
- Use **Depth Cuts**.
- Enable **Break through**.
- Set the depth according to the drawing.

Remove the material at the step using Dynamic Mill.
- Chain the outer profile in **Machining regions**.
- Enable **From outside**.
- Chain the outer ellipse in the **Avoidance regions**.
- Use the **1" Flat Endmill**.
- Enable **smoothing**.
- Disable **Depth cuts**.
- Set your **Entry method**.
- Disable **Break through**.
- Set the depth according to the drawing.

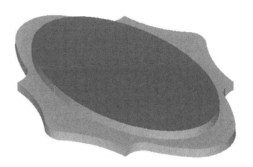

Pocket out the Center.
- Select the inner ellipse and the letters.
- Use a **1/4" Flat Endmill**.
- Choose the **Cutting method** to **Parallel Spiral Clean Corners**.
- Change the **Stepover percentage** to **25%**.
- Set the **Entry Motion**.
- Disable **Finishing**.
- Enable **Depth cuts** and set a **Max rough step** of **0.125"**.
- Set the depth according to the drawing.

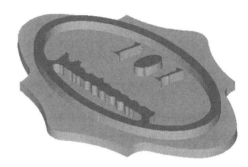

Remachine the Pocket.
- Use a **1/16" Flat Endmill**.
- Change the **Pocket Type** to **Remachining**.
- Enable **Machine complete finish passes**.
- Disable **Display stock**.
- Change the **Stepover percentage** to **55%**.
- Enable **Depth cuts** and set a **Max rough step** of **0.0625"**.
- Set the depth according to the drawing.

NOTES:

TUTORIAL #3 QUIZ

◆ What does Area Mill do?

◆ What does smoothing do?

◆ What does Pocket Remachining do?

TUTORIAL #4

OVERVIEW OF STEPS TAKEN TO CREATE THE FINAL PART:

From Drawing to CAD Model:
- The student should examine the drawing on the following page to understand what part is being created in the tutorial.
- From the drawing we can decide how to go about creating the geometry in Mastercam.

Create the 2D CAD Model used to generate Toolpaths from:
- The student will create the Top 2D geometry needed to create the toolpaths.
- Geometry creation commands such as Circle Center Point, Line Tangent, Mirror, Arc Tangent, Arc Polar, Trim, Fillet, Rotate, and Translate will be used.
- Create a solid using solid extrude command.

Create the necessary Toolpaths to machine the part:
- The student will set up the stock size and the clamping method used. Two setups will be used to machine the part from the top and then from the bottom.
- A 2D High Speed Area Mill toolpath will be created to remove the material inside of the step.
- A 2D High Speed Dynamic Mill toolpath will be created to remove the material inside of the deeper pockets.
- A 2D High Speed Area Mill toolpath will be created to remove the material inside of the smaller pocket.
- A Transform-Rotate toolpath will be created to machine the rest of the smaller pocket.
- A Pocket toolpath will be created to finish all the pockets.
- A Two Drill toolpath will be created to machine the holes.
- A Circle Mill toolpath will be created to remove the material inside of the center hole.
- A Contour-Chamfer toolpath will be created to chamfer all edges.
- A 2D High Speed Dynamic Mill toolpath will be created to remove the material inside of the part from the bottom.

Backplot and Verify the file:
- The Backplot will be used to simulate a step by step process of the tool's movements.
- The Verify will be used to watch a tool machine the part out of a solid model.

Post Process the file to generate the G-code:
- The student will then post process the file to obtain an NC file containing the necessary code for the machine.

 This tutorial takes approximately two hours to complete.

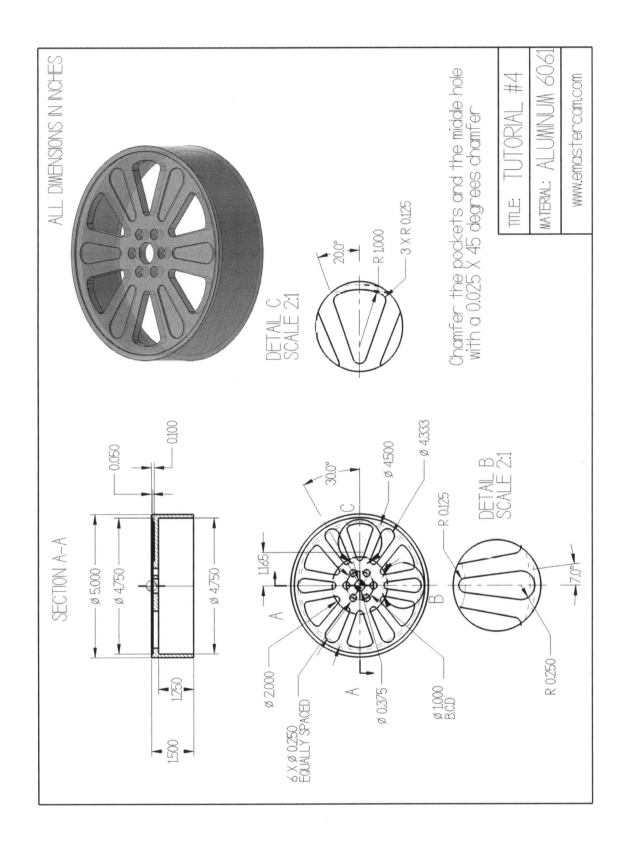

ALL DIMENSIONS IN INCHES

TITLE: TUTORIAL #4

MATERIAL: ALUMINUM 6061

www.emastercam.com

DETAIL C
SCALE 2:1

20.0°

R 1.000

3 X R 0.125

Chamfer the pockets and the middle hole
with a 0.025 X 45 degrees chamfer

SECTION A-A

0.050

0.100

Ø 5.000

Ø 4.750

Ø 4.750

1.250

1.500

30.0°

Ø 4.500

Ø 4.333

C

1.165

R 0.125

A

DETAIL B
SCALE 2:1

B

7.0°

Ø 2.000

A

R 0.250

6 X Ø 0.250
EQUALLY SPACED

Ø 0.375

Ø 1.000
B.C.D

2D GEOMETRY CREATION

STEP 1: SETTING UP THE GRAPHIC USER INTERFACE

Please refer to the Getting Started section to set up the graphical user interface.

STEP 2: CREATE ARCS

In this step you will create the arcs used for the main body of the part.

Step Preview:

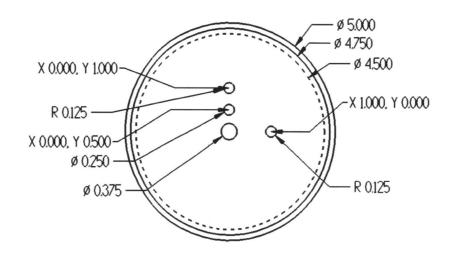

2.1 Create Circles

WIREFRAME

◆ From the **Arcs** group, select **Circle Center Point** as shown.

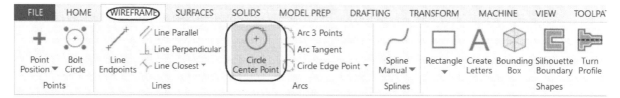

♦ In the **Circle Center Point** panel, type the **Diameter** of **5.0**. Press **Enter**.

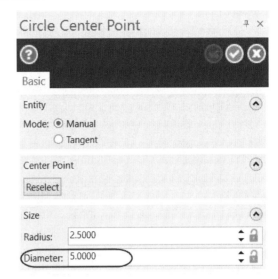

♦ [Enter the center point]: From the **General Selection** toolbar, click on the drop down arrow next to the **AutoCursor** as shown.

♦ From the fly-out menu, select **Origin**.

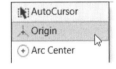

♦ Press **Alt** + **F1** to fit the geometry to the graphics window.
♦ Press **Enter** to continue in the same command.

NOTE: During the geometry creation of this tutorial, if you make a mistake you can undo the last step using the

Undo icon. ⤺ You can undo as many steps as needed. If you delete or undo a step by mistake, just use the

Redo icon. ⤼ To delete unwanted geometry, select it first and then press **Delete** from the keyboard.

• Move the cursor in the center of the circle and scroll down the mouse wheel to unzoom the geometry as shown.

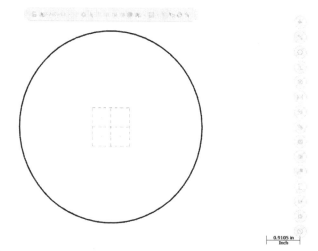

• Change the **Diameter** value to **4.75** and press **Enter**.

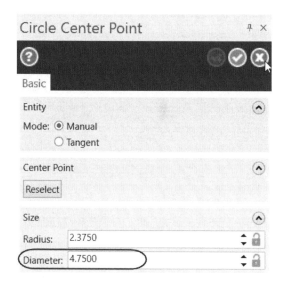

• [Enter the center point]: Select the **Origin**. The cursor may snap to the center of the first circle, which is also acceptable.

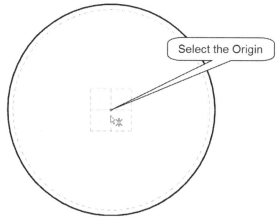

Select the Origin

• Press **Enter** to continue.
• Change the **Diameter** value to **0.375** and press **Enter**.

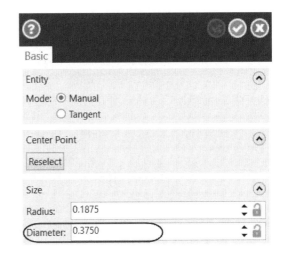

• [Enter the center point]: Select the **Origin** again.

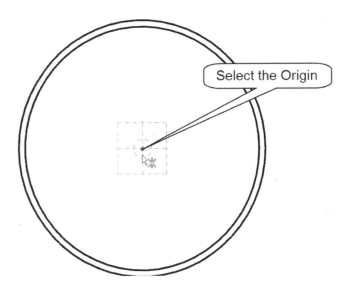

Select the Origin

• Press **Enter** to continue in the same command.
• Change the **Diameter** value to **0.25** and lock the value by selecting the lock icon as shown.

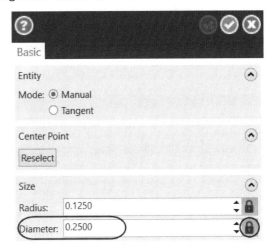

- [Enter the center point]: Press **Space bar** and the coordinate field appears at the upper left corner of the graphics window.
- Enter the coordinates as shown and hit **Enter** on your keyboard.

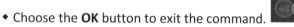

0,0.5

- Press **Enter** to continue in the same command.
- [Enter the center point]: Press **Space bar** again.
- Enter the coordinate values of **1, 0**and hit **Enter** on your keyboard.
- Press **Enter** to continue in the same command.
- [Enter the center point]: Press **Space bar** again.
- Enter the coordinate value of **0, 1** and hit **Enter** on your keyboard.

- Choose the **OK** button to exit the command.
- The geometry should look as shown.

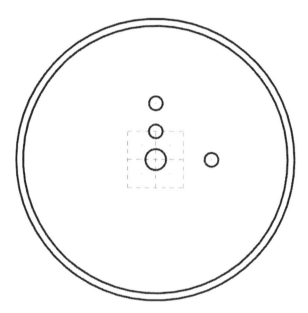

2.2 Change the Line Style and create the 4.5"diameter circle

HOME

• From the **Attributes** group, click on the arrow next to the **Line Style** options as shown in Figure: 2.2.1.

Figure: 2.2.1

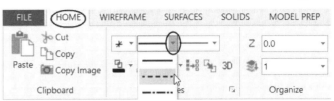

• Select from the list the **hidden line style** (2nd style in the list) as shown in Figure: 2.2.2.

Figure: 2.2.2

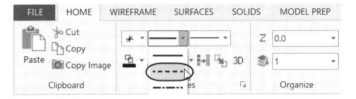

WIREFRAME

• From the **Arcs** group, select **Circle Center Point** as shown.

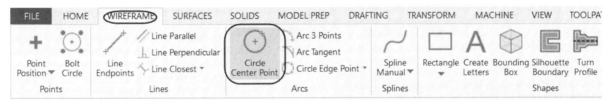

• In the **Circle Center Point**, change the **Diameter** to **4.5** and press **Enter**.

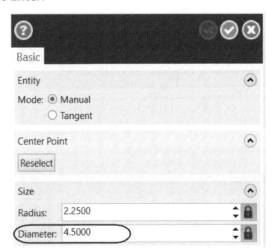

◆ [Select position for the center of the arc]: Select the **Origin**.

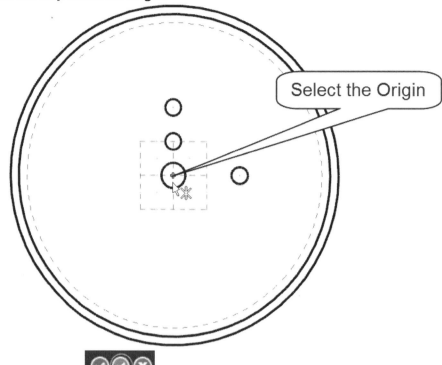

Select the Origin

◆ Choose the **OK** button to exit the command.

2.3 Change the Line Style back to Solid

HOME

• From the **Attributes** group, click on the arrow next to the **Line Style** options as shown in Figure: 2.3.1.

Figure: 2.3.1

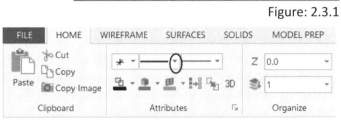

• Select from the list the **solid line style** (1st style in the list) as shown in Figure: 2.3.2.

Figure: 2.3.2

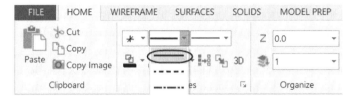

• The geometry should look as shown.

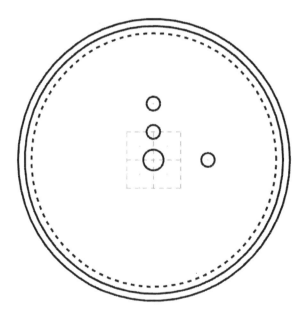

STEP 3: CREATE TANGENT LINES

In this step you will learn how to create tangent lines given the angle of the lines.

Step Preview:

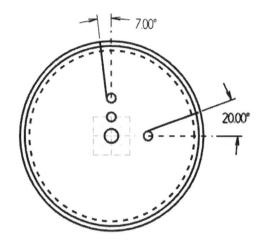

WIREFRAME

* From the **Lines** group, select **Line Endpoints** as shown.

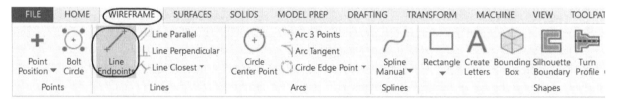

* In the **Line Endpoints** panel, ensure the **Tangent** option is enabled as shown.

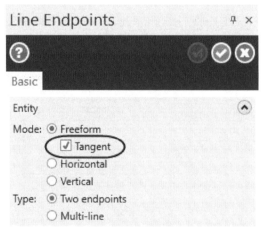

* Move the cursor to the right of the origin and scroll up the mouse wheel to zoom in as shown in Figure: 3.0.1.
* Select the arc as shown in Figure: 3.0.1.

NOTE: Make sure that you are not selecting any endpoints, midpoints or quadrants from the arc. If you select one of these points, Mastercam snaps to the points and disregards the tangent option.

Figure: 3.0.1

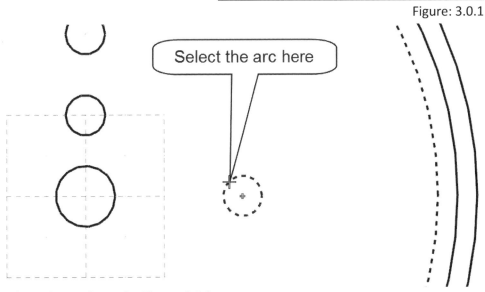

* Sketch a line at any angle to the point as shown in Figure: 3.0.2.

Figure: 3.0.2

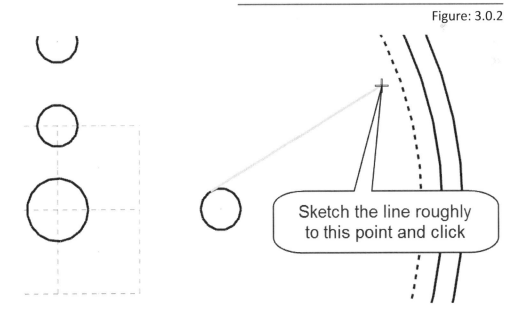

* In the panel, enter a line **Length** of **1.5** and an **Angle** of **20**.

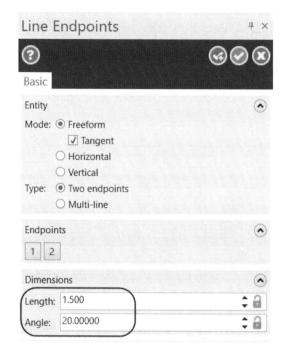

* Hit **Enter** on your keyboard to preview this line.
* Press again **Enter** to continue making lines.
* Press **Alt + F1** to fit the geometry to the graphics window.
* Move the cursor above the origin and scroll up the mouse wheel to zoom in on the area shown in Figure: 3.0.3.
* Select the arc as shown in Figure: 3.0.3.

NOTE: Make sure that you are not selecting any endpoints, midpoints or quadrants from the arc. If you select one of these points, Mastercam snaps to the points and disregards the tangent option.

Figure: 3.0.3

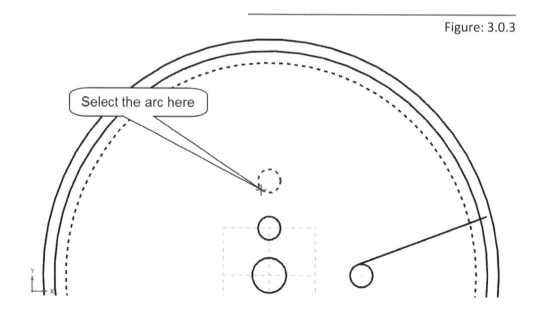

◆ Sketch a line at any angle to the point as shown in <u>Figure: 3.0.4</u>.

Figure: 3.0.4

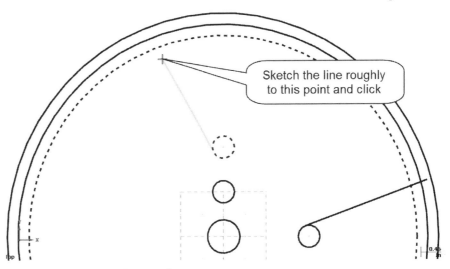

Sketch the line roughly to this point and click

◆ In the panel, enter a line **Length** of **1.5** and an **Angle** of **7+90** shown.

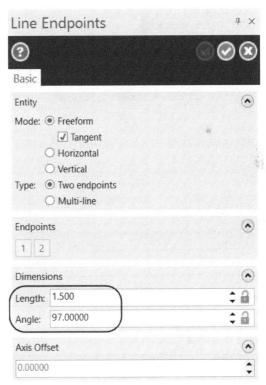

◆ Hit **Enter** to preview this line.

◆ Choose the **OK** button to exit the command.
◆ Press **Alt +F1** to fit the geometry in the graphics window.

◆ The drawing should appear as shown.

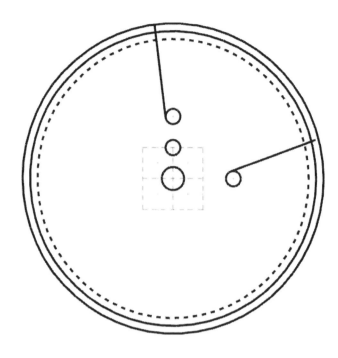

STEP 4: MIRROR THE TANGENT LINES

In this step you will learn how to Mirror the lines we created in the previous step.

Step Preview:

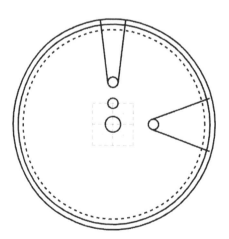

TRANSFORM

◆ From the **Position** group, select **Mirror** as shown.

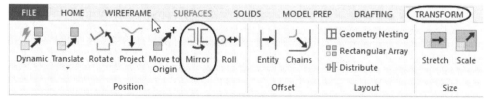

◆ [Mirror: select entities to mirror]: Select the line to mirror as shown in Figure: 4.0.1.

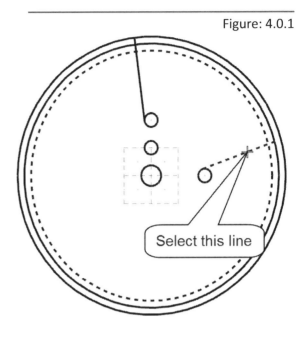

Figure: 4.0.1

Select this line

◆ Click on the **End Selection** button. End Selection
◆ In the **Mirror** dialog box, ensure **Copy** is enabled and pick the option to **Mirror about X axis** as shown in Figure: 4.0.2.

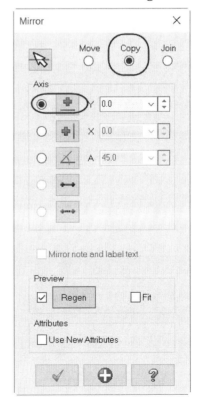

Figure: 4.0.2

* Pick the **Apply** button to select the next line to mirror.
* Select the line to mirror as shown in Figure: 4.0.3.

Figure: 4.0.3

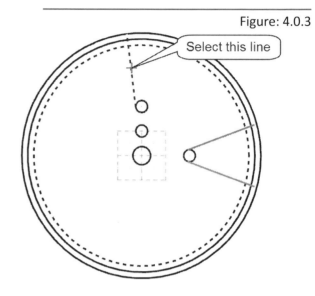

Select this line

* Click on the **End Selection** button. End Selection
* In the **Mirror** dialog box, ensure **Copy** is enabled and pick the option to **Mirror about Y axis** as shown in
  Figure: 4.0.4.

Figure: 4.0.4

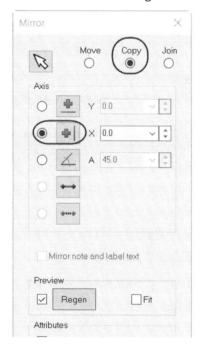

* Choose the **OK** button to exit the command.

◆ Right mouse click in the graphics window and from the **Mini Toolbar**, select **Clear Colors** to return the colors to the original system colors.

◆ The geometry should look as shown.

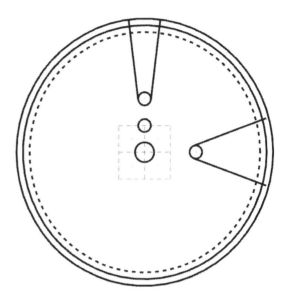

STEP 5: CREATE ARC TANGENT

In this step you will learn how to create an arc tangent to 3 entities.

Step Preview:

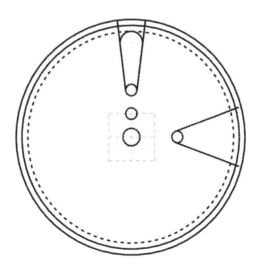

WIREFRAME

• From the **Arcs** group, select **Arc Tangent**.

• In the **Arc Tangent** panel, select the drop down arrow in the **Mode** field.
• Choose the **Arc three entities** as shown.

• Pick the entities in the order as shown in <u>Figure: 5.0.1</u>.

Figure: 5.0.1

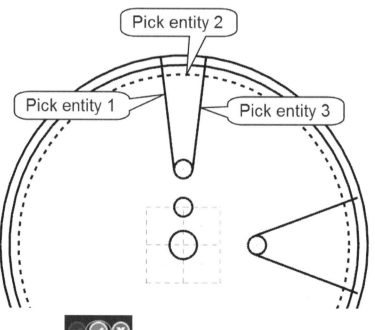

• Select the **OK** button to exit the **Arc Tangent** command.

STEP 6: CREATE ARC POLAR

In this step you will learn how to create an arc polar, given the center point, radius, start angle, and end angle.

Step Preview:

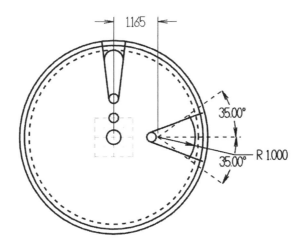

WIREFRAME

* From the **Arcs** group, click on the drop down arrow of the **Circle Edge Point** icon and select **Arc Polar** as shown.

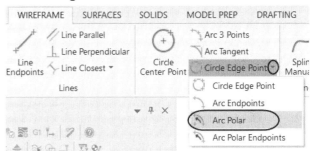

* [Enter center point]: Press **Space bar**.
* Input the coordinates **1.165, 0** as shown.

1.165,0

* Press **Enter**.

* Change the arc **Radius** to **1.0**, the **Start Angle** to **-35.0** degrees and the **End Angle** to **35.0**. Press **Enter** after each value.

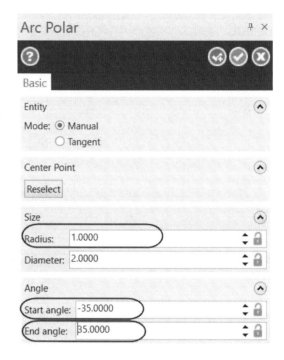

* Select the **OK** button to exit the command.

STEP 7: TRIM THE LINES

In this step you will learn how to Trim 3 entities and use the Divide function.

Step Preview:

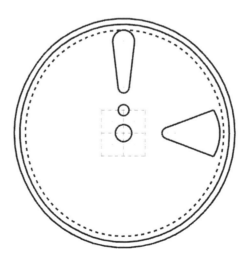

WIREFRAME
* From the **Modify** group, select **Trim Break Extend**.

◆ In the **Trim Break Extend** panel, enable **Trim 3 entities** as shown.

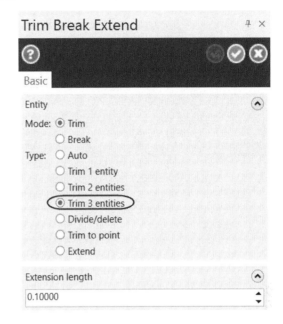

◆ Choose the entities in the order shown in <u>Figure: 7.0.1</u>.

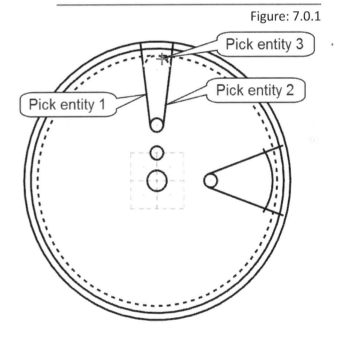

Figure: 7.0.1

◆ Repeat the step selecting the entities as shown in <u>Figure: 7.0.2</u>.

Figure: 7.0.2

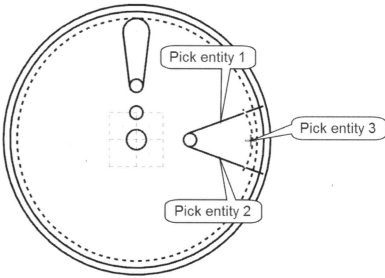

◆ Repeat the step selecting the entities as shown in <u>Figure: 7.0.3</u>.

Figure: 7.0.3

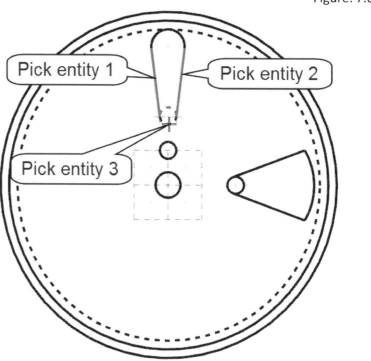

• In the **Trim Break Extend** panel, enable **Divide/delete** as shown.

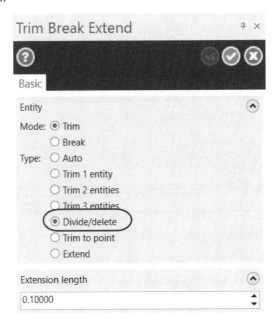

• Pick the arcs as shown in <u>Figure: 7.0.4</u>.

Figure: 7.0.4

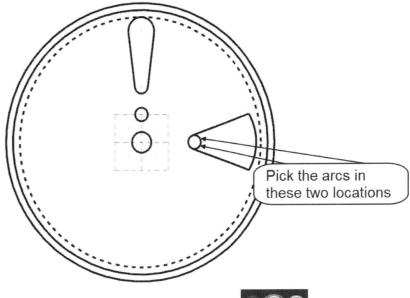

Pick the arcs in these two locations

• Once the arcs have been selected choose the **OK** button to exit the command.

◆ Your part up to this point will appear as shown.

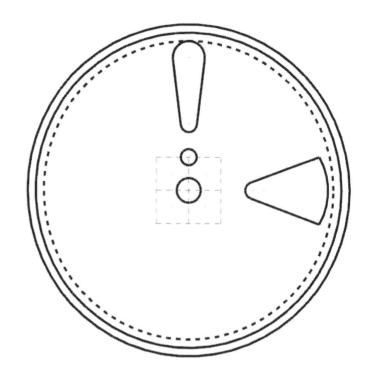

STEP 8: CREATE FILLETS

In this step you will learn how to create filleted corners. Filleted corners apply round corners to sharp corners.

Step Preview:

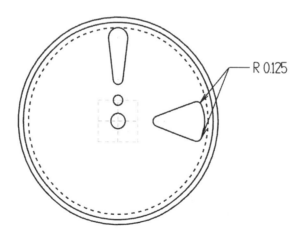

WIREFRAME

◆ From the **Modify** group, select **Fillet Entities**.

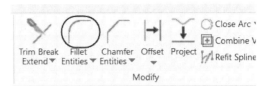

◆ In the **Fillet Entities** panel, input a **Radius** value of **0.125** as shown.

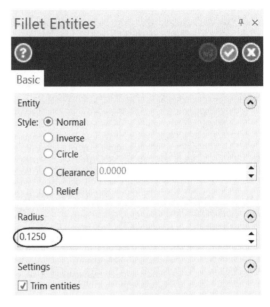

◆ Select the entities as shown in <u>Figure: 8.0.1</u>.

Figure: 8.0.1

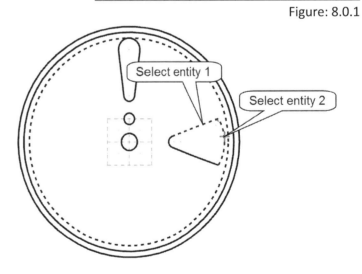

• Pick the entities as shown in <u>Figure: 8.0.2</u>.

Figure: 8.0.2

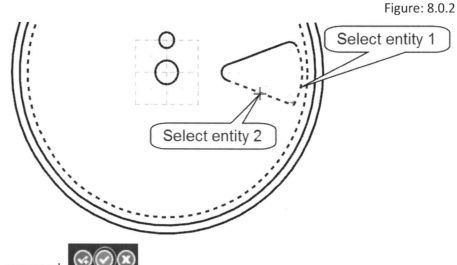

Select entity 1

Select entity 2

• Select the **OK** button to exit the command.

STEP 9: DELETE THE CONSTRUCTION ARC

In this step you will delete the arc.

Step Preview:

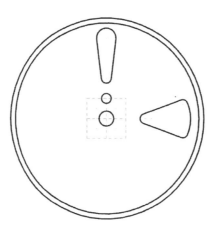

• Select the arc as shown in Figure: 9.0.1.

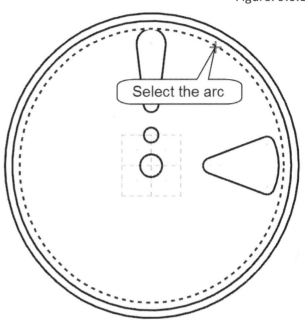

Select the arc

• Press **Delete** button from the keyboard.

STEP 10: ROTATE

In this step you will learn how to rotate entities around a center point by a specified angle.

Step Preview:

TRANSFORM

• From the **Position** group, select **Rotate**.

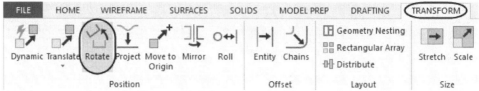

• Hold the **Shift** key and pick the shapes as shown in <u>Figure: 10.0.1</u>.

> **NOTE:** By holding down the **Shift** key and selecting one entity of a chain, Mastercam selects the whole chain.

Figure: 10.0.1

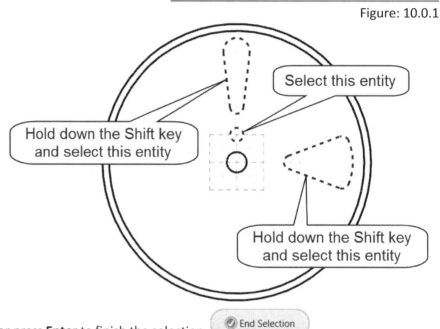

• Click on the **End Selection** button or press **Enter** to finish the selection.

- When the **Rotate** dialog box appears, ensure that **Copy** is enabled and the number of copies is set to **5** as shown in Figure: 10.0.2.
- Choose the option **Angle between** and input **360.0/6** and hit **Enter**.

Figure: 10.0.2

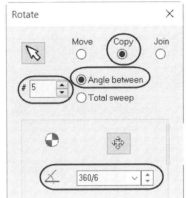

- Select the **OK** button to accept these parameters.
- Right mouse click in the graphics window and from the **Mini Toolbar,** select the **Clear Colors** icon to reset the colors back to the original colors.

- The geometry will appear as shown.

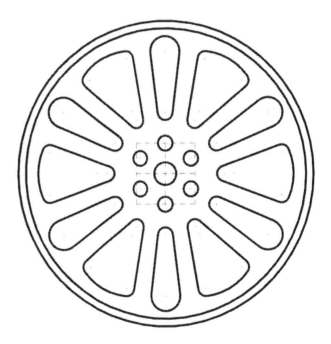

STEP 11: TRANSLATE

In this step you will learn how to translate entities to a different Z depth. This geometry will be used when creating a toolpath from the bottom of the part.

Step Preview:

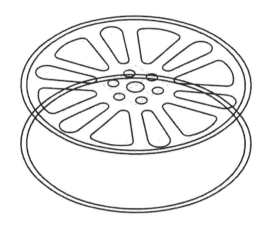

TRANSFORM

♦ From the **Position** group, select **Translate** and as shown.

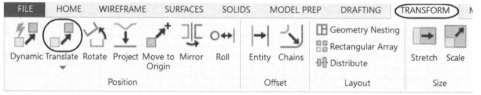

♦ Right mouse click in the graphics area, and select the graphic view **Isometric** as shown.

♦ [Translate: select entities to translate]: Select the two outer circles as shown in Figure: 11.0.1.

Figure: 11.0.1

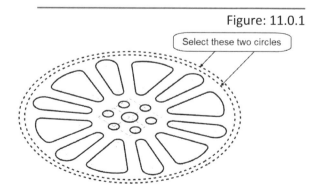

Select these two circles

- Click on the **End Selection** button.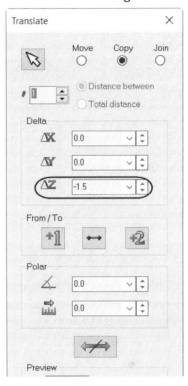
- When the **Translate** dialog box appears, ensure **Copy** is enabled and input a depth of **-1.5** as shown in Figure: 11.0.2.

Figure: 11.0.2

- Choose the **Apply** button to accept these parameters. ⊕
- Hold down the **Shift** key and click on all of the shapes within the top two circles as shown in Figure: 11.0.3.

Figure: 11.0.3

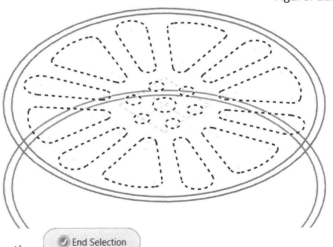

- Click on the **End Selection** button to finish the selection. ✓ End Selection

◆ When the **Translate** dialog box appears, ensure **Move** is enabled and input a depth of **-0.05** as shown in Figure: 11.0.4.

Figure: 11.0.4

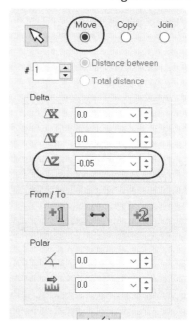

◆ Select the **OK** button to accept these parameters.
◆ Right mouse click in the graphics window and from the **Mini Toolbar,** select the **Clear Colors** icon to reset the colors back to the original colors.

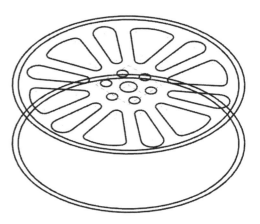

◆ Press **Alt + F1** to fit the entire geometry in the graphics window.
◆ The geometry should look as shown.

STEP 12: CHANGE THE SOLIDS COLOR TO RED AND THE VIEW TO ISOMETRIC

SOLID CREATION

A **Solid** is a geometric entity that occupies a region of space and consists of one or more faces, which define the closed boundary of the solid.

♦ Right mouse click in the graphics area, and from the **Mini Toolbar**, select the drop down arrow next to the **Solid Color** and select the color **Red** as shown.

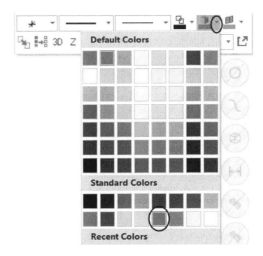

> **NOTE:** The construction plane or the graphics view do not affect the way in which the solid is generated.

STEP 13: CHANGE THE MAIN LEVEL TO 2

Levels are a primary organizational tool in Mastercam. A Mastercam file can contain separate levels for wireframe, surfaces, drafting entities, solids, and toolpaths. By organizing your files into levels, you can easily control which areas of the drawing are visible at any time and which parts are selectable. By doing so, you will not inadvertently make changes to areas of the drawing you do not want to change.
In this step we will change the **Main Level** to **2**, to create the solid on **Level 2**.

♦ Right mouse click in the graphics area and in the **Mini Toolbar**, change the **Level** number to **2** as shown.

♦ Press the **Enter** key on your keyboard.

STEP 14: CREATE THE SOLID BODY BY EXTRUDING A CLOSED CHAIN

Solid Extrude: Uses planar chains to create one or more solid bodies, create cuts in an existing solid or create bosses to an existing solid. Mastercam extrudes entities by driving the shapes of the entity along a linear path using a specified direction, distance, and other parameters that further define the results.

Step Preview:

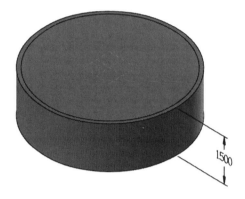

SOLIDS

• From the **Create** group, select **Extrude** as shown.

◆ Leave the default settings in the **Chaining** dialog box and select outside circle to create the chain as shown.

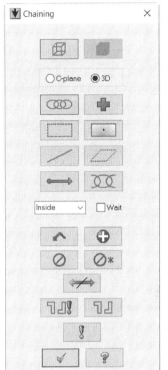

Chaining is the process of selecting and linking geometry entities such that they form the foundation of a toolpath, a surface, or a solid. When you chain the geometry, you can select one or more sets of curves (lines, arcs, and splines) that have adjoining endpoints.

Chaining differs from other selection methods because it assigns order and direction to the selected curves. Chaining order and direction determine how surfaces, solids, and toolpaths are generated.

◆ [Select chain(s) to extrude 1]: Select the outer circle as shown.

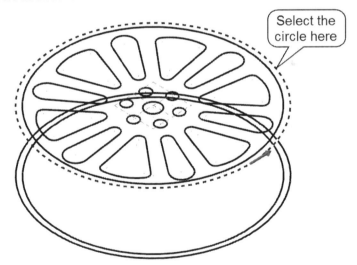

Select the circle here

NOTE: If you did not select the chain correctly, you can use the **Unselect** button ⊘ from the Chaining dialog box to undo the previous selection.

◆ Select the **OK** button to exit the **Chaining** dialog box.

◆ The **Solid Extrude** panel will display. An arrow will appear on the geometry. This arrow indicates the direction of the extrusion.

• Make sure that the arrow is pointing downward as shown.

• If the arrow appears upward, in the **Solid Extrude** panel, click on the **Reverse all** button.
• In the **Solid Extrude** panel, set the **Distance** to **1.5** as shown.

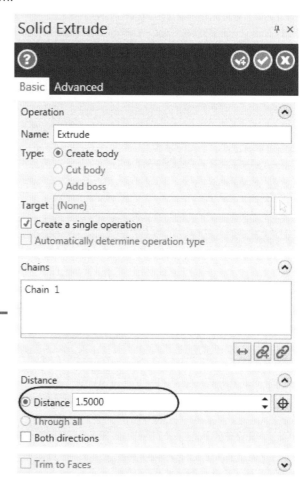

Extrusion Operation is used to create a solid body, cut a solid body, or add a boss to another solid.

Reverse Direction extrudes the solid in the opposite direction from the arrow on the chain indicating the extrusion direction.

Distance allows you to control the length of extrusion, by specifying a **Distance**, extending **Through all**, extending in **Both directions**, or trimming to selected faces.

- Press **Alt + S** to see the solid shaded if needed. Press **Alt + F1** to fit the geometry in the graphics window if needed.

- Select the **OK and Create a New Operation** button to remain in the same command .
- The geometry should now appear as shown in Figure: 14.0.1.

Figure: 14.0.1

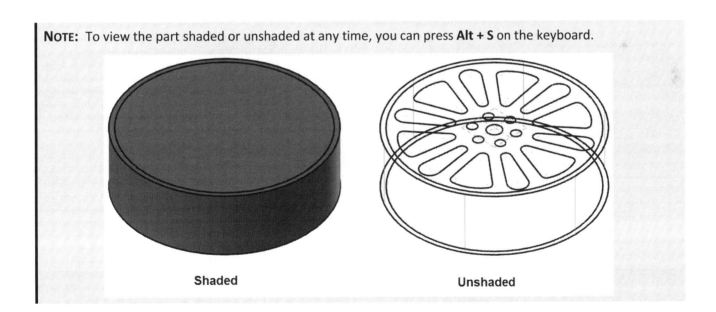

NOTE: To view the part shaded or unshaded at any time, you can press **Alt + S** on the keyboard.

Shaded   Unshaded

STEP 15: EXTRUDE CUT THE 0.05" DEEP POCKET

In this step you will cut the 0.05 deep pocket using the **Extrude** command with the type set to Cut.

Step Preview:

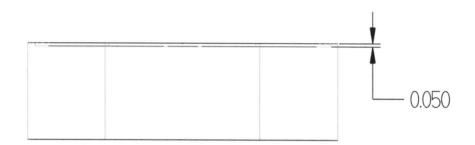

0.050

♦ Leave the default settings in the **Chaining** dialog box and select the circle as shown.

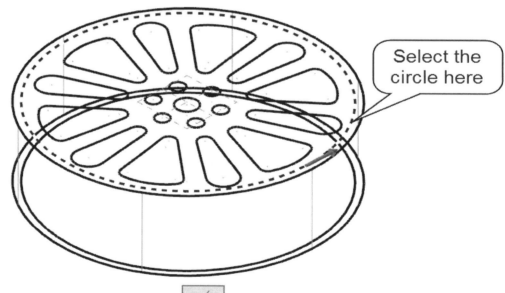

Select the circle here

♦ Select the **OK** button to exit the **Chaining** dialog box.

> **NOTE:** Make sure that the arrow points downwards, otherwise click on the **Reverse all**
> button.  .

• The **Solid Extrude** panel will appear. Change the **Type** to **Cut body** and enter the **Distance 0.05** as shown in Figure: 15.0.1.

Figure: 15.0.1

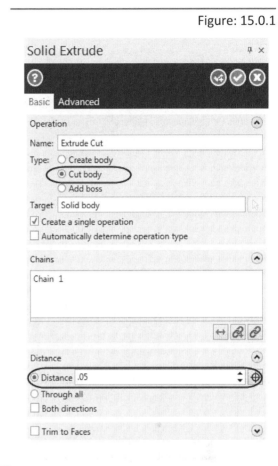

• Select the **OK** button to exit the **Extrude** panel.
• The part should appear as shown below.

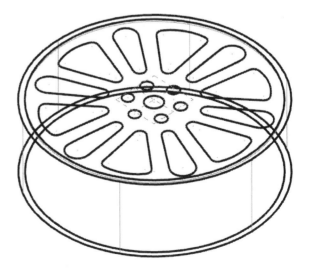

♦ To display the part in the shaded mode, press **Alt + S**.

♦ Click on the **Solids** tab at the bottom of the **Toolpaths Manager**.

♦ If the **Solids Manager** is not yet in display, select the **VIEW** tab, then from the **Managers** group, click on **Solids** as shown.

♦ In the **Solids Manager,** you should see one **Solid** as shown.

♦ To see the solid history with all the operations listed, click on the plus sign (+) in front of the **Solid**.

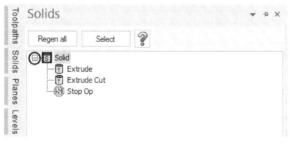

NOTE: To modify any of the solids operation, double click on the operation. The corresponding panel will appear on the screen, and hence the parameters can be modified. To update the solid after modifying the parameters, click on the **Regen all** button from the **Solids Manager**.

STEP 16: EXTRUDE CUT THE 1.25" DEEP POCKET

In this step another extrusion operation will be performed to cut the 1.25" deep pocket from the solid body to a specific depth.

Step Preview:

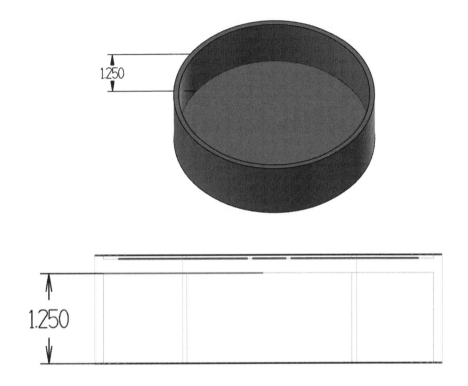

SOLIDS
- From the **Create** group, select **Extrude** as shown.

- Click in the graphics window and press **Alt + S** to display the solid in unshade mode.

◆ Leave the default settings in the **Chaining** dialog box and select the circle as shown.

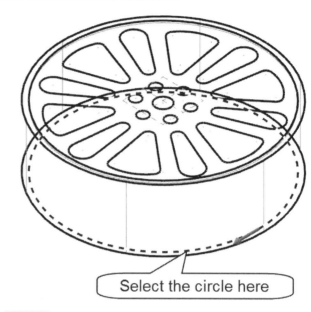

Select the circle here

◆ Select the **OK** button to exit the **Chaining** dialog box.

◆ Click on the **Reverse All** button, if needed, to change the arrow direction as shown.

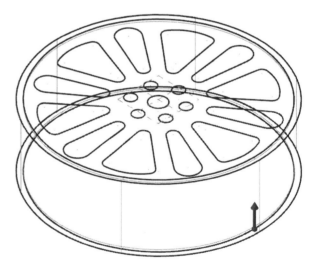

- The **Solid Extrude** panel will appear. Change the **Type** to **Cut Body** and enable **Distance** with the specified amount as shown.

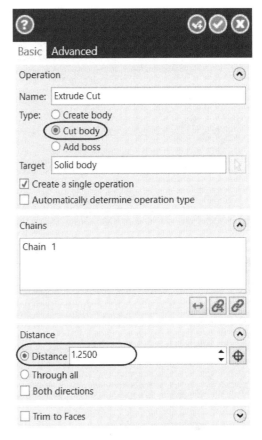

- Select the **OK and Create a New Operation** button to remain in the same command.
- The part should appear as shown in Figure: 16.0.1.

Figure: 16.0.1

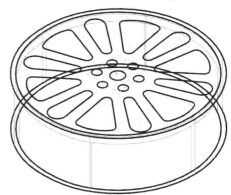

- Press **Alt + S** to shade the solid.

• Using the mouse wheel, click somewhere in the middle of the part and holding down the mouse wheel rotate the part to check the cut from the solid bottom as shown.

• Right mouse click in the graphics window and select the **Isometric** view.

🔲	Zoom Window
🔍	Unzoom 80%
🔄	Dynamic Rotation
🔲	Fit
🔳	Top (WCS)
🔳	Front (WCS)
🔳	Right (WCS)
🔳	Isometric (WCS)
✏	Delete Entities
⌐?	Analyze Distance...
⟍?	Analyze Entity Properties...

STEP 17: EXTRUDE THE CUT THROUGH POCKETS AND HOLES

In this step, another extrusion operation will be performed to cut all the cut through pockets and the holes from the solid.

Step Preview:

◆ Press **Alt+S** to display the solid in unshade mode.

• Leave the default settings in the **Chaining** dialog box and select the chains as shown.

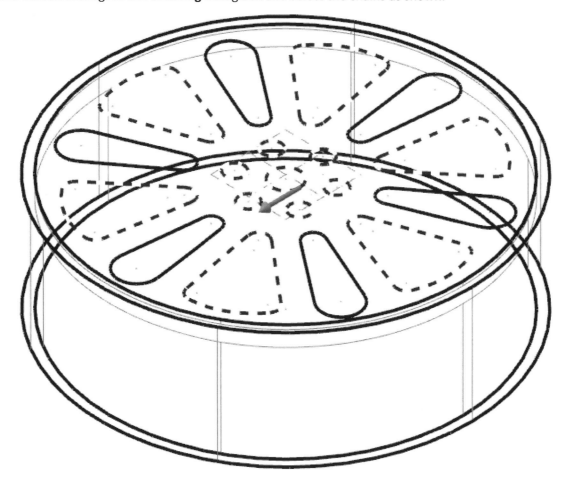

> **NOTE:** The chaining direction is not important in this case. The arrow showing the chaining direction disappears from the selected chain as you select the next chain.

• Select the **OK** button to exit the **Chaining** dialog box.

◆ Click on the **Reverse All** button, if needed, to change the arrow direction as shown.

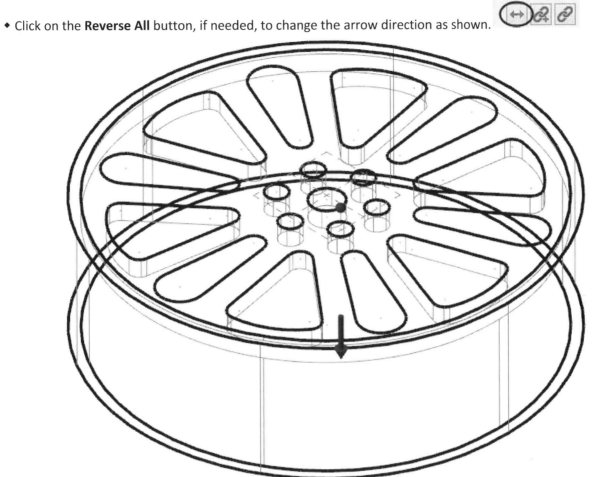

- The **Solid Extrude** panel will appear. Make sure that the **Type** to **Cut Body** is enabled and enable **Through all** as shown.

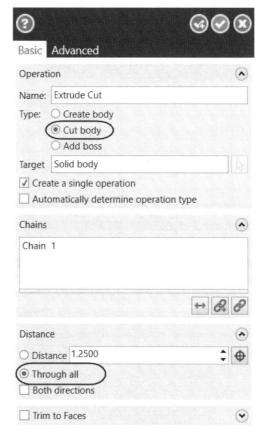

- Select the **OK and Create a New Operation** button to remain in the same command.
- The part should appear as shown in Figure: 17.0.1.

Figure: 17.0.1

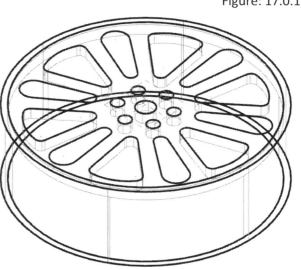

- Press **Alt + S** to shade the solid.

◆ Use the mouse wheel and rotate the part to check the cuts through as shown.

STEP 18: EXTRUDE THE 0.05" DEEP POCKETS

In this step another extrusion operation will be performed to cut the 0.05" deep pockets from the solid.

Step Preview:

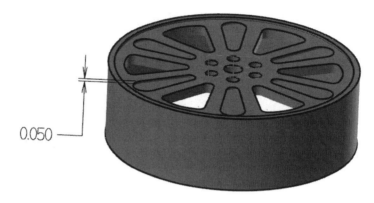

- Press **Alt + S** to display the solid in unshade mode.
- Leave the default settings in the **Chaining** dialog box and select the chains as shown.

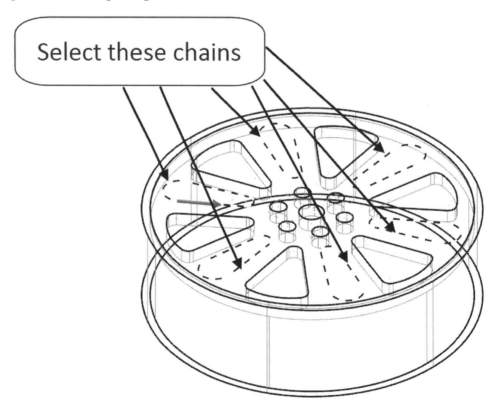

- Select the **OK** button to exit the **Chaining** dialog box.

• Click on the **Reverse All** button, if needed, to change the arrow direction as shown.

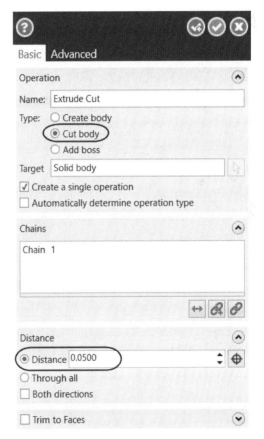

• The **Solid Extrude** panel will appear. Make sure that the **Type** to **Cut Body** is enabled and enable **Distance** and set the value as shown.

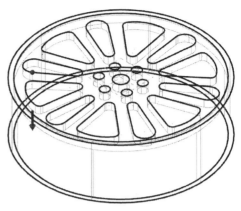

• Select the **OK** button to exit the **Extrude** panel.

◆ The part should appear as shown in <u>Figure: 18.0.1</u>.

Figure: 18.0.1

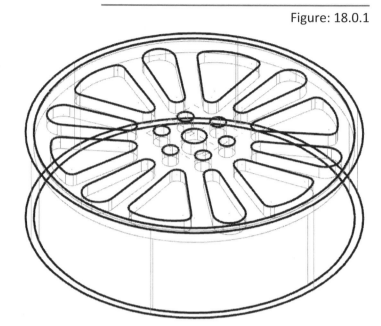

◆ Press **Alt** + **S** to shade the solid.

STEP 19: CHAMFER THE INSIDE POCKETS AND THE HOLES

One-Distance Chamfer uses edge blending to create a symmetrical beveled edge with the same chamfer distance for both edge faces.

In this step you will apply a 0.025" X 45° chamfer to the inside pockets and the center hole.

Step Preview:

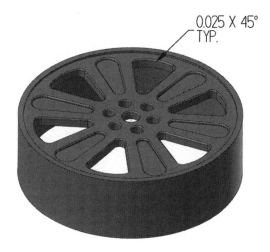

0.025 X 45°
TYP.

* To un-hide the **Levels** panel, from the left side of the graphics window click on the **Levels** tab as shown.

* Make **Level 1** invisible by clicking on the **X** under **Visible** column next to **Level 1** as shown. (The X indicates the selected level is visible.)

Num... ∧	Visible	Name	Entities	Level Set
1			71	
2	X		1	

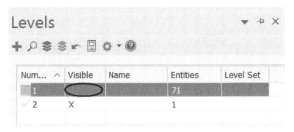

SOLIDS

- From the **Modify** group, select **One Distance Chamfer** as shown.

- In the **Solid Selection** panel, enable only the **Edge** button, and make sure that **Face**, **Body** and other buttons are disabled, as shown in the figure.

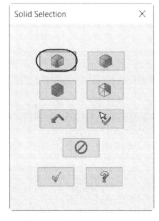

- [Select entities to chamfer]: Select one of the top edges from each pocket as shown in Figure: 19.0.1.

Figure: 19.0.1

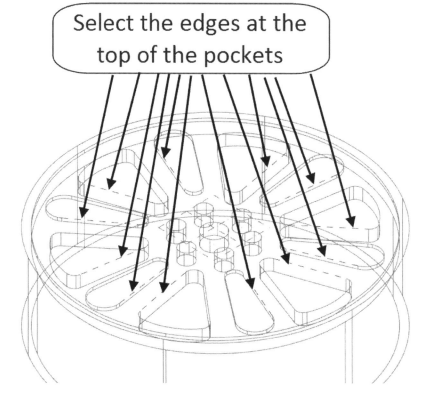

Select the edges at the top of the pockets

◆ [Select entities to chamfer]: Select all the edges of the holes as shown.

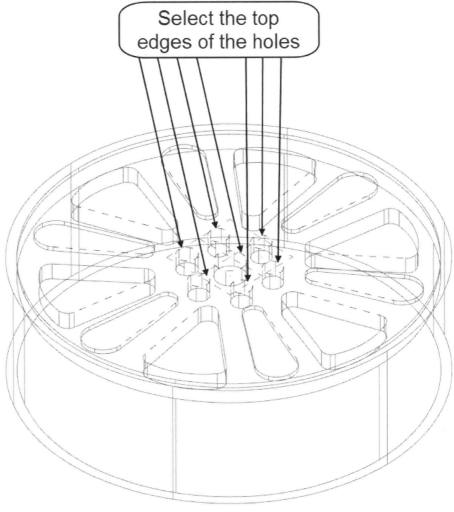

Select the top
edges of the holes

◆ Select the **OK** button to exit the **Solid Selection** panel.

• The **One-Distance Chamfer** panel will appear. Enable **Propagate along tangencies** and set the **Distance** as shown.

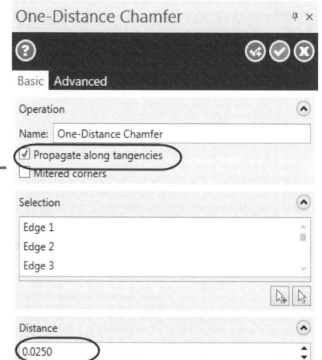

Distance sets the distance of the chamfer from the selected edge on the adjacent faces.

Mitered Corners Mastercam will extend each chamfer to the extent of the edge. Use this feature where three or more chamfered edges meet at a vertex. With this option disabled, a smooth face at the vertex where the chamfers meet will be created.

Propagate Along Tangencies extends the chamfer along all tangent edges until a non-tangent edge is reached.

• Select the **OK** button to exit the command.
• Press **Alt + S** to see the part in the shaded mode as shown.

STEP 20: SAVE THE FILE

FILE
- **Save As.**

- Click on the **Browse** icon as shown.
- Find a location on the computer to save your file.
- File name: "Your Name_4".

TOOLPATH CREATION - SETUP 1

SUGGESTED FIXTURE 1:

> **NOTE:** In order to machine this part, we will have 2 setups and output 2 NC files. To view the second setup, see **page 462**.

SETUP SHEET 1:

TOOL LIST

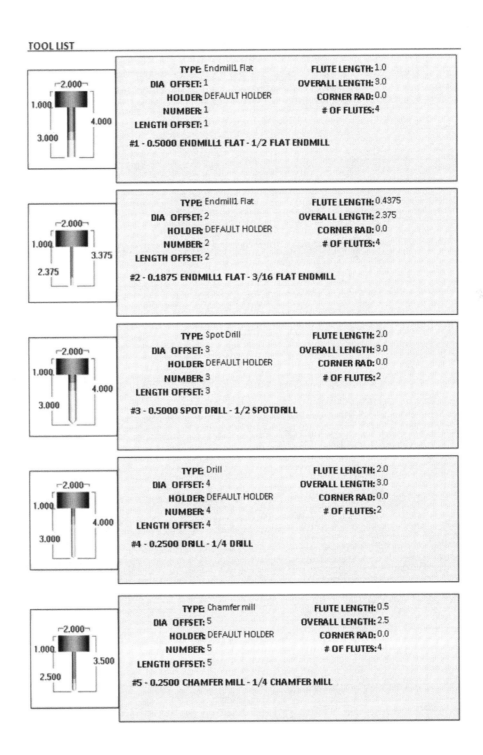

TYPE: Endmill1 Flat	**FLUTE LENGTH:** 1.0
DIA OFFSET: 1	**OVERALL LENGTH:** 3.0
HOLDER: DEFAULT HOLDER	**CORNER RAD:** 0.0
NUMBER: 1	**# OF FLUTES:** 4
LENGTH OFFSET: 1	

#1 - 0.5000 ENDMILL1 FLAT - 1/2 FLAT ENDMILL

TYPE: Endmill1 Flat	**FLUTE LENGTH:** 0.4375
DIA OFFSET: 2	**OVERALL LENGTH:** 2.375
HOLDER: DEFAULT HOLDER	**CORNER RAD:** 0.0
NUMBER: 2	**# OF FLUTES:** 4
LENGTH OFFSET: 2	

#2 - 0.1875 ENDMILL1 FLAT - 3/16 FLAT ENDMILL

TYPE: Spot Drill	**FLUTE LENGTH:** 2.0
DIA OFFSET: 3	**OVERALL LENGTH:** 3.0
HOLDER: DEFAULT HOLDER	**CORNER RAD:** 0.0
NUMBER: 3	**# OF FLUTES:** 2
LENGTH OFFSET: 3	

#3 - 0.5000 SPOT DRILL - 1/2 SPOTDRILL

TYPE: Drill	**FLUTE LENGTH:** 2.0
DIA OFFSET: 4	**OVERALL LENGTH:** 3.0
HOLDER: DEFAULT HOLDER	**CORNER RAD:** 0.0
NUMBER: 4	**# OF FLUTES:** 2
LENGTH OFFSET: 4	

#4 - 0.2500 DRILL - 1/4 DRILL

TYPE: Chamfer mill	**FLUTE LENGTH:** 0.5
DIA OFFSET: 5	**OVERALL LENGTH:** 2.5
HOLDER: DEFAULT HOLDER	**CORNER RAD:** 0.0
NUMBER: 5	**# OF FLUTES:** 4
LENGTH OFFSET: 5	

#5 - 0.2500 CHAMFER MILL - 1/4 CHAMFER MILL

STEP 21: SELECT THE MACHINE AND SET UP THE STOCK

In Mastercam, you select a **Machine Definition** before creating any toolpaths. The **Machine Definition** is a model of your machine's capabilities and features. It acts like a template for setting up your machine. The machine definition ties together three main components: the schematic model of your machines components, the control definition that models your control capabilities and the post processor that will generate the required machine code (G-code). For a Mill Level 1 exercise (2D toolpaths), we just need a basic machine definition.

> **NOTE:** For the purpose of this tutorial, we will be using the **Default Mill** machine.

21.1 Unhide the Toolpaths Manager panel

• From the left side of the graphics window, click on the **Toolpaths** tab as shown.

• Pin the **Toolpaths Manager** by clicking on the **Auto Hide** icon as shown.

21.2 Select the machine

MACHINE

• From the **Machine Type** group, click on the drop down arrow below **Mill** and select the **Default**.

> **NOTE:** Once you select the **Mill Default** the ribbon bar changes to reflect the toolpaths that could be used with **Mill Default**.

◆ Select the plus sign in front of **Properties** in the **Toolpaths Manager** to expand the **Toolpaths Group Properties.**

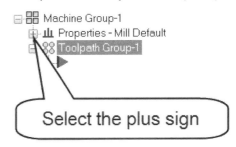

◆ Select **Tool settings** to set the tool parameters.

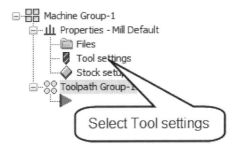

◆ Change the parameters to match the screen shot as shown in Figure: 21.2.1.

Figure: 21.2.1

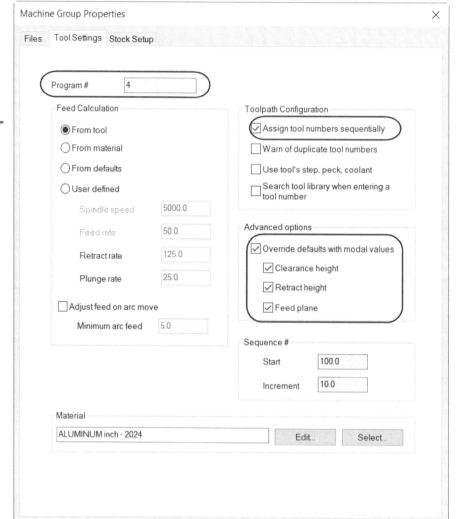

Program # is used to enter a number if your machine requires a number for a program name.

Assign tool numbers sequentially allows you to overwrite the tool number from the library with the next available tool number. (First operation tool number 1, Second operation tool number 2, etc.)

Warn of duplicate tool numbers allows you to get a warning if you enter two tools with the same number.

Override defaults with modal values enables the system to keep the values that you enter.

Feed Calculation set to **From tool** uses feed rate, plunge rate, retract rate and spindle speed from the tool definition.

- Select the **Stock Setup** tab to define the stock.
- Pick the **Cylindrical** shape option and the axis which the stock will be set to as **"Z"**.
- Pick the **All Entities** button to define the stock size as shown in Figure: 21.2.2.

Figure: 21.2.2

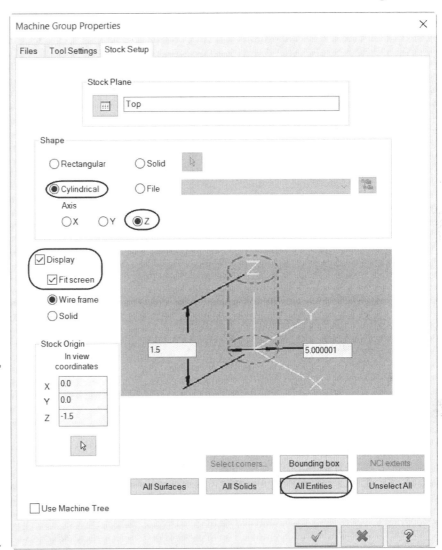

The **Stock Origin** values adjust the positioning of the stock, ensuring that you have an equal amount of extra stock around the finished part.

Display options allows you to set the stock as Wireframe and to fit the stock to the screen. (Fit Screen)

NOTE: The **stock** model that you create can be displayed with the part geometry when viewing the file or the toolpaths, during backplot, or while verifying toolpaths.

- Select the **OK** button to exit **Machine Group Properties**.

• Press **Alt** + **S** to see the part in the unshade mode.
• The stock model will appear as shown in Figure: 21.2.3.

Figure: 21.2.3

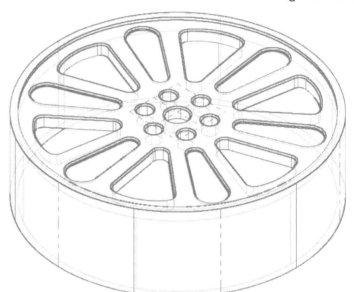

NOTE: The stock is not geometry and cannot be selected.
There will not be a facing toolpath because the stock is already to size.

STEP 22: 2D HIGH SPEED AREA MILL

2D High Speed Area Mill toolpath allows you to machine pockets, material that other toolpaths left behind, and standing bosses or cores using a smooth clean motion. Helical entries and tangent stepovers create efficient motion for your machine tools. Cut parameters let you control corner rounding to create the best toolpath, avoiding sharp corners or direction changes. You will machine the pocket keeping the tool inside the machining region by selecting **Stay inside** as your machining region strategy.

Toolpath Preview:

22.1 Chain Selection

TOOLPATHS

- From the **2D** group, select the **Expand gallery** arrow as shown.

- Select the **Area Mill** icon.

- When the new NC name panel appears select the **OK** button to accept the name.

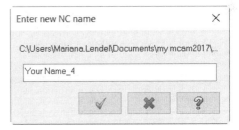

- In the **Chain Options,** make sure that **Stay inside** is enabled and click on the **Select Machining Chains** button in the **Machining regions** as shown.

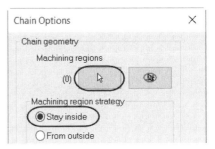

• In the **Chaining** dialog box, switch to **Solids** selection as shown.

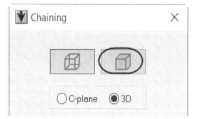

• Make sure that only the **Loop** button is enabled as shown.

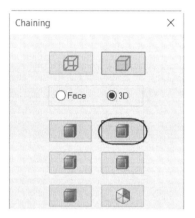

• Select the bottom of the pocket edge as shown in Figure: 22.1.1.

Figure: 22.1.1

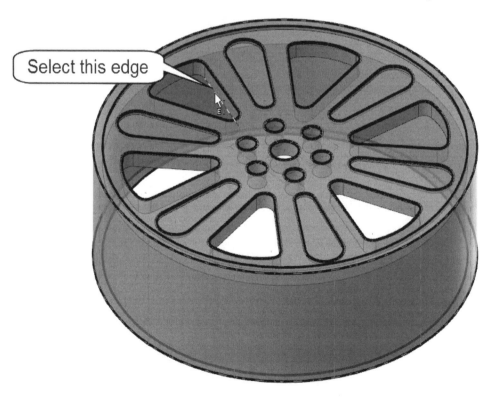

- The **Pick Reference Face** dialog appears, make sure that the bottom edge is selected and click on the **OK** button to continue.

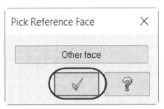

- Select the **OK** button to exit the **Chaining** dialog box.

- Select the **OK** button to exit the **Chain Options** dialog box.
- In the **Toolpath Type** page, **Area Mill** should be already selected as shown.

Dynamic Mill   Area Mill   Dynamic Contour   Peel Mill   Blend Mill

22.2 Preview Chains

The **Preview Chains** function is intended to give the user a quick visual representation of how Mastercam sees the various pieces of geometry that have been selected, how they interact with one another and a general overview of how the toolpath will be calculated with the selections presently made.

- Click on the **Color** icon to see the legend for **Preview chains** as shown.

- The **Preview Chains Colors** dialog box should look as shown.

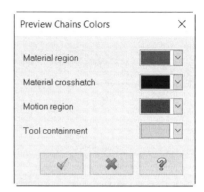

The **Material region** and **Material crosshatch** are the two colors that are used to define the material to be cut. The default colors are red for the background and black for the crosshatch.

The **Motion region** displays the area that Mastercam is making available to the toolpath for motion if it needs it. The color to represent it is dark blue. The primary reason for the display of the entire available (but not necessarily used) Motion region is to help the user visualize how the tool may move near or interact with any adjacent geometry.

The **Tool containment** is what you have selected as the Containment region in the chain geometry. If you have not selected a containment region, it will default to the outside of the Motion region since that is currently the default area the toolpath is being contained to. The color used to represent the Tool containment is yellow.

- Select the **OK** button to exit **Preview Chains Colors**.
- Select the **Preview chains** button as shown.

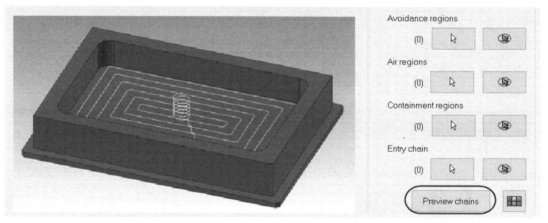

- Select the **Hide dialog** button to see the preview in the graphics window.

◆ The **Preview chains** should look as shown.

◆ Press **Esc** key to return to the toolpath parameters.
◆ Click on the **Preview chains** button again to clear the Preview chains display.

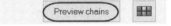

22.3 Select a 1/2" Flat Endmill from the Library and set the Tool Parameters

◆ Select **Tool** from the **Tree View list**.

◆ Click on the **Select library tool** button.
◆ Select the **Filter** button.

◆ Select the **None** button and then under **Tool Types** choose the **Flat Endmill** icon as shown.
◆ Under **Tool Diameter**, pick **Equal** and input a value of **0.5** as shown in Figure: 22.3.1.

Figure: 22.3.1

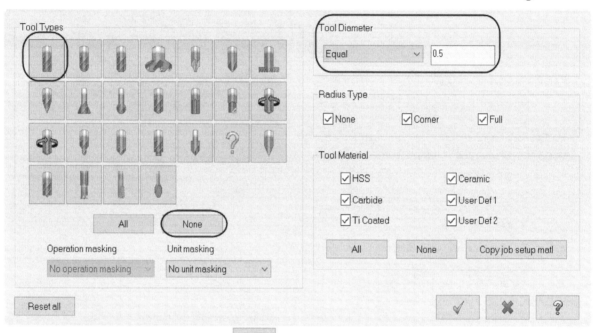

◆ Select the **OK** button to exit the **Tool List Filter.**
◆ In the **Tool Selection** panel you should only see a **1/2" Flat Endmill**.

#	Assembly...	Tool Name	Holder N...	Dia.	Cor. r...	Length	# Flut...	Type	Rad....
290	–	1/2 FLAT ENDMILL	–	0.5	0.0	1.0	4	End...	None

◆ Select the **1/2" Flat Endmill** in the **Tool Selection** page and then select the **OK** button to exit.

♦ Make all the necessary changes as shown in <u>Figure: 22.3.2</u>.

Figure: 22.3.2

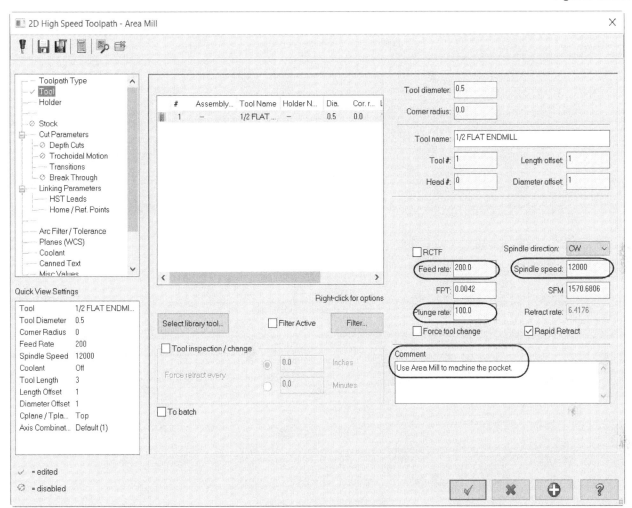

22.4 Set the Cut Parameters

♦ From the **Tree View list**, select **Cut Parameters**.
♦ Set the parameters as shown in Figure: 22.4.1.

Figure: 22.4.1

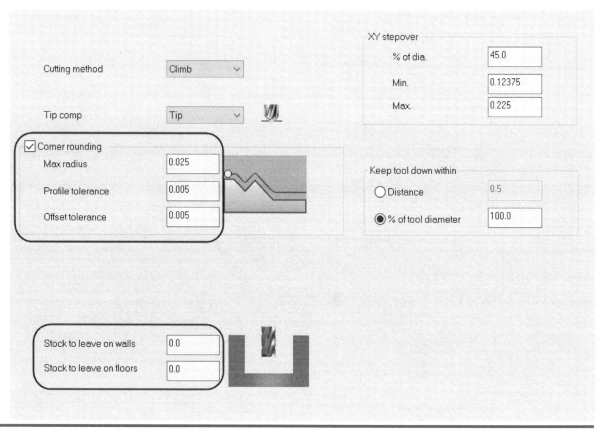

Cutting method set to **Climb** cuts in one direction with the tool rotating in the opposite direction of the tool motion.

XY stepover sets the distance between cutting passes in the X and Y axes.
% of diameter expresses the maximum XY stepover as a percentage of the tool diameter. The Max. XY stepover field will update automatically when you enter a value in this field. The actual stepover is calculated by Mastercam between the Min. and Max. values.

Corner rounding activates toolpath corner rounding, which replaces sharp corners with arcs for faster and smoother transitions in tool direction.

Profile tolerance represents the maximum distance that the outermost profile of a toolpath created with corner rounding can deviate from the original toolpath.

Offset tolerance represents the maximum distance that a profile of a toolpath created with corner rounding can deviate from the original toolpath. This is the same measurement as the profile tolerance but is applied to all the profiles except the outermost one.

22.5 Set the Depth Cuts Parameters

◆ From the **Tree View list**, select the **Depth Cuts** and disable it as shown.

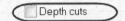
☐ Depth cuts

22.6 Set the Transitions

◆ From the **Tree View list**, select **Transitions** and make sure the parameters are set as shown.

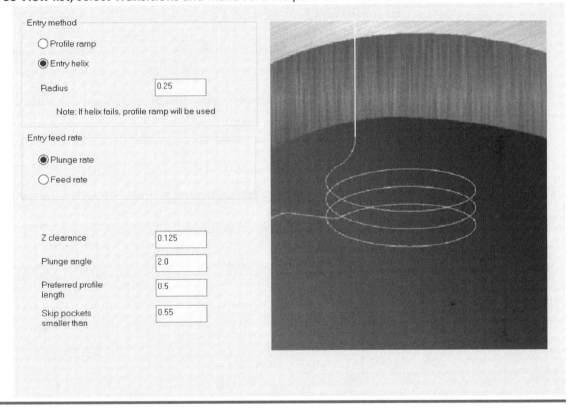

Entry helix creates a helical entry move.

Z clearance adds an extra height used in the ramping motion down from a top profile. It ensures that the tool has fully slowed down from rapid speeds before touching the material.

Plunge angle sets the angle of descent for the entry move and determines the pitch.

Skip pockets smaller than allows you to specify a minimum pocket size for which Mastercam will consider creating a cutting pass.

22.7 Set the Linking Parameters

• Select **Linking Parameters** and **Clearance** and set the value to **Absolute** and **1.0** as shown in Figure: 22.7.1.
• Make sure that the **Depth** is set to **Incremental** and **0.0** as shown in Figure: 22.7.1.

> **NOTE:** In this toolpath, you selected the bottom of the pocket and the incremental value for the depth is relative to the location of the chained geometry.

Figure: 22.7.1

22.8 Preview the Toolpath

- To quickly check how the toolpath will be generated, select the **Preview toolpath** icon as shown.

- To hide the dialog box, click on the **Hide dialog** icon as shown.
- To see the part from an **Isometric** view, right mouse click in the graphics window and select **Isometric** as shown.

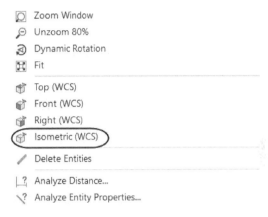

- The toolpath should look as shown.

- Press **Esc** key to exit the preview.

> **NOTE:** If the toolpath does not look as shown in the preview, check your parameters again.

- Select the **OK** button to generate the toolpath.

STEP 23: BACKPLOT THE TOOLPATHS

◆ Make sure that the toolpaths are selected (signified by the green check mark on the folder icon). If the operation is not selected, choose the **Select all operations** icon.

◆ Select the **Backplot selected operations** button.

◆ In the **Backplot** panel, enable **Display with color codes**, **Display tool** and **Display rapid moves** icons as shown.

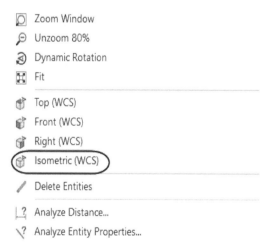

◆ To see the part from an **Isometric** view, right mouse click in the graphics window and select **Isometric** as shown.

Zoom Window
Unzoom 80%
Dynamic Rotation
Fit
Top (WCS)
Front (WCS)
Right (WCS)
Isometric (WCS)
Delete Entities
Analyze Distance...
Analyze Entity Properties...

◆ To fit the workpiece to the screen, if needed, right mouse click in the graphics window again and select **Fit**.

◆ You can step through the **Backplot** by using the **Step forward**  or **Step back** buttons.

◆ You can adjust the speed of the backplot.

◆ Select the **Play** button to run **Backplot**.

♦ The toolpath should look as shown.

♦ Select **Ok** button to exit the **Backplot**.

STEP 24: SIMULATE THE TOOLPATH IN VERIFY

♦ From the **Toolpaths Manager**, select the **Verify selected operations** icon as shown.

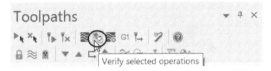

NOTE: Mastercam launches a new window that allows you to check the part using **Backplot** or **Verify**.

♦ From **Mastercam Backplot Home** tab, switch to **Verify** and change the settings for the **Visibility** and **Focus** as shown in Figure: 24.0.1.
♦ In the **Visibility** group, click on **Workpiece** twice to display it translucid as shown in Figure: 24.0.1.

Figure: 24.0.1

+ Select the **Play** button to run **Verify**.
+ The part will appear as shown.

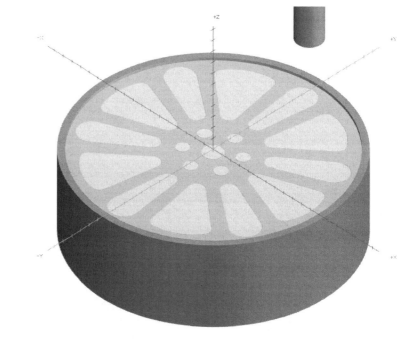

+ To go back to the Mastercam window, minimize the **Mastercam Simulator** window as shown.
+ Press **T** to remove the toolpath display.

STEP 25: 2D HIGH SPEED DYNAMIC MILL

2D High Speed Dynamic Mill utilizes the entire flute length of their cutting tools to produce the smoothest, most efficient tool motion for high speed pocketing. The toolpath supports a custom entry method and many others. Micro lifts further refine the dynamic milling motion and avoid excessive heat build up. Custom feeds and speeds optimize and generate safe tool motion. Dynamic Mill machines pockets using one or more chains to drive the toolpath. The outside chain contains the toolpath; all inside chains are considered islands.

In this step you will machine the six bigger pockets using 2D HS Dynamic Mill toolpath. To select all chains, you will use the **Chain Feature** option. You will have to make the wireframe geometry from Level 1 visible.

Toolpath Preview:

25.1 Chain selection using Chain Feature Option

♦ To make **Level 1** visible, right mouse click in the graphics window and from the **Mini Toolbar**, select the drop down arrow next to **Level** and click on **Level 1** as shown.

TOOLPATHS

• From the **2D** group, select the **Dynamic Mill** icon.

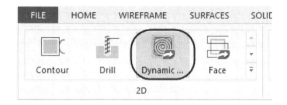

• In the **Chain Options,** make sure that **Stay inside** is enabled as the **Machining region strategy** and click on the **Select machining chains** button in the **Machining regions** as shown.

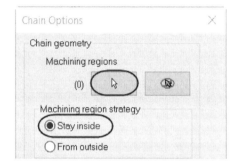

• In the **Chaining** dialog box, switch back to **Wireframe** selection as shown.
• Leave the default setting in the **Chaining** dialog box.

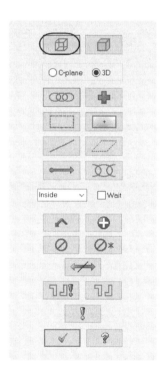

• If needed, press **Alt + S** to unshade the solid and then pick the chain as shown in <u>Figure: 25.1.1</u>.

Figure: 25.1.1

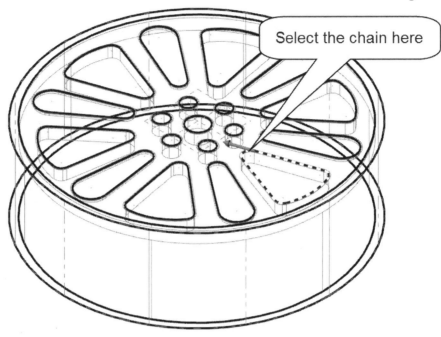

Select the chain here

• From the **Chaining** dialog box select the **Chain Feature** button.

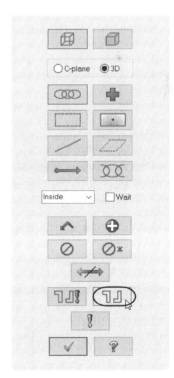

> **NOTE:** **Chain Feature** allows you to automatically select chains based on the initial chain. Chain Feature is most useful when you have a large number of chains in a part with groups of similar shapes and window chaining is not an option.

- All of the identical pockets should be selected as shown.

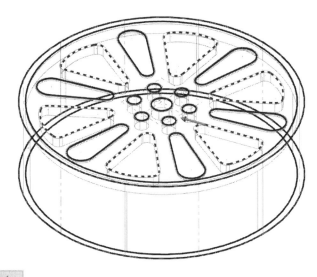

- Select the **OK** button to exit the **Chaining** dialog box.
- In the **Chain Options** panel, **Machining regions** will have 6 chains as shown.

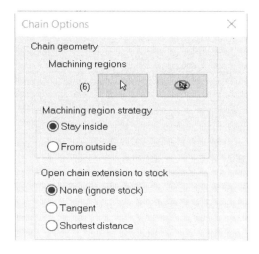

- Select the **OK** button to exit the **Chain Options** panel.
- In the **Toolpath Type** page, **Dynamic Mill** will be already selected as shown in Figure: 25.1.2.

Figure: 25.1.2

25.2 Preview Chains

♦ Select the **Preview chains** button as shown.

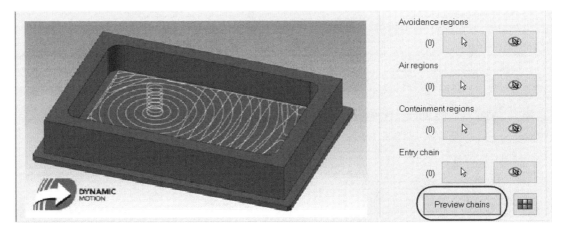

♦ See **page 383** to review the procedure.
♦ The **Preview chains** should look as shown.

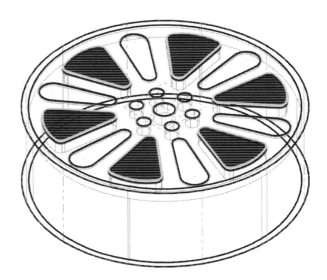

♦ Press **Esc** key to return to the toolpath parameters.
♦ Click on the **Preview chains** button again to clear the Preview chains display.

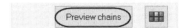

25.3 Select a 3/16" Flat Endmill from the library and set the Tool Parameters

◆ Select **Tool** from the **Tree View list**.

◆ Click on the **Select library tool** button.
◆ Select the **Filter** button.

◆ Select the **None** button and then under **Tool Types**, choose the **Flat Endmill** icon.
◆ Under **Tool Diameter**, pick **Equal** and input a value of **0.1875** as shown in Figure: 25.3.1.

Figure: 25.3.1

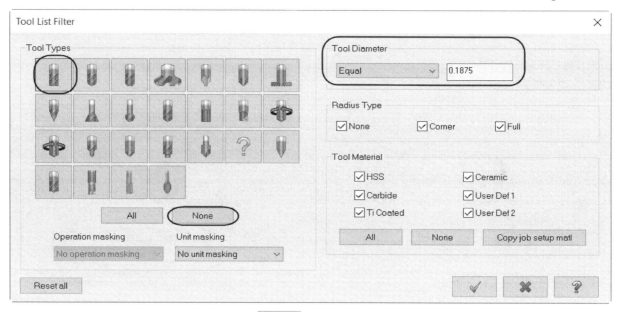

◆ Select the **OK** button to exit the **Tool List Filter**.
◆ In the **Tool Selection** panel you should only see a **3/16" Flat Endmill**.

#	Assembly...	Tool Name	Holder Name	Dia.	Cor. r...	Length	# Flut...	Type	Rad....
284	–	3/16 FLAT ENDMILL	–	0.1875	0.0	0.4375	4	End...	None

◆ Select the **3/16" Flat Endmill** in the **Tool Selection** page and then select the **OK** button to exit.

♦ Make all the necessary changes as shown in <u>Figure: 25.3.2</u>.

Figure: 25.3.2

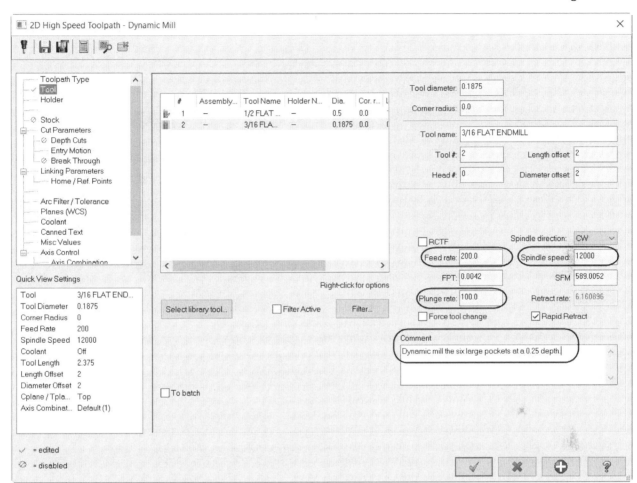

25.4 Set the Cut Parameters

♦ From the **Tree View list**, select **Cut Parameters**. The previously used settings will still be there.
♦ Change the settings for this second toolpath as shown in Figure: 25.4.1.

Figure: 25.4.1

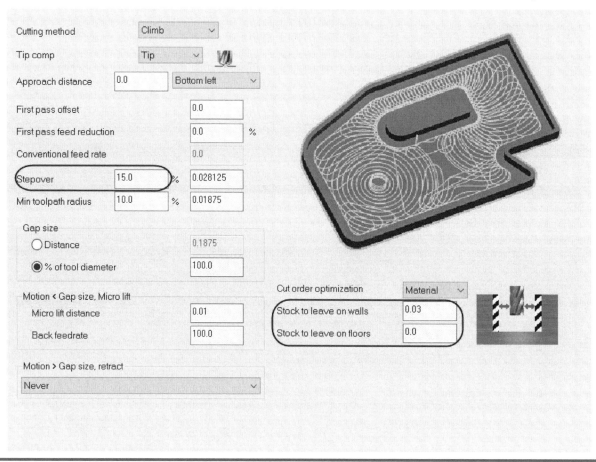

Stepover sets the distance between cutting passes in the X and Y axes.

Toolpath radius reduces sharp corner motion between cut passes.

Micro lift distance enters the distance the tool lifts off the part on the back moves. Microlifts are slight lifts that help clear chips and minimize excessive tool heating.

Back feedrate controls the speed of the backfeed movement of the tool.

Motion > Gap Size, retract controls retracts in the toolpath when making a non-cutting move within an area where the tool can be kept down or microlifted.

Cut order optimization defines the cut order Mastercam applies to different cutting passes in the dynamic mill toolpath.

Stock to leave on walls sets the stock left on the walls that has to be removed by another operation.

25.5 Set the Entry Motion

- ◆ Entry motion configures an entry method for the dynamic mill toolpath which determines not only how and where the tool enters the part, but the cutting method/machining strategy used by the toolpath.The previous settings will be saved.
- ◆ All we want to do is change the **Entry method** to **Profile** as shown in <u>Figure: 25.5.1</u>.

Figure: 25.5.1

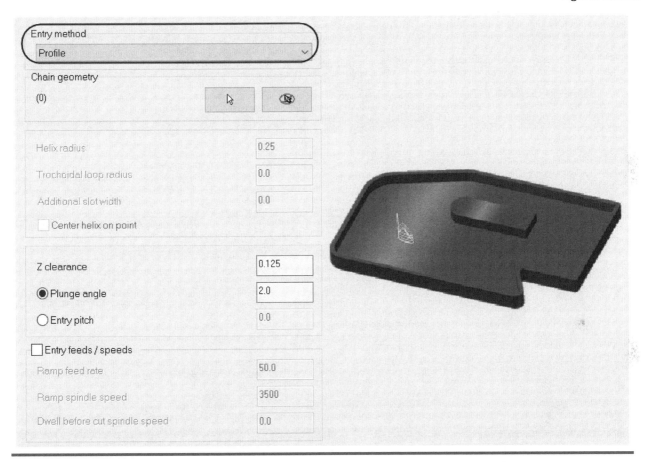

Entry method set to **Profile** creates a boundary based on the shape of the selected chain and uses the tool to ramp into the part. The slot is cleared by taking lighter cuts in the Z axis until the tool reaches the full depth.

Z clearance adds an extra height used in the ramping motion down from a top profile. It ensures that the tool has fully slowed down from rapid speeds before touching the material.

Plunge angle sets the angle of descent for the entry move and determines the pitch.

25.6 Set the Linking Parameters

◆ Select **Linking Parameters** and change the **Top of Stock** value to **0.0 Incremental** and the **Depth** to **-0.25 Incremental** as shown in <u>Figure: 25.6.1</u>.

Figure: 25.6.1

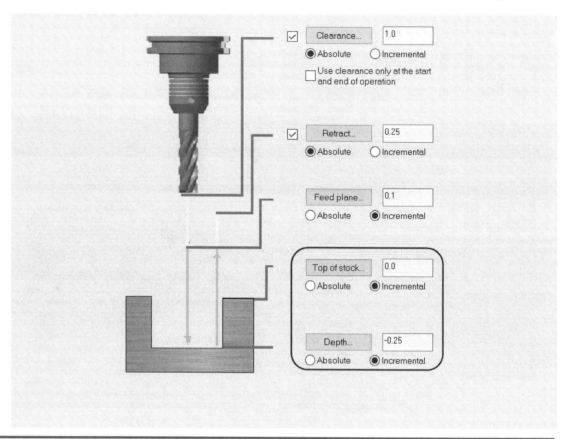

Incremental values are relative to other parameters or chained geometry. In this tutorial, the pocket chains were moved **0.05** along **Z** axis, below zero. The **Top of stock** and the **Depth** set to **Incremental** is measured from the Z depth of the chains. If you want to set the **Top of stock** and the **Depth** to **Absolute**, the values should be - **0.05** and -**0.3** respectively.

25.7 Preview the Toolpath

♦ To quickly check how the toolpath will be generated, select the **Preview toolpath** icon as shown.

♦ See **page 157** to review the procedure.
♦ The toolpath should look as shown. Press **Alt + S** to see the solid shaded if needed.

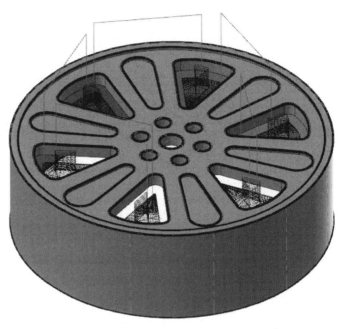

♦ Press **Esc** key to exit the preview.

> **NOTE:** If the toolpath does not look as shown in the preview, check your parameters again.

♦ Select the **OK** button to exit the toolpath parameters.

VIEW
♦ From the **Appearance** group, select **Translucency** as shown.

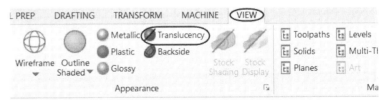

• **Backplot** the toolpath. See **page 158** to review this procedure.

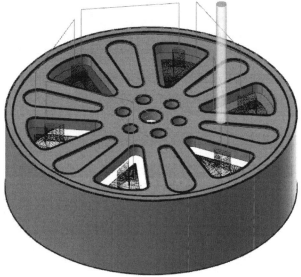

• Click again on the **Translucency** to see the solid opaque.

• Select the **OK** button to exit **Backplot**.

• To **Verify** the toolpaths make sure both operations are selected. To select both operations click on the **Select all operations** icon.

Toolpaths

• Select the **Verify selected operations** icon.

Toolpaths

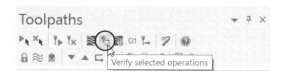

◆ See **page 160** for more information.

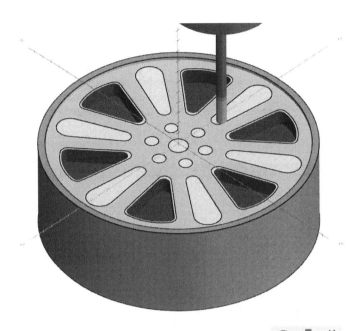

◆ To go back to the Mastercam window, minimize the Mastercam Simulator window as shown.
◆ Press **"T"** to remove the toolpath display.

STEP 26: TRANSFORM TOOLPATHS

Transform toolpaths are used when you want to run the same toolpath in different locations. You can transform a single toolpath or several at a time. In this step you will machine one of the smaller pockets using 2D HS Area Mill. Then, using the **Transform Rotate** toolpath, you will generate the toolpaths for the rest of the identical pockets.

NOTE: This step shows you a different way of machining the identical pockets. To machine the pockets, you can also use the method explained in **Step 25**.

26.1 Machine one of the smaller Pocket using 2D High Speed Area Mill

Toolpath Preview:

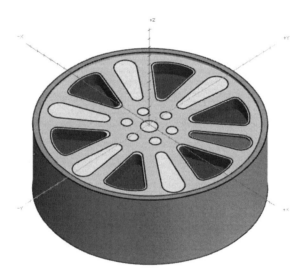

26.2 Chain Selection

TOOLPATHS

♦ From the **2D** group, select the **Expand gallery** arrow as shown.

◆ Select the **Area Mill** icon.

◆ In the **Chain Options** click on the **Select machining chains** button in the **Machining regions** as shown.

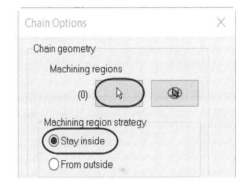

◆ Press **Alt + S** to unshade the part.
◆ Leave the default setting in the **Chaining** dialog box and pick the chain as shown in Figure: 26.2.1.

Figure: 26.2.1

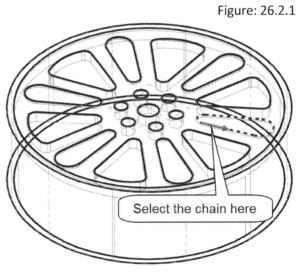

Select the chain here

◆ Select the **OK** button to exit the **Chaining** dialog box.

◆ Select the **OK** button to exit the **Chain Options** dialog box.

◆ In the **Toolpath Type**, **Area Mill** should be already selected as shown.

26.3 Preview Chains

◆ Select the **Preview chains** button as shown.

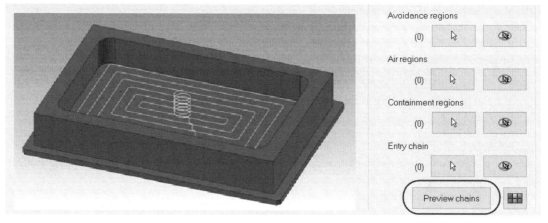

◆ See **page 164** to review the procedure.

◆ The **Preview chains** should look as shown.

◆ Press **Esc** key to return to the toolpath parameters.

◆ Click on the **Preview chains** button again to clear the Preview chains display.

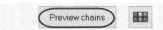

◆ From the **Tree View** list select **Tool**.
◆ Select the **3/16" Flat Endmill** and make all the necessary changes as shown in <u>Figure: 26.3.1</u>.

Figure: 26.3.1

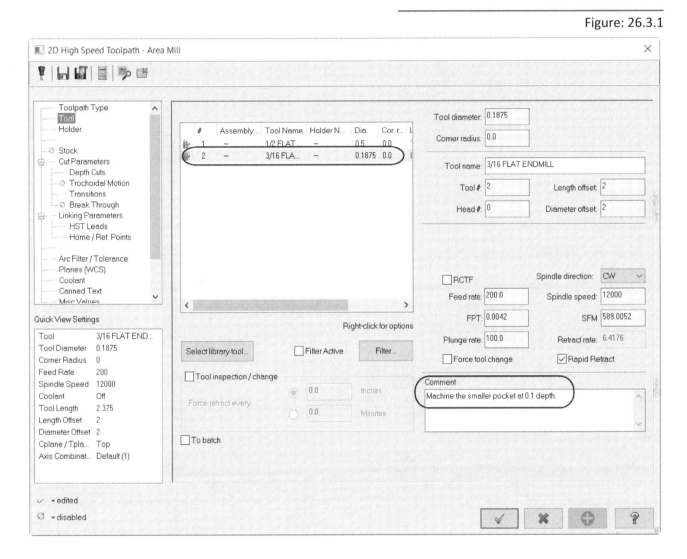

26.4 Set the Cut Parameters

◆ From the **Tree View** list, select **Cut Parameters**. The previously used settings will still be there. Leave stock on the walls as shown in <u>Figure: 26.4.1</u>.

Figure: 26.4.1

Cutting method	Climb ∨
Tip comp	Tip ∨

☑ Corner rounding

Max radius	0.025
Profile tolerance	0.001875
Offset tolerance	0.01875

XY stepover

% of dia.	45.0
Min.	0.046406
Max.	0.084375

Keep tool down within

○ Distance   0.5

◉ % of tool diameter   100.0

Stock to leave on walls	0.03
Stock to leave on floors	0.0

26.5 Set the Depth Cuts parameters

◆ From the **Tree View list**, select **Depth Cuts** and set the parameters as shown in <u>Figure: 26.5.1</u>.

Figure: 26.5.1

☑ Depth cuts	
Max rough step:	0.05
# Finish cuts:	1
Finish step:	0.01

☐ Use island depths

☐ Subprogram

◉ Absolute   ○ Incremental

☐ Tapered walls

Taper angle   0.0

Island taper angle   0.0

☐ Island facing

Overlap: 0.0   %   0.0

Stock above islands: 0.0

26.6 Set the Transitions

◆ From the **Tree View list**, select **Transitions** and leave the **Entry method** set to **Entry helix** as shown in
  <u>Figure: 26.6.1</u>.

Figure: 26.6.1

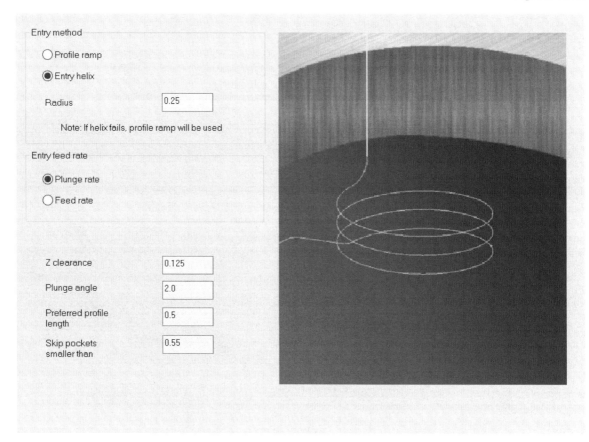

26.7 Set the Linking Parameters

♦ Select **Linking Parameters** and input the **Depth** as shown in Figure: 26.7.1.

Figure: 26.7.1

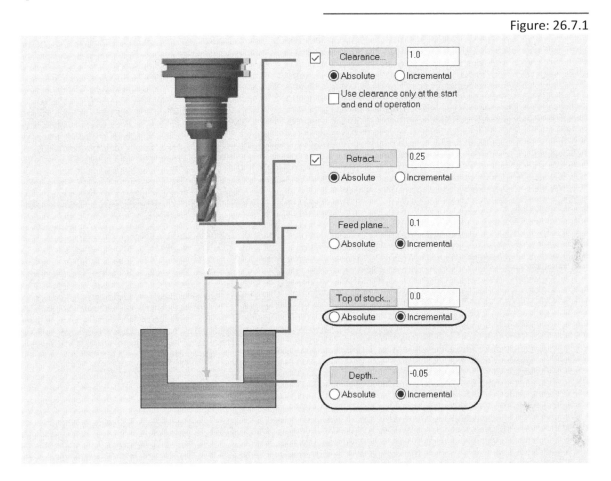

26.8 Preview the Toolpath

◆ To quickly check how the toolpath will be generated, select the **Preview toolpath** icon as shown.

◆ See **page 157** to review the procedure.
◆ The toolpath should look as shown.

◆ Press **Esc** key to exit the preview.

> **NOTE:** If the toolpath does not look as shown in the preview, check your parameters again.

◆ Select the **OK** button to exit the toolpath parameters.
◆ **Backplot** the toolpath as shown on **page 158**.

◆ Select the **OK** button to exit **Backplot**.
◆ To **Verify** the toolpaths, make sure all the operations are selected. To select all operations, click on the **Select all operations** icon.

◆ **Verify** the toolpaths as shown on **page 160**.

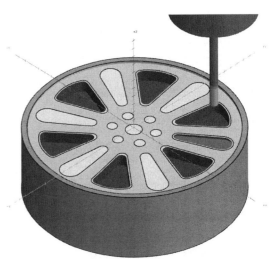

◆ To go back to the Mastercam window, minimize the **Mastercam Simulator** window as shown.

26.9 Transform-Rotate Toolpath

TOOLPATHS
◆ From the **Utilities** group, select the **Toolpath Transform**.

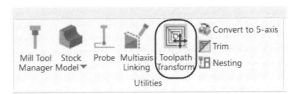

◆ For the **Type,** select **Rotate**, and select **Coordinate** for **Method.**
◆ Select **Operation 3.**

◆ In the **Group NCI output by** area select **Operation order** as shown in <u>Figure: 26.9.1</u>.

Figure: 26.9.1

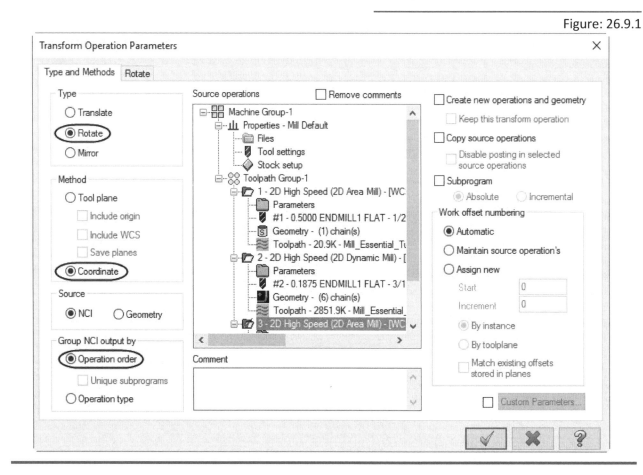

Rotate revolves the toolpath about the construction origin or a specified point. Activate the Rotate tab and you can set the rotation point and number of copies.

Coordinate creates new coordinate positions for the new toolpaths in the original tool plane.

Operation order sorts the transformed operations by the order they were selected. For example, if we choose the large pocket then small pocket. It will execute them in that order (large pocket, small pocket, large pocket, small pocket, etc.).

- ◆ Choose the **Rotate** tab.
- ◆ Input the **Number of steps 5,** a **Start angle** of **60.0** degrees, and a **Rotation angle** of **60.0** degrees as shown in Figure: 26.9.2.

Figure: 26.9.2

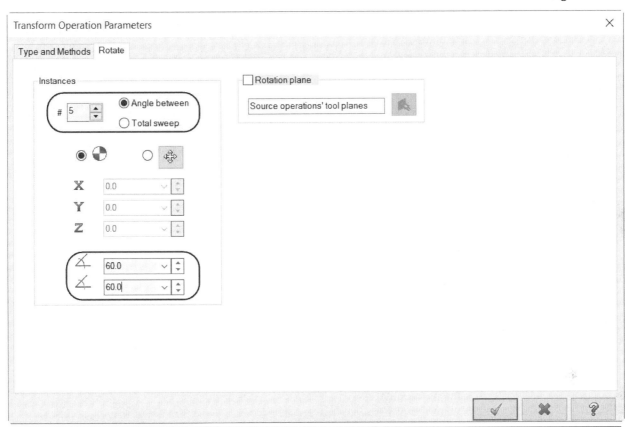

Number of steps is the number of times to rotate the toolpath.

Start angle sets the beginning angle for the rotate toolpath.

Rotation angle sets the angle of rotation for the transformed toolpath.

- ◆ Select the **OK** button to generate the toolpath.

- **Backplot** the toolpath as shown on **page 158**.

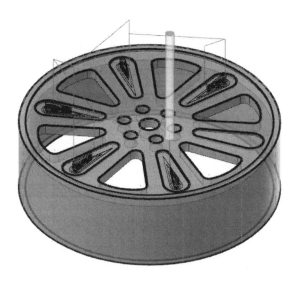

- Select the **OK** button to exit **Backplot**.
- Select all toolpaths to **Verify** them as shown on **page 160**.

- To go back to the Mastercam window, minimize the **Mastercam Simulator** window as shown.
- Press **Alt + S** to shade the solid.
- Press **"T"** to remove the toolpath display.

STEP 27: FINISH THE POCKETS USING A POCKET TOOLPATH

In this step you will use a pocket toolpath to finish the walls of all pockets. The High speed toolpaths do not have a finish wall option inside of their parameters. You will use the solid selections.

Step Preview:

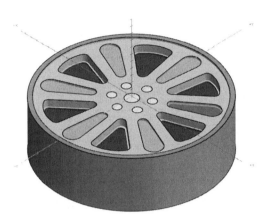

TOOLPATHS

• Select the **Expand gallery** drop down arrow from the **2D** group.

• Select the **Pocket** icon.

27.1 Select the pocket floors using solid Loop and solid Face selections

• In the **Chaining** dialog box, make sure to change to **Solid** selection as shown.

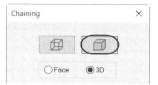

• In The **Chaining** dialog box, make sure that only the **Loop** button is selected as shown.

• [Select faces, edges, and/or loops]: Select one bottom edge of the pocket as shown.

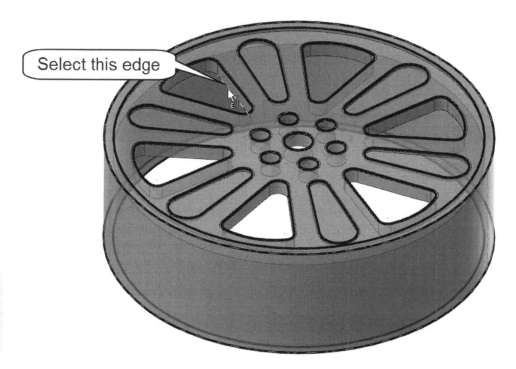

Select this edge

NOTE: The entire pocket bottom should be automatically selected.

- The **Pick Reference Face** panel appears. If the bottom chain is all selected, click on the **OK** button to continue.

- [Select faces, edges, and/or loops]: Select the next through cut pocket as shown.

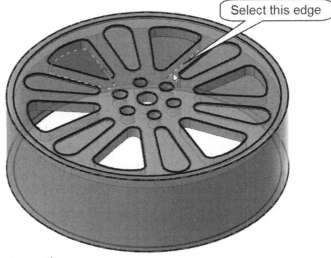

Select this edge

- From the **Pick Reference Face**, select the **OK** button to continue.
- Repeat these steps for the next 4 larger pockets.
- The selected geometry should look as shown.

- From the **Chaining** dialog box, enable the **Face** button and disable the **Loop** button as shown.

- Select the bottom faces of the smaller pockets as shown.

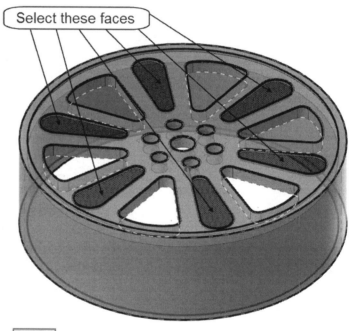

Select these faces

- Select the **OK** button to exit **Chaining** dialog box.
- In the **Toolpath Type,** the **Pocket** should already be selected as shown.

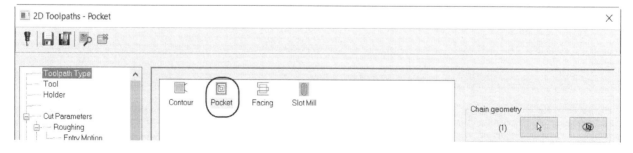

27.2 Select the tool and set the Tool parameters

- From the **Tree View list**, select **Tool.**
- From the **Tool display window**, select the **3/16" Flat Endmill.** Make all the necessary changes as shown.

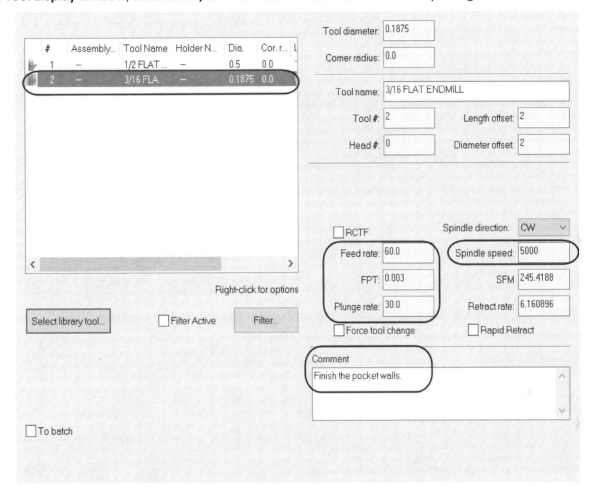

27.3 Set the Cut Parameters page

• From the **Tree View list**, select **Cut Parameters** and make the changes as shown.

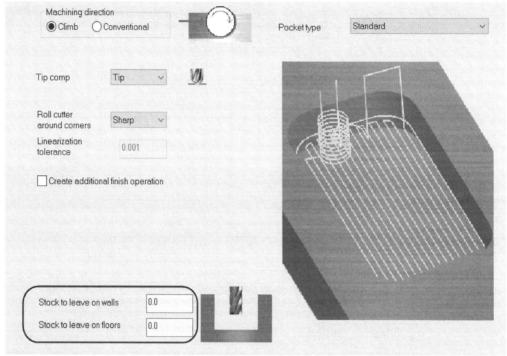

27.4 Disable Roughing page

• From the **Tree View list**, select **Roughing** and disable **Rough** as shown.

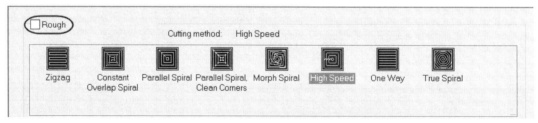

> **NOTE:** The **Roughing** option should be disabled as in this case you only want to finish the walls and not to machine again the pocket floors. For the same reason, you will turn the **Entry Motion** off.

27.5 Disable Entry Motion page

◆ From the **Tree View list**, select **Entry Motion** and enable **Off** to turn off any entry helix or ramp moves.

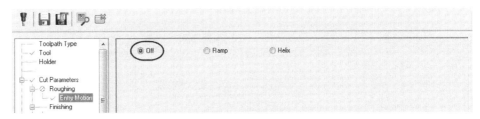

27.6 Set the Finishing page

◆ From the **Tree View list**, select **Finishing** and set the parameters as shown.

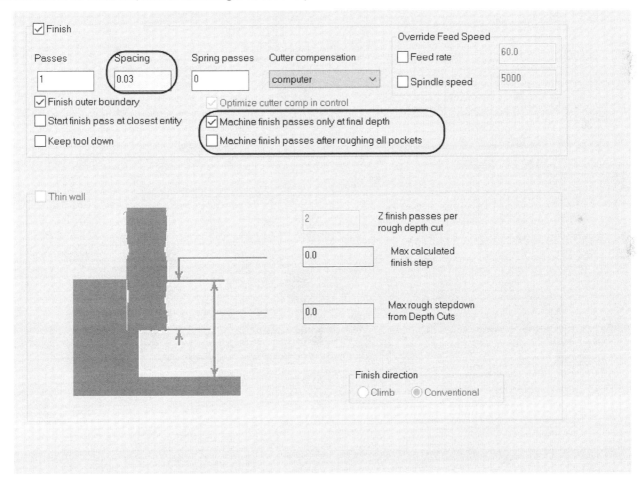

Passes sets the number of finish passes for the toolpath.

Spacing sets the amount of material to be removed with each cut.

27.7 Set the Lead In/Out page

• From the **Tree View list**, select **Lead In/Out** and make the changes to ensure smooth entry and exit moves to and from the part as shown.

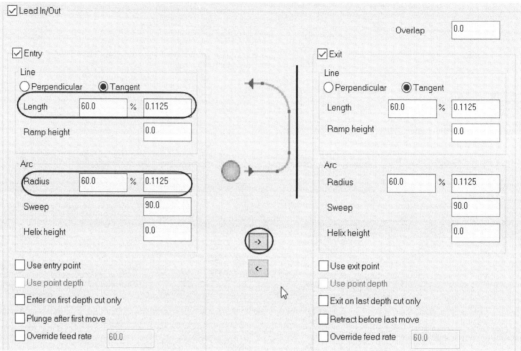

27.8 Set the Linking parameters page

• From the **Tree View list**, select **Linking** parameters and change the parameters as shown.

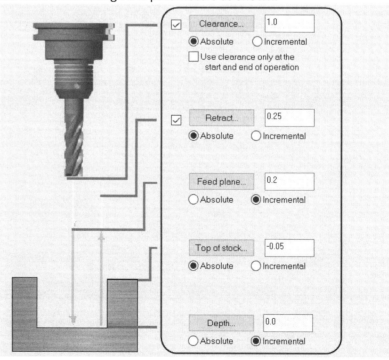

27.9 Preview the Toolpath

◆ To quickly check how the toolpath will be generated, select the **Preview toolpath** icon as shown.

◆ See **page 157** to review the procedure.
◆ The toolpath should look as shown.

◆ Press **Esc** key to exit the preview.

NOTE: If the toolpath does not look as shown in the preview, check your parameters again.

◆ Select the **OK** button to exit **Pocket** toolpath.

27.10 Verify the toolpath using both Backplot and Verify

♦ **Backplot** the toolpath as shown on **page 158**.

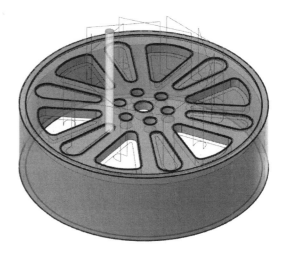

♦ Select the **OK** button to exit **Backplot**.
♦ To **Verify** the toolpaths make sure all the operations are selected. To select all operations click on the **Select all operations** icon.

Toolpaths

♦ **Verify** the toolpaths them as shown on **page 160**.

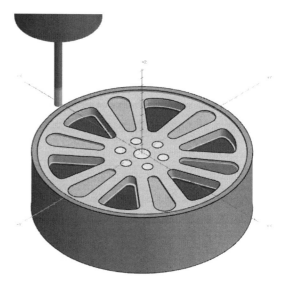

♦ To go back to the Mastercam window, minimize the Mastercam Simulator window as shown.
♦ Press **"T"** to remove the toolpath display.

STEP 28: SPOT DRILL THE HOLES

Spot Drilling the holes allows you to start the hole. In this operation, we will use the spot drill to chamfer the hole before drilling it.

Toolpath Preview:

TOOLPATHS

• From the **2D** group, select the **Expand gallery** drop down arrow.

• Select the **Drill** icon.

• In the **Drill Point Selection** dialog box, choose the option **Entities**.

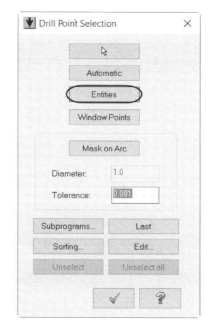

• Select the arcs as shown in <u>Figure: 28.0.1</u>.

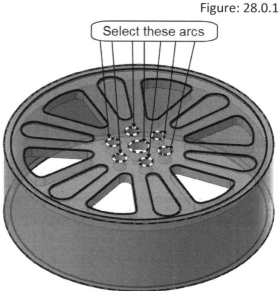

Figure: 28.0.1

• Click on the **End Selection** button or press **Enter** to finish the selection.

• Select the **OK** button to exit the **Drill Point Selection** dialog box.

• In the **Toolpath Type** page, the **Drill** toolpath will be selected.

Drill   Circle Mill   Point   Helix Bore   Thread Mill

28.1 Select a 1/2" Spot Drill from the Library and set the Tool Parameters

◆ Select **Tool** from the **Tree view list**.

◆ Click on the **Select library tool** button.

◆ To be able to see just the spot drill, select the **Filter** button.

◆ Under **Tool Types,** select the **None** button and then choose the **Spot drill** icon as shown in Figure: 28.1.1.

Figure: 28.1.1

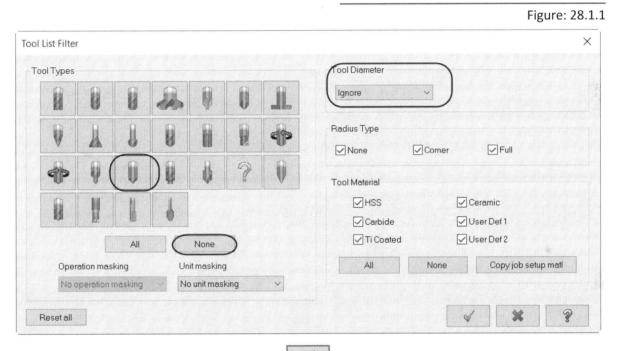

◆ Select **OK** button to exit the **Tool List Filter** dialog box.

◆ At this point you should only see **Spot Drills**.

◆ From that list select the **1/2" Spot Drill**.

#	Assembly Name	Tool Name	Holder Name	Dia.	Cor. rad.	Length	Type	Ra...	# Flutes
21	--	1/8 SPOTDRILL	--	0....	0.0	2.0	Sp...	No...	2
22	--	1/4 SPOTDRILL	--	0....	0.0	2.0	Sp...	No...	2
23	--	3/8 SPOTDRILL	--	0....	0.0	2.0	Sp...	No...	4
24	--	1/2 SPOTDRILL	--	0.5	0.0	2.0	Sp...	No...	2
25	--	3/4 SPOTDRILL	--	0....	0.0	2.0	Sp...	No...	4
26	--	1. SPOTDRILL	--	1.0	0.0	2.0	Sp...	No...	4

◆ Select the tool in the **Tool Selection** page and then select the **OK** button to exit.

• Make the necessary changes to the **Tool** page as shown in <u>Figure: 28.1.2</u>.

Figure: 28.1.2

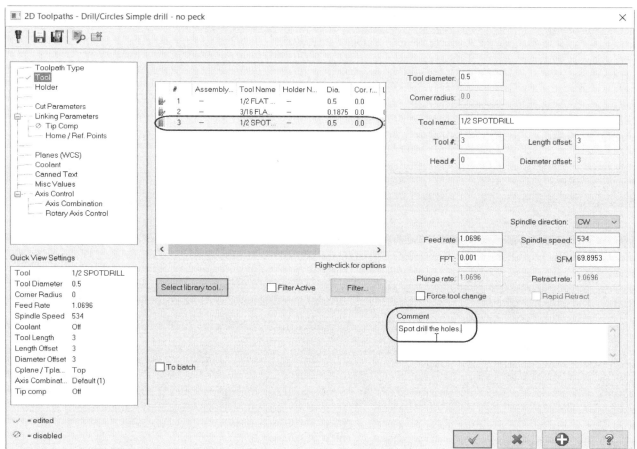

28.2 Set the Cut Parameters

◆ From the **Tree View list**, select **Cut Parameters** and make the necessary changes as shown in Figure: 28.2.1.

Figure: 28.2.1

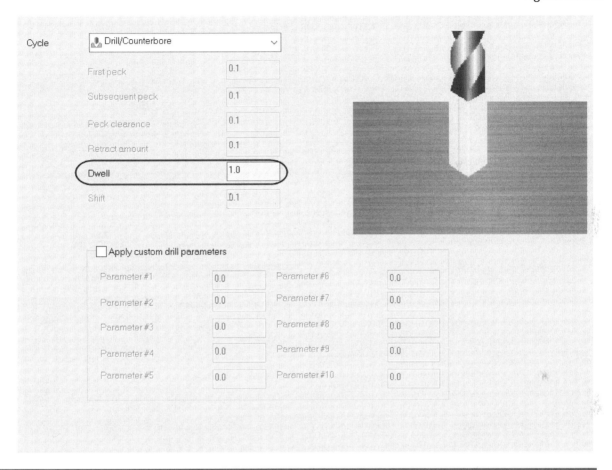

Cycle — Drill/Counterbore

First peck — 0.1
Subsequent peck — 0.1
Peck clearance — 0.1
Retract amount — 0.1
Dwell — 1.0
Shift — 0.1

☐ Apply custom drill parameters

Parameter #1	0.0	Parameter #6	0.0
Parameter #2	0.0	Parameter #7	0.0
Parameter #3	0.0	Parameter #8	0.0
Parameter #4	0.0	Parameter #9	0.0
Parameter #5	0.0	Parameter #10	0.0

Drill/Counterbore is recommended for drilling holes with depths of less than three times the tools diameter.

Dwell sets the amount of time in seconds that the tool remains at the bottom of a drilled hole.

28.3 Set the Linking Parameters

◆ Choose **Linking Parameters**, ensure **Clearance** is enabled and set to **Absolute** and **1.0** and the **Top of stock** is set to **Incremental** and **zero**.

◆ Set the **Depth** to **Incremental** and **zero** then select the **Calculator** icon.

◆ Input the following equation in the **Finish diameter** area **0.25+0.05** and hit **Enter** to calculate the **Depth** as shown in Figure: 28.3.1.

Figure: 28.3.1

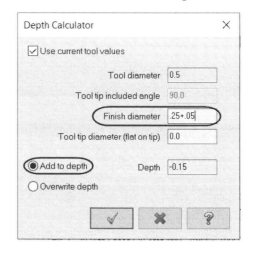

◆ Select the **OK** button to exit the **Depth Calculator**.

◆ You will now see the depth we calculated for the spot drilling operation set in the **Depth** field as shown in
<u>Figure: 28.3.2</u>.

Figure: 28.3.2

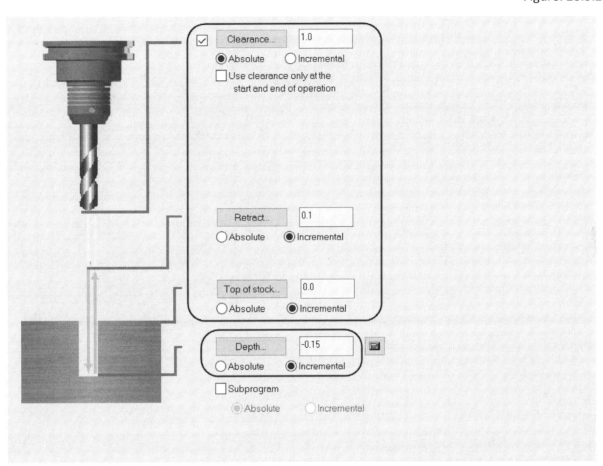

28.4 Preview the Toolpath

♦ To quickly check how the toolpath will be generated, select the **Preview toolpath** icon as shown.

♦ See **page 157** to review the procedure.
♦ The toolpath should look as shown.

♦ Press **Esc** key to exit the preview.

> **NOTE:** If the toolpath does not look as shown in the preview, check your parameters again.

♦ Select the **OK** button to exit the **2D Toolpaths - Drill/Circles Simple drill - no peck** parameters.
♦ **Backplot** and **Verify** the toolpaths. See **page 158** and **page 160** to review these procedures.

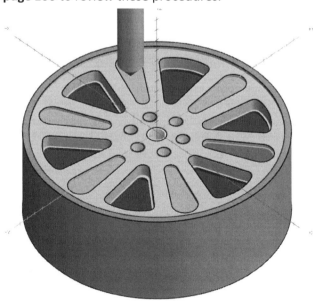

STEP 29: DRILL ALL HOLES

In this example, we will drill the 1/4" holes to a specified depth.

Toolpath Preview:

TOOLPATHS

◆ From the **2D** group, select **Drill** icon.

◆ In the **Drill Point Selection** dialog box, choose the option **Last**.

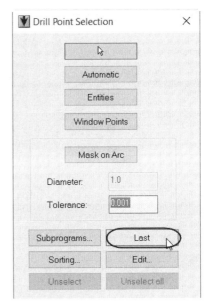

NOTE: This option will automatically select the hole for you based off the selection from the previous drill operation.

◆ Select the **OK** button in the **Drill Point Selection** panel to accept the 7 drill points.

* In the **Toolpath Type** page, the **Drill** toolpath will be selected.

Drill   Circle Mill   Point   Helix Bore   Thread Mill

29.1 Select a 1/4" Drill from the Library and set the Tool Parameters

* Select **Tool** from the **Tree View** list.

* Click on the **Select library tool** button. [Select library tool...]
* To be able to see just the drill, select the **Filter** button.

Filter...
☑ Filter Active
1 of 427 tools

* Under **Tool Types,** select the **None** button and then choose the drill icon.
* Under **Tool Diameter,** select **Equal** and enter **0.25** as shown in Figure: 29.1.1.

Figure: 29.1.1

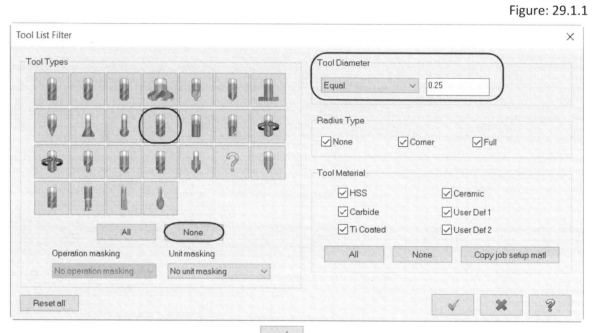

* Select the **OK** button to exit the **Tool List Filter** panel.
* From that list, select the **1/4" Drill.**

#	Assembly Name	Tool Name	Holder Name	Dia.	Cor. rad.	Length	# Flutes	Type	Ra...
124	--	1/4 DRILL	--	0....	0.0	2.0	2	Drill	No...

* Select the tool in the **Tool Selection** page and then choose the **OK** button to exit.

◆ Make the necessary changes to the **Tool** page as shown in <u>Figure: 29.1.2</u>.

Figure: 29.1.2

2D Toolpaths - Drill/Circles Simple drill - no peck ✕

- Toolpath Type
- ✓ Tool
- Holder

- Cut Parameters
- Linking Parameters
  - Tip Comp
  - Home / Ref. Points

- Planes (WCS)
- Coolant
- Canned Text
- Misc Values
- Axis Control
  - Axis Combination
  - Rotary Axis Control

#	Assembly...	Tool Name	Holder N...	Dia.	Cor. r...	L
1	--	1/2 FLAT ...	--	0.5	0.0	
2	--	3/16 FLA...	--	0.1875	0.0	0
3	--	1/2 SPOT...	--	0.5	0.0	
4	--	1/4 DRILL	--	0.25	0.0	2

Tool diameter: 0.25
Corner radius: 0.0
Tool name: 1/4 DRILL
Tool #: 4   Length offset: 4
Head #: 0   Diameter offset: 4

Spindle direction: CW

Feed rate 4.2784   Spindle speed: 1069
FPT: 0.002   SFM 69.9607
Plunge rate: 4.2784 Retract rate: 4.2784
☐ Force tool change ☐ Rapid Retract

Right-click for options

Select library tool...   ☐ Filter Active   Filter...

Comment
Drill the holes.

☐ To batch

Quick View Settings

Tool	1/4 DRILL
Tool Diameter	0.25
Corner Radius	0
Feed Rate	4.2784
Spindle Speed	1069
Coolant	Off
Tool Length	3
Length Offset	4
Diameter Offset	4
Cplane / Tpla...	Top
Axis Combinat...	Default (1)
Tip comp	Off

✓ = edited
◌ = disabled

29.2 Set the Cut Parameters

♦ Select **Cut Parameters**, change the drill **Cycle** to **Chip Break** and input a **Peck** value of **0.1** as shown in <u>Figure: 29.2.1</u>.

Figure: 29.2.1

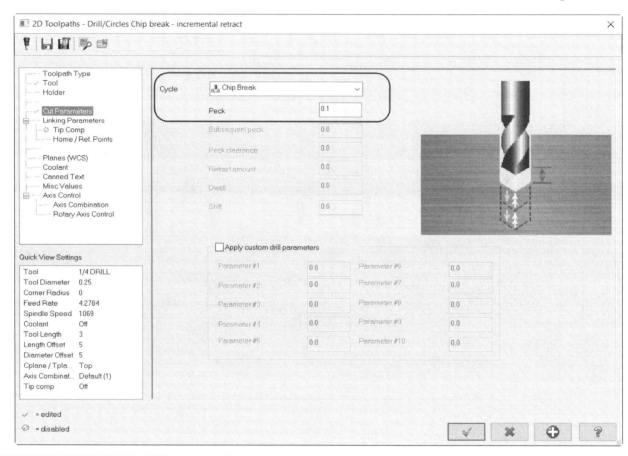

Chip Break drills holes with depths of more than three times the tool diameter. The tool retracts partially out of the drilled hole to break material chips.

Peck sets the depth for the first peck move which plunges in and out of the material to clear and break chips.

29.3 Set the Linking Parameters

♦ Choose **Linking Parameters** and input a **Top of Stock** value of **0.0 Incremental** and a **Depth** value of **-0.5 Incremental** as shown in <u>Figure: 29.3.1</u>.

Figure: 29.3.1

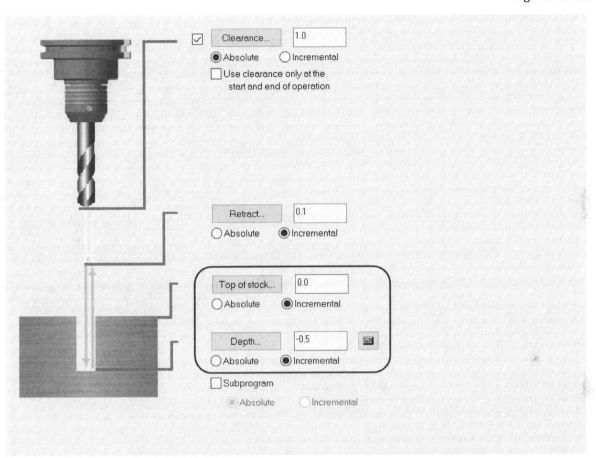

29.4 Preview the Toolpath

♦ To quickly check how the toolpath will be generated, select the **Preview toolpath** icon as shown.

♦ See **page 157** to review the procedure.
♦ The toolpath should look as shown.

♦ Press **Esc** key to exit the preview.

| **NOTE:** If the toolpath does not look as shown in the preview, check your parameters again.

♦ Select the **OK** button to exit the toolpath parameters.

♦ Select the **OK** button to exit the **2D Toolpaths - Drill/Circles Simple drill - no peck** parameters.

• **Backplot** and **Verify** your toolpath. See **page 158** and **page 160** to review these procedures.

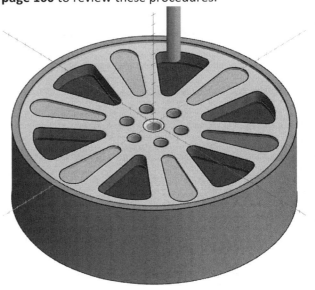

STEP 30: CIRCLE MILL THE CENTER HOLE

Circle mill toolpath is used to mill circular pockets based on a single point. Mastercam will pocket out a circular area of the diameter to the depth that you specify. After milling the center of the circle, Mastercam calculates an entry arc before approaching the perimeter and then a similar exit arc. You can add enhancements such as multiple passes, multiple depth cuts and helical plunge moves as well fine tuning the entry and exit arcs.

Toolpath Preview:

TOOLPATHS

• From the **2D** group, select **Circle Mill** as shown.

30.1 Select the Geometry

♦ When the **Drill Point Selection** dialog box, appears choose **Entities**.

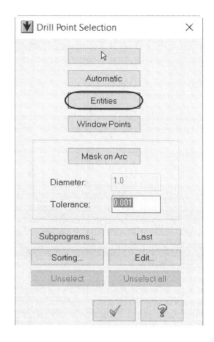

♦ Select the arc as shown in Figure: 30.1.1.

Figure: 30.1.1

Select this circle

♦ Click on the **End Selection** button or press **Enter** to finish the selection. End Selection

♦ Choose the **OK** button to exit the **Drill Point Selection** dialog box.

♦ On the **Toolpath Type** page, **Circle Mill** will be selected.

Drill   Circle Mill   Point   Helix Bore   Thread Mill

30.2 Select a 3/16" Flat Endmill from the Library and set the Tool Parameters

♦ Select **Tool** from the **Tree view** list.

♦ Click on **Select library tool** button.   Select library tool...

♦ To be able to see just the end mill select the **Filter** button.

Filter...

☑ Filter Active

1 of 427 tools

♦ Under **Tool Types** select the **None** button and then choose the **Flat Endmill** icon.

♦ Under **Tool Diameter** select **Equal** and enter **0.1875** as shown in Figure: 30.2.1.

Figure: 30.2.1

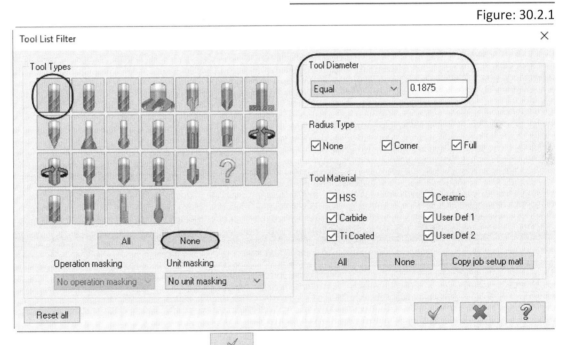

♦ Select **OK** button to exit the **Tool List Filter** panel.

♦ From that list select a **3/16" Flat Endmill**.

#	Assembly Na...	Tool Name	Holder Name	Dia.	Cor. rad.	Length	# Flutes	T:
284	--	3/16 FLAT ENDMILL	--	0.1875	0.0	0.4375	4	E

◆ Select the existing tool and change the parameters as shown in <u>Figure: 30.2.2</u>.

Figure: 30.2.2

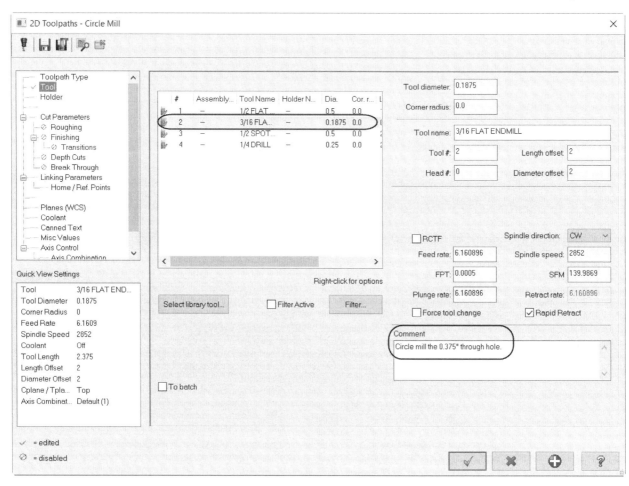

NOTE: Picking the 3/16" Flat Endmill will allow us to use the tool for this toolpath.

30.3 Set the Cut Parameters

◆ From the **Tree View** list, select **Cut Parameters** and ensure the parameters appear the same as shown in
Figure: 30.3.1.

Figure: 30.3.1

Compensation type	Computer		Circle diameter	0.0
Compensation direction	Left			
Tip comp:	Tip		Start angle	90.0

Stock to leave on walls 0.0
Stock to leave on floors 0.0

Start Angle sets the angle where the helix entry will start.

30.4 Set the Roughing Parameters

♦ Make sure the **Roughing** is disabled as shown.

30.5 Set the Finishing parameters

♦ From the **Tree View list**, select **Finishing** and enable it. Change the parameters as shown in Figure: 30.5.1.

Figure: 30.5.1

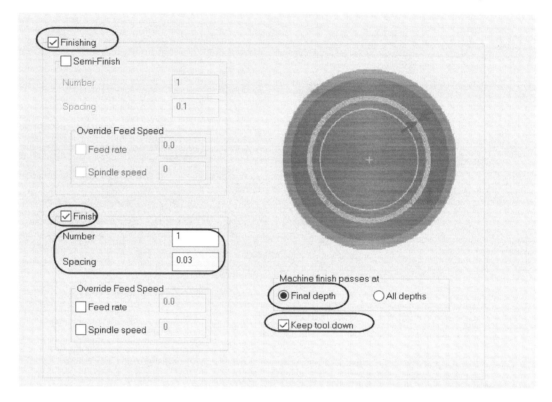

30.6 Set the Linking Parameters

♦ Select **Linking Parameters** from the **Tree View list.** Set the **Top of stock** and set the **Depth** as shown in
<u>Figure: 30.6.1</u>.

Figure: 30.6.1

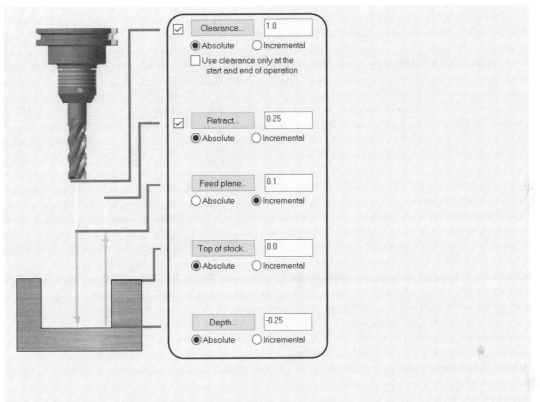

30.7 Preview the Toolpath

♦ To quickly check how the toolpath will be generated, select the **Preview toolpath** icon as shown.

♦ See **page 157** to review the procedure.
♦ The toolpath should look as shown.

♦ Press **Esc** key to exit the preview.

> **NOTE:** If the toolpath does not look as shown in the preview, check your parameters again.

♦ Select the **OK** button to exit the **Circle Mill** parameters.
♦ **Backplot** and **Verify** the toolpaths. See **page 158** and **page 160** to review these procedures.

STEP 31: CHAMFER THE PART

Contour - Chamfer toolpath automatically cuts a chamfer around a contour using a chamfer mill. The chamfer size you are machining in this step is 0.025" X 45 degrees.

Toolpath Preview:

TOOLPATHS

• From the **2D** group, using the **Expand gallery** arrow as shown.

• Select the **Contour** icon.

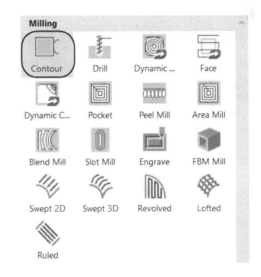

• In the **Chaining** dialog box, make sure that **Wireframe** selection is enabled and leave the defaults as shown in Figure: 31.0.1.

Figure: 31.0.1

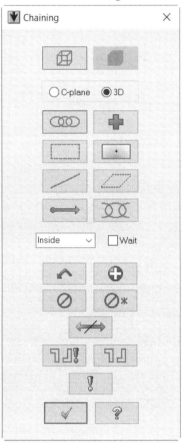

• The chaining direction should be **CounterClockWise** as shown.

Select the chain here

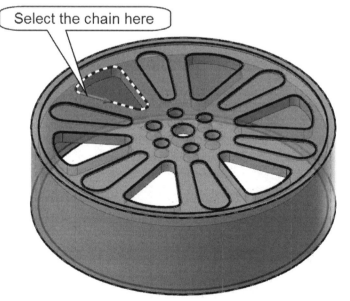

NOTE: It does not matter which contour you select first. However, the first contour you select will be the first contour cut. Make sure that all chains are selected in the CCW direction. Use the **Reverse** button to change the direction of the chain if needed.

♦ Repeat this step to select all the other pockets as shown.

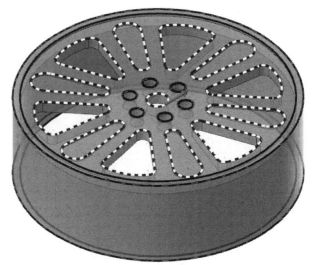

> **NOTE:** The arrows are used to show you the direction and where the starting point will be on each chain. The arrows disappear as you select a new chain.

♦ Select the **OK** button to exit the **Chaining** dialog box.
♦ In the **Toolpath Type** page, the **Contour** toolpath will be selected.

   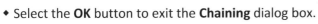

Contour   Pocket   Facing   Slot Mill

31.1 Select a 1/4" Chamfer Mill from the Library and set the Tool Parameters

♦ Select **Tool** from the **Tree View list**.

♦ Click on the **Select library tool** button. Select library tool...
♦ To be able to see just the chamfer mill, select the **Filter** button.

◆ Under **Tool Types**, select the **None** button and then choose the **Chamfer Mill** icon as shown in <u>Figure: 31.1.1</u>.

Figure: 31.1.1

◆ Select the **OK** button to exit the **Tool List Filter** panel.

> **NOTE:** You will only see a list of chamfer mills.

◆ From that list select the **1/4" Chamfer Mill**.

#	Assembly Name	Tool Name	Holder Name	Dia.	Cor. rad.	Length	Type	Ra...	# Flutes
318	--	1/4 CHAMFER MILL	--	0...	0.0	0.5	Ch...	No...	4

◆ Select the tool in the **Tool Selection** page and then choose the **OK** button to exit.

◆ Make all the necessary changes as shown in <u>Figure: 31.1.2</u>.

Figure: 31.1.2

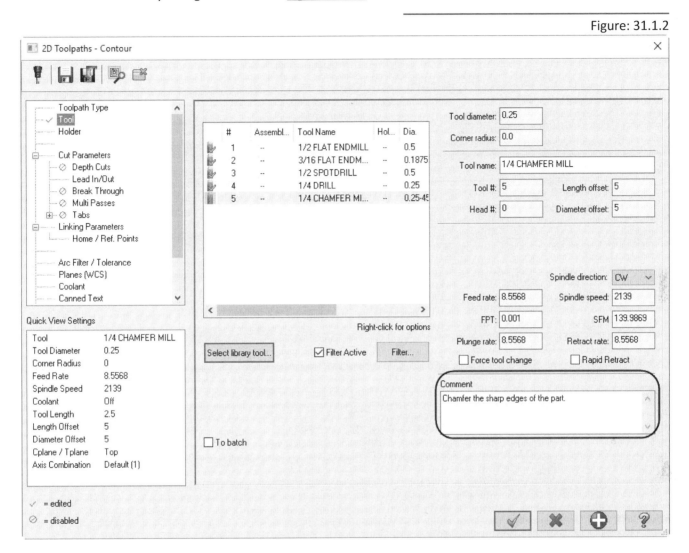

31.2 Set the Cut Parameters

♦ Select the **Cut Parameters** page and change the **Contour type** to **2D chamfer**.
♦ Input a **Width** of **0.025** and a **Tip offset** of **0.02** as shown in Figure: 31.2.1.

Figure: 31.2.1

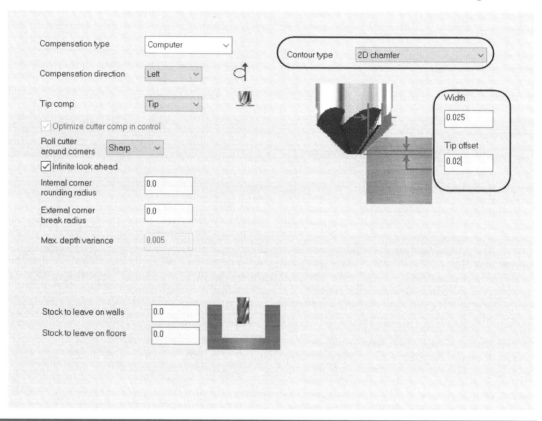

2D chamfer cuts chamfers around a contour.

Width sets the chamfer width. Mastercam measures the width from the chained geometry adjusted by the cut depths defined on the linking parameters page.

Tip offset is an amount to ensure that the tip of the tool clears the bottom of the chamfer.

31.3 Set the Lead In/Out Parameters

◆ Choose the option **Lead In/Out** and input an **Overlap** value.
◆ Make any other necessary changes as shown in <u>Figure: 31.3.1</u>.

Figure: 31.3.1

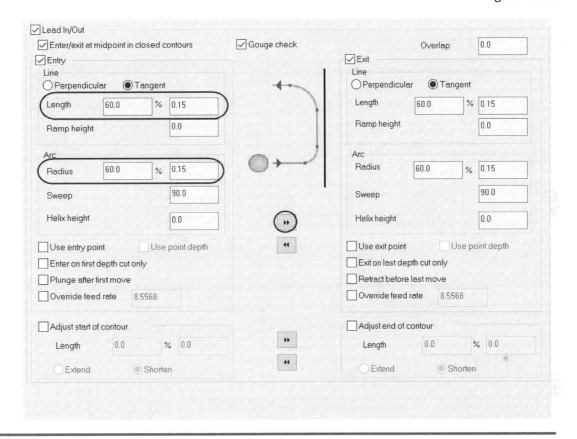

Lead In/Out allows you to create either entry moves, exit moves, or both. **Lead In/Out** moves can include both lines and arcs.

Enter/exit at midpoint in closed contours starts and ends a toolpath with closed chains at the midpoint of the first chained entity.

Gouge check ensures that the entry/exit moves do not gouge the part. If the entry/exit moves cause a gouge, they are removed from the toolpath.

31.4 Set the Linking Parameters

- Select the **Linking Parameters** from the **Tree View list**. Set the **Top of stock** to **0.0 Incremental** and the **Depth** to **0.0 Incremental** as shown in <u>Figure: 31.4.1</u>.

Figure: 31.4.1

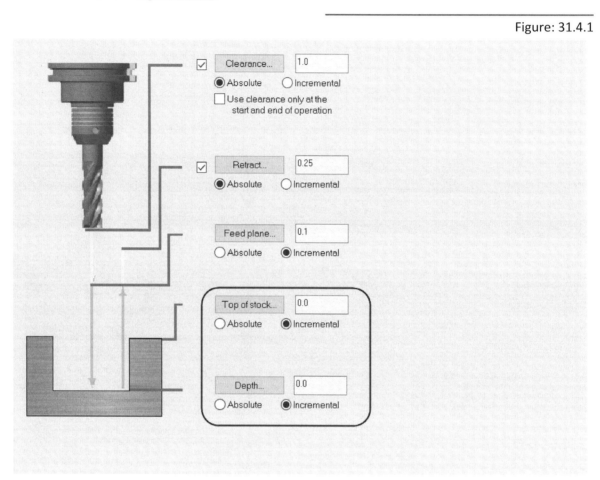

31.5 Preview the Toolpath

- To quickly check how the toolpath will be generated, select the **Preview toolpath** icon as shown.

- See **page 157** to review the procedure.

◆ The toolpath should look as shown.

◆ Press **Esc** key to exit the preview.

> NOTE: If the toolpath does not look as shown in the preview, check your parameters again.

◆ Select the **OK** button to exit the toolpath parameters.

> NOTE: The depth of the chamfer is based on the width and tip offset set in the **Cut Parameters** page. This is why we set the depth here to zero.

31.6 Backplot and Verify

◆ **Verify** the toolpath. See **page 160** to review the procedures.
◆ Your part will appear as shown.

TOOLPATH CREATION - SETUP 2

SUGGESTED FIXTURE 2:

> **NOTE:** The part is now flipped over and we will machine the part from the bottom.

SETUP SHEET 2:

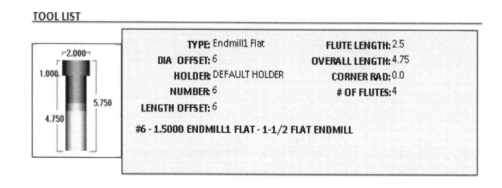

TOOL LIST

TYPE: Endmill1 Flat	**FLUTE LENGTH:** 2.5	
DIA OFFSET: 6	**OVERALL LENGTH:** 4.75	
HOLDER: DEFAULT HOLDER	**CORNER RAD:** 0.0	
NUMBER: 6	**# OF FLUTES:** 4	
LENGTH OFFSET: 6		

#6 - 1.5000 ENDMILL1 FLAT - 1-1/2 FLAT ENDMILL

STEP 32: CREATING AND RENAMING TOOLPATH GROUPS

To machine the part in two different setups, we will need to have two separate programs. To be able to post process the operations of each setup separately, we will create them under different toolpath groups with different NC names.

32.1 Rename the current Toolpath Group - 1 and the NC file

◆ Click on the **Toolpath Group - 1** to highlight and then click again on it and rename it "**Setup #1**."

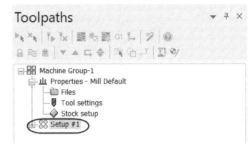

◆ Right mouse click on the toolpath group and select **Edit selected operations** and then select **Change NC file name** as shown in Figure: 32.1.1.

Figure: 32.1.1

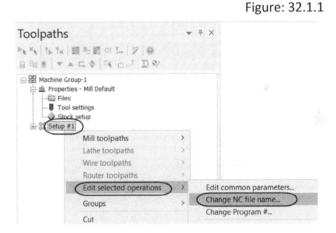

◆ Enter the new NC name: **Setup #1.**

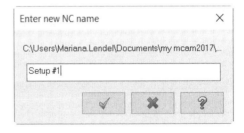

◆ Select the **OK** button to accept the new NC name.

32.2 Create a New Toolpath Group

◆ Right mouse click on the **Machine Group-1** and select **Groups** and then the **New Toolpath group.**

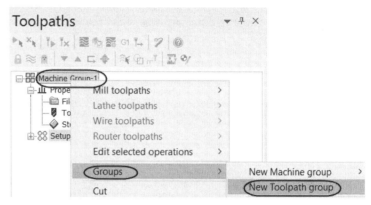

◆ Rename the toolpath group "**Setup #2**" as shown.

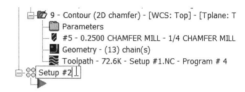

◆ Make sure that the **Insert arrow** is below the **Setup #2**, otherwise click on the **Move the insert arrow down an item** icon until the arrow is below the **Setup #2** group.

NOTE: The next operation is going to be generated at the insert arrow location.

STEP 33: SET THE WCS TO BOTTOM

Work coordinate system (WCS) is the active coordinate system in use by Mastercam at any given time. The **WCS** contains the orientation of the **X, Y, Z** axes plus the location of the zero point (the origin). This tells Mastercam how your part is positioned or orientated in the machine.

Construction plane (Cplane) is the plane in which the geometry is created.

Tool plane (Tplane) is the plane normal to Z or to the vertical tool axis in which the tool moves. When creating a toolpath, both **Cplane** and **Tplane** should be set to the same plane. If the Tplane is different then the **WCS**, the post will produce a rotary motion code. By setting the **Cplane**, **Tplane** and **WCS** to one plane, no rotary move will be generated in the code, which is what you want when machining parts with multiple setups.

In this step you are going to create a copy of the **Bottom** plane. This allows you to set a new origin for the plane and set **Z0** to the top of the flipped part.

♦ Select **Planes** tab located at the bottom left corner.

- To create a new plane based on existing geometry, click on the + sign as shown.

- To create a copy of the **Bottom** plane, select **Relative to WCS** and select **Bottom** as shown.

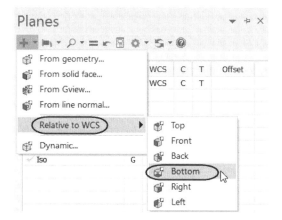

- Change the **Origin Z** value and enable **Set as WCS** as shown.

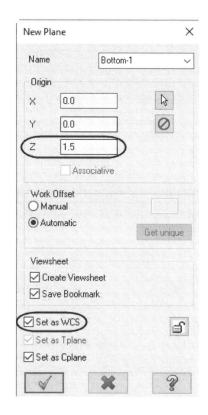

- Select the **OK** button to exit the **New Plane** dialog box.

◆ Right mouse click in the graphics window and select the **Isometric** view.

🔍	Zoom Window
🔎	Unzoom 80%
🔄	Dynamic Rotation
⛶	Fit
📦	Top (WCS)
📦	Front (WCS)
📦	Right (WCS)
📦	Isometric (WCS)
✏	Delete Entities
⌐?	Analyze Distance...
↘?	Analyze Entity Properties...

◆ Press **F9** on your keyboard to display the coordinate axes.

> **NOTE:** The dark blue axes are the original axes and the light blue axes are the current axes.

◆ Your part will appear as shown up to this point.

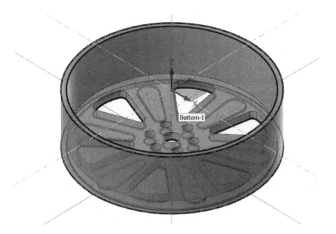

◆ Press **F9** to remove the axes display.
◆ Press **Alt + S** to unshade the model.

STEP 34: 2D HS DYNAMIC MILL

In this step we will utilize the 2D High Speed Dynamic Mill toolpath to remove the material in the middle of the part with the part now flipped over.

Toolpath Preview:

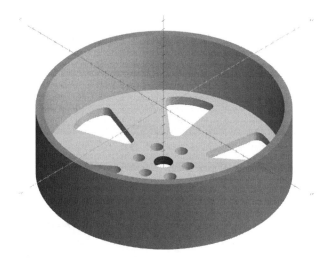

34.1 Chain Selection

TOOLPATHS

♦ From the **2D** group, select the **Dynamic Mill**.

♦ From the **Chain Options,** make sure that the **Stay inside** is enabled and then click on the **Select machining chains** button as shown.

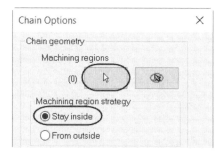

◆ Leave the default settings in the **Chaining** dialog box and pick the inner circle as shown in Figure: 34.1.1.

Figure: 34.1.1

Select the circle here

◆ Select the **OK** button to exit the **Chaining** dialog box.

◆ Select the **OK** button to exit the **Chain Options** dialog box.

◆ In the **Toolpath Type** page, **Dynamic Mill** will be selected.

34.2 Preview Chains

◆ Select the **Preview chains** button as shown.

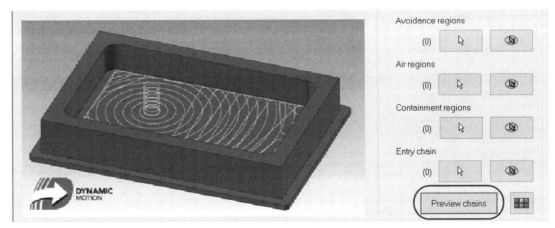

- See **page 164** to review the procedure.
- The **Preview chains** should look as shown.

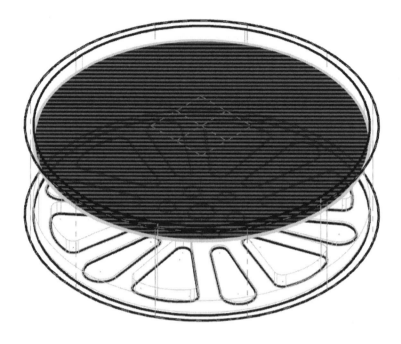

- Press **Esc** key to return to the toolpath parameters.
- Click on the **Preview chains** button again to clear the Preview chains display.

34.3 Select a 1 - 1/2" Flat Endmill from the Library and set the Tool parameters

◆ Select **Tool** from the **Tree View list**.

◆ Click on the **Select library tool** button.

◆ Select the **Filter** button as shown.

◆ Select the **None** button and then under **Tool Types** choose the **Flat Endmill** icon.
◆ Under tool diameter, pick **Greater than** and input a value **1.0** as shown in Figure: 34.3.1.

Figure: 34.3.1

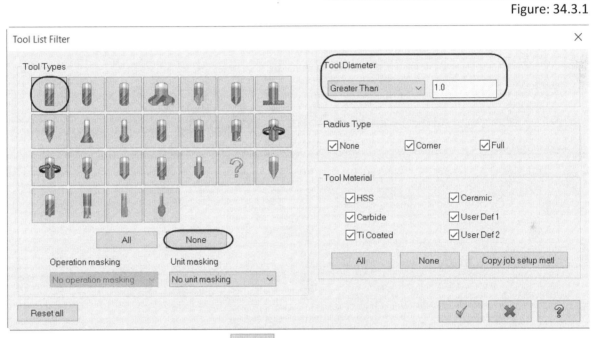

◆ Select the **OK** button to exit the **Tool List Filter**.
◆ In the **Tool Selection** panel you should only see **Flat Endmills** larger than **1.0"**.

#	Assembly Name	Tool Name	Holder Name	Dia.	Cor. rad.	Length	# Flutes	Type	Ra...
298	--	1-3/16 FLAT ENDMILL	--	1....	0.0	2.0	4	En...	No...
299	--	1-1/2 FLAT ENDMILL	--	1.5	0.0	2.5	4	En...	No...
300	--	2 INCH FLAT ENDMI...	--	2.0	0.0	2.75	4	En...	No...

◆ Select the **1 - 1/2" Flat Endmill** in the **Tool Selection** page.

◆ Select the **OK** button to exit.

◆ Make all the necessary changes as shown in <u>Figure: 34.3.2</u>.

Figure: 34.3.2

#	Assembly...	Tool Name	Holder N...	Dia.	Cor. r...	L
1	–	1/2 FLAT ...	–	0.5	0.0	
2	–	3/16 FLA...	–	0.1875	0.0	(
3	–	1/2 SPOT...	–	0.5	0.0	;
4	–	1/4 DRILL	–	0.25	0.0	;
5	–	1/4 CHA...	–	0.25-...	0.0	(
6	–	1-1/2 FLA...	–	1.5	0.0	;

Right-click for options

Select library tool...   ☐ Filter Active   Filter...

☐ To batch

Tool diameter: 1.5

Corner radius: 0.0

Tool name: 1-1/2 FLAT ENDMILL

Tool #: 6   Length offset: 6

Head #: 0   Diameter offset: 6

☐ RCTF   Spindle direction: CW

Feed rate: 6.4176   Spindle speed: 356

FPT: 0.0045   SFM 139.7906

Plunge rate: 6.4176   Retract rate: 6.4176

☐ Force tool change   ☑ Rapid Retract

Comment
Remove the material from the bottom of the part.

34.4 Set the Cut Parameters

◆ From the **Tree View list**, select **Cut Parameters**. Make sure that the parameters are set as shown
   <u>Figure: 34.4.1</u>**.**

Figure: 34.4.1

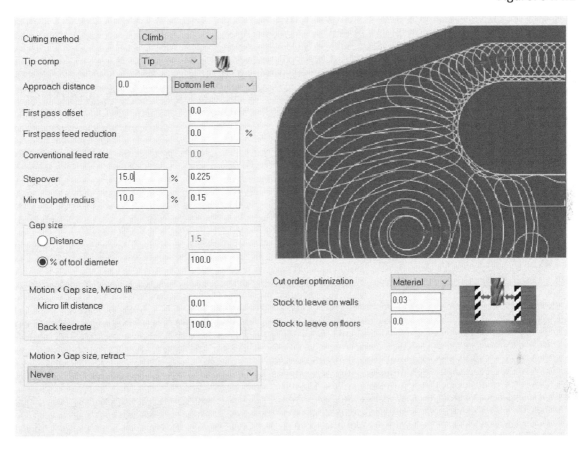

NOTE: For more information on these settings, see **page 402**.

34.5 Set the Depth Cuts Parameters

• From the **Tree View list**, disable the **Depth Cuts** if needed as shown.

☐ Depth cuts

34.6 Set the Entry Motion

• Set the **Entry method** to **Helix only**.
• Set the **Helix radius** to **0.75** and the rest of the parameters as shown in Figure: 34.6.1.
• Enable **Entry feeds / speeds** and set a **Ramp feed rate** of **10.0** Inches per minute, a **Ramp spindle speed** of **800** RPM and **Dwell before cut spindle speed** of **3.0** seconds as shown in Figure: 34.6.1.

Figure: 34.6.1

Entry method

| Helix only | ∨ |

Chain geometry

(0)

Helix radius	0.75
Trochoidal loop radius	0.0
Additional slot width	0.0

☐ Center helix on point

Z clearance	0.125
⦿ Plunge angle	2.0
◯ Entry pitch	0.0

☑ Entry feeds / speeds

Ramp feed rate	10.0
Ramp spindle speed	800
Dwell before cut spindle speed	3.0

NOTE: For more information on these settings, see **page 403**.

34.7 Set the Linking Parameters

◆ Select **Linking Parameters** and input the **Depth** of **-1.25** as shown in <u>Figure: 34.7.1</u>. Change any other parameters to match what is shown in <u>Figure: 34.7.1</u> if necessary.

Figure: 34.7.1

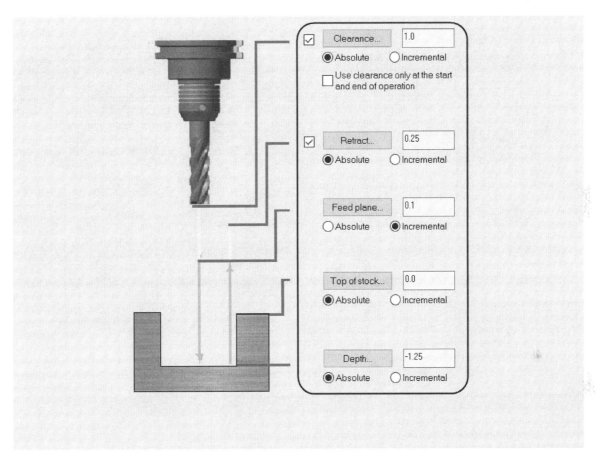

34.8 Preview the Toolpath

◆ To quickly check how the toolpath will be generated, select the **Preview toolpath** icon as shown.

◆ See **page 157** to review the procedure.
◆ The toolpath should look as shown.

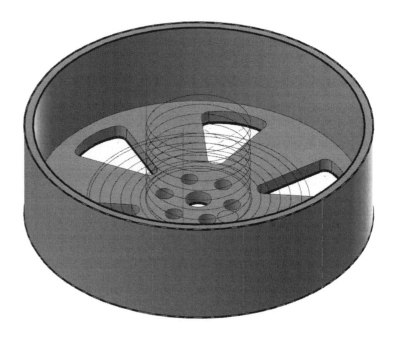

◆ Press **Esc** key to exit the preview.

> **NOTE:** If the toolpath does not look as shown in the preview, check your parameters again.

◆ Select the **OK** button to exit the toolpath parameters.
◆ Select the **Toolpaths** tab in the bottom left of the toolpaths manager.

• **Backplot** and **Verify** your toolpath. See **page 158** and **page 160** to review these procedures.

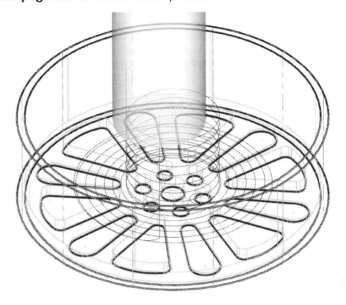

• Once complete, the part will appear as shown.

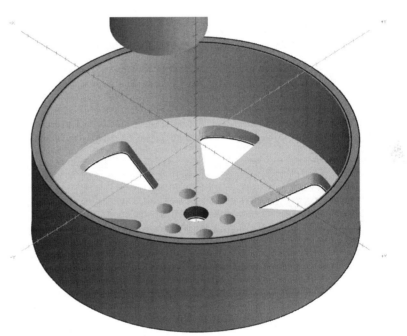

NOTE: The High Speed toolpaths do not have a finish wall option inside of their parameters. You need to finish the walls using a Contour toolpath.

STEP 35: FINISH THE POCKET WALL USING CONTOUR TOOLPATH

In this step we will utilize the Contour toolpath to finish the middle of the part with the part now flipped over. You will remove the 0.03" stock from the walls.

Toolpath Preview:

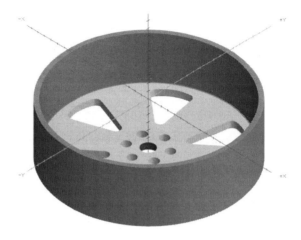

35.1 Chain Selection

TOOLPATHS

◆ From the **2D** group, select the **Contour** icon as shown.

◆ Leave the default settings in the **Chaining** dialog box and pick the inner circle as shown in Figure: 35.1.1.

Figure: 35.1.1

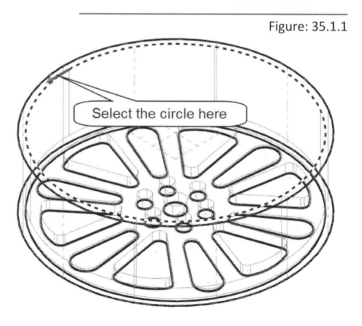

Select the circle here

♦ Select the **OK** button to exit the **Chaining** dialog box.
♦ In the **Toolpath Type** page, **Contour** will be selected.

35.2 Select a 1 - 1/2" Flat Endmill from Tool list window

♦ Select **Tool** from the **Tree View list**.
♦ Select the **1 - 1/2" Flat Endmill** in the **Tool list** window. Make all the necessary changes as shown in Figure: 35.2.1.

Figure: 35.2.1

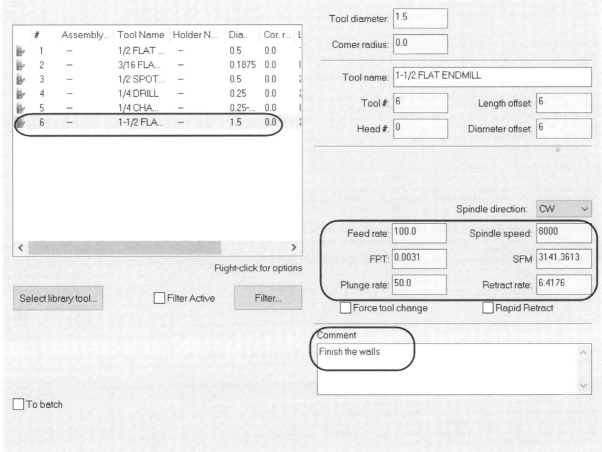

35.3 Set the Cut Parameters

♦ From the **Tree View list**, select **Cut Parameters** and make sure that the parameters are set as shown <u>Figure: 35.3.1</u>.

Figure: 35.3.1

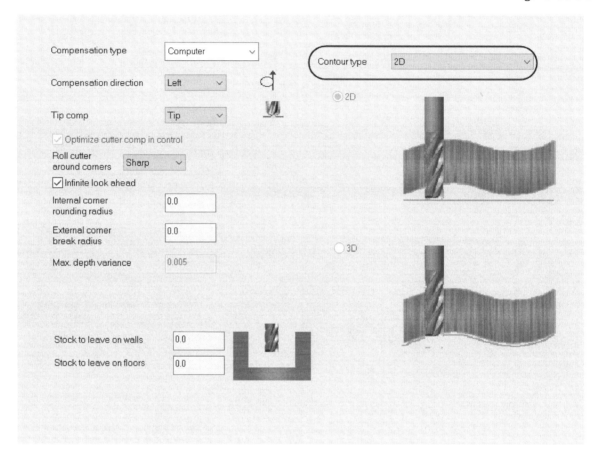

35.4 Set the Depth Cuts Parameters

◆ From the **Tree View list**, disable the **Depth Cuts** if needed as shown.

☐ Depth cuts

35.5 Set the Lead In/Out parameters

◆ Make sure that the parameters are set as shown in Figure: 35.5.1.

Figure: 35.5.1

NOTE: For more information on these settings, see **page 428**.

35.6 Set the Linking Parameters

◆ Select **Linking Parameters** and input the **Depth** of **-1.25** as shown in Figure: 35.6.1.

Figure: 35.6.1

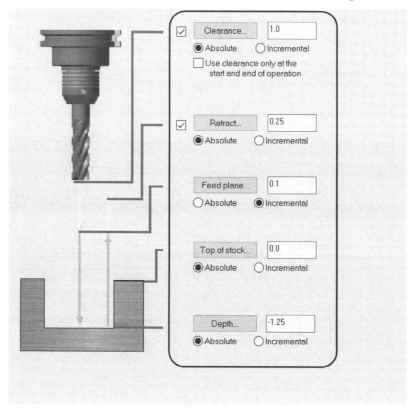

35.7 Preview the Toolpath

- ◆ To quickly check how the toolpath will be generated, select the **Preview toolpath** icon as shown.

- ◆ See **page 157** to review the procedure.
- ◆ The toolpath should look as shown.

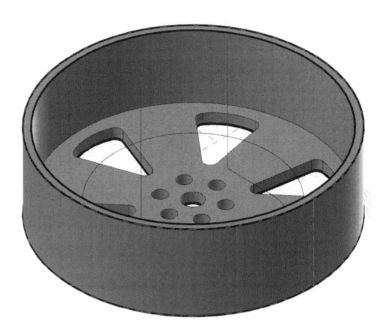

- ◆ Press **Esc** key to exit the preview.

> **NOTE:** If the toolpath does not look as shown in the preview, check your parameters again.

- ◆ Select the **OK** button to exit the toolpath parameters.
- ◆ **Backplot** and **Verify** your toolpath. See **page 158** and **page 160** to review these procedures.
- ◆ The part will appear as shown.

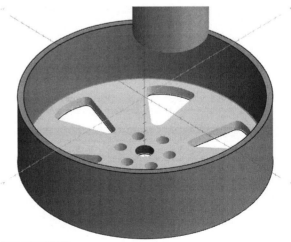

- ◆ To exit the Mastercam Simulator, click on the **Close** icon.

STEP 36: RENAME THE NC FILE

The **2D High Speed dynamic mill** operation in Setup #2 kept the NC name from Setup #1. We need to rename this operation so it will create 2 separate programs.

* Click on the **Setup #2** group to select only operation #10 and operation #11.
* Right click on **Setup #2**, choose the option **Edit selected operations** and then pick **Change NC file name**.

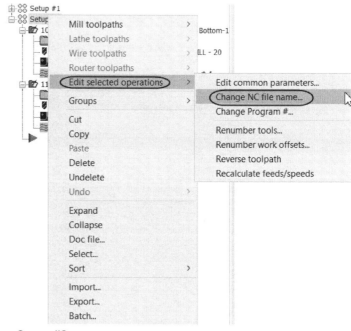

* When the **Enter new NC name** panel appears enter **Setup #2**.

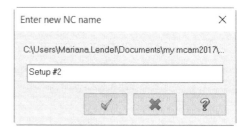

* Select the **OK** button to apply the changed **NC name** to operation **10** and **11**.
* As a result, you should see **Setup #2.NC** in the last item of text for operation **#10** and **#11**.

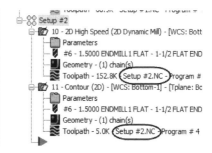

STEP 37: POST THE FILE

• Ensure all operations are selected. If they are not, use the button **Select all operations** in the **Toolpaths**

Manager.

• Select the **Post selected operations** button from the **Toolpaths Manager.**

• In the **Post processing** window, make the necessary changes as shown in <u>Figure: 37.0.1</u>.

Figure: 37.0.1

NC File enabled allows you to keep the NC file and to assign the same name as the MCAM file.

Edit enabled allows you to automatically launch the default editor.

• Select the **OK** button to continue.
• Save Setup #1 NC file.
• Save Setup #2 NC file.

♦ A window with **Mastercam Code Expert** will be launched and the NC program will appear as shown in Figure: 37.0.2.

Figure: 37.0.2

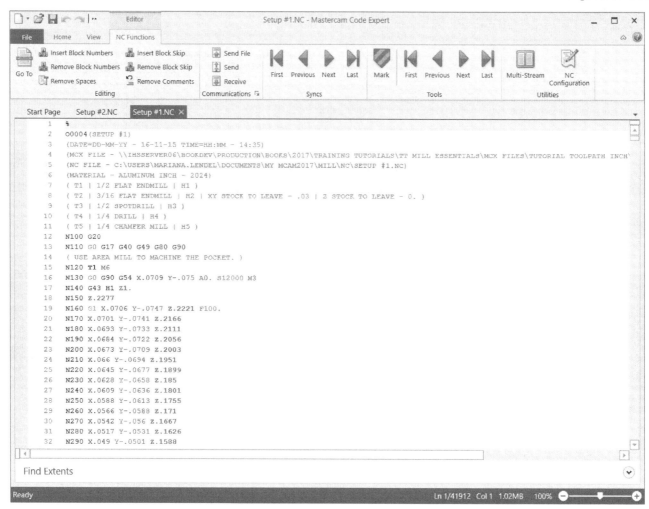

♦ Select the **"X"** box at the upper right corner to exit the editor.

STEP 38: SAVE THE UPDATED MCAM FILE

REVIEW EXERCISE - STUDENT PRACTICE

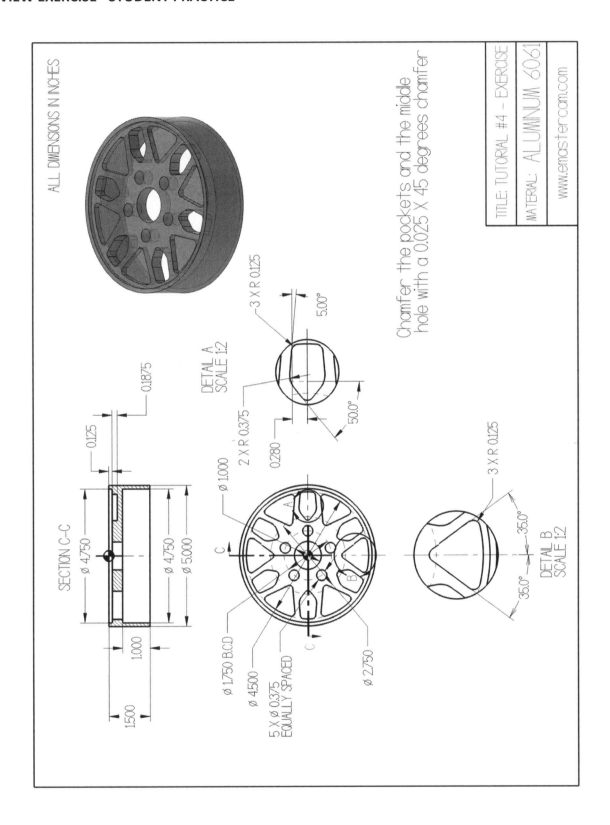

ALL DIMENSIONS IN INCHES

TITLE: TUTORIAL #4 – EXERCISE

MATERIAL: ALUMINUM 6061

www.emastercam.com

Chamfer the pockets and the middle
hole with a 0.025 X 45 degrees chamfer

DETAIL A
SCALE 1:2

3 X R 0.125

5.00°

50.0°

0.280

2 X R 0.375

Ø 1.000

DETAIL B
SCALE 1:2

3 X R 0.125

35.0°

35.0°

Ø 2.750

SECTION C-C

0.125

0.1875

Ø 4.750

Ø 4.750

Ø 5.000

1.000

1.500

Ø 1.750 B.C.D

Ø 4.500

5 X Ø 0.375
EQUALLY SPACED

CREATE THE 2D GEOMETRY FOR TUTORIAL #4 EXERCISE

Use these commands to create the geometry:

- ◆ Circle Center Point.
- ◆ Tangent Lines.
- ◆ Mirror.
- ◆ Arc Tangent.
- ◆ Arc Polar.
- ◆ Trim Break Extend.
- ◆ Fillets.
- ◆ Delete Entities.
- ◆ Rotate.
- ◆ Translate.

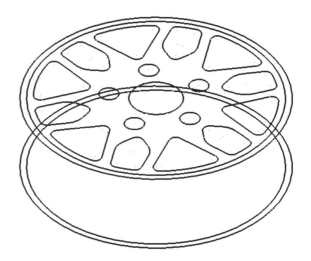

CREATE THE SOLID GEOMETRY FOR TUTORIAL #4 EXERCISE

Change the Main Level to Level 2

Use these commands to create the geometry:

- ◆ Solid Extrude Create body.
- ◆ Solid Extrude Cut body.

CREATE THE TOOLPATHS FOR TUTORIAL #4 EXERCISE

Create the Toolpaths for Tutorial #4 Exercise as per the instructions below.

Set the machine properties including the stock setup.

Remove the material in the center of the part.
- Use a **1" Flat Endmill**.
- Disable **Depth Cuts**.
- Set the **Entry Motion**.
- Set the **Depth** according to the drawing.

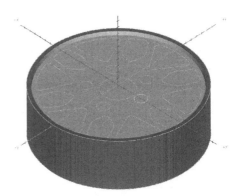

Area Mill one of the large pockets.
- Select one of the pockets.
- Use a **1/4" Flat Endmill**.
- **Stock to leave on the walls** = **0.03**.
- Enable **Depth Cuts**.
- Set the **Max rough step** to **0.05**.
- Set the **Transitions** to **Entry helix**.
- Set the **Top of Stock** and **Depth** according to the drawing.

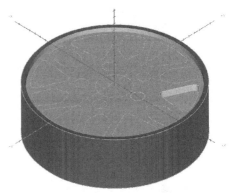

Dynamic Mill one of the small pockets.
- Select the chain and enable **Stay inside**.
- Use a **1/4" Flat Endmill**.
- **Stock to leave on the walls** = **0.03**.
- Disable **Depth Cuts**.
- Set the **Entry Motion** to **Helix only**.
- Set the **Top of Stock** and **Depth** according to the drawing.

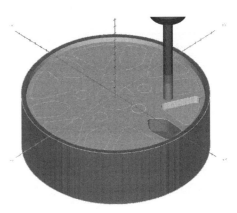

Transform Toolpaths.

♦ Choose **Rotate** and select **Operation #2** and **#3**.

♦ Select **Coordinate** and **Operation order**.

♦ Enable **Copy source operations**.

♦ Ensure disable posting in selected source operations is enabled.

♦ Select the **Rotate** tab.

♦ Input the number of steps # = **5**.

♦ **Start angle** = **60.0**.

♦ **Rotation angle** = **60.0**.

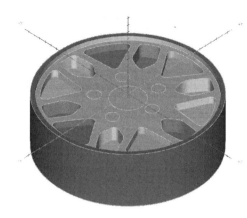

Use a pocket toolpath to finish the walls.

♦ Select the bottom of the pockets using **Solid** selections **Loop** and **Face**.

♦ Use the existing **1/4" Flat Endmill**.

♦ **Stock to leave on walls/floors** = **0.0**

♦ Disable **Roughing**.

♦ Turn **Off** the **Entry motion**.

♦ Finishing leave the default settings.

♦ In the **Lead In/Out** set the **Length** and the **Radius** to **60%** of the tool diameter.

♦ **Depth** to **Incremental** and **0.0**.

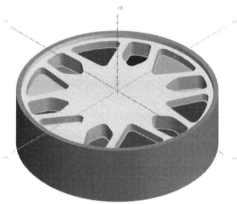

Spot Drill the holes.

♦ Use a **1/2" Spot Drill**.

♦ Set the **Cycle** and **Dwell**.

♦ Set the **Top of Stock** and **Depth** using the depth calculator.

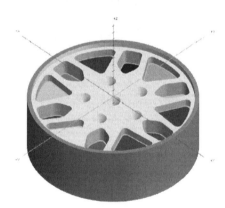

Drill the holes.

♦ Use a **3/8" Drill**.

♦ Set the **Cycle** to **Peck** and input your increments.

♦ Set the **Top of Stock** and **Depth** using the depth calculator.

Circle Mill the Center Hole.
- Use the **1/4" Flat Endmill.**
- Enable **Roughing**.
- Enable **Depth Cuts** and set **Max rough step** to **0.25"**.
- Enable **Multi Passes** and set **1 Finish** at a **Spacing** of **0.02"**.
- Set the depth to the appropriate depth.

Chamfer the sharp edges using Contour toolpath.
- Use **Wireframe** mode selection and select all the tops of the pockets and the center hole top.
- Select all the chains in CCW direction.
- Use a **1/4" Chamfer Mill.**
- **Contour type** set to **2D Chamfer; Width = 0.025; Tip offset = 0.02**.
- In the **Lead In/Out** set the **Length** and the **Radius** to **60%** of the tool diameter.
- **Top of stock and Depth** set to the depth of the top of the pockets.

Flip the part over Setup #2.

Set WCS to Bottom and input correct depth.
- Use **Dynamic Mill** and enable **Stay inside** to remove the material starting from the center.
- Use the **1" Flat Endmill.**
- Disable **Depth cuts**.
- Set the **Entry Motion**.
- Set the **Depth** according to the drawing.

- Your part should appear as shown once complete.

NOTES:

TUTORIAL #4 QUIZ

• What does the Solid Extrude command do?

• What does Circle Mill toolpath do?

• What does a "Dwell before cut spindle speed" do?

• What does a Transform toolpath operation do?

TUTORIAL #5

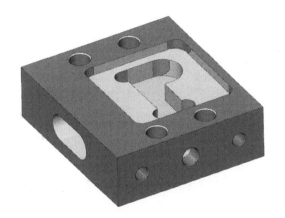

OVERVIEW OF STEPS TAKEN TO CREATE THE FINAL PART:

Import the 2D CAD Model and prepare it to generate Toolpaths from:
- The student will open the Solidworks file in Mastercam.

Create the necessary Toolpaths to machine the part:
- The student will set up the stock size and the clamping method. Three setups will be used to machine the part from the top and then from the bottom.
- A 2D High Speed Area Mill toolpath will be created to remove the material inside of the step.
- Two 2D High Speed Area Mill toolpaths will be created to remove the material inside of the pockets.
- Drill toolpaths will be created to machine the three holes in the front view.
- A Slot Mill toolpath will be created to remove the material inside of the slot from the left side view.

Backplot and Verify the file:
- The Backplot will be used to simulate a step-by-step process of the tool's movements.
- The Verify will be used to watch a tool machine the part out of a solid model.

Post Process the file to generate the G-code:
- The student will then post process the file to obtain an NC file containing the necessary code for the machine.

 This tutorial takes approximately two hours to complete.

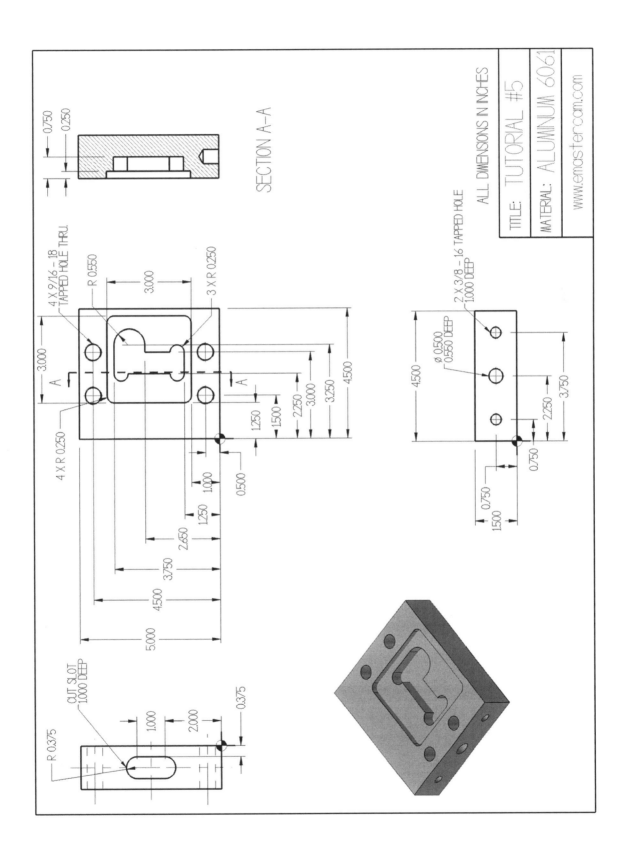

0.750
0.250

SECTION A-A

4 X 9/16 - 18
TAPPED HOLE THRU.

R 0.550

3 X R 0.250

3.000

3.000

A

4 X R 0.250

A

4.500

3.250

3.000

2.250

1.500

1.250

0.500

1.000

1.250

2.650

3.750

4.500

5.000

CUT SLOT
1.000 DEEP

R 0.375

1.000

2.000

0.375

2 X 3/8 - 16 TAPPED HOLE
1.000 DEEP

Ø 0.500
0.550 DEEP

4.500

3.750

2.250

0.750

0.750

1.500

ALL DIMENSIONS IN INCHES

TITLE: TUTORIAL #5

MATERIAL: ALUMINUM 6061

www.emastercam.com

GEOMETRY CREATION

STEP 1: SETTING UP THE GRAPHICAL USER INTERFACE

Please refer to the **Getting Started** section to set up the graphical user interface.

STEP 2: IMPORTING THE SOLIDWORKS FILE GEOMETRY

Mastercam lets you read (import) a variety of CAD file types into the Mastercam database. You can also write (export) Mastercam files to a variety of different file formats.

To import a SolidWorks file in Mastercam, you have to use the Open function and then select SolidWorks files from the File type list.

Download the files from www.emastercam.com/files.

Save the file at a preferred location.

FILE
* **Open**.
* In the file name extension, click on the drop down arrow as shown.

* From the file type list, select SOLIDWORKS Files (*.sldprt;*sldasm;*.slddrw) as shown.

Mastercam Files (*.mcam)
Mastercam X Files (*.mcx*)
Mastercam Edu X Files (*.emcx*)
All Mastercam Files (*.mc*;*.emc*)
IGES Files (*.igs;*.iges)
AutoCAD Files (*.dwg;*.dxf;*.dwf;*.dwfx)
Parasolid Files (*.x_t;*.x_b;*.xmt_txt)
ProE/Creo Files (*.prt;*.asm;*.prt.*;*.asm.*)
ACIS Kernel SAT Files (*.sat;*.sab)
STEP Files (*.stp;*.step)
VDA Files (*.vda)
Rhino 3D Files (*.3dm)
SOLIDWORKS Files (*.sldprt;*.sldasm;*.slddrw)
Solid Edge Files (*.par;*.psm;*.asm)
Autodesk Inventor Files (*.ipt;*.iam;*.idw)
KeyCreator Files (*.ckd)
Unigraphics/NX Files (*.prt)
ASCII Files (*.txt;*.csv)
StereoLithography Files (*.stl)
Catia Files (*.model;*.exp;*.catpart;*.CATProduct)
SpaceClaim Files (*.scdoc)
Alibre/Geomagic Design Files (*.ad_prt;*.ad_smp)
HPGL Plotter files (*.plt)
PostScript Files (*.eps;*.ai;*.ps)
All Files (*.*)

* Find and select **TUTORIAL #5.SLDPRT**. Note that you do not double-click on the file.

◆ Click on the **Options** button.

◆ Leave the **Solids** enabled to import the file as a solid and enable **Edge curves** for Mastercam to automatically create curves at the edges of the solid as shown.

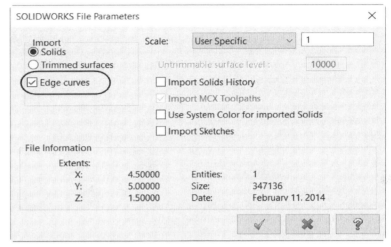

◆ Select the **OK** button to exit the **SolidWorks File Parameters** dialog box.
◆ Open the file.
◆ Press **Alt + S** to see the solid in a shaded mode.
◆ Right mouse click in the graphics area and select the graphic view **Isometric** as shown.

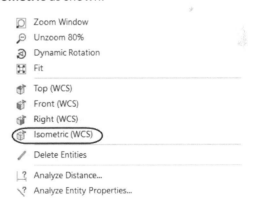

◆ Press **Alt + F1** to fit the geometry to the screen.
◆ Scroll the mouse wheel to zoom or unzoom as needed.

• The geometry should look as shown.

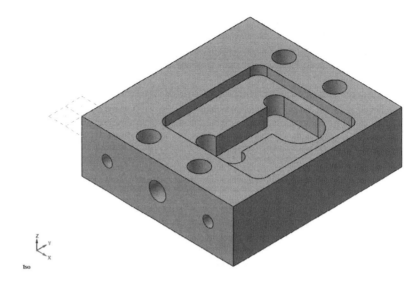

Iso

STEP 3: SAVE THE FILE

FILE
• **Save As.**

• Click on the **Browse** icon as shown.
• Find a location on the computer to save your file. File name: "Your Name_5".

TOOLPATH CREATION - SETUP 1

SUGGESTED FIXTURE:

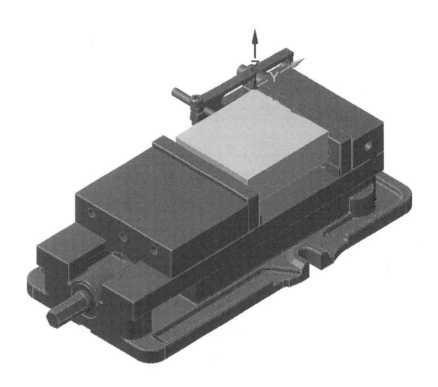

> **NOTE:** In order to machine this part, we will have 3 setups and output 3 NC files. To view the second setup, see **page 567** and to view the third setup, see **page 614**.

SETUP SHEET:

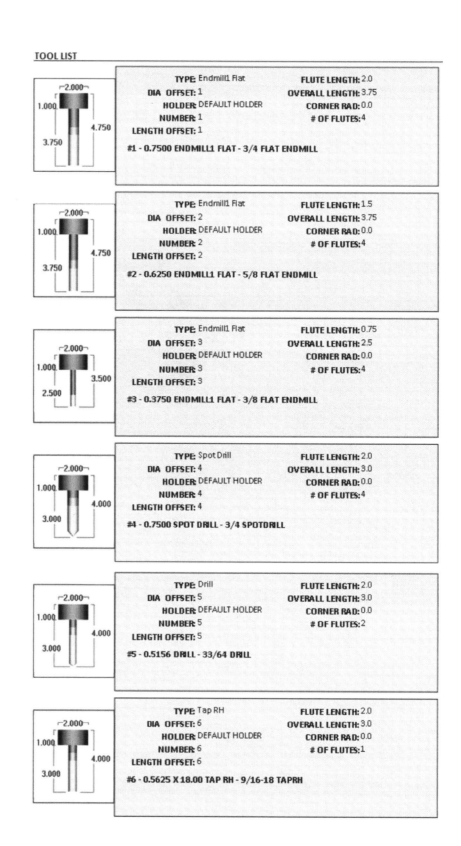

TOOL LIST

TYPE: Endmill1 Flat
DIA OFFSET: 1
HOLDER: DEFAULT HOLDER
NUMBER: 1
LENGTH OFFSET: 1
FLUTE LENGTH: 2.0
OVERALL LENGTH: 3.75
CORNER RAD: 0.0
 # OF FLUTES: 4

#1 - 0.7500 ENDMILL1 FLAT - 3/4 FLAT ENDMILL

TYPE: Endmill1 Flat
DIA OFFSET: 2
HOLDER: DEFAULT HOLDER
NUMBER: 2
LENGTH OFFSET: 2
FLUTE LENGTH: 1.5
OVERALL LENGTH: 3.75
CORNER RAD: 0.0
 # OF FLUTES: 4

#2 - 0.6250 ENDMILL1 FLAT - 5/8 FLAT ENDMILL

TYPE: Endmill1 Flat
DIA OFFSET: 3
HOLDER: DEFAULT HOLDER
NUMBER: 3
LENGTH OFFSET: 3
FLUTE LENGTH: 0.75
OVERALL LENGTH: 2.5
CORNER RAD: 0.0
 # OF FLUTES: 4

#3 - 0.3750 ENDMILL1 FLAT - 3/8 FLAT ENDMILL

TYPE: Spot Drill
DIA OFFSET: 4
HOLDER: DEFAULT HOLDER
NUMBER: 4
LENGTH OFFSET: 4
FLUTE LENGTH: 2.0
OVERALL LENGTH: 3.0
CORNER RAD: 0.0
 # OF FLUTES: 4

#4 - 0.7500 SPOT DRILL - 3/4 SPOTDRILL

TYPE: Drill
DIA OFFSET: 5
HOLDER: DEFAULT HOLDER
NUMBER: 5
LENGTH OFFSET: 5
FLUTE LENGTH: 2.0
OVERALL LENGTH: 3.0
CORNER RAD: 0.0
 # OF FLUTES: 2

#5 - 0.5156 DRILL - 33/64 DRILL

TYPE: Tap RH
DIA OFFSET: 6
HOLDER: DEFAULT HOLDER
NUMBER: 6
LENGTH OFFSET: 6
FLUTE LENGTH: 2.0
OVERALL LENGTH: 3.0
CORNER RAD: 0.0
 # OF FLUTES: 1

#6 - 0.5625 X 18.00 TAP RH - 9/16-18 TAPRH

STEP 4: SELECT THE MACHINE AND SET UP THE STOCK

In Mastercam, you select a **Machine Definition** before creating any toolpath. The **Machine Definition** is a model of your machine's capabilities and features. It acts like a template for setting up your machine. The machine definition ties together three main components: the schematic model of your machine's components, the control definition that models your control capabilities, and the post processor that will generate the required machine code (G-code). For a Mill Level 1 exercise (2D toolpaths), we just need a basic machine definition.

> **NOTE:** For the purpose of this tutorial, we will be using the Default milling machine.

4.1 Unhide the Toolpaths manager panel and lock it if needed

* From the left side of the graphics window, click on the **Toolpaths** tab as shown.

* Pin the **Toolpaths Manager** by clicking on the **Auto Hide** icon as shown.

4.2 Select the machine

MACHINE

* From the **Machine Type** area, click on the drop down arrow below **Mill** and select the **Default.**

> **NOTE:** Once you select the **Mill Default** the ribbon bar changes to reflect the toolpaths that could be used with **Mill Default**.

♦ Select the plus sign (+) in front of **Properties** in the **Toolpaths Manager** to expand the **Toolpaths Group Properties.**

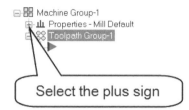

♦ Select **Tool settings** to set the tool parameters.

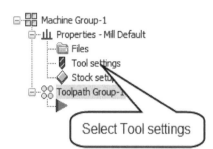

◆ Change the parameters to match <u>Figure: 4.2.1</u>.

Figure: 4.2.1

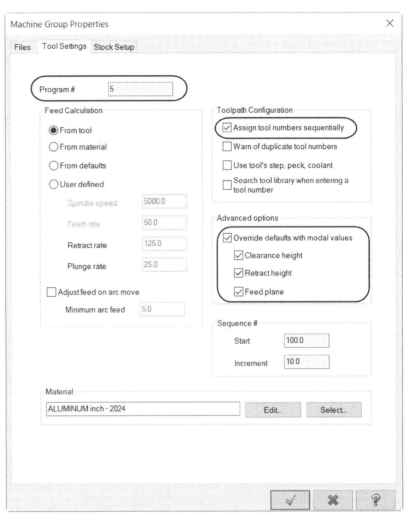

Program # is used to enter a number if your machine requires a number for a program name.

Assign tool numbers sequentially allows you to overwrite the tool number from the library with the next available tool number. (First operation tool number 1; Second operation tool number 2, etc.)

Warn of duplicate tool numbers allows you to get a warning if you enter two tools with the same number.

Override defaults with modal values enables the system to keep the values that you enter.

Feed Calculation set **From tool** uses feed rate, plunge rate, retract rate and spindle speed from the tool definition.

- Select the **Stock Setup** tab to define the stock.
- Select the **Rectangular** shape option.
- Select the **All Entities** button to define the stock size as shown in <u>Figure: 4.2.2</u>.

Figure: 4.2.2

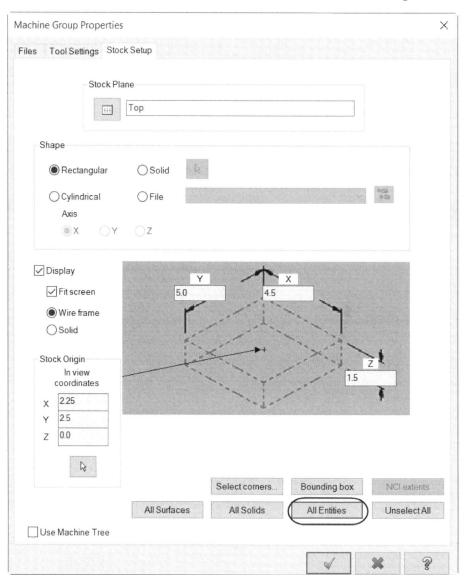

The **Stock Origin** values adjust the positioning of the stock, ensuring that you have equal amount of extra stock around the finished part.

Display options allow you to set the stock as **Wireframe** and to fit the stock to the screen. (Fit Screen)

NOTE: The **stock** model that you create can be displayed with the part geometry when viewing the file or the toolpaths, during backplot, or while verifying toolpaths. In the graphics, the plus sign (+) shows you where the stock origin is. The default position is the middle of the stock.

- Select the **OK** button to exit **Machine Group Properties**.

◆ The stock model will appear as shown.

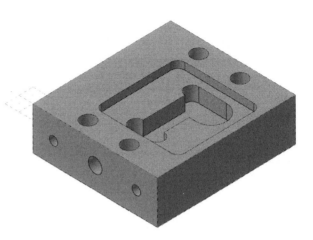

NOTE: You may not be able to see the stock very clearly due to the fact that the stock is the same size as the part. The stock is not geometry and cannot be selected. There will not be a facing toolpath because the stock is already to size.

STEP 5: 2D HIGH SPEED AREA MILL

2D High Speed Area Mill allows you to machine pockets, material that other toolpaths left behind, and standing bosses or cores. The toolpath depends on the **Machining strategy** that you choose in the **Chain Options**. If the strategy chosen is **From outside**, the toolpaths start at the outmost chain and works its way in taking on the final shape of the part as it approaches the final pass. You can also machine pockets, in which case the strategy selected is **Start inside**, which keeps the tool inside the machining region's helical entries and tangent stepovers create efficient motion for your machine. Cut parameters let you control smoothing to create the best toolpath, avoiding sharp corners or direction changes.

Toolpath Preview:

5.1 Chain Selection

TOOLPATHS

◆ From the **2D** group, click on the **Expand gallery** arrow as shown.

◆ Select the **Area Mill** icon as shown.

◆ When the new NC name dialog box appears, select the **OK** button to accept the name.

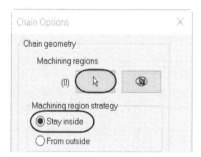

◆ From the **Chain Options**, click on the **Select machining chains** button.

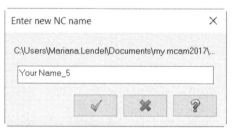

◆ When the chaining dialog box appears, select **C-plane** as shown.

◆ Leave the chaining method set to **Chain** as shown in <u>Figure: 5.1.1</u>.

Figure: 5.1.1

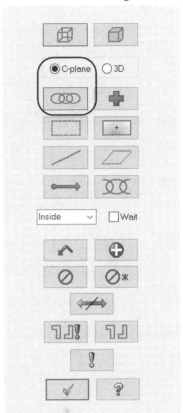

Cplane chains only the entities that are parallel to the current construction plane and at the same Z depth as the first entity you chain.

◆ [Select 2D HST machining chain 1]: Select the bottom of the pocket as shown in <u>Figure: 5.1.2</u>.

Figure: 5.1.2

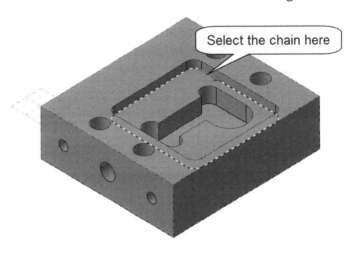

Select the chain here

◆ Select the **OK** button to exit the **Chaining** dialog box.

◆ Now the **Chain Options** dialog box should look as shown.

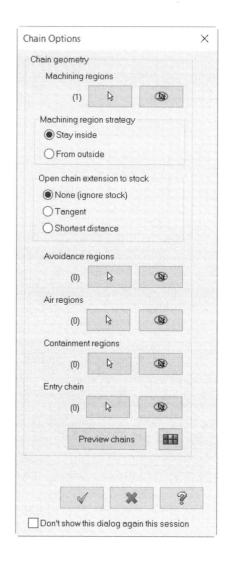

◆ Select the **OK** button to exit the **Chain Options**.
◆ In the **Toolpath Type** page, make sure that **Area Mill** is selected.

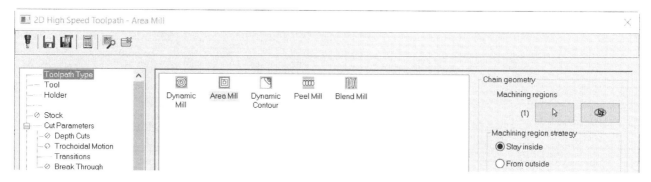

5.2 Preview Chains

The **Preview Chains** function is intended to give the user a quick visual representation of how Mastercam sees the various pieces of geometry that have been selected, how they interact with one another, and a general overview of how the toolpath will be calculated with the selections presently made.

♦ Click on the **Color** icon to see the legend for **Preview chains** as shown.

* The **Preview Chains Colors** dialog box should look as shown.

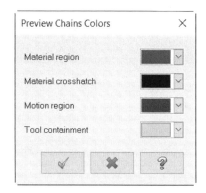

The **Material region** and **Material crosshatch** are the two colors that are used to define the material to be cut. The default colors are red for the background and black for the crosshatch.

The **Motion region** displays the area that Mastercam is making available to the toolpath for motion if it needs it. The color to represent it is dark blue. The primary reason for the display of the entire available (but not necessarily used) **Motion region** is to help the user visualize how the tool may move near or interact with any adjacent geometry.

The **Tool containment** is what you have selected as the containment region in the chain geometry. If you have not selected a containment region, it will default to the outside of the **Motion region** since that is currently the default area the toolpath is being contained to. The color used to represent the **Tool containment** is yellow.

* Select the **OK** button to exit **Preview Chains Colors**.
* Select the **Preview chains** button as shown.

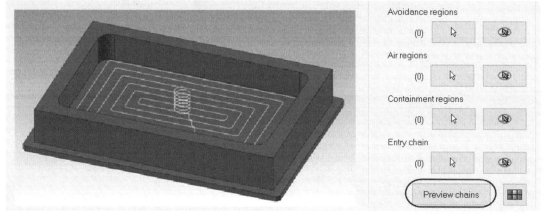

* Select the **Hide dialog** button to see the preview in the graphics window.

♦ The **Preview chains** should look as shown.

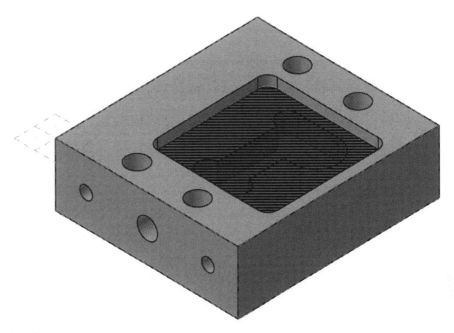

♦ Press **Esc** key to return to the toolpath parameters.
♦ Click on the **Preview chains** button again to clear the Preview chains display.

5.3 Select a 3/4" Flat Endmill from the library and set the Tool parameters

♦ Select **Tool** from the **Tree View list**.

♦ Click on the **Select library tool** button.
♦ Select the **Filter** button as shown.

♦ Select the **None** button and then under **Tool Types** choose the **Endmill1 Flat** icon.

◆ Under **Tool Diameter**, select **Equal** and input a value of **0.75** as shown in Figure: 5.3.1.

Figure: 5.3.1

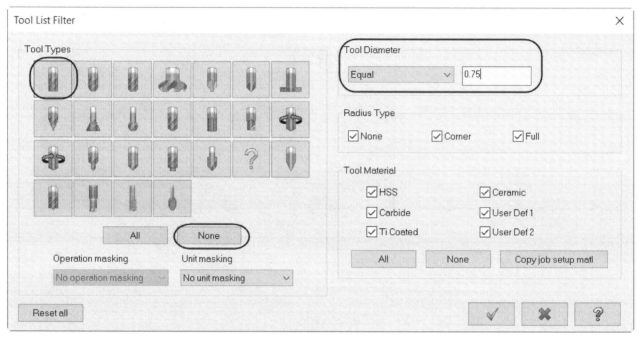

◆ Select the **OK** button to exit the **Tool List Filter.**
◆ In the **Tool Selection** dialog box you should only see a **3/4" Flat Endmill**.

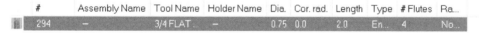

#	Assembly Name	Tool Name	Holder Name	Dia.	Cor. rad.	Length	Type	# Flutes	Ra...
294	–	3/4 FLAT ...	–	0.75	0.0	2.0	En...	4	No...

◆ Select the **3/4" Flat Endmill** in the **Tool Selection** page and then select the **OK** button to exit.

◆ Make all the necessary changes as shown in Figure: 5.3.2.

Figure: 5.3.2

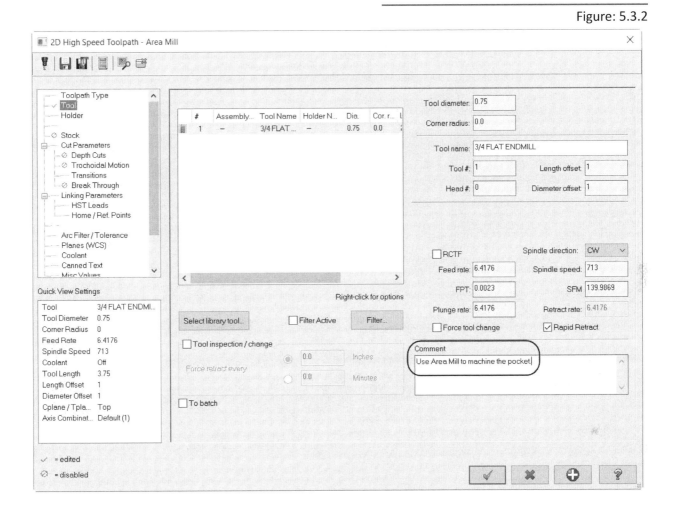

5.4 Set the Cut Parameters

◆ From the **Tree View list**, select **Cut Parameters**.
◆ Enable **Corner rounding** and ensure the settings appear as shown in Figure: 5.4.1.

Figure: 5.4.1

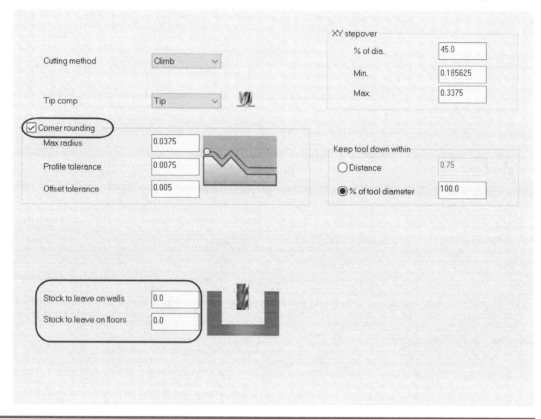

Corner rounding replaces sharp corners with arcs for faster and smoother transitions in tool direction. For more information on the parameters select the **Help** button ⌗. Once the **Mastercam Help** dialog box appears, click on the **Field definitions** tab to view more details.

Max radius inputs the radius of the largest arc that you will allow Mastercam to insert to replace a corner. Larger arcs will result in a smoother toolpath but with a greater deviation from the part corner.

Profile tolerance represents the maximum distance that the outermost profile of a toolpath with corner rounding can deviate from the original toolpath.

Offset tolerance represents the maximum distance that a profile of a toolpath created with corner rounding can deviate from the original toolpath.

5.5 Set the Depth Cuts Parameters

♦ From the **Tree View list**, select **Depth Cuts** and make sure it is disabled as shown in
Figure: 5.5.1.

Figure: 5.5.1

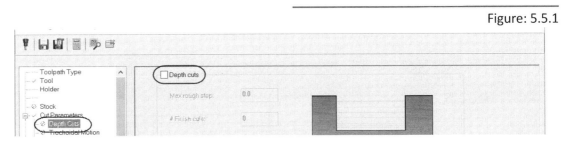

5.6 Set the Transitions

♦ From the **Tree View list**, select **Transitions**. Enable **Entry helix**, set the **Entry helix** to **0.500** and ensure the
parameters are the same as shown in Figure: 5.6.1.

Figure: 5.6.1

5.7 Set the Linking Parameters

♦ Select **Linking Parameters,** enable **Clearance** and input a value of **1.0**.
♦ You will notice the depth has been input based on the geometry we selected as shown in <u>Figure: 5.7.1</u>.

Figure: 5.7.1

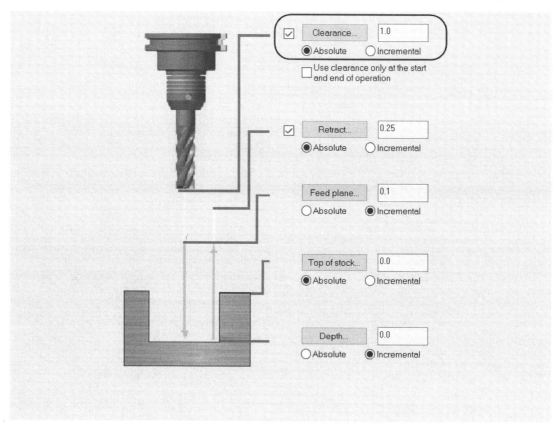

NOTE: The **Depth** set to **Incremental** and **0.0** is relative to the location of the chained geometry which was selected at the bottom of the pocket.

5.8 Preview the Toolpath

- To quickly check how the toolpath will be generated, select the **Preview toolpath** icon as shown.

- To hide the dialog box, click on the **Hide dialog** icon as shown.
- To see the part from an **Isometric** view, right mouse click in the graphics window and select **Isometric** as shown.

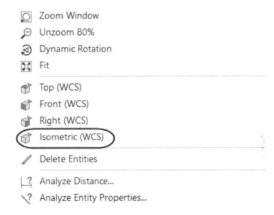

- The toolpath should look as shown.

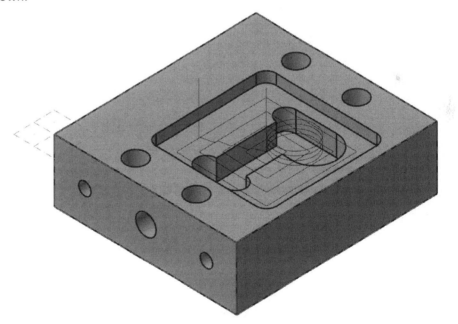

- Press **Esc** key to exit the preview.

> **NOTE:** If the toolpath does not look as shown in the preview, check your parameters again.

- Once complete, select the **OK** button to generate the toolpath.

STEP 6: BACKPLOT THE TOOLPATHS

Backplotting shows the path the tools take to cut the part. This display lets you spot errors in the program before you machine the part. As you backplot toolpaths, Mastercam displays additional information such as the X, Y, and Z coordinates, the path length, the minimum and maximum coordinates and the cycle time.

◆ Make sure that the toolpaths are selected (signified by the green check mark on the folder icon). If the operation is not selected choose the **Select all operations** icon.

◆ Select the **Backplot selected operations** button.

◆ In the **Backplot** dialog box, enable **Display with color codes**, **Display tool** and **Display rapid moves** icons as shown.

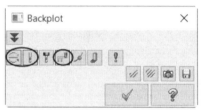

◆ Select the **Play** button to run **Backplot**.
◆ After **Backplot** is completed, the toolpath should look as shown.

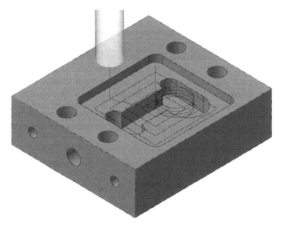

◆ Select the **OK** button to exit **Backplot**.

STEP 7: SIMULATE THE TOOLPATH IN VERIFY

Verify Mode shows the path the tools take to cut the part with material removal. This display lets you spot errors in the program before you machine the part. As you verify toolpaths, Mastercam displays additional information such as the X, Y, and Z coordinates, the path length, the minimum and maximum coordinates and the cycle time. It also shows any collision between the workpiece and the tool.

• From the **Toolpaths Manager**, select the **Verify selected operations** icon as shown.

NOTE: Mastercam launches a new window that allows you to check the part using **Verify.**

• Disable **Workpiece** in the **Visibility** group as shown in Figure: 7.0.1.

Figure: 7.0.1

• Select the **Play** button to run **Verify.**

• The part will appear as shown.

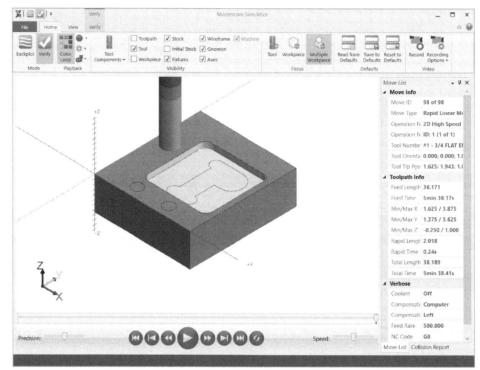

• To go back to the Mastercam window, minimize the **Mastercam Simulator** window as shown.

STEP 8: 2D HIGH SPEED AREA MILL

In this step you will learn how to copy a toolpath and reselect geometry. The main advantage of copying a toolpath is the parameters for the 1st toolpath remain intact for the second toolpath.

Toolpath Preview:

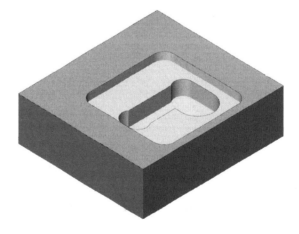

• To remove the toolpath display, from the **Toolpaths Manager**, click on the **Toggle display on selected operations** or press **T**.

8.1 Copy the Previous Toolpath

• Select Operation #1.

• Right click and hold the right mouse button down and drag the operation to a point below it as shown.

• Release the right mouse button and select the option **Copy After**.

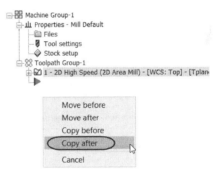

• Select the **Move insert arrow down one item** button to move the insert arrow down.

* The **Insert Arrow** should appear at the bottom of the list as shown in <u>Figure: 8.1.1</u>.

Figure: 8.1.1

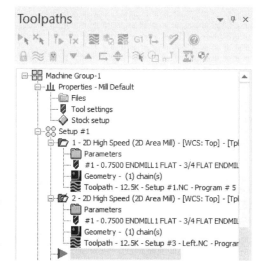

Insert Arrow controls where the new operation will be inserted.

8.2 Re-Chain the Geometry

* In Operation #2, select the **Geometry** as shown.

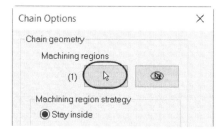

Select the Geometry

* Click on the **Select machining chains** button in the **Chain Options** dialog box as shown.

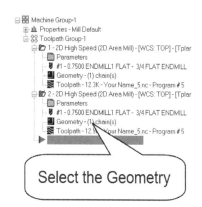

* When the **Chain Manager** appears, select **Chain 1**.

◆ Right click and select the option **Rechain all** as shown.

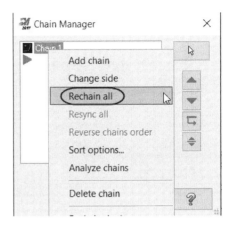

◆ When the **Chaining** dialog box appears, select **C-plane.**

◆ [Add chain 1]: Select the bottom of the pocket as shown in Figure: 8.2.1.

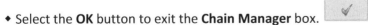

Figure: 8.2.1

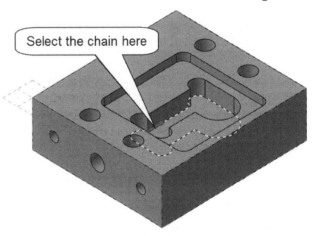

Select the chain here

◆ Once the geometry has been selected, choose the **OK** button to exit the **Chaining** dialog box.

◆ Select the **OK** button to exit the **Chain Manager** box.

◆ Select the **OK** button to exit the **Chain Options** box.

8.3 Preview Chains

♦ Select the **Preview chains** button as shown.

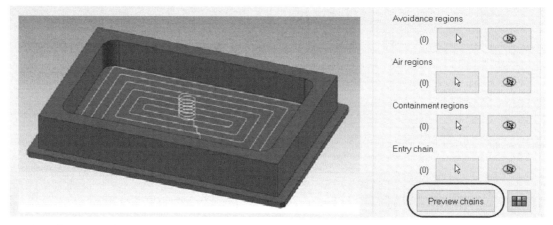

♦ See **page 164** to review the procedure.
♦ The **Preview chains** should look as shown.

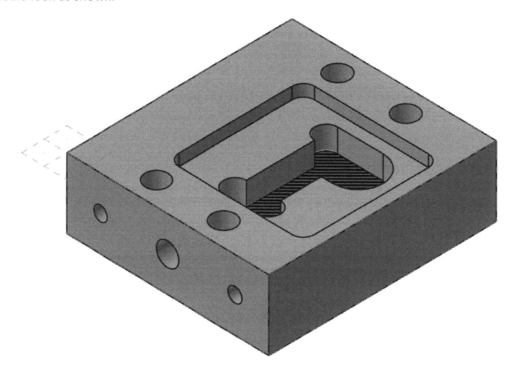

♦ Press **Esc** key to return to the toolpath parameters.
♦ Click on the **Preview chains** button again to clear the **Preview chains** display.

8.4 Select a 5/8" Flat Endmill from the Library and set the Tool Parameters

◆ Choose **Parameters** under Operation #2.

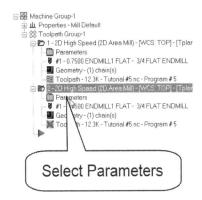

Select Parameters

◆ Select **Tool** from the **Tree View list**.

◆ Click on the **Select library tool** button. [Select library tool...]

◆ Select the **Filter** button as shown.

Filter...

☑ Filter Active

3 of 427 tools

◆ Select the **None** button and then under **Tool Types** choose the **Endmill1 Flat** icon.

◆ Under **Tool Diameter**, select **Equal** and input a value of **0.625** as shown in Figure: 8.4.1.

Figure: 8.4.1

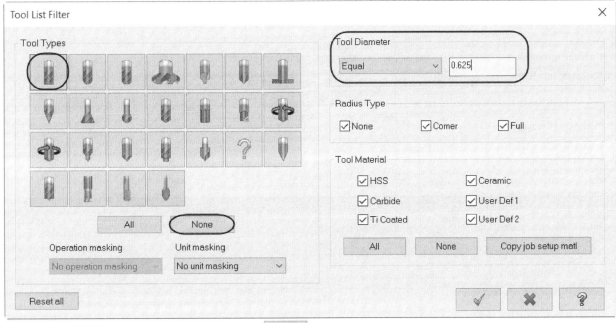

◆ Select the **OK** button to exit the **Tool List Filter.**

* In the **Tool Selection** dialog box, you should only see a **5/8" Flat Endmill**.

#	Assembly Name	Tool Name	Holder Name	Dia.	Cor. rad.	Length	# Flutes	Type	Ra...
292	–	5/8 FLAT ...	–	0...	0.0	1.5	4	En...	No...

* Select the **5/8" Flat Endmill** in the **Tool Selection** page and then select the **OK** button to exit.
* Make all the necessary changes as shown in Figure: 8.4.2.

Figure: 8.4.2

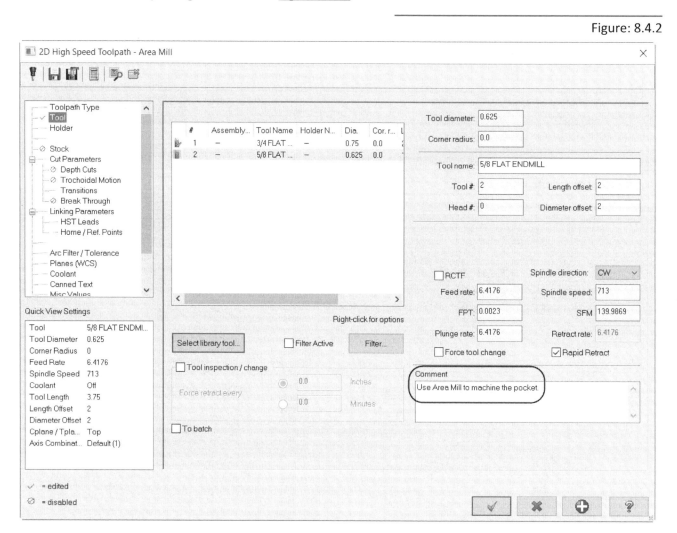

NOTE: Since this toolpath has been copied, all the parameters remain the same. Therefore the only parameters shown are the ones we will be changing.

8.5 Set the Depth Cuts parameters

- From the **Tree View list**, select the **Depth Cuts** and enable **Depth cuts**.
- Input a **Max rough step** of **0.2** as shown in Figure: 8.5.1.

Figure: 8.5.1

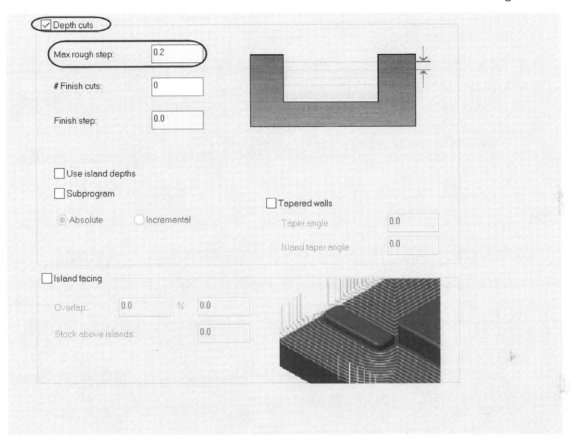

8.6 Set the Transitions

◆ From the **Tree View list**, select **Transitions**. Enable **Entry helix** and enter a **Radius** of **0.5** as shown in <u>Figure: 8.6.1</u>.

Figure: 8.6.1

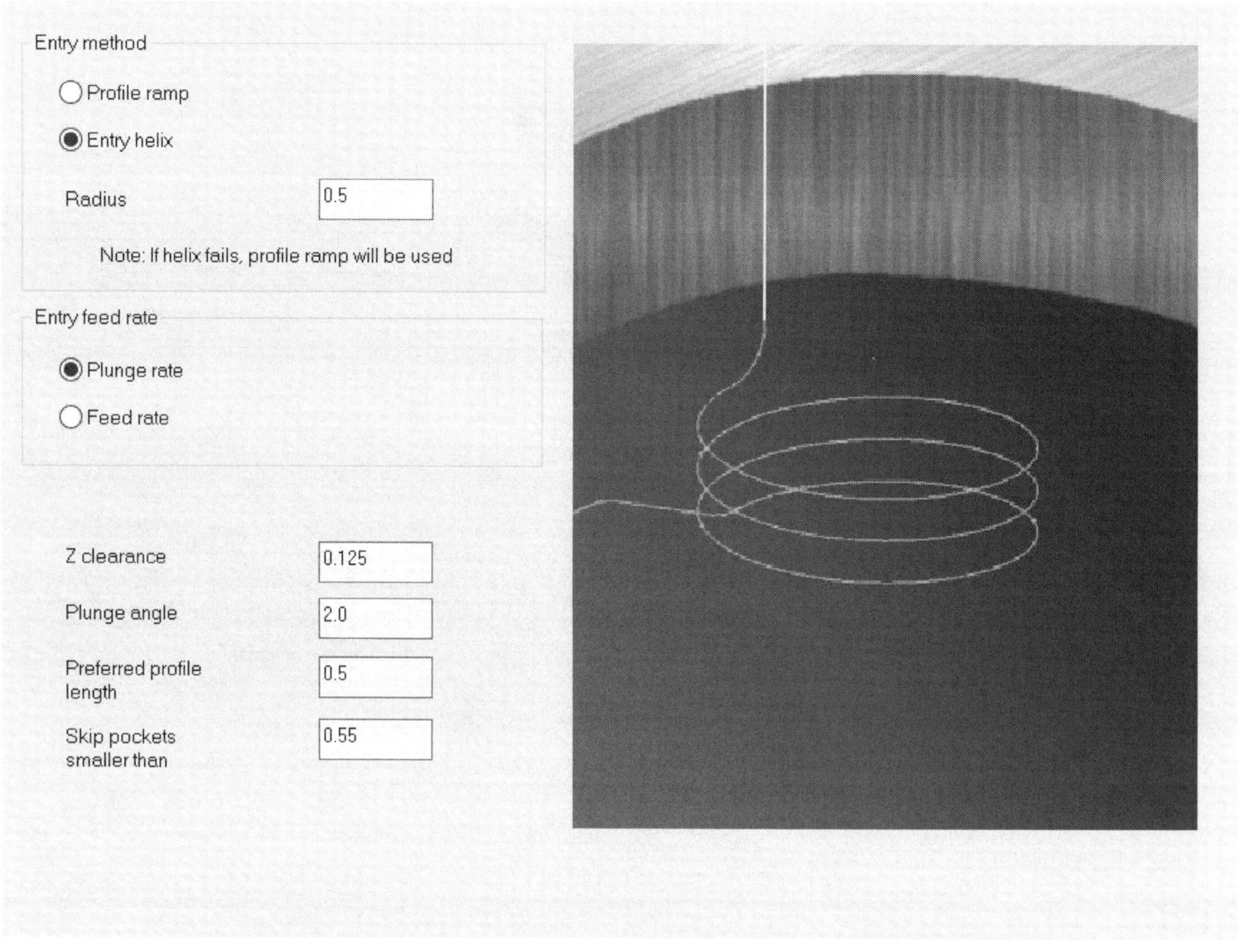

Entry method

○ Profile ramp

◉ Entry helix

Radius   `0.5`

Note: If helix fails, profile ramp will be used

Entry feed rate

◉ Plunge rate

○ Feed rate

Z clearance   `0.125`

Plunge angle   `2.0`

Preferred profile length   `0.5`

Skip pockets smaller than   `0.55`

Profile ramp creates a ramp motion to descend the tool.

Preferred profile length enters a minimum size for the profile in order for a ramp to be created.

8.7 Set the Linking Parameters

- Select **Linking Parameters** from the **Tree View list**.
- Set the **Top of Stock** and the **Depth** to **Absolute**.
- Select the **Top of stock** button (this will return you to the graphics screen).

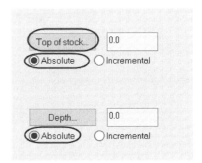

- Select the line endpoint as shown in Figure: 8.7.1.

Figure: 8.7.1

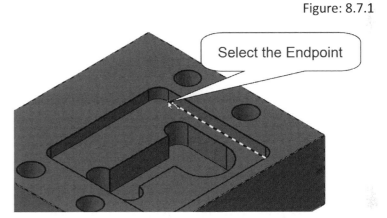

- Choose the **Depth** button (this will return you to the graphics screen).
- Select the line endpoint as shown in Figure: 8.7.2.

Figure: 8.7.2

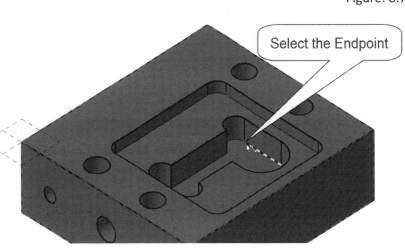

• **Top of stock** will be set to **-0.25** and the **Depth** set to **-0.75** as shown in <u>Figure: 8.7.3</u>.

Figure: 8.7.3

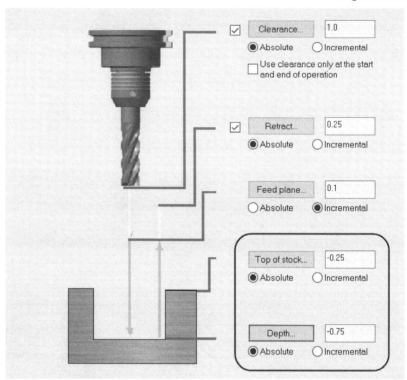

8.8 Preview the Toolpath

• To quickly check how the toolpath will be generated, select the **Preview toolpath** icon as shown.

• See **page 157** to review the procedure.
• The toolpath should look as shown.

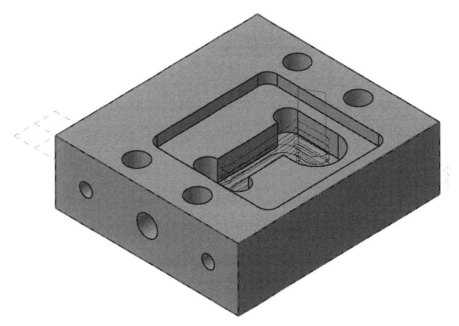

• Press **Esc** key to exit the preview.

> **NOTE:** If the toolpath does not look as shown in the preview, check your parameters again.

• Select the **OK** button to generate the **Area Mill** toolpath.
• Choose to **Regenerate all dirty operations**.

8.9 Backplot the toolpath

♦ Once the operation has been regenerated, **Backplot** the toolpath. See **page 518** to review these procedures.

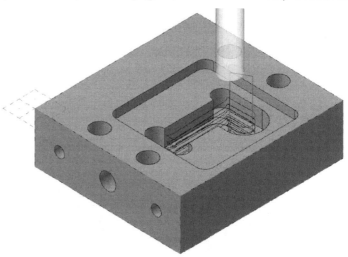

♦ Select the **OK** button to exit **Backplot**.

8.10 Verify the toolpaths

♦ To verify all toolpaths, from the **Toolpaths Manager**, choose the **Select all operations** icon.
♦ See **page 519** to review these procedures.

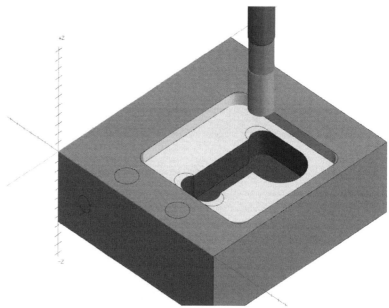

♦ To go back to the Mastercam window, minimize the **Mastercam Simulator** window as shown.

STEP 9: AREA MILL TO REMACHINE THE REMAINING MATERIAL

High Speed Area Mill toolpath with **Rest Material** options enabled targets material left behind by the previous toolpaths.

Toolpath Preview:

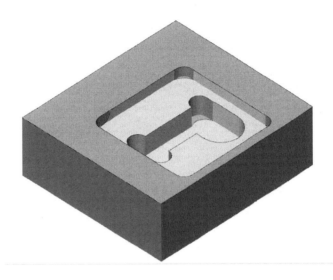

9.1 Copy the previous Toolpaths

♦ Select the **Select all operations** button.

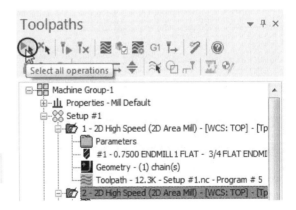

NOTE: Both toolpaths should be selected as shown.

◆ Right click and hold the right mouse button down and drag the operation to a point below it as shown in Figure: 9.1.1.

Figure: 9.1.1

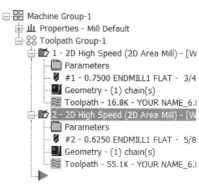

◆ Release the right mouse button and select the option **Copy after** as shown in Figure: 9.1.2.

Figure: 9.1.2

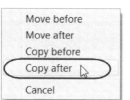

♦ Select the **Move insert arrow down one item** button twice to move the insert arrow down as shown.

♦ Choose **Parameters** under Operation #3.

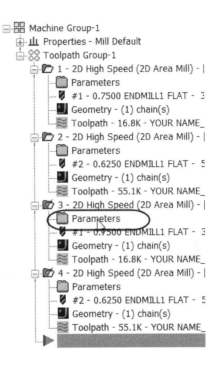

9.2 Preview Chains

♦ Select the **Preview chains** button as shown.

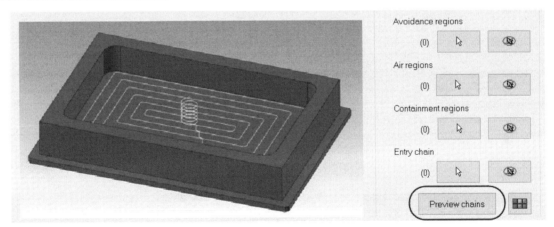

♦ See **page 164** to review the procedure.

◆ The **Preview chains** should look as shown.

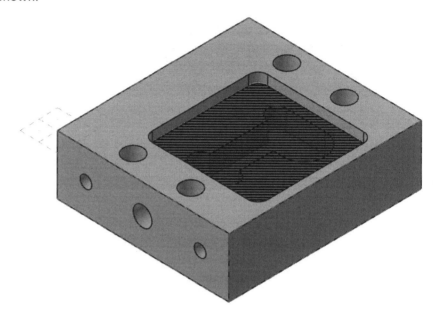

◆ Press **Esc** key to return to the toolpath parameters.
◆ Click on the **Preview chains** button again to clear the **Preview chains** display.

9.3 Select a 3/8" Flat Endmill from the Library and set the Tool parameters

◆ Select **Tool** from the **Tree View list**.

◆ Click on the **Select library tool** button.
◆ Select the **Filter** button.

◆ Select the **None** button and then under **Tool Types** choose the **Endmill1 Flat** icon.

♦ Under **Tool Diameter**, select **Equal** and input a value of **0.375** as shown in <u>Figure: 9.3.1</u>.

Figure: 9.3.1

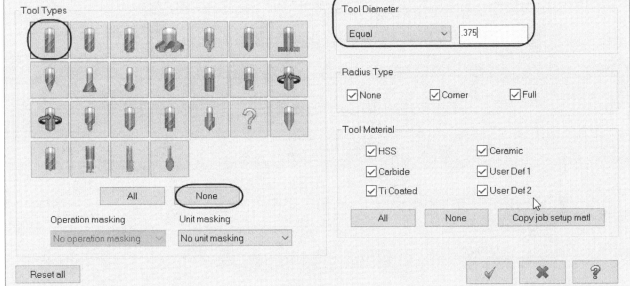

♦ Select the **OK** button to exit the **Tool List Filter.**
♦ In the **Tool Selection** dialog box you should only see a **3/8" Flat Endmill**.

#	Assembly Name	Tool Name	Holder Name	Dia.	Cor. rad.	Length	# Flutes	Ra...	Type
287	—	3/8 FLAT ...	—	0....	0.0	0.75	4	No...	En...

♦ Select the **3/8" Flat Endmill** in the **Tool Selection** page and then select the **OK** button to exit.

◆ Make the necessary changes as shown in <u>Figure: 9.3.2</u>.

Figure: 9.3.2

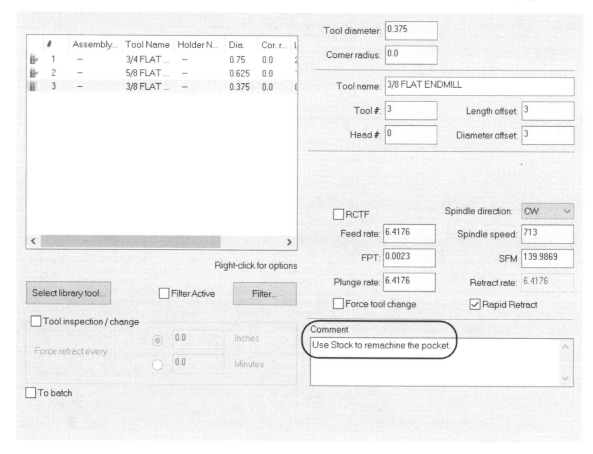

9.4 Set the Rest Material

◆ From the **Tree View list**, select **Stock**. Enable **Rest material** and set the parameters the same as shown in Figure: 9.4.1.

Figure: 9.4.1

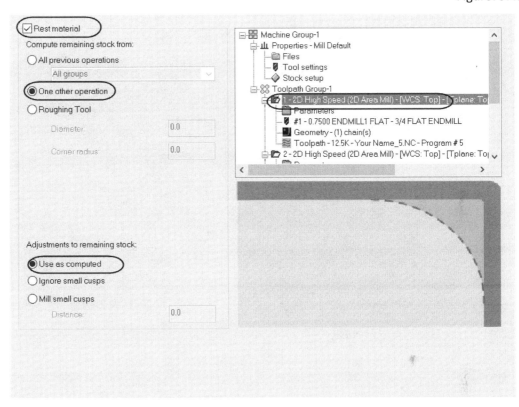

The **Rest material** page allows you to set how Mastercam calculates the remaining stock.

One other operation calculates the remaining stock from one source operation.

9.5 Preview the Toolpath

♦ To quickly check how the toolpath will be generated, select the **Preview toolpath** icon as shown.

♦ See **page 157** to review the procedure.
♦ The toolpath should look as shown.

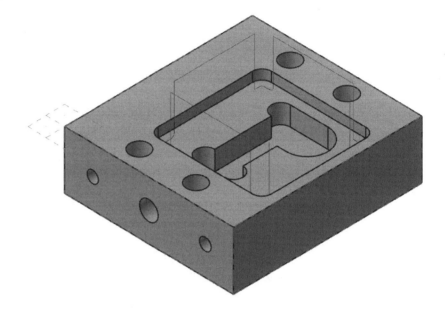

♦ Press **Esc** key to exit the preview.

NOTE: If the toolpath does not look as shown in the preview, check your parameters again.

♦ Choose the **OK** button to generate the toolpath.

NOTE: Since this toolpath has been copied, all the parameters remain the same. Therefore we do not have to view all the parameters.

9.6 Remachine the letter P pocket

◆ Select **Parameters** of Operation #4 as shown.

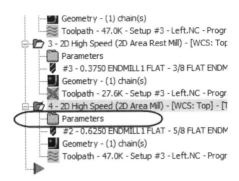

◆ In the **Toolpath Type** page, select the **Preview chains** button as shown.

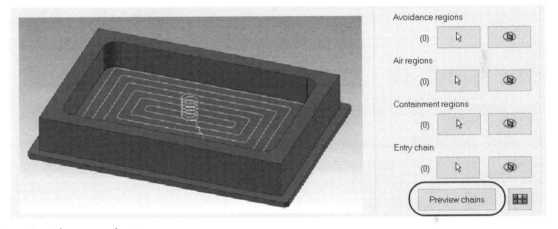

◆ See **page 164** to review the procedure.
◆ The **Preview chains** should look as shown.

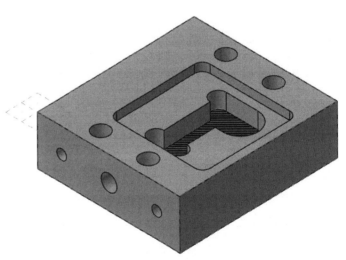

◆ Press **Esc** key to return to the toolpath parameters.
◆ Click on the **Preview chains** button again to clear the **Preview chains** display.

- In the **Tool** page, select the same tool used in Operation #3 and input a comment accordingly.
- Select **Stock** from the **Tree View list**. Similar to the previous **substep 9.4** on **page 539**, enable **Rest material**; check **One other operation** for **Compute remaining stock from** and then select Operation #2. Check **Use as computed**.
- To quickly check how the toolpath will be generated, select the **Preview toolpath** icon as shown.

- See **page 157** to review the procedure.
- The toolpath should look as shown.

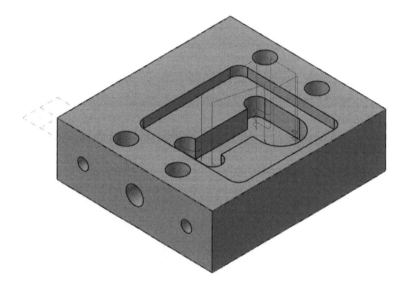

- Press **Esc** key to exit the preview.

> **NOTE:** If the toolpath does not look as shown in the preview, check your parameters again.

- Leave the rest parameters as they are and click on the **OK** button to generate the toolpath.
- Regenerate all dirty operations.

9.7 Backplot and Verify the toolpaths

◆ To **Backplot** both toolpaths see **page 518**.

◆ Hold down the **Ctrl** key and select only Operation #3 and #4.

◆ The toolpaths should look as shown.

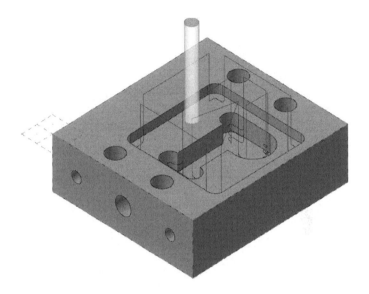

◆ Select the **OK** button to exit **Backplot**.

◆ To **Verify,** make sure that all toolpaths are selected by choosing the **Select all operations** icon.

◆ See **page 519** for more information.

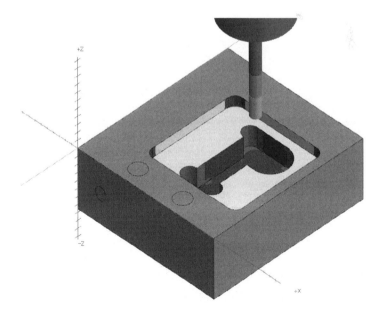

◆ To go back to the Mastercam window, minimize the **Mastercam Simulator** window as shown.

STEP 10: SPOT DRILL THE HOLE

Spot Drilling the holes allows you to start the hole. In this operation, we will use the spot drill to chamfer the hole before drilling it.

Toolpath Preview:

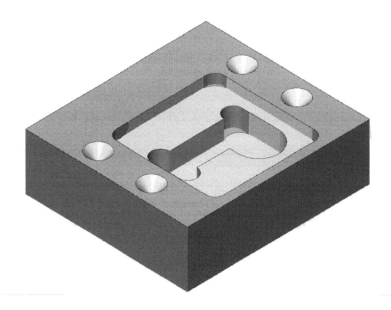

TOOLPATHS

* In the **2D** group, select the **Expand gallery** arrow and click on the **Drill** icon.

• In the **Drill Point Selection** dialog box, choose the option **Entities** as shown in Figure: 10.0.1.

Figure: 10.0.1

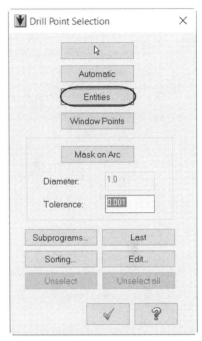

• Select the circles as shown in Figure: 10.0.2. The holes will be machined in same order in which you selected the circles.

Figure: 10.0.2

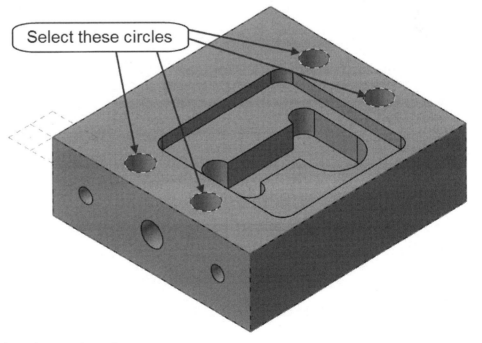

Select these circles

• Hit **Enter** once the entities have been selected.

* Select the **OK** button in the **Drill Point Selection** dialog box once you have selected the four circles.
* In the **Toolpath Type** page, the **Drill** toolpath will be selected.

| Drill | Circle Mill | Point | Helix Bore | Thread Mill |

10.1 Select a 3/4" Spot Drill from the Library and set the Tool Parameters

* Select **Tool** from the **Tree View list**.

* Click on the **Select library tool** button. `Select library tool...`
* To be able to see just the **Spot Drill**, select the **Filter** button.

* Under **Tool Types**, select the **None** button and then choose the **Spot Drill** icon.
* Ensure the **Total Diameter** is set to **0.75** as shown in Figure: 10.1.1.

Figure: 10.1.1

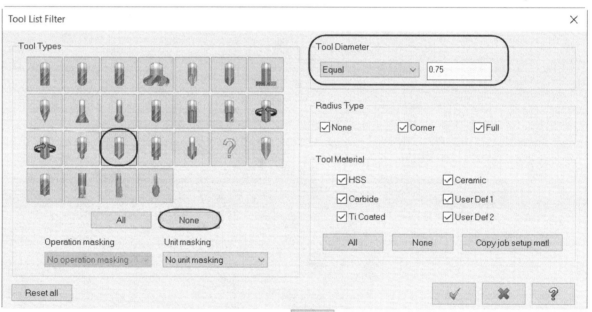

* Select the **OK** button to exit the **Tool List Filter** dialog box.
* Select the **3/4" Spot Drill**.

#	Assembly Name	Tool Name	Holder Name	Dia.	Cor. rad.	Length	Type	Ra...	# Flutes
25	–	3/4 SPOT...	–	0.75	0.0	2.0	Sp...	No...	4

* Select the **OK** button to exit.

◆ Make the necessary changes to the **Tool** page as shown in Figure: 10.1.2.

Figure: 10.1.2

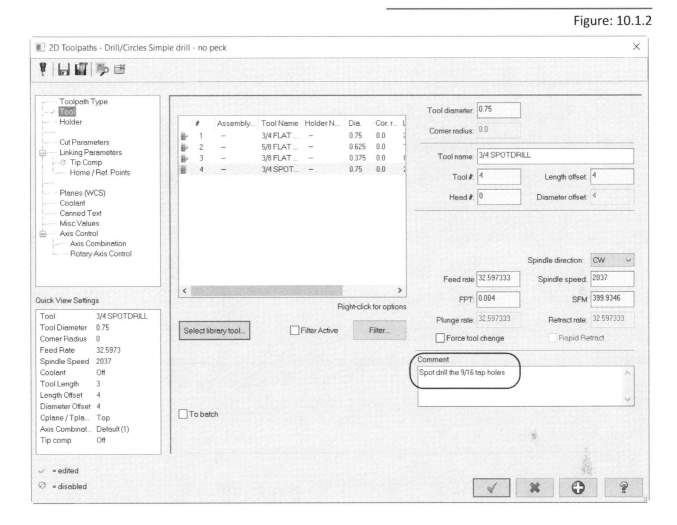

10.2 Set the Cut Parameters

♦ Select **Cut Parameters** and make the necessary changes as shown in Figure: 10.2.1.

Figure: 10.2.1

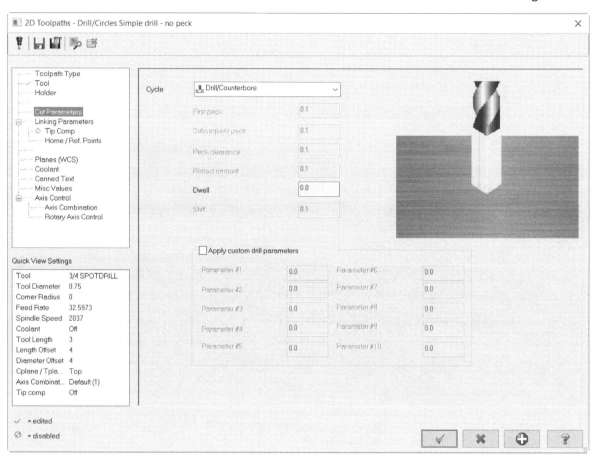

Drill/Counterbore is recommended for drilling holes with depths of less than three times the tool's diameter.

Dwell sets the amount of time in seconds that the tool remains at the bottom of a drilled hole.

10.3 Set the Linking Parameters

◆ Choose **Linking Parameters**, ensure clearance is enabled and set the **Top of stock** and the **Depth** to **Absolute** and **0.0**.

◆ To input the depth, select the **Calculator** icon.

◆ Input the following equation in the **Finish diameter** area: **9/16 + 0.05** (diameter of the finished hole + 2 X the chamfer size) as shown in Figure: 10.3.1 and hit **Enter** to calculate the **Depth.**

Figure: 10.3.1

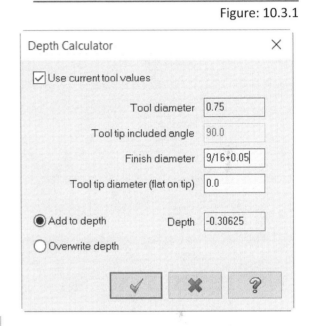

◆ Select the **OK** button to exit the **Depth Calculator**.

* You will now see the depth you calculated for the spot drilling operation set in the **Depth** field as shown in Figure: 10.3.2.
* This will chamfer the hole for the tapping operation.
* Change the **Clearance** value to **1.0**.

Figure: 10.3.2

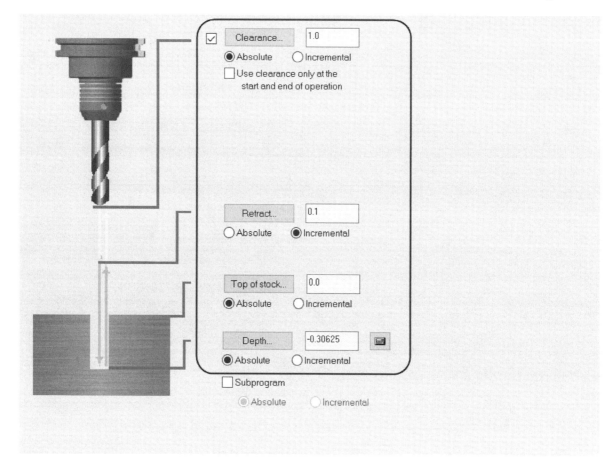

SPOT DRILL THE HOLE **TUTORIAL #5**

10.4 Preview the Toolpath

♦ To quickly check how the toolpath will be generated, select the **Preview toolpath** icon as shown.

♦ See **page 157** to review the procedure.
♦ The toolpath should look as shown.

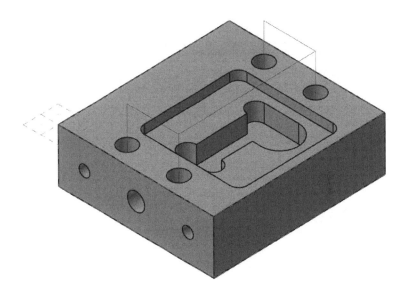

♦ Press **Esc** key to exit the preview.

> **NOTE:** If the toolpath does not look as shown in the preview, check your parameters again. The holes are machined in the order in which you selected the circles used in the toolpath.

♦ Select the **OK** button to exit the **2D Toolpaths - Drill/Circles Simple drill - no peck** parameters.

Mastercam 2017 — **Mill Essentials Training Tutorial** — Page|551

10.5 Backplot and Verify the toolpaths

◆ To **Backplot** and **Verify** your toolpaths, see **page 518** and **page 519**.

◆ To **Verify** all toolpaths, from the **Toolpaths Manager**, choose the **Select all operations** icon.

◆ The part should look as shown.

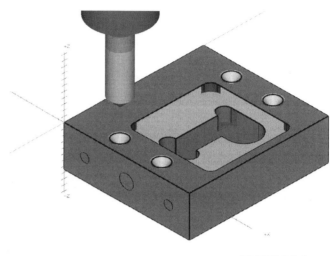

◆ To go back to the Mastercam window, minimize the **Mastercam Simulator** window as shown.

STEP 11: DRILL THE HOLES

In this example, we will drill the holes through the part.

Toolpath Preview:

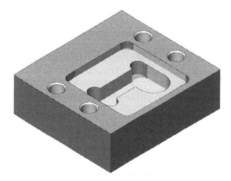

• In the **Toolpaths Manager,** select only the drilling operation as shown.

• As shown in previous steps, copy the drilling operation and move the insert arrow as shown.
• Select the **Parameters** in the second drilling operation as shown.

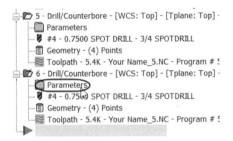

11.1 Select a 33/64" Drill from the Library and set the Tool Parameters

• Select **Tool** from the **Tree View list**.

• Click on the **Select library tool** button.

• To be able to see just the **Drill**, select the **Filter** button.

- Under **Tool Types**, select the **None** button and then choose the **Drill** icon as shown in <u>Figure: 11.1.1</u>.
- Under **Tool Diameter,** select **Equal** and enter the value **33/64** as shown in <u>Figure: 11.1.1</u>.

Figure: 11.1.1

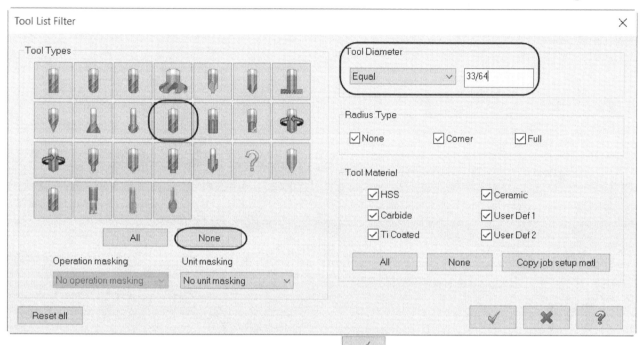

- Select the **OK** button to exit the **Tool List Filter** dialog box.
- At this point you should see only a **33/64" Drill**.
- From that list, select the **33/64"Drill** as shown in <u>Figure: 11.1.2</u>.

Figure: 11.1.2

#	Assembly Name	Tool Name	Holder Name	Dia.	Cor. rad.	Length	# Flutes	Type	Ra...
163	–	33/64 DRI...	–	0....	0.0	2.0	2	Drill	No...

- Select the tool in the **Tool Selection** page and then choose the **OK** button to exit.

♦ Make the necessary changes to the **Tool** page as shown in <u>Figure: 11.1.3</u>.

Figure: 11.1.3

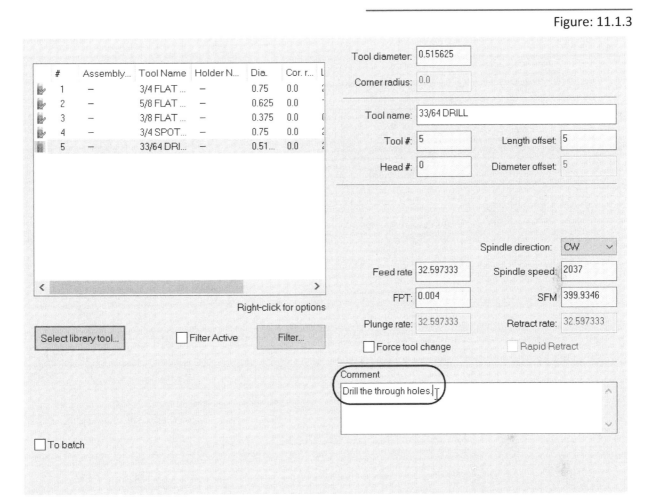

11.2 Set the Cut Parameters

- Select **Cut Parameters**, change the drill **Cycle** to **Peck Drill** and input a **Peck** value of **0.25** as shown in Figure: 11.2.1.

Figure: 11.2.1

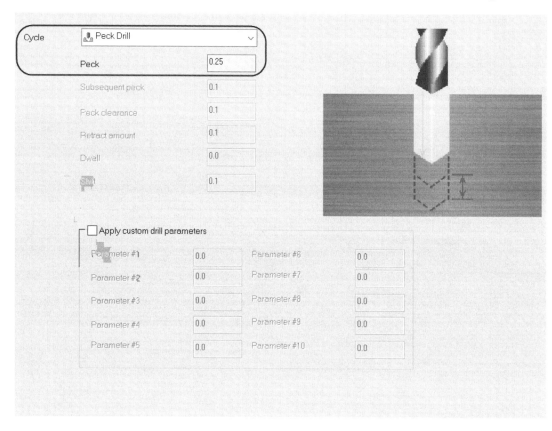

Peck Drill is recommended for drilling holes with depths of more than three times the tool's diameter. The drill retracts fully out of the drilled hole to remove material.

Peck sets the depth for the peck move.

11.3 Set the Linking Parameters

- Choose **Linking Parameters** and input a **Depth** value of **-1.5** as shown in <u>Figure: 11.3.1</u>.

Figure: 11.3.1

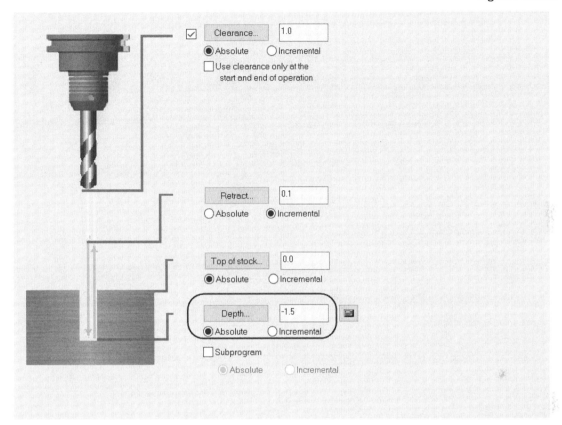

11.4 Set the Tip Comp Parameters

• Select **Tip Comp** and enable this option. Input a **Breakthrough amount** of **0.1** as shown in Figure: 11.4.1.

Figure: 11.4.1

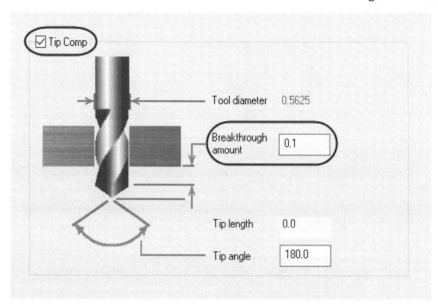

11.5 Preview the Toolpath

• To quickly check how the toolpath will be generated, select the **Preview toolpath** icon as shown.

• See **page 157** to review the procedure.
• The toolpath should look as shown.

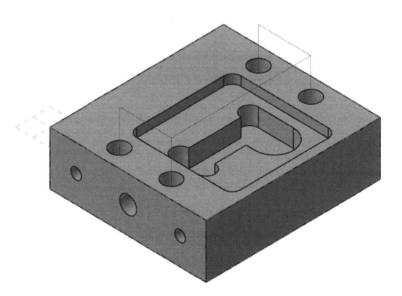

♦ Press **Esc** key to exit the preview.

> **NOTE:** If the toolpath does not look as shown in the preview, check your parameters again. The toolpath will be the same as the one in Operation #5 since Operation #6 is a copy.

♦ Select the **OK** button to exit the **Drill/Circles Simple drill - no peck** parameters.
♦ From the **Toolpaths Manager**, select the **Regenerate all dirty operations** icon.

11.6 Backplot and Verify

♦ To **Backplot** and **Verify** the toolpaths, see **page 518** and **page 519**.

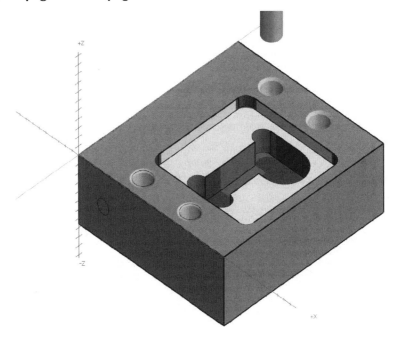

♦ To go back to the Mastercam window, minimize the **Mastercam Simulator** window as shown.

STEP 12: TAP THE HOLES

Tap cycle taps right or left internal threaded holes.

Toolpath Preview:

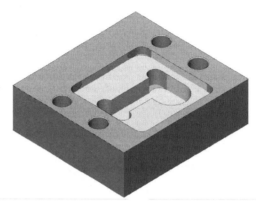

- In the **Toolpaths Manager,** select only the last drilling operation as shown.

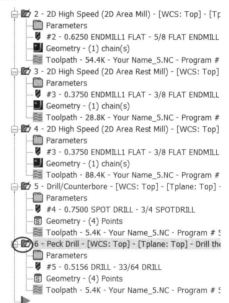

- As shown in previous steps copy the drilling operation and move the insert arrow as shown.
- Select the **Parameters** in the third drilling operation as shown.

12.1 Select a 9/16 - 18 RH Tap from the Library and set the Tool Parameters

• Select **Tool** from the **Tree View list**.

• Click on the **Select library tool** button.

• To be able to see just the **Tap RH drill**, select the **Filter** button.

• Under **Tool Types**, select the **None** button and then choose the **Tap RH** icon. Under **Tool Diameter**, select **Equal** and enter the value **9/16** as shown in Figure: 12.1.1.

Figure: 12.1.1

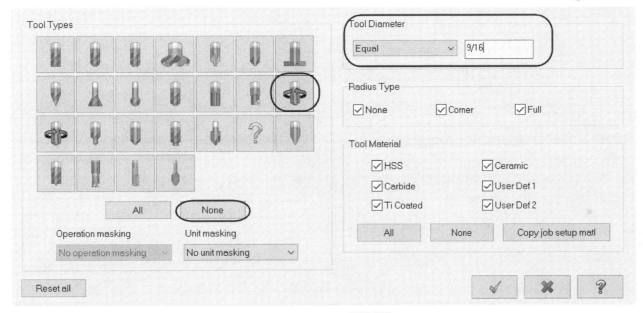

• Select the **OK** button to exit the **Tool List Filter** dialog box.

• At this point you should see a list full of taps.

• From that list, select the **9/16 - 18 Tap RH** as shown.

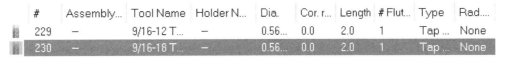

#	Assembly...	Tool Name	Holder N...	Dia.	Cor. r...	Length	# Flut...	Type	Rad....
229	–	9/16-12 T...	–	0.56...	0.0	2.0	1	Tap ...	None
230	–	9/16-18 T...	–	0.56...	0.0	2.0	1	Tap ...	None

• Select the tool in the **Tool Selection** page and then choose the **OK** button to exit.

◆ Make the necessary changes in the **Tool** page as shown in Figure: 12.1.2.

Figure: 12.1.2

2D Toolpaths - Drill/Circles Peck drill - full retract ✕

- Toolpath Type
- ✓ Tool
- Holder

- Cut Parameters
- Linking Parameters
  - Tip Comp
  - Home / Ref. Points

- Planes (WCS)
- Coolant
- Canned Text
- Misc Values
- Axis Control
  - Axis Combination
  - Rotary Axis Control

#	Assembly...	Tool Name	Holder N...	Dia.	Cor. r...	L
1	–	3/4 FLAT ...	–	0.75	0.0	
2	–	5/8 FLAT ...	–	0.625	0.0	
3	–	3/8 FLAT ...	–	0.375	0.0	
4	–	3/4 SPOT...	–	0.75	0.0	
5	–	33/64 DRI...	–	0.51...	0.0	
6	–	9/16-18 T...	–	0.56...	0.0	

Tool diameter: 0.5625

Corner radius: 0.0

Tool name: 9/16-18 TAPRH

Tool #: 6   Length offset: 6

Head #: 0   Diameter offset: 6

Spindle direction: CW

Feed rate 32.597333   Spindle speed: 2037

FPT: 0.008   SFM 274.955

Plunge rate: 32.597333   Retract rate: 32.597333

☐ Force tool change   ☐ Rapid Retract

Quick View Settings

Tool	9/16-18 TAPRH
Tool Diameter	0.5625
Corner Radius	0
Feed Rate	32.5973
Spindle Speed	2037
Coolant	Off
Tool Length	3
Length Offset	6
Diameter Offset	6
Cplane / Tpla...	Top
Axis Combinat...	Default (1)
Tip comp	On

‹ ›

Right-click for options

Select library tool...   ☐ Filter Active   Filter...

Comment

Tap the four holes.

☐ To batch

✓ = edited

⊘ = disabled

12.2 Set the Cut Parameters

◆ Select **Cut Parameters** and change the drill **Cycle** to **Tap** as shown in Figure: 12.2.1.

Figure: 12.2.1

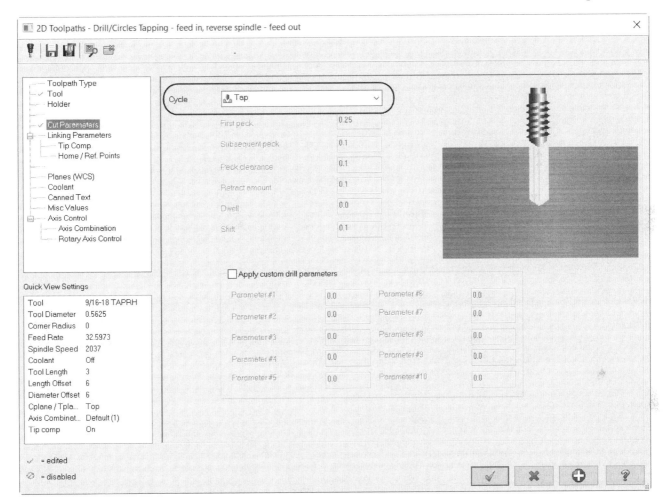

12.3 Set the Linking Parameters

• Choose **Linking Parameters** and make sure the **Depth** value is set to **-1.5** as shown in Figure: 12.3.1.

Figure: 12.3.1

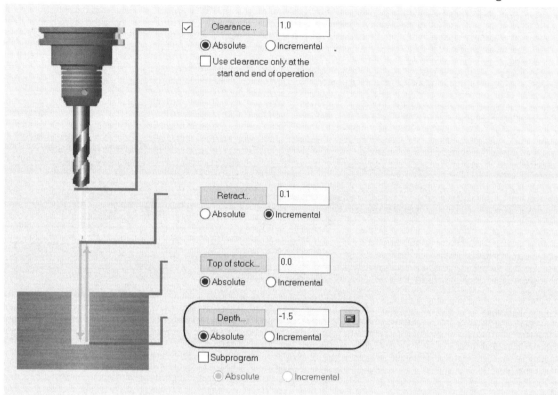

• Enable **Tip Comp**.

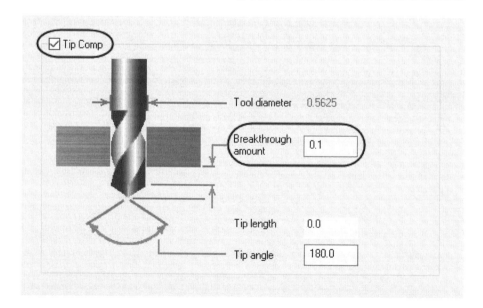

Mill Essentials Training Tutorial *Mastercam.* 2017

12.4 Preview the Toolpath

- To quickly check how the toolpath will be generated, select the **Preview toolpath** icon as shown.

- See **page 157** to review the procedure.
- The toolpath should look as shown.

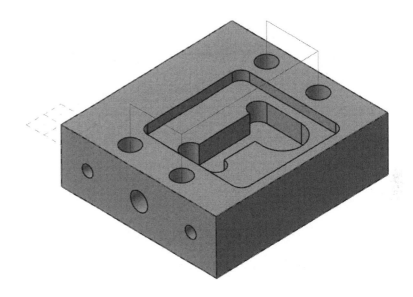

- Press **Esc** key to exit the preview.

> **NOTE:** If the toolpath does not look as shown in the preview, check your parameters again.

- Leave the rest of the parameters as they are and select the **OK** button to exit the **Drill/Circles Peck drill - full retract** parameters.
- From the **Toolpaths Manager**, select the **Regenerate all dirty operations** icon.

- To **Backplot** and **Verify** the toolpaths, see **page 518** and **page 519**.

- To make sure that all toolpaths are selected, choose the **Select all operations** icon.

♦ The part will appear as shown.

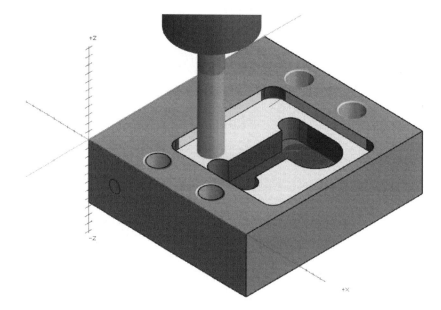

TOOLPATH CREATION - SETUP 2

SUGGESTED FIXTURE:

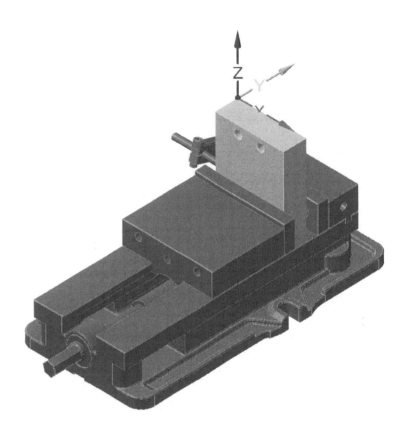

| NOTE: The part is now flipped over and you will machine the part from the **Front**.

SETUP SHEET:

TOOL LIST

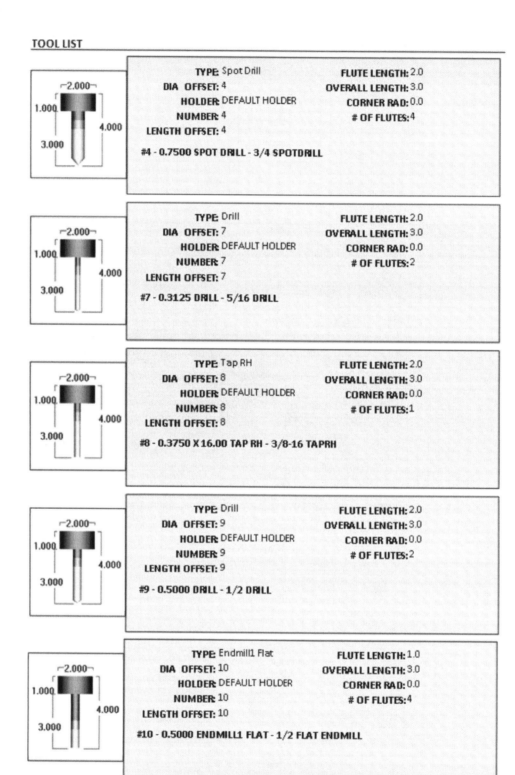

TYPE: Spot Drill
DIA OFFSET: 4
HOLDER: DEFAULT HOLDER
NUMBER: 4
LENGTH OFFSET: 4
FLUTE LENGTH: 2.0
OVERALL LENGTH: 3.0
CORNER RAD: 0.0
OF FLUTES: 4

#4 - 0.7500 SPOT DRILL - 3/4 SPOTDRILL

TYPE: Drill
DIA OFFSET: 7
HOLDER: DEFAULT HOLDER
NUMBER: 7
LENGTH OFFSET: 7
FLUTE LENGTH: 2.0
OVERALL LENGTH: 3.0
CORNER RAD: 0.0
OF FLUTES: 2

#7 - 0.3125 DRILL - 5/16 DRILL

TYPE: Tap RH
DIA OFFSET: 8
HOLDER: DEFAULT HOLDER
NUMBER: 8
LENGTH OFFSET: 8
FLUTE LENGTH: 2.0
OVERALL LENGTH: 3.0
CORNER RAD: 0.0
OF FLUTES: 1

#8 - 0.3750 X 16.00 TAP RH - 3/8-16 TAPRH

TYPE: Drill
DIA OFFSET: 9
HOLDER: DEFAULT HOLDER
NUMBER: 9
LENGTH OFFSET: 9
FLUTE LENGTH: 2.0
OVERALL LENGTH: 3.0
CORNER RAD: 0.0
OF FLUTES: 2

#9 - 0.5000 DRILL - 1/2 DRILL

TYPE: Endmill1 Flat
DIA OFFSET: 10
HOLDER: DEFAULT HOLDER
NUMBER: 10
LENGTH OFFSET: 10
FLUTE LENGTH: 1.0
OVERALL LENGTH: 3.0
CORNER RAD: 0.0
OF FLUTES: 4

#10 - 0.5000 ENDMILL1 FLAT - 1/2 FLAT ENDMILL

STEP 13: CREATING AND RENAMING TOOLPATH GROUPS

To machine the part in different setups, we will need to have separate programs. To be able to post the operations separate of each setup, we will create them under different toolpath groups with different NC names.

13.1 Rename the Current Toolpath Group-1 and NC File

♦ Click on the **Toolpath Group-1** to highlight it and then click again to rename it "**Setup #1.**"

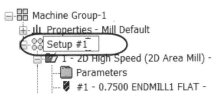

♦ Right mouse click on the toolpath group and select **Edit selected operations** and then select **Change NC file name.**

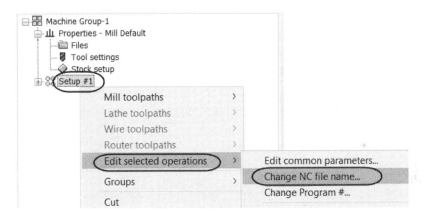

♦ Enter the new NC name: "**Setup #1.**"

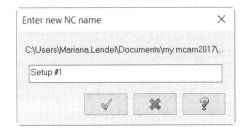

♦ Select the **OK** button to accept the new **NC name**.

13.2 Create a new Toolpath Group.

◆ Right mouse click on the **Machine Group-1.**
◆ From the list, select **Groups** and then **New Toolpath group** as shown.

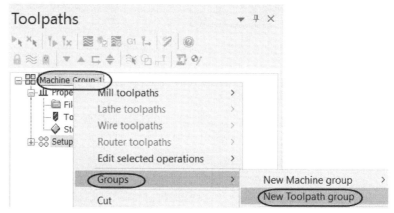

◆ Click on the new **Toolpath Group-1** and rename it "**Setup #2 - Front.**"

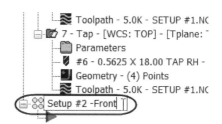

STEP 14: SET WCS TO FRONT

Work coordinate system (WCS) is the active coordinate system in use by Mastercam at any given time. The **WCS** contains the orientation of the X-Y-Z axes plus the location of the zero point (the origin). This tells Mastercam how your part is positioned or oriented in the machine.

Construction plane (Cplane) is the plane in which the geometry is created.

Tool plane (Tplane) is the plane normal to Z or to the vertical tool axis in which the tool moves. When creating a toolpath both **Cplane** and **Tplane** should be set to the same plane. If the Tplane is different than the **WCS**, the post will produce a rotary motion code. By setting the **Cplane, Tplane** and **WCS** to one plane, no rotary move will be generated in the code, which is what you want when machining parts with multiple setups.

In this step you will set the **WCS**, the **Construction plane (Cplane)** and the **Tool plane (Tplane)** to **Front**.

♦ Select the **Planes** tab located at the bottom left corner.

♦ Select the **Front** plane and click on the equal sign to set the **WCS**, **C**onstruction **Plane** and **T**ool **Plane** to the **Front** as shown.

♦ Right mouse click in the graphics window and select the **Isometric** view to see the part in the new orientation.

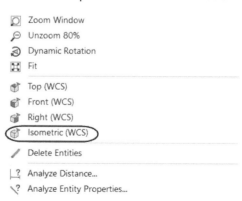

♦ Press **F9** on your keyboard to view the coordinate axes.

NOTE: The color of the coordinate axes remains the same because it is the same origin.

♦ Your part should look as shown.

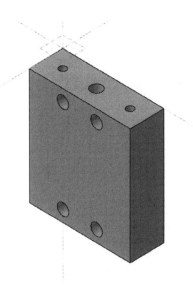

♦ Press **F9** again to remove the axes display.
♦ To open the **Toolpaths Manager**, select the **Toolpaths** tab from the lower left corner of the screen.

STEP 15: SPOT DRILL ALL 3 HOLES

Toolpath Preview:

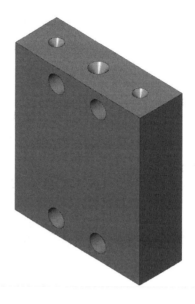

TOOLPATHS
- From the **2D** group, select the **Drill** icon.

- In the **Drill Point Selection** dialog box choose the option **Entities** as shown.

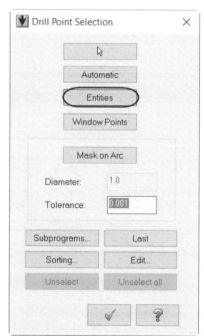

◆ Select the 3 circles as shown.

◆ Click on the **End Selection** button or press **Enter** to finish the selection.

◆ Select the **OK** button in the **Drill Point Selection** dialog box once you have selected the circles.

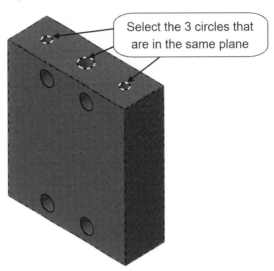

Select the 3 circles that
are in the same plane

◆ In the **Toolpath Type** page, the **Drill** toolpath will be selected.

Drill   Circle Mill   Point   Helix Bore   Thread Mill

♦ Select **Tool** from the **Tree View list**.
♦ Select the **3/4" Spot Drill** from the list.
♦ Make the necessary changes to the **Tool** page as shown in <u>Figure: 15.0.1</u>.

Figure: 15.0.1

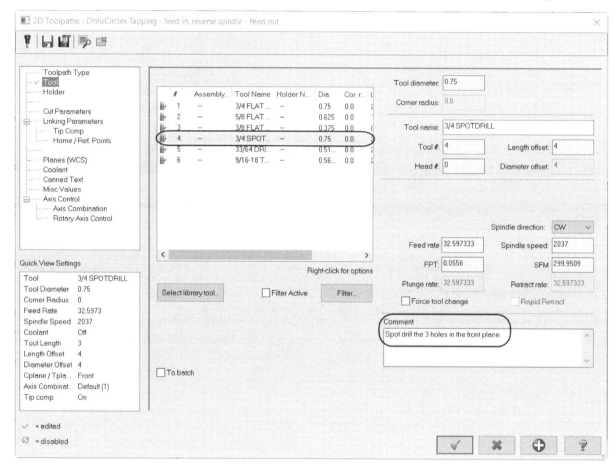

15.1 Set the Cut Parameters

• Select **Cut Parameters** and change the **Cycle** to **Drill/Counterbore** as shown in Figure: 15.1.1.

Figure: 15.1.1

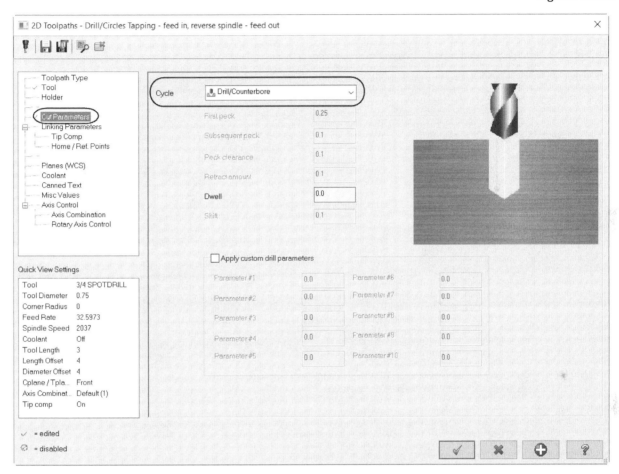

15.2 Set the Linking Parameters

♦ Choose **Linking Parameters**, ensure **Clearance** is enabled and the **Top of stock** and **Depth** is set to **Absolute** and **0.0**.

♦ To input the **Depth,** select the **Calculator** icon.

♦ Input the following equation in the **Finish diameter** area: **3/8+0.04** and hit **Enter** to calculate the **Depth** as shown in Figure: 15.2.1.

Figure: 15.2.1

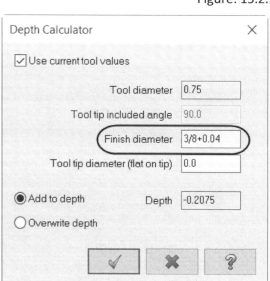

♦ Select the **OK** button to exit the **Depth Calculator**.

♦ You will now see the depth we calculated for the spot drilling operation set in the **Depth** field as shown in Figure: 15.2.2. This will chamfer the holes for the tapping operation.

Figure: 15.2.2

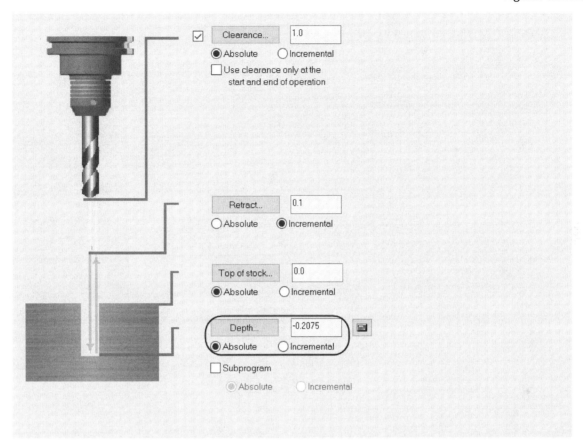

15.3 Set the Tip Comp

♦ Select **Tip Comp** and disable this option. If left enabled, the holes would be drilled much deeper as shown in Figure: 15.3.1.

Figure: 15.3.1

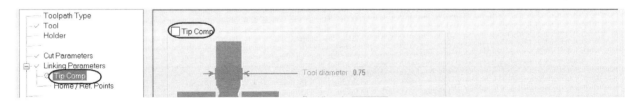

NOTE: All 3 holes are spot drilled to the same depth. The 0.5" diameter hole has to be drilled to a deeper depth.

15.4 Preview the Toolpath

* To quickly check how the toolpath will be generated, select the **Preview toolpath** icon as shown.

* See **page 157** to review the procedure.
* The toolpath should look as shown.

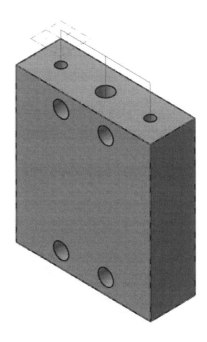

* Press **Esc** key to exit the preview.

> **NOTE:** If the toolpath does not look as shown in the preview, check your parameters again.

* Select the **OK** button to exit the **2D Toolpaths - Drill/Circles Simple drill - no peck** parameters.

SPOT DRILL ALL 3 HOLES **TUTORIAL #5**

15.5 Adjust the Depth of the Spot Drill

- Left click on **Geometry** in Operation #8.
- When the **Drill Point Manager** appears, select the point which represents the **0.5" diameter hole**.
- Then right click on it and select the option to **Change at point** as shown in Figure: 15.5.1.

Figure: 15.5.1

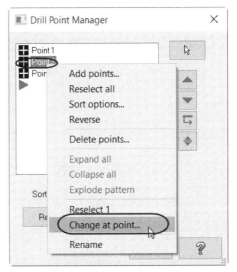

- When the **Drill change at point** dialog box appears, enable **Depth** and change the depth to **-0.27** as shown in Figure: 15.5.2.

Figure: 15.5.2

Drill Change at point allows you to make point-specific changes to a drill toolpath.

Depth changes the hole depth at the selected point. The coordinate you enter here will be output as either an absolute or incremental value, depending on the original settings for the operation.

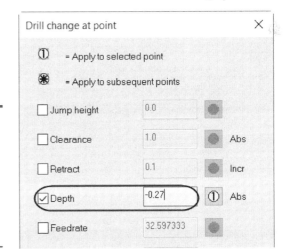

- Select the **OK** button to apply the changes and exit the **Drill change at point** dialog box.

- Choose the **OK** button to exit the **Drill Point Manager**.

◆ Select the button **Regenerate all dirty operations**.

15.6 Backplot and Verify the toolpaths

◆ To **Backplot** and **Verify** your toolpaths, see **page 518** and **page 519**.

◆ To make sure that all toolpaths are selected, choose the **Select all operations** icon.

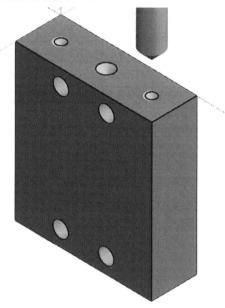

◆ To go back to the Mastercam window, minimize the **Mastercam Simulator** window as shown.
◆ When backplotting the toolpath, see if you can check the depth of the holes.
◆ Select the **Expand or contract this dialog** double arrow to expand the **Backplot** dialog box.

◆ Select the **Details** tab as shown below.

◆ You can step through the **Backplot** by using the **Step forward** or **Step back**.

• The coordinate values of the tip of the tool will be displayed with each step.

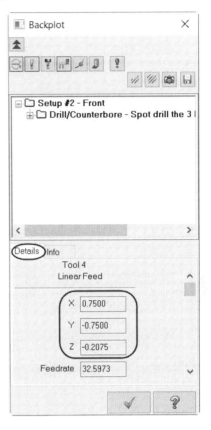

• Select the **OK** button to exit.

STEP 16: DRILL THE TWO 3/8" TAPPED HOLES

In this example, we will drill the holes to a specific depth.

Toolpath Preview:

TOOLPATHS

* From the **2D** group, select the **Drill** icon.

* In the **Drill Point Selection** dialog box, choose the option **Entities**.

NOTE: This option will let you select the circles we wish to drill.

◆ Select the circles as shown in <u>Figure: 16.0.1</u>.

Figure: 16.0.1

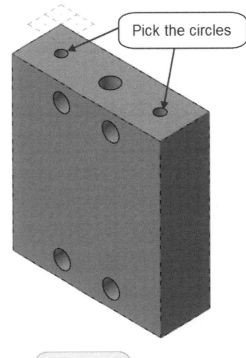

Pick the circles

◆ Click on the **End Selection** button or press **Enter** to finish the selection.

◆ Select the **OK** button in the **Drill Point Selection** dialog box to accept the 2 drill points.

◆ In the **Toolpath Type** page, the **Drill** toolpath will be selected.

Drill   Circle Mill   Point   Helix Bore   Thread Mill

16.1 Select a 5/16" Drill from the Library and set the Tool Parameters

◆ Select **Tool** from the **Tree View list**.

◆ Click on the **Select library tool** button. [Select library tool...]

◆ To be able to see just the **5/16" Drill,** select the **Filter** button.

◆ Under **Tool Types**, select the **None** button and then choose the **Drill** icon.

◆ Under **Tool Diameter,** select **Equal** and enter the value **5/16** as shown in Figure: 16.1.1.

Figure: 16.1.1

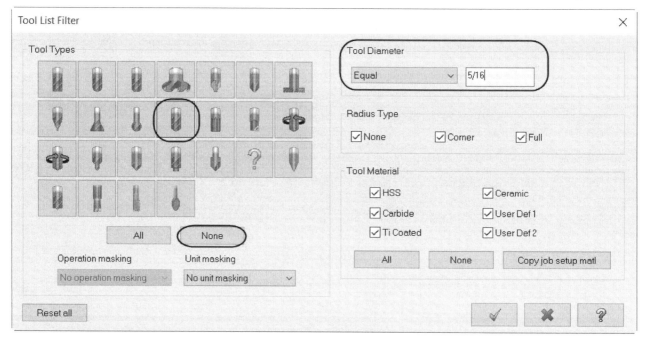

◆ Select the **OK** button to exit the **Tool List Filter** dialog box.

◆ At this point, you should see a **5/16" Drill**.

◆ Select the **5/16" Drill**.

#	Assembly Name	Tool Name	Holder Name	Dia.	Cor. rad.	Length	Type	# Flutes	Ra...
137	–	5/16 DRILL	–	0....	0.0	2.0	Drill	2	No...

◆ Select the tool in the **Tool Selection** page and then choose the **OK** button to exit.

♦ Make the necessary changes to the **Tool** page as shown in Figure: 16.1.2.

Figure: 16.1.2

2D Toolpaths - Drill/Circles Simple drill - no peck ✕

	#	Assembly...	Tool Name	Holder N...	Dia.	Cor. r...	L
	1	–	3/4 FLAT ...	–	0.75	0.0	
	2	–	5/8 FLAT ...	–	0.625	0.0	
	3	–	3/8 FLAT ...	–	0.375	0.0	
	4	–	3/4 SPOT...	–	0.75	0.0	
	5	–	33/64 DRI...	–	0.51...	0.0	
	6	–	9/16-18 T...	–	0.56...	0.0	
	7	–	5/16 DRILL	–	0.3125	0.0	

Toolpath Type
Tool
Holder

Cut Parameters
Linking Parameters
  Tip Comp
  Home / Ref. Points

Planes (WCS)
Coolant
Canned Text
Misc Values
Axis Control
  Axis Combination
  Rotary Axis Control

Tool diameter: 0.3125
Corner radius: 0.0

Tool name: 5/16 DRILL

Tool #: 7   Length offset: 7
Head #: 0   Diameter offset: 7

Spindle direction: CW

Feed rate 4.244173   Spindle speed: 855
FPT: 0.0025   SFM 69.9444
Plunge rate: 4.244173 Retract rate: 4.244173

☐ Force tool change   ☐ Rapid Retract

Quick View Settings

Tool	5/16 DRILL
Tool Diameter	0.3125
Corner Radius	0
Feed Rate	4.24417
Spindle Speed	855
Coolant	Off
Tool Length	3
Length Offset	7
Diameter Offset	7
Cplane / Tpla...	Front
Axis Combinat...	Default (1)
Tip comp	Off

Select library tool...   ☐ Filter Active   Filter...

Right-click for options

Comment
Drill the two 3/8 tap holes.

☐ To batch

✓ = edited
⊘ = disabled

16.2 Set the Cut Parameters

◆ Select **Cut Parameters**, change the drill **Cycle** to **Peck Drill** and input a **Peck** value of **0.25** as shown in Figure: 16.2.1.

Figure: 16.2.1

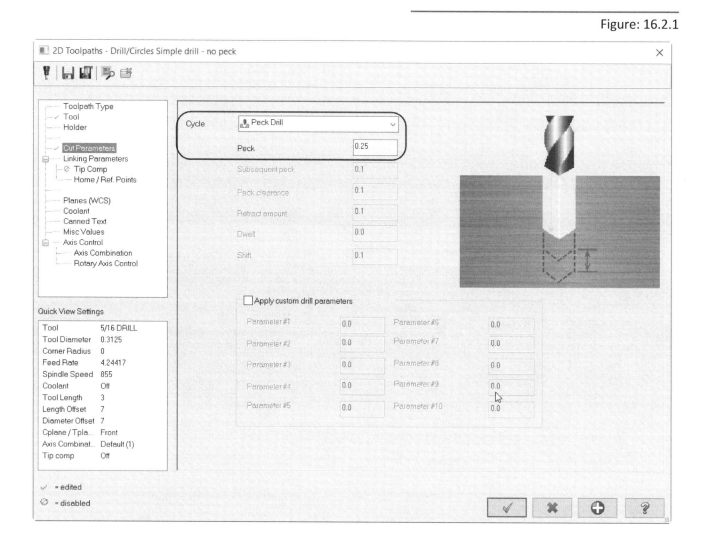

NOTE: For more information regarding the settings found on this page, see **page 556**.

16.3 Set the Linking Parameters

◆ Choose **Linking Parameters** and input a **Depth** value of **-1.25** as shown in <u>Figure: 16.3.1</u>.

Figure: 16.3.1

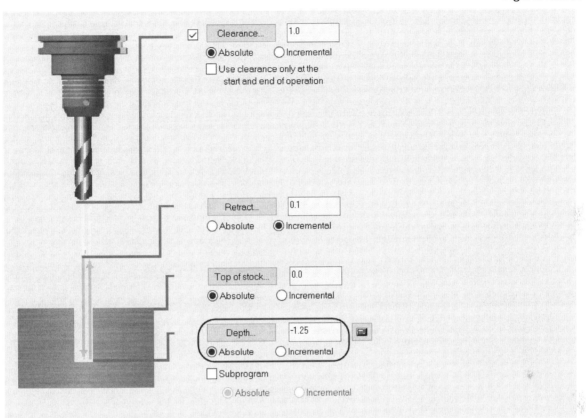

◆ Select **Tip Comp** and ensure this option is disabled.

16.4 Preview the Toolpath

◆ To quickly check how the toolpath will be generated, select the **Preview toolpath** icon as shown.

◆ See **page 157** to review the procedure.
◆ The toolpath should look as shown.

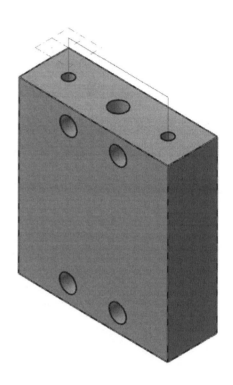

◆ Press **Esc** key to exit the preview.

> **NOTE:** If the toolpath does not look as shown in the preview, check your parameters again.

◆ Select the **OK** button to exit the **2D Toolpaths - Drill/Circles Simple drill - no peck** parameters.

16.5 Backplot and Verify

- To **Backplot** and **Verify** the toolpaths, see **page 518** and **page 519**.
- Use the mouse wheel to rotate the part as shown.

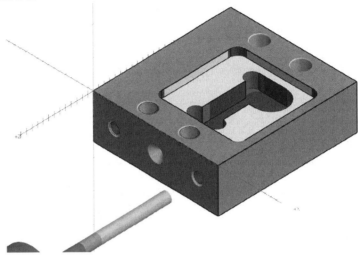

- To go back to the Mastercam window, minimize the **Mastercam Simulator** window as shown.

STEP 17: TAP THE TWO HOLES

Toolpath Preview:

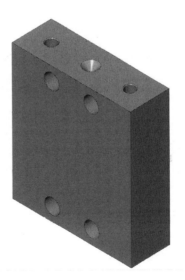

TOOLPATHS

- From the **2D** group, select the **Drill** icon.

• In the **Drill Point Selection** dialog box, choose the option **Entities**.

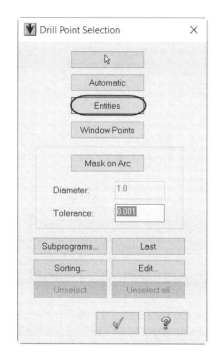

• Select the circles as shown in <u>Figure: 17.0.1</u>.

Figure: 17.0.1

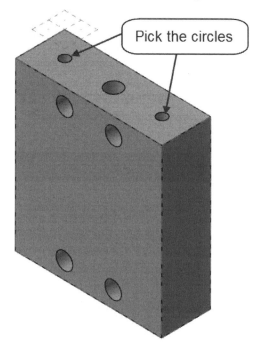

Pick the circles

• Click on the **End Selection** button or press **Enter** to finish the selection.

• Select the **OK** button in the **Drill Point Selection** dialog box to accept the **2 drill points**.

- In the **Toolpath Type** page, the **Drill** toolpath will be selected.

Drill   Circle Mill   Point   Helix Bore   Thread Mill

17.1 Select a 3/8 - 16RH Tap from the Library and set the Tool Parameters

- Select **Tool** from the **Tree View list**.

- Click on the **Select library tool** button. | Select library tool... |
- To be able to see just the **Tap RH drill**, select the **Filter** button.

- Under **Tool Types**, select the **None** button and then choose the **Tap RH** Icon. Under **Tool Diameter,** make sure the **Equal** option is selected and enter the diameter **3/8** as shown in Figure: 17.1.1.

Figure: 17.1.1

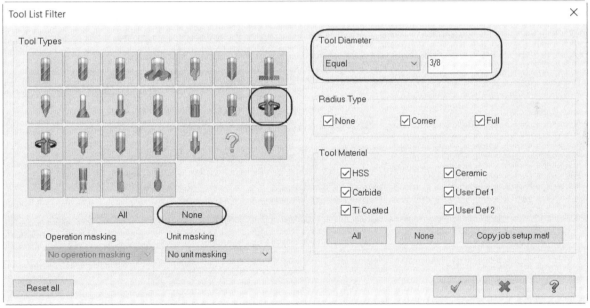

- Select the **OK** button to exit the **Tool List Filter** dialog box.
- From the list, select the **3/8 - 16 Tap RH** as shown in Figure: 17.1.2.

Figure: 17.1.2

#	Assembly Name	Tool Name	Holder Name	Dia.	Cor. rad.	Length	Type	Ra...
223	--	3/8-24 TAPRH	--	0....	0.0	2.0	Ta...	No...
224	--	3/8-16 TAPRH	--	0....	0.0	2.0	Ta...	No...

- Select the tool in the **Tool Selection** page and then choose the **OK** button to exit.

◆ Make the necessary changes to the **Tool** page as shown in <u>Figure: 17.1.3</u>.

Figure: 17.1.3

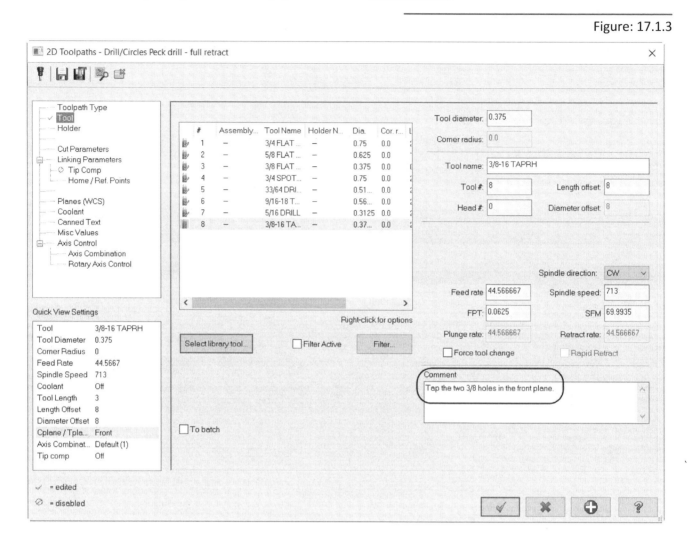

17.2 Set the Cut Parameters

◆ Select **Cut Parameters** from the **Tree View list** and change the drill **Cycle** to **Tap** as shown in <u>Figure: 17.2.1</u>.

Figure: 17.2.1

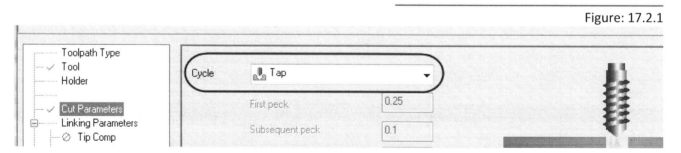

17.3 Set the Linking Parameters

◆ Choose **Linking Parameters** and input a **Depth** of **-1.0** as shown in <u>Figure: 17.3.1</u>.

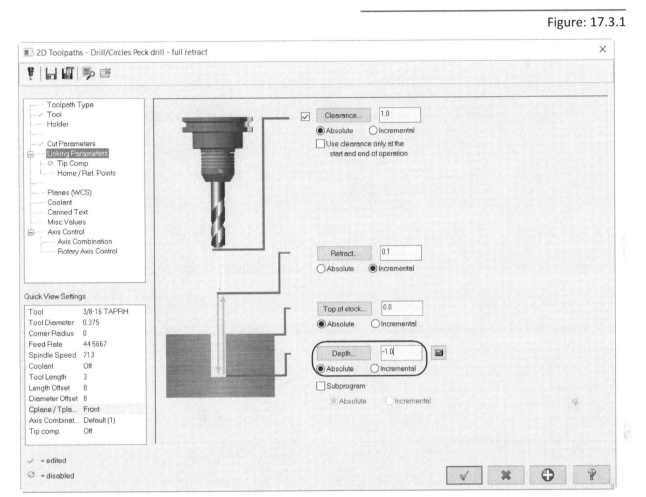

◆ Select **Tip Comp** and ensure this option is disabled. Thus, the **Depth** set in the **Linking Parameters** page is as deep as you would like the tap to go.

17.4 Preview the Toolpath

• To quickly check how the toolpath will be generated, select the **Preview toolpath** icon as shown.

• See **page 157** to review the procedure.
• The toolpath should look as shown.

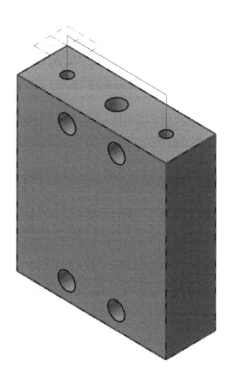

• Press **Esc** key to exit the preview.

> **NOTE:** If the toolpath does not look as shown in the preview, check your parameters again.

• Select the **OK** button to exit the **2D Toolpaths - Drill/Circles Peck drill - full retract** parameters.

• Select the **Regenerate all dirty operations** icon if necessary. ✗

17.5 Backplot and Verify

◆ To **Backplot** and **Verify** the toolpaths, see **page 518** and **page 519**.

◆ To make sure that all toolpaths are selected, choose the **Select all operations** icon.

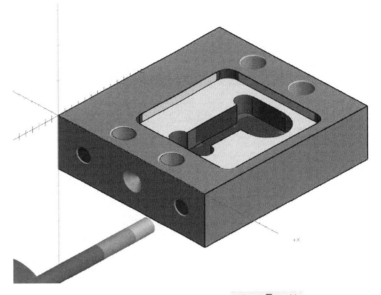

◆ To go back to the Mastercam window, minimize the **Mastercam Simulator** window.

STEP 18: DRILL THE 1/2" HOLE

You will drill the hole to a specific depth.

Toolpath Preview:

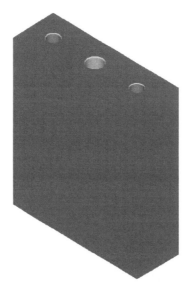

TOOLPATHS

♦ From the **2D** group, select the **Drill** icon.

♦ In the **Drill Point Selection** dialog box, choose the option **Entities** as shown in <u>Figure: 18.0.1</u>.

Figure: 18.0.1

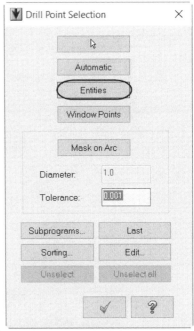

♦ This option will let you select the circles we wish to drill. Pick the circle as shown in <u>Figure: 18.0.2</u>.

Figure: 18.0.2

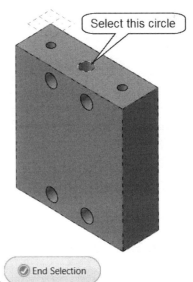

♦ Click on the **End Selection** button or press **Enter** to finish the selection.

♦ Select the **OK** button in the **Drill Point Selection** dialog box to accept the 1 drill point.

♦ In the **Toolpath Type** page, the **Drill** toolpath will be selected.

Drill   Circle Mill   Point   Helix Bore   Thread Mill

18.1 Select a 1/2" Drill from the Library and set the Tool Parameters

◆ Select **Tool** from the **Tree View list**.

◆ Click on **Select library tool** button.

◆ To be able to see just the **1/2" Drill**, select the **Filter** button.

◆ Under **Tool Types**, select the **None** button and then choose the **Drill** icon. Under **Tool Diameter,** select **Equal** and enter the value **0.5** as shown in Figure: 18.1.1.

Figure: 18.1.1

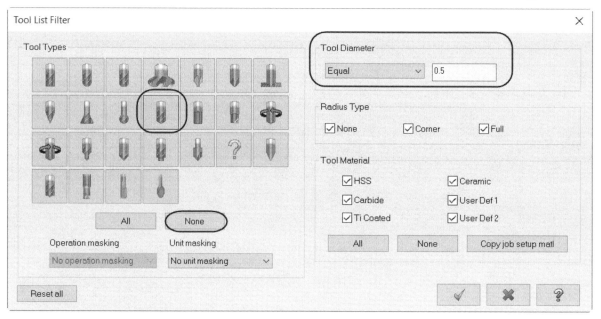

◆ Select the **OK** button to exit the **Tool List Filter** dialog box.

◆ Select the **1/2" Drill** tool.

#	Assembly Name	Tool Name	Holder Name	Dia.	Cor. rad.	Length	# Flutes	Type	Ra...
162	–	1/2 DRILL	–	0.5	0.0	2.0	2	Drill	No...

◆ Select the tool in the **Tool Selection** page and then choose the **OK** button to exit.

♦ Make the necessary changes to the **Tool** page as shown in Figure: 18.1.2.

Figure: 18.1.2

```
2D Toolpaths - Drill/Circles Tapping - feed in, reverse spindle - feed out          ✕
```

Toolpath Type
 Tool
 Holder

 Cut Parameters
 Linking Parameters
  ◇ Tip Comp
   Home / Ref. Points

 Planes (WCS)
 Coolant
 Canned Text
 Misc Values
 Axis Control
  Axis Combination
  Rotary Axis Control

#	Assembly...	Tool Name	Holder N...	Dia.	Cor. r...	L
1	–	3/4 FLAT ...	–	0.75	0.0	
2	–	5/8 FLAT ...	–	0.625	0.0	
3	–	3/8 FLAT ...	–	0.375	0.0	
4	–	3/4 SPOT...	–	0.75	0.0	
5	–	33/64 DRI...	–	0.51...	0.0	
6	–	9/16-18 T...	–	0.56...	0.0	
7	–	5/16 DRILL	–	0.3125	0.0	
8	–	3/8-16 TA...	–	0.37...	0.0	
9	–	1/2 DRILL	–	0.5	0.0	

Tool diameter: 0.5
Corner radius: 0.0
Tool name: 1/2 DRILL
Tool #: 9   Length offset: 9
Head #: 0   Diameter offset: 9

Right-click for options

Spindle direction: CW
Feed rate 4.2784   Spindle speed: 534
FPT: 0.004   SFM 69.8953
Plunge rate: 4.2784   Retract rate: 4.2784

Select library tool...   ☐ Filter Active   Filter...

☐ Force tool change   ☐ Rapid Retract

Comment
Drill the 1/2" hole in the front plane.

☐ To batch

Quick View Settings

Tool	1/2 DRILL
Tool Diameter	0.5
Corner Radius	0
Feed Rate	4.2784
Spindle Speed	534
Coolant	Off
Tool Length	3
Length Offset	9
Diameter Offset	9
Cplane / Tpla...	Front
Axis Combinat...	Default (1)
Tip comp	Off

✓ = edited
⊘ = disabled

18.2 Set the Cut Parameters

◆ Select **Cut Parameters**, change the drill **Cycle** to **Chip Break** and input a **Peck** of **0.25** as shown in Figure: 18.2.1.

Figure: 18.2.1

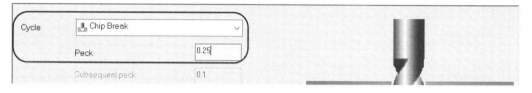

Chip Break retracts partially out of the drilled hole to break the material chips.

18.3 Set the Linking Parameters

◆ Choose **Linking Parameters** and input a **Depth** value of **-0.55** as shown in Figure: 18.3.1.

Figure: 18.3.1

Toolpath Type	
✓ Tool	
Holder	
✓ Cut Parameters	
✓ Linking Parameters	
⊘ Tip Comp	
Home / Ref. Points	
Planes (WCS)	
Coolant	
Canned Text	
Misc Values	
Axis Control	
Axis Combination	
Rotary Axis Control	

☑ Clearance... 1.0
● Absolute ○ Incremental
☐ Use clearance only at the start and end of operation

Retract... 0.1
○ Absolute ● Incremental

Top of stock... 0.0
● Absolute ○ Incremental

Depth... -0.55
● Absolute ○ Incremental
☐ Subprogram
● Absolute ○ Incremental

Quick View Settings

Tool	1/2 DRILL
Tool Diameter	0.5
Corner Radius	0
Feed Rate	4.2784
Spindle Speed	534
Coolant	Off
Tool Length	3
Length Offset	9
Diameter Offset	9
Cplane / Tpla...	Front

◆ Select **Tip Comp** and ensure this option is disabled.

18.4 Preview the Toolpath

♦ To quickly check how the toolpath will be generated, select the **Preview toolpath** icon as shown.

♦ See **page 157** to review the procedure.
♦ The toolpath should look as shown.

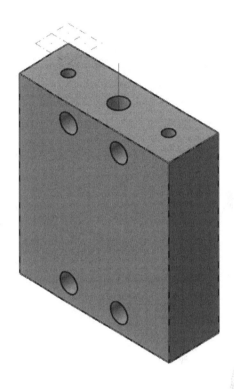

♦ Press **Esc** key to exit the preview.

NOTE: If the toolpath does not look as shown in the preview, check your parameters again.

♦ Select the **OK** button to exit the **2D Toolpaths - Drill/Circles Chip Break - incremental retract**

parameters.

18.5 Backplot and Verify

◆ To **Backplot** and **Verify** the toolpaths, see **page 518** and **page 519**.

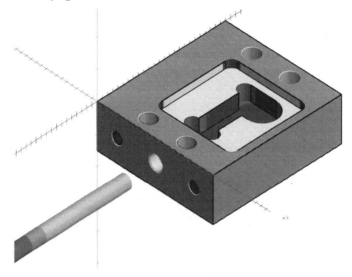

◆ To go back to the Mastercam window, minimize the **Mastercam Simulator** window.

STEP 19: COUNTERBORE THE 1/2" HOLE

In this step you will drill the holes to a specific depth using a **1/2" Flat Endmill** to give you a flat bottom hole.

Toolpath Preview:

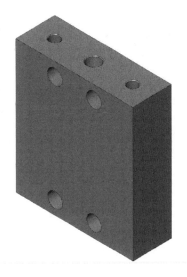

TOOLPATHS

* From the **2D** group, select the **Drill** icon.

* In the **Drill Point Selection** dialog box, choose the option **Entities** as shown in Figure: 19.0.1.

Figure: 19.0.1

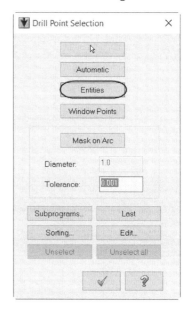

* Select the circle as shown in Figure: 19.0.2.

Figure: 19.0.2

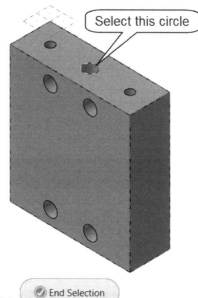

Select this circle

* Click on the **End Selection** button or press **Enter** to finish the selection.

* Select the **OK** button in the **Drill Point Selection** dialog box to accept the 1 drill point.

* In the **Toolpath Type** page, the **Drill** toolpath will be selected.

Drill   Circle Mill   Point   Helix Bore   Thread Mill

19.1 Select a 1/2" Flat Endmill from the Library and set the Tool Parameters

◆ Select **Tool** from the **Tree View list**.

◆ Click on the **Select library tool** button.

◆ To be able to see just the **Flat Endmill**, select the **Filter** button.

◆ Under **Tool Types**, select the **None** button and then choose the **Endmill1 Flat** icon. Under **Tool Diameter** select **Equal** and enter the value **0.5** as shown in Figure: 19.1.1.

Figure: 19.1.1

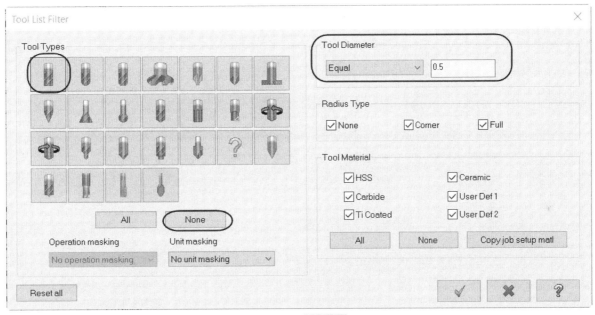

◆ Select the **OK** button to exit the **Tool List Filter** dialog box.

◆ Select the **1/2" Flat Endmill** as shown in Figure: 19.1.2.

Figure: 19.1.2

#	Assembly...	Tool Name	Holder Name	Dia.	Cor. r...	Length	# Flut...	Type	Rad....
290	–	1/2 FLAT ENDMILL	–	0.5	0.0	1.0	4	End...	None

◆ Select the tool in the **Tool Selection** page and then choose the **OK** button to exit.
◆ Make the necessary changes to the **Tool** page as shown in Figure: 19.1.3.

Figure: 19.1.3

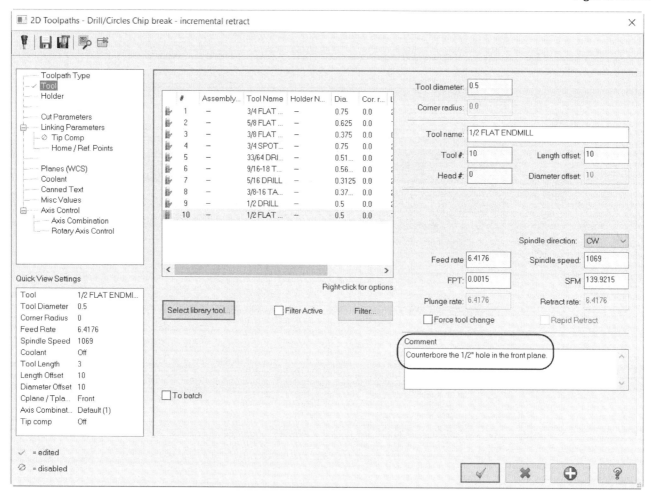

19.2 Set the Cut Parameters

◆ Select **Cut Parameters**, change the drill **Cycle** to **Drill/Counterbore** and input a **Dwell** of **1.0** second as shown in Figure: 19.2.1.

Figure: 19.2.1

19.3 Set the Linking Parameters

◆ Choose **Linking Parameters** and input a **Depth** value of **-0.55** as shown in Figure: 19.3.1.

Figure: 19.3.1

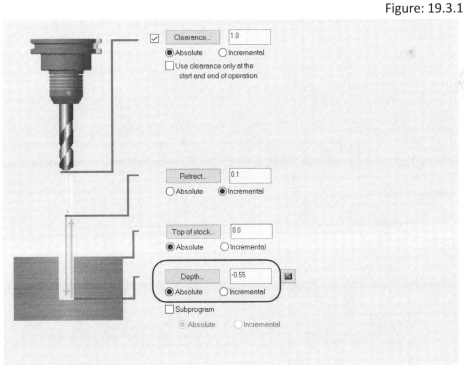

◆ Select **Tip Comp** and ensure this option is disabled.

19.4 Preview the Toolpath

◆ To quickly check how the toolpath will be generated, select the **Preview toolpath** icon as shown.

◆ See **page 157** to review the procedure.
◆ The toolpath should look as shown.

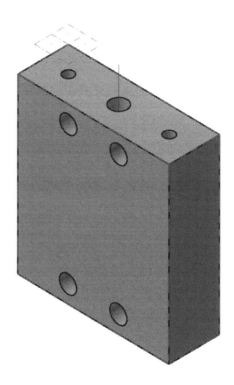

◆ Press **Esc** key to exit the preview.

| **NOTE:** If the toolpath does not look as shown in the preview, check your parameters again.

◆ Select the **OK** button to exit the **2D Toolpaths - Drill/Circles Simple drill - no peck** parameters and generate the

toolpath.

19.5 Backplot and Verify

◆ To **Backplot** and **Verify** the toolpaths, see **page 518** and **page 519**.

◆ To make sure that all toolpaths are selected, choose the **Select all operations** icon.

◆ The part should look as shown.

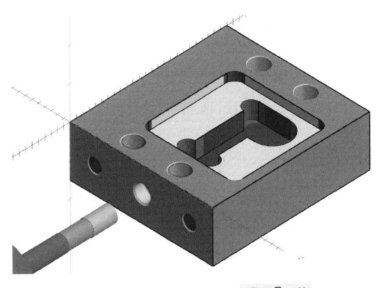

◆ To go back to the Mastercam window, minimize the **Mastercam Simulator** window.

STEP 20: RENAME NC FILE

The Drilling and Tapping operations in "Setup #2 - Front" kept the NC name from Setup #1. We need to rename this operation so it will create a separate program for this setup.

* Select "Setup #2 - Front" (make sure all the operations in Setup #2 are selected).
* Right click on the group, choose the option **Edit selected operations** and then select **Change NC file name**.

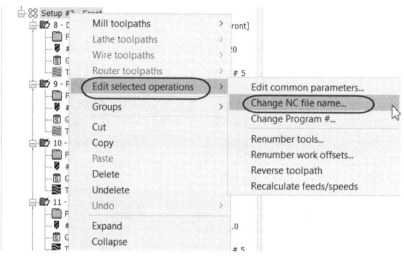

* When the **Enter new NC name** dialog box appears enter **"Setup #2 - Front"**.

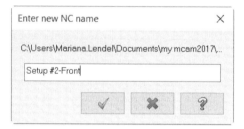

* Select the **OK** button to apply the changed NC name to all the operations in the second setup.

• The result you should see is **Setup #2 - Front.NC** in all of the operations in the second setup.

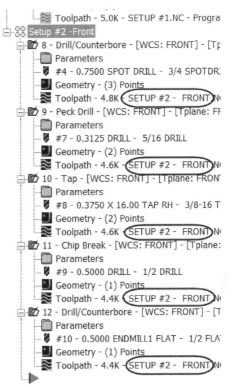

TOOLPATH CREATION - SETUP 3

SUGGESTED FIXTURE:

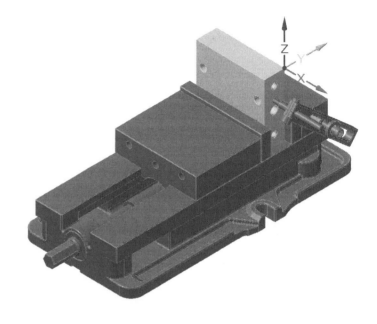

> **NOTE:** The part is now flipped and you will machine the part from the left side.

SETUP SHEET:

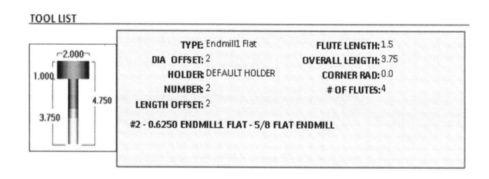

TOOL LIST

TYPE: Endmill1 Flat	**FLUTE LENGTH:** 1.5
DIA OFFSET: 2	**OVERALL LENGTH:** 3.75
HOLDER: DEFAULT HOLDER	**CORNER RAD:** 0.0
NUMBER: 2	**# OF FLUTES:** 4
LENGTH OFFSET: 2	

#2 - 0.6250 ENDMILL1 FLAT - 5/8 FLAT ENDMILL

STEP 21: CREATING AND RENAMING TOOLPATH GROUPS

To machine the part in different setups, you will need to have separate programs. To be able to post the operations separate of each setup, you will create them under different toolpath groups with different NC names.

21.1 Create Toolpath Group #3 (Setup #3 - Left)

◆ Right mouse click on the **Machine Group-1**.
◆ Select **Groups** and then **New Toolpath group** as shown in Figure: 21.1.1.

Figure: 21.1.1

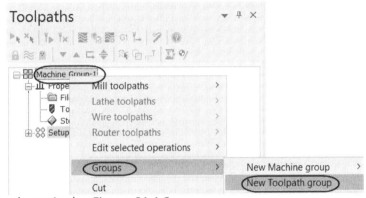

◆ Rename the toolpath group "**Setup #3 - Left**" as shown in the Figure: 21.1.2.

Figure: 21.1.2

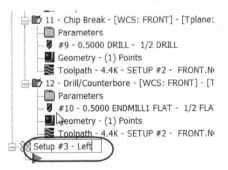

◆ Ensure the arrow is below "**Setup #3 - Left**".

STEP 22: SET THE WCS TO LEFT SIDE

Work coordinate system (WCS) is the active coordinate system in use by Mastercam at any given time. The WCS contains the orientation of the X-Y-Z axes plus the location of the zero point (the origin). This tells Mastercam how your part is positioned or oriented in the machine.

• Select **Planes** tab located in the bottom left corner.

Mill Essentials Training Tutorial   *Mastercam.* 2017

- Select the **Left side** plane and click on the **equal** sign to set the **WCS**, **C**onstruction **Plane** and Tool **Plane** to the **Left side** as shown.

- Right mouse click in the graphics window and select the **Isometric** view to see the part in the new orientation.

- Press **F9** on your keyboard to view the coordinate axes.

◆ Your part should look as shown.

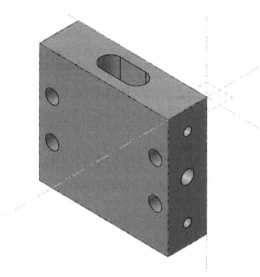

NOTE: The color of the coordinate axes remains the same because it is the same origin.

◆ Press **F9** to remove the axes display.
◆ To open the **Toolpaths Manager**, select the **Toolpaths** tab in the lower left corner of the screen.

STEP 23: MACHINE THE SLOT

Slot Mill efficiently machines obround slots. This toolpath automatically calculates plunge, entry and exit points appropriate for the slots.

Toolpath Preview:

TOOLPATHS

• From the **2D** group, click on the **Expand gallery** arrow and select **Slot Mill**.

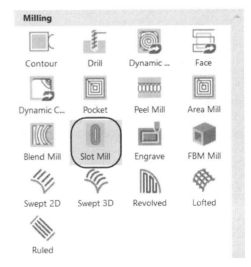

- When the **Chaining** dialog box appears, make sure that the **C-plane** is enabled as shown.

- Select the slot as shown in Figure: 23.0.1.

Figure: 23.0.1

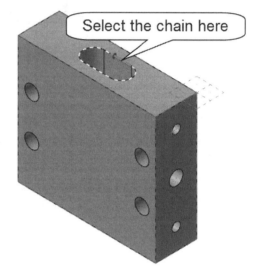

Select the chain here

- Select the **OK** button in the chaining dialog box to continue.
- In the **Toolpath Type** page, the **Slot Mill** toolpath will be selected as shown in Figure: 23.0.2.

Figure: 23.0.2

Contour   Pocket   Facing   Slot Mill

23.1 Select the 5/8" Flat Endmill from the Tool List

♦ Select **Tool** from the **Tree View list**.
♦ Select the **5/8" Flat Endmill** tool from the list.
♦ Make the necessary changes to the **Tool** page as shown in <u>Figure: 23.1.1</u>.

Figure: 23.1.1

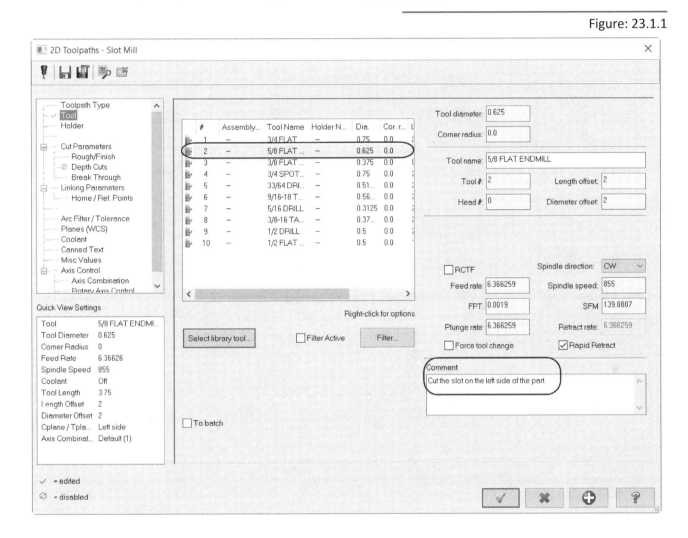

23.2 Set the Cut Parameters

♦ Select **Cut Parameters**, and add an **Overlap** of **0.2** as shown in <u>Figure: 23.2.1</u>.

Figure: 23.2.1

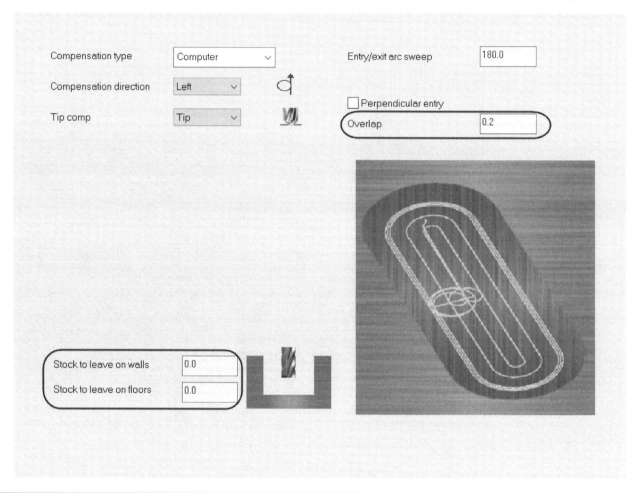

Entry/exit arc sweep sets the included angle of each entry and exit arc. If this value is set to less than 180 degrees, a line will be created.

Overlap sets how far the tool goes past the end of the toolpath before exiting for a cleaner finish.

23.3 Set the Rough/Finish Parameters

◆ Select **Rough/Finish** from the **Tree View list** and ensure your settings appear as shown in <u>Figure: 23.3.1</u>.

Figure: 23.3.1

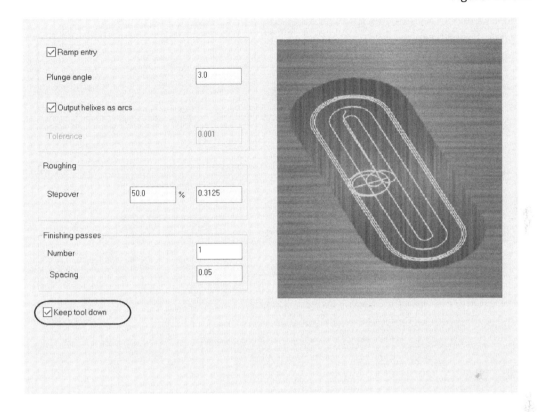

23.4 Set the Depth Cut Parameters

* Select **Depth Cuts** and input a **Max rough step** of **0.2** as shown in <u>Figure: 23.4.1</u>.
* Set the **Finish Cuts** to be **1** and a **Finish step** of **0.05**. Make sure the other parameters appear as shown in <u>Figure: 23.4.1</u>.

> **NOTE:** These settings instruct Mastercam to rough the slot leaving 0.05" and then create one lighter cut removing 0.1" of material for a finish pass.

Figure: 23.4.1

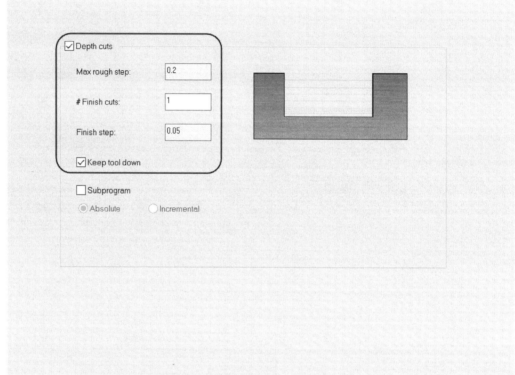

23.5 Set the Linking Parameters

• Select **Linking Parameters**, enable **Clearance**, set it to **1.0**, and input a **Depth** of **-1.0** as shown in <u>Figure: 23.5.1</u>.

Figure: 23.5.1

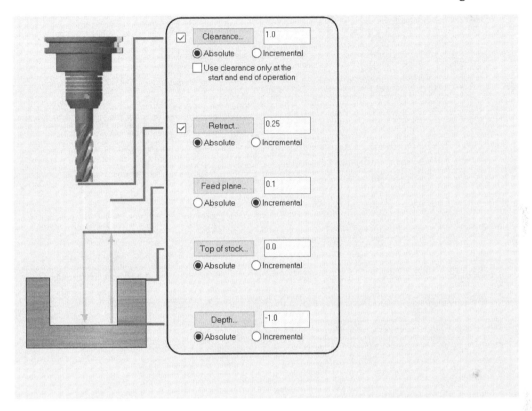

23.6 Preview the Toolpath

♦ To quickly check how the toolpath will be generated, select the **Preview toolpath** icon as shown.

♦ See **page 157** to review the procedure.
♦ The toolpath should look as shown.

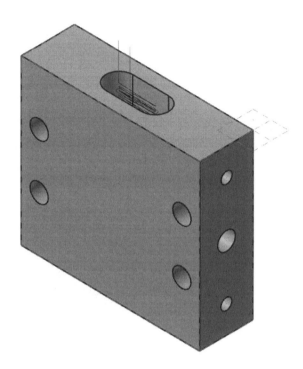

♦ Press **Esc** key to exit the preview.

> **NOTE:** If the toolpath does not look as shown in the preview, check your parameters again.

♦ Select the **OK** button to exit the **2D Toolpaths - Slot Mill** parameters and generate the toolpath.

23.7 Backplot and Verify

◆ To **Backplot** and **Verify** the toolpaths, see **page 518** and **page 519**.

◆ Ensure all operations are selected. If they are not, use the **Select all operations** icon from the **Toolpaths**

   Manager.

◆ The part should look as shown after it is verified.

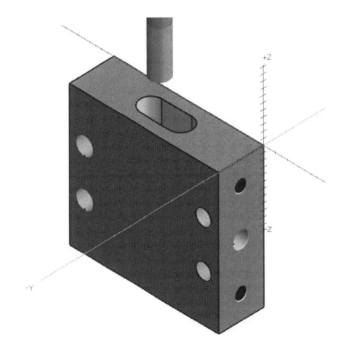

◆ Release the mouse wheel when the part is in the desired position.

◆ To exit the **Mastercam Simulator**, click on the **Close** icon.

STEP 24: RENAME THE NC FILE

The Slot milling operation in "Setup #3 - Left" kept the NC name from "Setup #2 - Front". We need to rename this operation so it will create a separate program for this setup.

♦ Select **"Setup #3 - Left"**, right click on the group (make sure all the operations in Setup #3 are selected), choose the option **Edit selected operations** and then select **Change NC file name** as shown in Figure: 24.0.1.

Figure: 24.0.1

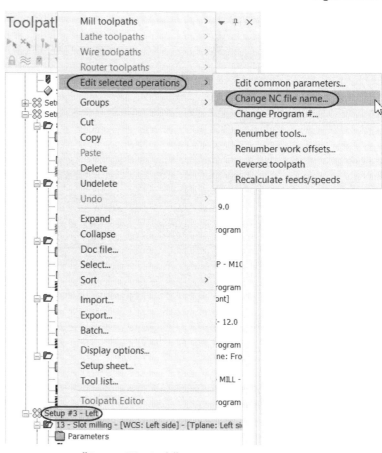

♦ When the **Enter new NC name** dialog box appears, enter **"Setup #3 - Left"**.

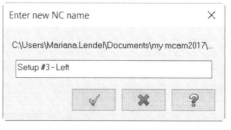

♦ Select the **OK** button to apply the changed **NC name** to all the operations in the third setup.

◆ The result you should see is **Setup #3 - Left.NC** in the last operation in the third setup as shown in Figure: 24.0.2.

Figure: 24.0.2

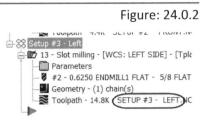

STEP 25: POST THE FILE

◆ Ensure all operations are selected. If they are not, use the button **Select all operations** from the **Toolpaths Manager.**

◆ Select the **Post selected operations** button from the **Toolpaths Manager.** G1

◆ In the **Post processing** window, make the necessary changes as shown in Figure: 25.0.1.

Figure: 25.0.1

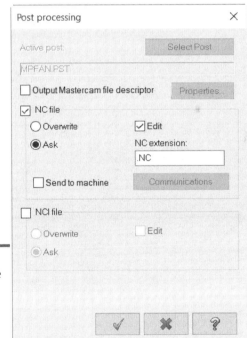

NC file enabled allows you to keep the NC file and to assign the same name as the MCAM file.

Edit enabled allows you to automatically launch the default editor.

◆ Select the **OK** button to continue.
◆ Save your file and name it Setup #1.NC.
◆ Save your file and name it Setup #2 - Front.NC.
◆ Save your file and name it Setup #3 - Left.NC.

♦ A window with **Mastercam Code Expert** will be launched and the NC program will appear as shown in <u>Figure: 25.0.2</u>.

Figure: 25.0.2

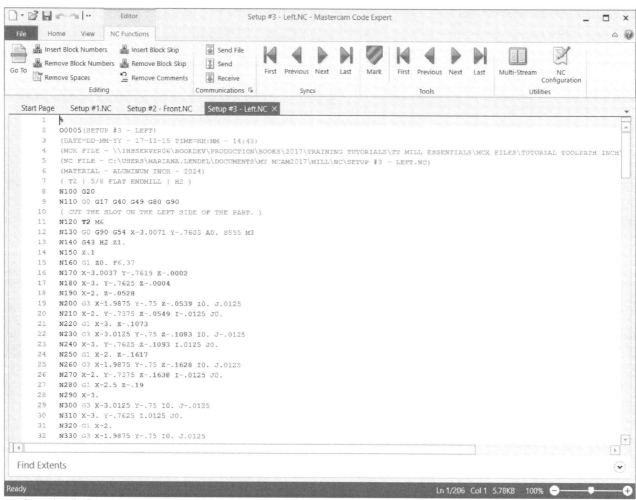

♦ Select the **"X"** box at the upper right corner to exit the editor.

STEP 26: SAVE THE UPDATED MCAM FILE

REVIEW EXERCISE - STUDENT PRACTICE

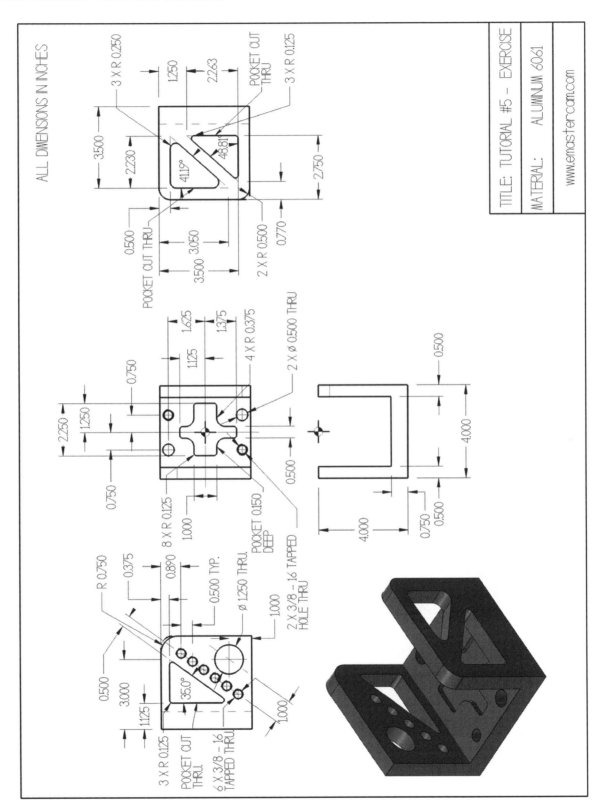

ALL DIMENSIONS IN INCHES

TITLE: TUTORIAL #5 – EXERCISE

MATERIAL: ALUMINUM 6061

www.emastercam.com

3 X R 0.250

1.250

2.263

POCKET CUT THRU

3 X R 0.125

3.500

2.230

41.9°

48.8°

POCKET CUT THRU

0.500

2 X R 0.500

2.750

0.770

3.500   3.050

1.625

1.375

1.125

4 X R 0.375

0.750

2 X Ø 0.500 THRU

2.250

1.250

0.500

0.750

8 X R 0.125

1.000

POCKET 0.150 DEEP

2 X 3/8 – 16 TAPPED HOLE THRU

0.500

4.000

0.750

0.500

4.000

R 0.750

0.375

0.890

0.500 TYP.

Ø 1.250 THRU

1.000

0.500

3.000

35.0°

1.125

1.000

3 X R 0.125

POCKET CUT THRU.

6 X 3/8 – 16 TAPPED THRU

IMPORT THE GEOMETRY FOR TUTORIAL #5 EXERCISE

Download the file from emastercam.com.
* Save the file to a known location.

Use File Open.
* Set the extension to SOLIDWORKS (*.sldprt; *.sldasm;*.slddrw).
* Select Tutorial #5 Exercise.SLDPRT.
* In **Options** enable **Solids**, **Edge curves**, and **Use System Color for imported Solids.**
* Open the file.
* The geometry should look as shown.

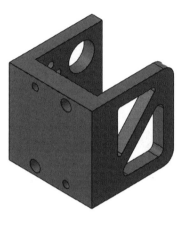

Use Transform Translate to Plane to rotate the part for machining.
* Make a Window around the entire part.
* **Transform.**
* **Translate to Plane.**
* Set the parameters and set the **Source** to **Back** and the **Destination** to **Top** view in the new layout, as shown below.

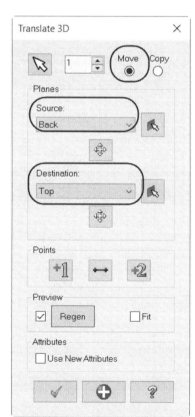

♦ The part should look as shown.

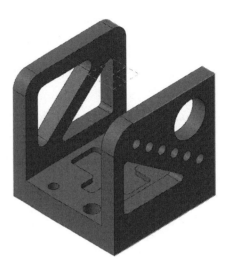

Save the file.
♦ Save the file as "Your Name_5 Exercise".

CREATE THE TOOLPATHS FOR TUTORIAL #5 EXERCISE

Create the Toolpaths for the Tutorial #5 Exercise as per the instructions below.

Select the Mill Default.
Set the machine properties including the stock setup.
• The stock will appear as shown.

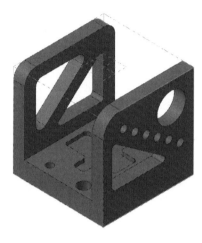

Remove the material in the center of the part using 2D HS Dynamic Mill.
• In **Machining regions**, select the bottom rectangle (enable **C-plane**).
• Enable **From outside**.

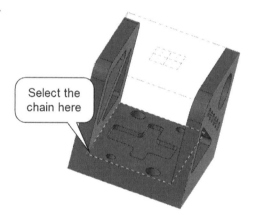

Select the chain here

◆ In **Avoidance regions,** switch in the **Chaining** dialog to **Solids** selection and enable only the **Face** button as shown.

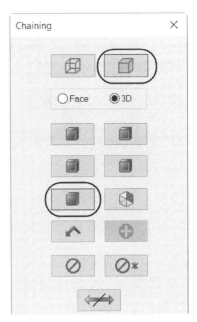

◆ Select the five faces as shown.

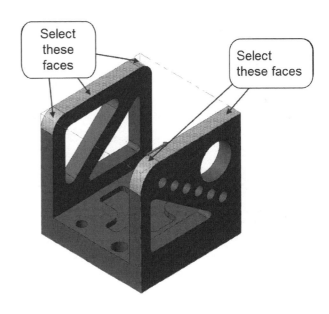

- Use a **1" Flat Endmill**.
- Ensure the **Cutting Method** is set to **Climb**.
- **Approach distance = 1.0.**
- **Stepover = 25%.**
- **Min toolpath radius = 10%.**
- **Gap size % of tool diameter = 100.**
- **Stock to leave on walls = 0.05.**
- **Stock to leave on floors = 0.0.**
- **Depth Cuts** set the **Max rough step = 1.0.**
- Choose an **Entry method Helix**.
- No **Break Through**.
- Set the depth according to the drawing.

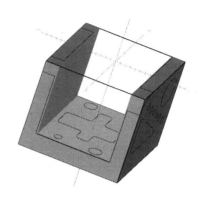

NOTE: Some of these toolpaths will require you to change the default tool's settings. Refer to **page 856** for more information on how to do this.

Change Tool Length.
- Select the tool under Operation #1.
- **Overall length = 6".**
- **Cutting length = 4".**
- Select **Finish**.

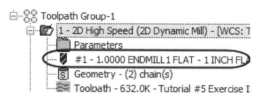

Use Contour toolpath to finish the vertical faces.
- Go back to **Wireframe** mode in the **Chaining** dialog box and use **Single** chain as shown.

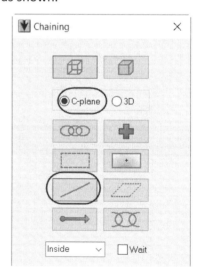

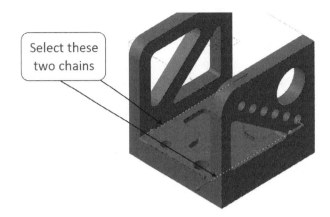

Select these two chains

◆ Select the two lines in the clockwise direction.

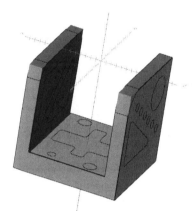

◆ Use a **3/4" Flat Endmill**.
◆ Increase the tool's **Cutting length** to **3.5"**.
◆ **Overall length** = **4"**.
◆ Set the **Compensation direction** to **Right**.
◆ **Depth cuts** set to **Max rough step** of **0.375**.
◆ **Lead In/Out** disable **Entry** and **Exit** and enable **Adjust start/end of contour** setting the **Length** to **Extend 100%**.
◆ Set the **Linking parameters** according to the drawing.

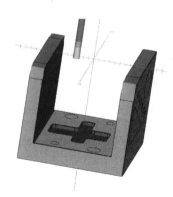

Machine the Pocket.
◆ Use a **1/4" Flat Endmill**
◆ Edit the tool's **Cutting length** to **4"** and the **Overall length** to **4.5"**.
◆ Ensure the **Machining direction** is set to **Climb**.
◆ **Stock to leave on walls/floors** = **0**.
◆ Select a desired **Cutting method**.
◆ Choose an **Entry motion**.
◆ Set the **Finishing** parameters.
◆ Enable **Lead In/Out**.
◆ Disable **Depth Cuts**, and **Break Through**.
◆ Set the **Top of stock** and the **Depth** according to the drawing.

Spot Drill the holes.

* Use a **3/4" Spot Drill.**
* Edit the tool **Cutting length** to **3"** and the **Overall length** to **4".**
* Set the **Drill Cycle** to **Drill/Counterbore.**
* Set the **Top of stock** according to the material.
* Set the **Depth** to leave a **0.05" Chamfer** on all the holes.
* Ensure to change the **Depth** for the two larger holes.

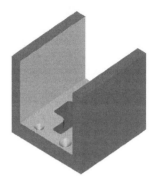

Drill the 1/2" Holes.

* Use a **1/2" Drill.**
* Edit the tool **Cutting length** to **3"** and the **Overall length** to **5".**
* Set the **Drill cycle** to **Drill/Counterbore.**
* Set the **Top of stock** according to the material.
* Set the **Depth** and include **Tip Comp.**

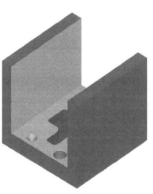

Drill the 3/8 Tapped Holes.

* Use a **5/16" Drill.**
* Edit the tool **Cutting length** to **3"** and the **Overall length** to **5".**
* Set the **Drill Cycle** to **Drill/Counterbore.**
* Set the **Top of stock** according to the material.
* Set the **Depth** and include **Tip Comp.**

Tap the 3/8 - 16 Holes.

* Use a **3/8 - 16NC Tap RH.**
* Edit the tool **Cutting length** to **3"** and the **Overall length** to **5".**
* Set the **Drill Cycle** to **Tap.**
* Set the **Top of stock** according to the material.
* Set the **Depth** and include **Tip Comp.**

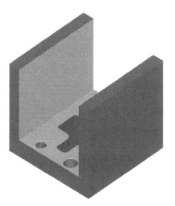

Set the WCS to a new plane defined by existing geometry.
* In the **Planes**, click on the **+** (plus sign) to create a new plane.
* From the list, select **From Geometry** as shown.

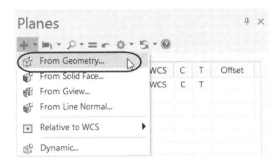

* Press **Alt** + **S** to see the solid in an wireframe mode.

> **NOTE:** You will select two lines that can define the plane.

* [Select an entity]: Select the lines in the order as shown.

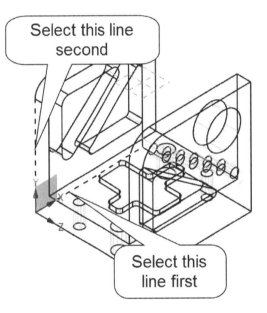

◆ To change the axes orientation from the **Select plane**, click on the **Next plane** button until the orientation looks as shown.

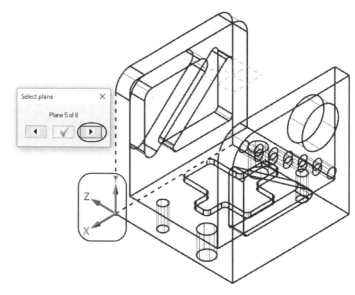

◆ From **Select plane** click on the **OK** button to continue.
◆ Name the plane, and enable **Set as WCS** as shown.

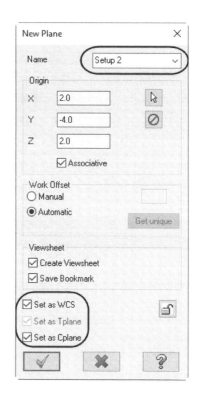

♦ The **Planes Manager** panel should look as shown.

♦ Right mouse click in the graphics window and select Isometric.
♦ Press **F9** to see where the axes and the origin is. The origin should be at the top of the part lower right corner.

Create a new Toolpath Group and rename the NC File name for the last toolpath group.
♦ **Pocket** the two cut through triangles.
♦ Use a **1/4" Flat Endmill**.
♦ **Stock to leave on walls** = **0.0**
♦ You may wish to use the original tool lengths from this point on as we no longer need to machine very deep pockets.

♦ Create a **Contour** toolpath around the two fillets.
♦ Use the **1/4" Flat Endmill**.
♦ Set the **Depth** according to the drawing.

Set the WCS to new plane based on existing geometry.
- Select the lines as shown.
- Select the **Next plane** button until the axes are oriented as shown.
- In the **New Plane** dialog box, change the plane name to **Setup 3** and enable **Set As WCS**.

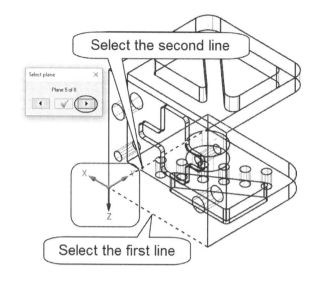

- Change the graphic view to Isometric and press **F9** to check for the **Origin**. It should be at the lower right top corner.

Create a new Toolpath Group and rename the NC File name for the last toolpath group.
- **Pocket** the cut through triangle.
- Use a **1/4" Flat Endmill**.
- **Stock to leave on walls/floors = 0.0**.

- **Drill** the 6 holes.
- Use the **5/16" Drill**.
- Set the **Drill Cycle** to **Drill/Counterbore**.

- **Tap** the 6 holes.
- Use the **3/8 - 16Tap**.
- Set the **Drill Cycle** to **Tap**.

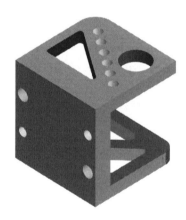

- **Circle Mill** the **1.25"** diameter hole.
- Use a **1/2" Flat Endmill**.
- **Stock to leave on walls/floors = 0.0**.
- Enable **Roughing**.
- Enable **Finishing** and set the **Finish Passes** to **2** with a spacing of **0.02"**.
- Set the depth according to the drawing.

- Create a **Contour** operation to remove the material around the fillet.
- Use a **1/2" Flat Endmill**.

Once complete, your part will appear as shown.

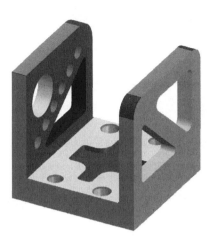

NOTES:

TUTORIAL #5 QUIZ

* What settings do you need to use to remachine a pocket using High Speed Area Mill Toolpath?

* What is the use of WCS in Mastercam?

* After creating a new toolpath group, why do you rename the NC file?

TUTORIAL #6

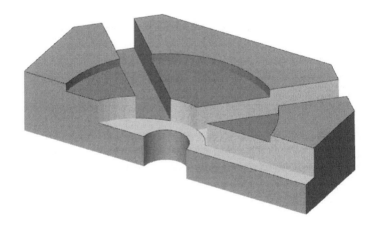

OVERVIEW OF STEPS TAKEN TO CREATE THE FINAL PART:

From Drawing to CAD Model:
- The student should examine the drawing on the following page to understand what part is being created in the tutorial.
- From the drawing we can decide how to create the geometry in Mastercam.

Create the 2D CAD Model used to generate Toolpaths from:
- The student will create the Top 2D geometry needed to create the toolpaths.
- Geometry creation commands such as Rectangle, Circle Center Point, Line Endpoints, and Line Parallel will be used.
- The student will also learn how to clean up the geometry using the trimming functions.

Create the necessary Toolpaths to machine the part:
- The student will set up the stock size to be used and the clamping method to be used.
- A 2D High Speed Dynamic Mill toolpath will be created to remove the material outside of the step.
- A 2D High Speed Mill toolpath will be created to machine the step.
- A 2D High Speed Blend Mill toolpath will be created to machine the semi arc shape pocket.
- Two 2D High Speed Peel Mill toolpaths will be created to machine the two slots.

Backplot and Verify the file:
- The Backplot will be used to simulate a step by step process of the tool's movements.
- The Verify will be used to watch a tool machine the part out of a solid model.

Post Process the file to generate the G-code:
- The student will then post process the file to obtain an NC file containing the necessary code for the machine.

 This tutorial takes approximately two hours to complete.

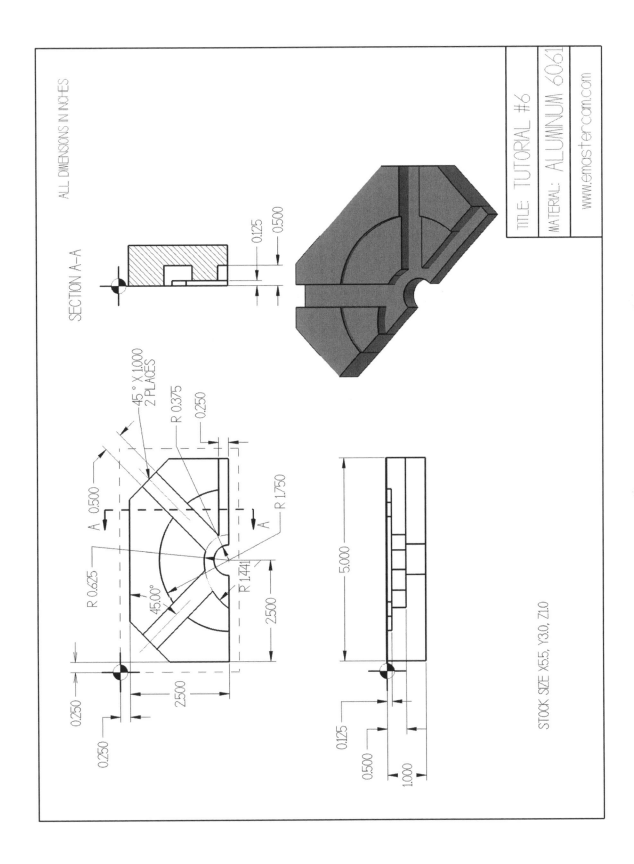

ALL DIMENSIONS IN INCHES

SECTION A-A

0.125
0.500

TITLE: TUTORIAL #6
MATERIAL: ALUMINUM 6061
www.emastercam.com

45° X 1.000
2 PLACES

R 0.375
0.250

A   0.500

R 0.625

R 1.750

45.00°

R 1.441

2.500

2.500

0.250

0.250

5.000

0.125
0.500
1.000

STOCK SIZE X5.5, Y3.0, Z1.0

GEOMETRY CREATION

STEP 1: SETTING UP THE GRAPHICAL USER INTERFACE

Please refer to the **Getting Started** section to set up the graphical user interface.

STEP 2: CREATE RECTANGLES

In this step you will create rectangles using the rectangular command. The rectangle you create will be based on the origin.

Step Preview:

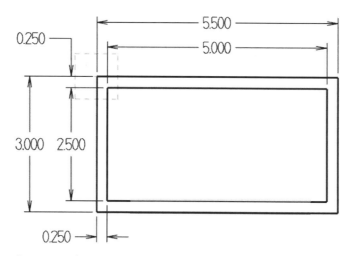

2.1 Create the 5.5" by 3.0" rectangle

WIREFRAME

* From the **Shapes** group, select **Rectangle**.

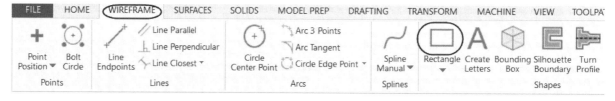

* To select the position of the base point, from the **General Selection** toolbar, click on the drop down arrow next to the **AutoCursor** as shown.

♦ From the fly-out menu, select **Origin**.

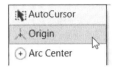

♦ [Select position of second corner]: Select a point to right of the origin and below it as shown in Figure: 2.1.1.

Figure: 2.1.1

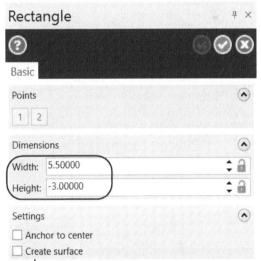

NOTE: You can make this rectangle as small or as large as you want. The entities are still live and therefore you can modify the values to get the size you want.

♦ Enter a **Width** of **5.5** and a **Height** of **-3.0** as shown in Figure: 2.1.2.

Figure: 2.1.2

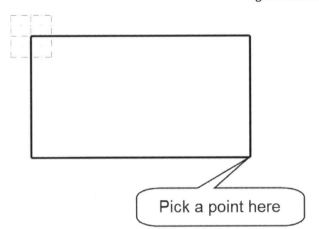

♦ Press **Enter** to finish the rectangle and continue in the same command.

NOTE: While creating the geometry for this tutorial, if you make a mistake, you can undo the last step using the **Undo** icon. ↶ You can undo as many steps as needed. If you delete or undo a step by mistake, just use the **Redo** icon. ↷ To delete unwanted geometry, select the geometry first and then press **Delete** from the keyboard.

◆ Press **Alt** + **F1** to fit the drawing to the graphics window.

2.2 Create the 5.0" by 2.5" rectangle

◆ [Select position of first corner]: Press **Space bar** from the keyboard.
◆ Enter the coordinate values of **0.25, -0.25** as shown.

0.25,-0.25|

◆ Hit **Enter** on your keyboard to set the first position of the corner.
◆ In the **Rectangle** panel, enter a **Width** of **5.0** and a **Height** of **-2.5** as shown.

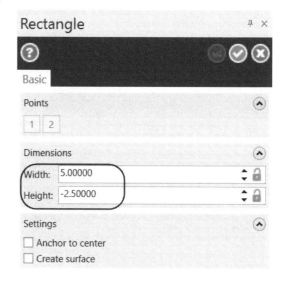

◆ Choose the **OK** button to exit the command.

STEP 3: CREATE CIRCLES AND ARC TANGENT

Create Circle Center Point lets you create circles given the center point and the radius or the diameter.
Create Arc Tangent 1 Entity lets you create an arc given the radius, the entity to which it is tangent and the tangency point.

Step Preview:

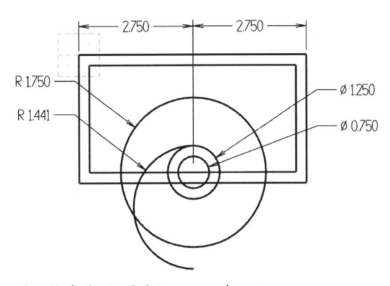

3.1 Create the Circles using Circle Center Point command

WIREFRAME

 ◆ From the **Arcs** group, select **Circle Center Point** as shown.

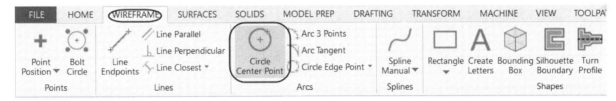

◆ In the **Circle Center Point** panel, enter a **Radius** value of **0.375** as shown. Press **Enter** and the diameter will be updated too.

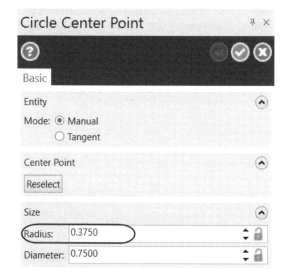

◆ [Enter the center point]: Select the line **Midpoint** as shown in Figure: 3.1.1.

Figure: 3.1.1

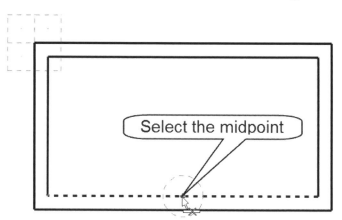

Select the midpoint

◆ Make sure that when selecting the center, the visual cue of the cursor changes as shown.
◆ Press **Enter** to continue.
◆ Change the **Radius** value to **0.625,** press **Enter** and select the same line midpoint.
◆ Press **Enter** to continue.
◆ Change the **Radius** value to **1.75** press **Enter** and select the same line midpoint.

◆ Choose the **OK** button to exit the command.
◆ Press **Alt + F1** to fit the geometry to the graphics window.

• The geometry should look as shown.

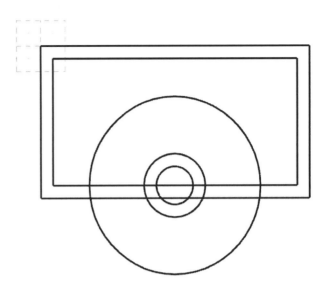

3.2 Create the Arc tangent to an entity

WIREFRAME

• From the **Arcs** group, select **Tangent** as shown.

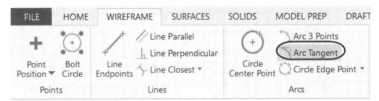

• In the **Arc Tangent** panel, in the **Mode** field, select **Arc one entity** as shown.
• Enter a **Radius** value of **1.441** and press **Enter**.

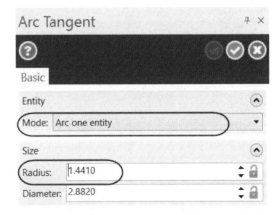

• [Select the entity that the arc is to be tangent to]: Select the arc as shown in Figure: 3.2.1.

Figure: 3.2.1

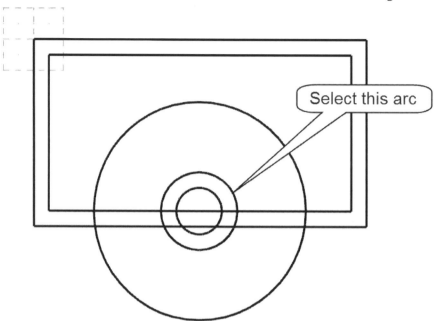

Select this arc

• [Specify the tangent point]: Select the **Quadrant** as shown in Figure: 3.2.2.

Figure: 3.2.2

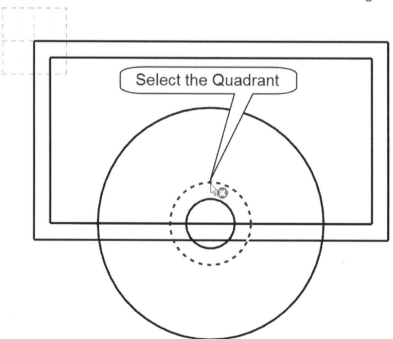

Select the Quadrant

◆ [Select an arc]: Select the arc as shown in <u>Figure: 3.2.3</u>.

Figure: 3.2.3

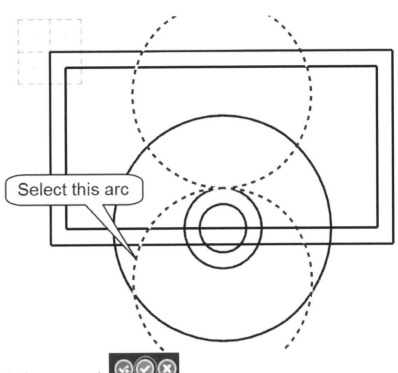

Select this arc

◆ Choose the **OK** button to exit the command.
◆ Press **Alt** + **F1** to fit the geometry to the graphics window.
◆ The geometry should look as shown.

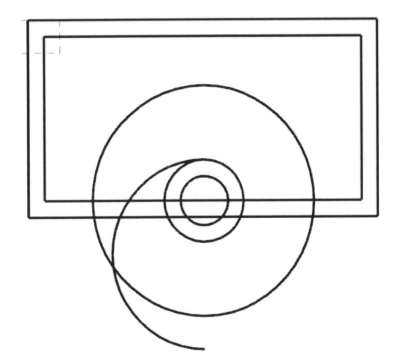

STEP 4: TRIM THE ARCS

Trim to point trims an entity to a point or any defined position in the graphics window. If the point you enter does not lie on the selected entity, Mastercam calculates the closest position on the entity and trims the entity to that point.

Step Preview:

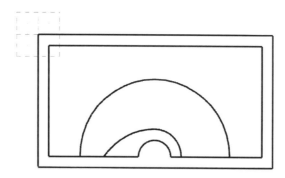

WIREFRAME

* From the **Modify** group, select **Trim Break Extend** as shown.

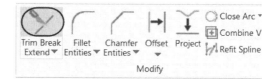

4.1 Trim the entities using Trim to point command

* Enable **Trim to point** in the panel as shown.

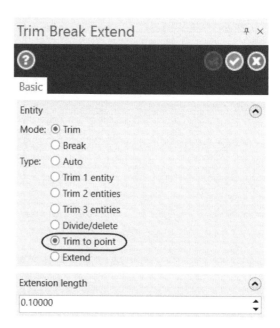

- ◆ [Select the entity to trim/extend]: Select the arc as shown in <u>Figure: 4.1.1</u>.
- ◆ [Indicate the trim/extend location]: Select the Endpoint as shown in <u>Figure: 4.1.1</u>.

Figure: 4.1.1

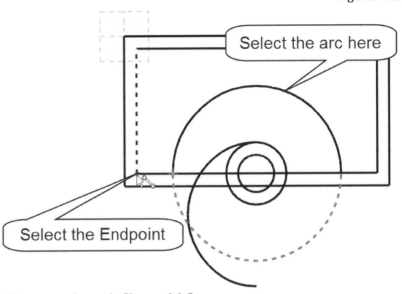

- ◆ [Select the entity to trim/extend]: Select the arc as shown in <u>Figure: 4.1.2</u>.
- ◆ [Indicate the trim/extend location]: Select the Intersection as shown in <u>Figure: 4.1.2</u>.

Figure: 4.1.2

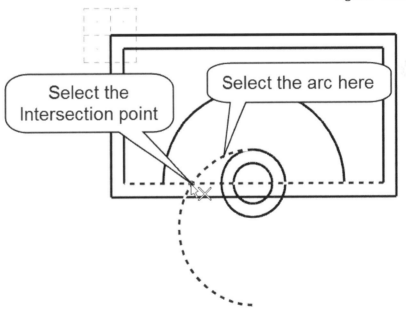

◆ [Select the entity to trim/extend]: Select the 0.375 radius circle as shown in <u>Figure: 4.1.3</u>.

◆ [Indicate the trim/extend location]: Select the Endpoint as shown in <u>Figure: 4.1.3</u>.

Figure: 4.1.3

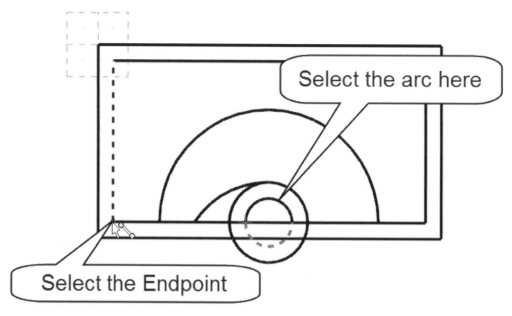

4.2 Trim the entities using Trim two entities

◆ In the **Trim Break Extend** panel, enable **Trim 2 entities** as shown.

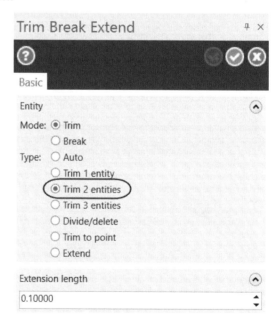

◆ [Select the entity to trim/extend]: Select Entity A as shown in <u>Figure: 4.2.1</u>.
◆ [Select the entity to trim/extend too]: Select Entity B as shown in <u>Figure: 4.2.1</u>.

Figure: 4.2.1

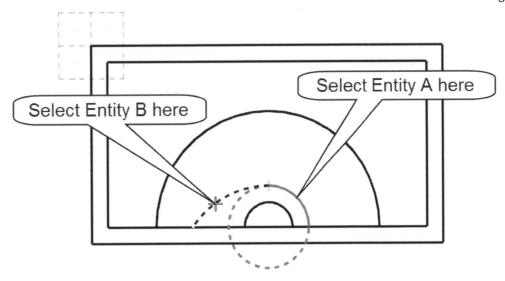

4.3 Trim Entities using Divide/Delete

◆ In the **Trim Break Extend** panel, enable **Divide/delete** as shown.

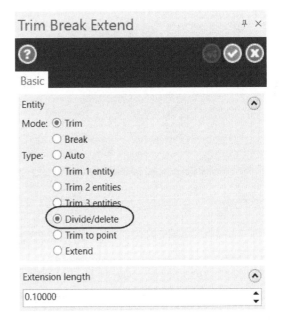

◆ Select the line in between the half circle endpoints as shown in <u>Figure: 4.3.1</u>.

Figure: 4.3.1

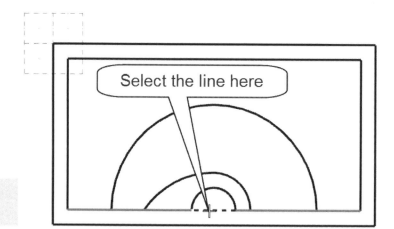

NOTE: Divide/Delete trims a line or arc to the intersection point between it.

◆ Select the **OK** button to exit the **Trim Break Extend** command.
◆ The part will appear as shown.

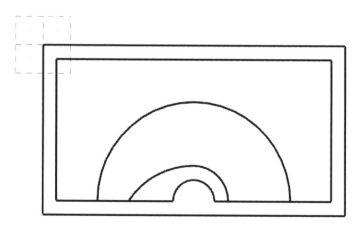

STEP 5: CREATE LINE PARALLEL

In this step you will learn how to create a line parallel given the distance and side on which to create the line.

Step Preview:

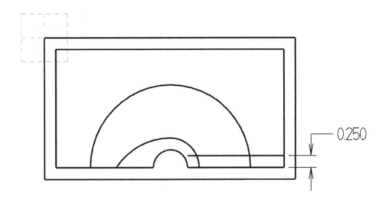

WIREFRAME

♦ From the **Lines** group, select **Line Parallel** as shown.

♦ [Select a line]: Select the line as shown in Figure: 5.0.1.

Figure: 5.0.1

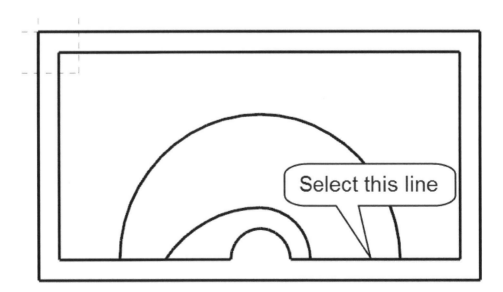

◆ [Select the point to place a parallel line through]: Select a point above that line as shown in <u>Figure: 5.0.2</u>.

Figure: 5.0.2

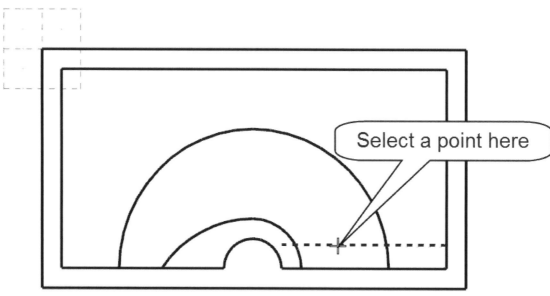

◆ In the **Line Parallel** panel, change the **Distance** to **0.25** as shown.

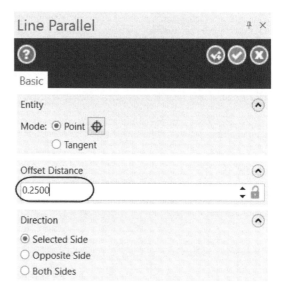

◆ Choose the **OK** button to exit the command.

STEP 6: CREATE CHAMFERS

In this step you will learn how to create a chamfer on two corners of the part. You will create this chamfer given the width and angle.

Step Preview:

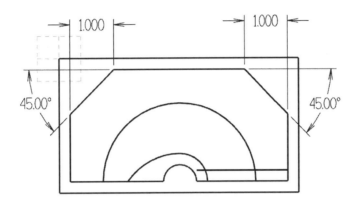

WIREFRAME
* From the **Modify** group, select **Chamfer Entities** as shown.

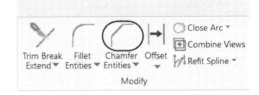

* In the **Chamfer Entities** panel, make sure the **Style** is set to **1 Distance**, the **Distance 1** is set to **1.0** and ensure **Trim entities** is enabled.

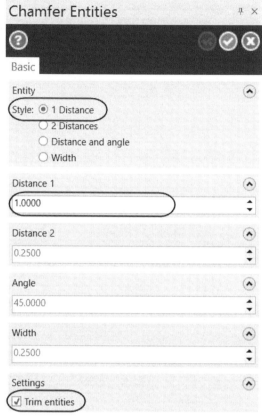

* Select the vertical line and then the horizontal line as shown in Figure: 6.0.1.

Figure: 6.0.1

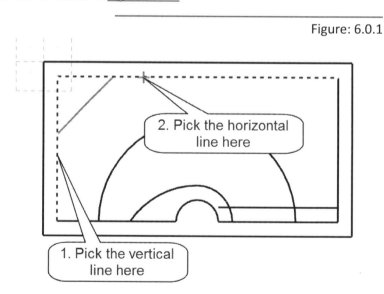

* Repeat this process for the opposite corner.

* Choose the **OK** button to exit the command.

STEP 7: CREATE POLAR LINES

In this step you will learn how to create a line given one endpoint and angle.

Step Preview:

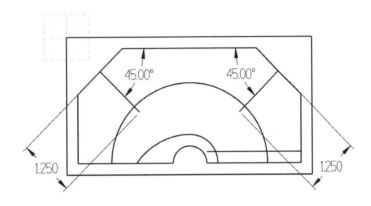

WIREFRAME

• From the **Lines** group, select **Endpoints** as shown.

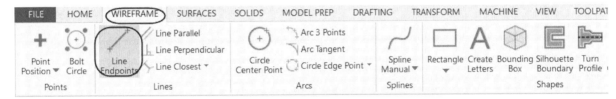

• [Specify the first endpoint]: Select the **Midpoint** of the left chamfer.

• Ensure the **AutoCursor** icon has changed to represent the line midpoint.

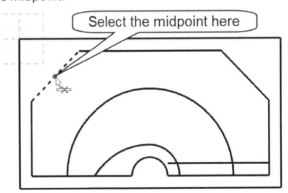

Select the midpoint here

◆ [Specify the second endpoint]: Sketch a line at any angle and any length as shown in <u>Figure: 7.0.1</u>.

Figure: 7.0.1

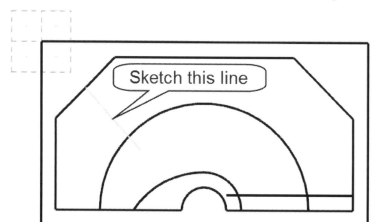

NOTE: At this point the line is still live and can be modified to any angle or length you desire.

◆ In the **Line Endpoints** panel, enter a **Length** of **1.25** and an **Angle** of **-45.0** degrees.

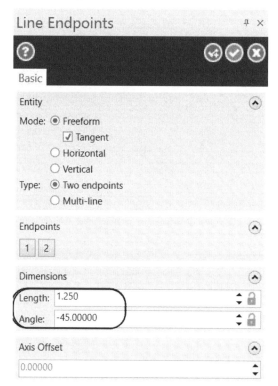

◆ Hit **Enter** on your keyboard to preview the line.
◆ Hit **Enter** again to continue in the same command.
◆ Select the midpoint of the opposite chamfer and sketch a line.

◆ Enter a **Length** of **1.25** and an **Angle** of **270-45.0** degrees as shown.

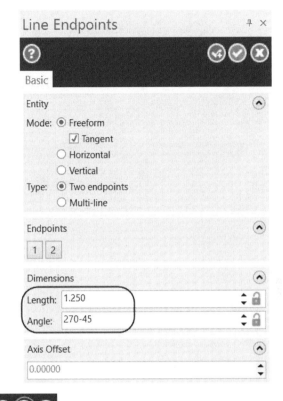

◆ Select the **OK** button to exit the **Line Endpoints** command.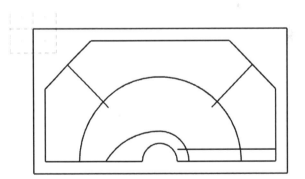
◆ The geometry should look as shown.

STEP 8: CREATE LINE PARALLEL

In this step you will learn how to create a line parallel given the distance and side on which to create the line.

Step Preview:

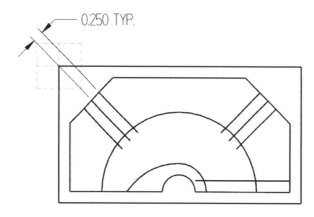

WIREFRAME

* From the **Lines** group, select **Line Parallel** as shown.

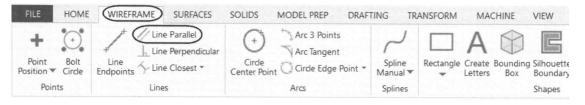

* Select the line as shown in Figure: 8.0.1.

Figure: 8.0.1

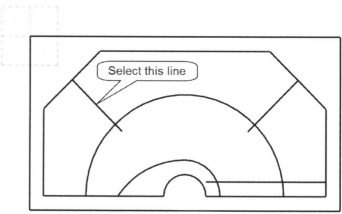

* Select a point on either side of this line.

♦ Input an **Offset Distance** of **0.25,** hit **Enter** on your keyboard and enable **Both sides** as shown.

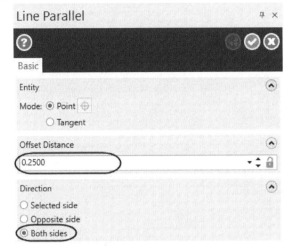

♦ This will position lines on either side of the originally selected entity as shown in <u>Figure: 8.0.2</u>.

Figure: 8.0.2

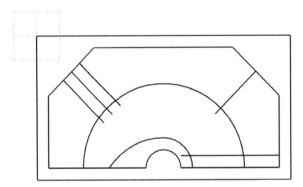

♦ Press **Enter** to continue in the same command and repeat the step for the opposite side of the part.
♦ The geometry should look as shown.

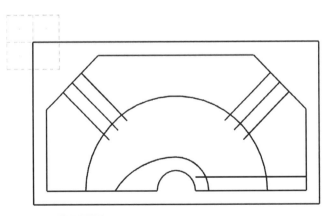

♦ Select the **OK** button to exit the **Line Parallel** command.

STEP 9: DELETE ENTITIES

Step Preview:

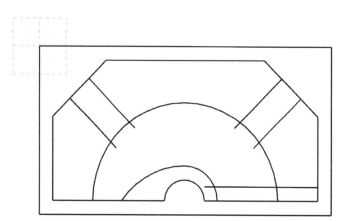

• Select the entities as shown in <u>Figure: 9.0.1</u>. Then press the **Delete** key from the keyboard.

Figure: 9.0.1

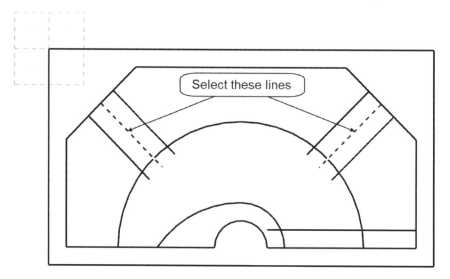

STEP 10: TRIM ENTITIES

To **Trim 1 entity**, select the entity you wish to trim, then select the entity you wish to trim to.

Step Preview:

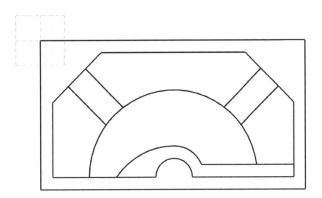

10.1 Trim entities using Trim 1 entity command

WIREFRAME
* From the **Modify** group, select the **Trim Break Extend** icon as shown.

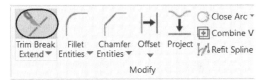

* In the **Trim Break Extend** panel, enable the **Trim 1 entity** as shown.

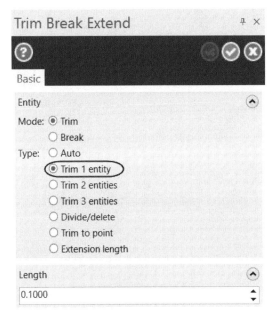

- [Select the entity to trim]: Select the line as shown in <u>Figure: 10.1.1</u>.
- [Select the entity to trim to]: Select the arc as shown in <u>Figure: 10.1.1</u>.

Figure: 10.1.1

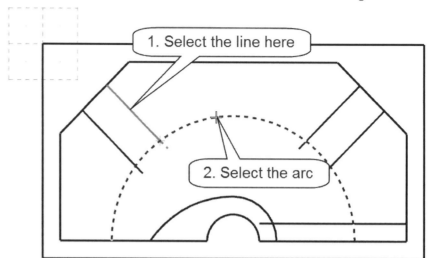

- Repeat the step for the other 4 lines.
- Your part should look as shown.

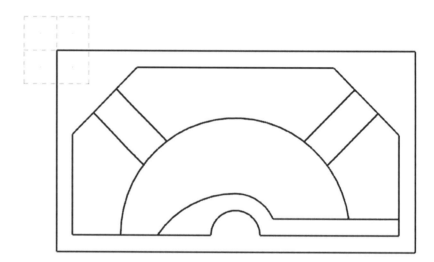

◆ Select the half circle and then select the line as shown in <u>Figure: 10.1.2</u>.

Figure: 10.1.2

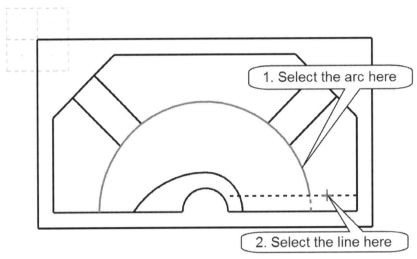

1. Select the arc here

2. Select the line here

10.2 Trim entities using Trim 2 entities

◆ In the **Trim Break Extend** panel, enable **Trim 2 entities** as shown.

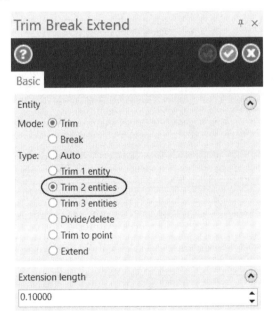

* Select the line and arc as shown in <u>Figure: 10.2.1</u>.

Figure: 10.2.1

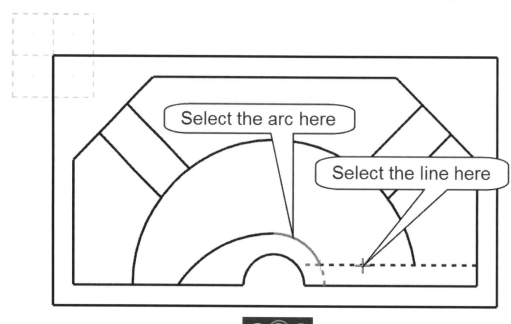

* Select the **OK** button to exit the **Trim Break Extend** command.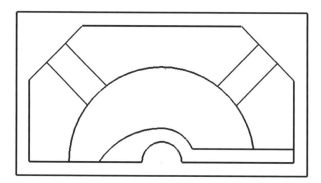
* The part will appear as shown once complete.

STEP 11: SAVE THE FILE

FILE
* **Save As.**

* Click on the **Browse** icon as shown.
* Find a location on the computer to save your file.
* File name: "Your Name_6".

TOOLPATH CREATION

SUGGESTED FIXTURE:

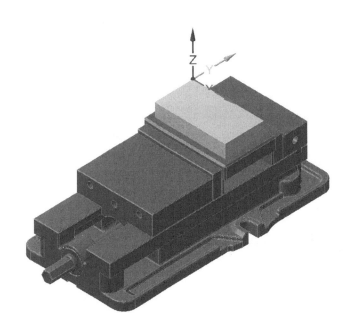

SETUP SHEET:

TOOL LIST

TYPE: Endmill1 Flat	**FLUTE LENGTH:** 1.0
DIA OFFSET: 1	**OVERALL LENGTH:** 3.0
HOLDER: DEFAULT HOLDER	**CORNER RAD:** 0.0
NUMBER: 1	**# OF FLUTES:** 4
LENGTH OFFSET: 1	

#1 - 0.5000 ENDMILL1 FLAT - 1/2 FLAT ENDMILL

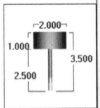

TYPE: Endmill1 Flat	**FLUTE LENGTH:** 0.5
DIA OFFSET: 2	**OVERALL LENGTH:** 2.5
HOLDER: DEFAULT HOLDER	**CORNER RAD:** 0.0
NUMBER: 2	**# OF FLUTES:** 4
LENGTH OFFSET: 2	

#2 - 0.2500 ENDMILL1 FLAT - 1/4 FLAT ENDMILL

STEP 12: SELECT THE MACHINE AND SET UP THE STOCK

In Mastercam, you select a **Machine Definition** before creating any toolpath. The **Machine Definition** is a model of your machine's capabilities and features. It acts like a template for setting up your machine. The machine definition ties together three main components: the schematic model of your machine's components, the control definition that models your control capabilities, and the post processor that will generate the required machine code (G-code). For a Mill Level 1 exercise (2D toolpaths), we just need a basic machine definition.

> **NOTE:** For the purpose of this tutorial, we will be using the **Default Mill** machine.

* Press **Alt + F1** to fit the drawing to the screen.
* From the left side of the graphics window, click on the **Toolpaths** tab as shown.

* Pin the **Toolpaths Manager** by clicking on the **Auto Hide** icon as shown.

12.1 Select the machine

MACHINE
* From the **Machine Type** group, click on the drop down arrow below **Mill** and select the **Default.**

> **NOTE:** Once you select the **Mill Default,** the ribbon bar changes to reflect the toolpaths that could be used with **Mill Default.**

◆ Select the plus sign (+) in front of **Properties** in the **Toolpaths Manager** to expand the **Toolpaths Group Properties.**

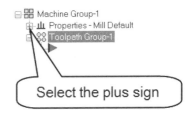

◆ Select **Tool settings** to set the tool parameters.

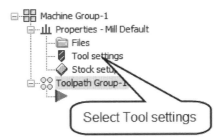

• Change the parameters to match the screen shot as shown in <u>Figure: 12.1.1</u>.

Figure: 12.1.1

Program # is used to enter a number if your machine requires a number for a program name.

Assign tool numbers sequentially allows you to overwrite the tool number from the library with the next available tool number. (First operation tool number 1, Second operation tool number 2, etc.)

Warn of duplicate tool numbers allows you to get a warning if you enter two tools with the same number.

Override defaults with modal values enables the system to keep the values that you enter.

Feed Calculation set **From tool** uses feed rate, plunge rate, retract rate and spindle speed from the tool definition.

◆ Select the **Stock Setup** tab to define the stock.
◆ Select the **Rectangular** shape option.
◆ Select the **All Entities** button and input a **Z** value of **1.0** as shown in <u>Figure: 12.1.2</u>.

Figure: 12.1.2

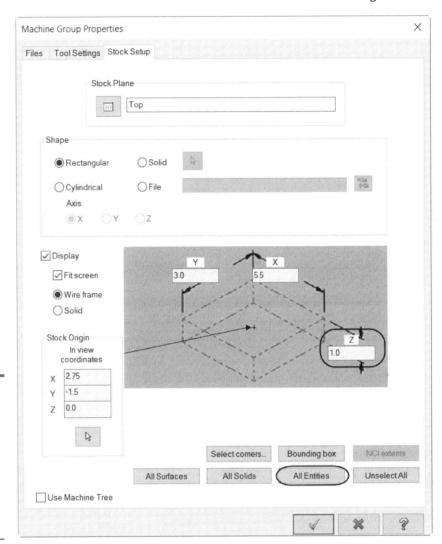

The **Stock Origin** values adjust the positioning of the stock, ensuring that you have an equal amount of extra stock around the finished part.

Display options allows you to set the stock as Wireframe and to fit the stock to the screen. (Fit Screen)

NOTE: The **stock** model that you create can be displayed with the part geometry when viewing the file or the toolpaths, during backplot, or while verifying toolpaths. In the graphics window, the plus sign (+) shows you where the stock origin is. The default position is the middle of the stock.

◆ Select the **OK** button to exit **Machine Group Properties**.

• Right mouse click in the graphics window and select the **Isometric** view to see the stock.

▢	Zoom Window
⊘	Unzoom 80%
⊙	Dynamic Rotation
▦	Fit
⬡	Top (WCS)
⬡	Front (WCS)
⬡	Right (WCS)
⬡	Isometric (WCS)
⟋	Delete Entities
⌐?	Analyze Distance...
⟍?	Analyze Entity Properties...

• Press **Alt + F1** to fit the drawing to the screen.
• The stock model should appear as shown in Figure: 12.1.3.

Figure: 12.1.3

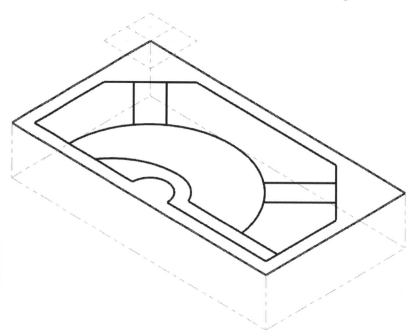

NOTE: The stock is not geometry and cannot be selected.
There will not be a facing toolpath because the stock is already to size.

STEP 13: 2D HIGH SPEED DYNAMIC MILL

2D High Speed Dynamic Mill utilizes the entire flute length of their cutting tools to produce the smoothest, most efficient tool motion for high speed pocketing and core milling. The **Dynamic Mill** toolpath machines pockets, material that other toolpaths left behind, and standing bosses or cores. The toolpath depends on the **Machining strategy** that you choose in the **Chain Options**. If the strategy chosen is **From outside**, the toolpath starts at the outmost chain and moves freely outside of this area; the inner chain defines the limit of the toolpath. You can also machine pockets, in which case the strategy selected is **Start inside**, which keeps the tool inside the machining regions.

Toolpath Preview:

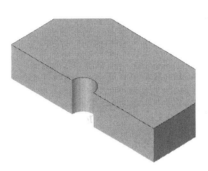

13.1 Break Lines prior to Chaining

> **NOTE:** We are breaking these pieces to be able to select the geometry chains required by the toolpath. This will ensure we cut the correct geometry.

WIREFRAME

- From the **Modify** group, select the drop down arrow below **Trim Break Extend** and select **Break Two Pieces** as shown.

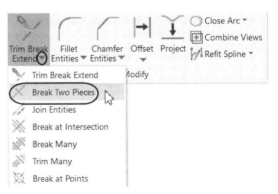

◆ [Select an entity to break]: Select the line as shown in <u>Figure: 13.1.1</u>.

◆ [Indicate the break position]: Select the line Endpoint which is where we want to break the line as shown in <u>Figure: 13.1.1</u>.

Figure: 13.1.1

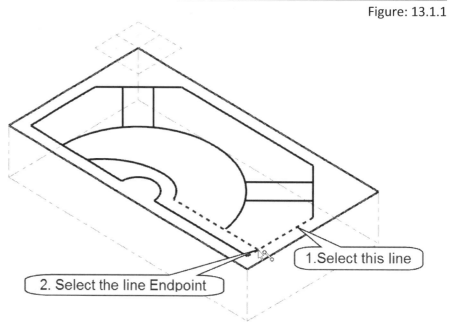

1.Select this line

2. Select the line Endpoint

◆ [Select an entity to break]: Select the line as shown in <u>Figure: 13.1.2</u>.

◆ [Indicate the break position]: Select the endpoint of the arc as shown in <u>Figure: 13.1.2</u>.

Figure: 13.1.2

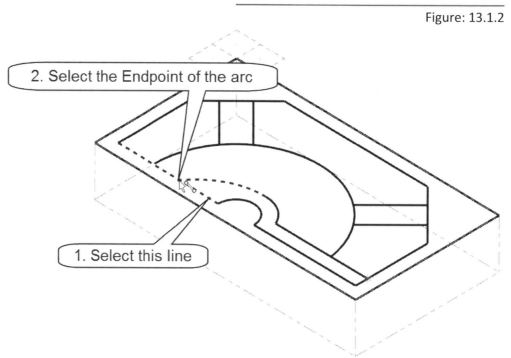

2. Select the Endpoint of the arc

1. Select this line

◆ Press **Esc** key to exit the command.

13.2 Chain Selection

TOOLPATHS

♦ From the **2D** group, select **Dynamic Mill** as shown.

♦ When the new **NC name** panel appears, select the **OK** button to accept the name.

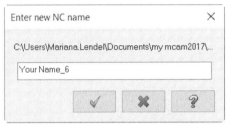

♦ In the **Chain Options**, **Machining region strategy**, enable **From outside** and click on the **Select machining chains** button as shown.

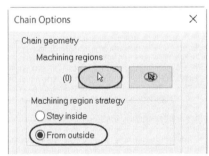

♦ When the **Chaining** dialog box appears, leave the default settings.
♦ [Select 2D HST machining chain 1]: Select the rectangle as shown in Figure: 13.2.1.

Figure: 13.2.1

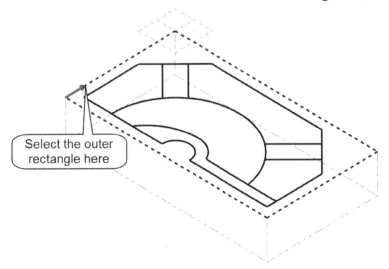

Select the outer rectangle here

* Select the **OK** button to exit the **Chaining** dialog box.
* In the **Chain Options**, **Avoidance regions**, click on the **Select avoidance chains** button as shown.

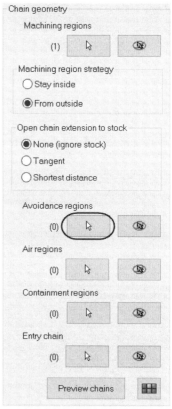

* [Select 2D HST avoidance chain 1]: Select the chain of the part as shown in <u>Figure: 13.2.2</u>.

Figure: 13.2.2

NOTE: The chain will stop at the branch point. A branch point in a chain is the point where the endpoints of three or more entities meet. Branch points indicate where there are different paths that the chain can take. When Mastercam encounters a branch point during chaining, it prompts you to choose the path for the chain to follow.

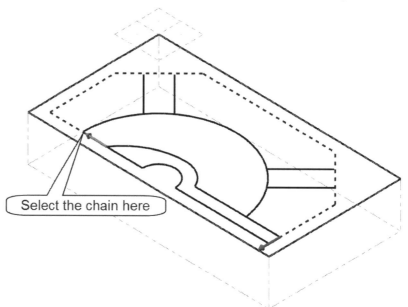

Select the chain here

◆ [Branch point reached]: Select the line past that point to continue the chain as shown in <u>Figure: 13.2.3</u>.

Figure: 13.2.3

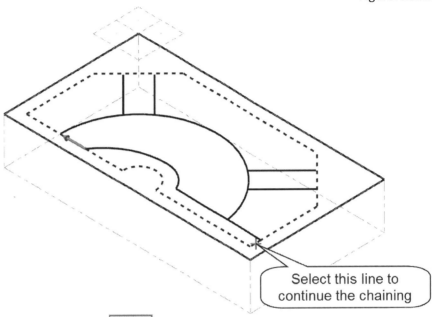

Select this line to
continue the chaining

◆ Select the **OK** button to exit the **Chaining** dialog box.

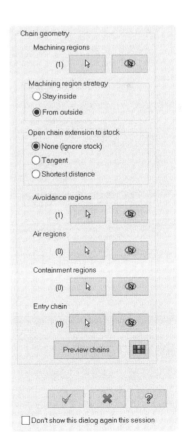

◆ Select the **OK** button to exit the **Chain Options** panel.
◆ In the **Toolpath Type** page, **Dynamic Mill** with **From outside** option should be already selected.

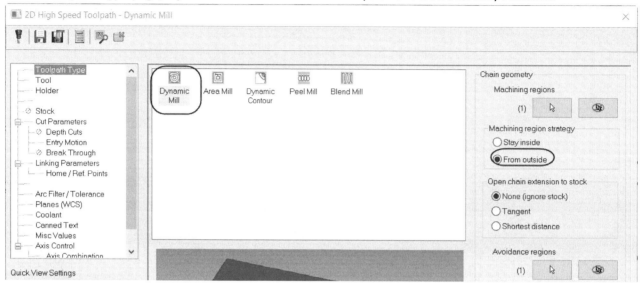

13.3 Preview Chains

The **Preview Chains** function is intended to give the user a quick visual representation of how Mastercam sees the various pieces of geometry that have been selected, how they interact with one another and a general overview of how the toolpath will be calculated with the selections presently made.

◆ Click on the **Color** icon to see the legend for **Preview chains** as shown.

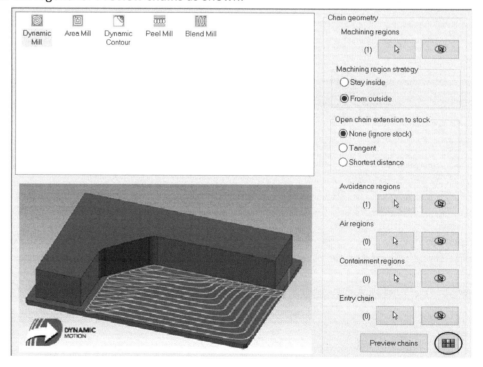

• The **Preview Chains Colors** dialog box should look as shown.

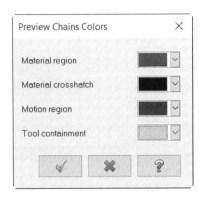

The **Material region** and **Material crosshatch** are the two colors that are used to define the material to be cut. The default colors are red for the background and black for the crosshatch.

The **Motion region** displays the area that Mastercam is making available to the toolpath for motion if it needs it. The color to represent it is dark blue. The primary reason for the display of the entire available (but not necessarily used) Motion region is to help the user visualize how the tool may move near or interact with any adjacent geometry.

The **Tool containment** is what you have selected as the Containment region in the chain geometry. If you have not selected a containment region, it will default to the outside of the Motion region since that is currently the default area the toolpath is being contained to. The color used to represent the Tool containment is yellow.

• Select the **OK** button to exit **Preview Chains Colors**.
• Select the **Preview chains** button as shown.

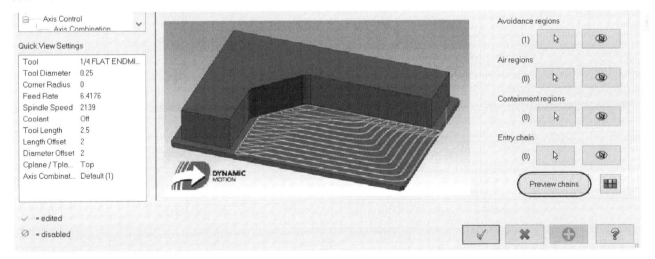

• Select the **Hide dialog** button to see the preview in the graphics window.

◆ The **Preview chains** should look as shown.

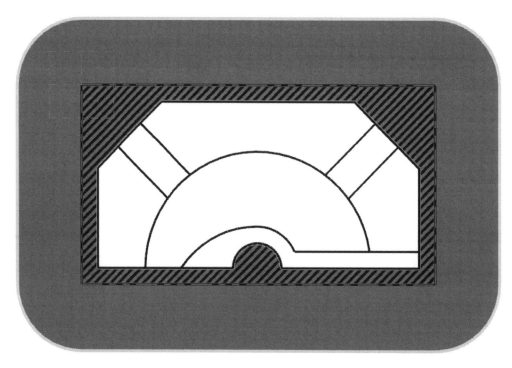

◆ Press **Esc** key to return to the toolpath parameters.
◆ Click on the **Preview chains** button again to clear the Preview chains display.

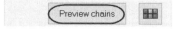

13.4 Select a 1/2" Flat Endmill from the Library and set the Tool Parameters

◆ Select **Tool** from the **Tree View list**.

◆ Click on the **Select library tool** button.
◆ Select the **Filter** button as shown.

◆ Select the **None** button and then under **Tool Types** choose the **Flat Endmill** icon.
◆ Under tool diameter, select **Equal** and input a value of **0.5** as shown in Figure: 13.4.1.

Figure: 13.4.1

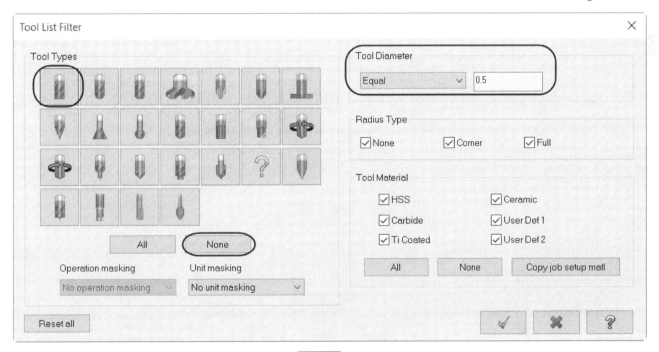

◆ Select the **OK** button to exit the **Tool List Filter.**
◆ In the **Tool Selection** panel you should only see a **1/2" Flat Endmill**.

#	Assembly...	Tool Name	Holder Name	Dia.	Cor. r...	Length	# Flut...	Type	Rad....
290	–	1/2 FLAT ENDMILL	–	0.5	0.0	1.0	4	End...	None

◆ Select the **1/2" Flat Endmill** in the **Tool Selection** page and then select the **OK** button to exit.

◆ Make all the necessary changes as shown in <u>Figure: 13.4.2</u>.

Figure: 13.4.2

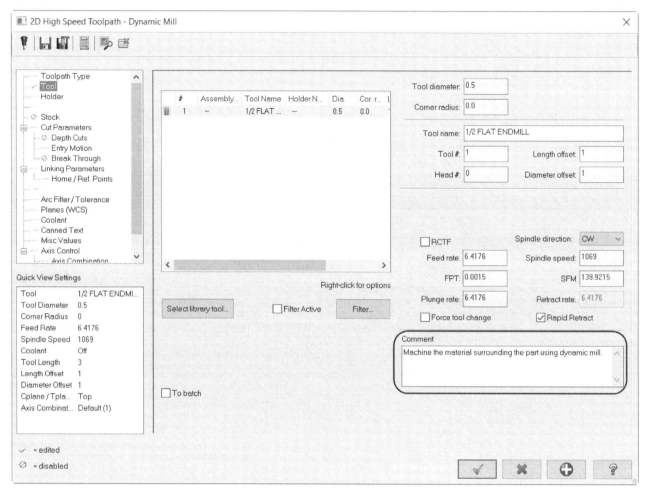

13.5 Set the Cut Parameters

◆ From the **Tree View list**, select **Cut Parameters** and ensure the parameters appear the same as shown in Figure: 13.5.1.

Figure: 13.5.1

Cutting method	Climb
Tip comp	Tip
Approach distance	0.5 Bottom left
First pass offset	0.0
First pass feed reduction	0.0 %
Conventional feed rate	0.0
Stepover	15.0 % 0.075
Min toolpath radius	10.0 % 0.05

Gap size
- ○ Distance   0.5
- ⦿ % of tool diameter   100.0

Motion < Gap size, Micro lift
- Micro lift distance   0.01
- Back feedrate   100.0

Motion > Gap size, retract

Never

Cut order optimization   Material

Stock to leave on walls   0.0

Stock to leave on floors   0.0

13.6 Set the Depth Cuts Parameters

◆ From the **Tree View list**, select **Depth Cuts** and disable **Depth cuts** if needed as shown in <u>Figure: 13.6.1</u>.

Figure: 13.6.1

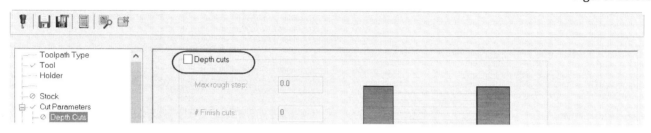

13.7 Set the Entry Motion

◆ From the **Tree View list**, select **Entry Motion**. Set the **Entry method** to **Helix only**. Input a **Helix radius** value of **0.25**, a **Z clearance** value of **0.05** and a **Plunge angle** of **2.0** degrees as shown in <u>Figure: 13.7.1</u>.

Figure: 13.7.1

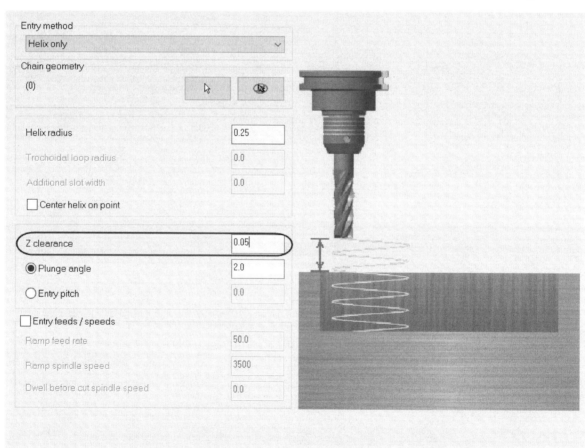

13.8 Set the Linking Parameters

- Select **Linking Parameters,** enable **Clearance**, input a value of **1.0 Absolute** and input a **Depth** value of **-1.0 Absolute** as shown in Figure: 13.8.1.

Figure: 13.8.1

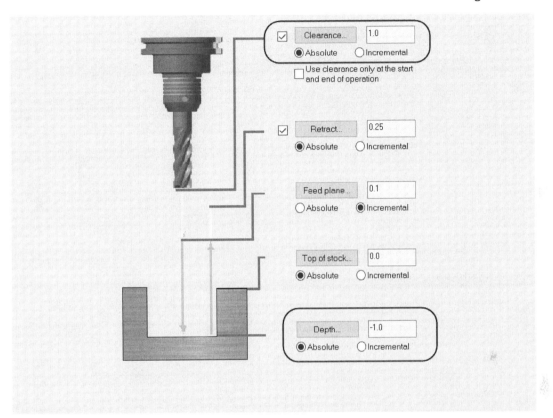

13.9 Preview the Toolpath

♦ To quickly check how the toolpath will be generated, select the **Preview toolpath** icon as shown.

♦ To hide the dialog box, click on the **Hide dialog** icon as shown.

♦ To see the part from an **Isometric** view, right mouse click in the graphics window and select **Isometric** as shown.

▢	Zoom Window
⊖	Unzoom 80%
⟳	Dynamic Rotation
⛶	Fit
⬢	Top (WCS)
⬢	Front (WCS)
⬢	Right (WCS)
⬢	(Isometric (WCS))
╱	Delete Entities
⌊?	Analyze Distance...
⟍?	Analyze Entity Properties...

♦ The toolpath should look as shown.

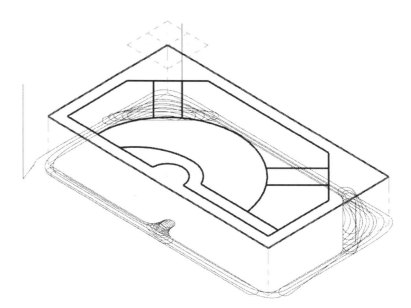

♦ Press **Esc** key to exit the preview.

> **NOTE:** If the toolpath does not look as shown in the preview, check your parameters again.

♦ Select the **OK** button to generate the toolpath.

STEP 14: BACKPLOT THE TOOLPATHS

Backplotting shows the path the tools take to cut the part. This display lets you spot errors in the program before you machine the part. As you backplot toolpaths, Mastercam displays additional information such as the X, Y, and Z coordinates, the path length, the minimum and maximum coordinates, and the cycle time.

◆ Make sure that the toolpaths are selected (signified by the green check mark on the folder icon). If the operation is not selected, choose the **Select all operations** icon.

◆ Select the **Backplot selected operations** button.

◆ Select the **Play** button run **Backplot**.
◆ After **Backplot** is completed, the toolpath should look as shown.

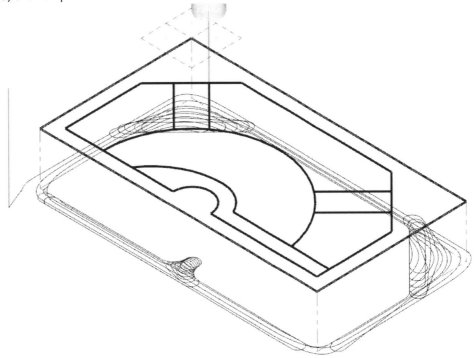

◆ Select the **OK** button to exit **Backplot**.

STEP 15: SIMULATE THE TOOLPATH IN VERIFY

Verify Mode shows the path the tools take to cut the part with material removal. This display lets you spot errors in the program before you machine the part. As you verify toolpaths, Mastercam displays additional information such as the X, Y, and Z coordinates, the path length, the minimum and maximum coordinates and the cycle time. It also shows any collisions between the workpiece and the tool.

• From the **Toolpaths Manager**, select **Verify selected operations** icon as shown.

NOTE: Mastercam launches a new window that allows you to check the part using **Backplot** or **Verify.**

• Select the **Play** button to run **Verify**.

• The part should appear as shown.

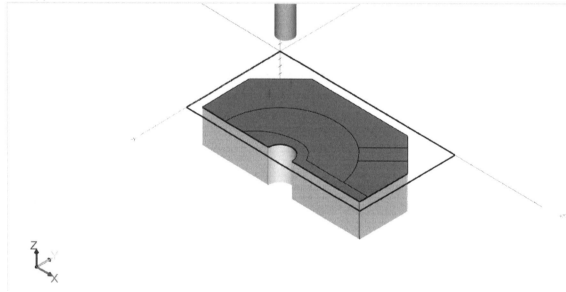

• To go back to the Mastercam window, minimize the **Mastercam Simulator** window as shown.

STEP 16: 2D HIGH SPEED AREA MILL

2D High Speed Area Mill toolpath machines pockets, material that other toolpaths left behind, and standing bosses or cores. Similarly **Dynamic Mill,** based on the **Machining strategy** selected, can generate the free flowing motion needed to machine features such as standing bosses and cores in a single operation. We need to chain the outer boundary of the part to define the machining region, and then chain the inner boundary which will be defined as the avoidance region and will not be machined.

Toolpath Preview:

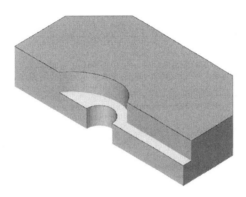

16.1 Chain the Entities

♦ Move the cursor in the **Toolpaths Manager** panel and press **T** to remove the toolpath display.

TOOLPATHS
♦ From the **2D** group, click on the **Expand gallery** icon.

♦ From the **Toolpath Gallery**, select **Area Mill** as shown.

♦ In the **Chain Options**, **Machining regions**, enable **From outside** and click on the **Select machining chains** button as shown.

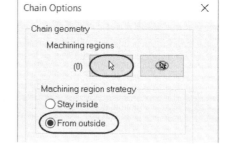

> **NOTE:** The **Machining regions** chain determines where the tool start to machine from.

♦ When the **Chaining** dialog box appears, leave the default settings.

◆ [Select 2D HST machining chain 1]: Select the rectangle as shown in <u>Figure: 16.1.1</u>.

Figure: 16.1.1

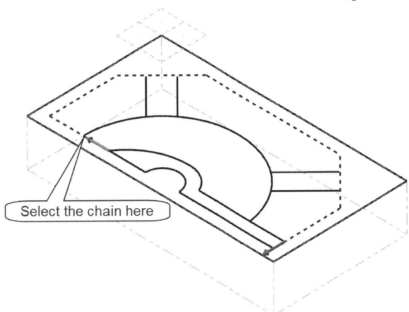

◆ [Branch point reached]: Select the line past that point to continue the chain as shown in <u>Figure: 16.1.2</u>.

Figure: 16.1.2

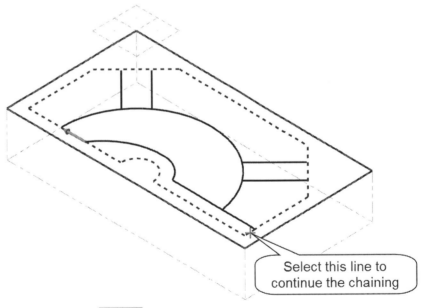

◆ Select the **OK** button to exit the **Chaining** dialog box.

◆ In the **Chain Options**, **Avoidance regions**, click on the **Select avoidance chains** button as shown.

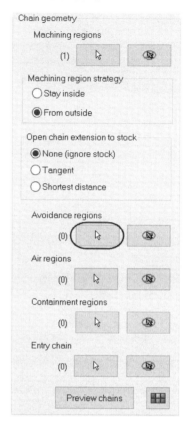

NOTE: The **Avoidance regions** are areas that will be avoided during machining. In our case the chain selected in the **Avoidance regions** is the chain up to where the tool needs to machine the part.

◆ [Select 2D HST avoidance chain 1]: Select the chain of the part as shown in Figure: 16.1.3.

Figure: 16.1.3

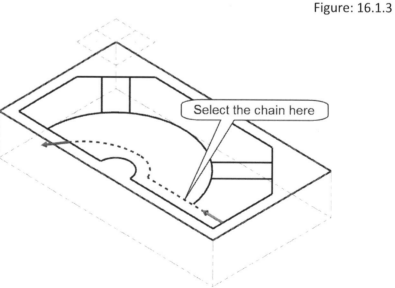

♦ [Branch point reached. Select next branch.]: Select the branch to complete the chain as shown in <u>Figure: 16.1.4</u>.

Figure: 16.1.4

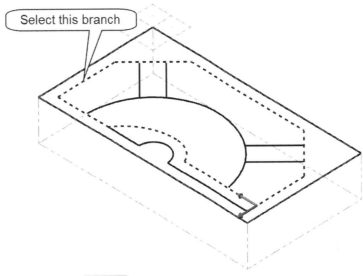

Select this branch

• Select the **OK** button to exit the **Chaining** dialog box.

• Select the **OK** button to exit the **Chain Options** panel.

♦ On the **Toolpath Type** page, **Area Mill** will be selected and **From outside** enabled as shown.

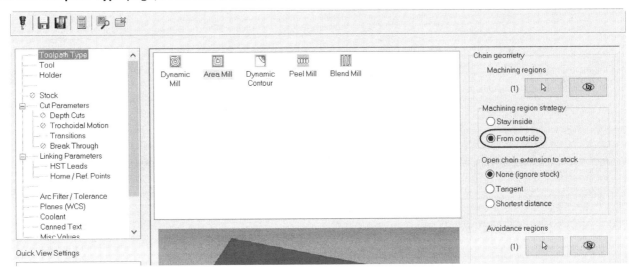

- Select the **Preview chains** button as shown.

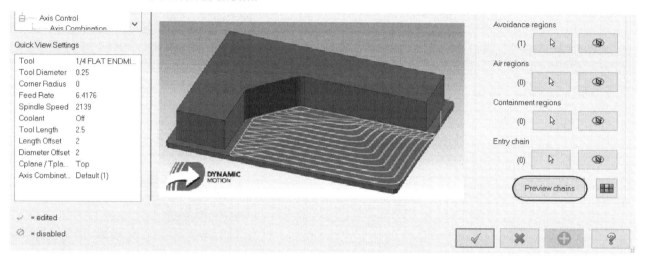

- See **page 164** to review the procedure.
- The **Preview chains** should look as shown.

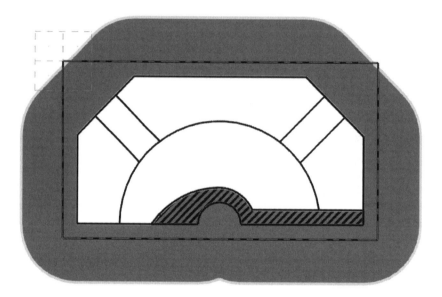

- Press **Esc** key to return to the toolpath parameters.
- Click on the **Preview chains** button again to clear the Preview chains display.

- Select the **Tool** page and make all the necessary changes as shown in <u>Figure: 16.1.5</u>.
- Select the **1/2" Flat Endmill** from the list.

Figure: 16.1.5

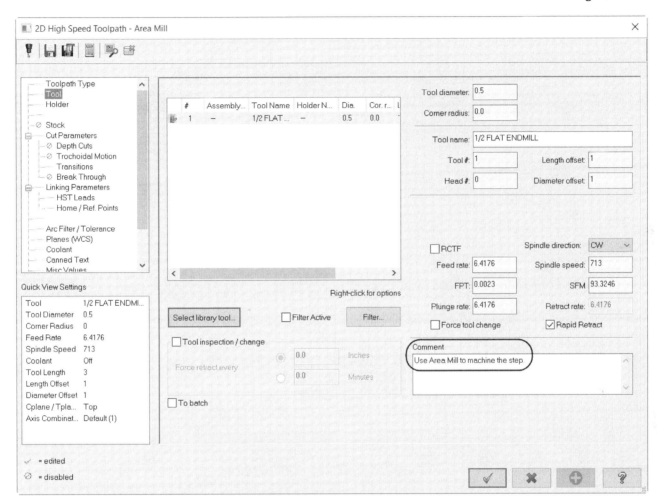

16.2 Set the Cut Parameters

♦ Choose **Cut Parameters** and enable **Corner rounding** as shown in Figure: 16.2.1.

Figure: 16.2.1

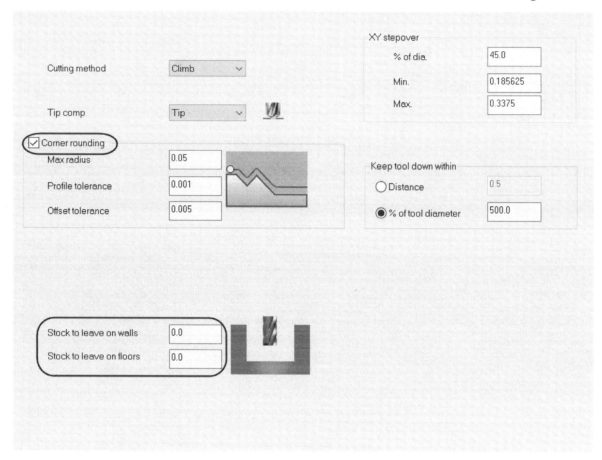

16.3 Set the Depth Cuts Parameters

◆ From the **Tree View list**, select **Depth Cuts**. Enable **Depth cuts** as shown in <u>Figure: 16.3.1</u>.

Figure: 16.3.1

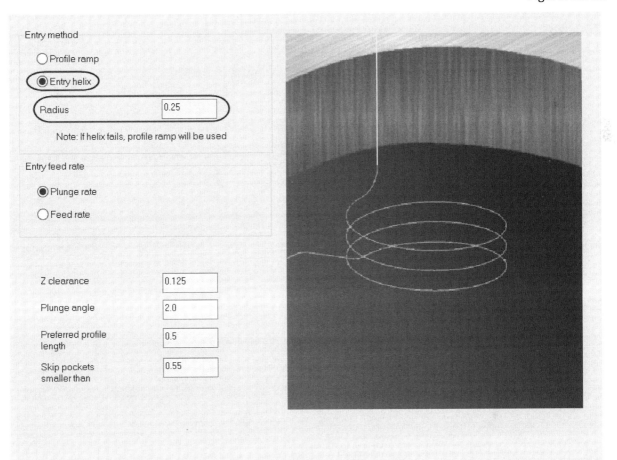

16.4 Set the Transitions

◆ From the **Tree View list**, select **Transitions**. Enable **Entry helix** and enter a **Radius** of **0.25**, as shown in <u>Figure: 16.4.1</u>.

Figure: 16.4.1

16.5 Set the Linking Parameters

♦ Select **Linking Parameters** and input a **Depth** of **-0.5 Absolute** as shown in Figure: 16.5.1.

Figure: 16.5.1

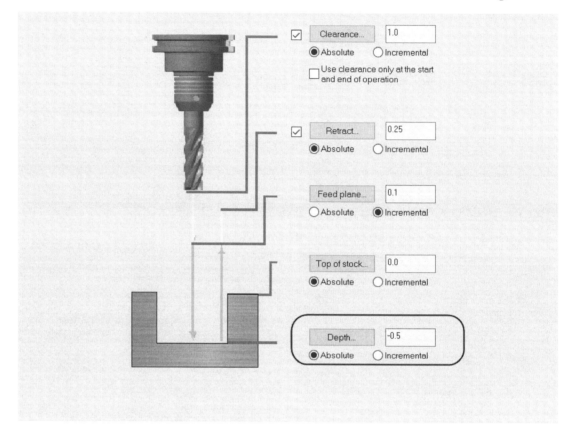

Mill Essentials Training Tutorial   *Mastercam.* 2017

16.6 Preview the Toolpath

◆ To quickly check how the toolpath will be generated, select the **Preview toolpath** icon as shown.

◆ See **page 157** to review the procedure.
◆ The toolpath should look as shown.

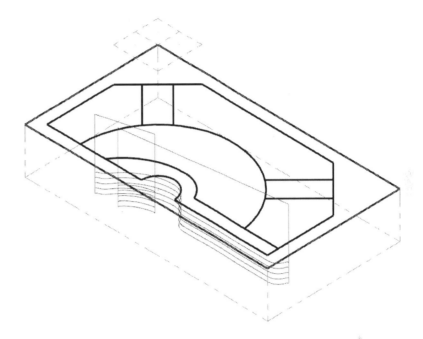

◆ Press **Esc** key to exit the preview.

| **NOTE:** If the toolpath does not look as shown in the preview, check your parameters again.

◆ Select the **OK** button to exit the **2D Area Mill** parameters.

16.7 Backplot the toolpath

♦ See **page 695** to review **Backplot** procedures.

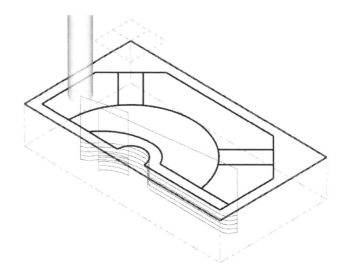

♦ Select the **OK** button to exit **Backplot**.

16.8 Verify both toolpaths

♦ See **page 696** for more info.

♦ To verify all toolpaths, from the **Toolpaths Manager**, choose the **Select all operations** icon.

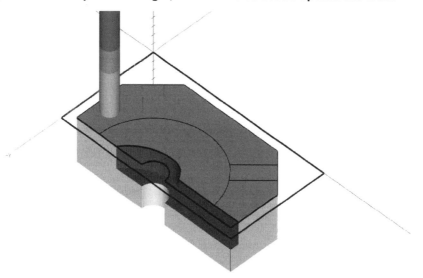

♦ To go back to the Mastercam window, minimize the **Mastercam Simulator** window as shown.
♦ Press **Alt + T** to remove the toolpath display.

STEP 17: 2D HIGH SPEED BLEND MILL

2D High Speed Blend Mill toolpath morphs smoothly between two open chains. You can create the toolpath along or across the selected chains. This machining strategy supports the full depth of cutting, utilizing more of the cutters flute length and resulting in less cycle time and tool wear.

Toolpath Preview:

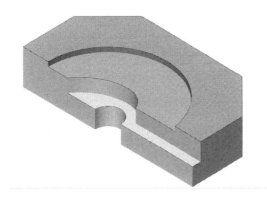

17.1 Chain the Entities

TOOLPATHS

• From the **2D** group, click on the **Expand gallery** icon as shown.

• Select the **Blend Mill** icon as shown.

♦ When the **Chaining** dialog box appears, select the **Single** button.

The **Single** button allows you to select one entity (a single line, arc, or spline) in a chain.

♦ [Blend: define chain 1]: Select the arc as shown in <u>Figure: 17.1.1</u>.

Figure: 17.1.1

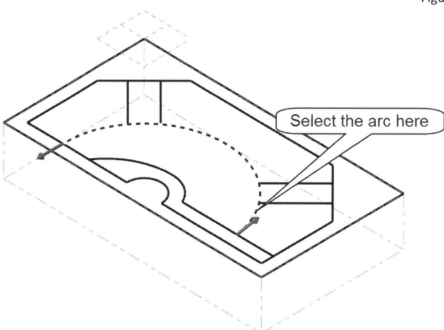

Select the arc here

◆ To chain the second arc, choose the **Partial** chaining method as shown in <u>Figure: 17.1.2</u>.

Figure: 17.1.2

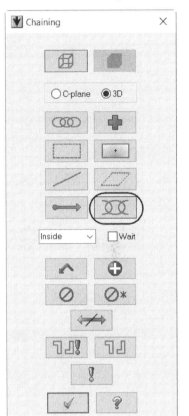

Partial creates an open chain with two mouse clicks. In the graphics window, click on the entity where you want to start the chain, then click where you want to end the chain.

◆ [Blend: define chain 2]: Select Entity A as shown in <u>Figure: 17.1.3</u>.

Figure: 17.1.3

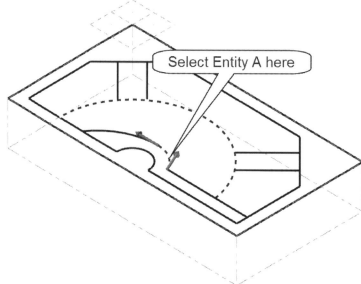

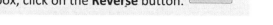

NOTE: Make sure the chain direction is as shown. Otherwise, in the **Chaining** dialog box, click on the **Reverse** button.

◆ [Select the last entity]: Select Entity B as shown in <u>Figure: 17.1.4</u>.

Figure: 17.1.4

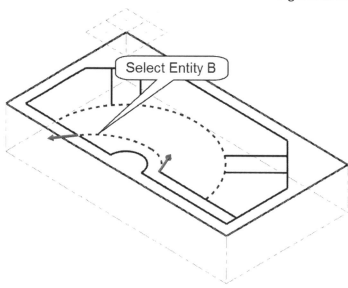

◆ Choose the **OK** button to exit the **Chaining** dialog box.
◆ Select **Toolpath Type** from the **Tree View list** and ensure that **Blend Mill** is enabled.

Dynamic Mill	Area Mill	Dynamic Contour	Peel Mill	Blend Mill

17.2 Select a 1/4" Flat Endmill from the Library and set the Tool Parameters

◆ Select **Tool** from the **Tree View list**.

◆ Click on the **Select library tool** button.

◆ Select the **Filter** button as shown.

◆ Select the **None** button and then under **Tool Types** choose the **Flat Endmill** Icon.

◆ Under **Tool Diameter**, select **Equal** and input a value **0.25** as shown in Figure: 17.2.1.

Figure: 17.2.1

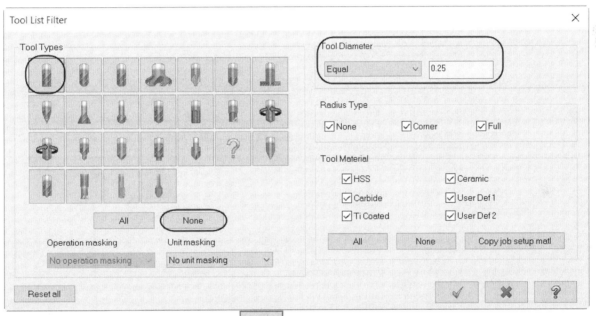

◆ Select the **OK** button to exit the **Tool List Filter.**

◆ In the **Tool Selection** panel you should only see a **1/4" Flat Endmill**.

#	Assembly Name	Tool Name	Holder Name	Dia.	Cor. rad.	Length	# Flutes	Ra..
285	--	1/4 FLAT ENDMILL	--	0....	0.0	0.5	4	No.

◆ Select the **1/4" Flat Endmill** in the **Tool Selection** page and then select the **OK** button to exit.

• Make the necessary changes as shown in Figure: 17.2.2.

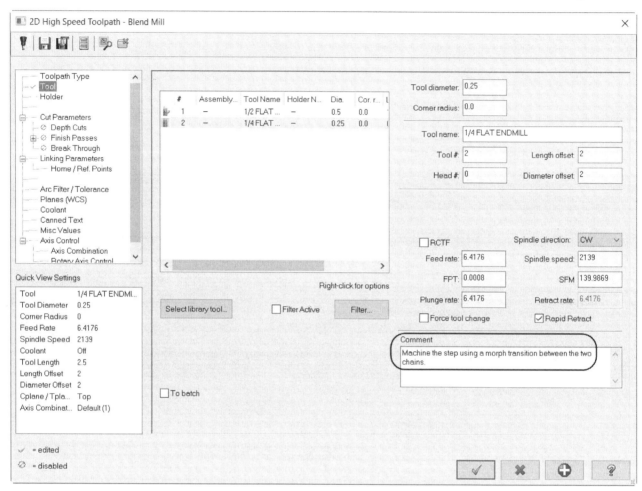

17.3 Set the Cut Parameters

♦ Select **Cut Parameters** from the **Tree View list**.
♦ Set the **Cutting method** to **Zigzag** and **Along** as shown in <u>Figure: 17.3.1</u>. This will start the cut along the first chain and then morph it towards the second chain.
♦ Make any other necessary changes as shown in <u>Figure: 17.3.1</u>.

Figure: 17.3.1

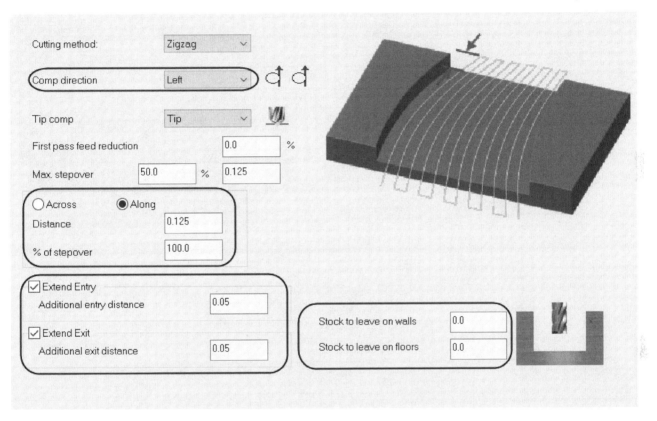

Compensation direction set to **Left** will allow the tool to travel to the left of the selected chains.

Along cuts in the along direction, stepping over in the across direction.

Max Stepover sets the distance between adjacent passes.

Distance/% of stepover sets the spacing between the temporary across moves. These moves are used to generate the final toolpath but are not included in the final toolpath.

17.4 Set Depth Cuts

♦ From the **Tree View list**, select **Depth Cuts** and ensure **Depth cuts** is disabled.

17.5 Finish passes

♦ From the **Tree View list** select **Finish Passes**. Enable **Finish pass** and change the parameters as shown in <u>Figure: 17.5.1</u>

Figure: 17.5.1

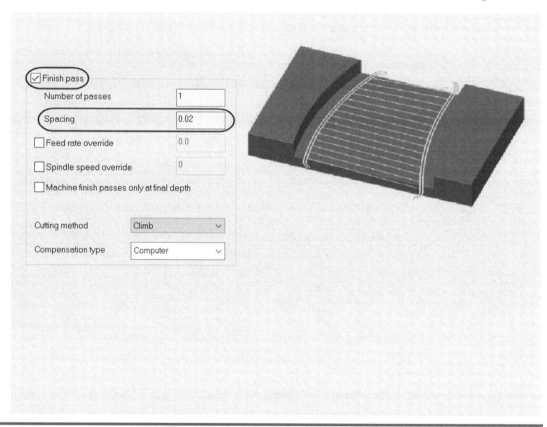

Finish pass page allows you to add finish passes along the selected chains of the toolpath.

Number of passes sets the number of finish passes.

Spacing sets the distance between the finish passes.

Machine finish passes only at final depth performs the finish passes only at the final cutting depth.

17.6 Set the Linking Parameters

◆ Select **Linking Parameters** and enter a **Depth** of **-0.125** as shown in <u>Figure: 17.6.1</u>.

Figure: 17.6.1

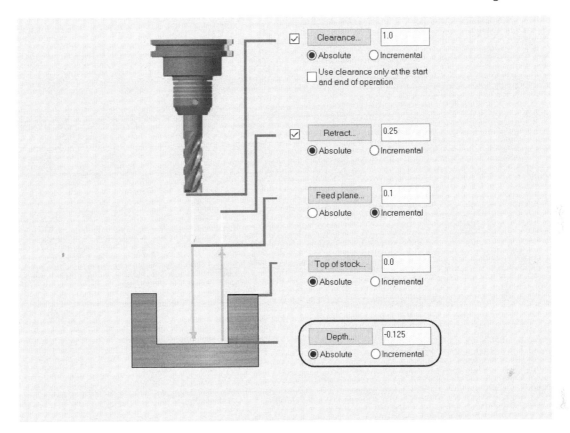

17.7 Preview the Toolpath

◆ To quickly check how the toolpath will be generated, select the **Preview toolpath** icon as shown.

◆ See **page 157** to review the procedure.
◆ The toolpath should look as shown.

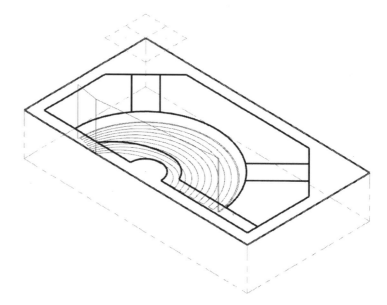

◆ Press **Esc** key to exit the preview.

> **NOTE:** If the toolpath does not look as shown in the preview, check your parameters again.

◆ Choose the **OK** button to generate the toolpath.

17.8 Backplot the toolpath

♦ **Backplot** the toolpath. See **page 695** for more information.

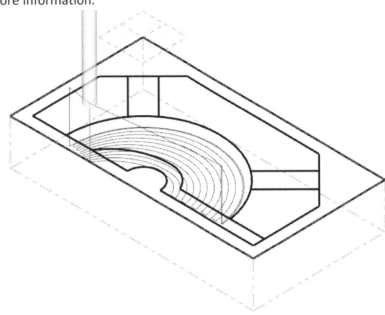

♦ Select the **OK** button to exit **Backplot**.

17.9 Verify the toolpaths

♦ **Verify** the toolpaths. See **page 696** for more information.

♦ To verify all toolpaths, from the **Toolpaths Manager**, choose the **Select all operations** icon.

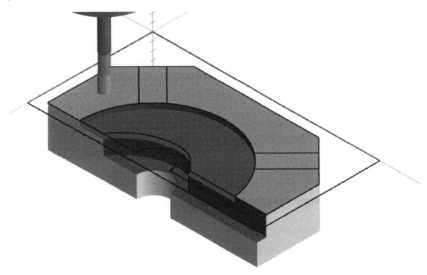

♦ To go back to the Mastercam window, minimize the **Mastercam Simulator** window.
♦ Press **Alt + T** to remove the toolpath display.

STEP 18: 2D HIGH SPEED PEEL MILL

2D High Speed Peel Mill toolpath allows for efficient constant climb milling between two selected contours or along a single contour. It uses a trochoidal style of motion to cut the slot. For single chains, you need to define the width of the cut. Otherwise, the width is defined by the area between the two contours.

Toolpath Preview:

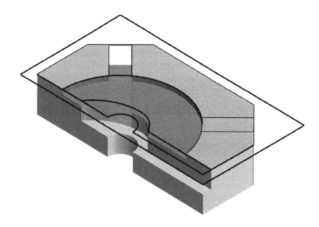

TOOLPATHS

◆ From the **2D** group, click on the **Expand gallery** icon as shown .

◆ Select the select the **Peel Mill** icon as shown.

◆ Leave the default chaining method and select the lines as shown. Ensure both chains go in the same direction as shown in Figure: 18.0.1.

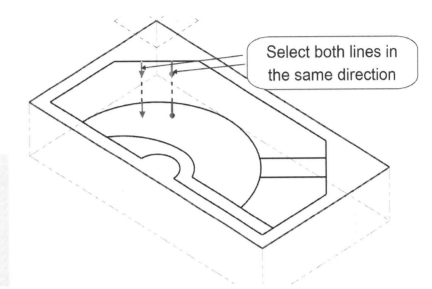

Select both lines in the same direction

NOTE: To change the direction of

chaining if needed, click on the

Reverse button from the **Chaining**

dialog box.

◆ Choose the **OK** button to exit the **Chaining** dialog box.
◆ In the **Toolpath Type**, **Peel Mill** should already be selected.

Dynamic Mill   Area Mill   Dynamic Contour   Peel Mill   Blend Mill

- Select the **Tool** page from the **Tree View list** and select the **1/4" Flat Endmill** from the list of tools.
- Make any necessary changes as shown in Figure: 18.0.2.

Figure: 18.0.2

2D High Speed Toolpath - Peel Mill   ✕

Toolpath Type
✓ Tool
    Holder

⊟   Cut Parameters
    ◇ Depth Cuts
⊞ ◇ Finish Passes
    ◇ Break Through
⊟   Linking Parameters
        Home / Ref. Points

    Arc Filter / Tolerance
    Planes (WCS)
    Coolant
    Canned Text
    Misc Values
⊟   Axis Control
        Axis Combination
        Rotary Axis Control

#	Assembly...	Tool Name	Holder N...	Dia.	Cor. r...	L
1	–	1/2 FLAT ...	–	0.5	0.0	
2	–	1/4 FLAT ...	–	0.25	0.0	

Right-click for options

Select library tool...   ☐ Filter Active   Filter...

☐ To batch

Tool diameter: 0.25

Corner radius: 0.0

Tool name: 1/4 FLAT ENDMILL

Tool #: 2   Length offset: 2

Head #: 0   Diameter offset: 2

☐ RCTF   Spindle direction: CW

Feed rate: 6.4176   Spindle speed: 2139

FPT: 0.0008   SFM: 139.9869

Plunge rate: 6.4176   Retract rate: 6.4176

☐ Force tool change   ☑ Rapid Retract

Comment
Machine the slot.

Quick View Settings

Tool	1/4 FLAT ENDMI...
Tool Diameter	0.25
Corner Radius	0
Feed Rate	6.4176
Spindle Speed	2139
Coolant	Off
Tool Length	2.5
Length Offset	2
Diameter Offset	2
Cplane / Tpla...	Top
Axis Combinat...	Default (1)

✓ = edited
⊘ = disabled

18.1 Set the Cut Parameters

- From the **Tree View list** select **Cut Parameters** and change the **Stepover** amount to **15%** as shown in Figure: 18.1.1.
- Enable the **Extend Entry** option and **Extend Exit** option. Input a value to extend the entry by **0.25** and to extend the exit by **1.25** as shown in Figure: 18.1.1.

Figure: 18.1.1

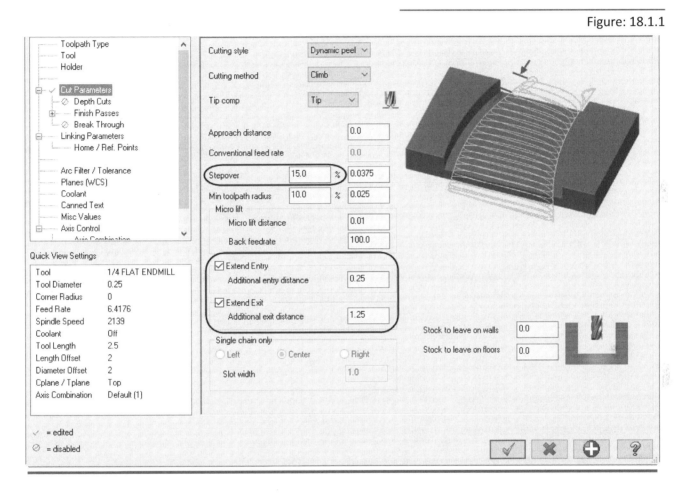

Stepover sets the distance between adjacent cuts of the toolpath.

Min toolpath radius defines the radius of the arc that the tool follows along its semi-circular path. This value must be greater than the stepover amount.

Micro lift distance enter the distance the tool lifts off of the part on back moves. Micro lifts are slight lifts that help clear chips and minimize excessive tool heating.

Back feedrate controls the speed (inches per minute or millimeters per minute) of the backfeed movement of the tool. This allows 3D arcs between cuts to have a different feed rate than the rest of the toolpath, which can help reduce cycle time.

Extend Entry/Exit allows you to adjust the initial and final tool engagement with the material.

18.2 Set the Depth Cuts

♦ Select **Depth Cuts** from the **Tree View list** and ensure **Depth cuts** is disabled.

18.3 Set the Finish Passes Parameters

♦ Select **Finish Passes** from the **Tree View list** and enable **Finish pass**. Ensure **Machine finish passes only at final depth** is checked and **Spacing** is set as shown in Figure: 18.3.1.

Figure: 18.3.1

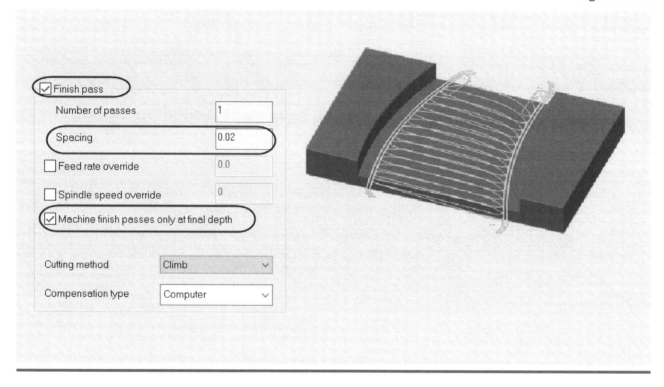

Finish Pass performs a high speed finish pass along the walls of the slot.

Machine finish passes only at final depth performs the finish passes at the final cutting depth only.

18.4 Set the Linking Parameters

◆ Select **Linking Parameters** from the **Tree View list** and set the **Depth** to **-0.5** as shown in <u>Figure: 18.4.1</u>.

Figure: 18.4.1

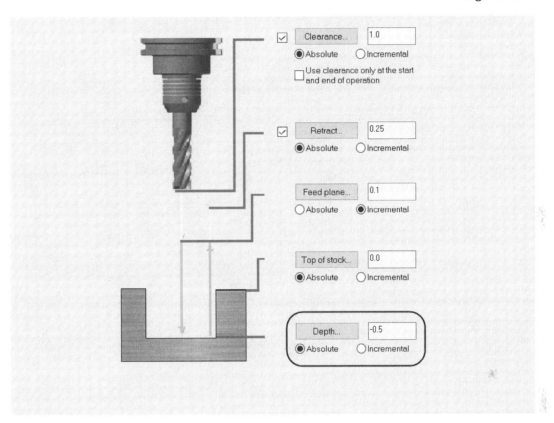

18.5 Preview the Toolpath

• To quickly check how the toolpath will be generated, select the **Preview toolpath** icon as shown.

• See **page 157** to review the procedure.
• The toolpath should look as shown.

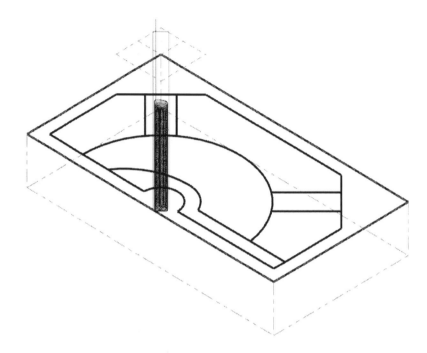

• Press **Esc** key to exit the preview.

| **NOTE:** If the toolpath does not look as shown in the preview, check your parameters again.

• Choose the **OK** button to generate the toolpath.

18.6 Backplot the toolpath

◆ See **page 695** for more information.

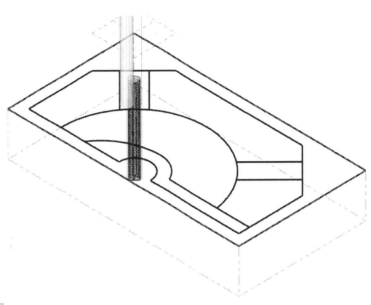

◆ Select the **OK** button to exit **Backplot**.

18.7 Verify all toolpaths

◆ See **page 696** for more information.

◆ To verify all toolpaths, from the **Toolpaths Manager**, choose the **Select all operations** icon.

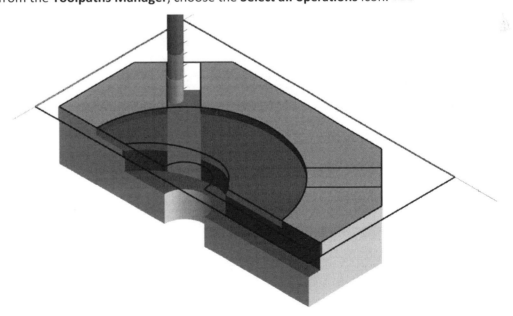

◆ To go back to the Mastercam window, minimize the **Mastercam Simulator** window as shown.
◆ Press **Alt + T** to remove the toolpath display.

STEP 19: 2D HIGH SPEED PEEL MILL

In this step you will review how to copy an existing toolpath in the **Toolpaths Manager**. You will also learn how to rechain the geometry used in the toolpath.

Toolpath Preview:

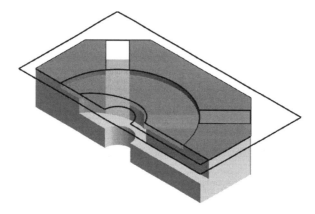

19.1 Copy the Previous Toolpath

• From the **Toolpaths Manager**, select only operation #4 (the peel mill toolpath).

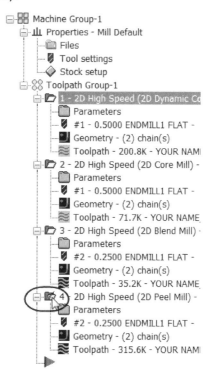

• Right click and hold the right mouse button down and drag the operation to a point below it as shown in Figure: 19.1.1.

Figure: 19.1.1

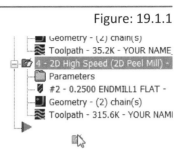

• Release the right mouse button and select the option **Copy after** as shown in Figure: 19.1.2.

Figure: 19.1.2

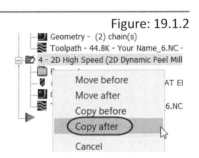

• Make sure that the insert arrow is below the last toolpath as shown in Figure: 19.1.3; otherwise, select the icon to move the insert arrow down.

Figure: 19.1.3

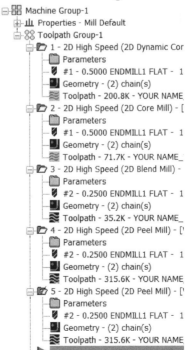

19.2 Re-Chain the Geometry

◆ In the operation #5, select **Geometry**.

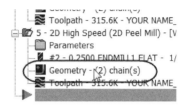

◆ Right mouse click in the **Chain Manager** and select **Rechain all** as shown.

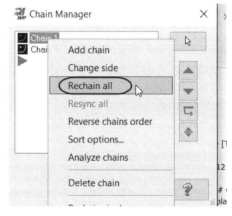

◆ When the **Chaining** dialog box appears, leave the default settings and choose the line as shown in Figure: 19.2.1 (this time we will chain one entity only to create the toolpath).

Figure: 19.2.1

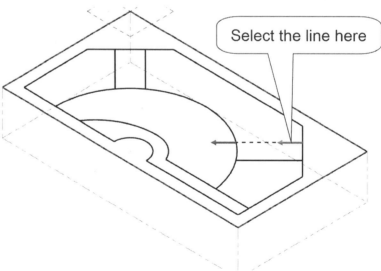

Select the line here

◆ Once the geometry has been selected, choose the **OK** button to exit the **Chaining** dialog box.

◆ Choose the **OK** button again to exit the **Chain Manager**.

• Select **Parameters** in **Operation #5.**

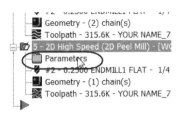

19.3 Set the Cut Parameters

• Select **Cut Parameters** and change **Single chain only** to **Left** and enter a **Slot width** of **0.5** as shown in
Figure: 19.3.1.

Figure: 19.3.1

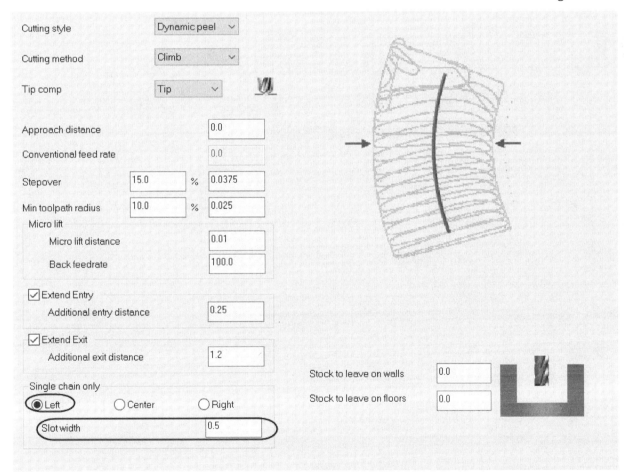

19.4 Set the Linking Parameters

♦ Select **Linking Parameters** and make sure that the **Depth** is set to **-0.5** as shown in <u>Figure: 19.4.1</u>.

Figure: 19.4.1

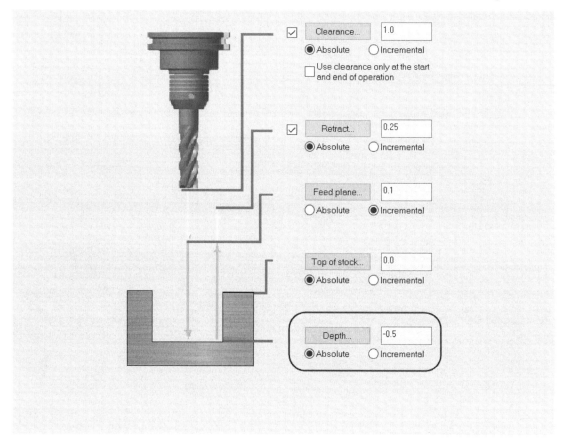

19.5 Preview the Toolpath

♦ To quickly check how the toolpath will be generated, select the **Preview toolpath** icon as shown.

♦ See **page 157** to review the procedure.
♦ The toolpath should look as shown.

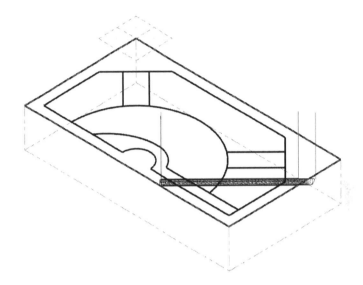

♦ Press **Esc** key to exit the preview.

> **NOTE:** If the toolpath does not look as shown in the preview, check your parameters again.

♦ Choose the **OK** button to exit the toolpath parameters.

♦ Select the button to **Regenerate all dirty operations**. ▮×

19.6 Backplot the toolpath

♦ **Backplot** the toolpath. See **page 695** for more information.

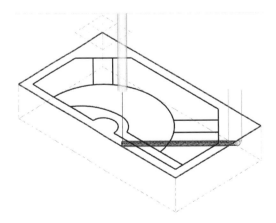

♦ Select the **OK** button to exit **Backplot**.

19.7 Verify all toolpaths

• **Verify** the toolpaths. See **page 696** for more information.

• To verify all toolpaths, from the **Toolpaths Manager**, choose the **Select all operations** icon.

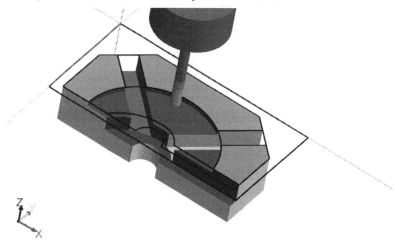

• To go back to the Mastercam window, minimize the **Mastercam Simulator** window as shown.

STEP 20: POST THE FILE

- Ensure all operations are selected; if they are not, use the **Select all operations** button in the **Toolpaths Manager.**

- Select the **Post selected operations** button from the **Toolpaths Manager.** G1
- In the **Post processing** window, make the necessary changes as shown in Figure: 20.0.1.

Figure: 20.0.1

NC File enabled allows you to keep the NC file and to assign the same name as the MCAM file.

Edit enabled allows you to automatically launch the default editor.

- Select the **OK** button to continue.
- Save your file and name it **YOUR NAME_6.NC**.

◆ A window with **Mastercam Code Expert** will be launched and the NC program will appear as shown.

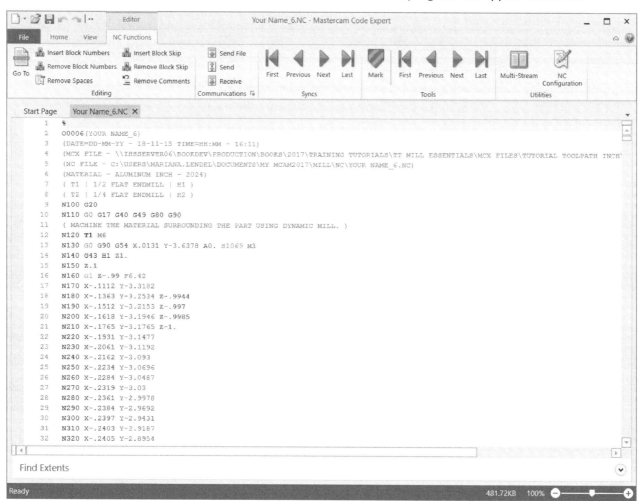

◆ Select the **"X"** box at the upper right corner to exit the editor.

STEP 21: SAVE THE UPDATED MCAM FILE

REVIEW EXERCISE - STUDENT PRACTICE

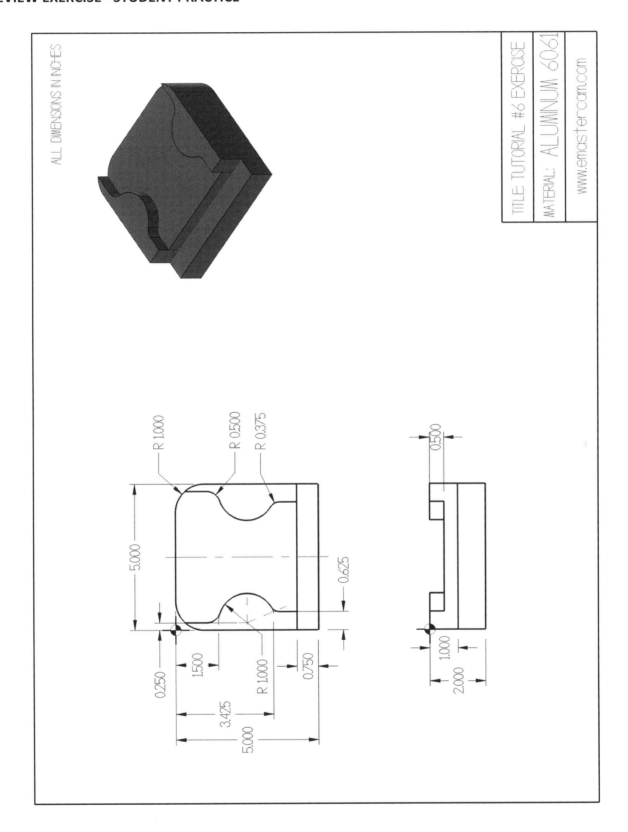

ALL DIMENSIONS IN INCHES

TITLE: TUTORIAL #6 EXERCISE

MATERIAL: ALUMINUM 6061

www.emastercam.com

R 1.000

R 0.500

R 0.375

5.000

0.625

0.250

1.500

R 1.000

0.750

3.425

5.000

0.500

1.000

2.000

CREATE THE GEOMETRY FOR TUTORIAL #6 EXERCISE

Use these commands to create the geometry:

* Rectangle.
* Line Endpoints.
* Circle Center Point.
* Arc Polar.
* Fillet Entities.

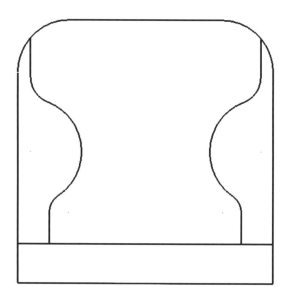

CREATE THE TOOLPATHS FOR TUTORIAL #6 EXERCISE

Create the Toolpaths for Tutorial #6 Exercise as per the instructions below.

Set the machine properties including the Stock Setup.
Remove the material on the step using Contour (2D).
- Use a **7/8" Flat Endmill**.
- Based on your chaining direction, ensure the **Compensation direction** is set correct.
- Enable **Depth Cuts**.
- **Lead In/Out**, ensure the **Arc Radius** is set to zero.
- No **Break Through**, **Multi Passes**.
- Set the depth according to the drawing.

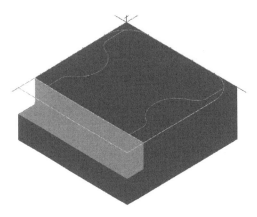

Remove the material around the fillets using Contour (2D).
- Use the **7/8" Flat Endmill**.
- Based on your chaining direction ensure the **Compensation direction** is set correct.
- Enable **Depth Cuts**.
- Set a **Lead In/Out** and **Break Through**.
- No **Multi Passes**.
- Set the depth according to the drawing.

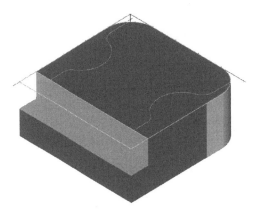

Create a 2D High Speed Blend Mill toolpath to remove the material in the center of the part.
- Select the two chains.
- Use a **1/2" Flat Endmill**.
- Set the **Compensation** direction to **Inside**.
- Select **Along** for the tool cutting direction.
- Set the **% of stepover** to **25**.
- **Extend Exit/Entry 0.5"**.
- Disable **Depth Cuts** and **Break Through**.
- Set the depth according to the drawing.
- Your part will appear as shown.

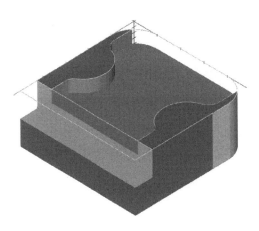

NOTES:

TUTORIAL #6 QUIZ

◆ What is the advantage of Dynamic Mill?

◆ What entities need to be chained to utilize Core Milling?

◆ How does a Blend Mill toolpath work?

TUTORIAL #7

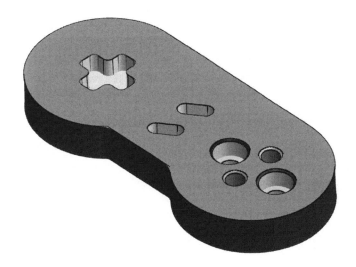

OVERVIEW OF STEPS TAKEN TO CREATE THE FINAL PART:

From Drawing to CAD Model:
* The student should examine the drawing on the following page to understand what part is being created in the tutorial.
* From the drawing we can decide how to go about creating the geometry in Mastercam.

Create the 2D CAD Model used to generate Toolpaths from:
* The student will create the Top 2D geometry needed to create the toolpaths.
* Geometry creation commands such as Circle Center Point, Line Tangent, Line Parallel, Rectangular Shapes, Trim, and Fillet Chains will be used.
* Create a solid using solid extrude, chamfer and fillet command.

Create the necessary Toolpaths to machine the part:
* The student will set up the stock size and the clamping method to be used.
* The 2D HS Dynamic Mill toolpath will be used to machine the pockets.
* The Feature Based Drill toolpath will be used to machine the four holes.
* The 2D HS Dynamic Mill toolpath will be used to machine the outside profile.
* The Pocket toolpath will be used to finish the pocket walls.
* The Contour toolpath will be used to finish the outside profile.

Backplot and Verify the file:
* The Backplot will be used to simulate a step-by-step process of the tool's movements.
* The Verify will be used to watch a tool machine the part out of a solid model.

Post Process the file to generate the G-code:
* The student will then post process the file to obtain an NC file containing the necessary code for the machine.

 This tutorial takes approximately one hour to complete.

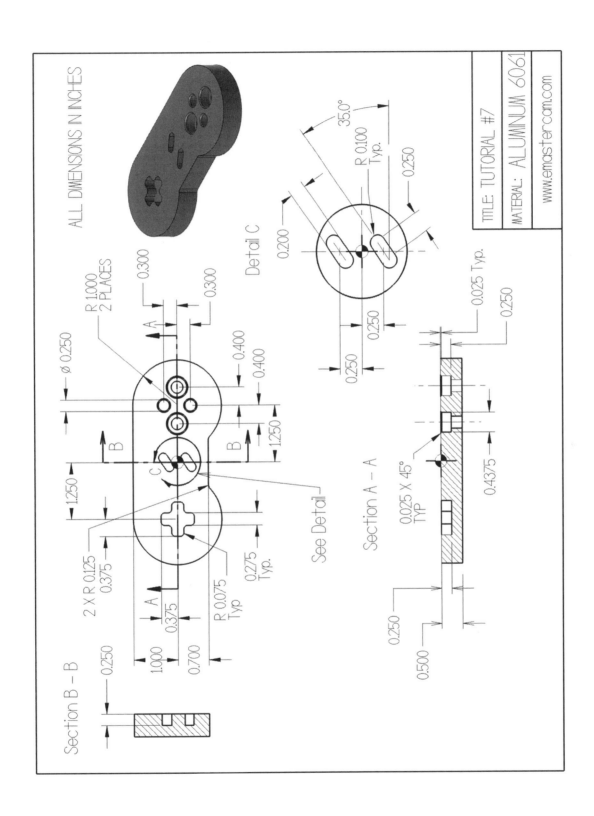

ALL DIMENSIONS IN INCHES

Detail C

35.0°

R 0.100
Typ.

0.250

0.200

0.250

0.250

0.025 Typ.

0.250

Section A – A

0.025 X 45°
TYP

0.4375

0.250

0.500

R 1.000
2 PLACES

0.300

A

0.300

Ø 0.250

0.400

0.400

B

1.250

B

1.250

See Detail

C

2 X R 0.125

0.375

A

0.375

R 0.075
Typ

0.275
Typ.

Section B – B

0.250

1.000

0.700

TITLE: TUTORIAL #7

MATERIAL: ALUMINUM 6061

www.emastercam.com

GEOMETRY CREATION

STEP 1: SETTING UP THE GRAPHICAL USER INTERFACE

Please refer to the **Getting Started** section to set up the graphical user interface.

◆ To hide the manager panels if needed, see **Tutorial 1 page 14**.

STEP 2: CREATE CIRCLE CENTER POINT

Create Circle Center Point lets you create circles knowing the center point and the radius or the diameter.

Step Preview:

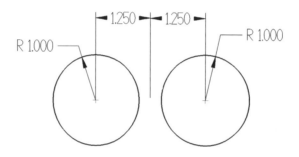

WIREFRAME
◆ From the **Arcs** group, select **Circle Center Point** as shown.

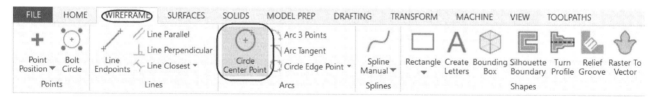

◆ In the **Ribbon Bar**, enter the **Radius** value of **1.0** and click on the radius icon to lock it as shown.

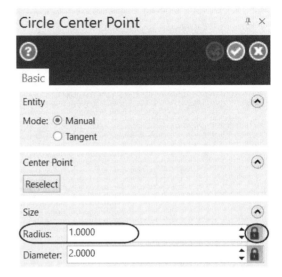

◆ Press the **Space bar** to enter coordinates for the center point as shown.

-1.25,0

◆ Press **Enter** to position the circle.
◆ Press **Enter** again to finish the circle.
◆ Press **Alt + F1** to fit the circle into the graphics window.
◆ Press the **Space bar** again to enter coordinates for the center point as shown.

1.25,0

◆ Choose the **OK** button to exit the command.
◆ Press **Alt + F1** to fit the geometry into the graphics window.
◆ The geometry should look as shown.

NOTE: During the geometry creation of this tutorial, if you make a mistake, you can undo the last step using the **Undo** icon. ⤾ You can undo as many steps as needed. If you delete or undo a step by mistake, just use the **Redo** icon. ⤿ To delete unwanted geometry, select it first and then press **Delete** from the keyboard.

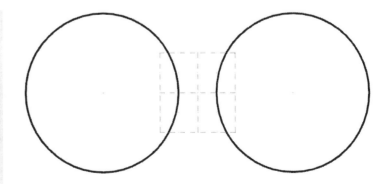

CREATE LINE TANGENT

You will create a line tangent to two arcs. You will use the **Create Line Endpoints** command with the tangent icon enabled.

Step Preview:

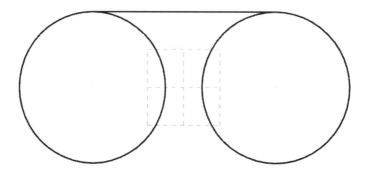

WIREFRAME

- From the **Lines** group, select **Line Endpoints** as shown.

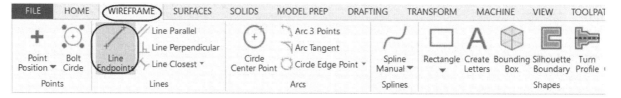

- In the **Line Endpoints** panel, make sure that **Freeform** and **Tangent** are enabled as shown.

NOTE: Make sure that you do not select the quadrant points while selecting the circles.

◆ [Specify the first endpoint]: Select Entity A as shown in <u>Figure: 2.0.1</u>.
◆ [Specify the second endpoint]: Select Entity B as shown in <u>Figure: 2.0.1</u>.

Figure: 2.0.1

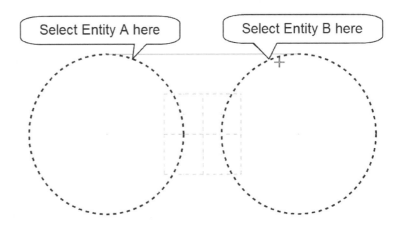

◆ Choose the **OK** button to exit the command.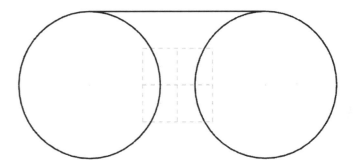
◆ The geometry should look as shown.

STEP 3: CREATE A LINE PARALLEL

Create a **Line Parallel** command knowing the distance between the lines.

Step Preview:

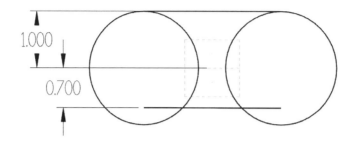

WIREFRAME

- From the **Lines** group, select **Line Parallel** as shown.

- [Select a line]: Select the line as shown in Figure: 3.0.1.
- [Select the point to place a parallel line through]: Click somewhere below the line as shown in Figure: 3.0.1.

Figure: 3.0.1

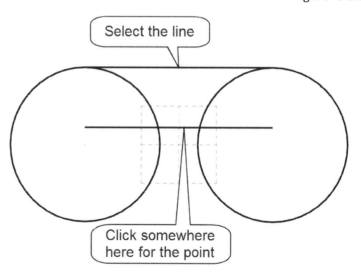

- In the **Line Parallel** panel, change the **Offset Distance** to **1.7**.

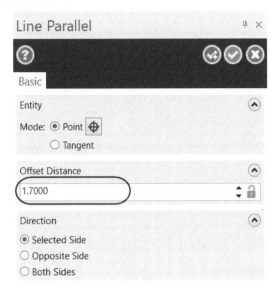

- Press **Enter** to position the line at the proper distance.

- Select the **OK** button to exit the command.
- The geometry should look as shown.

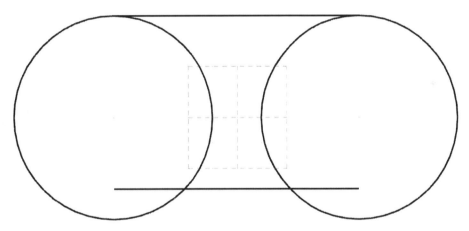

STEP 4: TRIM THE ENTITIES

You will trim the entities using the **Trim 3 entities** command. The first two entities that you select are trimmed to the third, which acts as a trimming curve. The third entity is then trimmed to the first two.

Step Preview:

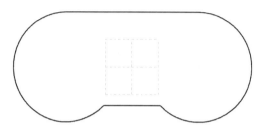

WIREFRAME

* From the **Modify** group, select **Trim Break Extend** as shown.

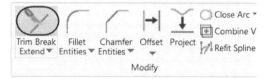

* In the **Trim Break Extend** panel, make sure that the **Trim Mode** and **Trim 3 entities** are enabled as shown.

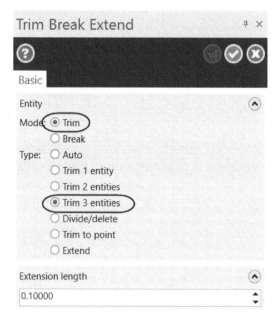

- ◆ [Select the first entity to trim/extend]: Select Entity A as shown in Figure: 4.0.1.
- ◆ [Select the second entity to trim/extend]: Select Entity B as shown in Figure: 4.0.1.
- ◆ [Select the entity to trim/extend to]: Select Entity C as shown in Figure: 4.0.1.

Figure: 4.0.1

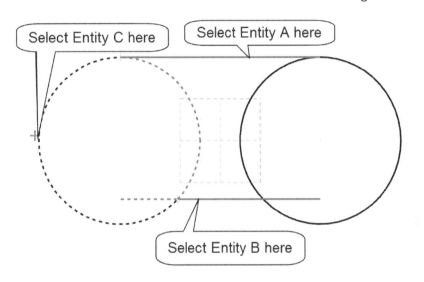

- ◆ [Select the first entity to trim/extend]: Select Entity A as shown in Figure: 4.0.2.
- ◆ [Select the second entity to trim/extend]: Select Entity B as shown in Figure: 4.0.2.
- ◆ [Select the entity to trim/extend to]: Select Entity C as shown in Figure: 4.0.2.

Figure: 4.0.2

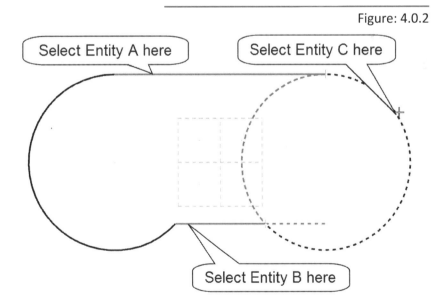

- ◆ Select the **OK** button to exit the command.

◆ The geometry should look as shown.

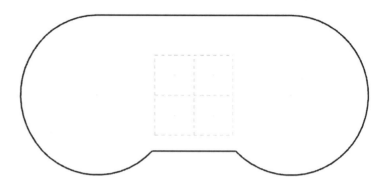

STEP 5: CREATE RECTANGULAR SHAPE

In this step you will create two rectangles using **Create Rectangular Shapes**.

Step Preview:

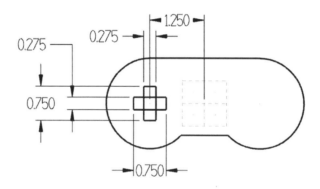

WIREFRAME

◆ From the **Shapes** group, select the drop down below **Rectangle** and select **Rectangular Shapes** as shown.

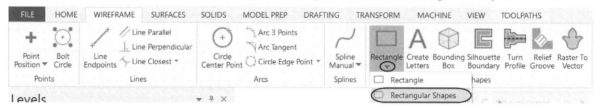

• Enter the **Width**, the **Height** and enable the **Anchor** location as shown in the Figure: 5.0.1.

Figure: 5.0.1

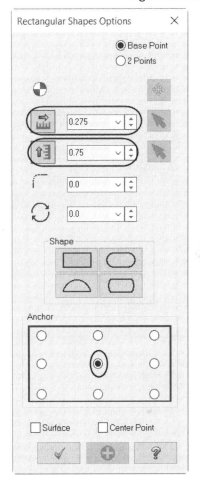

• Press **Enter** to see a preview of the rectangle while positioning it.
• [Select position of base point]: Select the circle center point as shown in Figure: 5.0.2.

Figure: 5.0.2

NOTE: Make sure that the center point icon appears while selecting the point.

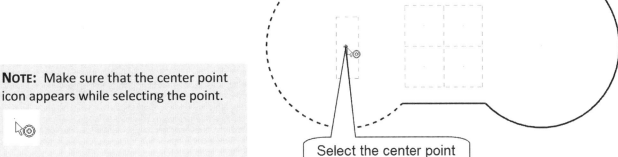

Select the center point

- Select the **Apply** button to continue in the same command.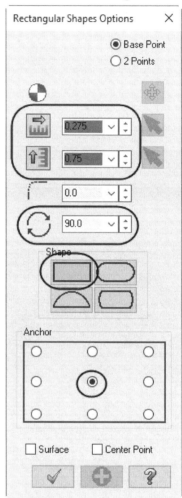
- In the **Rectangular Shapes Options** dialog box, click on the icons in front of the **Width 0.275** and **Height 0.75** to lock the rectangle values and enter **90** in the **Rotation** field as shown in Figure: 5.0.3.

Figure: 5.0.3

♦ [Select position of base point]: Select the same center point as shown in <u>Figure: 5.0.4</u>.

Figure: 5.0.4

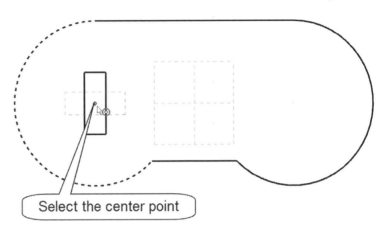

♦ Selected the **OK** button to exit the command.
♦ The geometry should look as shown.

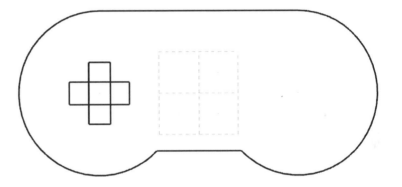

STEP 6: TRIM DIVIDE

In this step you will trim the entities using **Divide/delete** which trims a line, arc, or spline into two disjointed segments by removing the segment that lies between two dividing intersections. When you choose the **Divide/delete** function and select an entity in the graphics window, Mastercam uses the nearest two intersections on each end to divide the entity. If only one intersection exists, the selected entity is trimmed to the single intersection. If no intersection is found on the selected entity, or the point of intersection is an endpoint of the selected entity, the entity is deleted.

Step Preview:

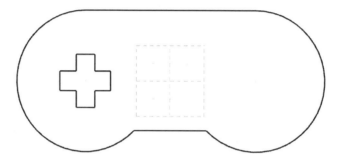

WIREFRAME

* From the **Modify** group, select **Trim Break Extend** as shown.

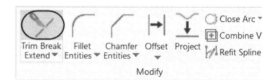

* In the **Trim Break Extend** panel, enable **Divide/delete** as shown.

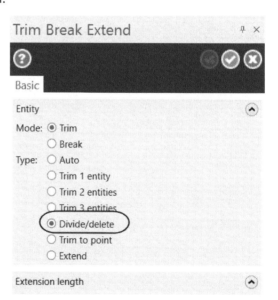

♦ [Select the entity to trim/extend]: Select the line as shown in Figure: 6.0.1.

Figure: 6.0.1

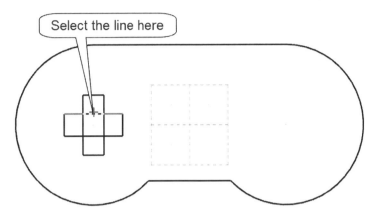

♦ Select the rest of the lines as shown in Figure: 6.0.2.

Figure: 6.0.2

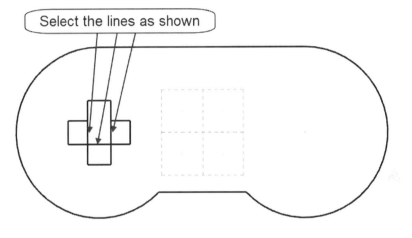

♦ Select the **OK** button to exit the command.
♦ The geometry should look as shown.

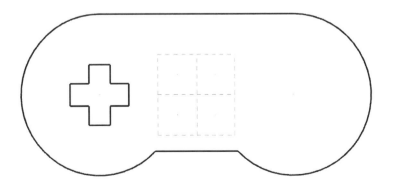

STEP 7: FILLET CHAINS

In this step we will fillet all the sharp edges of the shape using the **Fillet Chains** command.

Step Preview:

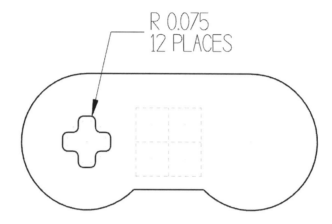

WIREFRAME

- From the **Modify** group, click on the drop down arrow next to **Fillet Entities** and select **Fillet Chain**s as shown.

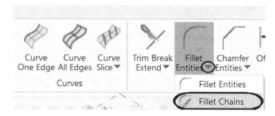

- Leave the **Chain** button enabled in the **Chaining** dialog box as shown.

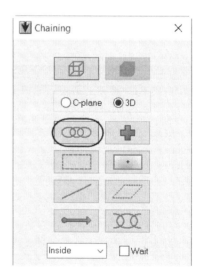

♦ Select the chain as shown.

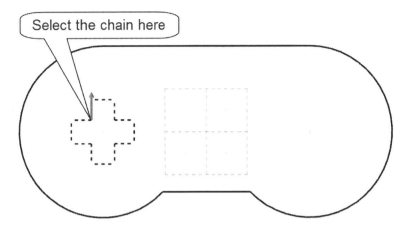

Select the chain here

♦ Select the **OK** button to exit the **Chaining** dialog box.
♦ In the **Fillet Chains** panel, change the **Radius** and make sure **Trim entities** is enabled as shown.
♦ Press **Enter** to apply the radius.

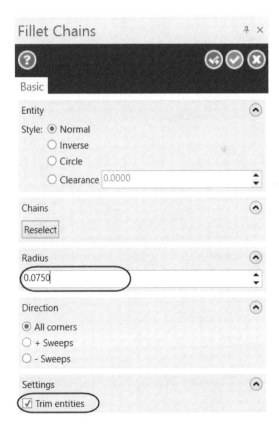

♦ Select the **OK** button to exit the **Fillet Chain** command.

* The geometry should look as shown.

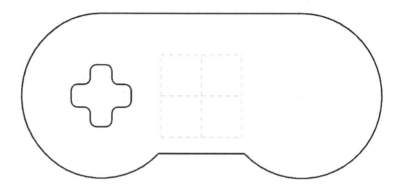

STEP 8: CREATE THE OBROUND SHAPES

In this step you will create the two **Obround** shapes using the **Rectangular Shapes** command.

Step Preview:

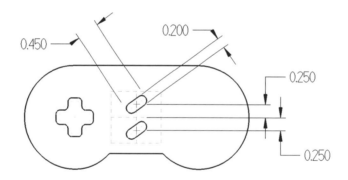

WIREFRAME

* From the **Shapes** group, select the drop down arrow below rectangle and select **Rectangular Shapes** as shown.

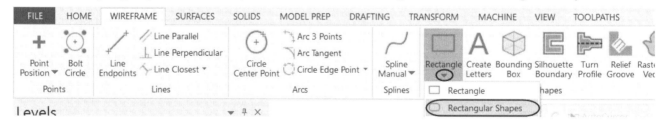

♦ In the **Rectangular Shapes,** enter a **Width 0.45,** the **Height 0.2, Angle 35** and enable the **Obround shape**.

Lock the values by clicking on the **Width** and **Height** icons in front of the value fields. Make sure that the **Anchor** location is in the center as shown in the Figure: 8.0.1.

Figure: 8.0.1

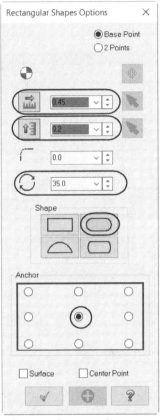

♦ [Select position of base point]: Press the **Space bar** to open the coordinates field and enter the coordinates as shown.

0,0.25

♦ Press **Enter.**

♦ Select the **Apply** button to continue in the same command. ⊕

♦ [Select position of base point]: Press the **Space bar** and enter the coordinates as shown.

0,-0.25

♦ Press **Enter.**

♦ Select the **OK** button to exit the **Rectangular Shapes Options** command. ✓

• The geometry should look as shown.

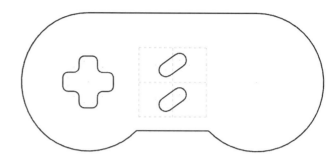

STEP 9: CREATE CIRCLES KNOWING THE CENTER POINT

In the step you will create the four 0.25" diameter holes knowing the diameter and the center points.

Step Preview:

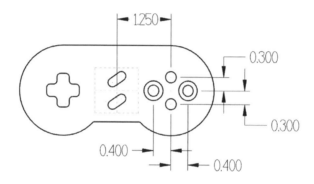

9.1 Create the 1/4" diameter circles

WIREFRAME
• From the **Arcs** group, select the **Circle Center Point** as shown.

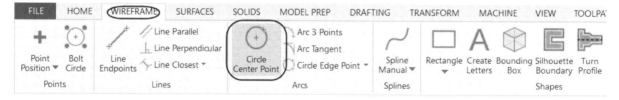

♦ In the **Circle Center Point**, enter the **Diameter** value of **0.25,** press **Enter** and make sure that the value is locked as shown.

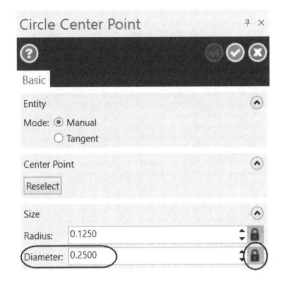

♦ Press the **Space bar** to enter coordinates for the center point **1.25-0.4, 0** as shown.

```
1.25-0.4,0
```

♦ Press **Enter** to position the circle.

NOTE: Mastercam lets you perform basic mathematical operations such as addition, substraction, multiplication or division.

♦ Press **Enter** to continue in the same command.
♦ Press the **Space bar** to enter coordinates for the center point **1.25+0.4, 0** as shown.

```
1.25+0.4,0
```

♦ Press **Enter** to position the circle.
♦ Press **Enter** to continue in the same command.
♦ Press the **Space bar** to enter coordinates for the center point **1.25, 0.3** as shown.

```
1.25,0.3
```

♦ Press **Enter** to position the circle.
♦ Press **Enter** to continue in the same command.
♦ Press the **Space bar** to enter coordinates for the center point **1.25, -0.3** as shown.

```
1.25,-0.3
```

♦ Press **Enter** to position the circle.
♦ Press **Enter** to continue in the same command.

◆ The geometry should look as shown.

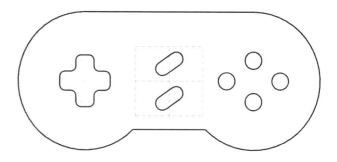

9.2 Create the 0.4375" diameter circles

◆ In the **Circle Center Point** panel, enter the **Diameter** value of **0.4375**, press **Enter** and make sure that the value is locked as shown.

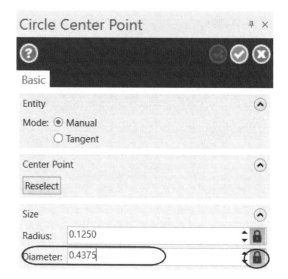

◆ [Enter the center point]: Select the center point of the circle as shown.

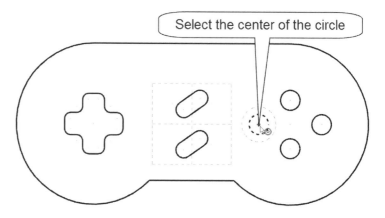

◆ Press **Enter** to continue in the same command.

♦ [Enter the center point]: Select the center point of the circle as shown.

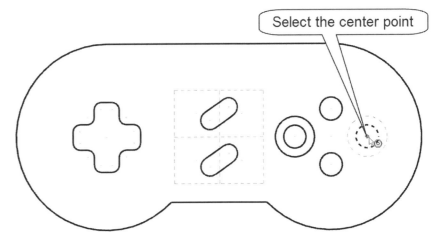

Select the center point

♦ Choose the **OK** button to exit the command.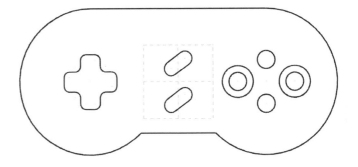
♦ The geometry should look as shown.

STEP 10: SET THE LEVEL

In this step you will change the solid color and the level on which the solid will be created on. This will be done to allow us to view our part easier.

* From the left side of the graphics window, click on the **Levels** tab as shown.

* When the **Levels Manager** appears, enter in the **Name** field "**Wireframe**" as shown in Figure: 10.0.1.

Figure: 10.0.1

Num... ^	Visible	Name	Entities	Level Set
✓ 1	X	Wireframe	42	

Number: 1

Name: Wireframe

Level Set

◆ In the **Number** field, input "**2**" and enter the name "**Solid**" as shown in Figure: 10.0.2.

Figure: 10.0.2

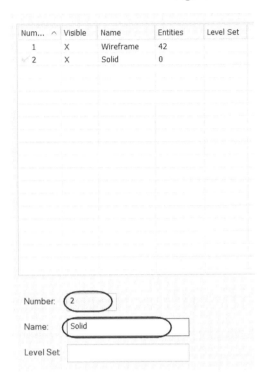

◆ In the **HOME** tab you should see the **Level** will be set to **2**.

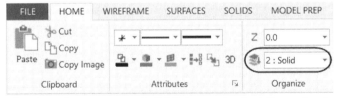

◆ To set the solid color, in the **Attributes** group, select the drop down next to **Solid Color** and select the red color as shown.

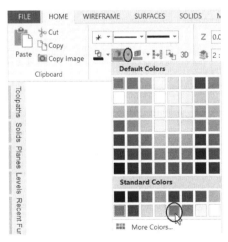

STEP 11: EXTRUDE THE BASE OF THE SOLID

Extrude function lets you extrude geometry to create one or more solid bodies, create cuts on an existing body or create bosses on an existing body.

Step Preview:

11.1 Create the body and the four holes

SOLIDS

• From the **Create** group, select **Extrude** as shown.

♦ When the **Chaining** dialog box appears, leave the default settings as shown.

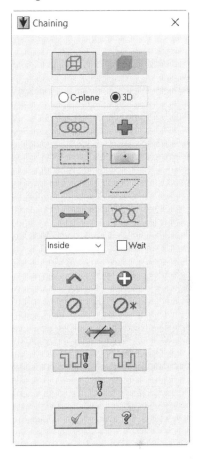

♦ Right mouse click in the graphics window and select **Isometric**.

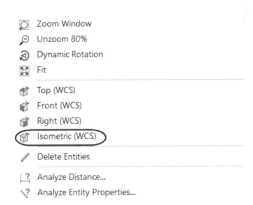

◆ Start selecting the outside profile of the part and then select the four holes in a clockwise direction as shown in <u>Figure: 11.1.1</u>.

Figure: 11.1.1

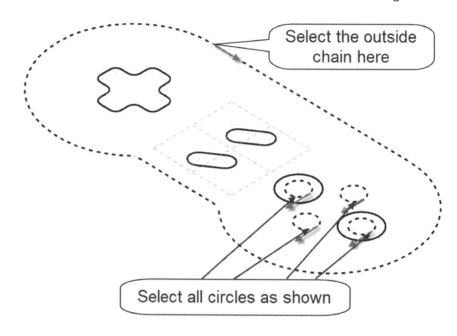

> Select the outside chain here

> Select all circles as shown

NOTE: The arrows will disappear as you select the next chain.

◆ Once the geometry has been chained, select the **OK** button.

◆ From the **Solid Extrude** panel, select the **Reverse All** button 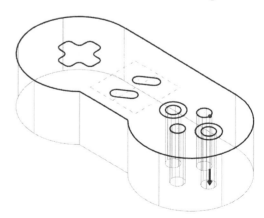 to ensure that the arrow is pointing in a negative or downward direction as shown in <u>Figure: 11.1.2</u>. Press **Alt + S** to see the solid in the unshaded mode.

Figure: 11.1.2

♦ In the **Solid Extrude** panel ensure **Create Body** and **Create a single operation** are enabled and input **0.5** to **Distance** as shown in <u>Figure: 11.1.3</u>.

Figure: 11.1.3

♦ Select the **OK** button to create the solid.
♦ Use the icons found in **VIEW Appearance** group to **Shade** or **Unshade** (Wireframe) the solid, or press **Alt + S** on your keyboard.

- Your part will appear as shown.

- Unshade the solid.

11.2 Cut the shapes

SOLIDS

- From the **Create** group, select **Extrude** as shown.

- When the **Chaining** dialog box appears, leave the default settings.
- Right mouse click in the graphics area and select **Top**.

- Press **Alt + F1** to fit the geometry into the graphics window.

♦ Select the five chains in a clockwise direction as shown in <u>Figure: 11.2.1</u>.

Figure: 11.2.1

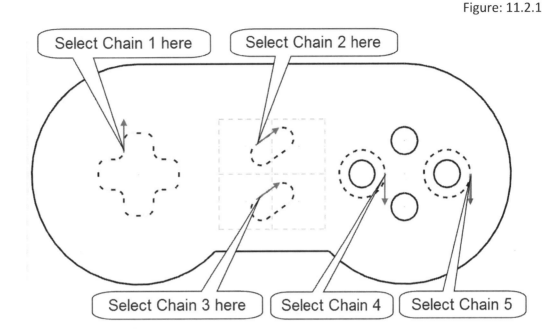

Select Chain 1 here

Select Chain 2 here

Select Chain 3 here

Select Chain 4

Select Chain 5

♦ Select the **OK** button in the **Chaining** dialog box.
♦ Right mouse click in the graphics window and select **Isometric**.

🔍	Zoom Window
🔍	Unzoom 80%
🔄	Dynamic Rotation
⊞	Fit
📦	Top (WCS)
📦	Front (WCS)
📦	Right (WCS)
📦	Isometric (WCS)
/	Delete Entities
⌐?	Analyze Distance...
∨?	Analyze Entity Properties...

♦ Make sure that the arrow is pointing downwards as shown in <u>Figure: 11.2.2</u>.

Figure: 11.2.2

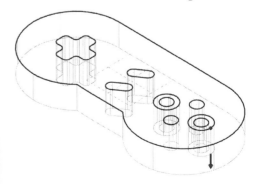

NOTE: To change the arrow direction, click on the chain closest
to the respective arrow.

♦ In the **Solid Extrude** dialog box enable **Cut body** and input a **Distance** of **0.25** as shown in <u>Figure: 11.2.3</u>.

Figure: 11.2.3

♦ Press **Enter** to preview the updated solid.

♦ Select the **OK** button to exit the **Solid Extrude** panel.

♦ Press **Alt + S** to shade the solid. The part will appear as shown.

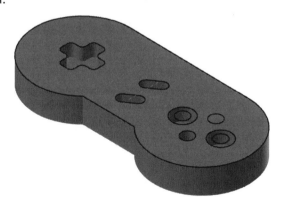

11.3 Make Level 1 Invisible

This will hide the 2D wireframe on your screen.

VIEW

◆ To have a better display of the solid, click on the **Outline Shaded**.

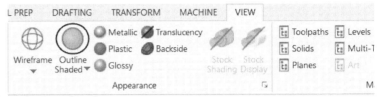

◆ From the left side of the graphics window, select the **Levels** tab.

◆ When the **Levels Manager** appears, left click in the **Visible** column and remove the "**X**" as shown in Figure: 11.3.1.

Figure: 11.3.1

- The part will appear as shown.

- From the left corner of the graphics window, select the **Solids** tab to open the **Solids Manager** panel.

- In the **Solids Manager** you should see a **Solid** body as shown.

- To see the solid operations that you created, in the **Solids Manager**, click on the plus in front of the **Solid** to expand the solid tree with two operations as shown.

NOTE: To modify the solid, you can double click on the operation and the respective **Solid Extrude** panel will appear and you can change the parameters as needed. Once you select the **OK** button to exit the **Solid Extrude** panel, click on the **Regen all** button to regenerate the solid.

STEP 12: CHAMFER THE HOLES

One Distance Chamfer uses edge blending to create a symmetrical beveled edge with the same chamfer distance for both edge faces.

In this step you will apply a 0.025" X 45°chamfer to the holes.

Step Preview:

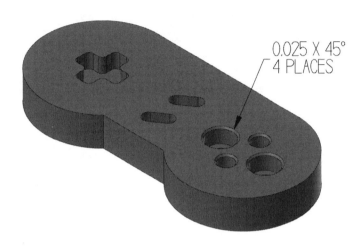

SOLIDS

• From the **Modify** group, select the **One Distance Chamfer**.

• In the **Solid Selection** dialog box, enable only the **Edge** button and make sure that **Face**, **Body** and other buttons are disabled, as shown in the figure.

♦ [Select entities to chamfer]: Select all the edges of the holes as shown in <u>Figure: 12.0.1</u>.

Figure: 12.0.1

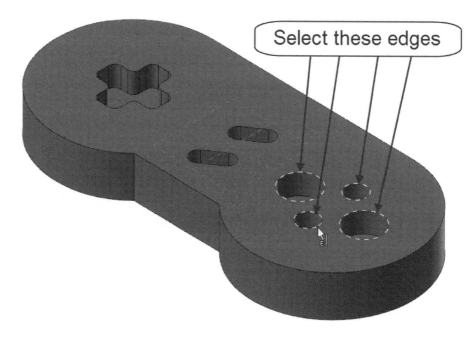

Select these edges

♦ Select the **OK** button to exit the **Solid Selection** dialog box.

♦ The **One Distance Chamfer** panel will appear. Enable **Propagate along tangencies** and set the **Distance** as shown.

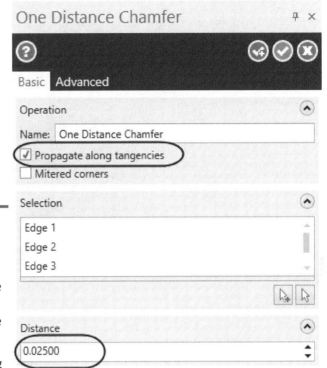

Distance sets the distance of the chamfer from the selected edge on the adjacent faces.

Mitered corners Mastercam will extend each chamfer to the extent of the edge. Use this feature where three or more chamfered edges meet at a vertex. With this option disabled, a smooth face at the vertex where the chamfers meet will be created.

Propagate along tangencies extends the chamfer along all tangent edges until a non-tangent edge is reached.

♦ Select the **OK** button to exit the command.
♦ The geometry should look as shown.

STEP 13: FILLET THE EDGES

Fillet - Constant Radius Fillet uses edge blending to produce a rounded edge.
In this step you will fillet the edges with a 1/8" radius.

Step Preview:

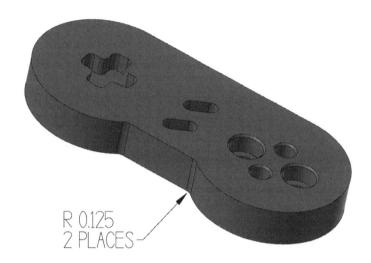

R 0.125
2 PLACES

SOLIDS
* From the **Create** group, select **Constant Fillet** as shown.

* In the **Solid Selection** dialog box, enable only the **Edge** button, and make sure that **Face**, **Body** and other buttons are disabled, as shown in the figure.

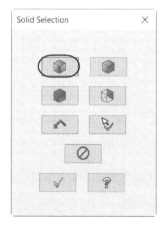

♦ [Select entities to fillet]: Click somewhere in the middle of the part, and holding down the mouse wheel slightly rotate the part as shown in Figure: 13.0.1.

♦ Select the two edges as shown in Figure: 13.0.1.

Figure: 13.0.1

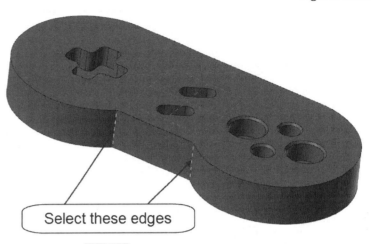

Select these edges

♦ Select the **OK** button to exit the **Solid Selection** dialog box.

♦ In the **Constant Radius Fillet** panel, change the **Radius** to **0.125** as shown.

Radius sets the radius of the fillet.

Propagate along tangencies extends the fillet along all tangent edges until a non-tangent edge is reached.

♦ Select the **OK** button to exit the command.

* The geometry should look as shown.

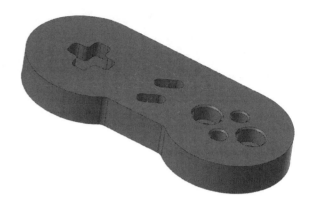

STEP 14: SAVE THE FILE

* Click on the **Browse** icon as shown.
* Find a location on the computer to save your file.
* File name: "Your Name_7".

TOOLPATH CREATION

SUGGESTED FIXTURE:

SETUP SHEET

TOOL LIST

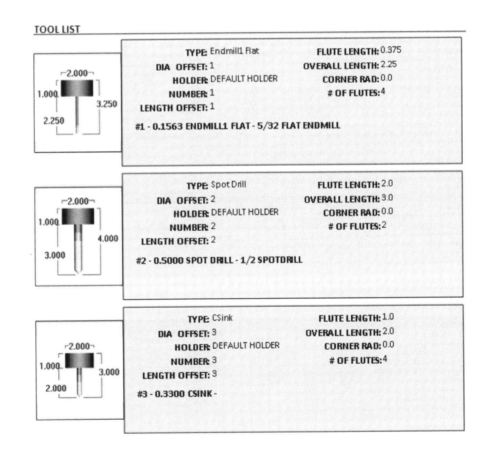

TYPE: Endmill1 Flat	**FLUTE LENGTH:** 0.375	
DIA OFFSET: 1	**OVERALL LENGTH:** 2.25	
HOLDER: DEFAULT HOLDER	**CORNER RAD:** 0.0	
NUMBER: 1	**# OF FLUTES:** 4	
LENGTH OFFSET: 1		

#1 - 0.1563 ENDMILL1 FLAT - 5/32 FLAT ENDMILL

TYPE: Spot Drill	**FLUTE LENGTH:** 2.0	
DIA OFFSET: 2	**OVERALL LENGTH:** 3.0	
HOLDER: DEFAULT HOLDER	**CORNER RAD:** 0.0	
NUMBER: 2	**# OF FLUTES:** 2	
LENGTH OFFSET: 2		

#2 - 0.5000 SPOT DRILL - 1/2 SPOTDRILL

TYPE: CSink	**FLUTE LENGTH:** 1.0	
DIA OFFSET: 3	**OVERALL LENGTH:** 2.0	
HOLDER: DEFAULT HOLDER	**CORNER RAD:** 0.0	
NUMBER: 3	**# OF FLUTES:** 4	
LENGTH OFFSET: 3		

#3 - 0.3300 CSINK -

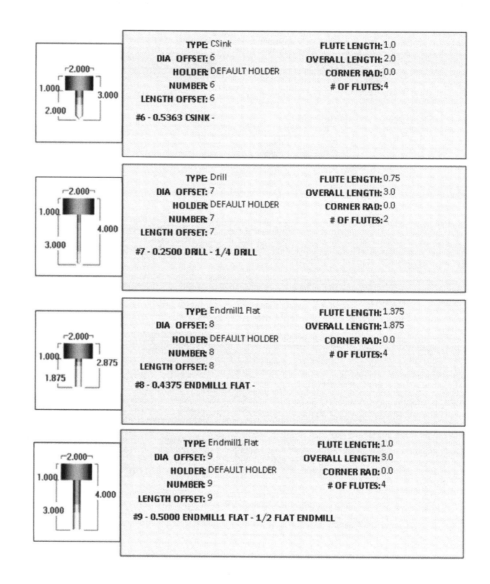

TYPE: CSink	**FLUTE LENGTH:** 1.0	
DIA OFFSET: 6	**OVERALL LENGTH:** 2.0	
HOLDER: DEFAULT HOLDER	**CORNER RAD:** 0.0	
NUMBER: 6	**# OF FLUTES:** 4	
LENGTH OFFSET: 6		

#6 - 0.5363 CSINK -

TYPE: Drill	**FLUTE LENGTH:** 0.75	
DIA OFFSET: 7	**OVERALL LENGTH:** 3.0	
HOLDER: DEFAULT HOLDER	**CORNER RAD:** 0.0	
NUMBER: 7	**# OF FLUTES:** 2	
LENGTH OFFSET: 7		

#7 - 0.2500 DRILL - 1/4 DRILL

TYPE: Endmill1 Flat	**FLUTE LENGTH:** 1.375	
DIA OFFSET: 8	**OVERALL LENGTH:** 1.875	
HOLDER: DEFAULT HOLDER	**CORNER RAD:** 0.0	
NUMBER: 8	**# OF FLUTES:** 4	
LENGTH OFFSET: 8		

#8 - 0.4375 ENDMILL1 FLAT -

TYPE: Endmill1 Flat	**FLUTE LENGTH:** 1.0	
DIA OFFSET: 9	**OVERALL LENGTH:** 3.0	
HOLDER: DEFAULT HOLDER	**CORNER RAD:** 0.0	
NUMBER: 9	**# OF FLUTES:** 4	
LENGTH OFFSET: 9		

#9 - 0.5000 ENDMILL1 FLAT - 1/2 FLAT ENDMILL

STEP 15: SELECT THE MACHINE AND SET UP THE STOCK

In Mastercam, you select a **Machine Definition** before creating any toolpath. The **Machine Definition** is a model of your machine's capabilities and features. It acts like a template for setting up your machine. The machine definition ties together three main components: the schematic model of your machine's components, the control definition that models your control capabilities, and the post processor that will generate the required machine code (G-code). For a Mill Level 1 exercise (2D toolpaths) we just need a basic machine definition.

NOTE: For the purpose of this tutorial, we will be using the **Default Mill** machine.

- To make sure that **3D** construction mode is enabled, right mouse click on the screen and check the mode as shown.
- If not just click on the **2D** to switch to **3D**.

- Press **Alt + F1** to fit the drawing to the screen.
- From the left side of the graphics window, click on the **Toolpaths** tab as shown.

- Pin the **Toolpaths Manager** by clicking on the **Auto Hide** icon as shown.

15.1 Select the machine

MACHINE

♦ From the **Machine Type** area, click on the drop down arrow below **Mill** and select the **Default**.

> **NOTE:** Once you select the **Mill Default**, the ribbon bar changes to reflect the toolpaths that could be used with **Mill Default**.

♦ Select the plus sign (+) in front of the **Properties** in the **Toolpaths Manager** to expand the **Toolpaths Group Properties.**

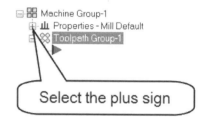

♦ Select the **Tool settings** to set the tool parameters.

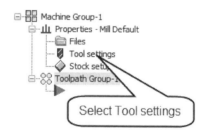

Mill Essentials Training Tutorial *Mastercam.* 2017

◆ Change the parameters to match the screen shot as shown in <u>Figure: 15.1.1</u>.

Figure: 15.1.1

Program # is used to enter a number if your machine requires a number for a program name.

Assign tool numbers sequentially allows you to overwrite the tool number from the library with the next available tool number. (First operation tool number 1; second operation tool number 2, etc.)

Warn of duplicate tool numbers allows you to get a warning if you enter two tools with the same number.

Override defaults with modal values enables the system to keep the values that you enter.

Feed Calculation set to **From tool** uses feed rate, plunge rate, retract rate and spindle speed from the tool definition.

* Select the **Stock Setup** tab to define the stock.
* Pick the **Rectangular** shape option.
* Choose the **All Solids** button and the stock size will be input as shown in <u>Figure: 15.1.2</u>.

Figure: 15.1.2

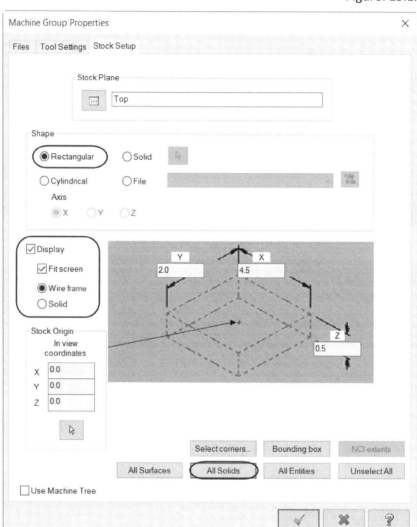

The **Stock Origin** values adjust the positioning of the stock, ensuring that you have an equal amount of extra stock around the finished part.

Display options allow you to set the stock as **Wireframe** and to fit the stock to the screen. (Fit Screen)

NOTE: The **stock** model that you create can be displayed with the part geometry when viewing the file or the toolpaths, during backplot, or while verifying toolpaths. In the graphics, the plus sign (+) shows you where the stock origin is. The default position is the middle of the stock.

* Select the **OK** button to exit **Machine Group Properties**.

◆ Right mouse click in the graphics window and select the **Isometric** view to see the stock.

⬚	Zoom Window
⊖	Unzoom 80%
⟳	Dynamic Rotation
⊡	Fit
⬢	Top (WCS)
⬢	Front (WCS)
⬢	Right (WCS)
⬢	Isometric (WCS)
✎	Delete Entities
⌐?	Analyze Distance...
✎?	Analyze Entity Properties...

◆ The stock model should appear as shown.

NOTE: The stock is not a geometry and cannot be selected.

STEP 16: 2D HIGH SPEED DYNAMIC MILL

2D High Speed Dynamic Mill utilizes the entire flute length of their cutting tools to produce the smoothest, most efficient tool motion for high speed pocketing. The toolpath supports a custom entry method and many others. **Micro lifts** further refine the dynamic milling motion and avoid excessive heat build up. Custom feeds and speeds optimize and generate safe tool motion. **Dynamic Mill** machines pockets, material that other toolpaths left behind, and standing bosses or cores. The toolpath depends on the **Machining strategy** that you choose in the **Chain Options**. The outside chain contains the toolpath; all inside chains are considered islands.

Toolpath Preview:

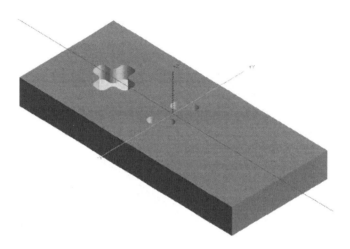

TOOLPATHS

• From the **2D** group, select **Dynamic Mill** as shown.

• When the new NC name dialog box appears, select the **OK** button to accept the name.

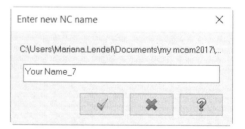

◆ From the **Chain Options** dialog box, click on the **Select machining chains** button in the **Machining regions** as shown.

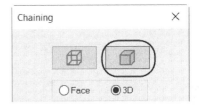

◆ In the **Chaining** dialog box, enable **Solids** selection as shown.

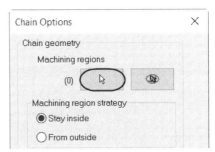

◆ In the **Chaining** dialog box, enable only the **Face** button and make sure that no other button is enabled as shown.

◆ Right mouse click in the graphics window and select the **Top** view as shown.

◆ Press **Alt + S** if needed to display the solid in shaded mode.

• Select the bottom of the pockets as shown.

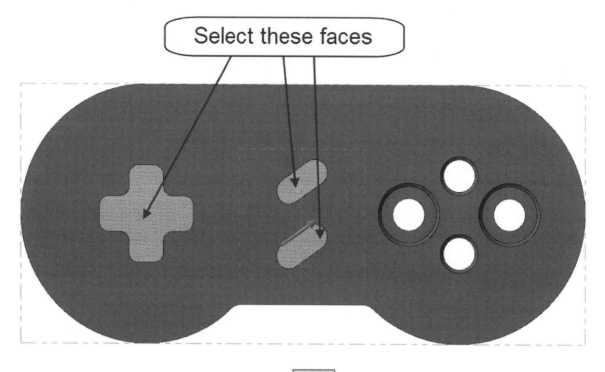

• Select the **OK** button to exit the **Chaining** dialog box.
• In the **Chain Options** dialog box, **Machining regions** will have 1 chain (solid selection displays one chain although all three chains are currently selected).
• Make sure that **Stay inside** is enabled as shown.

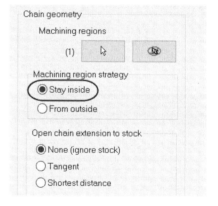

• Select the **OK** button to exit the **Chain Options** dialog box.
• In the **Toolpath Type** page, **Dynamic Mill** will be already selected as shown in Figure: 16.0.1.

Figure: 16.0.1

16.1 Preview Chains

The **Preview chains** function is intended to give the user a quick visual representation of how Mastercam sees the various pieces of geometry that have been selected, how they interact with one another, and a general overview of how the toolpath will be calculated with the selections presently made.

♦ Click on the **Color** icon to see the legend for **Preview chains** as shown.

♦ The **Preview Chains Colors** dialog box should look as shown.

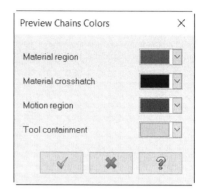

The **Material region** and **Material crosshatch** are the two colors that are used to define the material to be cut. The default colors are red for the background and black for the crosshatch.

The **Motion region** displays the area that Mastercam is making available to the toolpath for motion if it needs it. The color to represent it is dark blue. The primary reason for the display of the entire available (but not necessarily used) **Motion region** is to help the user visualize how the tool may move near or interact with any adjacent geometry.

The **Tool containment** is what you have selected as the containment region in the chain geometry. If you have not selected a containment region, it will default to the outside of the **Motion region** since that is currently the default area the toolpath is being contained to. The color used to represent the **Tool containment** is yellow.

♦ Select the **OK** button to exit **Preview Chains Colors**.
♦ Select the **Preview chains** button as shown.

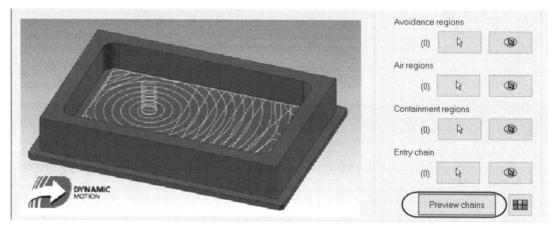

♦ Select the **Hide dialog** button to see the preview in the graphics window.

♦ The **Preview chains** should look as shown.

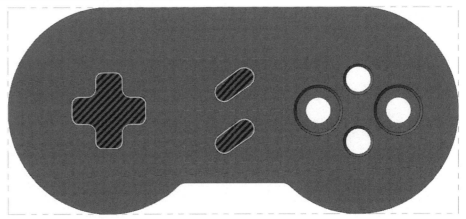

♦ Press **Esc** key to return to the toolpath parameters.
♦ Click on the **Preview chains** button again to clear the **Preview chains** display.

16.2 Select a 5/32" Flat Endmill from the library and set the Tool Parameters

♦ Select **Tool** from the **Tree View list**.

♦ Click on the **Select library tool** button.
♦ Select the **Filter** button.

♦ Select the **None** button and then under **Tool Types** choose the **Endmill1 Flat** icon.

◆ Under **Tool Diameter**, pick **Equal** and input a value of **5/32** as shown in <u>Figure: 16.2.1</u>.

Figure: 16.2.1

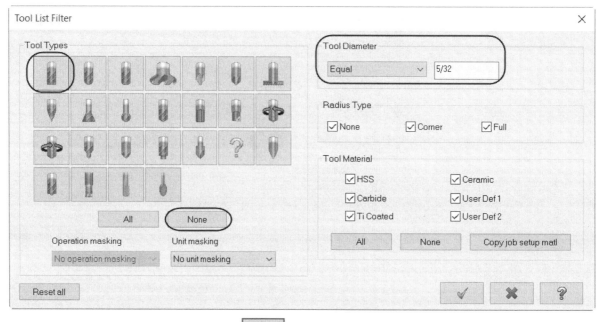

◆ Select the **OK** button to exit the **Tool List Filter.**

◆ In the **Tool Selection** dialog box you should only see a **5/32" Flat Endmill**.

#	Assembly...	Tool Name	Holder Name	Dia.	Cor. r...	Length	# Flut...	Type	Rad....
283	–	5/32 FLAT ENDMILL	–	0.15...	0.0	0.375	4	End...	None

◆ Select the **5/32" Flat Endmill** in the **Tool Selection** page and then select the **OK** button to exit.

♦ Make all the necessary changes as shown in <u>Figure: 16.2.2</u>.

Figure: 16.2.2

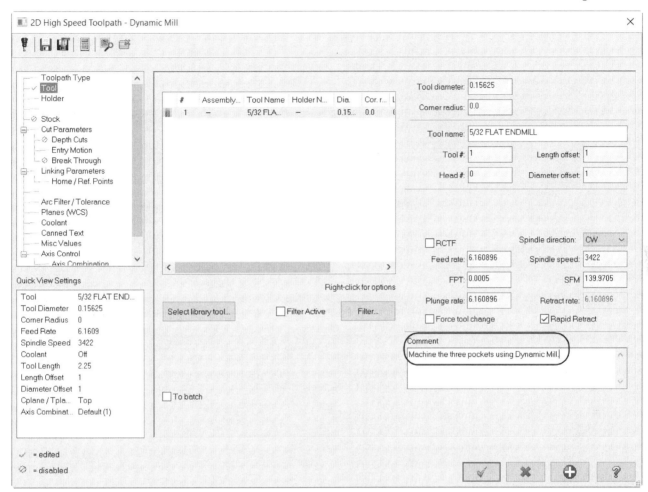

16.3 Set the Cut Parameters

◆ From the **Tree View list**, select **Cut Parameters**.
◆ Change the settings for this first toolpath as shown in Figure: 16.3.1.

Figure: 16.3.1

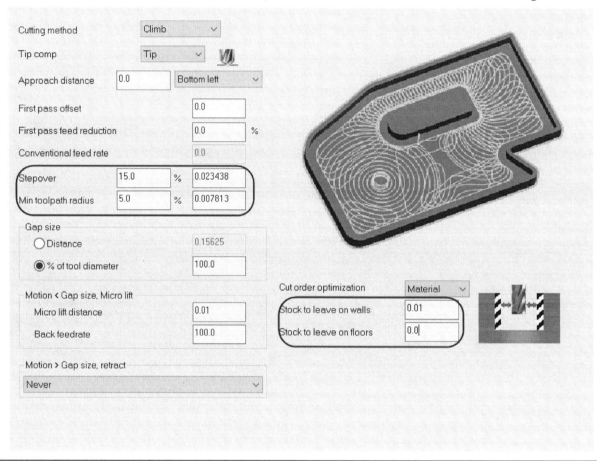

Stepover sets the distance between cutting passes in the X and Y axes.

Toolpath radius reduces sharp corner motion between cut passes.

Micro lift distance enters the distance the tool lifts off the part on the back moves. **Micro lifts** are slight lifts that help clear chips and minimize excessive tool heating.

Back feedrate controls the speed of the backfeed movement of the tool.

Motion > Gap Size, retract controls retracts in the toolpath when making a non-cutting move within an area where the tool can be kept down or microlifted.

Cut order optimization defines the cut order Mastercam applies to different cutting passes in the **Dynamic Mill** toolpath.

16.4 Set the Entry Motion

- **Entry Motion** configures an entry method for the **Dynamic Mill** toolpath which determines not only how and where the tool enters the part, but also the cutting method/machining strategy used by the toolpath. The previous settings will be saved.
- All we want to do is change the **Entry method** to **Profile** as shown in <u>Figure: 16.4.1</u>.

Figure: 16.4.1

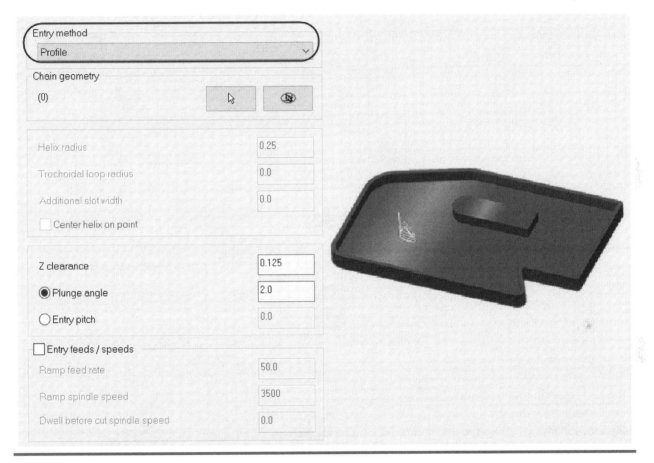

Entry method set to **Profile** creates a boundary based on the shape of the selected chain and uses the tool to ramp into the part. The slot is cleared by taking lighter cuts in the Z axis until the tool reaches the full depth.

Z clearance adds extra height used in the ramping motion down from a top profile. It ensures that the tool has fully slowed down from rapid speeds before touching the material.

Plunge angle sets the angle of descent for the entry move and determines the pitch.

16.5 Set the Linking Parameters

◆ Select **Linking Parameters,** enable **Clearance** and set it to **Absolute 1.0.** Change the **Top of stock** value to **Absolute 0.0** and the **Depth** to **Incremental 0.0** as shown in Figure: 16.5.1.

Figure: 16.5.1

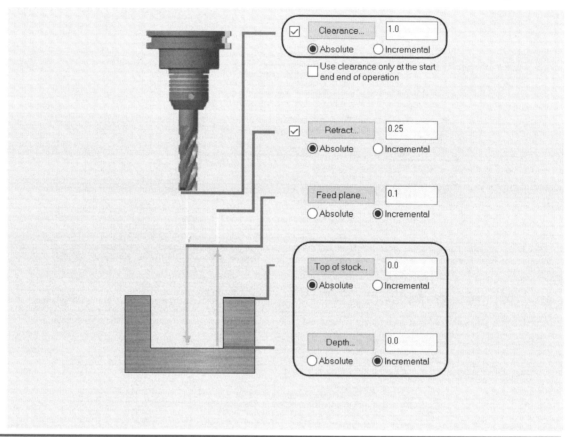

Incremental value for the **Depth** is measured at the chained geometry. In this tutorial, the pocket chains were selected at the bottom, which is their final depth.

16.6 Preview the Toolpath

♦ To quickly check how the toolpath will be generated, select the **Preview toolpath** icon as shown.

♦ To hide the dialog box, click on the **Hide dialog** icon as shown.

♦ To see the part from an **Isometric** view, right mouse click in the graphics window and select **Isometric** as shown.

⬚	Zoom Window
🔍	Unzoom 80%
🔄	Dynamic Rotation
⛶	Fit
📦	Top (WCS)
📦	Front (WCS)
📦	Right (WCS)
📦	(Isometric (WCS))
✏	Delete Entities
⌐?	Analyze Distance...
⌐?	Analyze Entity Properties...

♦ The toolpath should look as shown.

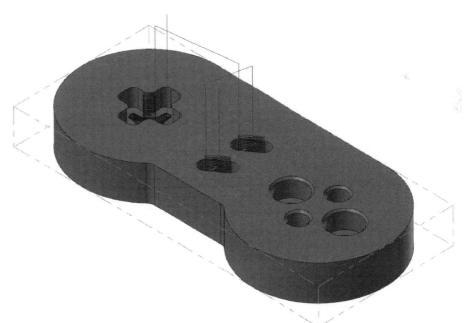

♦ Press **Esc** key to exit the preview.

> **NOTE:** If the toolpath does not look as shown in the preview, check your parameters again.

♦ Select the **OK** button to generate the toolpath.

STEP 17: BACKPLOT THE TOOLPATHS

Backplotting shows the path the tools take to cut the part. This display lets you spot errors in the program before you machine the part. As you backplot toolpaths, Mastercam displays additional information such as the X, Y, and Z coordinates, the path length, the minimum and maximum coordinates and the cycle time. It also shows any collision between the workpiece and the tool.

* Select the **Backplot selected operations** button.

* Right mouse click in the graphics window and select **Isometric** as shown.

VIEW

* From the **Appearance** group, select **Translucency** as shown.

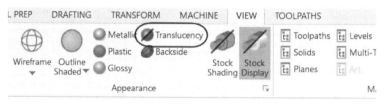

* Select the **Play** button to run **Backplot**.
* The toolpath should look as shown.

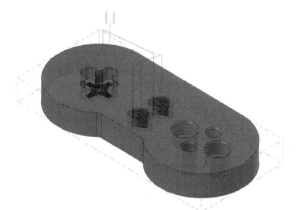

* Select the **OK** button to exit **Backplot**.

STEP 18: SIMULATE THE TOOLPATH IN VERIFY

Verify Mode shows the path the tools take to cut the part with material removal. This display lets you spot errors in the program before you machine the part. As you verify toolpaths, Mastercam displays additional information such as the X, Y, and Z coordinates, the path length, the minimum and maximum coordinates and the cycle time. It also shows any collision between the workpiece and the tool.

• From the **Toolpaths Manager**, select the **Verify selected operations** icon as shown.

NOTE: Mastercam launches a new window that allows you to check the part using **Backplot** or **Verify.**

• Select the **Play** button to run **Verify.**

• The part should appear as shown.

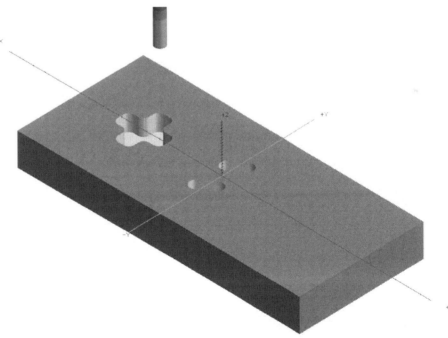

• To go back to the Mastercam window, minimize the **Mastercam Simulator** window as shown.
• Press **Alt + T** to remove the toolpath display.

STEP 19: DRILL THE HOLES USING FBM DRILL

FBM Drill automatically detects holes in a solid based on your specific criteria and generates a complete series of drilling and chamfering. **FBM Drill** also generates circle mill or helix bore operations for large-hole features when you activate these settings.

Toolpath Preview:

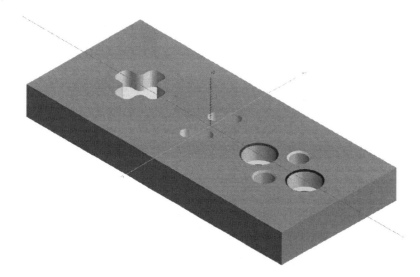

TOOLPATHS

♦ From the **2D** group, select the **Expand gallery** arrow as shown.

♦ From the **Toolpaths Gallery**, select the **FBM Drill**.

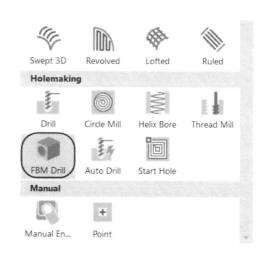

♦ When the **FBM Toolpaths - Setup** page appears, enable **Automatic initial hole detection.**
♦ Change the **Grouping** to **Plane** to group the operations by the plane in which the holes lie as shown in
Figure: 19.0.1.

Figure: 19.0.1

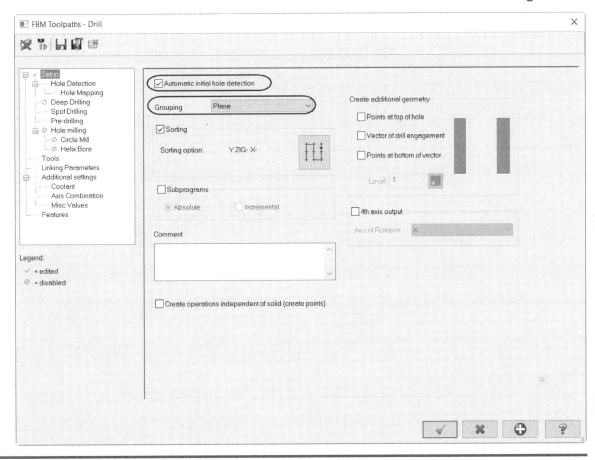

Automatic initial hole/feature detection when selected, Mastercam automatically detects features when you choose the FBM operation. If you save the settings to your toolpath. DEFAULTS file and use that final settings in the active machine group, Mastercam automatically detects features every time you choose the FBM operation.

Grouping controls how the drill cycles that **FBM Drill** creates are organized in the **Toolpaths Manager**. Mastercam orders operations within groups into subgroups by operation type.

Plane groups all operations based on the plane of the hole.

Create additional geometry selects one or more options to create geometry for detected hole features without generating toolpaths. The geometry is saved to a level you choose in this section and is non-associative.

19.1 Hole Detection

♦ Choose **Hole Detection** to control the types of holes **FBM Drill** detects. Enable/disable the options as shown in <u>Figure: 19.1.1</u>.

Figure: 19.1.1

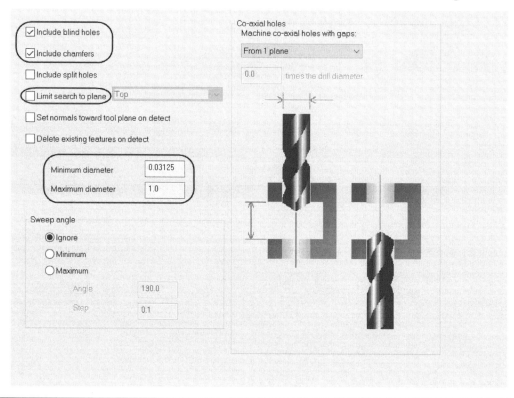

Include blind holes will search your part for blind holes (holes that do not go through the entire solid).

Include chamfers searches for holes with chamfers.

Include split holes searches the part for holes that are incomplete.

Limit search to plane detects features that can only be machined in the selected plane.

Minimum diameter finds holes which are equal to or greater than this value.

Maximum diameter finds holes which are equal to or less than this value.

Sweep angle lets you set a tolerance for how complete holes need to be in terms of their included angle to be detected by and included in the **FBM Drill** operation.

Machine co-axial holes with gaps determines whether Mastercam treats multiple holes that share a common axis as a single hole, or as multiple holes from different planes.

19.2 Spot Drilling

◆ Select **Spot Drilling** to activate and define the spot drilling toolpaths for the **FBM Drill** operation.
◆ Enable the option **Use this tool for all spot drill operations** as shown in <u>Figure: 19.2.1</u>.

> **NOTE:** It takes couple of minutes to enable **Use this tool for all spot drill operations.**

Figure: 19.2.1

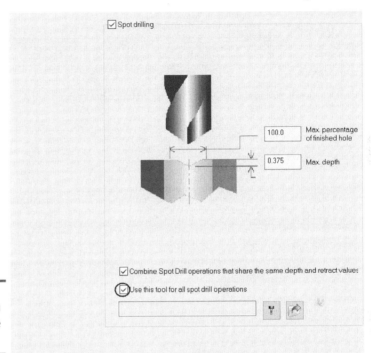

Use this tool for all spot drill operations allows you to choose a specific spot drill cycle generated by the **FBM Drill** operation.

◆ Pick the button **Select tool from library.** 📷
◆ This will let you choose a tool from the current tool library.
◆ Find and select the **1/2" Spot Drill** from the list.

#	Assembly...	Tool Name	Holder Name	Dia.	Cor. r...	Length	# Flut...	Type	Rad....
22	–	1/4 SPOTDRILL	–	0.25	0.0	2.0	2	Spot...	None
23	–	3/8 SPOTDRILL	–	0.375	0.0	2.0	4	Spot...	None
24	–	1/2 SPOTDRILL	–	0.5	0.0	2.0	2	Spot...	None
25	–	3/4 SPOTDRILL	–	0.75	0.0	2.0	4	Spot...	None
26	–	1. SPOTDRILL	–	1.0	0.0	2.0	4	Spot...	None
27	–	1/64 DRILL	–	0.01...	0.0	1.0	2	Drill	None
28	–	NO. 78 DRILL	–	0.016	0.0	1.0	2	Drill	None

◆ Select the **OK** button and the **Spot Drill** will appear in the box to the left of the buttons. ✓

19.3 Pre-Drilling

This page defines pre-drilling cycles that rough out the drilled holes before the finish drill cycle.

♦ Select **Pre-drilling** from the **Tree View list**. Leave **Pre-drilling** settings as shown in Figure: 19.3.1.

Figure: 19.3.1

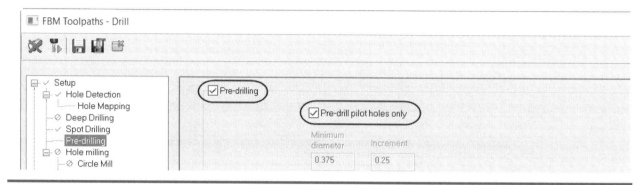

Pre-drilling creates pre-drilling operations that rough out the detected holes before creating any finished drill and chamfer operation.

Pre-drill pilot holes only deactivates all pre-drill roughing cycles except for assigned pilot holes cycles. This also deactivates the parameters for minimum diameter, increment and stock to leave on the page because they are not applicable. **FBM Drill** generates only pilot holes pre-drill cycles followed by finish hole cycles.

19.4 Tools

This page controls the tools Mastercam selects for the drill cycles that the **FBM Drill** operation creates.

◆ Select **Tools** from the **Tree View list**. Enable/disable the parameters as shown in Figure: 19.4.1.

Figure: 19.4.1

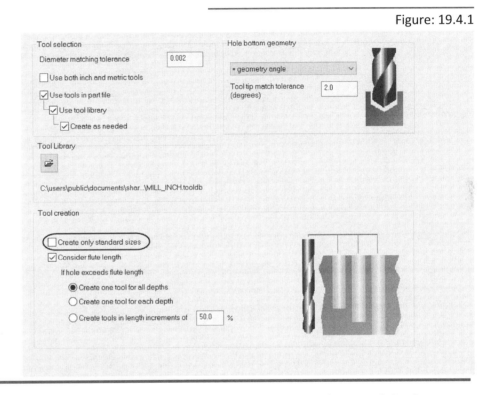

Tool selection lets you pick one or more of the following options to tell Mastercam where to locate tools for the FBM-generated toolpaths.

Diameter matching tolerance uses this value to determine how closely the diameter of the tool and the hole must match before selecting an appropriate tool.

Use tools in part file looks in the current Mastercam file for an appropriate tool. The tools do not have to be used in previous operations to be available to the FBM operations.

Use tool library searches the selected tool library for the necessary tools.

Create as needed creates the necessary tools using the tool creation parameters you define.

Hole bottom geometry defines the relationship of the bottom hole geometry to the tool tip geometry.

= geometry angle the tool tip angle must match the hole bottom geometry within the specified tool tip match tolerance.

> geometry angle the tool tip must be greater than the floor angle geometry.

< geometry angle the tool tip must be less than the floor angle geometry.

19.5 Linking Parameters

This page defines how **FBM Drill** calculates clearance height and retract height for the drilling cycles.

◆ Select **Linking Parameters** from the **Tree View list**. Set the parameters as shown in <u>Figure: 19.5.1</u>.

Figure: 19.5.1

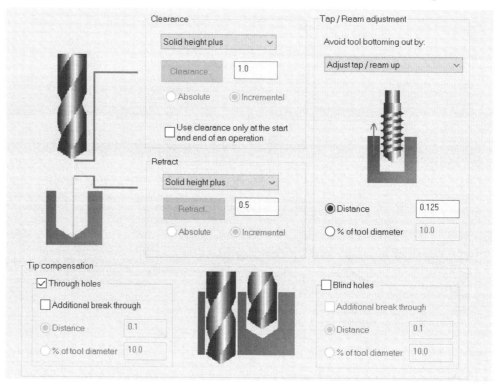

Clearance is the height at which the tool moves to and from the part. There are several options available from where the height is measured:

Solid height plus adds a fixed height above the highest point of the solid model.

Stock model plus adds a specified height above the stock model.

Top of hole plus adds clearance distance above the top of each hole.

Top of coaxial holes plus sets the clearance above the highest hole on the shared axis for holes that share the same axis

Manual allows you to set the clearance using all options in any combination.

Retract is the height at which the tool moves before the next tool pass. The same options are available as the **Clearance** height.

Tap/Ream adjustment determines whether tapped and reamed holes are fully finished.

Tip compensation compensates for the tool tip.

19.6 Features

This page allows you to manage the list of hole features that **FBM Drill** detects in the solid model.

◆ Select **Features** from the **Tree View list**.

◆ Choose the button to **Detect the Features** on the top left corner of the dialog box for Mastercam to detect the holes as shown in Figure: 19.6.1.

Figure: 19.6.1

FBM Toolpaths - Drill

Setup
  Hole Detection
      Hole Mapping
    Deep Drilling
    Spot Drilling
    Pre-drilling
  Hole milling
      Circle Mill
      Helix Bore
  Tools
  Linking Parameters
  Additional settings
      Coolant
      Axis Combination
      Misc Values
    Features

Legend:
✓ = edited
⊘ = disabled
🚩 = Hole can be created
⚠ = Warning - check tool
🔩 = SOLIDWORKS defined hole
🚩 = Feature suppressed

☐ Display all normals   10 features, 0 selected

State	Hole type	Dia.	Plane	Z 1	Depth	CB	CS	Blind	Split	Finish tool
🚩	Drill	0.25	Top	-0.25	0.25					SLDPRT: DRILL
🚩	Drill	0.25	Top	-0.25	0.25					SLDPRT: DRILL
🚩	Drill	0.25	Top	-0.025	0.475					SLDPRT: DRILL
🚩	Drill	0.25	Top	-0.025	0.475					SLDPRT: DRILL
🚩	Counter bore	0.4375	Top	-0.025	0.225	X		X		SLDPRT: ENDM
🚩	Counter bore	0.4375	Top	-0.025	0.225	X		X		SLDPRT: ENDM
🚩	Chamfer (90.0)	0.3	Top	0.015	0.165		X			SLDPRT: CSINI
🚩	Chamfer (90.0)	0.3	Top	0.015	0.165		X			SLDPRT: CSINI
🚩	Chamfer (90.0)	0.4875	Top	0.024375	0.268125		X			SLDPRT: CSINI
🚩	Chamfer (90.0)	0.4875	Top	0.024375	0.268125		X			SLDPRT: CSINI

☐ Select common features   ☐ Select coaxial features

◆ Choose the **OK** button to exit the **FBM Toolpaths - Drill** parameters.

19.7 Backplot the toolpaths

- Click on the **Select all operations** icon in the **Operations Manager**.
- **Backplot** the toolpaths. See **page 802** to review the procedure.
- The toolpaths should look as shown.

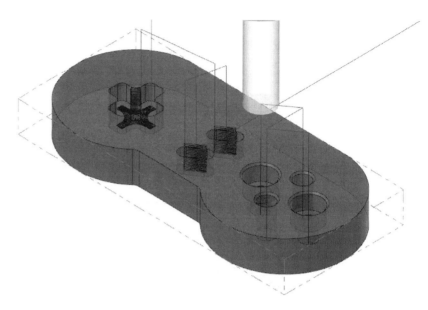

- Select the **OK** button to exit **Backplot**.

19.8 Verify the toolpaths

- **Verify** the toolpaths. See **page 803** to review the procedure.
- The part should look as shown.

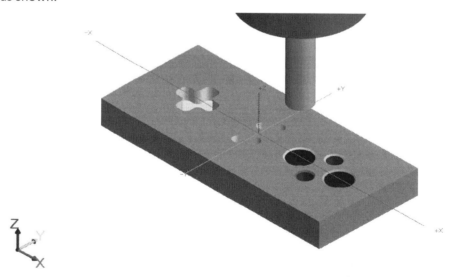

- To go back to the Mastercam window, minimize the **Mastercam Simulator** window as shown.

STEP 20: MACHINE THE OUTSIDE OF THE PART USING DYNAMIC MILL-ING

2D High Speed Dynamic Mill utilizes the entire flute length of their cutting tools to produce the smoothest, most efficient tool motion for high speed pocketing and core milling.

The **Dynamic Mill** toolpath machines pockets, material that other toolpaths left behind, and standing bosses or cores. The toolpath depends on the **Machining strategy** that you choose in the **Chain Options.** If the strategy chosen is **From outside**, the toolpath starts at the outmost chain and moves freely outside of this area; the inner chain defines the limit of the toolpath. You can also machine pockets, in which case the strategy selected is **Start inside**, which keeps the tool inside the machining regions.

Toolpath Preview:

* Click on the **Move insert arrow down one item** icon to move the arrow at the end of the toolpaths as shown in

  <u>Figure: 20.0.1</u>.

Figure: 20.0.1

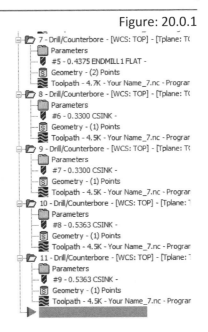

- In the **Toolpaths Manager**, click **Select all operations.**
- Press **Alt** + **T** until you remove the toolpath display.

TOOLPATHS

- From the **2D** group, select the **Expand gallery** arrow and then from the **Toolpath Gallery** select **Dynamic Mill**.

- In the **Chain Options**, **Machining regions**, enable **From outside** and in the **Open chain extension to stock**, enable **Shortest distance** as shown in Figure: 20.0.2.
- Click on the **Select avoidance chains** button in the **Avoidance regions** as shown in Figure: 20.0.2.

Figure: 20.0.2

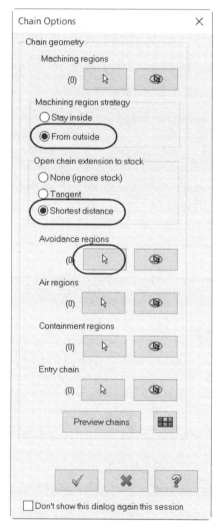

♦ Enable **Loop** in the **Chaining** dialog box and make sure that all the other buttons are not selected as shown.

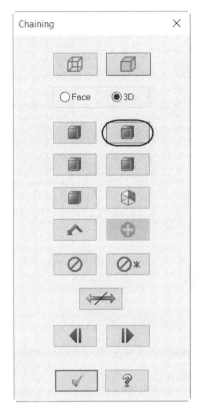

♦ Right mouse click in the graphics window and select the **Isometric** view as shown.

- Zoom Window
- Unzoom 80%
- Dynamic Rotation
- Fit

- Top (WCS)
- Front (WCS)
- Right (WCS)
- Isometric (WCS)

- Delete Entities

- Analyze Distance...
- Analyze Entity Properties...

◆ [Select faces, edges, and/or loops]: Select the edge as shown.

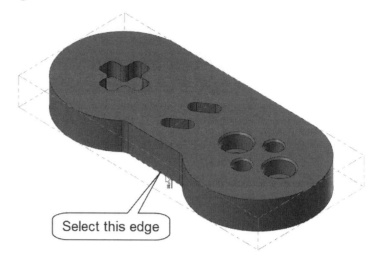

Select this edge

◆ The entire profile will be selected as shown.

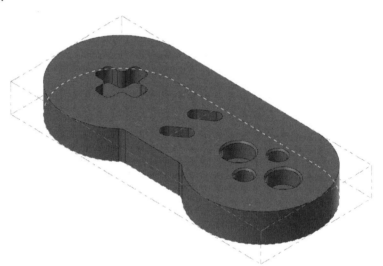

◆ In the **Pick Reference Face** dialog box, select the **OK** button to accept this face.

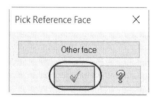

◆ Select the **OK** button to exit the **Chaining** dialog box.

◆ The **Chain Options** dialog box should look as shown.

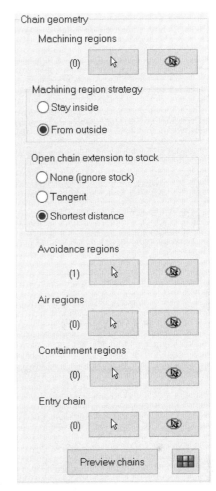

From outside enabled ensures that the tool will approached the part from the outside.

Open chain extension to stock set to the **Shortest distance** sets how the system calculates the amount of the material that has to be removed based on the shortest distance from the chain to the edge of the stock.

Avoidance regions allows you to select the profile that describes the shape up to where the material will be removed.

◆ Select the **OK** button to exit the **Chain Options** dialog box.
◆ In the **Toolpath Type** page, **Dynamic Mill** with **From outside** option should be already selected.

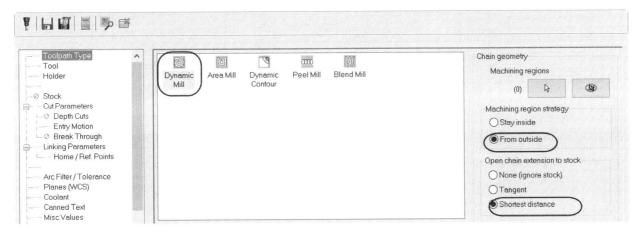

20.1 Preview Chains

♦ Select the **Preview chains** button as shown.

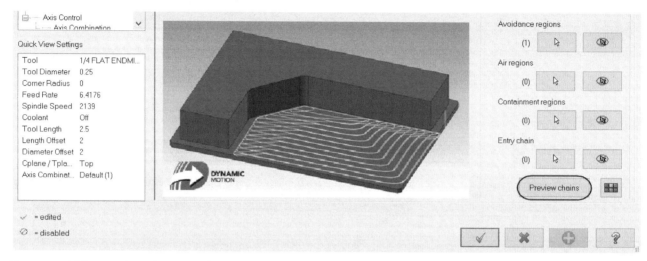

♦ See **page 164** to review the procedure.
♦ The **Preview chains** should look as shown.

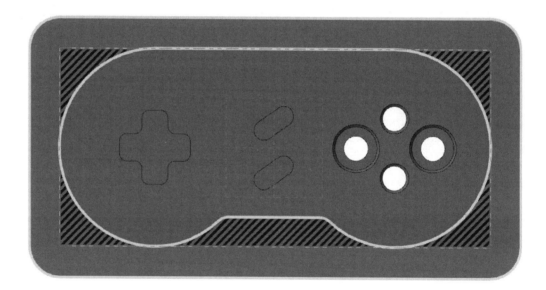

♦ Press **Esc** key to return to the toolpath parameters.
♦ Click on the **Preview chains** button again to clear the **Preview chains** display.

20.2 Select a 0.5" Flat Endmill from the Library and set the Tool Parameters

◆ Select **Tool** from the **Tree View list**.

◆ Click on the **Select library tool** button.
◆ Select the **Filter** button.

◆ Select the **None** button and then under **Tool Types** choose the **Endmill1 Flat** icon.
◆ Under **Tool Diameter**, pick **Equal** and input a value of **0.5** as shown in Figure: 20.2.1.

Figure: 20.2.1

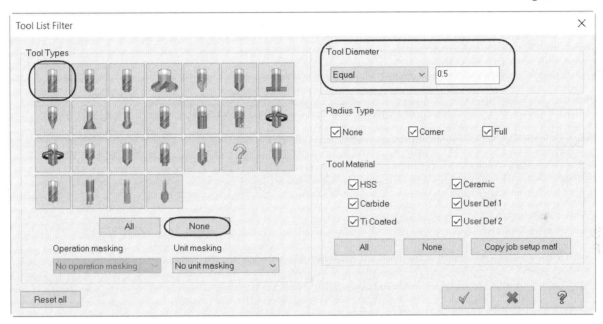

◆ Select the **OK** button to exit the **Tool List Filter.**
◆ In the **Tool Selection** dialog box you should only see a **1/2" Flat Endmill**.

#	Assembly...	Tool Name	Holder Name	Dia.	Cor. r...	Length	# Flut...	Type	Rad....
290	--	1/2 FLAT ENDMILL	--	0.5	0.0	1.0	4	End...	None

◆ Select the **1/2" Flat Endmill** in the **Tool Selection** page and then select the **OK** button to exit.

◆ Make all the necessary changes as shown in Figure: 20.2.2.

Figure: 20.2.2

#	Assembly...	Tool Name	Holder N...	Dia.	Cor. r...	L
1	–	5/32 FLA...	–	0.15...	0.0	
2	–	1/2 SPOT...	–	0.5	0.0	
3	–		–	0.33	0.0	
4	–		–	0.33	0.0	
5	–		–	0.53...	0.0	
6	–		–	0.53...	0.0	
7	–	1/4 DRILL	–	0.25	0.0	
8	–		–	0.4375	0.0	
9	–	1/2 FLAT ...	–	0.5	0.0	

2D High Speed Toolpath - Dynamic Mill

Toolpath Type
Tool
Holder

Stock
Cut Parameters
  Depth Cuts
  Entry Motion
  Break Through
Linking Parameters
  Home / Ref. Points

Arc Filter / Tolerance
Planes (WCS)
Coolant
Canned Text
Misc Values
Axis Control
  Axis Combination

Quick View Settings

Tool	1/2 FLAT ENDMI...
Tool Diameter	0.5
Corner Radius	0
Feed Rate	150
Spindle Speed	8000
Coolant	Off
Tool Length	3
Length Offset	9
Diameter Offset	9
Cplane / Tpla...	Top
Axis Combinat...	Default (1)

✓ = edited
⊘ = disabled

Tool diameter: 0.5
Corner radius: 0.0

Tool name: 1/2 FLAT ENDMILL
Tool #: 9   Length offset: 9
Head #: 0   Diameter offset: 9

☐ RCTF   Spindle direction: CW
Feed rate: 150.0   Spindle speed: 8000
FPT: 0.0047   SFM: 1047.1204
Plunge rate: 50.0   Retract rate: 6.4176
☐ Force tool change   ☑ Rapid Retract

Comment
Machine the outside profile.

Right-click for options

Select library tool...   ☐ Filter Active   Filter...

☐ To batch

20.3 Set the Cut Parameters

• From the **Tree View list**, select **Cut Parameters** and ensure the parameters appear the same as shown in
  Figure: 20.3.1.

Figure: 20.3.1

Cutting method	Climb
Tip comp	Tip
Approach distance	0.0 Bottom left

First pass offset	0.1
First pass feed reduction	0.0 %
Conventional feed rate	0.0
Stepover	15.0 % 0.075
Min toolpath radius	5.0 % 0.025

Gap size
  ○ Distance   0.5
  ◉ % of tool diameter 100.0

Motion < Gap size, Micro lift
  Micro lift distance   0.01
  Back feedrate   100.0

Motion > Gap size, retract
  Never

Cut order optimization   Material
Stock to leave on walls   0.03
Stock to leave on floors 0.0

20.4 Set the Depth Cuts Parameters

* From the **Tree View list**, select **Depth Cuts** and disable **Depth cuts** as shown in Figure: 20.4.1.

Figure: 20.4.1

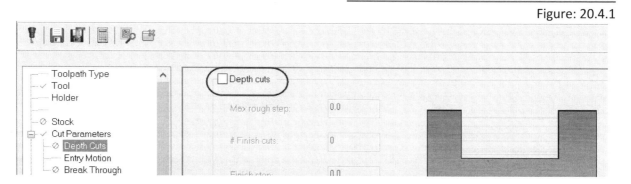

20.5 Set the Entry Motion

* Set the **Entry method** to **Helix only**. Input a **Z clearance** value of **0.05** and a **Plunge angle** of **2.0** degrees as shown in Figure: 20.5.1.

Figure: 20.5.1

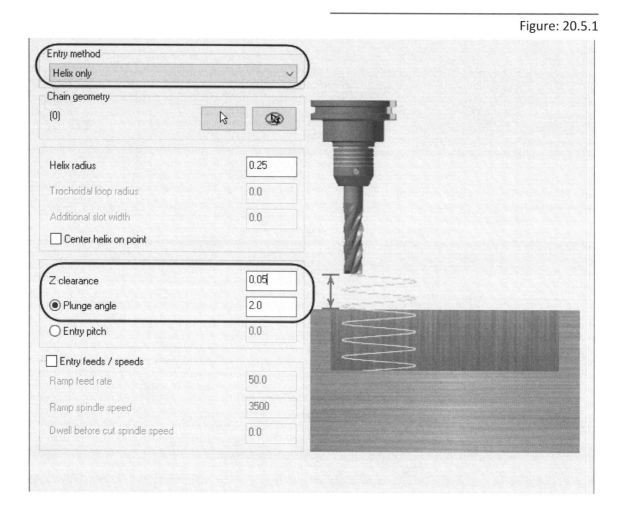

20.6 Set the Linking Parameters

♦ Select **Linking Parameters**, enable **Clearance**, input a value of **1.0** and input a **Depth** value of **-0.5** as shown in
Figure: 20.6.1.

Figure: 20.6.1

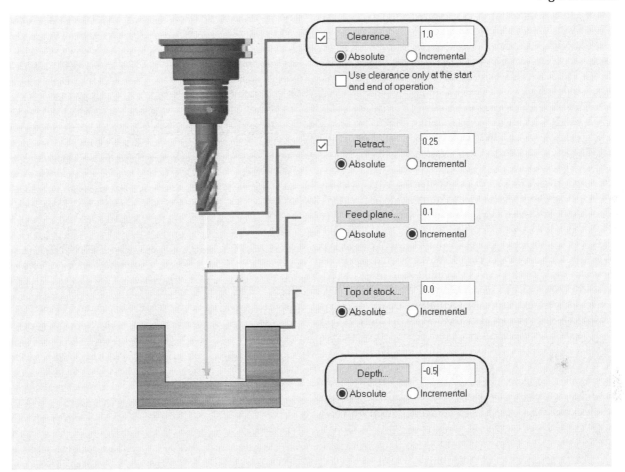

20.7 Preview the Toolpath

♦ To quickly check how the toolpath will be generated, select the **Preview toolpath** icon as shown.

♦ See **page 157** to review the procedure.
♦ The toolpath should look as shown.

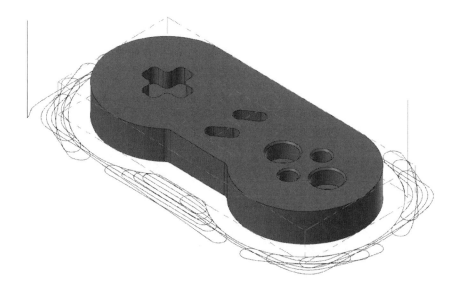

♦ Press **Esc** key to exit the preview.

| **NOTE:** If the toolpath does not look as shown in the preview, check your parameters again.

♦ Select the **OK** button to generate the toolpath.

20.8 Backplot the toolpath

• **Backplot** the toolpath. See **page 158** for more information.

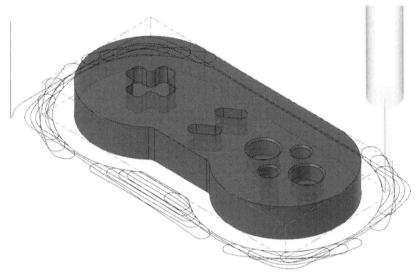

• Select the **OK** button to exit **Backplot**.

20.9 Verify the toolpaths

• **Verify** the toolpaths. See **page 160** for more information.

• To **Verify** all toolpaths, from the **Toolpaths** Manager, choose the **Select all operations** icon.

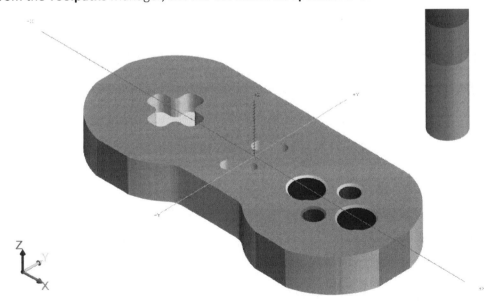

• To go back to the Mastercam window, minimize the **Mastercam Simulator** window as shown.

STEP 21: FINISH THE POCKETS USING A POCKET TOOLPATH

In this step you will use a pocket toolpath to finish the walls of all pockets. The high speed toolpaths do not have a finish wall option inside of their parameters. You will use the solid selections.

Step Preview:

TOOLPATHS

 From the **2D** group, select the **Expand gallery** arrow and in the **Toolpath Gallery** select **Pocket** as shown.

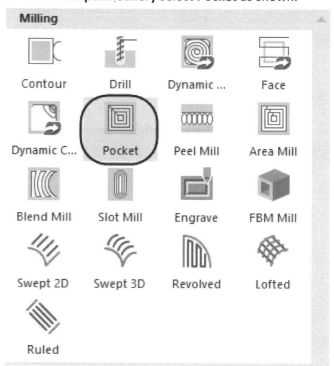

Mill Essentials Training Tutorial *Mastercam.* 2017

21.1 Select the pocket floors using Solid Face selections

♦ From the **Chaining** dialog box, enable the **Face** button and make sure all the other buttons are unselected as shown.

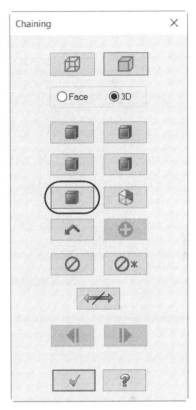

♦ Right mouse click in the graphics window and select the **Top** graphics view.

♦ Select the bottom of the pockets as shown.

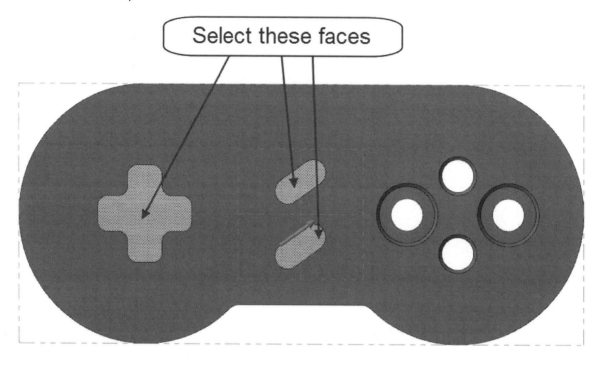

Select these faces

♦ Select the **OK** button to exit the **Chaining** dialog box.
♦ In the **Toolpath Type**, **Pocket** should already be selected as shown.

Contour   Pocket   Facing   Slot Mill

21.2 Select the tool and set the Tool parameters

- From the **Tree View list**, select **Tool.**
- From the **Tool display window**, select the **5/32" Flat Endmill.** Make all the necessary changes as shown.

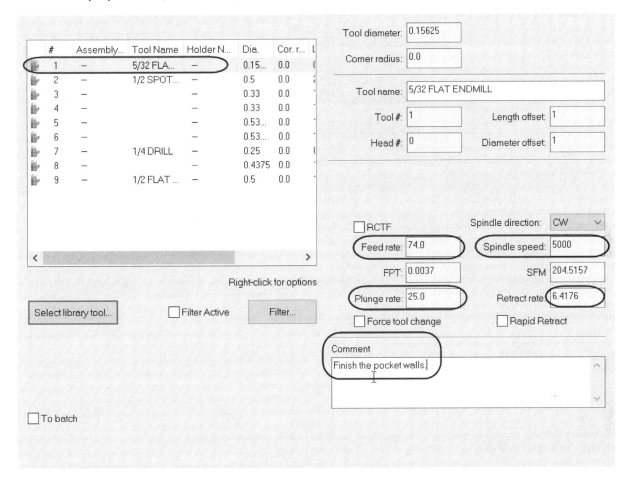

21.3 Set the Cut Parameters page

♦ From the **Tree View list**, select **Cut Parameters** and make the changes as shown.

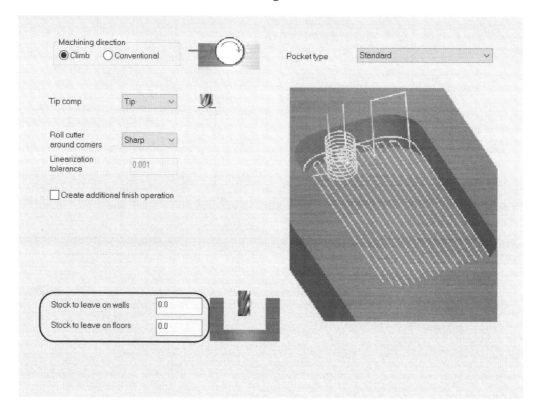

21.4 Disable Roughing page

♦ From the **Tree View list**, select **Roughing** and disable **Rough** as shown.

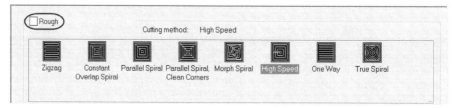

NOTE: The **Roughing** option should be disabled as in this case you only want to finish the walls and not to machine again the pocket floors. For the same reason, you will turn the **Entry Motion** off.

21.5 Disable Entry Motion page

• From the **Tree View list**, select **Entry Motion** and enable **Off** to turn off any entry helix or ramp move.

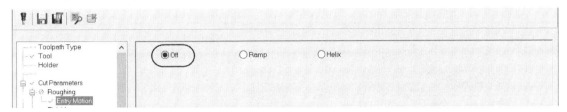

21.6 Set the Finishing page

• From the **Tree View list**, select **Finishing** and set the parameters as shown.

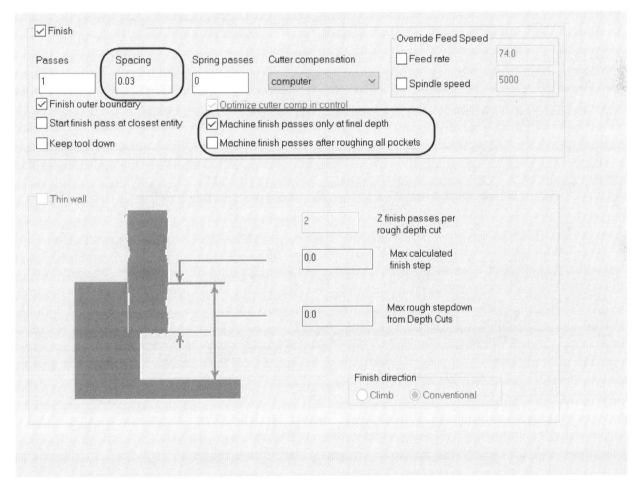

Passes sets the number of finish passes for the toolpath.

Spacing sets the amount of material to be removed with each cut.

21.7 Set the Lead In/Out page

- From the **Tree View list**, select **Lead In/Out** and make the changes to ensure smooth entry and exit moves to and from the part as shown.

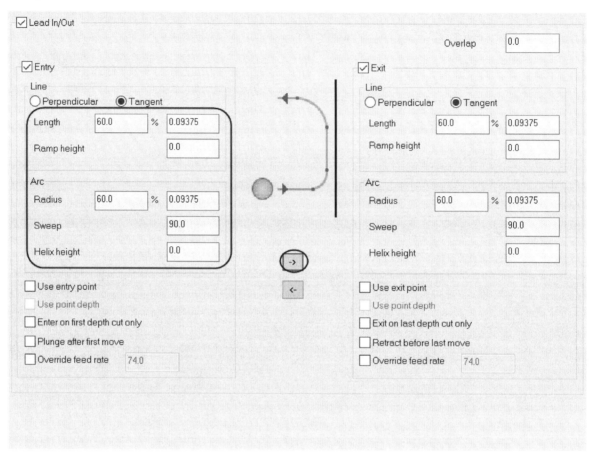

21.8 Set the Linking Parameters page

◆ From the **Tree View list**, select **Linking Parameters** and make sure the parameters are set as shown.

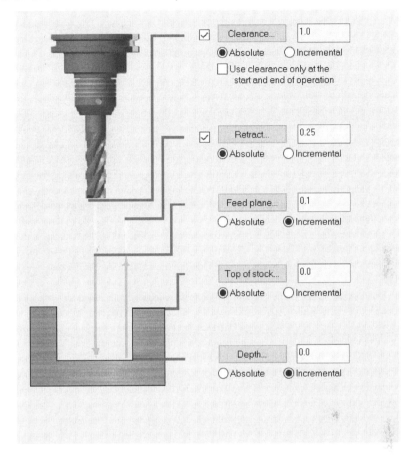

21.9 Preview the Toolpath

◆ To quickly check how the toolpath will be generated, select the **Preview toolpath** icon as shown.

◆ See **page 157** to review the procedure.
◆ The toolpath should look as shown.

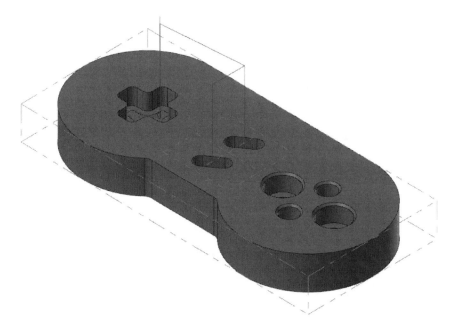

◆ Press **Esc** key to exit the preview.

> **NOTE:** If the toolpath does not look as shown in the preview, check your parameters again.

◆ Select the **OK** button to exit the **2D Toolpaths - Pocket** parameters.
◆ Right mouse click in the graphics window and change the graphics view back to **Isometric**.

21.10 Verify the toolpath using both Backplot and Verify

• Select the last toolpath only and run **Backplot**.
• The toolpath should look as shown.

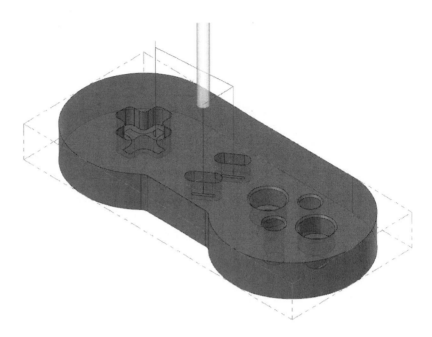

• Select the **OK** button to exit **Backplot**.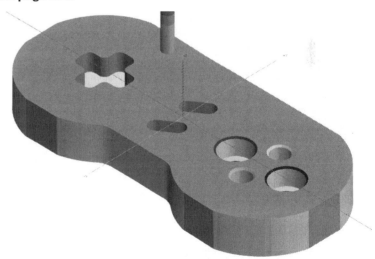
• Select all toolpaths to **Verify** them as shown on **page 160**.

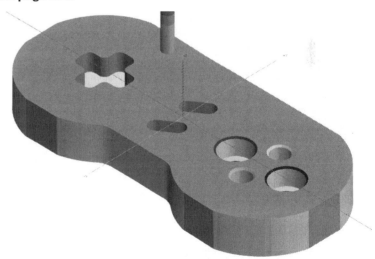

• To go back to the Mastercam window, minimize the **Mastercam Simulator** window as shown.

STEP 22: CONTOUR TOOLPATH

A **Contour** toolpath removes material along a path defined by a chain of curves. A **Contour** toolpath only follows a chain; it does not clean out an enclosed area. You will use this toolpath to finish the outside profile.

Toolpath Preview:

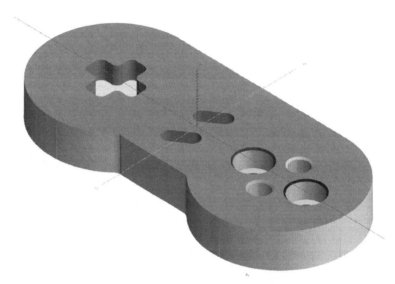

• Hover the cursor in the **Toolpaths Manager** and press **T** to remove the toolpath display if needed.

TOOLPATHS

• From the **2D** group, select the **Expand gallery** arrow and from the **Toolpath Gallery** select **Contour** as shown.

◆ First enable **Solids** selection. Then check only the **Loop** button in the **Chaining** dialog box as shown.

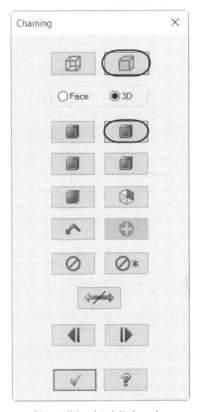

◆ Click on somewhere along the edge of the lower outside profile and the entire profile will be highlighted as shown.

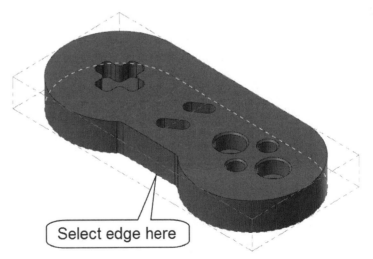

Select edge here

♦ In the **Pick Reference Face** dialog box, select the **OK** button to accept this face.

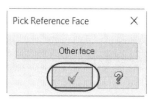

♦ Make sure the chaining direction is **Clockwise** as shown in Figure: 22.0.1. Otherwise, from the **Chaining** dialog

box, select the **Reverse** button.

Figure: 22.0.1

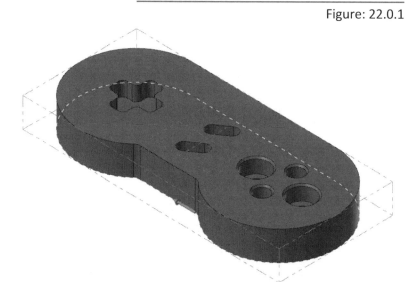

♦ Select the **OK** button to exit the **Chaining** dialog box.
♦ In the **Toolpath Type** page, the **Contour** toolpath will be selected.

Contour   Pocket   Facing   Slot Mill

22.1 Select the 5/32" Flat Endmill from the library and set the Tool Parameters

- Select **Tool** from **Tree View list**.
- Select the **5/32" Flat Endmill**. You may need to use the tool library to select this tool.
- Make all the necessary changes as shown in Figure: 22.1.1.

Figure: 22.1.1

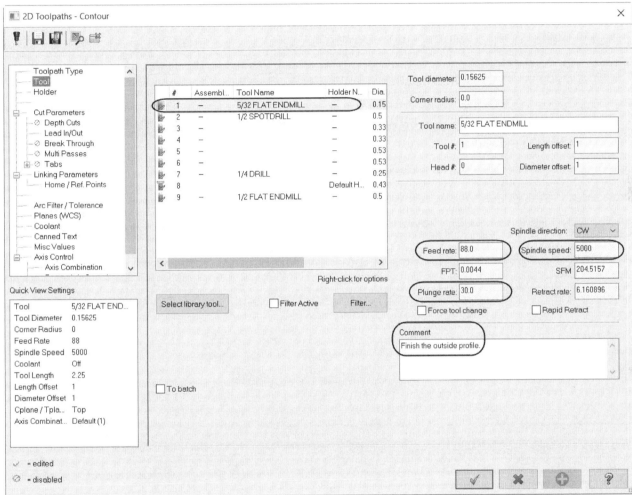

22.2 Cut Parameters

• Select the **Cut Parameters** and make the necessary changes as shown in <u>Figure: 22.2.1</u>.

Figure: 22.2.1

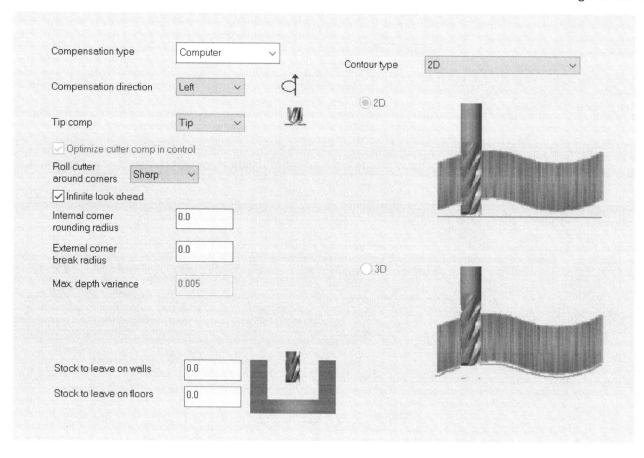

Roll cutter around corners inserts arc moves around corners in the toolpath.

None guarantees all sharp corners.

Sharp rolls the tool around sharp corners (135 degrees or less).

All rolls the tool around all corners and creates smooth tool movement.

22.3 Depth Cuts

• Select **Depth Cuts** and make sure it is disabled as shown.

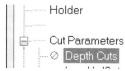

22.4 Lead In/Out

◆ Choose the option **Lead In/Out** and input an **Overlap** value. Make any other necessary changes as shown in
Figure: 22.4.1.

Figure: 22.4.1

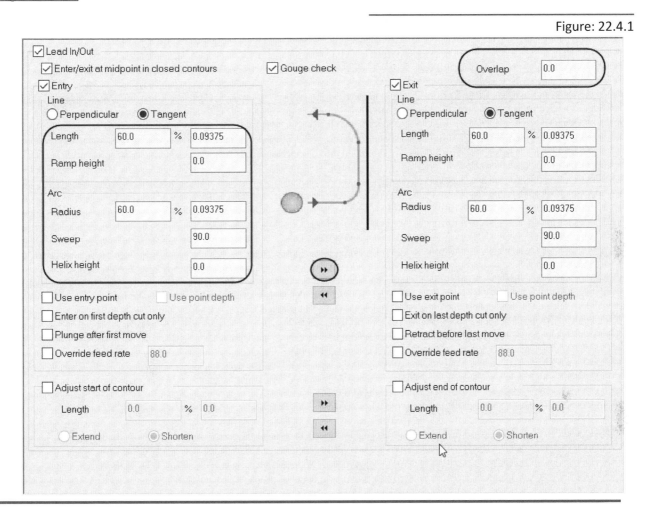

Lead In/Out allows you to select a combination of a Line and an Arc at the beginning and/or end of the contour
toolpath for a smooth entry/exit while cutting the part.

Length set to 60% of the tool diameter ensures that the linear movement is bigger than the tool radius in case **Cutter
Compensation** in **Control** was used.

Radius set to 60% of the tool diameter ensures that the arc movement is bigger than the tool radius to generate an arc
output.

Overlap sets how far the tool goes past the end of the toolpath before exiting for a cleaner finish.

22.5 Linking Parameters

♦ Select **Linking Parameters** from the **Tree View list**. Set the **Top of stock** to **0.0** and the **Depth** to **Incremental** and **0.0** as shown in <u>Figure: 22.5.1</u>.

Figure: 22.5.1

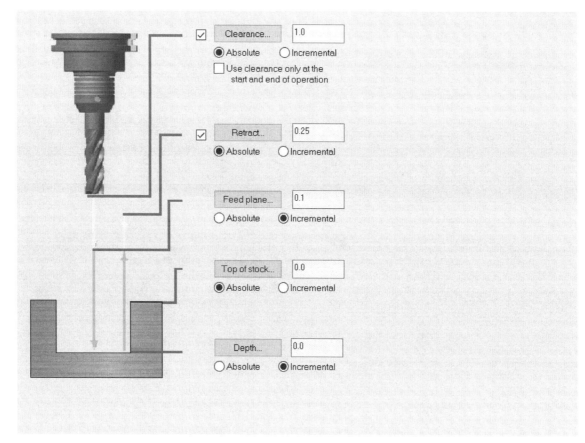

22.6 Preview the Toolpath

♦ To quickly check how the toolpath will be generated, select the **Preview toolpath** icon as shown.

♦ See **page 157** to review the procedure.
♦ The toolpath should look as shown.

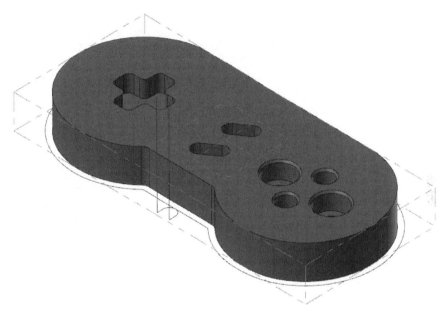

♦ Press **Esc** key to exit the preview.

> **NOTE:** If the toolpath does not look as shown in the preview, check your parameters again.

♦ Select the **OK** button to exit the **2D Toolpaths - Contour** parameters.

22.7 Verify the toolpaths

♦ **Select all operations.**

♦ Click on the **Verify selected operations** icon.
♦ For information on how to set the verify parameters and to simulate the toolpath, check **page 160**.

♦ The finished part will appear as shown in <u>Figure: 22.7.1</u>.

Figure: 22.7.1

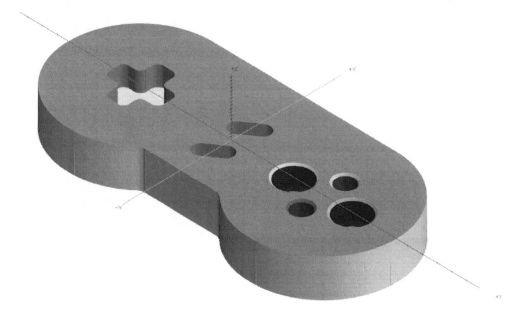

♦ To go back to the Mastercam window, minimize the **Mastercam Simulator** window as shown.

STEP 23: POST THE FILE

◆ Ensure all operations are selected. If they are not, use the button **Select all operations** in the **Operations Manager.**

◆ Select the **Post selected operations** button from the **Toolpaths Manager.** G1
◆ In the **Post processing** window, make the necessary changes as shown in Figure: 23.0.1.

Figure: 23.0.1

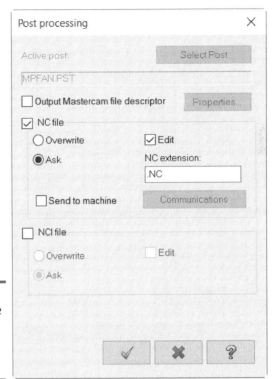

NC File enabled allows you to keep the NC file and to assign the same name as the MCAM file.

Edit enabled allows you to automatically launch the default editor.

◆ Select the **OK** button to continue.

◆ Save "Your Name_7.NC" file.

♦ A window with **Mastercam Code Expert** will be launched and the NC programs will appear as shown in
<u>Figure: 23.0.2</u>.

Figure: 23.0.2

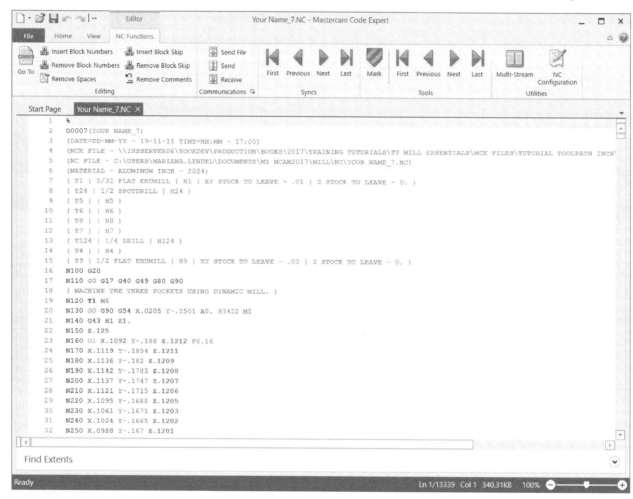

♦ Select the **"X"** box at the upper right corner to exit the editor.

STEP 24: SAVE THE UPDATED MCAM FILE

REVIEW EXERCISE - STUDENT PRACTICE

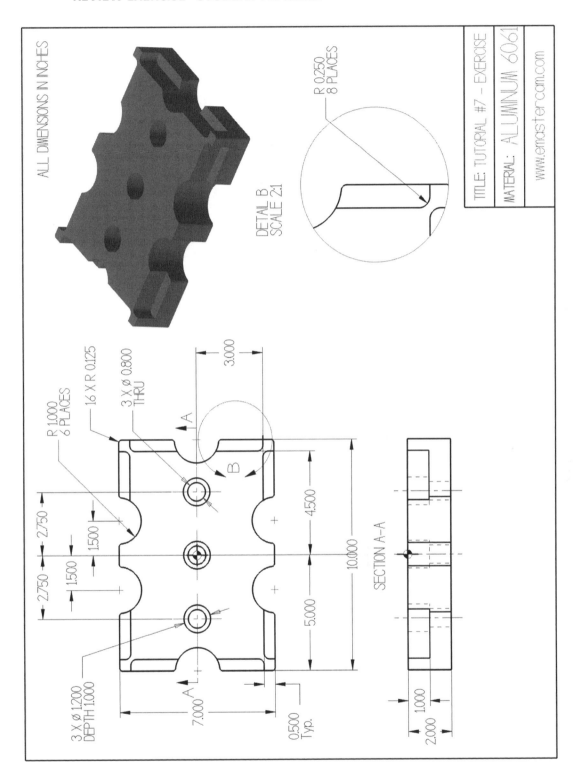

ALL DIMENSIONS IN INCHES

R 0.250
8 PLACES

DETAIL B
SCALE 2:1

TITLE: TUTORIAL #7 – EXERCISE

MATERIAL: ALUMINUM 6061

www.emastercam.com

R 1.000
6 PLACES

16 X R 0.125

3 X Ø 0.800
THRU

3.000

2.750

2.750

1.500

1.500

4.500

10.000

5.000

7.000

0.500
Typ.

SECTION A-A

1.000

2.000

3 X Ø 1.200
DEPTH 1.000

CREATE THE 2D GEOMETRY FOR TUTORIAL #7 EXERCISE

Use these commands to create the geometry:
- Rectangle.
- Arc Polar.
- Break Two Pieces.
- Mirror.
- Translate.
- Join.
- Circle Center Point.
- Trim Break Extend.

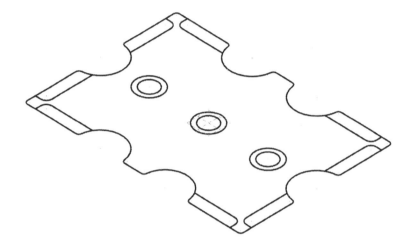

CREATE THE SOLID GEOMETRY FOR TUTORIAL #7 EXERCISE

Change the Main Level to Level 2.

Use these commands to create the geometry
- Solid Extrude Create body.
- Solid Extrude Cut body.

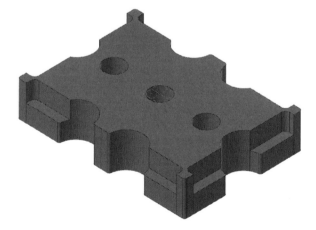

CREATE THE TOOLPATHS FOR TUTORIAL #7 EXERCISE

Create the Toolpaths for Tutorial #7 Exercise as per the instructions below.

Set the machine properties including the Stock.

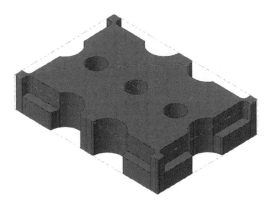

FBM Drill.
* Enable **Automatic initial hole detection**.
* **Grouping** set to **Plane**.
* Under **Hole Detection Include blind holes**.
* **Include chamfers**.
* **Maximum diameter** set to **1.625**.
* **Spot drilling** and **Combine Spot Drill operations that share the same depth and retract values** enabled.
* **Max percentage of finished hole** set to **100%** and **Max depth** set to **0.375**.
* **Pre-drilling** and **Pre-drill pilot holes only** enabled.
* In **Tool selection**, have **Use tools in part file**, **Use tool library** and **Create as needed** enabled.
* In **Tool creation**, disable **Create only standard sizes**, enable **Consider flute length** and **Create one tool for all depths**.
* In the **Linking Parameters**, have **Clearance** set to **Solid height plus** and **1.0** and **Retract** set to **Solid height plus** and **0.5**.
* Enable **Through holes**.
* Click on **Detect** the **features**.

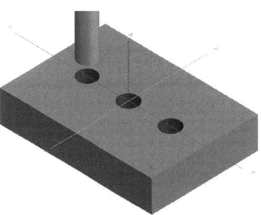

Machine the outside profile using 2D HS Dynamic Mill.

- In the **Chain Options**, enable **From outside**, **Shortest distance** for **open chain extension to stock**.
- Click on the **Select avoidance chains** button in the **Avoidance regions**. In the **Chaining** dialog box, enable **Solids** mode and select **Loop**. Then select the bottom edge of the solid.

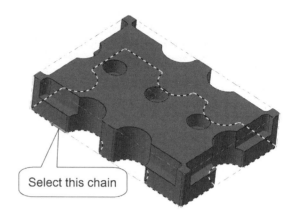

Select this chain

- Select the **1/2" Flat Endmill**.
- **First pass offset** = **0.1**.
- **Stepover** = **25%**.
- **Min toolpath radius** = **10%**.
- **Micro lift distance** = **0.01**.
- **Stock to leave on walls** = **0.03**.
- **Stock to leave on floors** = **0.0**.
- **Entry motion Helix only**; **Radius 0.25**.
- **Clearance** = **1.0** (Absolute).
- **Retract** = **0.25** (Absolute).
- **Feed plane** = **0.1** (Incremental).
- **Depth** = **-2.0**(Absolute).

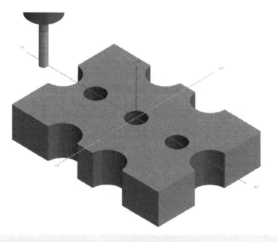

NOTE: Change the **Cutting length** and **Overall length** as needed. To change the default tool properties, in the tool list, right mouse click on the tool and select **Edit tool** to set tool parameters.

Machine the steps using 2D HS Dynamic Mill.

* In the **Chain Options**, enable **From outside**, **None** for **Open chain extension to stock**.
* Click on the **Select machining chains** button in the **Machining regions**. In the **Chaining** dialog box, enable **Solids** mode and select only **Loop**. Select the bottom edges as a contour.

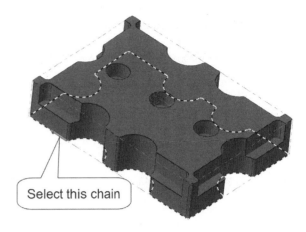

Select this chain

* Click on the **Select avoidance chains** button in the **Avoidance regions** and stay in the **Solids** mode. Enable **Loop** and select the top edges as a contour.

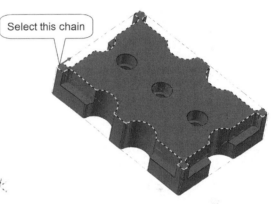

Select this chain

* Select the same **1/2" Flat Endmill**.
* **First pass offset** = **0.1**.
* **Stepover** = **25%**.
* **Min toolpath radius** = **10%**.
* **Micro lift distance** = **0.01**.
* **Stock to leave on walls** = **0.03**.
* **Stock to leave on floors** = **0.0**.
* **Entry motion Helix only; Radius 0.25**.
* **Clearance** = **1.0** (Absolute).
* **Retract** = **0.25** (Absolute).
* **Feed plane** = **0.1** (Incremental).
* **Top of stock** = **0.0** (Absolute).
* **Depth** = **-1.0** (Absolute).

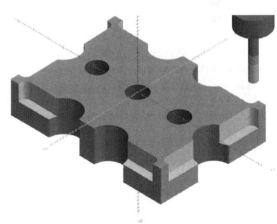

Finish the bottom profile using Contour toolpath.

- Enable **Solids** selection, then check **Loop** button and select the bottom profile as shown before in the **Clockwise** direction.
- Select a **3/8" Flat Endmill**.
- **Contour type 2D**.
- **Compensation type** in **Computer**.
- **Compensation direction** set to **Left**.
- **Stock to leave on walls** and **floors** = **0.0**.
- **Lead In/Out** set to defaults.
- **Clearance = 1.0** (Absolute).
- **Retract = 0.25** (Absolute).
- **Feed plane =0.1** (Incremental).
- **Top of stock = 0.0** (Absolute).
- **Depth = 0.0** (Incremental).

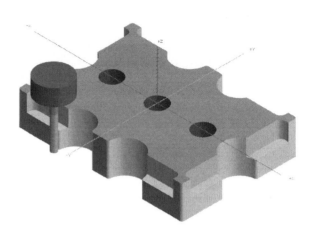

NOTE: Change the **Cutting length** and **Overall length** as needed. To change the default tool properties, in the tool list, right mouse click on the tool and select **Edit tool** to set tool parameters.

Finish the step profile using Contour toolpath.

- Enable **Solids** selection, then check **Partial loop** button and select the bottom profiles of the 8 steps in the **Counter-clockwise** direction.
- Use the same **3/8" Flat Endmill**.
- **Contour type 2D**.
- **Compensation type** in **Computer**.
- **Compensation direction** set to **Left**.
- **Stock to leave on walls** and **floors** = **0.0**.
- **Lead In/Out** set to defaults.
- **Clearance = 1.0** (Absolute).
- **Retract = 0.25** (Absolute).
- **Feed plane = 0.1** (Incremental).
- **Top of stock = 0.0** (Absolute).
- **Depth = -1.0** (Absolute).

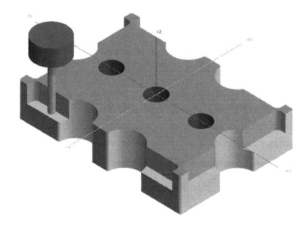

NOTES:

TUTORIAL #7 QUIZ

◆ What does FBM Drill allow you to do?

◆ What does Open chain extension to stock set to Shortest distance do?

◆ What does Avoidance regions selection do?

CREATING/EDITING TOOLS

Objectives:

✓ The student will learn how to create and modify tools.

CREATING AND EDITING A MILL TOOL LIBRARY

NOTE: The purpose of tool libraries is to hold the tool data. The libraries can be edited or added to by following the directions below. Each time the **Tool Type** or **Cutter diameter** is changed in the **Toolpath parameters**, the tool library recalculates the feed rate and spindle speed. The following menu selections will allow you to create a new tool.

CREATING A NEW TOOL

MACHINE
* **Default.**

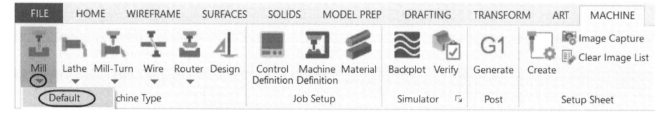

NOTE: Once you select the **Mill Default** the ribbon bar changes to reflect the toolpaths that could be used with **Mill Default**.

Option 1: Create a new tool using Mill Tool Manager

TOOLPATHS
* From the **Utilities** group, select **Tool Manager** as shown.

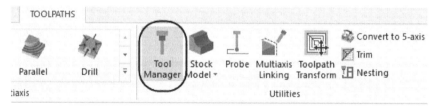

◆ Right click in the tool display area.
◆ Select **Create new tool** as shown.

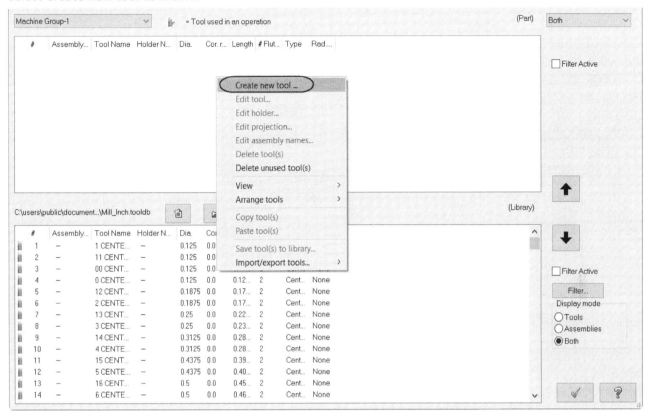

Option 2: Create a new tool inside of the Toolpath Parameters

Close the Tool Manager.
Create a rectangle.

TOOLPATHS
- From the **2D** area, select **Contour**.
- Chain the rectangle.
- From the **Tree View list,** select **Tool**.
- Right click in the tool display area.
- Select **Create new tool** as shown.

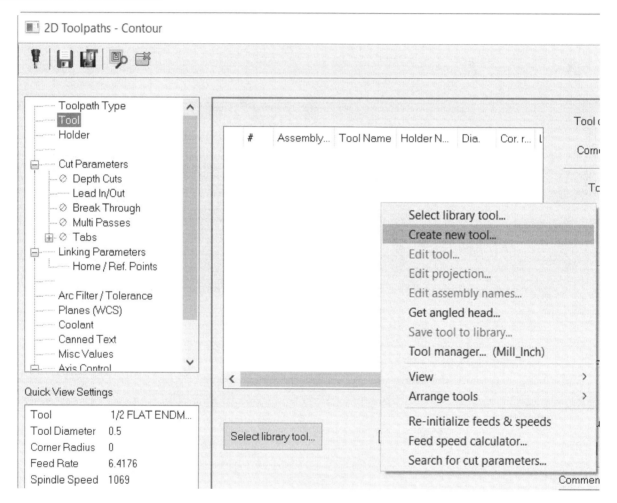

1. What type of tool would you like to create?

The **Create New Tool** dialog box displays all the default tool type options in Mastercam.

◆ The **Define Tool** screen will appear as shown.

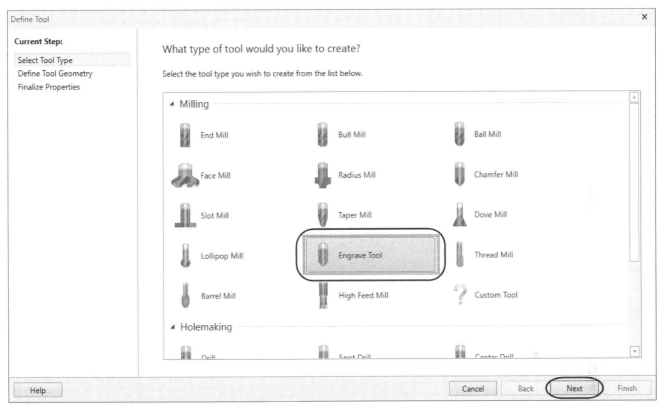

◆ Choose the tool type you wish to modify and then select the **Next** button.

2. Define geometric tool parameters.

Define geometric tool parameters lets you enter new parameters or edit current parameters of Mill tools. A description of each parameter in the **Define geometric tool parameters** is listed below.

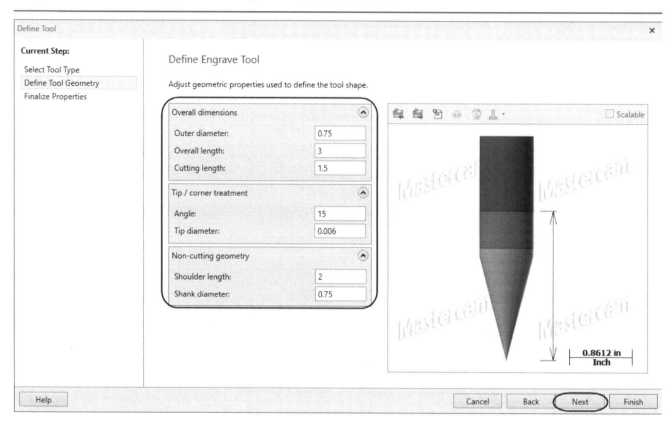

NOTE: The fields on the tabs change depending on the type of tool you are creating.

Overall Dimensions

Outer Diameter - sets the diameter of the tool.

Overall Length - sets the length of the tool.

Cutting Length - sets the length from the top of the flutes to the tip of the tool.

Tip/Corner Treatment

Corner Type - allows you to choose between None, Chamfer, Corner radius and Full radius.

Angle - measures the angle from the center line of the tool to the outer angle of the tool.

Tip Diameter - sets the tool tip diameter.

Non-Cutting Geometry

Shoulder Length - sets the distance from the top of the shoulder to the tip of the tool.

Shank Diameter - sets the diameter of the tool shank.

◆ Set the dimension values and then select the **Next** button.

3. Finalize miscellaneous properties

This area allows you to type information such as Name, Manufacturer Name and Manufacturer's tool code. It also allows you to enter the tool offset numbers, the feeds and speeds, the material, coolant settings and other settings.

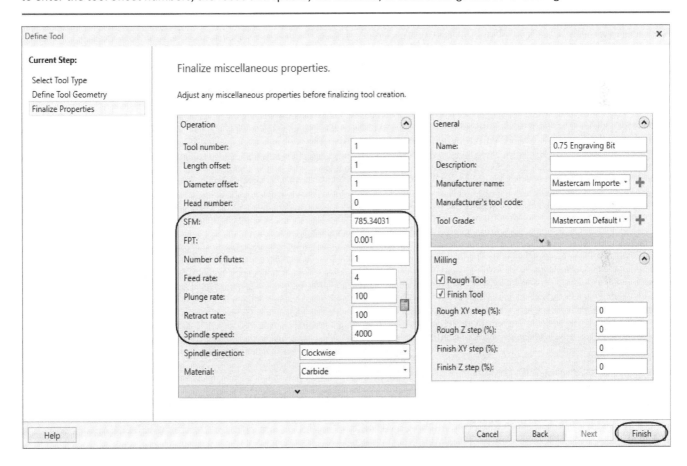

NOTE: To set up the coolant, click on the drop down arrow.

◆ Make any necessary changes as shown and select the **Finish** button to complete the tool creation.

Operation

Tool Number - sets the default tool assembly number.

Length Offset - sets the number that corresponds to a register in the machine that compensates for the tool length.

Diameter Offset - sets the number that corresponds to a register in the machine that offsets the diameter.

Number of Flutes - specifies the number of flutes on the tool which is used to calculate the feed rate.

Feed Rate - sets the default feed rate.

Plunge Rate - sets the default plunge rate.

Retract Rate - sets the default retract rate.

Spindle Speed - sets the spindle speed in RPM.

Spindle Direction - allows you to choose the spindle direction between Clockwise, Counterclockwise and Static.

Material - displays the tool material.

Coolant - allows you to set the canned text coolant options.

Metric - allows you to enable metric tools.

General

Name - allows you to type the name of the tool.

Description - displays additional info.

Manufacturer Name - allows you to type the name of the Manufacturer.

Manufacturer's Tool Code - allows you to type the tool code.

Milling

Rough XY step (%)- allows you to set the size of a roughing step in the X and Y axes for the tool. The system measures this distance as a percentage of the tool diameter.

Rough Z step (%) - allows you to set the size of a roughing step in the Z axis for the tool. The system measures this distance as a percentage of the tool diameter.

Finish XY step (%) - allows you to set the size of a finish step in the X and Y axes for the tool. The system measures this distance as a percentage of the tool diameter.

Finish Z step (%) - allows you to set the size of a step in the Z axis for finish the tool. The system measures this distance as a percentage of the tool diameter.

EDITING AN EXISTING TOOL

Option 1: Edit an existing tool using the Tool Manager

MACHINE
• From the **Machine Type** area, click on the drop down arrow below **Mill** and select the **Default.**

TOOLPATHS
• From the **Utilities** group, select **Tool Manager** as shown.

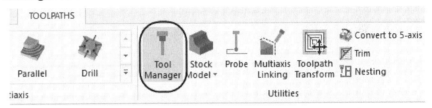

• Find the **3/8" Ball Endmill (#309)** from the library list and click on the upward arrow to move it in the current tool list as shown.

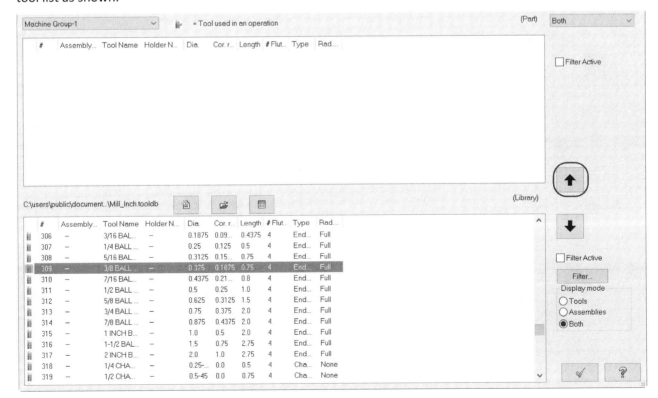

- Right click on the existing tool.
- Select **Edit tool** as shown.

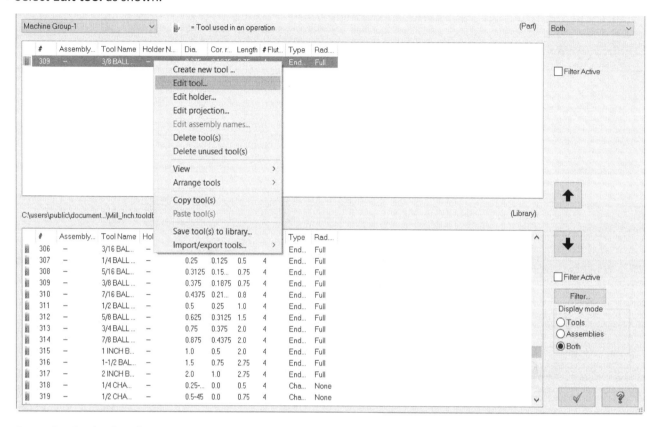

- Once the **Tool Wizard** opens, you can change any of the dimensions or properties of the tool that you want.

Option 2: Editing an existing tool inside of the toolpath parameters

◆ In the **Tool** dialog box, right click on the existing tool and then select **Edit tool** as shown.

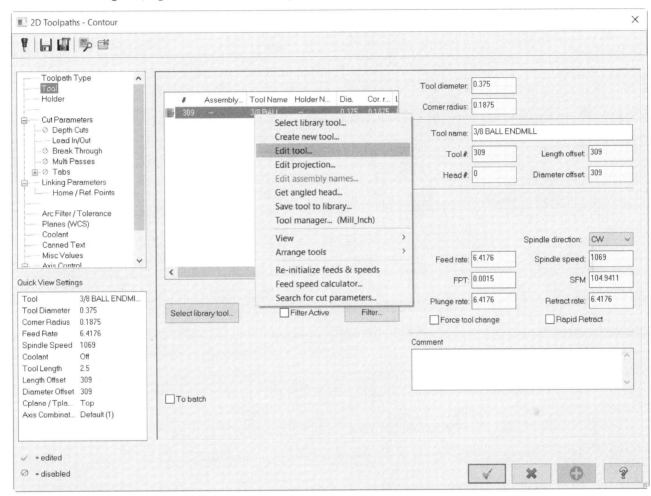

◆ Make the changes to the tool.
◆ Once you select the **OK** button, the tool will be automatically saved with the new changes.

QUIZ ANSWERS

Objectives:

✓ The answers to the 7 Tutorial quizzes.

MILL LEVEL 1 TUTORIAL QUIZ ANSWERS

Tutorial # 1 Answers

◆ What is a Contour Toolpath used for?
◆ **Contour toolpath** removes the material along a path defined by a chain of curves. Contour toolpaths only follow a chain; they do not clean out an enclosed area.

◆ What is a Facing Toolpath used for?
◆ **Facing toolpath** quickly removes material from the top of the part to create an even surface for future operations.

◆ What does a Circle Mill toolpath do?
◆ **Circle Mill toolpath** is used to mill circular pockets based on a single point. Mastercam will pocket out a circular area of the diameter and to the depth that you specify.

◆ What does Backplot do?
◆ **Backplotting** shows the path the tools take to cut the part. This display lets you spot errors in the program before you machine the part. As you backplot toolpaths, Mastercam displays the current X, Y, and Z coordinates in the lower left corner of the screen.

◆ What does Verify allow you to do?
◆ **Verify** allows you to use a solid model to simulate the machining of a part. The model created by verification represents the surface finish, and shows collisions, if any exist.

Tutorial # 2 Answers

◆ What does Slot Mill toolpath do?
◆ **Slot Mill** toolpath allows Mastercam to efficiently machine oblong slots. These are slots that consist of 2 straight lines and two 180-degree arcs at the ends.

◆ What does 2D HS Dynamic Mill do?
◆ **2D HS Dynamic** machines, utilizing the entire flute length of their cutting tools, to machine open pocket shapes, standing core shapes or pockets. To machine standing cores the toolpath uses the outmost chain as the stock boundary. The tool moves freely outside of this area; the inner chain defines the limit of the toolpath.

◆ What does 2D HS Dynamic Contour Mill do?
◆ **2D HS Dynamic Contour** toolpath utilizes the entire flute length of the cutting tools and is used to mill material off walls. It does support both closed or open chains.

◆ What is the process used to be able to post different operations as different programs?
◆ Create a new toolpath group and then rename it.

Tutorial # 3 Answers

◆ What does Area Mill do?

◆ **Area Mill** takes small cuts to machine open pocket shapes, standing core shapes or pockets based on the machining region strategies.

◆ What does smoothing do?

◆ **Smoothing** replaces sharp corners with arcs for faster and smoother transitions in tool direction.

◆ What does Pocket Remachining do?

◆ **Pocket Remachining** calculates areas where the pocket roughing tool could not machine the stock and creates a remachining pocket toolpath to clear the remaining material.

Tutorial # 4 Answers

◆ What does the Solid Extrude command do?

◆ The **Solid Extrude** command creates one or more solid bodies, cuts in an existing solid or create bosses to an existing solid.

◆ What does a **Dwell before cut spindle speed** do?

◆ It adds a dwell after the entry ramp into the cut. This pause allows the spindle to ramp up to the desired spindle speed before starting the cutting passes.

◆ What does a Transform toolpath operation do?

◆ It allows you to run the same toolpath in different locations. You can transform a single toolpath or several at a time.

Tutorial # 5 Answers

◆ What settings do you need to use to remachine a pocket using High Speed Area Mill Toolpath?

◆ **2D High Speed Area Mill toolpath** with the **Rest Material** enabled targets material left behind by previous toolpaths.

◆ What is the use of WCS in Mastercam?

◆ This tells Mastercam how your part is position or orientated in the machine.

◆ After creating a new toolpath group, why do you rename the NC file?

◆ You rename the NC file to create two separate programs.

Tutorial # 6 Answers

◆ What does the Translate 3D do?

◆ **Translate 3D** allows you to move the geometry between views (from one plane to another).

◆ How does a Blend Mill toolpath work?

◆ **2D High Speed Blend Mill** toolpath morph smoothly between two open chains.

◆ What does Peel Mill toolpath do?

◆ **2D High Speed Peel Mill toolpath** allows for efficient constant climb milling between two selected contours or along a single contour. It uses a trochodial style of motion to cut the slot.

Tutorial # 7 Answers

◆ What does FBM Drill do?

◆ **FBM Drill** automatically detects holes in a solid based on your specific criteria and to generate a complete series of drilling and chamfering. FBM drill also generates circle mill or helix bore operations for large-hole features when you activate these settings.

◆ What does Open chain extension to stock set to Shortest distance do?

◆ **Open chain extension to stock** set to **Shortest distance** sets how the system calculates the amount of the material that has to be removed based on the defined stock.

◆ What does Avoidance regions selection do?

◆ **Avoidance regions** allows you to select the profile that describes the shape up to where the material will be removed.